A HISTORY

OF

THE UNITED STATES

BY

EDWARD CHANNING

VOLUME II

A CENTURY OF COLONIAL HISTORY

1660–1760

New York

THE MACMILLAN COMPANY

1918

All rights reserved

Norwood Press
J. S. Cushing Co. — Berwick & Smith Co.
Norwood, Mass., U.S.A.

CONTENTS

v

MAPS

A HISTORY OF THE UNITED STATES

CHAPTER I

THE COLONIAL POLICY OF THE RESTORATION

THE restoration of the second Charles to the English throne on the 29th of May, 1660, marks a turning-point in the history of the American colonies, as well as in that of England itself. King and courtiers returned from exile poorer in purse even than they were in morals; their financial needs determined the course of events in the next few years. They possessed large landed estates, but these had been confiscated by the Puritans in the day of their triumph, and were now restored without compensation for waste and demolitions, and without repayment of arrears of rent. The returned owners could not exact increased rentals from their tenants, because that would turn the tenantry against them, and possibly bring on another civil war. Charles and his followers were burdened with debts, and were under heavy obligations; they had had to live even in exile, and he had been obliged to make promises that must be fulfilled. Ordinary means of taxation would provide for the needs of government and leave something over, but the requirements of the king and his court were far in excess of anything that could be raised by ordinary taxation. New means of supply must be sought in every direction.

The king and his advisers at once seized upon colonial

enterprise as one means of providing the necessary funds. They built upon the foundations of the Puritan time, and by a series of navigation acts monopolized colonial commerce in the interests of English subjects and the royal exchequer. They seized Dutch New Netherland, and founded the colonies of Carolina and New Jersey. They interested themselves in the formation of the Royal African Company, and in the company for the exploitation of the fur trade of Hudson Bay.[1]

The time was propitious for the inauguration of new ventures in colonization and commerce. The political and mental upheaval of the Puritan epoch had aroused a spirit of unrest among Englishmen, and had opened their eyes to the possibilities of profits to be gained in the outer parts of the world. The seizure of the island of Jamaica in Cromwell's time was the beginning of a new page in the history of England's dominion in the West Indies. Commercial capital had accumulated in England, and was now seeking investment outside of the home land. Among the defeated Puritans and the impoverished cavaliers there were many persons who were anxious to secure a new start in life, and were willing to brave the unknown hardships of the wilderness of the New World to gain subsistence for themselves and their posterity.

Politically, in England, the Restoration marked a return to the institutions and political methods of the days before the meeting of the Long Parliament; in America, institutions and political methods went on developing on the lines that had already been laid down. The planting of the colonies had drawn from the British Islands very many of

---

[1] Charles sent an expedition under Sir John Narborough to establish intercourse with the natives in the vicinity of Magellan Strait in the hope of finding another Peru. See Walter's *Anson's Voyage of Discovery* (ed. 1765), p. 93 ; Weddell's *Voyage towards the South Pole* (ed. 1827), p. 208.

their sturdiest and most radical inhabitants, and others had perished on both sides in the battles of the Civil Wars. In the rank and file of the contending armies there were many persons whose death on the battlefield or in the hospital was a gain to the nation rather than a loss; but the officers of the opposing forces, and many of the privates in Cromwell's Ironsides and Rupert's Cavalier horse regiments, were men whom any nation could ill afford to spare. For a century after 1660 there was a constant remodeling of institutions in America to adapt them to the needs of growing communities living on the fringe of a wilderness, while the same period in England saw a positive retrogression politically, institutionally, and socially.

The second Charles [1] was an example of the reappearance in children and grandchildren, and even great-grandchildren, of the salient qualities of their forebears. Through his father, he was descended from the first James and from Mary, Queen of Scots; he possessed the cunning of one and the moral obliquity of both. Through his mother, he traced his descent back to Henry of Navarre, who had turned from Protestantism to Catholicism because, as he declared, Paris was worth a mass, and whose morals were a reproach to both his religions. In the Islip Chapel at Westminster Abbey may still be seen the waxen effigy that was borne in the funeral pageant of Charles the Second. The form is that of a strong athletic man to whom the fatigues of court and camp were a pleasure rather than a burden. The face is that of one who had known sorrow as well as joy, of one who gained his ends whether they were good or evil. Charles possessed ability and tenacity of purpose and effectually concealed these ad-

---

[1] Osmund Airy's *Charles II* gives an excellent idea of the "Merry Monarch" and his surroundings. It was originally published in Goupil's illustrated historical series, but has been reprinted in octavo form (London, 1904).

mirable qualities under a frivolous exterior. He surrounded himself with advisers and companions whose characters and careers too often matched his own; with them were intimately associated his brother, James, Duke of York and Albany, and his cousin, Prince Rupert. King, courtiers, and princes formed a well-marked group which is noteworthy for the stimulus that its members gave to colonial enterprises.

Of Charles's advisers the first in place and respectability was Edward Hyde, Earl of Clarendon, now lord chancellor. He had abandoned the cause of reform and had gone into exile because he could not sanction Puritan attacks on the Established Church. His daughter, Anne, married James, Duke of York, much against the wish of her father, who begged the king to put her into the Tower for her presumption. She became the mother of the Princesses Mary and Anne. The former married William of Orange and with him ascended the English throne at the "Glorious Revolution"; the latter was the Queen Anne of the eighteenth century; their cousin, Clarendon's grandson, Lord Cornbury, earned notoriety in American history by being the most disreputable governor that New York has ever known.

Other men of importance in court and colonization were George Monk, Duke of Albemarle, who had brought about the Restoration; Anthony Ashley Cooper, Lord Ashley, and later Earl of Shaftesbury, who secured the passage of the Habeas Corpus Act; Henry Bennet, Lord Arlington, who managed colonial affairs in the first years of the reign; John, Baron Berkeley of Stratton, brother of Sir William Berkeley, governor of Virginia; Sir George Carteret, the stubborn defender of the isle of Jersey; and William, Lord Craven, the companion of Charles's aunt,

Elizabeth, once Queen of Bohemia.　These six men, with Clarendon, Sir William Berkeley, and Sir John Colleton, a planter of Barbados, were the proprietors of Carolina and the Bahama Islands.　They, or members of their families, held stock in the Royal African Company and the Hudson Bay Company, and two of them were the proprietors of New Jersey.　With them in official life were associated Henry Jermyn, Earl of St. Albans, the favorite of the dowager queen, Henrietta Maria ; Admiral Penn, father of the founder of Pennsylvania; and Sir George Downing, who introduced the practice of making specific appropriations of public money, and played a prominent part in the passage of the Navigation Act of 1660, and in urging on the conquest of New Netherland.　The history of England and America in the next thirty years was determined by the necessities [1] of these men, rather than by their avarice and moral turpitude.

The government of the Restoration denied the validity of laws which had been made during the Interregnum, but they built upon the precedents of the Puritan period. During the Protectorate colonial affairs had been in the hands of the Lord Protector and the Council.　In 1660 Charles continued this arrangement by leaving the actual management of colonial affairs to a committee of the Privy Council.　At the same time he appointed two advisory councils, one a Council for Trade, the other a Council for Foreign Plantations.[2]　These councils included in their membership leading ministers, important members

---

[1] Bishop Burnet (*History of my Own Times*, ii, 111, ed. of 1900) states that on one occasion the king accepted money for espousing an evil cause, acknowledging that the cause was bad, but that he had good money for taking the part that he did. This is only one example of what undoubtedly was a constant practice.

[2] On the organization of the Council for Foreign Plantations see *New York Colonial Documents*, iii, pp. xiii–xix; the commissions are noted in *Calendars of State Papers, Colonial, 1574–1660*, p. 492. Many of the official papers are printed at length in *New York Colonial Documents*, iii, 30–37.

of the peerage, persons versed in mercantile affairs, and a few men of social prominence. These councils were entirely advisory : the former having to do with the trade and commerce of the home land; the latter having in charge matters relating to the government, trade, and commerce of the colonies. The actual direction of colonial affairs remained with the Privy Council and the ministers, especially one of the secretaries of state. The Council for Foreign Plantations soon showed a hopeless incapacity for the management of business and a proneness to seize upon power which it had no authority to exercise. The enemies of Massachusetts at once presented in person or in writing their complaints against the rulers of that colony.[1] The Councilors for Foreign Plantations listened to these plaints with sympathetic ears, and drew up a threatening letter in which they admonished the men of the Bay Colony to mend their ways, and that right speedily. When the epistle came before the Privy Council, the inadvisability of using such vigorous language to the New Englanders at that moment was made clear, and the letter was never sent. In another instance, the Councilors for Foreign Plantations, without any examination into the facts, advised the king to take into his own hands the government of the proprietary provinces. They even assumed power in ordering the Virginia government to send agents to England.[2] As a result of this precipitancy and lack of tact the Council for Foreign Plantations soon lost whatever of authority and respect it had at one time enjoyed. The actual representatives of the royal government in dealing with the colonies were successive .

[1] See *Calendars of State Papers, America and West Indies, 1661–1668,* Nos. 33, 45, 46, 48, 49, 50, 51, 53, 64, 75, 78, 80.

[2] *Calendars of State Papers, America and West Indies, 1661–1668,* p. 11.

secretaries of state, Sir Henry Bennet, Sir William Morrice, and Sir Joseph Williamson.

The policy of the regulation of trade for the benefit of English industry goes back to the days of Richard II. In the time of the Puritan Commonwealth, Parliament, following the lead of Sir Henry Vane, had passed a Navigation Ordinance,[1] systematizing the practice of preceding years. The Convention Parliament in 1660 reënacted this measure with some important modifications,[2] and their action was confirmed by the first regular Parliament which came together in the next year. The moving spirit in this new legislation was Sir George Downing,[3] " the second graduate " of Harvard College and nephew of John Winthrop, governor of Massachusetts. In the period of the Civil Wars, Downing returned to England and found favor with the leaders of the Puritan forces. In 1650 he was scout-master-general of Cromwell's army in Scotland and in 1657 was one of those who tried to place the crown upon the Protector's head. Downing had gone to France in 1655 to protest against the massacre of Protestants in Switzerland, and, two years later, had been appointed minister resident to the Netherlands. When the return of Charles to England became certain, he abandoned his Puritan friends and employers and offered his services to the king. Not only this, he delivered two regicides into the hands of the English government, one of them being his old leader, Colonel Okey.[4] For some years after

---

[1] See the present work, i, 490.

[2] 12 Charles II, Cap. 18. The provisions of the navigation acts are summarized in Note II on page 27.

[3] On Downing, see Sibley's *Harvard Graduates*, i, 28; Massachusetts Historical Society's *Collections*, Fifth Series, i, Preface; Hunt's *Merchants' Magazine*, iv, 407; and *Dictionary of National Biography*. See also *Colonial Records of North Carolina*, i, 267.

[4] The evidence on this point is contained in the *Brief Narrative of Colonel Okey, Col. Barkstead, and Miles Corbet, Esq.*; and in Ludlow's *Memoirs* (Bern, 1699), iii, 100, 237.

1660 Downing continued to act as English minister at the Hague, and also to represent the financial policy of the government in the House of Commons.[1] He took a leading part in the passage of the Navigation Act, introducing the most important amendment to it which required colonial staples to be landed in England.[2]

The prompt action of the new government and the Convention Parliament in pushing on the passage of the Navigation Act was due to the financial straits of the new rulers, and to the pressure which the mercantile and industrial classes put upon them.[3] In those days, merchants, land owners, and men of education were united in believing that the exploitation of colonists for the benefit of the people of the mother country was right and proper. Such a policy does not indicate that they were actuated by a spirit of despotism or disregard of colonial interests, but simply that they were living in the days when the existence of colonies could only be defended on business grounds. Moreover, the system that comes to be outlined in the navigation laws and acts of trade was a system of intra-imperial free trade and preference for English products, which reminds one of the policy of the United States two hundred and fifty years later.

[1] At one time, Sir George Downing was practically the minister of finance. In his house were held the meetings of the treasury board. His name was attached to the street upon which his house was situated, and "Downing Street," even to this day, is often used as synonymous with the English government, since there is situated the official residence of the head of the treasury who is usually prime minister.

[2] *Commons Journal*, viii, 120.

[3] The interest of English merchants in the carrying out of the navigation system and perhaps in its inception may be gathered from a petition which they presented to the Council in 1662, complaining of the violations of the law of 1660 which had been permitted by the Council and praying that any dispensations which had been issued might be recalled. See *Calendars of State Papers, America and West Indies, 1661–1668*, p. 10, and *Commons Journals*, viii, 521. An Order in Council, modifying the customs regulations as to certain classes of colonial shipping, is printed in Massachusetts Historical Society's *Collections*, Fourth Series, ii, 279.

The underlying idea of the navigation system was to make the empire self-supporting and to confine the carrying trade of English lands to ships built within the empire, owned by the people thereof, and navigated by officers and crews who were subjects of the English king.[1] Furthermore, trade in colonial products was to pass through England. This was provided in the last section of the Act of 1660, which required tobacco, sugar, and other colonial staples to " be laid on the shore " of England, Ireland, or of some plantation other than that of production, before they were shipped for an alien port. These commodities were enumerated in the act itself and are always referred to as the " enumerated goods."

By the Act of 1660 the colonists were permitted to import European goods directly from the place of production, and these might even be carried to the colonies by ships of the producing country. Ships belonging to aliens were by no means excluded from colonial ports ; but the presence of French and Dutch vessels in colonial waters defeated the purpose of the navigation system. It is true that these vessels could not legally carry colonial staples from the plantations, but they did it constantly and were thus able to earn freights both ways, carrying goods on as favorable terms as English ships. Permitting the colonists to import European goods directly from the producing countries also was found to defeat the purpose of the act, because such

---

[1] In the acts the phrase used always is " English," but this was inclusive and descriptive of lands and people within the limits of the English empire, as appears by an act passed in the 13, 14 Charles II, Cap. 11 (*Statutes of the Realm*, v, 394), which defines foreign-built ships as those " not built in any of His Majesties Dominions of Asia, Africa or America," and of course in England, and " His Majesties subjects of England, Ireland, and the Plantations " are to be accounted English. That this was the interpretation placed on the phrase for many years to come is shown by the constant demand in the petitions and arguments of the sugar planters in the middle of the eighteenth century that the ships and crews engaged in the sugar trade should be owned and navigated by residents of Great Britain and not by British subjects, no matter where they might dwell.

goods could be sold much more cheaply in the colonies than those which were imported through England. To do away with these "inconveniences," Parliament passed a supplemental act in 1663 for maintaining "a greater correspondence and kindness" between England and the colonies and keeping the latter "in a firmer dependence upon it [England] and rendering them yet more beneficial and advantageous unto it." This law provided that European goods should be carried to the colonies from England alone and in "English" ships, the only exceptions being salt for the New England fisheries, wine of Madeira and the Azores, and a few other unimportant commodities. The Act of 1660 was designed to make England the entrepôt for colonial staples; that of 1663 was intended to give to her merchants the profits of handling all European goods that were consumed in the plantations.[1]

The navigation system further sought to confine commercial operations within the empire to subjects of the English crown; the Scots, equally with the Dutch and the French, were excluded from participation in the profits of colonial trade. At the moment, Parliament felt well disposed toward Ireland, as is shown by the fact that the enumerated goods might be unladen on the shore of that island, and an Irishman, in common with English colonists, was accounted as English when reckoning up the crews of vessels navigated under the provisions of the act. In 1670[2] the privilege of the direct importation of enumerated commodities into Ireland was removed, but it required much legislation effectually to enforce this prohibition. As long as Scotland remained a separate country, none of the enu-

---

[1] This is well summed up by S. C. Bell in his *Colonial Administration of Great Britain*, 45-47.

[2] See 22, 23 Charles II, Cap. 26, § 6 (*Statutes of the Realm*, v, 748).

merated goods could be taken directly to it from the colonies,
no European goods could be carried from it to the colonies,
and no Scot could act as merchant or factor in the plantations.

Besides the Navigation Act, Parliament, in 1660, passed a
Tonnage and Poundage Act.[1] This authorized the collection
of duties on goods imported into or exported out of England
and the dominions thereunto belonging ; but it was never
enforced in the colonies. The law itself was not complicated, the details of taxation were set forth in a supplementary " Book of Rates." This was authenticated with
the signature of Sir Harbottle Grimston, Bart., Speaker of
the House of Commons, and was filed with the enrolled
copy of the act. The " Book of Rates " occupies twenty-two
double-columned pages in the great folio edition of the
" Statutes of the Realm." It covers almost every conceiv-
able object from " babies or puppets for children " to tobacco for men, and wearing apparel for both sexes and all
ages. Goods imported or exported by " Merchant Aliens "
or " Strangers "[2] were to pay increased duties sometimes
as high as fifty per cent extra. Tobacco was the most important colonial staple at that time, and the provisions of
the " Book of Rates " as to its importation are many and

[1] 12 Charles II, Cap. 4 (*Statutes of the Realm*, v, 181, 189, note at end of cate-gory of drugs, 190, 192, 198, 199, 202).

[2] The word " foreign " is not used here because in those days it implied distance in a geographical and not racial or gov-ernmental sense. An example of this is to be found in the title of the Council for Foreign Plantations whose business it was to advise the government as to the English colonies. The use of the word " foreign " in the fourth section of the Navigation Act of 1660 has given rise to some debate. At first sight it would seem to include Europe, but D. O

McGovney has pointed out that the judges and law officers of the crown declared it not to extend to Europe. McGovney's article is in *American His-torical Review*, ix, 727. His authority is Reeves's *History of the Law of Shipping and Navigation*. Reeves (pp. 159, 160, of the London edition) gives a decision of Chief Baron Hale in 1668. On the other hand, the ninth section of the act, threatening colonial governors with dis-missal if uncertified " foreign vessels " were found unloading in their ports, clearly includes European ships within its scope.

puzzling. Tobacco of alien production was taxed ten shillings per pound upon importation; that of English production one shilling, ninepence on importation, and one penny per pound nine months later. If the tobacco was exported within twelve months of importation, one half of the import duty and all of the penny tax were repaid.[1] The net result was that each pound of Virginia tobacco that was taken to foreign markets through England contributed tenpence halfpenny to the royal treasury in addition to the profits of merchants and warehousemen and the extra freight involved in a double voyage.

The loose wording of the navigation laws, and the inefficient machinery which was provided for carrying them out, made evasion so easy that they brought little revenue to the English treasury or profits to English merchants. The framers of these laws evidently expected them to be self-enforcing. A few customs officials were sent to America, but the government relied on the activity and goodwill of colonial governors to carry out its policy. No definite instructions were sent to them, and few governors, if any, had an adequate conception of what was expected of them. None of them exerted themselves to enforce the navigation acts. In New England, they could not have done so had they wished. In Virginia, Sir William Berkeley, the governor, was himself a tobacco planter, and naturally had no desire to enforce laws taxing his staple crop. Instead, he went to England and tried, unsuccessfully, to secure a modification of the acts.[2]

In 1672 Parliament passed another navigation act[3] to

---

[1] 12 Charles II, Cap. 4 (*Statutes of the Realm*, v, 203).

[2] *Virginia Magazine of History*, i, 141. Giles Bland, son of a London merchant of the same name, came out to Virginia as collector of customs and was well received until the purpose of his visit was understood. *Calendars of State Papers, America and West Indies, 1675-1676*, p. 385.

[3] 25 Charles II, Cap. 7 (*Statutes of the Realm*, v, 792).

remedy the defects of the law of 1660 as to the enumerated commodities, and to secure a greater share of the revenue from the tobacco trade for England. It was now provided that whenever a ship captain loaded any tobacco, sugar, or other enumerated commodity in the colony of its production, he must give bonds to land it in England, or else pay a duty of one penny on every pound of tobacco, and corresponding duties on other enumerated goods in the colony where they were produced. This act closed the legislation as to navigation and trade in the time of Charles II. The system brought some revenue to the royal coffers, but did not directly benefit the courtiers : their enrichment was expected from colonizing enterprises, the greatest of which was the founding of Carolina.

Sir John Colleton, an Englishman, had acquired lands and riches in Barbados. Returning home, he called Lord Ashley's attention to the probability of profit to be made from the exploitation of the resources of the country between English Virginia and Spanish Florida. Ashley interested Albemarle, Clarendon, Berkeley, Carteret, and Craven in the scheme, and together they secured a grant of Carolina[1] from the king in the early spring of 1663. The limits of the new colony were coextensive with those of the Carolana of 1629,[2] extending from the thirty-first to the thirty-sixth parallel, and from the Atlantic to the Pacific. There had been settlements in this region before 1663, possibly as early as 1650.[3] Especially the Cape

[1] The Carolina Charter of 1663 is in *Colonial Records of North Carolina*, i, 20 ; Cooper's *Statutes of South Carolina*, i, 22] ; *Charters and Constitutions*, ii, 1382.

[2] The Carolana Patent is printed at length in *Colonial Records of North Carolina*, i, 5–13. Sir Robert Heath, the first grantee, had intended to send a colony of French Protestants from Ro-

chelle, but this had not been done and Charles II declared the patent forfeited on the ground that it had not been used. See *Calendars of State Papers, America and West Indies, 1574–1660*, pp. 109–112 and South Carolina Historical Society's *Collections*, v, 8 (" Shaftesbury Papers ").

[3] See Saunders's " Introduction " to the first volume of the *Colonial Records of North Carolina*.

Fear River had attracted the attention of prospecting settlers, some of whom had come from England, others from New England. They had experimented with the soil and the Indians in the vicinity, but neither proving congenial, had abandoned their enterprises before 1663. The first permanent English settlers in Carolina came from Virginia, and cleared lands on the Chowan River and its neighborhood. These were living there in 1663, but it was not perfectly clear whether they were within the limits which the king had assigned to the grantees of Carolina. In 1665, therefore, they procured from him a new charter [1] extending their lands on the north to thirty-six degrees thirty minutes, which would clearly include the Chowan settlements within their province. They also secured an extension on the south to the twenty-ninth parallel. This was done possibly with a view to future negotiations with Spain. Five years later, in 1670,[2] England and Spain came to an agreement, by which each confirmed the other in its possessions in the New World; but no statement was made in the treaty as to the boundary between Carolina and Florida. Even this enormous extent of territory did not satisfy the land hunger of the Carolina proprietors. They asked the king for the Bahama Islands, that they might guard the passage from Barbados to their province, and he acceded to their request.[3]

The Carolina patents conferred upon the proprietors rights of jurisdiction similar to those which had been given to Lord Baltimore by the first Charles; but the fact that in Maryland there was one proprietor and in Carolina eight, made the execution of these powers very dissimilar.

---

[1] *Charters and Constitutions*, ii, 1390; *Colonial Records of North Carolina*, i, 102; Cooper's *Statutes of South Carolina*, i, 31.

[2] Chalmers's *Treaties*, ii, 37.
[3] *Calendars of State Papers, America and West Indies, 1669–1674*, p. 122.

The single proprietor of Maryland exercised direct personal control; the business of Carolina could be transacted only after a good deal of conference. At first the Carolina proprietors formed a reasonably homogeneous body, but later their heterogeneity became most marked.

At the outset Clarendon was the principal man among the Carolina proprietors. Devotion to the Established Church was his leading characteristic, so much so, indeed, that the religious laws of the first years of Charles's reign are often referred to as the "Clarendon Code."[1] The first Carolina charter, however, authorized the proprietors to grant indulgences and dispensations to those of their colonists who could not conform to the liturgy of the Church of England with such limitations and restrictions as they might think fit and reasonable on condition that such persons declare their obedience to the king and to the laws of the province and do not disturb the peace thereof, or scandalize the established religion. Two years later, in the Charter of 1665, the king went farther and himself granted liberty of conscience in matters of religious concernment to all colonists of Carolina who should live peaceably and commanded that all such were to enjoy their judgments and consciences without being called in question. These provisions of the Carolina charters reflect the belief of the proprietors that available settlers for their broad domains were not in general faithful members of the Church; irreligion, indeed, appears to be a marked characteristic of the early Carolinians.

[1] The Act of Uniformity (14 Charles II, Cap. 4) established the Book of Common Prayer as the only legal service book; the Conventicle Act (16 Charles II, Cap. 4) defined a conventicle as a religious meeting not held according to the rites of the Established Church and provided penalties for being present at such a meeting; the Five Mile Act (17 Charles II, Cap. 2) forbade dissenting clergymen from living within five miles of any town in which they had exercised their holy function.

The first settlers on the Chowan and other affluents of Albemarle Sound came from Virginia in search of " fertile bottom lands." [1]   William Edmundson, a Quaker missionary, visited the colony in 1671. He reported that there was only one Quaker family there, — and Methodists, Presbyterians, and Baptists were equally scarce in those days. The presence of the settlers in northernmost Carolina induced the proprietors to establish a government for that part of their province. They placed the matter in the hands of Governor Berkeley of Virginia, who sent William Drummond to rule over these settlements [2] and to grant lands on a quit-rent tenure.

The northern Carolinians soon showed themselves to be indisposed to any kind of government or to paying taxes or dues of any nature. Isolated planters living in a wilderness, they were self-assertive and constantly rebelled against those who were sent out from England to govern them and quite as readily fought among themselves over question of land or other property. They were especially dissatisfied with the ever changing policy of the proprietors as to granting land. In 1668, to quiet them, if possible, these authorized the then governor of Albemarle, [3] as the northern settlements were called, to grant lands on the same terms and conditions that prevailed in Virginia. The instrument containing this authorization, the colonists always referred to as the " Great Deed of Grant," and

---

[1] On this general subject, see Saunders's " Introduction " to the *Colonial Records of North Carolina*, i, p. xxi, and extracts from Edmundson's and Fox's journals in *ibid.*, 215, 217. In 1708 the Quakers formed at least one tenth of the total population, *ibid.*, i, pp. xix, 686. Saunders asserts that the Quakers bore arms in Cary's Rebellion, *ibid.*, i, p. xxix. An account of religious conditions from an Episcopalian standpoint is in *ibid.*, i, 708.

[2] *Calendars of State Papers, America and West Indies, 1661–1668*, pp. 159, 160.

[3] *Colonial Records of North Carolina*, i, 175; the governor of Albemarle was generally called governor or deputy-governor of North Carolina, *ibid.*, i, p. xxiv.

promised liberty of conscience. In 1667 Clarendon was impeached, among other things he was charged with having introduced an arbitrary form of government into the plantations and imprisoned those who petitioned the King and Council for relief.[1] This charge refers to the conduct of affairs in Barbados and not to Clarendon's connection with Carolina, and was never proved. For reasons not at all connected with the colonies, Clarendon was induced to flee from England and passed the rest of his life in exile. From this time Lord Ashley becomes the leading man among the Carolina grantees.

Lord Ashley began political life as an adherent of Charles I, and deserted his royal master because he deemed his policy destructive of religion. Twelve years later, as an exponent of democratic principles, he opposed Cromwell, and was one of those who powerfully aided General Monk to bring about the restoration of the old monarchy. For a dozen years or so, Ashley, or Shaftesbury,[2] to give him his later title, was in favor with the second Charles; he then deserted him to head the radical forces in favor of excluding the Duke of York from the throne. Shaftesbury was essentially an experimentalist in government, and was greatly aided in putting his theories into writing by John Locke,[3] his confidential secretary, who served as clerk to the Carolina proprietors. Locke

[1] Howell's *State Trials*, vi, 332; Clarendon's statement is in *ibid.*, vi, 422; see also *Life of Clarendon by Himself* (ed. 1827), iii, 407.

[2] H. D. Traill has stated the most important facts of Shaftesbury's career in his volume in the series of "English Worthies." Of the longer books, W. D. Christie's *Life of Shaftesbury* is by far the best.

[3] See H. R. Fox Bourne's *Life of John Locke*, i, 239. The editor of the "Shaftesbury Papers" (South Carolina Historical Society's *Collections*, v, 117) speaks of the Constitutions as "conceived by Shaftesbury and drawn by Locke," but gives no authority for the surmise. In recognition of his services to the Carolina proprietors, Locke was appointed a landgrave with a grant of forty-eight thousand acres in the province; see *Calendars of State Papers, America and West Indies, 1669–1674*, p. 312. At the same time James Carteret was likewise made a landgrave with the same amount of land.

regarded as a species of Magna Charta, but Secr
Popple[1] of the Board of Trade held that it was a
porary letter of attorney which was revokable at w

The settlements farther south on the Cape Fear River
the shores of Charleston Harbor were connected with
fortunes of Sir John Colleton, Sir John Yeamans, a
other planters of the island of Barbados where disconte
was rife, because the government of the Restoration ha
questioned the titles to the lands of the planters there
Many of these estates were held by squatter right only
and grantees from the king were disposed to push their
advantages. Many Barbadian settlers wished to leave that
island and try their fortunes elsewhere. In 1665 and 1666
two expeditions, led by Sir John Yeamans and Captain
Robert Sandford, sailed for the Carolina coast, explored
it more or less carefully, made a trial of its possibilities,
and returned to older settled colonies. In 1667 there were
no settlers in Carolina south of Albemarle Sound.[2]

The political history of Carolina begins with the pro-
mulgation by the proprietors of certain " Declarations and
Proposals "[3] that were issued in 1663 and formed the first
organic law of the province. In this document the proprietors declared that laws should be made by two deputies to be chosen by the freeholders out of every parish.
These laws were to go into force at once and so remain
until repealed in England — which might be done at any
time. Liberal quantities of land were offered to those
who should emigrate within five years and all settlers were

---

[1] *Ibid.*, iii, 354.

[2] On the Cape Fear settlements, see *Colonial Records of North Carolina*, i, Introduction, pp. x, 148–151, 157–159, 177–208. The documents printed in these pages show conclusively that the colony was abandoned in 1667 and that the statement to the contrary by Chalmers and other early writers was a mistake.

[3] *Colonial Records of North Carolina*, i, 43. The editor of these records states that the so-called " Constitution of 1667 " was merely a transcript of this document.

was now thirty-six years of age, and up to this time had not exhibited any of those great qualities which afterward made him famous as a philosopher, writer on political theory, and economist. Shaftesbury and Locke formulated a new organic law for Carolina, which possessed an archaic character, and an extravagance of language and provision not to be found in any other document of the kind that was intended to be put into actual, everyday practice. They conceived a government for feeble plantations in an American wilderness, which might possibly have been appropriate to European society in the time of Philip Augustus. The name of this instrument was " The Fundamental Constitutions of Carolina." [1] According to its provisions, the senior proprietor was to hold the office of Lord Palatine, the others being gratified with the titles of Admiral, Chamberlain, Chancellor, Constable, Chief Justice, High Steward, and Treasurer. The province was to be divided into counties, seigniories, baronies, and precincts — each of the last-named divisions containing six colonies. Each seigniory, barony, and colony contained twelve thousand acres of land; the seigniories were reserved for the eight proprietors; the baronies for the proposed colonial nobility; the colonies for the commonalty. The charter provided for the granting of titles of nobility if such titles were not like those used in England. The Carolina nobility were, therefore, to bear German or American designations as landgrave and cazique; of the first there were to be as

[1] The "Fundamental Constitutions" as they were published in 1669 are printed in *Colonial Records of North Carolina*, i, 187; Cooper's *Statutes of South Carolina*, i, 43; and *Charters and Constitutions*, ii, 1397. The "First Set of the Constitutions," with the interlineations and corrections of the original, is printed in the *Forty-third Report of the Deputy Keeper of the Public Records* (1872), Appendix, 258, and in South Carolina Historical Society's *Collections*, v, 93–117. The colonial view of the "Constitutions" in 1688 is noted in a "Representation of the People of Carolina" in *Calendars of State Papers, America and West Indies, 1685–1688*, p. 623.

many as there were counties, and of caziques, twice as many. Both landgraves and caziques were members of the parliament of the province.

A portentous scheme of government was elaborated in the Constitutions, including eight supreme courts, one grand council, various colleges, and a parliament. The last comprised the proprietors, or their deputies, the landgraves and caziques, and one freeholder out of every precinct to be chosen by the freeholders of the said precinct, and to have not less than five hundred acres of freehold within the precinct. The members of parliament were to sit in one house, after the Scottish manner, each having one vote. Bills were to be prepared by the grand council, the members of parliament merely expressing their assent or dissent, as was the case in Penn's later Frame of Government. All laws came to an end in one hundred years without being repealed. There was to be no manner of comment or exposition on any part of the Fundamental Constitutions or of the laws of the province, and it should be accounted a base and vile thing to plead in court for money or reward. Transfers of land must be registered, and so, also, births, marriages, and deaths. No atheist could acquire lands or inhabit in Carolina. The Church of England was recognized as the Established Church of the province ; but persons of other faiths might gather themselves into other churches or professions, and no person above the age of seventeen years should have any benefit or protection of the law who was not a member of some church or religious profession. These are some of the leading provisions of this famous instrument; but it is not necessary to analyze it further, as it never had the force of law within the province.

In 1669 the proprietors sent an expedition to Carolina

from England by way of Barbados. The securing of the charters and the expenses of organization cost about six hundred pounds, mainly expended in fees.[1] Now, five of the proprietors, not including Clarendon or the two Berkeleys, contributed two thousand six hundred and forty-five pounds to fit out a fleet. In addition, they spent about fifteen hundred pounds more in sending another vessel with supplies to the colonies, but the total expenditure of the proprietors on the province did not exceed six thousand pounds.[2] Three vessels were bought and renamed *Carolina*, *Albemarle*, and *Port Royal*. They sailed from the Thames with more than one hundred colonists, among whom were fifteen women, one of them bearing the historic name of Margaret Tudor. Contrary winds detained the vessels in the Downs so long that the emigrants were placed on short rations while yet within one hundred miles of the docks of London. They had sailed with fifteen tons of beer and thirty gallons of brandy on board, but this long delay forced them to drink water before they lost sight of the British Isles.[3] The fleet called at Kinsale in Ireland to take on board seventy Irish servants. Only ten could be obtained, and some of the passengers, who had come from England, seized the opportunity to desert. The vessels followed the extreme southern route across the Atlantic, arriving at Barbados in October. There the *Albemarle* was wrecked in a storm, but another vessel was procured and the fleet sailed north-

[1] *Calendars of State Papers, America and West Indies, 1661–1668,* p. 379.

[2] *Ibid., 1669–1674,* p. 19; "Shaftesbury Papers" in South Carolina Historical Society's *Collections,* v, 137–152.

[3] South Carolina Historical Society's *Collections,* v, 137. The original papers are printed in this volume from the "Shaftesbury Papers." The best secondary account is Mayor Courtenay's "Address on the Centennial of the Incorporation of Charleston" in the *Year-Book* for 1883, which is also printed separately. McCrady's account is largely based on this.

ward. Sir John Yeamans also joined the expedition at that point with a few recruits, and at once assumed chief command in the place of Joseph West, who had occupied that office during the voyage. Another storm cast the *Port Royal* ashore on one of the Bahamas. Most of her passengers were saved, but the *Carolina* and the Barbadian sloop were driven far out of their course to Bermuda. Yeamans abandoned the ill-fated expedition at this place, assigning the command to a Bermudian planter, William Sayle,[1] who had already explored the coasts of Carolina. Procuring a sloop at Bermuda, the expedition again headed for Carolina and reached the coast in the vicinity of the Sea Islands, north of the Savannah River (March, 1670). The sea-worn adventurers had intended to settle near the modern Port Royal; but the Indians told them of a better site farther north and they made one more voyage to Charleston Harbor, where they landed in April, 1670. The selection of this location was fortunate, because the peninsula between the Ashley and Cooper rivers was the destined center of commerce of the region south of the Chesapeake Bay throughout the colonial period. It also had the advantage of being farther from the Spanish settlements and, therefore, safer.[2] Charleston Harbor is defended from the sea by dangerous sand bars, but the passage of these was comparatively easy for the small vessels of the early day. The land all about was low and in places sandy, but in general the soil was rich and the climate at first was free from malaria.

The first settlement was made on the southern side of Ashley River at Albemarle Point, which could be easily

[1] South Carolina Historical Society's *Collections*, v, 117.

[2] In 1670 the Spaniards captured a party of immigrants bound to Carolina, *Colonial Records of North Carolina*, i, 207.

defended from Indian attacks. Food was procured from
Virginia and Barbados and, although the colonists were
often on short allowance, there was no suffering like that
which is associated with the earlier settlements in Virginia
and New England. Other immigrants joined the first
comers and in 1672 Lord Ashley estimated that three hundred and ninety-nine persons, including sixty-two children,
had reached Charleston Harbor; but of these forty-eight
were dead and sixteen were "absent."[1] The latest historian of South Carolina, General Edward McCrady, declines
to accept the evidence of a contemporary that the first
colonists were "persons of the most desperate fortunes,"
but he says, nevertheless, that they were "adventurers"
who had come to the New World to seek riches they
could not achieve at home. They were certainly much
given to disputation and to writing home of each other's
failings. Probably, the hardships of the voyage, the
unusual climate, and the difficulties of life in the new
plantation brought out the worst qualities of their natures.
Within three years of the settlement on Albemarle Point,
some of the colonists had moved across the Ashley River
to the tongue of land between that stream and the Cooper.
In 1680 the formal settlement of Charleston was begun.[2]
From this time southern Carolina constantly grew, but the
rate of progress was very slow.

The proprietors sent out no more expeditions after the
early years, but colonists were constantly arriving. Among
these was a party of French Protestants or Huguenots, who
came in 1680. The first band was only forty-five in number, but they were later joined by many others of their
faith. They formed an interesting group in Charleston and

[1] *Charleston Year-Book*, 1883, p. 379.
[2] The name was spelled Charles Towne or Charlestown throughout the colonial period.

on the Santee River, and were looked upon with great favor by the rulers of the province. They had come over to introduce the production of silk, olives, and wine, but they soon gave over that enterprise. In 1683 a band of Scots founded Stewarts Town in the vicinity of Port Royal; but this settlement was viewed with jealousy by the Charleston people because it enjoyed a separate government. In 1686 the Spaniards attacked the Scots, killed some of them, and carried others away into captivity, treating them with great cruelty. The survivors found refuge in the town on the bank of the Cooper River.

The Fundamental Constitutions were declared to be unalterable and irrevocable, but the proprietors revised them at least twice and each time ordered the colonists to obey them. The Carolina charters authorized the proprietors to legislate with the consent of the freemen of the province; but as the Constitutions were never consented to by a legislative body in the colony, they cannot be regarded as having ever been of binding force except as to those settlers who had actually subscribed to them. The proprietors were constantly regulating the elections to the assemblies and changing the constitution of that body. At one time they proposed to have one parliament for all Carolina. Almost no attention was paid to these changing requirements by the colonists in Carolina, north or south. They assembled and enacted laws to suit themselves, but the proprietors on their part used their veto power with such goodwill that at one time there was not a local law of southern Carolina in force in that province.[1]

In 1700 the population of Carolina as a whole was

---

[1] These disputations are related with abundant detail by McCrady in his *South Carolina under the Proprietary Government* and by Saunders in his Introduction to the first volume of the *Colonial Records of North Carolina*.

about eight thousand of whom not far from five thousand
lived in the southern part. Among these were a few
negro slaves. In the northern part of the province there
were even fewer slaves, the people there living on farms
or small plantations; in the southern colony, settlement
was concentrated at Charleston and its neighborhood.
Clarendon and Shaftesbury and their associates expended
money and thought in the Carolina enterprise for which
they never received any adequate return, pecuniary or
otherwise. (This part of the colonial policy of the
Restoration was a failure from the standpoint of king
and courtier. In the larger view it was completely successful since it resulted in the founding of two of the
original thirteen states. A further step in the same policy
led to the conquest of New Netherland and the establishment of three more of the "original thirteen,"—Delaware,
New Jersey, and New York.

NOTES

I. General Bibliography. — There is no good secondary work on the period between 1660 and 1760. The publication of the English *Calendars*[1] has reached the end of the seventeenth century only, at the present time (1908); but the collections of documents which have been published by the states of New York and North Carolina in some measure fill this gap. The *Calendars* themselves hardly meet the need of the student, especially since the later volumes are not edited by Mr. Sainsbury. Moreover, no calendar can long satisfy the legitimate desires of delvers into American history for the "Journal of the Lords of Trade" in full, so far at least as it relates to the Continental Colonies, with excerpts from the "Papers." The Pennsylvania Historical Society has a transcript of these records which are referred to in the present volume as "Philadelphia Transcripts."

George Chalmers used the official papers in the preparation of his *Annals*,[2] *Introduction*,[3] and *Opinions*.[4] The *Introduction* is written in a dogmatic style and reflects the author's theory of the inherent wickedness of colonists; but one is impressed with the accuracy of his reading of the records when the same sentence comes under the eye in the "Journals" and "Papers" of the Board of Trade. Chalmers also made a *Collection of Treaties between Great Britain and other Powers*[5] which is serviceable to the student of colonial history.

George Bancroft's volumes,[6] covering this period, are not very

[1] *Calendars of State Papers, Colonial Series, America and West Indies, Preserved in the Public Record Office.*

[2] George Chalmers, *Political Annals of the Present United Colonies from their Settlement to the Peace of 1763* (London, 1780). This volume brings the story down to the Revolution of 1688–89. Three supplementary chapters dealing with the period of William's reign were found among Chalmers's papers after his death and were printed by the New York Historical Society in its *Collections* for 1868, 1–176.

[3] George Chalmers, *An Introduction to the History of the Revolt of the American Colonies.* This was printed in 1782 and suppressed; and was reprinted sixty years later under the editorship of Jared Sparks and J. L. Sibley with a continua-

tion from a manuscript that had come into Mr. Sparks's hands. Two volumes, often bound in one (Boston, 1845).

[4] George Chalmers, *Opinions of Eminent Lawyers on various points of English Jurisprudence chiefly concerning the Colonies, Fisheries, and Commerce . . . from the originals in the Board of Trade.* 2 vols. (London, 1814); reprinted in 1 vol. (Burlington, Vt., 1858).

[5] 2 vols. (London, 1790).

[6] George Bancroft's *History of the United States* (vols. ii–iv of the original edition, Boston). The later editions of this work were not revised after a new study of the sources and are not so useful to the student as the earlier editions.

detailed. They are written from the sources, but the author was so prejudiced in favor of theoretical democracy that his comments upon the facts must be received with caution. He was a thorough and conscientious seeker and used in manuscript much material that has since been printed, and also a good deal of matter that has not yet appeared in book form. It is a good plan to read Chalmers and Bancroft on the same subjects, as one corrects the other. The "Critical Essays" in Winsor's *Narrative and Critical History of America* are mines of information, but it is not always easy to get at particular points, owing to limited indexes. The narrative portions of this part of the work are not so well done as those in the earlier and later volumes, and some of them are now rather out of date. Professor C. M. Andrews's volume on *Colonial Self-Government* and Professor Evarts B. Greene's on *Colonial Commonwealths* in the "American Nation Series" are based on studies of the sources, and Professor Andrews, especially, has used manuscript material to advantage.

II. Navigation Laws. — The Navigation Act of 1660 stands on the statute book as 12 Charles II, Chapter 18.[1] Sections 1 and 3 provide that no goods shall be imported into or exported out of any English plantations in Asia, Africa, or America, except in vessels belonging to the people of England, Ireland, Wales, Berwick-upon-Tweed, or of the English plantations whereof the master and three fourths of the mariners shall be English; and that no goods of the growth, production, or manufacture of any part of Asia, Africa, or America shall be imported into England, Ireland, Wales, the Channel Islands, or Berwick-upon-Tweed except in vessels belonging to the people of the place of shipment or belonging to English subjects. Section 4 provides that no foreign goods which are to be brought into the last-mentioned places in English vessels shall be shipped from any other port than that of their production or manufacture except that they might be brought from those ports where the particular goods are ordinarily first shipped for transportation. Section 8 provides that no goods of the production or manufacture of Russia or Turkey, no "masts, timber, or board, no foreign salt, pitch, tar, rosin, hemp or flax, raisins, figs, prunes, olive oils, no sort of corn or grain, sugar, potashes, wines, vinegar, or spirits called aqua-vitæ or brandy wine" shall be brought into England except in ships that belong to the people thereof. All such goods otherwise imported shall be

---

[1] *Statutes of the Realm*, v, 246.

regarded as "alien goods" and pay higher duties accordingly. Section 18 provides that sugar, tobacco, cotton wool, indigo, fustick, or other dyeing wood of the production or manufacture of any English plantation must be laid on the shore of some other English plantation or of England, Ireland, Wales, or the town of Berwick-upon-Tweed. Section 2 of the same act provides that no alien or person born without the allegiance of the king and not naturalized or given the rights of a free denizen could trade in the plantations.

The Act for Preventing Frauds and Regulating Abuses in His Majesty's Customs was enacted in 1662 and is cited as 14 Charles II, Chapter 11.[1] The fifth section provides that no foreign-built ship "(that is to say) not built in any of His Majesties dominions of Asia, Africa, or America" except some expressly named as being privileged, shall enjoy the advantages of ships belonging to England but shall be deemed "Alien's Ships." Furthermore, the requirement that the master and three fourths of the mariners of English ships shall be likewise English is to be interpreted as including "His Majesties subjects of England, Ireland, and his plantations."

In 1663 the Act of 15 Charles II, Chapter 7,[2] provided that no European goods should be brought into the plantations but what shall be shipped in England, Wales, or Berwick-upon-Tweed in English built ships navigated according to law and shall be carried directly thence to the plantations and from no other place or places whatsoever.

The Act of 1672[3] which is cited as 25 Charles II, Chapter 7, provided that the "enumerated goods" must be brought to England, Wales, or Berwick-upon-Tweed, or that certain imposts must be paid in the colony producing the goods before the shipping thereof. Among these duties was one of five shillings on every hundred weight of white sugar, one shilling sixpence on every hundred weight of brown sugar, and one penny per pound on tobacco.

Extracts and abstracts of these laws are in William MacDonald's *Select Charters and Other Documents illustrative of American History, 1606–1775,* and *American History Leaflets, No. 19.* The legislative

---

[1] *Statutes of the Realm*, v, 394.
[2] *Statutes of the Realm*, v, 449.
[3] *Statutes of the Realm*, v, 792. Besides these acts, there are numerous

entries in the *Commons Journals* as to "improving" the navigation laws; as, for instance, in vol. ix, pp. 108, 158.

history of the acts can be unraveled in the "Journals" of the House of Lords and House of Commons. The colonial system is described in G. L. Beer's "Commercial Policy of England toward the American Colonies" in *Columbia University Studies*, ii, pt. ii, and Channing's "Navigation Laws" in American Antiquarian Society's *Proceedings* for 1889–1890, pp. 165 and fol. The subject is very briefly treated in the general works on English commerce by Cunningham, Lindsay, and Leone Levi.

III. Bibliography of Carolina. — Edward McCrady's *History of South Carolina*, in three volumes, supplants all earlier works. It is written from the point of view of a Charleston lawyer and a soldier in the Confederate armies, and a warden of St. Philip's Church, Charleston; but this does not in any way lessen the value of the work to the student, although the author's religious and local sympathies need to be understood that they may be guarded against. The first volume, dealing with the proprietary period, was printed before the publication of the "Shaftesbury Papers." In a note to p. 128, General McCrady states that his "account of the voyage of the colonists has been collated principally from the Centennial Address of Major W. A. Courtenay, Year Book City of Charleston, 1883, and by him compiled from MS. Shaftesbury Papers of the So. Ca. Hist. Society, now about to be published." Were it not for this statement, one would hesitate to suggest that the latest historian of South Carolina had not used these manuscripts.

Mrs. St. Julien Ravenel's *Charleston, the Place and the People*, also written by a loyal South Carolinian, is virtually a history of the colony in the early years. It is in some respects the best book on the subject and contains excellent illustrations. Of the older books, William J. Rivers's *Sketch of the History of South Carolina* and *A Chapter in the Early History of South Carolina* are the most satisfactory. The running title of both publications is "Early History of South Carolina," and they are often so cited. William A. Courtenay, for years mayor of Charleston, was deeply interested in historical research and printed much valuable material in the *Year Books* of that city. His "Centennial Address"[1] is a sketch of the early history of the colony and has much useful information not easily attainable elsewhere. It also contains a facsimile of an old map showing the early settlements. W. A. Schaper's "Section-

---

[1] *Charleston Year Book for 1883;* also issued separately.

alism and Representation in South Carolina" in the American Historical Association's *Reports* (1900, i, 237) deals mainly with the later period, but has some interesting information on the earlier time.

There is no good secondary book describing the pre-Revolutionary history of North Carolina. William L. Saunders's "Prefatory Notes" to the successive volumes of the *Colonial Records* are admirable bits of historical work ; they might well be printed separately in one volume. D. H. Hill's *Young People's History of North Carolina* (Charlotte, N.C., 1907) is designed for children, but in the absence of a more formal work may well be used by older persons, and Collier Cobb's brief sketch in the North Carolina State Normal School's *Publications*, entitled "The Schoolteacher" (Winston, N.C.), is also the result of recent study. The titles of older books are given in Winsor's *America*.

The principal collection of documents relating to the history of Carolina is the *Colonial Records of North Carolina*. The first ten volumes covering the period to 1776 were edited by William L. Saunders, secretary of state of North Carolina. Volumes xi–xxvi were edited by Walter Clark, chief justice of the state supreme court. These volumes cover the period 1776–90 and bear the title *State Records of North Carolina*. The two series form one publication and will eventually have an index in a separate volume. The papers are arranged chronologically, but documents which were found after the printing of a volume are given in appendices to later volumes, and volume xi includes papers of the years 1730–76, which were obtained after the publication of the first ten volumes. For South Carolina, there is no similar work, but the fifth volume of the *Collections* of the state historical society contains the "Shaftesbury Papers" relating to that province *in extenso*. Many of these are also printed in the *Colonial Records of North Carolina*, and most of them and many other documents are noted in the *Calendars of State Papers*. The appendices to Rivers' books contain many papers of value, and the *South Carolina Historical Magazine*, which was begun in 1900, has also some interesting matter.

CHAPTER II

THE alien colony of New Netherland, situated between New England and the tobacco plantations on Chesapeake Bay, was distinctly disadvantageous to the growth of English interests on the American continent. The men about the restored monarch also perceived that its acquisition by England would provide another prosperous English colony to yield new revenue for the royal family and indirectly for themselves, and also facilitate the carrying out of the reorganized colonial system.

There were abundant reasons for ill-feeling and war between the English and the Dutch, for they were commercial rivals in the Indies and on the African coast. James, Duke of York, the king's brother and heir-presumptive to the English throne, was Lord High Admiral of England, and was the nominal head of an association of merchants which sought to monopolize the trade of the west coast of Africa, and ultimately formed the Royal African Company. English and Dutch traders did not get on well together. The English sufferers had powerful advocates at court, but Sir George Downing's strongest remonstrances to the Dutch authorities at the Hague brought no redress.[1] In defiance of the navigation acts, Dutch shipmasters persisted in carrying tobacco from the Chesapeake

---

[1] The course of this controversy can be followed in the *New York Colonial Documents*, vol. iii ("Holland Documents") and vol. iv ("London Documents"), using the tables of contents and the "General Index" to the first ten volumes.

31

plantations to European ports, either directly or by way of New Amsterdam, at an annual loss to the English exchequer of ten thousand pounds.[1] English shipowners complained of this clandestine trade and asked the government to put an end to it.   Goods were also brought to the Dutch colony from Asia, Africa, and other parts of America, and thence distributed by coasting vessels to the English plantations.

In the early days of New Netherland, the English representative at the Hague had called the attention of the Dutch government to the fact that the traders and settlers on the banks of the Hudson River were intruders on English territory. The Pilgrims and the Massachusetts authorities had also warned the Dutch that they were trespassing on land claimed by England.[2] In 1654 Cromwell had sent an expedition across the Atlantic to conquer the Dutch colonists, but peace in Europe had been declared in time to divert this force to another direction.[3] The river valleys occupied by the Dutch in America had been included within the limits of the first Virginia charter, and also within the boundaries of New England, as set forth in the patent of 1620. Among other Englishmen who claimed lands under grants from the Council for New England within the Dutch colony was William Alexander, Earl of Stirling.[4] His heirs now conveyed their claims to the king. Moreover, the English settlers on Long Island also complained to Charles of "their cruel and rapacious neighbors," the Dutch,[5] and asked for relief.   All these things gave point to a report of the

[1] *Calendars of State Papers, America and West Indies, 1661–1668,* p. 172; there is much other material on the general subject of Dutch competition which can easily be reached through the index.

[2] As to the Dutch title, see Fowler's "Historical Introduction" to the Grolier Club's reprint of Bradford's *Laws and Acts of New York,* pp. ii–xvi.

[3] See the present work, i, 483.

[4] *New York Colonial Documents,* iii, 42.

[5] Scott to Williamson in *Calendars of State Papers, America and West Indies, 1661–1668,* p. 173.

defenseless condition of New Netherland, which was drawn
up by Berkeley, Carteret, and Sir William Coventry.[1] It
is doubtful if the royal brothers needed much urging: at
all events, they determined to undertake the conquest.

On March 12, 1664, Charles, by letters patent under the
great seal, granted to his brother James, his heirs and
assigns, "all that part of the Main Land of New England"
extending from the St. Croix River westward to Pemaquid and the Kennebec and northward to the River of
Canada, together with Long Island and other islands on
the southern New England coast and lands between the
Connecticut River and the Delaware. In the warrant
directing the law officers of the crown to prepare a patent,
the last block of land extended from the west side of the
Hudson to the east side of the Delaware; why the limits
were enlarged eastwardly to the Connecticut is not
known.[2] The king further gave the Duke of York "absolute power and authority to correct, punish, pardon, govern and rule" all English subjects living within these limits according to "such laws, orders, ordinances, directions,
and instruments as by our said dearest brother or his assigns
shall be established . . . in all causes and matters, . . . so
always as the said statutes, ordinances, and proceedings be
not contrary to but as near as conveniently may be agreeable
to the laws, statutes, and government of this our realm of
England."[3] The right of appeal to the king touching any
judgment to be there made or given was expressly reserved.

[1] *Ibid.*, p. 183.

[2] *Magazine of American History*, viii,
Part i, 26. The bill with the signet
attached has the limits of the patent;
see also *Calendars of State Papers,
America and West Indies, 1661–1668*,
pp. 190, 191. For the forms used in issuing letters patent, see the *Magazine of
American History*, as above, and an

elaborate paper by Charles Deane in the
Massachusetts Historical Society's *Proceedings*, 1871, pp. 166–196.

[3] *Charters and Constitutions of the
United States*, i, 783; another text following the copy in the office of the Secretary of State at Albany is in *Boundaries
of New York*, i, 12, 14.

Some two weeks after the date of the patent, the Duke of York commissioned Colonel Richard Nicolls to be deputy governor of his lands in New England, including New Netherland within these limits, with all the powers of government which had been given to him by his brother. At about the same time the king issued a commission to Nicolls, Sir Robert Carr, Colonel George Cartwright, and Samuel Maverick, directing them, in addition to settling disputes in New England, to take possession of New Netherland for the Duke of York.[1] To accomplish the latter purpose, they were given three war vessels, a hired transport, a few hundred soldiers, and four thousand pounds sterling.[2] Stuyvesant received ample notice of this new attempt on the Dutch colony from those who were friendly to him in New England. The burghers of New Amsterdam, one third at a time, and also the company's negroes, were at once set to work on the fortifications. The inhabitants of Manhattan Island were also directed to equip themselves for military service, and the brewers were forbidden to malt any hard grain for eight days, in order to preserve it for food. In making these somewhat inadequate preparations for defense, Stuyvesant, doubtless, counted upon the New Englanders occupying the commissioners' time and attention; but he reckoned without knowledge of the energetic character of Colonel Richard Nicolls, who crossed the Atlantic, made a brief stay at Boston, and anchored off Coney Island on August 18, 1664, within less than five months after the date of his commission. At that point, John Winthrop and other leading men from Connecticut,

---

[1] See "Private Instructions to Coll. R. Nicolls" in *New York Colonial Documents*, iii, 57. His commission is lost, see *Colonial Laws of New York* (ed. of 1896), i, p. xi.

[2] *Calendars of State Papers, America and West Indies, 1661–1668*, p. 190.

Thomas Willett from Plymouth, and Captain John Scott with soldiers from New Haven joined the expedition. The English settlers on the eastern end of Long Island were arming, and Massachusetts was busily engaged in raising her contingent for the conquest of the Dutch colony. Against this array of ships and soldiers, and the certainty of numerous reënforcements from New England, Stuyvesant had little to offer in the way of resistance. Fort Amsterdam, on the southern end of Manhattan Island, was out of repair and poorly supplied with ammunition, while the inhabitants of the Dutch settlements were either lukewarm in their allegiance to Stuyvesant or were prepared to welcome the invaders whenever that should be reasonably safe. To gain time, and also to ascertain the numbers and condition of the enemy's forces, the Dutch governor sent four men to inquire as to the object of the coming of the squadron.[1] Nicolls frankly informed them that he had come to reduce New Netherland to English authority and would not argue as to the rights and wrongs of his errand. The next day, Saturday, August 20, four Englishmen appeared at New Amsterdam with a letter from Nicolls. In this he asserted that the right of England to the soil of New Netherland was unquestionable and required the surrender of New Amsterdam and its fort. He assured the Dutch inhabitants that they should enjoy security of life, liberty, and property, " with all other privileges with his Majesty's English subjects." [2] Nicolls had sent the summons unsigned, and Stuyvesant, striving for time, returned it in order that every formality might be

---

[1] An interesting account of these transactions is in the *Records of New Amsterdam*, v, 114; many documents are noted in the *Calendars of State Papers, America and West Indies, 1661–1668*, pp.

xxii, 225 and fol., which the editor, William Noel Sainsbury, states are not printed in the *New York Colonial Documents*.

[2] O'Callaghan's *New Netherland*, ii, 522 note.

observed. The following Monday, the letter reappeared, this time duly authenticated. The town's people demanded to know what terms were offered, and information was conveyed to Winthrop and Willett that they would compel Stuyvesant to surrender if they could be assured of free intercourse with Holland. The negotiation now assumed a roundabout course : Nicolls wrote to Winthrop that if Manhattan were surrendered, the people might enjoy intercourse with the Netherlands ; Winthrop wrote to Stuyvesant and his council advising them to accept the liberal terms which were offered and which he stated at length. He also threatened them with an avalanche of troops from Massachusetts and Connecticut in case the negotiations should be protracted. Winthrop and other New England men then sought Stuyvesant and consulted with him and his advisers. After the Englishmen had gone back to their ships, the burgomasters of New Amsterdam appeared in the council room and insisted on seeing Winthrop's letter. Stuyvesant became very angry, declared that he "had much rather be carried out dead "[1] than surrender, and tore the letter into bits. Ultimately, he was obliged to have the fragments reassembled and transcribed for the benefit of his rebellious subjects. When Stuyvesant again tried to protract the negotiations by justifying the Dutch occupation, Nicolls cut him short by declaring that if the terms were not accepted within forty-eight hours, he would come up to the city with his ships and men. Still further to quicken him, English soldiers were landed on Long Island and marched to Brooklyn, and the fleet proceeded up the bay to Governor's Island. On this Stuyvesant ordered the fort to open fire, but he was led away from the ramparts by Domines

---

[1] Brodhead's *New York*, ii, 35.

John and Samuel Megapolensis before a gun was discharged. Three days later, on August 29, 1664, old style, or September 8, according to the modern method, Fort Amsterdam was surrendered without a shot having been fired on either side. Nicolls sent Sir Robert Carr to take possession of the Swedish-Dutch settlements on the Delaware. This was easily accomplished, but not without bloodshed, robbery, and brutality.[1]

Richard Nicolls[2] came of a distinguished family and had the blood of the Bruces in his veins. He had followed the Stuart fortunes in camp and exile since the beginning of the Civil Wars. In 1664 he was groom of the bed chamber to James and had recently received the degree of doctor of civil law from Oxford University. He was a man of ability, learning, and varied accomplishments, and beneath the exterior of a courtier concealed a power of will unmatched among English rulers in America in his day. On paper, Nicolls's powers[3] were almost unlimited; in reality, they were greatly restricted by a lack of funds which continued to the end of his career as governor. He could not tax the Dutch or English settlers for fear that they would rebel; and, in the unsettled conditions then prevailing, imposts on merchandise imported into the colony produced little revenue. He was obliged to put his hand into his own pocket and use in the Duke's service funds which he had brought from England for his own benefit[4] — in his will he strictly charged his executors to collect whatever sums were still remaining

[1] Papers relating to this part of the conquest of New Netherland are in *New York Colonial Documents*, xii, 457–669.

[2] The best accounts of Nicolls are in *Notes and Queries*, Second Series, iii, 214; Fifth Series, i, 503; Eighth Series, x, 296, 421. O'Callaghan's "Note" to Gowan's edition of Wooley's *Journal*

(p. 71) and Doyle's article in the *Dictionary of National Biography* tell about the same story.

[3] His commission is noted in *Calendars of State Papers, America and West Indies, 1661–1668*, p. 196.

[4] *New York Colonial Documents*, iii, 69, 104, 114.

unpaid. Nicolls's authority was also diminished by the terms of the Articles of Capitulation [1] which were regarded as binding, although they were never formally ratified in England. According to them, the Dutch West India Company was permitted to enjoy its property in the colony and to have six months in which to transport arms and ammunition out of the country. The inhabitants should have a year and six months in which to move, if they wished, and if they remained were to be regarded as free denizens under English law. Moreover, they should have liberty of commerce [2] and of conscience, should not be pressed into service in time of war, nor have soldiers billeted upon them, and should enjoy their own customs concerning inheritances. As to inferior officers, these were to continue to hold their positions until the time for new elections, when the outgoing officers might choose their successors as was customary in Dutch municipalities; but the new officers must take the oath of allegiance to the English king.

The geographical distribution of the settlements under Nicolls's government, the diversity of race which prevailed therein, and the religious heterogeneity of the settlers greatly intensified the difficulties of his position. Leaving out of account, for the present, all consideration of the affairs of the eastern part of what is now the state of

[1] *New York Colonial Documents*, ii, 250; *Revised Laws of New York* (ed. 1813), vol. ii, Appendix I.

[2] There was some confusion regarding commerce in the Articles of Capitulation. The words of the sixth article are "Dutch vessels may freely come thither, and any of the Dutch may freely return home, or send any merchandise home in vessels of their own country"; the seventh section provides that Dutch ships or other ships and goods therein shall be received here and sent hence "after the manner which formerly they were before our coming hither for six months next ensuing." In 1667, on petition of Peter Stuyvesant, the King in Council ordered that three Dutch ships yearly for seven years should be permitted to trade direct with New Netherland; but upon the protest of English merchants trading to the plantations this privilege was withdrawn in the next year. *New York Colonial Documents*, iii, 163, 166, 177.

Maine and of the islands of Martha's Vineyard and Nantucket, in none of which did Nicolls exercise effective authority, we can consider the condition of affairs in what are now the states of New York and New Jersey with some slight attention to the outlying settlements on the Delaware.   The colonists of this part of Nicolls's domain lived in three widely separated regions, the central point being Manhattan Island.   On the Delaware there were feeble settlements of Swedish and Dutch farmers and fur traders.   On the Hudson, the Dutch hamlets and farms extended northward to the Mohawk River and Albany.   On Long Island, the settlements on the western end had been made by Dutchmen, those on the eastern end by Englishmen, while in the central portion of the island the inhabitants belonged to both races.   On the Delaware and the Hudson, except in the immediate vicinity of Manhattan Island, strong executive authority was necessary; for years, therefore, these portions of the Duke of York's province were ruled by successive military governments.[1]

In the central part of his government, at Manhattan Island and in the Long Island towns, military rule was out of the question.   The Articles of Capitulation protected the settlers of New Amsterdam and the Dutch towns

[1] Nicolls's adroitness is well shown in the settlement of disputes which arose between the inhabitants of Esopus and English soldiers who were stationed there. He sent three commissioners with private instructions as to what they should do. Upon inquiry, they were to find that Captain Brodhead, the English commander of the post, did only offer to fling a dirk at a certain brewer, but did not fling it, that he offered to draw his sword, but did not draw it, and that the brewer struck the first blow. The commissioners were then to declare that a king's officer is not of so mean a quality as to be struck by a burgher. They were to inform those inhabitants who had participated in the riot that their action was treason, listen to no excuses on their part, and send the six ringleaders to him, who pardoned them after he thought they were sufficiently terrified. The commissioners were further to find that Captain Brodhead had broken his instructions and were to suspend him from his employment. *New York Colonial Documents*, iii, 149.

on Long Island, while the strength and political training of the English there made military rule impossible. The capitulation required the continuance of the Dutch magistrates in office for the time being; but Nicolls imparted an English aspect to the map by changing the names to suit the fact of conquest. The colony of New Netherland now becomes the Province of New York, and New Amsterdam also takes that name. The West India Company's post near Rensselaerswyck becomes Albany from the Duke's second title. The names of the Dutch towns on Long Island were also changed, Midwout becoming Flatbush, Middelburgh, Newtowne, and Folestone, Oyster Bay.

In the settlement of affairs at New Amsterdam, now become New York, Nicolls pursued a policy which was truly Machiavellian. For the time being, the Dutch officials retained their places until the expiration of their terms, and were allowed to elect their successors,[1] all in strict accordance with the terms of surrender. This election was held in February, 1665. In the following June, Nicolls, in obedience to the directions of the Duke of York, discharged "the form of Government late in practice" and instituted a government by mayor, aldermen, and sheriffs. At the same time, he introduced a vigorous leaven of English officials, Thomas Willett being the first mayor.[2] Nicolls then directed the new officials to swear to be obedient to the orders of the Duke of York.[3] In the preceding October the Dutch colonial leaders had asked that the words "Conformable to the Articles concluded on the Surrender of this place" be inserted in

---

[1] *Records of New Amsterdam*, v, 183.
[2] Willett's commission is printed in *Minutes of the Common Council of New York*, ii, 53.

[3] *Records of New Amsterdam*, v. 249, 251.

this oath because they feared that otherwise the articles would become void, but Nicolls declared the contrary to be the case, and the oath was taken [1] in the form which he had prescribed.   This whole procedure savors of despotism and ill faith, but Nicolls was able to assert that he had carried out the Articles of Capitulation to the letter ; he said nothing about the spirit.   He continued the commercial rights of the residents of New Amsterdam, the trade in that city being reserved to the freemen of the corporation who in this way represented the burghers of the Dutch period.

Nicolls now turned his attention to revamping the institutions of Long Island.   The colonists living in the towns on the eastern part of the island were Englishmen who had come originally from Connecticut with the consent of the rulers of that colony.   They had bought their lands of the Indians and had never submitted to the authority of the Dutch governor general.   According to constitutional maxims, they were entitled to enjoy the fundamental rights of Englishmen and could not in any way be treated as a conquered people.   Nicolls, therefore, was constrained to give them a form of government in which the precepts of English constitutional precedents should at least appear to be complied with.   Procuring the printed laws of Massachusetts and New Haven, he promulgated a legal code which is known as the " Duke of York's Laws," or more simply as the " Duke's Laws." [2] In these, he sought to give a New England semblance to

---

[1] *Records of New Amsterdam*, v, 142–145.

[2] The set preserved in manuscript at East Hampton, Long Island, is printed in full in the New York Historical Society's *Collections*, i, 305–428, and is reprinted thence in the volume entitled *Charter of William Penn and Laws of Pennsylvania*, which was edited by Staughton George and others and published by that state, since this code was the fundamental law of Delaware and Pennsylvania as well as of New York.

local institutions while preserving the actual power of government almost intact in the hands of those whom the Duke appointed to administer the affairs of his province.

In place of the New England town system, Nicolls provided a local organization in which elected officials called constables and overseers were to exercise local authority; there were to be no town meetings. These town officials were practically accountable to the governor, although they were chosen by the freeholders in the several towns. In place of the religious system of New England he established freedom of conscience and religion, but at the same time provided that every town must build a church and support religion.

Nicolls reserved to the governor the appointment of the justices who held office during pleasure and, besides executing the judicial functions which naturally belonged to their position, also exercised legislative power. They held Courts of Assizes [1] and adopted regulations which, with the governor's consent, became the law of the province. This was not in any sense a representative system, for the people had no voice in the appointment of the justices, nor were the justices representative men from the several parts of the colony; often they might even be newcomers from England, who were entirely ignorant of the needs and wishes of the people. An important change in legal institutions was the introduction of trial by jury.

At first the new system was confined to " Yorkshire," as Long Island was termed; but when affairs quieted down in the other parts of the province, the Duke's Laws were extended to them so that by the time of the Dutch re-conquest, the Duke's Laws were the fundamental

[1] The records of the Court of Assizes   Historian's *Report* for 1897.
are largely printed in New York State

laws of the whole province and the Court of Assizes included justices from the Delaware [1] and the Hudson as well as from "Yorkshire." In addition to these regulations for the political organization, the Duke's Laws also contained a good deal of legislation on other matters, such, for example, as the punishment of crime; in these respects they were distinctly liberal in comparison with the existing practice in England. Upon the whole, one is compelled to admire the mode in which Nicolls combined his duty to the Duke of York with the necessity for keeping up the appearance of justice to the New England settlers on Long Island.

On the 28th of February, 1664–65, Nicolls held a general meeting at Hempstead on Long Island of two deputies from each of the Long Island towns and from West Chester on the mainland. To them he presented his code, which did not seem to some of them to square with his promise of "equal (if not greater) freedoms and immunities than any of his Majesty's colonies in New England," [2] or with his promise that deputies should be summoned to give their advice in all matters tending to the peace and good of Long Island.[3] But when they objected and requested that they be allowed to have a hand in making the laws, he replied that if the people desired other arrangements than those which he had devised, they must petition the king. In the end the deputies accepted the Duke's Laws and issued a declaration in which they asserted their cheerful submission to whatever he should do for them, — such was the influence exerted by the presence and tact of Colonel Richard Nicolls.

[1] The "Duke's Laws" were established at Newcastle on the Delaware by order of Andros in 1676. *Records of the Court of Newcastle*, p. 6.

[2] Printed in O'Callaghan's "Histori-cal Introduction" to *Journal of the Legislative Council of the Colony of New York*, p. iv.

[3] See *Colonial Laws of New York* (ed. 1896), i, p. xii.

Returning home the deputies met with a cold reception from their fellow-townsmen, and some of them signed a "Narrative and Remonstrance," declaring that they meant no more by "cheerful submission" than that they would obey his Majesty's letters patent according to their duty and allegiance.[1] The strenuous John Underhill was then residing at Oyster Bay; he characterized Nicolls's arrangements as an example of "arbitrary power," and discreetly retired with all speed to Connecticut. In the following autumn, the Court of Assizes decreed that those who reproached the Hempstead deputies or vilified their proceedings should be punished as guilty of slander. The stocks and pecuniary fines for three of the most outspoken put an end, for the time being, to open complaining.[2]

While Nicolls was crossing the Atlantic, Lord Berkeley and Sir George Carteret sought out the Duke of York and asked for a share of the spoils of anticipated victory, and he, with Stuart prodigality, at once assigned to them lands that were still within the government of Peter Stuyvesant. This he did (June 24, 1664) by a curious form of conveyance,[3] which is known in English law as "lease and re-lease." In the "lease" for the sum of ten shillings paid to him by the grantees James bargained and sold to them a described tract of land, while the "re-lease" stated that for a competent sum of money he had bar-

[1] *New York Colonial Documents*, iii, 91.

[2] Nicolls's demand that the Long Islanders should secure confirmations of the title to their lands especially aroused their resentment. There was a good deal to be said in favor of his policy as these lands had been obtained either by purchase from the Indians or grant from the Dutch authorities and not at all from those who claimed title from the Council for New England. The money paid for confirmation would go far to make the government independent, which was the last thing that the Long Islanders desired. The Court of Assizes, however, put an end to the disputation by decreeing that, after a certain date, the old deeds could not be regarded as evidence in the courts of the colony. New York Historical Society's *Collections*, i, 419.

[3] *New Jersey Archives*, i, 8; *Boundaries of the State of New York*, i, 23.

gained, sold, re-leased, and confirmed to the grantees certain lands "in as full and ample manner as the same is granted to the said Duke in the said letters patent," namely, the grant by Charles II to his brother. The exact words of the passage which has just been quoted are worth bearing in mind in view of the disputes which later arose over the question as to whether James had parted with his rights of jurisdiction to Berkeley and Carteret. The territory [1] which was thus lavishly bestowed comprised what is now known as the state of New Jersey, which was so called in honor of Sir George Carteret's gallant and determined defense of the Island of Jersey against the forces of the Puritans. [2]

The knowledge of this grant reached Nicolls shortly after the completion of the conquest and aroused his indignation. He at once wrote letters to England stating that the Duke had parted with the most improvable lands in the province, [3] the only lands, indeed, on which it was possible to settle "men well affected to monarchy." The rest of the conquered colony, he said, was so impoverished that one hundred pounds would be all the money that he could raise in any one year without danger of arousing rebellion. [4] This protest from his trusted lieutenant came too late to secure the reversal of the grant; but Nicolls both before and after the action of the Duke came to his attention was active in sending colonists to New Jersey. On the mainland on the western shore of New York Harbor there were already some Dutch settlers who held

[1] For the details as to the boundaries and the disputes which arose over them, see *Boundaries of the State of New York*, ii, 598.

[2] Clarendon, in his *History of the Great Rebellion* (ed. 1826, vi, 608, 609), states that Carteret's stronghold, Elizabeth Fort, was the last garrison to lower the royal banner.

[3] *New York Colonial Documents*, iii, 105; *Calendars of State Papers, America and West Indies, 1661–1668*, p. 337.

[4] New York Historical Society's *Collections*, ii, 74–77.

their lands from the West India Company and some of them by grant from the Indians. Nicolls induced several other groups of settlers to go to the eastern part of New Jersey from Long Island and New England. These people settled at Monmouth, Middletown, and vicinity, and began the formation of that strong New England community which dominated the eastern and northern part of the province.[1] They were soon joined by other colonists who came from England under the auspices of the grantees.

Berkeley and Carteret in England had at once taken energetic steps to provide settlers for their new domain. On the 10th of February, 1664–65, they issued a "Concession and Agreement,"[2] offering lands to colonists on liberal terms. They also promised liberty of conscience and of worship, and an allowance of two hundred acres in each parish for the maintenance of the minister who should be chosen by the settlers. The governmental ideas of the proprietors were equally liberal. They proposed to appoint a governor and council who should legislate with twelve representatives annually elected by the freemen of the province. The laws must be in harmony with those of England ; they were to go into force at once upon their passage, but might be annulled by the proprietors, in England. Armed with these Concessions and accompanied by a few emigrants from the Channel Islands,[3] Philip Carteret, a

[1] The names and former residence of the first settlers are given in E. Salter's *Monmouth and Ocean Counties*, p. 18. On the value of their land titles see "Opinions of Council [including Holt and Pollexfen] concerning Col. Nicols' patent and Indian purchases in New Jersey," in New York State Historian's *Report*, 1897, p. 215.

[2] "The Concession and Agreement of the Lords Proprietors of the Province of New Cæsarea, or New Jersey, to and with all and every the Adventurers and all such as shall settle and plant there." Leaming and Spicer's *Grants and Concessions of New Jersey*, p. 12.

[3] Their names are printed in Hatfield's *Elizabeth, New Jersey*, p. 58. Doyle (*The Middle Colonies*, p. 160) says that "the whole body of emigrants who accompanied Philip Carteret numbered only thirty, most of them German salt-refiners," but he gives no authority for the statement.

kinsman of Sir George, came over to New Jersey as governor in 1665.

New Haven and Connecticut have always been prolific of pioneers. In May, 1666, a considerable body of settlers came to New Jersey from these colonies and from other parts of New England. The proprietors' representative granted them land in the northeastern part of the province, and they also took the precaution to purchase the title to these tracts from the Indians. Their lands lay in the region now included in Newark and the Oranges, and they soon became the site of a prosperous settlement in which everything was done on the strict New England model that required profession of faith in a Congregational church as a condition for voting in town meeting. Their coming increased the New England complexion of the colony which must have been exceedingly irksome to Philip Carteret and even more so to Richard Nicolls, whose headquarters were not far away on the other side of the North River. In 1668 the first New Jersey Assembly met at Elizabethtown and promptly passed twelve capital laws which bore a strong resemblance to those of the Eaton Code of New Haven, and made other provisions of a distinctively Puritan cast. Philip Carteret reprobated these doings, and the Assembly after another session broke up in an exceedingly bad humor. The Nicolls colonists were even more outspoken; they refused to pay any taxes or to take any oaths to the proprietors, stating that they held their lands by grant from the Duke of York and by purchase from the natives and therefore owed no obligation of any sort to Berkeley and Carteret. In 1672 matters came to a crisis, when the colonists chose an assembly without any authorization from the governor. They elected as president, James Carteret, a son of Sir George and a landgrave of Carolina who happened to be in the colony at the time. Unable to make head against this movement, Philip Carteret went to England where the proprietors, the duke, and the king, warmly espoused his cause.[1] They issued orders which sent James Carteret out of the colony and induced the settlers to give obedience to the proprietors' representative.

War between England and the Netherlands followed on the seizure of the Dutch colony on the Hudson, although how far this was a contributory cause of the outbreak of hostilities is not entirely clear. In this contest the English navy showed at its very worst. The administration was honeycombed with corruption, owing to the avarice of Admiral Penn, Sir George Carteret, Mr. Samuel Pepys, and those below them. On the ships insubordination was rife from the highest to the lowest ranks, owing to slack discipline, lack of pay, and scarcity of food. On the other hand, the Dutch navy was never in better condition than it was at this moment, and it was under the command of two of the greatest of the Netherlands' naval heroes, Michel Adriaanszoon de Ruyter and Cornelis van Tromp. In 1665 the fleets fought an indecisive battle off Lowestoft and again in 1666 off the North Foreland. These two years also witnessed the greatest visitation of the plague which London ever experienced and the most disastrous fire in her history. During the next year (June, 1667) the Dutch blockaded the Thames, destroyed the docks and shipping at Sheerness, and escaped unharmed. Naturally, Nicolls and his employers in England felt nervous as to the Dutch in New York and apprehended an attack on Manhattan Island by a naval force from the mother country. Nothing

[1] See order of Charles II commanding "all persons to yield obedience to the laws and government there [in New Jersey] established by said Lord Proprietors." *Calendars of State Papers, America and West Indies, Addenda, 1675–1676*, p. 151.

of the kind happened at that time. Dutch privateers appeared in the Chesapeake and there was some fighting between them and Virginia vessels. Sir William Berkeley, governor of Virginia, displayed great energy. He enlisted a formidable force to oppose the Dutch in case they landed on the shores of the Old Dominion ; but they clung resolutely to their ships.[1] In July, 1667, the turn of European politics impelled the Dutch to make a treaty of peace with England in which, among other things, the possession of New Netherland was confirmed to its English conquerors.

To a man of Nicolls's experience with court life, his position in New York must have been intolerable.[2] Upon the close of hostilities, he was relieved from his arduous task to resume his attendance upon James and was killed by a cannon ball in an action with the Dutch fleet at Solebay in the next war. His successor as governor of New York was Colonel Francis Lovelace, who was also a military man and a friend of Charles and James. He belonged to a family which had long been concerned in colonial affairs, and he himself had already visited Long Island.[3] His instructions forbade him to make any alterations in the government, the Duke reserving all changes in Nicolls's arrangements to himself. On his arrival, Lovelace at once became involved in disputations with the Long Islanders, who demanded the performance of Nicolls's promise that they should enjoy the privileges of other English subjects, by which they meant local self-government. Lovelace stated that he could do nothing for them because his instructions obliged him to

---

[1] On this conflict in the colonies, see Brodhead's *New York*, ii, 126; *Calendars of State Papers, America and West Indies, 1661–1668*, pp. 315, 316, 474; New York Historical Society's *Collections*, ii, 122.

[2] *Calendars of State Papers, America and West Indies, 1661–1668*, p. 337.

[3] On Lovelace's family connections, see American Historical Association's *Reports*, 1891, p. 269; the article deals mainly with John, Lord Lovelace, grandson of Francis, who became governor of New York after Cornbury, and died five months after his arrival.

continue the constitution as he found it.   Thereupon the
dwellers in the eastern towns refused to pay their share of
a levy which he made for the reparation of the fort on
Manhattan Island.   They stated that they could not be
compelled to pay taxes to which their consent had not
been given by their representatives.   Lovelace asserted
that this was sedition and in 1670 caused the Court of
Assizes to declare that all titles which should not at once
be confirmed should be regarded as invalid.   But the colonists stood firm and refused payment of customs which
were levied by the Duke's orders on all goods that were
brought into the colony.   The time was not favorable for
compulsion, and they were perforce permitted to have their
way.

In 1670 there was signed at Dover in England a secret
treaty by which Charles II bound himself to serve the
ends of Louis XIV of France in consideration of financial
assistance from that monarch.   This alliance led to an
unprovoked attack on the Netherlands in the year 1672.
In 1673 fifteen vessels under the command of the. Dutch
captain, Cornelis Evertsen, reached the West Indies.   There
they met other Dutch vessels and the combined fleets visited Chesapeake Bay, where they "took eight and burned
five Virginia tobacco ships" and also gained knowledge
of the defenseless condition of New York.[1]   Up to that
moment they do not seem to have had any intention of re-
conquering New Netherland.   What with their captures and
their original vessels, the Dutch fleet now numbered twenty-
three ships with about twelve hundred fighting men.   In
the summer this force appeared in lower New York Bay.
Lovelace was absent in Connecticut, where he was in con-

[1] See accounts of the surrender in *New York Colonial Documents*, iii, 199, 200, 205, 213; Brodhead's *New York*, ii, 205; *Calendars of State Papers, America and West Indies, 1669–1674*, pp. 520–522.

ference with John Winthrop, and the command at New York was in the hands of Captain Manning.   He permitted the Dutch ships to anchor in front of the fort without firing on them and asked for delay.   Evertsen gave him only half an hour, after which he opened on the fort, landed a force on the island, and advanced to the assault.   Manning replied to the Dutch fire in a feeble way and, without waiting the attack on the fort, surrendered with the loss of only one man.   After the surrender, Lovelace, venturing into the city to attend to private matters, was seized by the Dutch, but was later released.[1]

For fifteen months, New York remained in the hands of the Dutch, when it was restored to the English by the Treaty of Westminster (1674) as a part of the price which the Dutch paid to England for peace.   While they were in occupation of the reconquered New Netherland, they restored the old Dutch forms of government by burgomasters and schepens.   All officials swore to maintain the true Christian religion conformably to the word of God and the order of the Synod of Dort and as taught in the churches of the Netherlands.[2]   This requirement, of course, disqualified all Englishmen from official position. The name of the city of New York was changed to New Orange and not to its old designation of New Amsterdam. The restored Dutch authorities were especially mindful as to the observance of the Lord's Day — a circumstance which leads one to infer that there had been a good deal of laxity in that respect during the time of English rule.   They forbade mechanic employments and commerce, drunkenness, gambling, dancing, and fishing on Sunday, and

[1] Upon his return to England, Lovelace was committed to the Tower and, at one time, was in danger of banishment. An attack of dropsy secured his release and he disappeared from historic sight. *Calendars of State Papers, America and West Indies, 1675–1676*, pp. 176, 211.

[2] *Records of New Amsterdam*, vi, 398.

paid especial attention to the children, forbidding them to play and shout in the street; from all who disobeyed the officer might take their hats or upper garments — leaving an irate parent to do the rest.[1]

Upon the restoration of New York to the English in 1674, new letters patent and deeds were issued.[2] The king made a fresh grant to the Duke of York, and he in turn executed new deeds of lease and release of northern New Jersey in the terms of the earlier documents. In the preceding year, Lord Berkeley had sold his half of New Jersey for one thousand pounds to two Quakers, John Fenwick and Edward Byllynge.[3] The Duke did not confirm this sale, but the grantees proceeded on the assumption that the Treaty of Westminster had revived all the rights of Berkeley and Carteret.

In selecting a governor for New York, James picked out Edmund Andros, or Andrews, to spell the name as it was pronounced at the time. He came of gentle English blood, which had combined with the stock of the "fighting Sausmarez" of the Island of Guernsey. His family had remained loyal to the Stuart cause throughout the Civil Wars. Upon the Restoration he was appointed Gentleman in Ordinary to the king's aunt, Elizabeth of the Palatinate. From that time his advancement was rapid, especially after his marriage with Lord Craven's cousin, Lady Mary Craven. In 1666 Andros was appointed

[1] *Records of New Amsterdam*, vi, 405. The article could be redeemed by payment of two guilders.

[2] This was probably done to remove all doubts as to the title, because the earlier grant of 1664 had been made while New Netherland was still in the possession of the Dutch. See on this subject Fowler's "Introduction" to the Grolier Club's reprint of Bradford's *New York Laws*, p. lx.

[3] The conveyance of 1673 is not printed in the *New Jersey Archives;* the recital given in the text is based on that in the "Quintipartite Deed" of 1676 in *ibid.*, i, 209. In 1680 James conveyed West Jersey to Penn and others, who administered the territory which Berkeley had conveyed to Fenwick and Byllynge. *New Jersey Archives*, i, 324.

major of a regiment of foot and served in the West Indies.
Through Craven's influence he was made a Carolina landgrave with a grant of forty-eight thousand acres to support
his dignity.[1] In 1674 he succeeded to his father's estates
and title of Bailly of the Island of Guernsey. From this
brief biography it is clear that Edmund Andros was no
adventurer. He possessed fair abilities, but these were
coupled with an old-fashioned temper and an absence of
tact which unfitted him for the performance of the delicate tasks to which he was assigned. His commission[2] as
governor of New York was like that which had been
issued to Lovelace, but his instructions were more detailed.
He was directed to appoint a council of not more than
ten members. These were to hold office during James's
pleasure and Andros was to be guided by their advice on
extraordinary occasions. The Duke's Laws, as they were
already established, were to be followed except in cases of
" emergent necessities," or " apparent inconveniencies."
In such cases, Andros, with the advice of his Council and
other grave inhabitants, might make new laws, but they
must be confirmed by the proprietor. All the inhabitants
of the province were to enjoy freedom of conscience and
worship, but no one should " disquiet others in the free
exercise of their religion." The Duke of York also established certain customs duties[3] by commission and instructions[4] to William Dyer as collector of the province.
These were moderate in amount so far as goods imported
from England or the other plantations were concerned;

---

[1] The fullest sketch of Andros is
that prefixed to Whitmore's edition of
" Andros Tracts " in the publications of
the Prince Society. The Carolina land-
graviate is noted in *Calendars of State
Papers, America and West Indies, 1669–
1674*, p. 312.

[2] *New York Colonial Documents*, iii,
215; the instructions are in *ibid.*, p. 216.
[3] *Ibid.*, iii, 217.
[4] *Ibid.*, iii, 221, 222.

but they were heavy on goods that were brought in from
other parts of the world. Moreover, an extra duty was
levied on all articles taken up the Hudson River. Furs
and tobacco exported from the colony were also to be
taxed. These customs duties were established for three
years until 1677, when they were continued for three
years more, or until 1680. The internal taxes were to remain as they had been arranged by Nicolls and Lovelace.
Besides these general levies, the towns and other administrative districts raised money for local needs. In the
beginning, the customs and excise produced sufficient funds
only to pay the necessary costs of the general government; but later, they returned a small surplus which was
probably used by the proprietor for the payment of his
personal expenses. These rates were not excessive in
amount; but the fact that they were made by an absentee
proprietor without the consent of the inhabitants could
not fail sooner or later to be regarded as a grievance.

At the time of the Dutch reconquest of New York, the
inhabitants of the old English towns on the eastern end of
Long Island had maintained their independence and had
again joined the colony of Connecticut. They now asked
to be allowed to continue under that jurisdiction; but
Andros ordered them to recognize his authority or to be
declared rebels. As the Connecticut government did not
wish to have any unnecessary friction with the English
authorities, they declined to give the islanders any assistance, and these were forced to comply with Andros's
demand;[1] but not before John Burroughs, clerk of Newtown, had stood an hour at the whipping-post before the
city hall in New York with a paper pinned to his breast,
setting forth that he had signed seditious documents.

[1] New York State Historian's *Report*, 1897, p. 241.

In his dealings with the people of the Long Island towns, Andros only followed his orders, although he may have been unduly harsh in his treatment of offenders; but his letters to the Duke do not give one the impression of a despotically inclined ruler. For instance, he called his master's attention to the fact that the people of the province desired to have an assembly. This idea did not approve itself to James. He replied to Andros that the assembling of such a body would not be consistent with the form of government already established in the province; if the people had any grievances, they could present them at the Court of Assizes, which would be composed of the same persons who would naturally be elected as representatives. In a later letter,[1] James declared that assemblies were of dangerous consequence in that they often assumed privileges which were destructive of government or very disturbing to it — all of which was true enough and was the precise reason why the people desired to have a representative assembly summoned.

Andros soon realized that James had given to Berkeley and Carteret one of the most valuable parts of his province. He did what he could to compensate for the ill effects of this gift by compelling all vessels carrying goods to New Jersey to pay duties at New York, and denied absolutely the right of Fenwick to exercise any sort of jurisdiction in western New Jersey, to which region the latter had led a band of Quaker colonists.[2] Andros caused him to be seized and brought to New York, and only released him on his giving bond not to meddle with the government of that part of New Jersey.

Andros next came into collision with a more influential

---

[1] *New York Colonial Documents*, iii, 235.

[2] On Fenwick and his settlement at Salem, see R. G. Johnson's *Historical Account of the Settlement of Salem in West Jersey*, Philadelphia, 1839.

person than any of the early proprietors of New Jersey.
This was none other than William Penn, the son of James's
old friend the Admiral and later the founder of Pennsylvania. The younger Penn had become interested in
American colonization as arbiter in a dispute between
Fenwick and Byllynge, and, later, as a trustee for the
latter's creditors. In 1676, Penn with three other Quakers
and Sir George Carteret executed a "quintipartite deed"
between the last named, on one side, and the four
Quakers, on the other, for the division of New Jersey.
The legal standing of this document, as well as its origin,
are very doubtful; the result of it was to encourage Penn
and his partners to proceed with the settlement of the
southern and western part of the province, which was
allotted to them by its provisions. They formulated
Concessions and Agreements[1] which shadow forth the
spirit of democracy that actuated the Quakers. They
proposed to grant lands in full right to those who should
purchase them, each one of these proprietors having in
full the rights of the original grantees from James.
Annually the resident proprietors were to elect by ballot
ten men to perform executive functions and another set to
serve as an assembly. This representative legislative body
had full control of its organization and discipline except
that every member had the right of protest, and the
assembly could not exclude their constituents from their
deliberations. Freedom of religion, equal justice, and self-
taxation were guaranteed. Criminal offenders were to be
tried by juries of twelve men, and all trials were to be
public "that justice may not be done in a corner." The

---

[1] The document is dated 3rd March, 1676, and bears the signatures of about one hundred and fifty persons, among them William Penn. It is printed in Smith's *New Jersey*, Appendix ii.

Quakers were well aware of the limitations of human nature and provided that any person who gave or promised to give to an elector "any meat, drink, money, or money's worth for procurement of their choice or consent" should themselves be disqualified from office. The colonization of West New Jersey now went merrily on.[1] Andros felt obliged to give his aid, but not without declamations as to the rights of his master and sundry layings of his hand on his sword. The new proprietors, to make matters certain, accepted commissions from him. In 1678 Andros again interfered with Fenwick[2] and appointed a governor of his own for that part of New Jersey.

For some years the people of East New Jersey paid duties to the collector at New York, but in 1679 the Assembly at Elizabeth promised indemnity to the owners of any vessel that should come directly to New Jersey in violation of Andros's orders. This brought from him a formal demand that Philip Carteret, who was still acting as governor of East New Jersey, should forbear to exercise any power in that region. Andros also published a proclamation, commanding all persons in East New Jersey to submit to his government. Andros and Carteret were kinsmen, but this did not save the latter from the humiliation of an arrest in the middle of the night and a trial at New York for riotously presuming to exercise government within the limits of the Duke of York's territory. Andros himself presided at this trial; but the jury, notwithstand-

---

[1] Two letters from John Riresby, deputy lieutenant of the West Riding of Yorkshire, show the jealousy with which emigration to the colonies was regarded by some of the local authorities in England. He caused the arrest of Richard Matthews, one of the proprietors, for enticing his Majesty's subjects to leave the realm to go to "the island" of West Jersey, and suggested that an embargo should be laid on all vessels leaving Hull and other ports with emigrants. See *American Historical Review*, ii, 472.

[2] Brodhead's *New York*, ii, 320.

ing his utmost efforts, persisted in acquitting Carteret.[1] For the time being, however, Andros's officers exercised jurisdiction in East New Jersey and justices from that colony attended the New York Courts of Assizes.

The proprietors of the Jerseys now combined to secure redress from James. Penn stated the case of the Quakers with ability and tact and appealed to his friend's circumstances and hopes. The great lawyer, Sir William Jones,[2] on being applied to, declared that James had parted with the jurisdiction and profit of New Jersey because he had made no reservation of these in his deeds. Upon this James transferred to the West Jersey Associates all the rights of jurisdiction in that part of the province which had been granted to him by Charles. Furthermore, he declared that Andros had acted without orders and issued a deed confirming East Jersey with the jurisdiction thereof to the heirs of Sir George Carteret. In 1681–82 William Penn and eleven other Quakers purchased the rights of the Carteret heirs in East New Jersey and a few months later bought Fenwick's claims to the southwestern part of the province, and thus all of New Jersey was at last again in the hands of one group of proprietors.

From what has been said as to the settlement of New Jersey, it will be seen that the colonists of that province differed materially from those of New York. The Dutch

---

[1] Brodhead's *New York*, ii, 333, 334; Leaming and Spicer's *Grants, Concessions of New Jersey*, 673–674; *New York Colonial Documents*, iii, 284, 350.

[2] *New York Colonial Documents*, iii, 285. On February 13, 1692–93, Solicitor General Thomas Trevor gave his opinion that "The Proprietor of New York may assign his propriety in New Jersey, which is part of New York, to others, but cannot by any such grant or assignment absolutely sever New Jersey from New York, but that still it remains a part thereof and dependent on the Government of New York and liable to contribute men and provisions for the support and protection of New York against any enemies." *Ibid.*, iv, 1 note. Trevor and Hawles declared in 1697 (October 18) that the right to constitute ports is in the Commissioners of the Customs, and that the Duke of York did not have it and could not have conferred it on Berkeley and Carteret. "Board of Trade Papers," *Proprieties*, B 1 ("Philadelphia Transcripts," vol. ii).

element was insignificant in New Jersey; in the northern
and eastern part, New Englanders formed the bulk of the
early settlers, while the southern and western portion was
colonized by English Quakers. As was to be expected
from the manner of its founding, the people of New
Jersey have been distinguished for sobriety and industry
and have always enjoyed deserved prosperity.

While Andros was thus embroiling himself with his
neighbors on the west, he was also trying to enforce the
Duke's claims to portions of Connecticut and Massachusetts on the east. The charter of Connecticut of 1662 and
the New York grants of 1664 and 1674 included within
the limit of the respective colonies the lands from the west
side of Connecticut River to the east side of Delaware.
Desirous of the aid of Connecticut, Nicolls had agreed to a
line which would have included the central Hudson Valley
within the limits of that colony.[1] Andros claimed that
all of Connecticut west of the river of that name was
within the limits of New York. He chose the time of
King Philip's War to press his case, going to Saybrook
with an armed force. The Connecticut authorities, warned
of his coming, sent a detachment of troops to that point.
Andros landed, showed a copy of the Duke's patent and
other papers to the Connecticut commander, and then
reëmbarked. Ultimately, in Dongan's time, the boundary
between the two colonies was agreed upon as it at
present exists, although it was not actually surveyed on
the ground until half a century later.

[1] At the same time there seems to have
been some understanding between Nicolls
and the Connecticut people that the
boundary between the two colonies
should not approach within twenty miles
of the Hudson River. There is a good
account of this boundary dispute in C.
W. Baird's *History of Rye*, ch. xiii; see
also C. W. Bowen's *Boundary Disputes
of Connecticut*, pt. iv. There is an excellent map in Baird, p. 105, which is reproduced in Bowen, p. 17.

New York was very prosperous,[1] but the returns to James were small. There were many complaints of Andros and suggestions of peculation and extravagance on the part of New York officials. In 1680 James sent an agent to New York to investigate[2] these charges and directed Andros to return to England to render an account of his stewardship. In the confusion attendant upon his sudden departure, Andros forgot to renew the customs duties, which expired by limitation in that year. Discovering this, the merchants refused to pay the imposts which William Dyer, the Duke's collector, continued to levy. Seizing a vessel with its cargo, Dyer was sued by the owner for unlawfully detaining property which was not his own. He was cast in damages, was indicted on a charge of high treason, and appealing his case to England was sent home to stand trial.[3] The indictment charged Dyer with having "contrived innovations in government and the subversion and change of the known, ancient, and fundamental laws of the Realm of England . . . contrary to the great Charter of Liberties, contrary to the Petition of Right, and contrary to other statutes in these cases made and provided."[4] Dyer and Andros easily cleared themselves in England; but the New Yorkers continued to act independently of the Duke's officers, refusing to pay duties levied by his command. This movement was the first colonial rebellion against taxation from England, and the words of Dyer's indictment carry one backward to the times of the Puritan Rebellion in England and forward to the days of Otis, Henry, and Dickinson in America.

[1] In 1678 Andros informed the Lords of Trade that there were 24 settlements in the colony; that the militia numbered 2000, and that the province might be valued at £150,000; see *New York Colonial Documents*, iii, 260.

[2] His commission and instructions are in *New York Colonial Documents*, iii, 279.

[3] Dyer's tribulations are set forth in *New York Colonial Documents*, iii, 287.

[4] *American Historical Register*, i, 40.

NOTE

Bibliography. — The original material on this portion of New York history is ample and accessible. Most important is the set entitled *Documents relative to the Colonial History of the State of New York*. Papers dealing with the period covered in this chapter are printed in the following volumes: ii, "Holland Documents"; iii, "London Documents"; xii, xiii, xiv, "Documents from New York Archives." Each volume in lieu of a table of contents has a brief calendar of the papers printed in that volume. A detailed index to the first ten volumes is printed in a separate volume, each of the last three volumes of the series has an index of its own. The *Documentary History of New York*, in four volumes, contains papers which are not printed in the first-named series. Other papers are printed in the *Annual Reports of the State Historian, Colonial Series*,[1] and in the *New York State Library Bulletin*,[2] "History No. 2," and *Bulletin of the New York [City] Library*.[3] Matter of local interest is contained in the *Records of New Amsterdam* and in the *Minutes of the Common Council of the City of New York, 1675–1776* (15 vols., New York, 1905). The *Annals of Albany* (10 vols., Albany, 1850–59), and local histories and records, especially those of the Long Island towns, are useful.[4] Many of the papers printed in the *New York Colonial Documents* are minuted in the *Calendars of State Papers*. The New York Historical Society has printed much valuable material in its *Collections* and its "Fund Publication" series. Brodhead's *New York*, vol. ii, and Fiske's *Dutch and Quaker Colonies* (ii, chs. x, xi), tell the story in detail; A. E. McKinley narrated in a more modern way the "Transition from Dutch to English Rule" in *American Historical Review*, vi, 693.

The documentary history of New Jersey is printed at length in the *Archives of the State of New Jersey*. The first ten volumes

[1] Vol. i, Appendix G, "Transcription from the Records in the State Library," 1664–1673; Appendix H, "Muster Rolls of a Century," 1664–1760, vol. ii, Appendix L, "Transcription of the Records," 1673–1675; Appendix M, "Colonial Muster Rolls," 1686–1775.

[2] University of the State of New York, *State Library Bulletin, History*, Nos. 1-5.

[3] *Bulletin of the New York Public Library, Astor, Lenox, and Tilden Foundations;* there is no separate series devoted to historical material, but valuable papers are printed in connection with the book lists.

[4] Among them Furman's *Antiquities of Long Island;* B. F. Thompson's *History of Long Island* (2 vols., 2d ed., "greatly enlarged," 1843); *Records of the Town of East-Hampton* (Sag Harbor, 1887); C. W. Baird's *History of Rye*.

have a second title: *Documents relating to the Colonial History of the State of New Jersey,* with an index volume. The state historical society has also printed original matter and a useful *Analytical Index* to New Jersey documents in the State Paper Office at London. Aaron Leaming and Jacob Spicer edited in 1752 a volume entitled *Grants, Concessions, and Original Constitutions of the Province of New Jersey* (reprinted at Somerville, N.J., 1881). It contains the deeds and agreements of the proprietary period and Lord Cornbury's commission and instructions as royal governor, together with the laws passed before the surrender of the province to Queen Anne. Samuel Smith's *History of the Colony of Nova-Cæsaria or New Jersey* (Burlington, N.J., 1765) is in reality a constitutional history of the province and gives the important documents in considerable detail. There are many excellent histories of portions of New Jersey and of separate towns, especially those which are associated with the name of William A. Whitehead.

CHAPTER III

VIRGINIA AND NEW ENGLAND, 1660–1680

VIRGINIA deserved well of the Stuarts ; but she offered a safe field for the spoiler and paid the penalty. Some of the leading men of Virginia had invited the fugitive monarch to come to the colony with his companions, but he had preferred the penury and pleasure of European life to the chaster delights of an American wilderness. He did not come, but instead granted the northern part of the colony (1649) to some of his favorites, among them Sir John, afterward Lord Berkeley. Again in 1669 he confirmed this grant,[1] giving to its holders important rights of jurisdiction and commanded Governor Berkeley to assist the grantees. This action aroused infinite discontent, but the complaints[2] of the Virginians had no other effect than to induce Charles to grant to Lord Arlington and Lord Culpeper[3] all of Virginia, with the quitrents and escheated lands. They were to enjoy this patent for thirty-one years and, to protect themselves, were given the power to appoint sheriffs. Governor Berkeley, Thomas Ludwell, the secretary, and Robert Wynne, Speaker of the Burgesses, presented a protest against this grant in the name of the people of Virginia[4] (1674). Thomas Lud-

---

[1] *Calendars of State Papers, America and West Indies, 1669–1674*, pp. 23, 151. This patent included the land between the Potomac and the Rappahannock which was known locally as the Great Neck.

[2] *Calendars of State Papers, America and West Indies, 1669–1674*, p. 23.

[3] *Ibid., 1669–1674*, p. 334; Hening's *Statutes*, ii, 569.

[4] Royal Historical Manuscripts Commission's *Reports*, iv, 237; Burk's *Virginia*, ii, Appendix, p. xxxiii. The latter contains other material on this negotiation.

well and Francis Moryson proceeded to England to negotiate with the king and the patentees. Upon their representations the king consented to the incorporation of the
governor, council, and burgesses of Virginia for the purpose
of receiving quitrents and profits from escheated lands with
which to satisfy the demands of Arlington and Culpeper.[1]
He also gave his consent to the drawing up of a document
to protect the Virginians from any further grants, like
those which have been described, provided that the king's
power should not be lessened " for the New England disease is very catching." [2]   The commotions in Virginia
deferred the granting of this charter until later and its
exact wording is not known.[3]

The tobacco of the Chesapeake, like the vacant lands of
Virginia, seemed to afford a probable source of profit to
the English exchequer. In the navigation acts and the
laws raising revenue, tobacco was regulated and taxed with
great thoroughness ; but the government sought to equalize
matters by prohibiting its production in England, Ireland,
and the Channel Islands.[4]   The price of tobacco on the

[1] *Calendars of State Papers, America
and West Indies, 1675–1676,* p. 298.

[2] *Ibid., 1675–1676,* p. 153. Burk's *Virginia,* ii, Appendix, p. xl.

[3] The report of the Lords Committee
for Foreign Plantations, advising the is-
suance of such a charter as the Virginians
desired, was presented at a meeting of the
Privy Council, which was held on November 19, 1675 (Burk's *Virginia,* ii, Appendix, p. lv) ; *Calendars of State Papers,
America and West Indies, 1675–1676,* p.
356. Virginia writers often refer to a
document that bears date October, 1676
(Burk's *Virginia,* ii, Appendix, p. lxi ;
Hening's *Statutes,* ii, 532), as the charter
granted by Charles II. This document
states that Virginians shall be under the
immediate dependence upon the crown
under the rule of such officers as the
king might appoint. It confirms Virginians in the possession of their lands

and declares that the existing system of
fifty-acre head rights shall continue.
It also states that treason, felony, and
murder shall in the future be tried by the
governor or deputy governor and council.
On the repeal of the New York " Bill of
Rights " of 1691 in 1697, it was proposed
to issue a similar document for New
York; but this does not appear to have
been done. The record, however,
mentions the Virginia Charter granted
by Charles II and is therefore additional
proof that such a document was issued ;
see *New York Colonial Documents,* iv,
264. Moreover, in 1717, it was stated that
trial in criminal causes was confirmed
to the people of Virginia by the " Royal
Charter of 10th Oct., 1676," *Virginia
Magazine of History,* v, 272, from " Ludwell MSS."

[4] 12 Charles II, Cap. 34 (*Statutes of the
Realm,* v, 297).

plantations was lower at this time than at any other period in Virginia's history. There had been a large emigration to the dominion between 1656 and 1670, and the production of tobacco had been greatly increased.[1] Various attempts were made to diminish the amount grown by limiting[2] the period of planting, but Virginia and Maryland could never agree on any one plan.[3] To save themselves from bankruptcy, the planters systematically evaded the navigation laws and were assisted in this by the highest officials in the colony.[4] They also experimented with other commodities, notably with silk. Governor Berkeley sent three hundred pounds of it to Charles, who had it wrought into bed furniture; but the production of silk was never commercially profitable in the Old Dominion.[5] There was distress in Virginia, and the home government treated the planters with anything but gratitude; on the other hand, they were quite circumspect in their dealings with the New Englanders.

"New England is in a peevish and touchy humor,"[6] wrote John Evelyn in 1671, and so it had been for eleven years. The government of the Restoration hesitated to vex the people of Massachusetts lest they should declare the independence of the Puritan Commonwealth.[7] That colony then contained one third of all the inhabitants of English North America. Her government was energetic and autocratic. It had declined to proclaim Richard

[1] *Calendars of State Papers, America and West Indies, 1661–1668*, pp. 384, 394.

[2] *Ibid., 1661–1668*, pp. 90, 132, 222, 257, 391; *Colonial Records of North Carolina*, i, 117, 139, 141, 152.

[3] "Newsletter" noted in Royal Historical Manuscript Commission's *Reports*, xii, Part vii, 53.

[4] *Calendars of State Papers, America and West Indies, 1675–1676*, p. 385.

[5] *Ibid., 1661–1668*, p. 594, "News-

letters" noted in Royal Historical Manuscripts Commission's *Reports*, xii, Part vii, 60.

[6] Evelyn's *Diary*, ii, 261, 262, 264, 273; the quotation is on p. 262.

[7] See Toppan's *Edward Randolph*, i, 41 note; Hutchinson's *Collection of Original Papers*, 320–331; *Calendars of State Papers, America and West Indies, 1661–1668*, p. 30.

Cromwell and might refuse to acknowledge the restoration of the old monarchy.[1] Military men declared that a few warships by interfering with the trade of New England could bring the colonists to terms without making any direct attack on them; but the king had no ships of war to spare for that service in the first half of his reign and for the present took no decisive action. The sentiment of racial unity and personal loyalty to the royal family kept Massachusetts within the empire in 1660.

Captain Breedon, an Englishman, then residing at Boston, recognized two of the regicides on the streets of that town. These were Edward Whalley and William Goffe. They were marked men, having served as " Major Generals " in the Protectorate, and Goffe had led Cromwell's own regiment of Ironsides at the battle of Dunbar and had urged severity in dealing with Charles I.[2] They speedily disappeared from Massachusetts, and John Endicott who was then governor appointed two agents to seek them out and bring them back to Boston. These agents followed them to Hartford and New Haven and there losing the scent went on to New Amsterdam. Stuyvesant assured them that there were no regicides in his government and that if any appeared, he would send them to Boston. The agents returned and reported their doings and their failure, which Governor Endicott lost no time in sending to England. Whalley and Goffe had been sheltered at New Haven. At a later period they moved northward to the new settle-

---

[1] They would have been entirely justified in doing this according to the theories by which John Locke defended the English Revolution of 1688–89 and Thomas Jefferson the American Revolution of 1776.

[2] Carlyle's *Cromwell*, Letter xcii.

F. B. Dexter's " Memoranda respecting Whalley and Goffe " (New Haven Historical Society's *Papers*, ii, 117) gives many details as to the early careers of these regicides and also of their movements in New Haven Colony.

ment of Hadley in Massachusetts and there lived in obscurity for many years.[1]

Meantime, in December, 1660, the General Court of Massachusetts Bay had formulated and sent to England an address to the king. In this they prayed his gracious protection in the continuance of the privileges and religion [2] which had been granted to them by his royal father and declared that their "liberty to walk in the faith of the gospel with all good conscience . . . was the cause of their transporting themselves . . . from that pleasant land over the ocean into this vast and waste wilderness." Again, in the following August, they addressed a "gratulatory and lowly " petition to him, begging that they might still be permitted to sing the Lord's song in their strange land, and expressing the hope that the Lord would "make the throne of King Charles the Second both greater and better than the throne of King David or than the throne of any of your royal progenitors." [3]

Charles, doubtless, would have been glad to accept the submission of the Massachusetts authorities and put off any inquiry into their doings until a more convenient season ; but the enemies of the Bay Colony brought forward one complaint after another. On May 17, 1661, the king ap-

[1] On the regicides in New England, see Stiles's *The Three Judges of Charles I;* Goffe's "Journal" is in Massachusetts Historical Society's *Proceedings* for 1863–64, p. 281, and there are papers relating to this subject in the *Collections* of that same society (Third Series, vii, 123). Franklin B. Dexter has printed other documents in New Haven Colony Historical Society's *Papers,* ii, 117; many papers are noted in *Calendars of State Papers, America and West Indies, 1661–1668,* among them Endicott's instructions to his agents, Kirke and Kellond (p. 27). Their report is in Hutchinson's *Collections of Original Papers,* 334.

[2] *Calendars of State Papers, America and West Indies, 1574–1660,* p. 495; Hutchinson's *Collection of Original Papers,* 325. The royal letter of February 15, 1660–61, announcing the restoration of Charles (Hutchinson's *Collection,* 333) was probably written while this letter was on its way to England. It is significant that these letters should have been written more than six months after Charles's accession to power.

[3] *Calendars of State Papers, America and West Indies, 1661–1668,* p. 51; Hutchinson's *Collection of Original Papers,* 341; *Massachusetts Colony Records,* iv; Part ii, 33.

pointed a committee of the Privy Council to consider "the settlement of the Government of New England." [1] Upon their advice, he sent a royal letter,[2] directing the government at Boston to send to England for trial all Quakers who were then in prison. This missive reached Massachusetts at a moment when the prison doors had temporarily been thrown open.[3] The General Court suspended [4] the execution of the laws against the Quakers until further order. Later, an address [5] was sent to the king describing the Quakers as "open capital blasphemers, open seducers from the glorious Trinitie, the Lords Christ, our Lord Jesus Christ, the blessed gospel, and from the holy Scriptures as the rule of life, open enemies to government itself as established in the hands of any but men of their own principles, malignant and assiduous promoters of doctrines directly tending to subvert both our Churches and State . . . The Quakers died not because of their other crimes how capital soever, but upon their superadded presumptuous and incorrigible contempt of authority." Had they promised to depart and not return, "we should have bene glad of such an oportunitie to have said they should not dye." [6]

[1] *Calendars of State Papers, America and West Indies, 1661–1668*, p. 30. The Council for Foreign Plantations summarized their objections to the course pursued by the government of Massachusetts in a report dated April 30, 1661 (*ibid., 1661–1668*, p. 24).

[2] *Ibid., 1661–1668*, p. 55 (September 9, 1661).

[3] Order of the General Court, May 22, 1661; *ibid., 1661–1668*, p. 33; *Massachusetts Colony Records*, iv, Part ii, 24. As to the significance of this so-called "King's Missive," see G. E. Ellis in Massachusetts Historical Society's *Proceedings*, xviii, 357, and J. G. Whittier in *ibid.*, xviii, 387. Dr. Ellis notes the *ex parte* nature of much of the evidence on the Quaker side as the well-known

works of Sewel and Bishop. It is the same as to the persecutions of the Quakers in the other colonies and in England.

[4] *Massachusetts Colony Records*, iv, Part ii, 34 (November 27, 1661).

[5] *Calendars of State Papers, America and West Indies, 1661–1668*, p. 8 (February 11, 1661–62).

[6] To the Quakers the action of the Massachusetts magistrates assumed a distinctly different guise, and seemed harsh and unjust, as can be seen by reading the title of a book which was published at London in 1659, with the name of Francis Howgil on the title page: "The Popish Inquisition newly erected in New England, whereby their Church is manifested to be a Daughter of Mys-

Massachusetts sent Simon Bradstreet and John Norton, the latter a clergyman, to represent the colony at London and, if possible, to mitigate the complaints of her enemies. They returned with another royal missive,[1] asserting that the Quakers' principles being inconsistent with government, the king had made a sharp law against them and was content that Massachusetts should do the like. So far, the letter was satisfactory, but it went on to require that persons of good estate and mode of life should be admitted to the right to vote, although they were not members of any approved Massachusetts religious organization. After an interval, the General Court passed a law to meet the king's demands; but as the orthodoxy of the candidate for admission to the company would be certified to by one of the settled ministers of the colony, the law did not accomplish much in the way of broadening the franchise.[2]

tery — Babylon, Which did drink the Blood of the Saints, who bears the express Image of her Mother, demonstrated by her Fruits . . . manifest by their wicked compulsory Laws against the Lamb and his Followers, and their cruel and bloody Practices against the Dear Servants of the Lord." The next year he published another book entitled "The Deceiver of the Nations Discovered . . . More especially *his Cruel Works of Darkness* laid open & reprov'd in *Mariland* in *Virginia*, and the *Sad Sufferings* of the *Servants of the Lord* there by his *Cruel Instruments*." In this work he is especially severe on the rulers of Maryland who, according to him, confiscated the Quakers' goods, tortured, imprisoned, whipped, and scourged them. "How have they grinded the Faces of the poor," he asks, "And yet not for Evil-doing, it may be for not doffing a hat, or because they cannot learn to be swift to shed blood," — all of which applies to Massachusetts as well as to Maryland. Howgil was himself to be a victim of the universality of the intolerance toward Quakers

among English-speaking people; for refusing to take the oath he was committed to jail by the justices of Kendal in Westmoreland, England, and there died in 1669, after four and a half years' imprisonment.

[1] *Calendars of State Papers, America and West Indies, 1661–1668*, p. 93.

[2] This law provided that a man over twenty-four years of age who was orthodox in religion and of good conversation and paid ten shillings in any one rate might be considered for admission to the Massachusetts Bay Company; but his name would have to be voted on by the members of the corporation. Whitmore's *Laws of 1672*, p. 56. It is said that not three per cent of the men in the colony paid as much as ten shillings in a single rate. *Calendars of State Papers, America and West Indies, 1661–1668*, p. 344. The General Court in 1675 refused to permit a deputy to take his seat because they suspected him of being "prelatical in his principles." Felt's *Ecclesiastical History of New England*, ii, 566.

While Massachusetts was fencing with royal authorities, Connecticut and Rhode Island were seeking privileges at the hands of the king. These colonies had no authorization for government from any Stuart monarch. For some time, Dr. John Clarke of Rhode Island had been in England seeking protection for the weak settlements on Narragansett Bay against the encroachment of her powerful neighbors of the New England Confederation. He had solicited one government after another, but had not accomplished much when John Winthrop, Jr., came to London to secure a royal charter, giving rights of jurisdiction to the voters of Connecticut.[1] The younger Winthrop enjoyed peculiar facilities in approaching the second Charles. Besides being a cousin of Sir George Downing, he had been a faithful servant to Lord Say and Sele, both were now in favor at court. Winthrop is said to have made presents to some of the leading men, and a little money well distributed would have gone a long way with Sir George Carteret and the other restored courtiers in the year 1662. There is a picturesque story of the presentation to the king by the Connecticut negotiator of a ring which the first Charles is said to have given to the first Winthrop while the latter was still in good repute with Buckingham and his master. By whatever means he accomplished it, John Winthrop, Jr., secured for himself and his fellow-colonists of Connecticut a most liberal grant of rights of jurisdiction. He also gained a confirmation of their claims to land so extensive in its scope that it included New Haven Colony and the greater part of the

[1] The petitions of Clarke on the behalf of Rhode Island and of Winthrop for Connecticut are noted in *Calendars of State Papers, America and West Indies, 1661-1668*, pp. 4, 5, 74; for Clarke, see *Dictionary of National Biography*; for Winthrop, see "Sketch of John Winthrop the Younger" by T. F. Waters in Ipswich Historical Society's *Publications*, No. vii; and American Antiquarian Society's *Proceedings*, 1898, p. 295. A good life of him is greatly to be desired.

mainland of Rhode Island within the chartered limits of
Connecticut. Winthrop could scarcely have done anything else than secure a confirmation of the deed from
the Saybrook grantees;[1] but the inclusion of New Haven
within the limits of its more powerful and less holy
neighbor appeared to the people of the smaller colony
rank treachery on his part. For a time civil war between
two members of the New England Confederation seemed
probable; but wiser counsels prevailed and the New
Havenites submitted to the inevitable.[2]

In the Connecticut charter the eastern limit was stated
to be the "Narragansett River." This phrase contained
the seed for trouble with Rhode Island, for if the Narragansett Bay was the same thing as the river, the greater
part of the mainland of the present state of Rhode Island
would have been included within the limits of Connecticut.
Dr. Clarke at once protested; but he and Winthrop, realizing the ill consequences of such a disputation at the
moment, submitted the matter to arbiters in England.
These decided that the phrase "Narragansett River," as
it was used in the charter, should be interpreted to mean
Pawcatuck River,[3] because that stream might be described
as the river of the Narragansett country. This interpretation was incorporated in the text of the Rhode Island
patent which was issued in the next year (1663).[4] Connecticut repudiated Winthrop's acceptance of the arbitra-
tion, and proceeded to take possession of the land between

---

[1] See vol. i, p. 401, of the present
work.

[2] This matter is summarized in Palfrey's *New England*, ii, 543. Longer
accounts are in Trumbull's *History of
Connecticut*, i, 250–278; Atwater's *History of New Haven*, chs. xx, xxi; many
documents are printed in *New Haven
Colonial Records*, iii, 467–557.

[3] *Calendars of State Papers, America
and West Indies, 1661–1668*, p. 127; *1677–
1680*, pp. 575, 578, 592; C. W. Bowen's
Boundary Disputes of Connecticut, 33.

[4] *Charters and Constitutions of the
United States*, ii, 1602.

the Pawcatuck River and Narragansett Bay. The Rhode Islanders vehemently objected. Early in 1665 the Royal Commissioners who had come out in the preceding year to conquer New Netherland and settle disputations in New England visited this region. They took the coveted tract from the jurisdiction of both colonies, called it the King's Province, and then appointed the Rhode Island magistrates to act as commissioners therein.[1] Nevertheless, Connecticut continued from time to time, as opportunity or occasion offered, to exercise power within the disputed region. For instance, in August, 1672, a Commissioners' Court was held at " Wickford in Connecticut Colony." At that time and place, John Johnson prosecuted the wife of Edmund Cosons for feloniously taking divers goods from his house. " Presently," so the record reads, " there came a writing . . . sent by the magistrates of Rhode Island " warning the Commissioner in the name of his Majesty not to exercise jurisdiction within the King's Province.[2] And so the dispute went on, until Sir Edmund Andros took possession of both colonies. Ultimately, the King's Province fell to Rhode Island.

In 1663 John Clarke obtained a charter for Rhode Island. This and the Connecticut patent bore a close resemblance to each other, although there are a few differences to be noted. In each of them certain persons, who are mentioned by name, are incorporated with an official residence in the colony and with power to admit others to share in their rights. The effect was to incorporate the voters of each colony and to give them rights of self-

---

[1] *Calendars of State Papers, America and West Indies, 1661–1668*, pp. 275, 342.

[2] " Fones Records," Mss. in the office of the Secretary of State of Rhode Island. The best account of this dispute is in Bowen's *Boundary Disputes of Connecticut*, Part ii. See also S. G. Arnold's *Rhode Island*, 315; Palfrey's *New England*, ii, 603.

government. The laws of Connecticut and Rhode Island were to be like those of England, so far as was convenient, but they were not submitted to the king for his approbation or disallowance. The framework of government resembled that which had been worked out in the New England colonies. It consisted of a governor, a board of assistants, and an assembly — all chosen by the voters. The governor of these " charter colonies " possessed less power and dignity than did the chief magistrates of the royal and proprietary provinces ; he was, indeed, hardly more than the first among the assistants. The franchise was left to the determination of the legislature in each colony ; but the apportionment of representation was partly arranged in the charters, and gave in Rhode Island what turned out to be an undue amount of power to the older towns as against the commercial and industrial centers developed by changing economic conditions. Apart from the sweeping grant of power the most notable clause in the Rhode Island patent is that which confirmed the policy of that colony as to religious freedom. So liberal were these charters that they survived the Revolution and remained the fundamental laws of Connecticut and Rhode Island until 1818 and 1842, respectively.[1]

Among the most influential and persistent of the enemies of Massachusetts was Samuel Maverick. He was one of the first to settle on the shores of Boston Harbor and had been admitted to the Massachusetts Bay Company in spite of the fact that he was an Episcopalian. Later, he had fallen out with the rulers and had removed to New Amsterdam. He now wrote to Clarendon and to other lead-

[1] These charters may be found in any of the early compilations of the laws of Connecticut and Rhode Island, or in the governmental publication entitled *Charters and Constitutions of the United States.*

ing men in England [1] that for thirty years he with some thousands of loyal subjects had been deprived of civil and religious liberty by the Massachusetts government. He suggested that all of the old New England, as it existed in 1620, should be annexed to the crown; if this were not feasible, a royal commission might be sent out to "regulate all things." [2]

The plan of sending a commission to New England had already been under discussion, but it was not until 1664 that the Commissioners sailed for America and they then had the twofold task of conquering New Netherland as well as regulating New England. They were Colonel Richard Nicolls, Sir Robert Carr, Colonel George Cartwright, and Mr. Samuel Maverick.[3] They had two sets of instructions, one to be shown to the Massachusetts authorities, the other to guide them in the performance of their tasks.[4] According to the latter, they were to endeavor to ingratiate themselves with Massachusetts people by attending their churches and by not appearing solicitous as to religion, and were to ascertain the true condition of the New England colonies.[5] Their public instructions directed them to assure the government of Massachusetts of the king's good intentions and directed them to exercise great discretion in the performance of their task, that the colonists might realize the king's "singular affection" for them. Clarendon tried to enforce discretion by writing

[1] "Clarendon Papers" in New York Historical Society's *Collections* for 1869, pp. 19, 35.

[2] *Calendars of State Papers, America and West Indies, 1661–1668*, pp. 151, 157.

[3] The last three named commissioners were second-rate characters. It was provided, therefore, that they could not act unless all three of them were present. Colonel Nicolls could act with the aid of only one of his colleagues. *Calendars of*

State Papers, America and West Indies, 1661–1668, pp. 110, 128.

[4] *New York Colonial Documents*, iii, 51, 55, 57, 64.

[5] See letter of Charles II of January 28, 1664, to Nicolls and the other commissioners in "Winslow Papers" in the cabinet of the Massachusetts Historical Society; there are several letters on this episode which have never been printed.

a personal note to Maverick;[1] but that worthy at once suggested to Captain Breedon[2] that he should advise the Governor and Company of Massachusetts Bay to take care what they do in view of the coming of his Majesty's Commissioners.

On learning what was in store for them, the Massachusetts rulers confided the charter to the care of a committee, placed a garrison in the fort at the entrance to the harbor, mounted new guns on its ramparts, and supplied it with ammunition. The Commissioners made a brief visit to Boston on their way to New Netherland, and after the conquest of that colony, Cartwright, Maverick, and Carr returned to New England. They had no trouble with the Connecticut and Rhode Island colonists, and going to Plymouth suggested that the settlers there might get their lands confirmed without cost, provided they would receive a royal governor; but the men of Plymouth replied that they preferred to remain as they were. The Massachusetts government petitioned the king in loyal phrase to " let our Government live, our patent live, our magistrates live, our laws and liberties live, our religious enjoyments live, so shall we all have yet further cause to say from our heart, ' Let the King live for ever,' and the blessing of them that were ready to perish shall come upon your Majesty, having delivered the poor that crieth and such as had none to help them."[3] If the king were not merciful, they added, they would be obliged to seek new habitations or faint under intolerable burdens.

In dealing with the Commissioners, the Massachusetts

[1] *New York Colonial Documents*, iii, 92; *Calendars of State Papers, America and West Indies, 1661–1668*, p. 288.

[2] *Ibid.*, p. 221.

[3] *Massachusetts Colony Records*, iv, Part ii, 129; the greater part of the petition is also printed in Palfrey's *New England*, ii, 588; the answer by Secretary Morrice is noted in *Calendars of State Papers, America and West Indies, 1661–1668*, p. 282.

authorities also expressed great loyalty, calling attention
to the fact that they held their lands and governed the
people by virtue of a charter from his Majesty's royal
father, the first Charles. This patent obliged them to safeguard the interests of the people of Massachusetts Bay, and
this they proposed to do. The Commissioners tried to get
them to acknowledge their authority, but the reply was
that the charter did not require them to give an opinion
as to the validity of a royal commission. Even the at-
tracting presence of Colonel Nicolls could not budge the
men of Massachusetts from this position. The Commissioners then opened a court of inquiry,[1] but the magistrates
sent a trumpeter around the town warning all persons
upon their allegiance to the king and duty to God to refrain
from heeding the call of the Commissioners. After this
rebuff, Nicolls returned to New York, and the others, after
an unsatisfactory visit to Maine followed him.[2] Massachusetts did what it could to salve the wounded feelings of
majesty by more petitions,[3] by a present of a shipload of
great masts, and by sending provisions to the West Indies
to refresh the crews of the English ships in those waters.[4]
For the present nothing further could be done; the king
could only thank Massachusetts for the masts and the
seasonable succor and bide his time.

The policy of the New England colonists toward the
aboriginal inhabitants of that region had been enlightened

[1] New York Historical Society's *Collections*, 1869, pp. 62, 68.

[2] *Calendars of State Papers, America
and West Indies, 1661–1668*, pp. 305, 310,
333, 341. Cartwright sailed for England
with the official papers, but was captured
by a Dutch privateer. Carr, thereupon,
drew up a report from memory, and later
going to England to report in person,
died at Bristol, the day after he landed.
In 1671 Cartwright, having regained Eng-

land, drew up a "recollection of his
thoughts." See also Brodhead's *New
York*, ii, 113 note.

[3] Massachusetts Historical Society's
Proceedings, Second Series, vi, 469; the
oaths of allegiance adopted in 1665 are
in *ibid.*, 1873, 233.

[4] *Calendars of State Papers, America
and West Indies, 1661–1668*, p. 497; *1669–
1674*, p. 20.

and humane from the beginning, that is if any policy which deprived the Indians of their hunting grounds could be so considered. They recognized that the natives possessed a right of occupancy of the soil which it was their business to extinguish.[1] This they had generally done by purchase; but when the savages became restive and attacked the settlers, they had meted out to them that severity of treatment which the prestige of the white man seems to require. The colonists through their legislatures had usually forbidden the sale of spirituous liquors to the Indians. They had provided the natives with many useful implements, and in private disputes between the whites and the Indians had endeavored to render justice to the aborigines. Meantime the Dutch and English rulers of the Hudson Valley fostered the members of the Iroquois confederacy, providing them with firearms and ammunition. The white settlers were constantly pressing inland from the seacoast, killing the game and destroying the wilderness which sheltered it, and the Iroquois barred the way to the interior of the continent. The Indians of southeastern New England made one desperate attempt to regain their lost hunting grounds by driving the whites into the sea or killing them where they lived. Conditions similar to these existed in Virginia and Maryland, for the power of the Iroquois extended southward to the Ohio; they were constantly forcing the coast tribes upon the frontier settlements of the tobacco colonies. These Indians, like those of New England, must fight or die. In June, 1675, the Indians attacked the farmers of Swanzey in New Plymouth Colony and killed a planter in Stafford County, Virginia.

The Indian war of 1675–76 in New England is known

[1] See the present work, vol. i, pp. 338–341.

as King Philip's War, from the name of Massasoit's son, the chief of the Wompanoags.[1] He resented the contemptuous attitude of the Plymouth magistrates, who seemed to regard him as being in a state of pupilage. A series of murders and executions aroused the Indians' fears and led to hostilities while both whites and reds were unprepared. The contest spread from the seacoast to the Connecticut Valley,[2] and then eastwardly to the province of Maine. The whites had taught the natives the use of firearms and had converted many of them to Christianity. The converts generally relapsed and the Indians used their firearms against the nearest white settlers. The red men had been so intimate with the colonists that they knew their peculiar habits. They were thus enabled to choose the best time for attack, especially when the settlers were attending divine service. At the outset, victory usually was with the Indians, who were more mobile and better able to endure hardships and hunger. After the war had gone on for a few months, however, the tide of success changed.

The Narragansetts, living to the west of the bay of that name, were the strongest tribe in New England east of the Connecticut River. Their chief sachem was Canonchet. He was aroused by the success of the early Indian attacks to play a somewhat doubtful and defiant part. The authorities of Massachusetts, Connecticut, and New Plymouth thought that the easiest way to solve the problem would be to crush the power of the Narragansetts, once for all. A combined force sought out their fortified village in what is now Kingston, R. I. In the

---

[1] His Indian name was Metacom; the whites always called him Philip.

[2] Grindall Reynolds' essay on "King Philip's War," in his *Collection of Historical and Other Papers*, deals especially with Brookfield, but many of his suggestions as to the war in general show historical acumen.

midst of the cold and snow of a New England winter, they attacked it in broad daylight, carried it by storm, and slew the inhabitants, December 19, 1675. How many Indians were killed, how many were wounded, how many were captured, will never be known : it is certain that, on that day, the military power of the Narragansett tribe was broken. The course of the conflict now turned more and more in favor of the whites, although there were many disasters still to be suffered. With the killing of King Philip on August 12, 1676, the war in southern New England came practically to an end ; but it continued for some time in the eastern settlements, where it had begun later.

King Philip's War greatly weakened New England. Of the five thousand men of military age in Massachusetts and New Plymouth, one in ten had been killed or captured. Of the eighty or ninety towns in eastern New England, forty were badly damaged by fire and a dozen were totally destroyed. More than one hundred thousand pounds were spent by the colonists on their military forces, a sum which was stated to exceed in amount the personal property of the inhabitants.

The conflict in the colonies on the Chesapeake involved both Virginia and Maryland. In its course, a body of Susquehanna Indians was blockaded in an abandoned fort by Marylanders under Major Thomas Truman and Virginians under Colonel John Washington. Five chiefs came from the fort to negotiate with the whites. After some debate they were led away and killed. For this act, Major Truman was impeached by the lower house of the Maryland Assembly and was convicted by the council. He was never punished because the two houses could not agree as to the penalty, the delegates arguing for a fine only on the ground that the Virginians had consented to the execution.[1] The outcome of this slaying of the envoys was a fierce and desperate Indian war, in which Virginia especially suffered. Governor Berkeley seemed to the colonists to be lukewarm in their defense. The murder by the Indians of an overseer on Nathaniel Bacon's frontier plantation gave the signal for an attempt by the settlers to take matters into their own hands, which in turn led to an insurrection that is known in Virginia history as Bacon's Rebellion.

There were many other reasons for discontent in the Old Dominion. Among these was the autocratic nature of the government. The chief magistrate, Sir William Berkeley, had occupied that office ever since 1642, excepting for a few years in the time of the Puritan supremacy. He was now old and marriage to a young wife had converted his earlier desire for the public good into a " covetous foolage."[3] His temper, which was never stable, had not improved with years, so that he was now " peevish and brittle." [2] He was no longer popular, but the Assembly was helpless to control him, because he took his salary of twelve hundred pounds sterling from permanent revenues.[3] In the later royal provinces the council acted as a curb upon the governor, and this had been the intention of those who drew up Berkeley's commission and instructions.[4] His long tenure of office, his powerful connections in England, and his manipulation of appointments in

[1] *William and Mary Quarterly*, ii, 39; *Maryland Archives* (Assembly, May 27, 1676), ii, 494. Truman's impeachment was the first in colonial history.

[2] *Journal of the Life, Travels, Sufferings, and Labour of Love of William Edmundson* (2d ed., London, 1774), 70.

[3] This was the two-shilling impost on each hogshead of tobacco exported.

Hening's *Statutes*, ii, 130. There were also fees and perquisites.

[4] For the commission of 1641, see vol. i of the present work, p. 232. The instructions of 1662 are noted in Royal Historical Manuscripts Commission's *Reports*, iv, 237, and *Calendars of State Papers, America and West Indies, 1661-1668*, p. 110.

Virginia had made him practically absolute. The councilors were leading planters in the colony and were banded
together by class interests. They performed all kinds of
functions, legislative, judicial, and executive, and secured
most of the lucrative appointments in the colony.

The system of local government which prevailed in
Virginia made for the exaltation of the councilors and
other leading planters. The principal administrative division was the county which was ruled by the justices
sitting as a county court. These not only acted in a
judicial capacity, but laid the taxes and voted expenditures without the assistance of the humbler inhabitants
of the county. As they were appointed by the governor,
they were but slightly amenable to the action of public
opinion and sometimes closed the doors when discussing
financial questions.[1] The other administrative unit was
the parish which was ruled by the vestry. Originally, the
vestrymen had been elected by the parishioners, but now
they filled the vacancies in their own number. As a rule
the justices of the county courts sat on the vestries of
their parishes. On their own plantations they were supreme, as was well expressed by one of their number
when he asserted that a Quaker "might as well go naked
into a hot oven as set his foot on my plantation."

The land system of Virginia also greatly assisted in
the building up of an aristocracy. Each importer of labor
was entitled to fifty acres of land for each person whom
he imported, but the land must be "seated" within a
short time. These technical requirements meant little in
practice. In 1697 the attorney general of the province
informed the Lords of Trade that head rights could be
bought for twelve pence each and declared that Colonel

---

[1] "Surry County Grievances," 1676, in *Virginia Magazine of History*, ii, 170.

Ludlow, having a certificate for forty rights, added a cipher to the record and thus secured twenty thousand acres.[1] Land was granted subject to a quitrent and was forfeited if it was not "seated" within the appointed time and the quitrents paid when due. The planters combined to evade these requirements by buying forfeited estates for nominal prices and deeding them back to the first holder.[2] In these and other devious ways, thousands of acres were secured by the richer planters.

Of the forty thousand persons living within the settled area of Virginia in 1670, six thousand were white servants and two thousand negro slaves. The servants were indentured for varying terms of years, — three, five, seven, fourteen, or twenty-one. Those who were bound for the longest period were convicts who were now coming to Virginia in appreciable numbers.[3] Those who were bound for the briefer terms were often respectable persons whose poverty had compelled them to sell their services for a term of years to pay the expenses of emigration to the New World. Upon receiving their freedom, the erstwhile servants were given small amounts of land and, in a short time, might themselves become employers of labor. They formed a class of small landowners who had no capital except their personal energy and experience and were, therefore, severely affected by the recurring low prices of the staple products of their farms. The growth of the

---

[1] "Board of Trade Journals," Ms., September 1, September 20, 1697 ("Philadelphia Transcripts," x, 228, 265).

[2] An interesting account of this process is given in Bassett's "Introduction" to his edition of *The Writings of William Byrd of Westover.* Commissary Blair testified in 1697 that this Colonel Byrd's father, who was at that time deputy auditor and also a member of the council, sold the "quitrent tobacco" to himself and the governor. "Board of Trade Journals," Ms., August 25, 1697 ("Philadelphia Transcripts," x, 220).

[3] In 1670 the "General Court" by order prohibited the landing of felons. *Calendars of State Papers, America and West Indies, 1669–1674,* p. 63; Hening's *Statutes,* ii, 509.

landed aristocracy also made them restless and led to
abortive insurrections in 1673 and 1674.[1]   Fifteen hundred
servants came in annually, but only three slave ships had
visited the colony in the seven years ending in 1670.[2]   The
increasing number of the laboring class made possible the
large plantations which were the mark of this period.

The condition of religion and education also was unfavorable to the smaller planters.   It was easy for rich
men to hire private tutors for their children ; but this was
out of the question with the small farmers, who also were
often denied the consolations of religion.   The parishes
were of vast extent, many of them were without churches
and more without ministers.   The ecclesiastics exercised
little influence and were often inefficient in the discharge
of their duties.   A contemporary writer states that two
thirds of the preachers were " leaden lay readers " and
that even laymen usurped the office of minister.[3]   In his
famous report,[4] which was presented to the Lords of Trade
in 1671, Governor Berkeley declared that " we have forty-
eight parishes, and our ministers are well paid, and by my
consent should be better *if they would pray oftener and
preach less.*   But of all other commodities, so of this, *the
worst are sent us,* and we had few that we could boast of,
since the persecution in Cromwell's tiranny drove divers
worthy men hither.   But I thank God, *there are no free
schools,* nor *printing,* and I hope we shall not have, these
hundred years ; for *learning* has brought disobedience, and
heresy, and sects into the world, and *printing* has divulged
them, and libels against the best of government.   God
keep us from both ! "

---

[1] Charles Campbell's *History of the
Colony and Ancient Dominion of Virginia,* 275.

[2] Hening's *Statutes,* ii, 515.

[3] Campbell's *Virginia,* 277.

[4] This is printed in many places as
in Hening's *Statutes,* ii ; Neill's *Virginia
Carolorum,* 330; the quoted matter is on
p. 338 of Neill and ii, 517, of Hening.

The years immediately following 1670 saw a succession of poor harvests. The spring of 1673 had been preceded by "an unexperimented hard winter," in which half of the live stock had perished.[1] Wheat and corn were so scarce in Virginia in 1676 that Governor Berkeley felt obliged to prohibit the exportation of food from the province to supply the New Englanders whom King Philip's War had placed on short commons.[2] Poverty and a sense of unredressed grievances were now combined with Indian massacres to work the people to highest indignation. It was at this moment that a leader appeared in the person of Nathaniel Bacon.

The new leader came of that famous English family[3] which had given lord chancellors to Elizabeth and to her successor, the first James. He was connected by marriage with Sir William Berkeley and with Lord Culpeper, and it is not impossible that a dispute over property or some other family matter was the cause of the violent hatred which Berkeley displayed toward his wife's kinsman.[4] Bacon had come to Virginia after 1670[5] and had settled on the western frontier.[6] When his plantation was attacked by the Indians and his overseer killed,[7] he led a force

---

[1] *Calendars of State Papers, America and West Indies, 1669–1674*, p. 474.

[2] *Ibid., 1675–1676*, pp. 301, 366.

[3] See *Virginia Magazine of History* (ii, 125) for notes on the Bacons of England and Virginia, from which John Fiske constructed the genealogy which is printed on p. 64 of the second volume of his *Old Virginia*.

[4] In letters written in 1680, Culpeper speaks of "our Cousin Nat Bacon, the Rebel's widow." Again he writes: "My Lady Berkeley is married to Mr. Ludwell and thinks no more of our world. I shall now marry Cate as soone as I can and then shall reckon myself to be a Freeman without clogge or charge." Maxwell's *Virginia Historical Register*,

iii, 190, 193. Lady Berkeley was probably the sister of Alexander Culpeper and niece or cousin of Thomas, Lord Culpeper, governor of Virginia.

[5] William Sherwood, writing in 1676, states that Bacon had been two years in the country. *Virginia Magazine of History*, i, 169.

[6] There was another Nathaniel Bacon in Virginia, an older settler, and a kinsman of the more famous man. The elder is generally referred to as Nathaniel Bacon, Senior.

[7] As to these outrages, see a letter from Mrs. Nathaniel Bacon, Jr., to her sister, in *Virginia Magazine of History*, v, 219.

against the savages and dealt them a vigorous blow. A priori, one would suppose that a provincial governor would hail with delight such a display of vigor ; but Berkeley declared that Bacon was little better than a rebel and set forth to arrest him for fighting the Indians without a commission. Upon this, the inhabitants of York Peninsula burst into open revolt against the government. Berkeley abandoned his expedition and, realizing that some concession to the people was necessary, dissolved the assembly that had been in existence since October, 1660, and issued writs[1] for a new election (May 10, 1676). The new assembly was controlled by the reformers who passed a series of acts which are ordinarily known as Bacon's Laws, although there is no evidence that he had anything to do with them.[2] These acts were all repealed by order of the king,[3] but succeeding assemblies reënacted some of the more important provisions. In 1677 they provided that the freeholders of each parish might appoint six of their number to sit and vote with the vestrymen " at the assessing of the parish taxes,"[4] and two years later provided that four or more representatives in each county should sit with the justices when they made new by-laws.[5] In 1677, also, the holding of more than one office was forbidden by law.[6] These acts would have gone far to redress the political grievances of the Virginians; but, although they remained unrepealed for many years, probably little attention was paid to them.

Nathaniel Bacon, Jr., had been chosen a member of the Assembly of 1676, although he already had a seat in the

[1] Berkeley's proclamation is in *Calendars of State Papers, America and West Indies, 1675–1676*, p. 391.

[2] Hening's *Statutes*, ii, 341–365.

[3] *Calendars of State Papers, America and West Indies, 1675–1676*, p. 468.

[4] Hening's *Statutes*, ii, 396.

[5] *Ibid.*, ii, 441.

[6] *Ibid.*, ii, 390.

Council.[1] He came to Jamestown in an armed sloop to attend the session; but before he reached the little capital of the Old Dominion he and his boat were captured by Captain Gardner of the armed ship *Adam and Eve.* Upon receiving his submission and upon his making acknowledgment of his late crimes and disobediences, Berkeley set Bacon at liberty and readmitted him to the Council. Bacon resented the interference of the commander of the *Adam and Eve* and caused him to be fined seventy pounds for the unwarranted seizure of his sloop and himself and imprisoned in default of payment.

At this stage of the proceedings, Bacon fled from Jamestown, although why he should have done this is as shrouded in mystery as many other acts of his career. With seventy men, or with six hundred, according to whether one follows the estimate of Baconians or Berkeleyans, he reappeared, marched to the house where the Assembly was in session, and demanded a commission to lead his men against the Indians. Berkeley came out from the Assembly, bared his ancient bosom, and bade the rebels shoot. Bacon replied that he wanted a commission to fight the Indians, and not the life of the senile ruler. He would not harm a hair of Berkeley's head, he said, but must be authorized to fight the heathen, who were daily spilling Christian blood. While this scene was enacting, some of the soldiers pointed their guns at overcurious burgesses who were looking on from the windows of the building in which the sessions of the

[1] It had been the regular practice for councilors to take part in the work of the House of Burgesses, apparently without being elected thereto. On the other hand, the burgesses reviewed the judicial decisions of the council according to Berkeley's Report of 1671 : " Every year, at least, the assembly is called, before whom lye appeals and this assembly is composed of two burgesses out of every county," Hening's *Statutes*, ii, 512. An interesting description of the government of Virginia in 1666 by Thomas Ludwell is in *Virginia Magazine of History*, v, 54.

Assembly were held; but the legislators displayed a white handkerchief, and nothing further was done.

Having extracted a commission by this show of force, Bacon marched with a thousand men to chastise the Indians. His back was hardly turned when Berkeley proclaimed him and his followers rebels and traitors, but public opinion was so clearly against Berkeley that the governor abandoned Jamestown and fled to the loyal settlements at Accomac, across the Chesapeake. Bacon then held a convention at Middle Plantation, where Williamsburg now stands, and obliged his followers to swear "to oppose what forces shall be sent out of England by his Majesty against me, till such time I have acquainted the King with the state of this country, and have had an answer."[1] It was probably at this time that Bacon held a conversation with John Goode, which the latter described to Berkeley.[2] In this conversation Bacon is said to have argued that English soldiers could be successfully resisted, and to have suggested that Virginia might achieve her independence. Moreover, Maryland and Carolina might join the Old Dominion in a concerted movement and in the future choose their own governors and manage their own affairs. Our knowledge of this supposed project of Bacon's rests upon a single piece of ex parte evidence; but the condition of popular feeling in Carolina and in Maryland might well have encouraged him to advocate some such action.

It was while at Middle Plantation, or, perhaps, at some later date, that Bacon issued a proclamation and appeal for support. The proclamation[3] begins: "If virtue be sin,

---

[1] See Fiske's *Virginia*, ii, 83; and in summary in J. A. Doyle's *English in America*, i, 331.

[2] G. Brown Goode's *Virginia Cousins*,

30–B. The same author's article in *Magazine of American History*, xviii, 418, is well worth reading.

[3] *Virginia Magazine of History*, i, 55.

if piety be guilt, all the principles of morality, goodness, and justice be perverted, We must confess that those who are now called rebels may be in danger of those high imputations." If, however, there be a just God, let him judge "since we cannot in our hearts find one single spot of rebellion or treason." The proclamation then denounced those in power as sponges that have sucked up the public treasure as unworthy favorites and juggling parasites, and as forming a powerful cabal. Then follows a declaration of the people in which the surrender of Sir William Berkeley and nineteen other persons was demanded, and those who shelter them declared to be "traitors to the people." The declaration purported to be in the name of "the Commons of Virginia" and was signed "Nath Bacon, Gen'l. By the Consent of ye People." From the use of the phrases the "Commons of Virginia" and "the people," it is not unlikely that Bacon and those who abetted him represented the democratic elements in Virginia society as opposed to the aristocratic desires of Berkeley and his followers. This impression is confirmed by contemporary statements in letters from persons who were more or less prominent on the governor's side. William Sherwood, in one of the interesting letters which came from his pen, informed his correspondent that now "tag, rag, and bobtail carry a high hand" in Virginia.[1] It has frequently been stated that there were "Cromwell's men" among the Baconians, and the lapse of the Virginians from aristocratic ideas has been traced to this source. There may have been a few veterans of the "New Model" in Virginia ; but their numbers must have been insignificant if one may argue from the speedy collapse of the rebellion after Bacon's death.

[1] *Calendars of State Papers, America and West Indies, 1675–1676*, p. 416.

The later portion of the conflict had a curious see-saw character, first Berkeley and then Bacon occupying Jamestown, and then seeking safety across the Chesapeake in Accomac or marching to the frontier to fight the natives. One episode is well avouched. Bacon besieging Jamestown brought forward his artillery, and then taking "the wives and female relations of such gentlemen as were in the governor's service against him (whom he had caused to be brought to the works) places them in the face of his enemy as bulwarks for their battery." On this Berkeley's forces rapidly disintegrated, and the Baconians taking Jamestown set fire to that village that it might not again furnish shelter to their enemy.

From this time on Bacon assumed more and more the air of a successful revolutionist; he hanged one of his followers for attempted desertion; he confiscated property of the Berkeleyans, and he provided for the government of the colony by a system of committees. However, before he concluded his task, "Providence did that which no other hand durst (or at least did) do and cut him off." Fever and dysentery, hard work, and worry killed this first successful American rebel. His followers placed his body in a weighted coffin and sunk it beyond recovery in one of Virginia's many rivers, or, possibly, hid it away in the woods.[1]

With Bacon out of the way, the insurrection rapidly ran to its close. The rebels were hunted down, the leaders were captured and executed, and their property confiscated. One of these, Richard Lawrence, disappeared into the wilderness. Another of them, William Drummond, once governor of Chowan, was warmly received by Governor Berkeley. " Mr. Drummond," he said, " you are very welcome,

---

[1] It is interesting to note that Massachusetts magistrates issued a proclamation for the apprehension of Bacon. *Virginia Magazine of History*, ix, 47.

I am more glad to see you than any man in Virginia. Mr. Drummond, you shall be hanged in half an hour." He was hanged as soon as a council of war could be held and a gibbet erected.[1] A year later his widow sued Berkeley's widow for the unlawful conversion of the crop growing on the executed rebel's estate, and won.

Meantime the wildest rumors were current in England: at one time Berkeley was said to have retired to Nevis in the West Indies;[2] again he was reported to be dead, "Bacon hath hang'd, drawn, and quartered Sir Bartlet, they say, in Virginia."[3] When the king heard of the insurrection, he appointed three commissioners to go to Virginia with one thousand soldiers to crush the rebels,[4] but when the expedition reached the Chesapeake, it was found that the commissioners' principal task was to curb the sanguinary fury of the aged governor. The king's instructions[5] to Berkeley gave him a good deal of discretion, and his powerful connections in England induced the commissioners to act with great caution. Returning to England, Berkeley speedily died without seeing the king.

For a year after Berkeley's retirement, Captain or Colonel Herbert Jeffreys acted as governor. He had many difficulties to contend with, among others the rapacity of the triumphant Berkeleyans, the poverty of the country, and the necessity of supporting the useless soldiers whom he had brought from England. Among the royalists was Philip Ludwell, brother of the secretary of the colony.

---

[1] See *Colonial Records of North Carolina*, i, Introduction, p. xiii. The story of the interview rests upon the narrative which is signed with the initials " T. M.," as is most of the dramatic information relating to the insurrection.

[2] Royal Historical Manuscripts Commission's *Reports*, xii, Part vii, 129.

[3] *Ibid.*, xii., Part v, 32.

[4] *Calendars of State Papers, America and West Indies, 1675–1676*, pp. 449, 455, 457, 460, 461, 476, 483. The estimated cost of the force for one year was sixteen thousand pounds sterling, which would naturally be extracted from the unhappy Virginians. See *ibid.*, 462.

[5] *Ibid., 1675–1676*, pp. 457, 468.

He sued one of the Baconians for damages, and Jeffreys, being appealed to, protected the ex-rebel. Upon this Ludwell declared that the governor was a worse rebel than Bacon, that he was perjured, that he was not worth a groat, "and that if every pitiful little fellow with a periwig that came in governor to this country made the laws as he chose, no one could be safe."[1] The governor laid the matter before the council, which bound Ludwell over in the sum of fifteen hundred pounds sterling to abide the decision of the King in Council and, meantime, to behave properly before the governor. Jeffreys died before the matter came to a decision and three years later Ludwell married Sir William Berkeley's widow. Thomas, Lord Culpeper, had been appointed governor of Virginia for life in 1675,[2] his term of office to begin with the retirement of Sir William Berkeley. Culpeper did not come to the colony until 1679 and his career in Virginia was marked by rapacity and extortion. He came armed, however, with a general pardon which the Assembly enacted as a law and thus put an end to the Baconian troubles. From this time on Virginia is given over to a series of greedy governors and continued to be severely taxed for the benefit of the royal exchequer. Insurrection and riot followed one another with brief intervals of repose. From this picture of royal oppression it is pleasant to turn to the attempts of humbler men to right the ills of humanity by governing through love instead of through fear.

---

[1] The Ludwells were not alone in the use of seventeenth-century language, for Giles Bland, heated with drink, to be sure, told one of them that he was a "pitifull fellow, Puppy . . . mechanic fellow . . . coward." The phrases which Randolph, Quary, Nicholson, Bellomont, and other officials of that time used as to each other and as to those against whom they made charges were couched in such violent language that one is obliged to conclude that their words meant to them no more than the harmless adverbs and adjectives of the present day mean to us. In short, to understand their letters we must translate them into modern English.

[2] *Calendars of State Papers, America and West Indies, 1675-1676*, p. 247.

NOTES

I. Massachusetts and the Commissioners. — The letters and other documents relating to Massachusetts in this period are noted in the volume of *Calendars of State Papers, Colonial Series, America and the West Indies*, for the years 1661–1668. Some of them are printed at length in the *New York Colonial Documents*, iii. The *Records of the Governor and Company of Massachusetts Bay* contain the votes of the General Court and doings of the magistrates. Hutchinson's *History of Massachusetts* and his supplementary volume of " Original Papers " are very helpful. Palfrey's *New England* was written after an examination of the manuscripts, most of which have since been either calendared or printed in full. His account of this episode is full and reliable, although somewhat biased.

II. King Philip's War. — George W. Ellis and John E. Morris collaborated in the production of a volume entitled *King Philip's War* in the " Grafton Historical Series " (New York, 1906). They used the original papers and their volume is amply annotated. G. M. Bodges's *Soldiers of King Philip's War* contains a concise account of the conflict as a whole (pp. 24–43) and a mass of detail as to the war in parts. Palfrey's *New England* is sufficiently detailed for most readers, but is now somewhat antiquated. Among contemporary narratives may be mentioned Increase Mather's *Brief History of the War with the Indians* (Boston, 1676). This with other matter is reprinted in S. G. Drake's *Old Indian Chronicle*. There is a long and important letter from William Harris in the *Calendars of State Papers, America and West Indies, 1675–1676*, pp. 441–444, printed in full in the " Harris Papers " in Rhode Island Historical Society's *Collections*, x. Other papers may be found in the Calendar through the Index under " Philip," especially a letter with inclosures from Governor Leverett of Massachusetts (p. 317). See also American Antiquarian Society's *Proceedings*, 1887, p. 77. Many other references may be found in Winsor's *Memorial History of Boston*, i, 327, and his *America*, iii, 360.

III. Bacon's Rebellion. — So much new matter relating to Bacon's Rebellion and the reason thereof has been brought to light in recent years that the older accounts of that important movement are necessarily obsolete. The most complete modern dissertation is Osgood's *American Colonies in the Seventeenth Century*, iii, ch. viii. John

Fiske (*Old Virginia and her Neighbours*) used much of the new material; his account is scholarly and interesting. The *Virginia Magazine of History*[1] and the *William and Mary Quarterly*[2] contain valuable documents and others are noted in the *Calendars of State Papers, America and West Indies, 1675–1676*. The documents contained in the "Aspinwall Papers,"[3] Force's *Tracts*, Burk's *Virginia*, (ii, Appendix), Hening's *Statutes*, and *Virginia Historical Collections* xi, 177) must still be consulted. For other matter, see Winsor's *America*, iii, 164. The most vivid account of Bacon's Rebellion from which nearly all the interesting anecdotes are taken is "The Beginning, Progress, and Conclusion of Bacon's Rebellion in Virginia, in the Years 1675 and 1676." The dedication, signed "T. M.," is dated July 13, 1705, and states that the author had obliged his pen "to step aside from its habitual element of figures into this little treatise of history." It would seem, therefore, that the tract was written twenty-five or thirty years after the event when age and long-sustained recollection had confirmed the author in the reality of his remembrances. It is unfortunate that so many of the stories which have given life to the popular accounts of Bacon's Rebellion should be contained only in this belated narrative by "a contemporary." It was first printed from a copy made by President Jefferson with his own hand, in the *Richmond Enquirer*, September 1, 5, 8, 1804; it is also in Force's *Tracts*, i, No. viii, and Maxwell's *Virginia Historical Register*, iii.

[1] *Virginia Magazine of History*, i, 55, Bacon's Proclamations; i, 167, accounts by Sherwood and Ludwell; v, 64, letter of Mrs. Bacon; vi, 139, vindication of Governor Berkeley. Other papers are also scattered through vols. ii, iv, and v.

[2] Vol. ii, 68, 129; iii, 121; iv, 3.

[3] Massachusetts Historical Society's *Collections*, Fourth Series, ix, 162–184.

CHAPTER IV

THE FOUNDING OF PENNSYLVANIA, 1681–1690

GEORGE FOX, the first Quaker, had a highly emotional nature which led him to strange actions, and he clothed his ideas in mystical language that is sometimes hard to interpret. None the less a sureness of reasoning gave to his thoughts and his conclusions a degree of stability and permanence that has seldom been allotted to men of modern times.[1] He was born of respectable parents in the year 1624 and early gave way to introspection, for which his youthful occupations of tending sheep and cobbling shoes afforded opportunity. At the age of nineteen years or so, intercourse with his fellow-men proved to be so unsatisfactory that he thought he must forsake all people and be a stranger unto them.[2] For a time he wandered about the country and then sought the advice of men whose business it was to heal disorders of the soul. One of these conversed with him and then made use of the lad's ideas in his sermons. Another swore at him when he inadvertently stepped on his flower beds. A third, an "ancient priest," advised him to take tobacco

---

[1] Fox possessed some means, as he maintained himself, and gave away in charity besides. Carlyle's picture of the "man in leathern breeches" is not true to the fact; although in common with other Englishmen of his time and our own, he wore leathern garments of one sort or another — on occasion.

[2] This account of Fox is based upon a reading of his " Journal " as given in his

Works and Thomas Hodgkin's *George Fox*. The " Journal " is remarkable and stimulating; but as it was edited by Barclay and Penn before publication, it possibly does not give the exact words of its original writer. Hodgkin's memoir is written in the spirit of modern historical inquiry and also in full sympathy with the aspirations and deeds of a remarkable man.

and sing psalms; but tobacco, says Fox, " was a thing I did not love, and psalms I was not in a state to sing." Finally, " one Macham, a priest in high account," believing the youngster to be suffering from brain fever, endeavored to bleed him, but " could not get one drop of blood from me, either in arms or head, though they endeavored it, my body being, as it were, dried up with sorrows, griefs, and troubles."[1] Priests, old and young, humble or high-placed, were miserable comforters, and Fox once more had recourse to nature for inspiration.

It was while walking in a field one Sunday morning that his first great conclusion came to him. It was that " being bred at Oxford or Cambridge was not enough to fit or qualify men to be ministers of Christ." A second conclusion followed easily upon this, that God " did not dwell in temples made with hands "; but that the Church was " the pillar and ground of truth, made up of living stones, living members, a spiritual household, which Christ was the head of."[2] The Savior, indeed, is constantly teaching men through the Spirit, — the " Inner light," which comes to the humble and to the poor as well as to the proud and the rich, to the ignorant as well as to those of education. It comes freely and must be given freely. There were, therefore, no paid ministers in Fox's spiritual household; there was no need of an educated ministry. Nor were there rites and ceremonies; for " the baptism which saves is not the putting away of the filth of the flesh, but is the answer of a good conscience toward God."

Fox had strong convictions, he cared nothing at all for the feelings of those whose souls he sought to save; what matter was a little inconvenience and annoyance in this life compared to eternal salvation? Entering a " steeple-

---

[1] **Fox's** *Works* (ed. of 1831), i, 68–71.   [2] *Ibid.* i, 83.

house," he would interrupt the minister, contradict him, overbear him to silence, and then preach in his stead, until the officers could be summoned to take him away. As Fox described the process, " the Lord's power was so mighty upon me, and so strong in me that I could not hold, but was made to cry out and say ' Oh no, it is not the scriptures '; and I told them what it was, namely, the Holy Spirit. . . . As I spake thus amongst them, the officers came and took me away and put me into a nasty stinking prison, the smell whereof got so into my nose and throat that it very much annoyed me." At another time the sight of the three spires of the great " steeple-house " at Lichfield imbued him with a threefold vigor, although he was fresh from a year's imprisonment at Derby. Taking off his shoes, he entered the city and went up and down the streets, crying with a loud voice, " Woe to the bloody city of Lichfield." He went to the market place with the same cry and marveled that no one laid hands on him — and so do we.

The time was propitious for the founding of new faiths. The "New Model Army" was a body of radical Englishmen who were bent on reforms in Church and State, as well as a wonderful military machine. In its ranks were men like Lilburne, who believed in the equality of man, and like Oliver Cromwell, who believed in nothing of the kind. Outside of the army there were those who disbelieved in everything, but were intent on reforming the world and bringing back simplicity to daily life.[1] Soon Fox's followers numbered hundreds and thousands. Then his task was to moderate their extravagances so that at one time he appears almost in the light of a conservative.

[1] Lewis H. Berens makes the interesting suggestion that one of these, " Gerrard Winstanly, was the spiritual founder of the Quakers." *The Digger Movement in the Days of the Commonwealth.*

The essential feature of George Fox's faith was the action of God on the human soul; all true believers, whether Protestants or Papists, rich or poor, high-born or of low estate, were children of God ; all were equal in the sight of God — why not in the sight of man ?   Fox, therefore, refused to give to human agents those titles of respect with which men and women usually greeted them. He addressed them by their first names, called them thee and thou, and forebore doffing his hat when in their presence.[1] Recalling the greatest of all sermons, Fox saw the words " Swear not at all " written in characters of fire and would not swear even at the bidding of king and Parliament. He saw no difference between what might be termed private swearing and swearing by command of a human magistrate. Oath taking was regarded as a safeguard against one's enemies.   Whoever refused to take the oath of allegiance to Charles II was presumably a Roman Catholic, and it was a dangerous thing in those days to be suspected of leanings to the old faith, since it exposed one to the penalties of præmunire, which were loss of property and imprisonment for life or for some considerable term.   Three thousand Quakers are said to have been imprisoned in England between the execution of Charles I in 1649 and 1660 ; after the Restoration[2] they felt the full burden of

[1] The ceremonial importance of the covering and uncovering of the head is shown by the fact that in 1633 Strafford, then Lord Deputy of Ireland, prohibited any one to put on his hat in the cathedral at Dublin until the preacher had read his text and permitted none under the degree of Esquire, except certain church dignitaries, to wear head covering of any sort in time of sermon. *Calendars of State Papers, Ireland, 1633-1647*, p. 31. The Canons of 1604 (Article xviii) directed that " no man shall cover his head in the church or chapel in the time of divine service except he had some

infirmity."   Bishop Wrenn also in his " Particular Orders . . . given in the diocese of Warwick " in 1636 directed that " no man presume to have his hat on his head in the time of service or sermon in the Church."   See Cardwell's *Documentary Annals of the Reformed Church of England* (2nd ed., Oxford, 1844), ii, 254. Dr. Roland G. Usher very kindly called my attention to these entries.

[2] On religious questions in general at this epoch, see J. Stoughton's *Religion in England* (vols. iii, iv, " The Church of the Restoration ").

persecution, three thousand and sixty-eight of them being imprisoned in the first twenty-four months of Charles's reign.[1]   In May, 1662,[2] that "Merrie Monarch" assented to an act providing fine, imprisonment, and transportation for those who refused to take an oath, or with four or more fellow-Quakers assembled for religious purposes.   The persecution of the Quakers now went on with redoubled vigor; they were imprisoned by the thousands and transported by the hundreds.[3]   Fox himself was imprisoned for two years and nine months (January, 1664–September, 1666), a part of the time under circumstances of extreme cruelty, being deprived of a fire and exposed to the winds and rain.

The trials and sufferings of Fox and the Friends are almost exclusively told by Quaker writers; the other side has never been stated with anything like the dramatic power which attends these autobiographic portrayals. The magistrates and constables were respectable men; they had solemnly sworn to perform the duties that had been intrusted to their keeping by the king or by the great officers of state.   The county justice was the person designated by the law to put into execution the acts against the Quakers and other religious dissenters. Moreover, the attitude of Fox and his followers was far from conciliatory.   In a century when Sir Edward Coke could find no better way to express his malignant contempt for Sir Walter Ralegh

[1] Hodgkin's *George Fox*, 183, from Quaker statistics. See also Royal Historical Manuscripts Commission's *Reports*, xii, Part vii, 32 and fol.

[2] 14 Charles II, Cap. 1 (*Statutes of the Realm*, v, 350). The penalty for the infraction of the law was for the first offense, five pounds sterling or three months in prison; for the second offense, ten pounds or six months' imprisonment without bail; for the third offense, the convict should abjure the realm or be transported to the colonies.

The laws against the Quakers are summarized in C. G. Crump's "Introduction" to the *History of the Life of Thomas Ellwood . . . written by his own hand* (London, 1900); the text of this work gives a convincing picture of the life of an English Quaker in the thirty years preceding the founding of Pennsylvania.

[3] A warrant for enforcing the transportation of Quakers is noted in *Calendars of State Papers, America and West Indies, 1661-1668*, p. 287.

than to "thee" and "thou" him, and when Ralegh started at the salutation to exclaim "I will thou thee, thou traitor," the Quakers persisted in thus addressing the judges before whom they were brought. In an age when the Commons and the Lords disputed as to whether the former should wear their hats in the presence of the latter, the Quaker when brought into court charged with unlawful acts refused to doff his headgear. Country magistrates and clerks were often ignorant of the law and disposed to be harsh and overbearing. The Quakers from dire experience had gained expert knowledge of the laws relating to themselves and were thus able to dispute and argue with magistrate and clerk, often to the discomfiture of those functionaries. It was usually under these circumstances that the judicial authorities bethought themselves of the oath of allegiance and ordered it to be tendered to the contumacious Quaker, knowing full well that he would refuse to take it and thereby expose himself to the penalties of præmunire.[1]

"Love your enemies" was the command of Christ. Interpreting this literally, Fox and his followers refused to defend themselves against those who came to break up their meetings and to arrest their persons ; as between the commands of God and man, they obeyed the former at no matter what cost. The constables drove them from their meeting houses, they went back through the windows ; the constables pulled down the meeting houses, they met on the ruins ; the constables bore the adults off to prison, the children met by themselves and worshiped in silence. The Quakers declined to fight as soldiers or to pay for the employment or training of others in that capacity. In England and in the non-Quaker colonies it was feasible

[1] The Friends refused to use the ecclesiastics and ritual of the Established Church in marriage or burial services; this also frequently led to excommunication and imprisonment.

enough to refuse to use "carnal weapons," because the government there protected Quakers with other people from the attacks of alien enemies and from the assaults of evil-disposed persons among their countrymen. When the Friends crossed the Atlantic and planted a colony of their own in the wilderness, their goods and persons were at the mercy of wrongdoers. So they "drew a line between police and military measures"; they established an efficient constabulary to put down thieving in Philadelphia; they refused aid to protect their farms from invading Frenchmen. In 1740 the Pennsylvania Assembly voted it to be "easy to discover the Difference between killing a Soldier, fighting (perhaps) in Obedience to the Commands of his Sovereign . . . and executing a Burglar who broke into our Houses . . . who must know at the Time of the Commission of the Fact, It was in violation of Laws humane and divine." [1] The difference was not always discernible to even the most eminent colonists. In 1702 James Logan, Penn's agent in the province, with the sheriff of Philadelphia and other persons with firearms in their hands, "for the greater awe of such as should attempt to oppose," drove a Jersey man from one of the islands in the Delaware. He was obliged to beg pardon of the Philadelphia Monthly Meeting and ask God to enlighten him better in the future. [2]

[1] *Minutes of the Council*, iv, 373.

[2] *Pennsylvania Magazine of History*, **xxi**, 122. President Sharpless (*Quaker Government*, i, 189 and fol.) gives other instances, among them he tells of a Wilmington man who gave way to a "warmth of temper" and put a fellow-Quaker into a pond as to whose bounds the two were disputing. Another, a Rhode Island merchant, voyaged to the West Indies expressly to cowhide a man who had slandered him, and accomplished his purpose long after his blood must have cooled. J. P. Hazard in *Narragansett Register*, i, 296.

In 1716 the Rhode Island Quakers paid twenty-three pounds sterling for not bearing arms. Earlier, William Smith, a prominent Rhode Island Quaker, paying fines for not training to avoid the seizure of his property, was informed that until "he be or can be convinced" of the wrongfulness of complying with the law, he cannot be a member of the Yearly Meeting. *Records of the Rhode Island Yearly Meeting (Ms.)*, 16, 92.

The Society of Friends enforced a discipline among its members that was subversive of freedom of thought and of action. The central governing body was the Yearly Meeting, which was attended by delegates from all England, and later two Yearly Meetings were established in America,— one in Pennsylvania, the other in Rhode Island. Under the Yearly Meetings were Quarterly Meetings and under them Monthly Meetings, the last forming the actual working organization of the Society. The Friends did not entirely reproduce the polity of any other religious body ; but the Monthly Meeting performed many of the functions which in New England fell to the " church," while the Yearly Meeting answered fairly well to the synod of the Presbyterian organization. The Quakers keenly scrutinized the private affairs of the members of their society, examining the accounts of those who were suspected of backwardness in their business relations [1] and inquiring into their drinking habits. They interposed in the most delicate relations of life, as, for instance, when Thomas Story gave his testimony of " the displeasure of God . . . against mixed marriages between them [the Friends] and the world," namely, non-Quakers, and prevented the marriage of the son of a prominent Virginia Quaker with a woman who was outside the fold.[2] Friends were not even permitted to be present at such a marriage.[3]

[1] Sharpless's *Quaker Government*, i, 26 note.

[2] See Story's *Journal* (ed. 1747), p. 156.

[3] This prohibition long persisted as is seen in the well-known anecdote of the marriage of Angelina Grimké, a South Carolina Quakeress and an Abolitionist, to Mr. Weld, a non-Quaker. It is related that Whittier accompanied a young lady to the door of the house, where the ceremony was to be performed, but turned back because Mr. Weld was "out of Society." Pickard's *Whittier*, i, 236. See also *Rules of Discipline of the Yearly Meeting, held on Rhode Island for New England*, New Bedford, 1809, p. 123. An edition containing this prohibition was printed as late as 1856. Now, Friends are permitted to marry outside and remain members of the Society, *Constitution and Discipline for the American Yearly Meetings*, 1901.

Such interferences with personal freedom were every-day occurrences in Quaker communities.

No character in American colonial history has been more fiercely assailed than William Penn. His settlers disliked him in his lifetime, and after his death the Pennsylvania colonists attacked his sons even more fiercely than they had the "founder."[1] His colonizing schemes threatened Maryland, and her writers have been unfavorable to him, one of them going so far as to say that his life furnished no fit model for an honorable career.[2] Lord Macaulay disliked him because he was a friend of James; he declared him to be "a poor, shallow, half-crazed creature,"[3] although he was satisfied that he was not "a papist." In a life full of care and dealing with many determined men, William Penn inevitably made enemies and mistakes; but there is much in his career that is hard to reconcile with the uprightness of character and scrupulousness of dealing which one has a right to expect in a leader of a religious sect. The circumstances of his birth and parentage brought him within the court circles of the Restoration and he made good use of his friendship with the royal brothers to secure mercy for his fellow-Quakers. His activity in urging on the surrender of the charters of the English corporations, when Charles and James were remodeling them in order to pack the House of Commons, lends confirmation to this view; for it was of this that Penn wrote "when a few towns are done we may expect to hear of a Parliament to render our case legal, that our poor posterity may be preserved from the cruelty of wicked per-

[1] This is shown at its worst in *An Historical Review of the Constitution and Government of Pennsylvania*, which was written by Benjamin Franklin and published at London in 1759.

[2] Dr. George W. Archer in Maryland Historical Society's *Fund Publications*, No. 30, i, p. 135.

[3] *American Catholic Historical Researches*, viii, 75. Some of Penn's enemies declared him to be a Jesuit. Shepherd's *Pennsylvania*, 273.

secutors."[1] This way of looking at the case is surely not far removed from the acceptation of the Declaration of Indulgence by New England Puritans. Even so straight-laced a man as Increase Mather endeavored to gain the good will of James and failed where Penn succeeded — "Ye cannot serve God and Mammon" was not the rule in those days, at least not in public life. In point of fact, Penn should not be judged as a man of affairs. He was an idealist whom chance placed at the head of a great business enterprise, and he experienced the fate that befalls the dreamer when he has to do with actualities.

William Penn, the Founder, was the son of Admiral Sir William Penn, who had achieved the feat of standing well with two masters at the same time, Oliver Cromwell and Charles the Second. At the Restoration he became one of the Commissioners of the Navy and acted as chief of staff to the Duke of York in the naval campaign which ended in the battle of Lowestoft. In 1668 he was impeached on a charge of the unlawful conversion of government property to his own use,[2] but was not convicted. In 1644 the younger William Penn saw the light of day. In due course of time, as his years and his father's fortune increased, he went to college that he might gain some useful knowledge and make valuable acquaintances — for much the same reasons that sons of many self-made men seek the universities at the present time. At Oxford he learned something, perhaps more than most young men of his period, and also made acquaintances. One of these was a Quaker minister, Thomas Loe. His preaching

---

[1] Royal Historical Manuscripts Commission's *Reports*, xiii, Part ii, 52. Other interesting matter is noted in *ibid.*, "Portland Manuscripts," v, 17; xi, Part v, 170 ; xv, Part iv, 19, 30, 79, 316, 326.

[2] Royal Historical Manuscripts Commission's *Reports*, xiii, 106, 107; *Lords Journals*, xii, 233, 237; Pepys's *Diary*, vii, 374 and fol.

made so great an impression on the plastic mind of the
lad that the college authorities sent him home. The ad
miral beat his son, turned him out of doors, and then
thought better of it. He gave him letters of introduction
to those high in the gay world at Paris and sent him there
to lose in that school some of the seriousness which he had
gained at Oxford. This plan succeeding, the youth next
went to Ireland to look after his father's property there.
As fortune would have it, one day, he again listened to
the exhortations of Thomas Loe. The text was, "There
is a faith which overcometh the world, and there is a faith
which is overcome by the world." From that providential moment to his death, William Penn was a Quaker.
Returning to London, he wore his hat in his father's presence, "thee'd" and "thou'd" him, and was again turned
out of doors.

It was in 1667 or 1668 that William Penn definitely
announced his conversion to the Quaker faith. He was
not long in finding the inside of a prison. He wrote a
pamphlet entitled the "Sandy Foundation Shaken," denying three "generally believed and applauded doctrines;
first of one God, subsisting in three distinct and separate
persons; second, of the impossibility of divine pardon
without the making of a complete satisfaction; and third,
of the justification of impure persons by an imputed
righteousness." Thereupon, the Bishop of London placed
him in the Tower. Possibly Penn had no distinct idea as
to what he meant to convey in the theses which made up
his pamphlet; certainly one modern reader has not acquired definiteness of impression from its perusal. After
some residence in the Tower and a rather apologetic
pamphlet, "Innocency with her Open Face," he was set
at liberty.

In 1670 William Penn was arrested for being present at an unlawful and tumultuous assembly in Gracechurch Street and there addressing a great concourse and tumult of people in contempt of the king and of his law and against the peace of the king, his crown, and dignity. In court Penn desired to know upon what law the indictment was grounded. The Common Law was the answer. "Where is that Common Law?" demanded Penn; but the judge declined to produce it. Upon which Penn declared that such law could not be very common, if it was so hard to find. He then claimed for himself the rights of Englishmen as set forth in the Great Charter and its confirmations. The magistrates answered his arguments with epithets, calling him "a saucy fellow," "an impertinent fellow," "a troublesome fellow," "a pestilent fellow." Steadfast courage and appeals to the fundamental rights of Englishmen had their inevitable effect upon the jury. They refused to convict in manner and form as indicted. Instead, they found the accused "guilty of speaking in Gracechurch Street," or to "an assembly in Gracechurch Street." They were then locked up over night without meat, drink, fire, or any other accommodation, but this produced only two more verdicts of "guilty of speaking in Gracechurch Street." Finally, after the judge had threatened to stake Penn to the ground and to cut the nose of one of the jurymen, they brought in a verdict of "not guilty," for which they were fined forty marks apiece and imprisoned until the fine should be paid.[1] In due course one of the imprisoned jurymen, Edward Bushel by name, sued out a writ of habeas corpus and was brought before Sir John Vaughan, Chief Justice of Common Pleas. He and his companions were set at

---

[1] Howell's *State Trials*, vi, 951.

liberty on the ground that the finding of a verdict against the evidence or contrary to the direction of the court was no sufficient cause for fine and imprisonment.[1] The young man's stout defense was the one thing in his career during these years that his fighting father could understand. He paid his son's fine, welcomed him to the side of his deathbed, and then passed away to that part of the unseen world which was appropriated for the eternal residence of the second Charles and his companions.

Penn's connection with the New Jersey settlements has already been described. He now conceived the project, or it was suggested to him,[2] of getting land on the west side of Delaware, where the Quakers might try experiments in government and society with more freedom than they could in New Jersey — with its doubtful government and diverse population. On June 1, 1680, William Penn, in consideration of "the debts due to him and his father from the Crown," petitioned the king[3] to grant him land in America, west of the Delaware and north of Maryland, and thence northward "as far as plantable, which is altogether Indian." Charles favored the project and James, Duke of York, added to the royal gift his own claim to lands west and south of Delaware Bay and River.[4] The intention of Charles and James, undoubtedly, was to give Penn lands

---

[1] Howell's *State Trials*, vi, 999.

[2] It is sometimes stated that Penn in his "holy experiment" was carrying out his father's wishes. The admiral died September 16, 1670; the son's petition for land is dated June 1, 1680, which would seem to show scant respect for the father's wishes, if he ever made such a suggestion. Fox is also regarded as the originator of the enterprise. As early as 1660-61 the purchase of lands on the Susquehanna is mentioned in Fox's cor-respondence. Letter from Josiah Cole to Fox quoted in Jenkins's *Pennsylvania*, i, 193.

[3] Journal of the Lords of Trade, June 14, 1680 ("Philadelphia Transcripts," iii, 173); *Calendars of State Papers, America and West Indies, 1677–1680*, pp. 544, 553, 554, and also 623, 633, 634.

[4] The Duke of York's three deeds are printed in the *Votes of Pennsylvania*, i, p. xxxv; *Pennsylvania Archives*, ii, 202; Hazard's *Historical Register*, i, 429; ii, 27.

to which no other subject had a valid title; but the prevailing ignorance of American geography and of previous
grants gave Penn a claim on lands to which Lord Baltimore and even James himself had pretensions. As soon
as surveyors tried to lay out the limits according to Penn's
deeds and letters patent, it was at once apparent that they
included lands to which Baltimore had the better title and
did not include lands which were clearly Baltimore's, but
the possession of which was essential to the carrying out
of Penn's plans. Instead of adopting a policy of frankness
and readiness to make mutual concessions, Penn and Baltimore went at the matter like a pair of special pleaders,
each examining the other's patents, seeking to pick flaws
in the other's titles. The phrases used in the documents
were themselves confusing. Take the clause in the Maryland charter describing that province as extending "unto
that part of the Bay of Delaware on the north, which lyeth
under the fortieth degree of north latitude from the æqui-
noctial, where New England is terminated," or the clauses
of the Pennsylvania patent describing that province as
stretching "from twelve miles Northwards of New Castle
Towne unto the three and fortieth degree of Northerne
Latitude," and bounding it on the south "by a circle
drawne at twelve miles distance from New Castle Northward and Westward unto the beginning of the fortieth
degree of Northern Latitude." Lands which "lyeth under"
a degree of latitude, lands which extend "unto" a degree
of latitude or "unto the beginning" thereof: What do
these phrases mean? Penn and Baltimore and their children fought over the matter until 1760, when a final agreement was entered into. A few years later in accordance
with this arrangement two English surveyors, Charles
Mason and Jeremiah Dixon, located the southern boundary

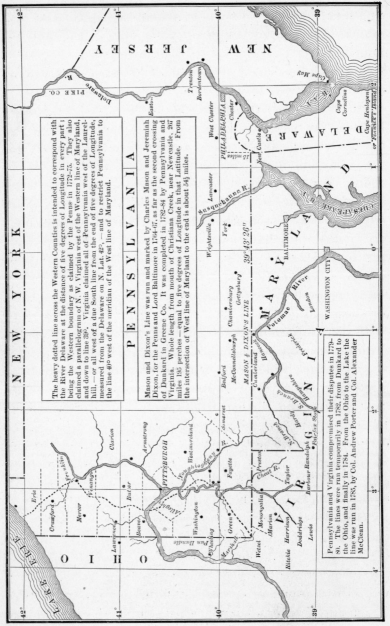

PENNSYLVANIA BOUNDARIES

of Pennsylvania at thirty-nine degrees and forty-four minutes, or nineteen miles south of forty degrees and drew the boundaries of Delaware as they are to-day.[1]

The intention of the makers of the Pennsylvania charter undoubtedly was to give Penn three degrees of latitude north of the fortieth parallel; but when he tried to buy lands on the Susquehanna from the Iroquois, the New York fur traders became alarmed. Colonel Thomas Dongan had just come out as representative of the Duke of York and upheld his master's rights with his accustomed vigor. Technically, the territory belonging to the Duke of York extended only to the Delaware; but Dongan secured from the Iroquois an acknowledgment of the Duke of York's jurisdiction and a deed of the contested lands on the Susquehanna. Penn must have felt sorely annoyed at Dongan's interference, but considering his relations with the royal brothers and how important it was to keep on good terms with them, he could not express his feelings too strongly. Years afterward, when James was in exile, Dongan deeded the tract back to Penn.[2] When it came to arranging the boundaries with New York, the arguments which the Penns had put forward in their disputation with Maryland were

[1] The southern limit of the Duke of York's deed of the Territories to Penn was Cape Henlopen. As this point had an unpleasant habit of shifting its position, it was decided, for purposes of this agreement, to regard it as twenty miles south of the existing cape of that name. From the point ascertained in this arbitrary way, a line should be run due west to Chesapeake Bay. The middle point of this line would be the southwestern corner of Penn's Territories on the Delaware. From this middle point a line should be run tangent to a twelve-mile circle to be drawn around New Castle. From the point where this line impinged upon the circle, a line should be run due north to the parallel of a point sixteen miles south of the southernmost street of Philadelphia, and from where this due north line intersected this parallel a line should be run due west to the western limit of Maryland. This arrangement gave nineteen miles south of the fortieth parallel to Pennsylvania for the whole length of her southern frontier. Moreover, the point selected to stand for Cape Henlopen turned out to be at the widest part of the peninsula between the Chesapeake and the Atlantic. Maryland thus lost in every direction. For the authorities on the boundary disputes of Pennsylvania, see Note III, p. 128.

[2] In 1696, see *Pennsylvania Archives*, i, 122.

used against them so that the northern boundary of Pennsylvania is the forty-second and not the forty-third parallel of latitude.

Penn had originally intended that the province which he received by charter from the king should be called New Wales; but this proving distasteful to some of the members of the government, he suggested Sylvania. By a happy chance, the king prefixed to this " Penn," in honor of the father of the grantee. The addition troubled the " founder " because he feared that it would be attributed to his un-Quakerlike vanity by those who did not know the true reason. He offered twenty guineas to an under secretary to vary the name, which that official declined to do. Pennsylvania was the name of the " province," which Penn held from the king by reason of the royal letters patent and also by a quitclaim deed from the Duke of York. The lands included in the present state of Delaware he held by reason of deeds of lease and release similar to the New Jersey deeds that have already been described; they are referred to as the " Territories " or the " Lower Counties."

There were settlers — Swedes, Dutchmen, and Englishmen — already living on Penn's newly acquired possessions. He assured them by letter that he had an honest mind to deal with them uprightly; that they would be governed by laws of their own making, and live a free, sober, and industrious people. Penn regarded himself as occupying the position of a trustee and sincerely wished to divest himself of all power to do mischief and so to serve God and man " that an example might be set to the nations." For the moment, his mind was intent upon trying a " holy experiment " in government and society, for which he thought there might be room in America far removed from the temptations and conventionalities of the Old World. In the history of modern times, there are few examples of such disinterestedness; it remained to be seen whether Penn's high ideals could be put in practice.

Penn published an "Account of the Province of Pennsylvania,"[1] which was translated into Dutch, German, and French, and spread far and wide over the British Isles and the continent of Europe. In this paper he described Pennsylvania with a moderation[2] that was often lacking in similar prospectuses and stated carefully the kind of colonist he desired : industrious husbandmen, carpenters, masons, weavers, shoemakers, and other mechanics, industrious spirits that are oppressed about a livelihood, younger brothers and men of universal spirits who understood the promotion of a just government among a plain and well-intending people. As a man of the world, Penn desired to establish in his new plantation persons of substance as well as godliness. He induced Quakers of family and fortune to embark in the enterprise by granting them large estates at low rates. He offered lots of five thousand acres each for one hundred pounds down and an annual quitrent of one shilling for each hundred acres, the purchaser to have a lot in the "great town" which was to be built on the banks of the Delaware. He wished to have the lands seated in townships of three thousand acres, with a space two hundred feet broad left as "a highway in the township, for the future good and great benefit of the country."[3]

---

[1] "A Further Account of the Province of Pennsylvania and its Improvements," dated 1685, 10th month, also by Penn, is reprinted in *Pennsylvania Magazine of History*, ix, 63.

[2] In 1701, however, he wrote to Sir John Lowther that silk would be a staple product of Pennsylvania, Royal Histori-

cal Manuscripts Commission's *Reports*, xiii, Part vii, 246.

[3] *Breviate for the Plaintiffs*, 56. Penn's land system is fully described in Shepherd's *Pennsylvania* ; the same author also has an article on the subject in American Historical Association *Reports*, 1895, p. 117.

In 1681 Penn sent his cousin, William Markham, to rule the people living in his new domain, as deputy governor. In August of the next year (1682) he himself sailed from the Thames for the Delaware in the ship *Welcome*, with one hundred emigrants — more or less.   October 27, 1682, he landed at Newcastle.   There agents of the Duke of York awaited him; they handed him the key of the fort that he might "lock upon himself alone the door, which being opened by him again they did deliver also unto him one turf, with a twig upon it, a porringer with river water and soil," — and thus with feudal ceremony the Quaker proprietor took possession of the lands which the Duke of York had given him.   Proceeding up the river, Penn went ashore at the old Swedish settlement of Upland, which name he now changed to Chester.   Later he explored the stream as far as the site of Philadelphia.

One of Penn's ideas which turned into solid reality was that of building a "capital city" on the banks of the Delaware.   The best site for such a "great town" would be where a river flowed into the Delaware from the west and where deep water close to the shore would enable vessels to unload without the necessity of building expensive wharves and docks.   Near the confluence of the Schuylkill and the Delaware the banks were so steep that vessels swept the boughs of trees on shore with their yards as they passed. There the streets of the city were marked out on a checkerboard pattern and named with Quaker simplicity "First," "Second," etc., for those running parallel to the river, and "Pine," "Spruce," etc., for those extending from the Delaware to the Schuylkill.   Penn intended that the water front should remain common property — the top of the bank serving as an exchange; but this idea was gradually lost sight of and many other open spaces were also built over. At first the inhabitants dwelt in log huts and in caves dug in the bank of the river; but in a few years Philadelphia[1] gave that impression of regularity and stability which has been its chief characteristic ever since.

The Pennsylvania settlers had none of those struggles with famine and disease which give an enduring interest to the early history of Jamestown and Plymouth. On the contrary, in ten years' time they were exporting food to Barbados and Jamaica.[2] The earlier colonists had farmed to good purpose and were producing a surplus which they were quite willing to sell to the newcomers, who also procured supplies from other colonies, especially from New York. The Indians of the neighborhood brought such store of corn as they could spare and such game and venison as the chase provided, which they sold to the whites. Sometimes, indeed, they even endeavored to take advantage of the ignorance of Penn's followers : one of the natives tried to sell an eagle to Pastorius under the guise of a turkey, but the German pioneer had already been long enough in the country not to be caught by any such wile.

The Indians of the southern and western bank of the Delaware had been very well treated by the whites. The Swedes and the Dutch had lived in harmony with them and the Duke of York's agents had done what they could to protect them from the consequences of contact with civi-

---

[1] The name of the new city was derived either from that of an ancient town of Asia Minor or because when translated into English it meant " brotherly love." Mr. H. Addington Bruce makes the interesting suggestion that possibly the name may have come to Penn from that of Philadelphia Wharton, or from some other English lady with the same baptismal name. What is generally regarded as the first charter of Philadelphia (1691) is printed in *Pennsylvania Magazine of History*,

xviii, 504; but the earlier grant of rights of government in 1683 may well be looked upon as the " first charter."

[2] Letter of John Goodson written at Philadelphia in 1690, *Some Letters from Pennsylvania* (London, 1691). Robert Quary, writing in 1700, states that in Pennsylvania " they have improved tilledge to that degree that they have made bread, flower and Beer a drugg in all the Markets in the West Indies." *Pennsylvania Magazine of History*, xxiv, 63.

lization.[1] Penn always insisted upon fair dealing with the aborigines, so that they should not be cheated in their trafficking with the whites. He even refused to sell the monopoly of the Indian trade between the Delaware and the Susquehanna rivers for the sum of six thousand pounds, lest the natives should be ill-used. He also desired to have them tried by mixed juries, but this plan soon became unworkable.[2] In fact, notwithstanding the efforts of Penn and the Friends, the coming of the whites was inevitably a curse to the natives. Justus Falckner, writing from Germantown in 1701, declared that the Indians learned drunkardness and stealing and other vices from the whites [3] and were not converted to Christianity.

Soon after the sealing of the charter, Penn addressed a letter to the Indian chiefs, assuring them of his good intention. Upon his arrival in the province, he entertained them hospitably and repeated these assurances. He also made many treaties with them for the purchase of lands. Some of these Indian deeds were very vague; in one of them the tract conveyed extended backward from the river as far as a man could ride on horseback in two days; the consideration was "so much wampum, so many guns, shoes, stockings, looking-glasses, blankets, and other goods as he the sd. William Penn shall please to give unto us."[4] It is

---

[1] In the Duke of York's Laws, Nicolls repeated the prohibition of the Massachusetts code against selling liquor to the natives; but he modified it by the addition of a clause permitting the governor to grant licenses for the sale of spirits to the natives. The first formal law on the subject was made by the Pennsylvania Assembly in 1701, but the discipline among the Friends was so rigid that probably little liquor was sold or given to the Indians after the earliest years. See Sharpless, *Quaker Government*, i, 166; *Pennsylvania Magazine of History*, xxi, 218; xxvii, 225.

[2] Sharpless, *Quaker Government*, i, 158. On this whole subject see *Conrad Weiser and the Indian Policy of Colonial Pennsylvania*. The younger Penns did not carry out their father's beneficent intentions. See Sharpless, i, 173, and Buck's *The Walking Purchase*.

[3] *Pennsylvania Magazine of History*, xxi, 218, 221.

[4] *Pennsylvania Archives*, i, 63. On p. 47 of the same volume is a list of articles actually given for a tract of land. Rum was one of the commodities paid for land in 1682. Sharpless, *Quaker Government*, i, 166.

impossible to identify any one of these transactions as "Penn's Treaty with the Indians" which has been so celebrated in prose and picture.[1]

The persecutions of the Quakers in England had aroused within them a desire for a more peaceful life in some other part of the English empire. Penn easily enlisted in his design many of the richer English Friends. Some of these did not come to Pennsylvania; but the fact that they invested money in the undertaking, encouraged many men of smaller means to emigrate. Besides being well known in England, Penn was popular among the Quakers of Wales and Ireland. Many of the best-known names in early Pennsylvania are of these immigrants, as Thomas and David Lloyd, among Welshmen, and James Logan among those who were born in Ireland.[2] Penn also attracted immigrants from Germany, which country he had visited with Fox and Barclay in 1677.[3] In Germany the followers of Menno Simon or Mennonites held many doctrines which were similar to those of the Quakers. Indeed, it is sometimes said that Fox unconsciously reproduced some of these.[4] The Mennonites were persecuted, even in Switzerland, especially on account of their refusal to bear arms. In Germany, also, were the "Pietists," [5] who thought that religion should be brought into everyday life. The news that the Quakers were founding a colony in America attracted much attention in Germany ; a longing to see more of the world and a desire to share in the profits [6] of colonial enterprise, also

[1] Shepherd's *Pennsylvania*, ch. vi.

[2] A. C. Myers's *Immigration of the Irish Quakers into Pennsylvania, 1682–1750.*

[3] In the party was Benjamin Furly, an English merchant, resident in the Netherlands. He acted as Penn's agent, and to his house many English exiles resorted in the years 1670–89. See *Pennsylvania Magazine of History*, xix, 277.

[4] As late as 1710 William Penn contracted to grant lands in Pennsylvania to fifty or sixty "Swissers," called Mennonists ; Royal Historical Manuscripts Commission's *Reports*, xi, Part iv, p. 63.

[5] See J. F. Sachse's *Pietists*, 49.

[6] See, for instance, "Articles of Agreement between the Members of the Frankfort Company," 1686, in *Pennsylvania Magazine of History*, xv, 205.

actuated some of those who now came forward to found a German settlement in Pennsylvania. The best-known figure in this movement was Francis Daniel Pastorius, who had already visited England and was a man of learning. In 1683 he landed at Philadelphia, was cordially welcomed by the proprietor, and founded a settlement to which he gave the name of Germantown;[1] but the great German migration began at a later time and was due to other causes.

From a material point of view, the holy experiment was successful beyond the dreams of its promoters; but politically the enterprise was not so happy, although equally instructive. Penn's political ideals were pure and noble, and his enunciations of them were full of striking passages, breathing faith in humanity and in Christian endeavor; but he was inconstant in the pursuit of ideals and inconsistent in his dealings with his opponents, often forgetting the teachings of his own precepts. While the words of the various fundamental laws which are connected with his name shadow forth many ideas of recognized value, the working of these schemes in actual everyday practice proved that they were not suited to the task immediately in hand.

By the royal letters patent,[2] Pennsylvania was erected

[1] Pennypacker's *Germantown* (Pennsylvania German Society's *Proceedings*, ix, 98 and fol.).

[2] The royal charter of Pennsylvania, authenticated by the great seal, has disappeared from sight. The document which is preserved at Harrisburg is a copy made for purposes of record or possibly is an "exemplification." It is this copy of the original letters patent which is reproduced in facsimile in the *Laws of Pennsylvania* (ed. 1879), edited by Staughton George and others. See *Pennsylvania Magazine of History*, xvi, 86.

There is some confusion as to the date of the Pennsylvania charter. For example, in the book of laws just mentioned it is referred to as the charter of 1682. The confusion has arisen from the printing of the copy as the original, for the former has under it the words "John Shaler, chirer. xxvij die Janry, 1682, Fir." In the text itself, the charter is said to have been issued on the "fourth day of March, in the three and thirtieth year of our reign." The copies printed by Proud (*Pennsylvania*, i, 187) and by Franklin (*Votes of Pennsylvania*, i, p.

into a province with powers similar to those enjoyed by the proprietor of Maryland. There were, however, some important limitations of the powers of the Pennsylvania proprietor which do not appear in any earlier grant. The legislative supremacy of Parliament is distinctly recognized in the Pennsylvania patent and obedience to the navigation acts expressly required. Moreover, the laws of Pennsylvania were to be submitted to the king within five years of their passage, who had six months thereafter in which to confirm or reject them. Appeals must also be allowed to England from the decision of the provincial courts. There is no guarantee of religious freedom, for anything of the kind was needless; but there is a clause providing that the Bishop of London might send a minister of the Established Church to the province whenever twenty members of that faith should make application and that this minister must not be interfered with in any way. It is not uninteresting to note that by this requirement the Quaker proprietor of Pennsylvania is expressly obliged to tolerate in his province the religion established by act of Parliament.

As soon as the charter had been engrossed, or perhaps before, Penn set to work to draw up a fundamental law or frame of government for his province. To his mind "the good of the people" was the end of government

xxiv) have the words "Annoque Domini one thousand six hundred and eighty-one"; by whom added is not stated. In each of the three books is Charles's "Declaration to the Inhabitants and Planters of the Province of Pennsylvania," in which the king states that he has granted a charter to Penn. This document is dated the "second day of April, 1681." Charles I was beheaded on January 30, 1648, Old Style. His son dated his reign from the moment of the execution. It follows, therefore, that the first year of the reign of Charles II extended from January 30, 1648, to January 29, 1649, Old Style, inclusive, and the three and thirtieth year extended from January 30, 1680, to January 29, 1681, Old Style. The English year then began on March 25. March 4 in the "three and thirtieth year of our reign" was, therefore, March 4, 1680, Old Style, or March 14, 1681, New Style. The charter may, therefore, be called the charter of 1680 or the charter of 1681, but should never be called the charter of 1682.

which owed its existence to the necessity of the "good ordering of the people in society," and he thought to put these precepts into practice.   In the library of the Historical Society at Philadelphia there is a volume of manuscript drafts of fundamental laws.   These are in various handwritings and are impossible of identification.[1]   It is supposed that Penn consulted Algernon Sidney in the preparation of his first constitution, but there is no means of ascertaining how far he followed Sidney's advice, if, indeed, he followed it at all. Penn's original plan was probably much more democratic than that which was adopted, owing to the advice of those Friends who were proposing to risk their money in the colony.   The document, as we have it, consists of a preamble and a framework setting forth Penn's ideas of a working constitution.

" When the great and wise God had made the world, of all his creatures, it pleased him to choose man his deputy to rule it."   Thus runs the preamble, which proceeds with the observation that " governments, like clocks, go from the motion men give them ; and as governments are made and moved by men, so, by them they are ruined, too. Wherefore, governments rather depend on men than men upon governments."   After this style, the preamble goes on for three printed octavo pages.   Six more set forth the fundamental law, but its leading points are easily described.   Penn proposed to confide the actual government of the province to a council of seventy-two members, in which he preserved three votes for himself.   This body was to consist of the persons of the most note for wis-

[1] One of the early states of the Frame of Government, entitled "Fundamental Constitutions of Pennsylvania," is printed in *Pennsylvania Magazine of History*, xx, 283. The Frame as adopted is in *Charters and Constitutions of the United States ;* Proud's *Pennsylvania,* i, Appendix, 15; *Votes of Pennsylvania,* i, p. xviii.

dom, virtue, and ability in the province. These should be chosen by the freemen from their own number, and one third of them should be elected in each year. It was the business of the council to prepare all laws, which should be posted in the most noted places in the province thirty days before the meeting of the general assembly. As was the case in Maryland and Carolina, so in Pennsylvania, Penn was obliged to secure the consent of the "freemen" of the province to all "laws,"[1] but he could assemble them for this purpose in such manner and form as should seem best to him. He proposed that the freemen should elect two hundred of their number to act as a general assembly and give their assent or dissent to the laws which had been drawn up and promulgated by the council. This plan left no room for amendments or discussion by the members of the assembly.

In order to understand Penn's ideas, the Frame of Government should be read in connection with the "Laws Agreed upon in England." The code begins by defining "freeman" as a person who owns land or pays taxes. As the freemen held the electoral power, this is equivalent to a property franchise. As to courts, lawyers, and moral problems, these laws have a distinctly Puritanical flavor. In the treatment of convicts, however, there was a distinct advance. Ten thousand Quakers had tasted the horrors of English prisons; in Pennsylvania the houses of detention were to be free as to fees, food, and lodging, and were to be places of reformation. The thirty-fifth article of this code is memorable as setting forth the Friends' ideas on religious freedom. It provides that all persons who acknowledge the "one Almighty and Eternal God to

[1] He could make "ordinances" for the regulation of minor affairs without the consent of the freemen; but these should not extend to harm a man in limb or property.

be the Creator, Upholder, and Ruler of the world " should
in no ways be molested for their religious persuasion or
practice, or be compelled to frequent or maintain any
religious worship or ministry whatsoever. Nevertheless,
they must live peaceably and abstain from common daily
labor on the first day of the week, and Christians only
could have any share in the government.

On his arrival in America, Penn proceeded to organize
the government without paying the slightest attention to
his own fundamental law. He directed the freeholders of
the several parts of the Province and of the Territories[1] to
elect out of their number seven persons to serve as their
representatives in General Assembly. Accordingly, about
forty persons came together at Chester in December, 1682,
and proceeded to act as a one-chambered legislative body.
They adopted sixty-one bills and then adjourned. These
laws followed closely those which had been drawn up
in England, but there were some additional measures.
Among these was an act uniting the Territories with the
Province, which is called the " Act of Union." In February, 1683, Penn sent out writs for the election of another
assembly. This time he directed the freemen of Pennsylvania and of the Territories to choose seventy-two persons
to serve as a Provincial Council[2] and ordered that the freemen should assemble in a body with the Council for the
purpose of giving their assent to such laws as might be
proposed. Before the Provincial Council came together,
he either suggested or acquiesced in another arrangement
by which of the twelve persons chosen in each of the six

---

[1] What is now the state of Pennsylvania was usually termed "the Province," while what is now the state of
Delaware was called "the Territories."
It will be convenient to use these terms
in the following pages.

[2] For one of these writs, see *Charter
and Laws of Pennsylvania*, 483; also in
Proud's *Pennsylvania*, i, 234 note.

counties of the Province and Territories three should serve
as councilors and nine as members of the Assembly. Up
to this time, little or no regard has been paid to the
Frame of Government which Penn had so laboriously
compiled in England. Now, however, the representatives
requested the proprietor to see to it that these neglects of
the fundamental law should not deprive the colonists of
the other rights which they enjoyed under that document.
They passed a law, March 19, 1682–83,[1] which is called
the Act of Settlement, and ratified the arrangements
which had been made as to the council and assembly. In
the next month, a new Frame of Government was adopted,[2]
which provided that the council should consist of not less
than eighteen members and the assembly of not less than
thirty-six. Moreover, the full and secure possession of
lands was guaranteed to the holders upon payment of
rents and services to the proprietor. Finally, the sole
power of appointing to office was limited to the lifetime
of the present proprietor. In all these constitutional
arrangements there is shown a singular lack of regard for
the royal charter under which Penn and his tenants held
their lands. Moreover, the constitutional position of these
various organic laws is also open to doubt. According to
the charter, the laws of the province were to be submitted
to the king, but there is no evidence that any of the
Frames of Government were laid before the royal authorities. Moreover, Penn's personal attitude toward these fundamental laws is interesting, for he seems to have felt
entirely at liberty to disregard all or any of their provisions. Nor did the colonists look upon them with favor.

---

[1] *Laws of Pennsylvania* (ed. 1879),
p. 123; *Votes of Pennsylvania*, i, Part i,
p. 11.
[2] *Laws of Pennsylvania* (ed. 1879),
p. 155; *Votes of Pennsylvania*, i, Part i,
p. 21; *Minutes of the Council of Pennsylvania*, i, p. xxxiv.

The Quakers were "a peculiar people," so far as religion and social institutions were concerned; but as to politics, they were ordinary, everyday Englishmen. They had that distrust of parental and theoretical government which has ever been the mainstay of the Anglo-Saxon race and preferred the "Constitution of England" to the political theories of Harrington, Sidney, and Penn.

Had the proprietor been able to live in the colony, affairs might have gone well, for at this time he had the confidence of the colonists, and the power to act promptly and with vigor; but the dispute with Baltimore obliged him to sail for home in August, 1684. Before his departure he confided the executive power to the Council as a whole. For a while affairs progressed peacefully, but in May, 1685,[1] the Assembly met for the first time since Penn's departure, and at once the disputations began. Among the leading men in the province was Nicholas More. He had been chairman of the first Assembly and Speaker of the second and was now Chief Justice and also a member of the Assembly. He was accused of acting illegally and arbitrarily. The Assembly expelled him from his seat, voting him "a public enemy to the Province and Territories, and a violator of the privileges of the freemen." They impeached him as an "aspiring and corrupt minister of state" and asked the President and Council to remove him from his position as Chief Justice, but nothing was done.

The President of the Council at this time was Thomas Lloyd, perhaps the most eminent of the settlers of Pennsylvania. He and his colleagues magnified their office and caused the laws to be promulgated "by the authority of the President and Council." Moreover, for some rea-

Votes of Pennsylvania, i, Part i, p. 30.

son, the bills to which the Assembly were asked to assent had not been posted, as the Frame required. These infractions of the organic law were bitterly resented by the Assembly, which, nevertheless, was quite willing itself to break the Frame by initiating legislation, amending bills, and indulging in oral discussion. It assented to ten bills, but the ill feeling which had been aroused continued for many years.

The noise of these proceedings reached the ears of the proprietor in England and troubled him. He wrote letter after letter to his friends in Pennsylvania, imploring them to "let all old sores be forgotten as well as forgiven." At another time he besought them to be more amicable: "For the love of God, me, and the poor country, be not so governmentish, so noisy, and open, in your dissatisfactions."[1] In 1686 he revoked his appointment of the council as deputy governor and confided the powers of that office to five commissioners of state, any three of whom could act. In his instructions[2] to the commissioners, Penn passed from beseechings to threatenings. He authorized them to work with the Provincial Council, if possible, or to appoint such a council as they thought convenient, "for I will no more endure their most slothful and dishonorable attendance, but dissolve the frame without any more ado." He ordered them to curiously inspect the proceedings of the council and assembly and inform him in what particulars they had broken the Frame. They were to declare everything null and void which had been done since his departure. Finally, and in a somewhat contrary spirit, they were to have a tender regard to peace: "Love, forgive, help, and serve one another, and let the people learn by your example, as well as by your power, the happy life of concord."

---

[1] Proud's *Pennsylvania*, i, 297 ncte. [2] *Ibid.*, i, 305.

Concord, however, was out of the question. On the contrary, discord began with the meeting of the Assembly in May, 1688, when that body neglected to present the Speaker to the Commissioners of Government for their approval. Furthermore, the Assembly for the first time in the history of that body sat with closed doors. The Commissioners and the councilors themselves were by no means conciliatory. They reminded the Assembly that they were to consider the promulgated bills only, and informed them that immediate dissolution would follow the transaction of any other business. The two branches of the legislature, having begun their work in this unhappy spirit, proceeded with ever increasing lack of harmony. Especially they came to loggerheads on the question of money. Under the Frame of Government, the drawing up of money bills, like other laws, was in the hands of the Provincial Council; but the Assembly was very sensitive on this point, since the initiative as to money bills was one of the matters on which the House of Commons in England had recently won a great victory. The Assembly proposed to vote money by resolution, which being assented to by the governor and council would have the effect of a law. In the end, the Assembly accepted five of the seven bills which had been promulgated by the council, but refused to pass the other two, one of which was a money bill.

The times were now stormy in England, for it was in November of this year (1688) that William of Orange landed at Torbay and speedily occupied his father-in-law's kingdom. On the 10th of the following December, William Penn was summoned before the Privy Council and questioned as to his relations with the fugitive James. In this critical condition of affairs, Penn bethought him of intrusting the government of his American territories to one who was not a member of the Society of Friends. He chose Captain John Blackwell, a Cromwellian veteran, whom he described as "a grave, sober, wise man." He instructed [1] Blackwell to pass under the great seal of the province all commissions which had been properly signed in England; to collect all the laws and send them over to him and, in general, to "rule the meek, meekly: and those that will not be ruled, rule with authority." Blackwell found none of meek disposition in Penn's domain, and the task of ruling the others "with authority" proved to be hopeless. This portion of Pennsylvania history is unusually difficult to understand. We find, for instance, so strong and intelligent a man as Thomas Lloyd declining to obey what appear to be reasonable and legal directions on the part of the proprietor. As keeper of the great seal of the province, Lloyd refused point blank to affix that emblem of authenticity to commissions which Blackwell presented to him. The governor, thereupon, sought to keep him out of the Council. Blackwell also came into collision with David Lloyd, who was deputy master of the rolls, clerk of the courts, and clerk of the Assembly, and who in these capacities declined to deliver to Blackwell documents which the governor demanded.

By the time that the Assembly met in May, 1689,[2] these wranglings had progressed so far that the deputy governor was deprived of the support which under ordinary circumstances the holder of this office might have expected from the Council. Blackwell, in opening the Assembly, declared that the royal charter required all laws to be authenticated by the great seal of the province, but that none of the en-

---

[1] Proud's *Pennsylvania*, i, 339.
[2] *Votes of Pennsylvania*, i, Part i, p. 50; *Minutes of the Council of Pennsylvania*, i, 244.

grossed laws, except the Frame of Government and Act of Union, had been so attested. It followed from this and from other considerations, to which he adverted, that none of the existing acts of assembly could be regarded as laws ; he thought, however, that so far as they were not contrary to the laws of England, they might be looked upon in the light of instructions from the proprietor until his pleasure, or that of the king, could be ascertained. In reply, the Speaker of the Assembly declared that the Frame of Government made no provision for the use of the great seal of the province in authenticating laws, omitting to mention the fact that the royal charter contained this requirement. After thirteen months, Blackwell was relieved of his office at his own request and thankfully turned over the government to the Provincial Council, which promptly elected Thomas Lloyd its president. Such was the working of the " holy experiment " in the first decades of Pennsylvania.

NOTES

I. William Penn. — Penn's career has attracted the attention of students and writers, but a detailed scientific survey of his life free from adulation and controversy remains to be written. George Hodges's little volume, entitled *William Penn,* in the Riverside Biographical Series, best represents the creditable side of his career. The strictly colonial side of his life is admirably set forth in W. J. Buck's *William Penn in America. Giving, as far as possible, his every-day occurrences while in the Province.* This contains in convenient form a mass of material, largely quoted; but the edition was limited to three hundred copies and the book is, therefore, not always accessible. S. G. Fisher's *The True William Penn* contains some valuable matter and does not conceal the "founder's" shortcomings. Of the older works, the memoirs by S. M. Janney, W. H. Dixon, and Thomas Clarkson are statements from the Quaker side. There is a valuable series of articles on the "Family of William Penn" in the *Pennsylvania Magazine of History,* xxi, xxii. Shepherd in his *Pennsylvania as a Proprietary Province* devotes much attention to Penn as a political reformer, and the opening chapters of Egle's *Pennsylvania* contain a résumé of his career.

The best way to gauge Penn's ideas is to read his letters and state papers. These are scattered far and wide in the *Pennsylvania Magazine,* the *Penn-Logan Correspondence,* the memoirs above noted, the histories of Pennsylvania, especially Proud's, and the legislative records of the assembly and the council. Penn's letters to his second wife before their marriage are interesting from a personal point of view (*Pennsylvania Magazine of History,* xxvii, 296). There are also several important letters in the *New England Historical Genealogical Register,* xxvi, 423. The collected works of William Penn, of which there are two sets, are rather disappointing for his American career.

II. Pennsylvania. — In the Pennsylvania Historical Society's rooms at Philadelphia are some one hundred volumes of "Penn Papers." A patient perusal of these formed the groundwork of William R. Shepherd's *Pennsylvania as a Proprietary Province.* This book is unfortunately arranged, but contains a mass of matter not elsewhere in print. Proud's *Pennsylvania,* although it was written long ago and is strongly biased in favor of the Quakers, is still an indispensable book. Isaac Sharpless's *Quaker Government in Pennsylvania*[1] is based on the study of Quaker manuscript records and is extremely instructive. The same author's *Two Centuries of Pennsylvania History* is an excellent brief book on the subject.

The records of Pennsylvania have been largely printed. First in importance are the six folio volumes entitled *Votes and Proceedings of the House of Representatives of the Province of Pennsylvania.* The *Minutes of the Provincial Council of Pennsylvania* form the first ten volumes of the *Colonial Records.* They are often cited under the latter title, but in the present work the former title is used. Staughton George and others compiled a volume of official papers before 1701, which is herein cited as *Laws of Pennsylvania* (ed. 1879).[2] In the absence of the first volume of the collected *Colonial Laws of Pennsylvania* this work is indispensable to the student. The *Pennsylvania Archives* compiled by Samuel Hazard are also important. Notwithstanding this mass of original matter and the documents printed in the *Pennsylvania Magazine* and Proud's *Pennsylvania,* it will be impossible to treat the history of that state in a scholarly way until the "Penn Papers" are published and the *Penn-Logan Correspondence* is printed in its entirety.

III. Southern Boundaries of Pennsylvania. — The best brief account is in Shepherd's *Proprietary Government,* 117–168; it is not long and is discriminating. The rabid partisan statements of Dr. George W. Archer[3] and Sidney George Fisher[4] best retain the spirit of the original disputants; a perusal of them both gives one a good idea of the merits and demerits of this controversy. The documents are enumerated in Winsor's *America* (iii, 513; v, 272). Among them may be mentioned Penn's letter to the Lords of the Committee of Plantations, dated Philadelphia the 14th of the Sixthmonth, 1683.[5] The "Breviate . . . for the Plaintiffs. Upon a Bill to compell a *Specifick Execution* of *Articles* of *Agreement* entred into between the Partys for setling the Boundarys of the

---

[1] The first volume was originally printed as *Quaker Experiments in Government.*

[2] *Charter to William Penn and Laws of the Province of Pennsylvania passed between the years 1682 and 1700; preceded by the Duke of York's Laws . . . with an Appendix containing laws relating to the organization of the provincial* courts and historical matter (Harrisburg, 1879).

[3] Maryland Historical Society's *Fund Publications,* No. 30, i.

[4] *The Making of Pennsylvania,* ch. xi.

[5] Printed in Proud's *Pennsylvania,* i, 267–274.

Province of *Pensilvania,* the *Three Lower Countys,* and the Province of *Maryland,* and for perpetuating Testimony, etc.," which was printed for use of counsel in the proceedings in Chancery in 1742 contains a long summary of evidence from the Penn side and three curious maps. One of these is given in facsimile in Maryland Historical Society's *Fund Publications,* No. 34, p. 134. This number of the *Fund Publications* is entitled "the Calvert Papers, Number Two. Selections from Correspondence." It contains (pp. 132, 165, etc.) interesting letters from Cæcilius Calvert written in 1752. Of the special secondary accounts, the titles of which are given in Winsor, James Veech's *Mason and Dixon's Line* (Pittsburg, 1857) may be mentioned. There is a paper on the "General Title of the Penns to Pennsylvania" in *Pennsylvania Magazine of History,* xxiii, 60.

(From Richard Blome's *Present State of His Majesties Isles and Territories in America*, London, 1687.)

CHAPTER V

THE GALLIC PERIL, 1664-1689

In the spring of 1689 the opponents of the Stuart government in Massachusetts, New York, and Maryland raised the cry of danger from French invasion, danger from the alliance between the French and the Indians, and danger from the Roman Catholics. It has been the habit of historical writers to make light of these alarms and to regard them as party shibboleths which were used by colonial agitators to further their evil designs or to hide their infamous doings. A careful consideration of all the facts leads irresistibly to the conclusion that the Gallic peril was more real than has generally been thought to have been the case.

Until 1660 the French settlements in Canada had developed with painful slowness owing to the ineptitude of Frenchmen for colonial enterprise and the active hostility of the Indian nations composing the League of the Iroquois. This powerful confederation had always been hostile to the French, but had also maintained its independence of Dutch control. The coming to power of Louis XIV infused new vigor into French colonization, with the unexpected result of frightening the Iroquois into the outstretched arms of the English. At this time the English towns and plantations stretched for hundreds of miles from north to south, along the Atlantic seaboard. As yet they clung to the tide water and the banks of navigable streams; up to 1660 they had not passed the foot hills of the Alleghanies. In the far south the Spaniards had formerly explored the inland part of the country; but in 1660 the hinterland, from the Lakes to the Gulf, lay open to French enterprise, limited only by the persistent hostility of the Iroquois tribes.

French missionaries, fur traders, and explorers searched out the great valleys of the interior and penetrated to the heart of the continent by the way of the St. Lawrence and the Great Lakes. Before 1640 Jean Nicolet ascended the Fox River, an affluent of Lake Michigan, and gained the Wisconsin, down which he voyaged toward the Mississippi, but did not come within sight of the " Father of Waters." In 1659 Radisson and Groseilliers camped on the banks of a stream which is believed to have been one of the head waters of that great river. In 1669–70 La Salle reached the Ohio and the Illinois, but probably did not follow either of them to the Mississippi.

Of all the great Frenchmen who held high station in the government of Canada, none seems to have had clearer vision than Jean Talon, the Intendant of New France. The Jesuit fathers were eager to save souls and to extend the influence of Christianity and of their order; La Salle was full of enthusiasm for wilderness exploration and for the establishment of centers of French influence in the interior; Talon, with a statesman's imaginative prescience, saw that the speedy control of the lake region and the country to the southward was essential to the successful prosecution of the conquest of North America from the colonists of England and the soldiers of Spain.[1] In 1670 he sent Daumont de Saint-Lusson to take formal possession of the great inland basin for the king of France.

---

[1] See on this subject Thomas Chapais' *Jean Talon, Intendant de la Nouvelle France*, 356.

Saint-Lusson, with whom went Nicholas Perrot, performed his task with abundant formality in the presence of representatives of fourteen Indian tribes at Saut Ste. Marie in June, 1671.[1] Two years later, Joliet and Marquette reached the Mississippi by way of the Wisconsin, and voyaged on its waters as far south as the mouth of the Arkansas. They wondered at what point it reached the salt sea; but fear of the Spaniards impelled them to return to New France with the knowledge they had already attained, lest by attempting too much they might lose all. Returning, they ascended the Illinois and by a short portage gained Lake Michigan. From this point the exploration of the Mississippi Valley was bound up with the life of La Salle.

Few figures stand forth in history in truer heroic proportions than does that of Robert Cavelier, Sieur de La Salle. The insufficiency of his means for the accomplishment of the ends which his ardent imagination placed before him, the absolute ignorance of the value of money which was one of his distinguishing characteristics, the constant misfortunes that dogged his steps, and the tragic death that overtook him, all combine to give him a place in our annals which a plain, successful, everyday explorer might not have found. La Salle's conception was an immense one; with a license from the king and a few hundred thousand francs from his relatives and friends, he essayed a systematic and continuous exploration of half a continent and proposed to make this work pay for itself by means of the fur trade of the unknown western regions. Unfortunately, he was a bitter enemy of the Jesuits and a firm friend of Frontenac, governor of Canada, who was at swords' points with nearly every one else in New France, and

1 Thwaites's *Jesuit Relations*, lv, 105–115.

the exploitation of the fur trade which La Salle proposed was contrary to the interests of many merchants of Montreal and Quebec.   The Jesuits and the fur traders poisoned the minds of the authorities at home against La Salle and Frontenac, and, in America, incited his men to mutiny. They also aroused the Indians by circulating reports that La Salle was striving to bring the dreaded Iroquois upon them.   His designs were so far-reaching in scope and the results attained were so great, that even in their partial fulfillment his plans and performances are of exceeding interest.   The plan was to establish defensive posts and fur-trading stations on the shores of the Great Lakes and of the rivers flowing into the Mississippi; to build vessels for the navigation of these interior waters and by means of them to conduct the fur trade and carry out extensive explorations.

From beginning to end, affairs went hard with La Salle, the very winds fought against him : [1] the *Griffin* which he built to navigate the lakes disappeared with all on board, and a vessel bringing him supplies from France went to the bottom in the lower St. Lawrence.   The years from 1677 to 1681 form a period of stress in his life to which his biographer necessarily devotes large attention, but which in the chronicle of exploration may be passed over briefly.   At the end of 1680, in addition to rebuilding Fort Frontenac, which he took over from the government, he had accomplished little except to establish a post on the St. Joseph River, which enters Lake Michigan nearly opposite Chicago, and to send an exploring expedition to the upper Mississippi under the command of the adventurous and

[1] On these early expeditions, see M. B. Anderson's *Relations of the Discoveries and Voyages of Cavelier de La Salle from 1679 to 1681;* this is a translation of the "Relation des descouvertes" in Margry's *Découvertes des Français.* See also Ogg's *Opening of the Mississippi.*

untruthful Father Louis Hennepin. In the winter of 1681–82, La Salle himself set out upon the exploration of the Mississippi.

It was in December, 1681, that La Salle left the southern end of Lake Michigan to follow the great river to its mouth. He had with him twenty-two Frenchmen and thirty-one Indians ; of the latter ten were women and three were children — in all fifty-four persons. \ The second in command of the expedition was the Chevalier Henri de Tonty. He was La Salle's most faithful follower. Born in Italy, he had become domesticated in France and for years followed the fortunes of his great leader and was steadfast even after the latter's tragic death. Another tried companion was Father Zenobe Membré, who kept a journal of the voyage and possibly wrote what is sometimes regarded as La Salle's official report of the expedition.[1])

Leaving St. Joseph, the explorers passed " toward the divine river, called by the Indians Checagou." [2] From it they crossed to the Illinois and dragged their sleds over the frozen course of that stream until the ice gave way to open water, then launching their canoes they voyaged down the Illinois to the Mississippi to which La Salle now gave the name Colbert. The drift-ice was coming down the Mississippi in such great quantities that they were obliged to remain in camp for a week until the stream became safe for their canoes. Then they paddled and drifted downward by the mouth of the Missouri, the site of the later city of

[1] " Relation de la Découverte de l'Embouchure de la Rivière Mississippi, " in R. Thomassy's *Geologie Pratique de la Louisiane ;* this portion is printed separately as *De la Salle et ses Relations Inédites de la découverte du Mississippi* (Paris, 1859). A fuller narrative by Membré, containing long extracts from the above, is printed in Le Clercq's *First Establishment of the Faith* (Shea's translation), ii, 161–195. There is no authentic portrait of La Salle, see Winsor's *America*, iv, 242, 244 notes.

[2] Le Clercq's *First Establishment of the Faith* (Shea's translation), ii, 162.

St. Louis, and the confluence of the Ohio. The muddy water of the Missouri astonished them and caused them some anxiety on the supposition that it had made the Mississippi water undrinkable. Near the Third Chickasaw Bluffs, about midway between the mouths of the Ohio and Arkansas and not very far from the site of the modern city of Memphis, the explorers built a fort which they named Prudhomme, for one of their number who nearly lost his life wandering in the wilderness in that region. Then down stream they went until they came to a village of the Arkansas Indians. These treated the explorers with great kindness, which La Salle requited by taking formal possession of their country in the name of the king of France, greatly to the Indians' joy, so Membré relates.[1] Then on and on they passed, by the sites of Vicksburg, Natchez, and New Orleans, until the river split into three channels. Dividing, they floated down the several streams to the Gulf, April 6, 1682. Three days later, after some further explorations, the reunited parties landed on a bit of firm ground inside the river's mouth, erected a pillar, buried a leaden plate, and chanted the hymn of the church, "Vexilla Regis" and the "Te Deum." Then La Salle took possession of the country under the name of Louisiana, together with " all the nations, peoples, provinces, cities, towns, villages, mines, minerals, fisheries, streams, and rivers " from the mouth of the Ohio to the sea and to the River of Palms, or Rio Grande. This he did " upon the assurance we have had from the natives of these countries that we are the first Europeans who have descended or ascended the said river Colbert," or Mississippi. The statement is interesting, both on account of the ignorance which La Salle displayed as to the earlier Spanish explorations and also because of the fact that priority

[1] Le Clercq's *First Establishment of the Faith* (Shea's translation), ii, 169.

of discovery seemed to him to be the basis of a good title. The return journey was safely accomplished, with the loss of a few men who deserted to the Indians.   In due season La Salle regained Quebec to find Frontenac recalled and a lukewarm governor installed in his place.   He then sailed for France, whence some years afterward he embarked on his ill-fated expedition to the Gulf of Mexico.

The French in Canada and in the interior were never formidable in numbers; in 1688, at the end of the period which we are now considering, there were twenty times as many people in the English colonies on the seaboard as there were in all of New France.   These figures, however, have no relation to the comparative military resources of the two groups of colonists.   The French lived under a despotic government in State and Church : politically, they were all under one ruler; religiously, they were all of one faith. Whatever strength for offense or defense they possessed, could be thrown effectively at any one given point at any one moment.   In the epoch under consideration began that contest between the two races in America which was to continue for nearly one hundred years until it ended disastrously for France on the Plains of Abraham.

The first effective limitation to the expansion of New France was the establishment of the Hudson Bay Company by Charles II in the year 1670.[1]   The mode in which this was brought about well illustrates the intimate relations that existed between England and France in the reigns of the second Charles and James.   Among the French explorers and fur traders were Pierre Radisson and Medard Chouart, who took the title of des Groseilliers from a

---

[1] See Beckles Wilson's *The Great Company* (Toronto, 1899); George Bryce's *Remarkable History of the Hudson Bay Company* (London, 1900). The important documents are enumerated in Winsor's *America*.

little estate which he had inherited from his father. Groseilliers's wife was Radisson's sister. Radisson himself, a Huguenot, had married an Englishwoman, the daughter of Sir John Kirke, kinsman of the Kirkes who had seized Quebec a generation earlier in the time of Champlain. After years of successful fur trading and exploration, these brothers-in-law learned from the Indians of the existence of an easy line of communication between Lake Superior and Hudson Bay. They were carrying on their fur-trading operations against the wishes of the Jesuits, and now hit upon the scheme of approaching the fur-yielding preserves of the interior by some other route than that which lay through the settled parts of New France. Without the means of providing the funds for so great a scheme, they first sought to interest merchants and shipowners of Boston, New England, in the plan. That failing, they next tried Paris also ineffectually, and finally induced the colonizing group of courtiers at London to provide the necessary funds.

Of those near relatives who deserved well of the restored Stuart king, his cousin, Prince Rupert, had so far been unprovided for. This was partly due to the fact that this prince possessed certain funds which he had saved from the proceeds of his buccaneering career in the West Indies during the Protectorate. With his money and with that furnished by others interested in hazardous commerce, the two Frenchmen and a Boston ship captain sailed from London for Hudson Bay in the year 1668, in the good ship *Nonsuch*. The voyage was prosperous and led to the chartering of the Hudson Bay Company by Charles II in 1670 with Prince Rupert as its first governor. Among the other charter members were two of the proprietors of Carolina, Lord Craven and Lord Ashley, and three members of the families of other Carolina proprietors, — Sir Peter Colleton, Sir Philip Carteret, and Christopher, second Duke of Albemarle, while still another was Lord Arlington who had interests in Virginia. Up to 1688 the Hudson Bay Company had not assumed formidable proportions ; but the fact that Englishmen had made good a foothold on the southwestern shore of Hudson Bay was an important event in the history of the contest for the continent. Possibly its most important result was the making connections between the English and the Indians of the Great Lake system. At nearly the same time, Colonel Thomas Dongan brought the Indians of the Iroquois Confederation clearly within the scope of English policy.

The League of the Iroquois occupied the region which extends from the mountains of western New England to Lake Erie. In addition, from time to time they established their villages north of that lake and Lake Ontario. Their power extended westward of these limits and southward as far as the Ohio. Their hold on these western and southern tributary tribes was exposed to constant risk. When they were successful in war, the western tribes were submissive; but when the Five Nations suffered defeats, the westerners were prone to throw off the yoke. The easternmost tribe of the Iroquois was the Mohawk ; next to them were the Oneidas, and then in order came the Onondagas, Cayugas, and Senecas. Their political organization was the most perfect of any Indian power in North America, and they were reputed to be the most bloodthirsty of Indian tribes.

The friendship or hostility of the Iroquois was the key to the reasonably peaceful possession of the region north of the Potomac and the Ohio and east of the Mississippi. Were the Iroquois English Indians or were they French

Indians? and what, in any case, were the boundaries of their domains? For years, French governors and church-men had sought to overcome the hostility of the members of this formidable Indian confederacy by converting them to Christianity of the French type. One Jesuit missionary after another had gone to them and with slight success. The Jesuit fathers stand high in the roll of heroes and martyrs; they were sincere, high-minded, unselfish men; but their heroism and the unhappy fates of some of them must not blind us to the dangers of their doings. Had they converted the Iroquois to Christianity and made them spiritual and military allies of France, the bounds of New France would have extended southward at least as far as the Mohawk River and probably into Pennsylvania; French military power would have enveloped the English colonies and would inevitably have conquered Virginia and New England. Fortunately the Iroquois did not take kindly to French blandishments and, moreover, they had become accustomed to Dutch and English goods which could be laid down at Albany cheaper than French commodities could be transported to Montreal. Like all Indians, they were fond of intoxicating beverages which could be ob-tained from Albany cheaply and in abundance, while the French brandy was dear in price and difficult to procure, owing to the efforts of the Jesuit fathers to suppress drunk-enness among the natives. The Dutch and the English had no scruples against supplying the Indians with rum or even with firearms, and considering the imperfectability of human nature, it is not to be wondered at that the Iroquois preferred friendship with Dutch and English traders to becoming the subjects of French priests and governors.

Louis XIV took a personal interest in the expansion of

French power and exercised a paternal solicitude as to the welfare of Catholic Frenchmen. The perilous condition of affairs in New France led him, in 1665, to send a body of trained soldiers to Canada. This regiment of some thousand men had originally been recruited by the Prince of Carignan, but at this time was commanded by Colonel de Salières and is known as the Carignan-Salières regiment. The object of sending this formidable body of veteran fighters to America was to deal a blow at the eastern tribes of the Five Nations and thus to secure immunity from attack to the French settlements in the St. Lawrence Valley for many years to come. Under the direction of the Marquis de Tracy, Lieutenant General of New France, and Daniel de Rémy, Sieur de Courcelles, the governor of the province, three hundred of these veterans and one hundred Canadian frontiersmen marched to the attack of the Iroquois strongholds in January, 1666. The distance from Quebec, the starting point to the Mohawk villages, was a little over four hundred miles, and was made through the forests and over the frozen surface of lake and river by men, most of whom, up to that time, had been accustomed only to the conditions which obtained on the continent of Europe. They lost their way and instead of reaching the villages of the Mohawks found themselves encamped within two miles of the settlement of Schenectady. To their dismay they found that the village was no longer in the possession of the Dutch, who were momentarily the allies of France ; but, with the rest of New Netherland, had been conquered by the English with whom France was then at war. In the wilderness, however, there were no hostilities between whites at this time. After securing needed supplies the French returned to Canada, losing some of their number on the homeward march. In the autumn of 1666 the French

again came south with an even stronger force.[1] This time
they reached the Mohawk castles, whose defenders fled at
the sound of twenty French drums, for they thought that
the noise was the roaring of some strange and terrible
beast. The Frenchmen destroyed a few villages and ruined
much of the winter supply of food, but did not accomplish
anything else. The most pregnant outcome of these expeditions was the discovery of the route from the St. Lawrence to the middle Hudson Valley, which was to be used
on many later occasions in the campaigns against the English colonies. Why Tracy and Courcelles did not at once
turn the Carignan-Salières regiment upon the defenseless
Dutch-English frontier posts, is one of the mysteries of
the time ; but their failure to do so was one of those
providential events which have so conspicuously marked
the course of American history. This was the Frenchman's opportunity and once lost was never to recur ; New
England might then have been isolated from the Chesapeake colonies with a fair prospect of its ultimate conquest.
Returning to Quebec, Tracy was recalled to France with
the greater part of the Carignan-Salières regiment. The
soldiers who remained behind were ultimately colonized
under their officers in the valley of the Richelieu River ;[2]
they and their descendants became the nucleus of expedition
after expedition which ravaged the English frontier settlements.

Colonel Richard Nicolls better understood the possibilities of action and tried to induce the New Englanders to
bestir themselves for an attack upon the French villages
in the St. Lawrence Valley. But the people of Massa-

[1] Parkman's *Old Régime*, 246–261;
Faillon's *Histoire de la Colonie Fran-
çaise en Canada*, iii, 129–147; Thwaites's
Jesuit Relations, l, 131–147.

[2] W. B. Munro's *Seigniorial System
in Canada*, 72.

chusetts and Connecticut were not at all inclined to further the ambitious projects of James's representative in New York; they alleged want of time and strength. Nicolls, however, fitted out a privateer which cruised against Dutch and French commerce and with some success. Among other booty to be captured was an Indian who was sold into slavery in the West Indies by order of the authorities at Manhattan Island. In 1667, by the treaty of Breda, peace was made between England, on the one side, and France and the Netherlands, on the other. Acadia, which had been captured by Sedgwick and the New Englanders in the time of the Protectorate, was now returned to France. Ten years later (1677) Sir Edmund Andros was governor of New York, which was still under the proprietorship of James. Relying, perhaps, on the Duke's fidelity to the Faith and the king's financial obligations to Louis XIV, the French government in Canada informed Andros that the Iroquois country lay within the French sphere of action in America. Andros replied with a declaration that the English dominion extended northward to the St. Lawrence and the Great Lakes,[1] but his situation in New York was so insecure that he had to content himself with this assertion of his master's rights.

Saturday, the 25th of August, 1683, was a memorable day in the history of America, for it was then that Colonel Thomas Dongan arrived at New York overland from Boston, where he had disembarked from the frigate *Constant Warwick*. With his coming a new epoch opened in the history of the province of New York, in the history of English-American colonies, and in the history of the international relations of England and France. The Dutch and Swedish colonists on the Hudson and Delaware had

---

[1] Brodhead's *New York*, ii, 306; *Historical Magazine*, x, 268.

been an alien element on the continent, but they had always been so feeble in numbers in comparison with the English settlements to the north and to the south of them that their coming and staying had been no menace to English colonial life, although their presence was, no doubt, inconvenient from several points of view. Moreover, the Dutch and Swedes were Protestants and their institutions were, in most respects, similar to those of their English neighbors. The French power in the St. Lawrence Valley was on an entirely different footing. The French Canadians were not only alien in blood, but they were almost all of them Roman Catholics and faithful subjects of the ruler who had revoked the Edict of Nantes. Moreover, their institutions were of a distinctly feudal cast, while those of the English colonists were the farthest removed from the mediæval mode of government of any institutions within the limit of Christendom.

Thomas Dongan[1] was an Irishman of good family, as is shown by the fact that in 1698, long after his retirement from colonial affairs, he succeeded to the Earldom of Limerick. He had commanded an Irish regiment in the service of the king of France and was well versed in the ways of Frenchmen, although he did not use their language with ease, at least not when excited. He was a Roman Catholic and enjoyed to the full the confidence of the royal brothers. There is little left to us as to the personal qualities of Governor Dongan, but he must have been a man of forceful disposition and personal magnetism. He possessed the Irish instinct for political dis-

[1] Brodhead's *History of New York,* ii, 370; O'Callaghan's "Historical Introduction" to the *Journal of the Council of New York,* i, p. xxiii, note. Owing to the varying forms in which Dongan's name appears as Duncan, Duggan, Dungan, and Dongan, it is difficult to trace his life in the diaries and letters of the time. The name was pronounced Duggan, or Dungan.

putation and the power to ingratiate himself with various classes of people. He also enjoyed distinct advantages over any earlier governor of New York, because he was authorized by the Duke to summon a representative assembly and to give favorable charters to the cities of New York and Albany.[1] Finally, he was directed not to interfere with the government of New Jersey and was thus freed from danger of attack from Penn and the other proprietors of that province. The constitutional history of his time will be taken up in another place;[2] here it is only necessary to say that he had a contented people behind him as no other governor of New York had for a hundred years. The one difficulty in Dongan's position lay in the fact that he had no definite instructions from the English government as to the management of negotiations with the French in Canada, except to be careful not to embroil himself with the French governor.[3] He must have often felt very doubtful as to how his doings would be regarded in England; but with an Irishman's optimism, he acted as if no such thought ever crossed his mind. An example of his masterful way of doing business has already been related in connection with Pennsylvania. In that case, without instructions from home and directly contrary to the wording of the king's grants to the Duke of York and to William Penn, he had pushed the limits of the ducal domains indefinitely westward and southward, and Penn had been obliged to submit.[4]

---

[1] Dr. J. A. Fairlie's paper on "Municipal Corporations in the Colonies" in *Municipal Affairs*, ii, 341, gives the facts as to the growth of boroughs and cities before the Revolution; the subject will be considered in a later volume of the present work.

[2] See the present volume, ch. x.

[3] *Calendars of State Papers, America*

and *West Indies, 1681–1685*, pp. 604, 740; *New York Colonial Documents*, iii, 340, 353.

[4] James's secretary, Sir John Werden, urged Dongan to keep the Pennsylvanians and New Jerseyites from the Susquehanna. *New York Colonial Documents*, iii, 350.

Since the time of Courcelles, the Iroquois had risen to the height of their power; time and again they had attacked the French in the north and often successfully; they had also extended their sway to the south and through their tributary tribes had ravaged the frontiers of Maryland and Virginia. In July and August, 1684, Governor Dongan and Lord Howard of Effingham, governor of Virginia, held a conference at Albany with sundry chiefs of the Five Nations.[1] Two most important objects were accomplished: the Iroquois were induced to desist from attacking the back settlements of the Chesapeake colonies and acknowledged themselves subjects of England. As a token of their amicable intentions, five axes were buried in the southeast corner of the courtyard of the fort, "one in Behalf of Virginia and their Indians, another in Behalf of Maryland and theirs, and three for the Onnondagas, Oneydoes, and Cayugas." To emphasize the fact that the Indians and their territories were under the protection of the king of England, the arms of the Duke of York were affixed to the walls of the Iroquois fortified towns or castles, with the consent of their inhabitants and defenders.

Dongan now began a correspondence with the French authorities at Quebec which was destined to continue for some years. In 1684 he informed Count Le Febvre de La Barre, who was at the head of the administration of New France, that the Iroquois were under the government of New York and had traded with the people of that province for about forty years and with no one else except secretly. Moreover, he informed the French governor that

---

[1] *New York Colonial Documents*, iii, 347; Cadwallader Colden's *History of the Five Nations* (London, 1747), pp. 44-56; Wraxall's *Abridgment of Indian Affairs*, Ms., p. 3. Colden often follows Wraxall very closely.

the province of New York included all the territory south
and southwest of the Lake of Canada.[1] On his side,
La Barre denied that the Iroquois were British subjects.
This Dongan would not admit for one moment and reit-
erated the declaration that they were subjects of the
British crown and under the government of New York.

La Barre now organized an expedition to punish the
Senecas for their repeated assaults upon Frenchmen and
their disregard of French interests. Upon learning of this
threatened attack on the subjects of England, Dongan
wrote that he should be very sorry to hear that La Barre
had invaded the " Duke's Territories " after his promises
and expostulations. As an additional dissuasive, he told
the Frenchman that he had caused the Duke's escutcheon
to be displayed on the Indian forts. La Barre replied
that French missionaries had labored among the Iroquois
for twenty years ; that he was about to punish evildoers among them ; and that he hoped Dongan did not
desire to protect robbers, assassins, and traitors, since in
that case he " could not distinguish their protector from
themselves." [2] The expedition was undertaken, but
turned out badly, owing to the advanced age and incapacity of La Barre and the lack of coöperation of those under
him. His soldiers sickened and starved, and, making a
disgraceful treaty with the Senecas, he returned precipi-
tately to Montreal and Quebec and was soon afterward
recalled to France. His successor was Jacques René de
Brisay, Marquis de Denonville.

The new governor had scarcely arrived in his province
before Dongan opened a vigorous correspondence with him.
The New York magistrate began by complaining of the

---

[1] *New York Colonial Documents*, iii,   [2] *Ibid.*, iii, 450.
447, 448.

doings of La Barre and said that he hoped he would live on better terms with Denonville than he had with the other gentleman.   He then went on to warn the newcomer not to interfere with the Iroquois, who were English subjects and under the protection of the English government.   They were, it is true, fighting with the " farr Indians " southwest of the Great Lakes, but Dongan thought that Denonville should not engage himself in Indian quarrels ; in fact, he could not believe that a person of the French governor's " reputation in the world " would follow in his predecessor's footsteps.[1]   On his side Denonville was inclined to take a high tone, but Dongan met arrogance with arrogance and sometimes assumed an ironical tone which his correspondent did not fully understand.   On one occasion he lamented " that Monsr de Nonville has so soon forgot the orders he had from his Master to live well with the King of England's subjects, but I find the air of Canada has strange effects on all the Governors boddys."[2]   The Frenchmen sought to appeal to the Irishman's religious sense as a fellow Roman Catholic and implored him to check the insolence of " the enemies of the Faith, who by their wars and customary cruelties blast the fruit of our Missionaries among the most distant tribes," and the Jesuit priest Lamberville, who had lived among the Iroquois, added his efforts to those of Denonville. Dongan, however, felt that he was as good a Catholic as any Frenchman ; he replied that he would import English or Irish Roman Catholic priests to convert the savages to the true religion.   He did import a few, but they did not take kindly to life in the wilderness and refused to play the part which had been assigned to them.   Again Denonville wrote : " Think you, Sir, that Religion will make

---

[1] *New York Colonial Documents*, iii, 455.   [2] *Ibid.*, iii, 472.

any progress whilst your Merchants will supply, as they do, *Eau de Vie* in abundance which, as you ought to know, converts the Savages into Demons and their Cabins into counterparts and theatres of Hell."[1] To this Dongan answered that when the English missionaries arrived " care would then be taken to dissuade them [the Iroquois] from their drunken debouches though certainly our Rum doth as little hurt as your Brandy and in the opinion of Christians is much more wholesome."[2] At times Dongan tried to cajole his opponent, as when he sent him "some Oranges hearing they are a rarity in your partes." Denonville, however, declared that the New Yorker's intentions did not at all correspond with his fine words, and as for his oranges, " it was a great pity that they should have been all rotten."[3] Such were some of the amenities of international colonial politics in the seventeenth century.

November 16, 1686, representatives of France and England assembled at Whitehall, London, and put their names to an instrument which is generally known as the Treaty of Neutrality.[4] In this it was provided that there should be peace and good correspondence upon the lands and seas of America, and that neither of the parties to the compact should violate the territories of the other on the western side of the Atlantic, no matter whether there was war or peace in Europe. The expectation of the French king doubtless was that this would deliver the Iroquois into the hands of his representative in New France. Copies of the treaty were sent to Dongan and to Denonville with orders from their respective masters that it

---

[1] *New York Colonial Documents*, iii, 462.

[2] *Ibid.*, iii, 463.

[3] *Ibid.*, iii, 472.

[4] Du Mont's *Corps Universel Diplomatique*, vii, Part ii, p. 141, see Note at end of the present chapter.

should be duly observed and executed. The reading of this document must have been disheartening to Dongan, but the Irish governor at once put on a bold front. He sent a copy to Denonville with a request that he would "not seek any correspondence with our Indians on this side of the Great Lake."[1] On his part, with Louis's approval, the governor of New France prepared a great expedition to conquer the Iroquois, but not to attack the English.[2] With nearly a thousand regulars, he set out for the country of the Senecas. He captured a party of English traders, had an indecisive conflict with the Indians, destroyed their corn and some of their villages, and returned to the St. Lawrence. Dongan met this attack as if the Treaty of Neutrality had no application to the Iroquois. He supplied them with arms and ammunition to defend themselves against French aggression and wrote vigorous letters to the French governor, demanding the return of the captives. In the following winter the Iroquois took matters into their own hands, marched to the banks of the St. Lawrence, and destroyed French settlements within sight of Montreal. Dongan informed his master of the doings of the Frenchmen and pointed out the financial value of the beaver trade. Louis complained to the English king and asked him to order Dongan to desist from his opposition. James, who had now succeeded his brother, declared in reply that the Iroquois were English subjects and had acknowledged themselves to be such before the governors of Virginia and New York in July, 1684.[3] He informed Louis that he was very much

---

[1] *New York Colonial Documents*, iii, 469.

[2] See Désiré Girouard's "L'expedition du Marquis de Denonville" in Royal Society of Canada's *Proceedings and Transactions*, Second Series, v, 5 (" Memoirs," section i, pp. 87–101); *Documentary History of New York*, i, 191–278.

[3] *New York Colonial Documents*, iii, 509.

surprised at the French complaints as he was obliged to protect his subjects; he directed Dongan to inform Denonville that the Iroquois were English subjects and to take the necessary measures for protecting them against French attack and to call upon the neighboring English colonies for assistance.[1] Orders were also sent to Andros, who was now governor of New England, and to the other English colonial governors to give Dongan such help as he might require.

The danger to English interests in America was very real. As long as the colonies were under separate governments, it was difficult to bring about concerted action even when the governors of New York and New England were both appointed by James and governed without the necessity of consulting elected representative bodies. The imminence of danger from the side of New France was the one thing needed to induce James to take the final step of consolidating all the colonies north of Pennsylvania into one government with Andros as governor general and Francis Nicholson as lieutenant governor, April 7, 1688. In recalling Dongan, he was informed that the king was entirely satisfied with his actions as governor of New York and that he might expect marks of royal favor.[2] While removing Dongan from his position, James ordered his successor to protect the Iroquois as subjects of England and defined the eastern limit of

[1] *New York Colonial Documents*, iii, 503.

[2] *Ibid.*, iii, 550; *Calendars of State Papers, America and West Indies, 1685–1688*, p. 533. Precisely why Andros was preferred to Dongan as governor of the consolidated dominion is not at all clear. While Andros was a knight, Dongan came of a noble Irish family. They were both good administrators and intensely loyal to James. As a Roman Catholic, it would seem that Dongan would have appealed to his royal master's religious zeal. It is not unlikely that the opposition of Penn, whose schemes had been interfered with by the New York governor, may have been the determining cause which led to the preference of Andros. Besides it was natural that he should continue to be governor of New England, and the removal of Dongan was pleasing to the French king.

the Dominion of New England as the St. Croix River and also declared that that dominion extended northward to the River of Canada,[1] as the St. Lawrence was then known to Englishmen.

In upholding the rights of England on the continent of North America, James Stuart, his Roman Catholic governor of New York, and his arbitrary ruler of New England acted as high-minded, patriotic Englishmen. In constitutional and political affairs, the actions of James and Andros stirred against them the wrath of the English colonists. These suspected the good faith of both of them: Dongan's good work in New York was not sufficient to balance Andros's misrule in New England. In the long series of wars which followed on the Glorious Revolution, the English colonists suffered severely; but in the end, by the Treaty of Utrecht, the Iroquois were acknowledged to be English subjects. This meant that English territory extended as far north as Lake Ontario. Such an outcome was the direct result of the firm stand that Dongan had taken. To him must be given the credit for first seeing the importance of the position of New York and the Iroquois in the international politics of North America.

[1] This phrase occurs in Andros's commission and also in his instructions. *New York Colonial Documents*, iii, 537, 543. The order to protect the Iroquois is on p. 548 of the same volume.

NOTES

I. Bibliography. — The foregoing account of Dongan's administration is based on the papers printed in the third volume of the *Documents Relative to the Colonial History of the State of New York.* Most of these papers are noted in the *Calendars of State Papers, America and West Indies, 1685–1688,* and there are many additional letters noticed in that volume. Brodhead's *New York* contains a good account of this part of Dongan's administration, but the importance of his policy from the international standpoint is not clearly brought out.

The subject-matter of the preceding chapter is treated by Francis Parkman at great length in three volumes of his *France and England in North America,* as follows: *La Salle and the Discovery of the Great West,* 1–321; *The Old Régime in Canada,* chs. x–xii, xv, xviii; *Count Frontenac and New France under Louis XIV,* chs. vi ("La Barre and the Iroquois"), vii ("Denonville and Dongan"), viii–x (the Iroquois attack on Canada). The courage of priest, soldier, and savage appealed powerfully to Parkman, whose own life was an exemplar of heroism rarely seen in this world. He described his sufferings and the ill conditions under which he labored in a paper that was read after his death and was printed in the Massachusetts Historical Society's *Proceedings* for 1893 and reprinted in the appendix of Sedgwick's *Francis Parkman.*

II. Treaty of Neutrality. — Following are the paragraphs from the treaty of November 16, 1686, relating to North America: —

I. Il a esté conclu & accordé, que du jour du present Traité il y aura entre la Nation Françoise & la Nation Angloise, une ferme Paix, Union, Concorde, & bonne Correspondance, tant sur Mer, que sur Terre, dans l'Amerique Septentrionale & Meridionale, & dans les Isles, Colonies, Forts & Villes, sans aucune distinction de lieux, scises dans les Etats de Sa Majesté Tres-Chrêtienne, & de Sa Majesté Britannique, & gouvernées par les Commandans de leursdites Majestez respectivement.

II. Qu' aucuns Vaisseaux, ou Bastimens, grands ou petits, appartenans aux Sujets de Sa Majesté Tres-Chrêtienne, ne seront équipez, ni employez dans lesdites Isles, Colonies, Forteresses, Villes & Gouvernemens des Etats de Sadite Majesté, pour attaquer les Sujets de Sa Majesté Britannique, dans les Isles, Colonies, Forteresses,

Villes, & Gouvernemens de Sadite Majesté, ou pour leur faire aucun tort ni dommage. Et pareillement qu'aucuns Vaisseaux ou Bastimens, grands ou petits, appartenans aux Sujets de Sa Majesté Britannique, ne seront équipez ou employez dans les Isles, Colonies, Forteresses, Villes, & Gouvernemens de Sadite Majesté, pour attaquer les Sujers de Sa Majesté Tres-Chrêtienne dans les Isles, Colonies, Forteresses, Villes, & Gouvernemens de Sadite Majesté, ou pour leur faire aucun tort ni dommage.

IV. Il a esté convenu que chacun desdits Rois aura & tiendra les Domaines, Droits & Prééminences dans les Mers, Détroits, & autres Eaux de l'Amerique, & avec la même étendué qui leur appartient de Droit, & en la même maniere qu'ils en jouïssent à present. Du Mont's *Corps Universel Diplomatique*, vii, Part ii, pp. 141, 142.

CHAPTER VI

THE STUART DOMINATION IN NEW ENGLAND, 1680–1689

THE last fourteen years (1670–85) of the reign of the second Charles were very different in character and purpose from the ten years which preceded them. The king continued to lead a dissolute life, but his merriment was more tempered by business than it had been in the earlier part of his reign. At his death he was an absolute monarch. The leading character in this second period was Sir Thomas Osborne. He is better known by his later title of Earl of Danby, and occupied the office of lord treasurer during most of these years. He had a positive talent for financial affairs, possessed sound political judgment, and was absolutely unscrupulous as to the means by which he filled his pockets and those of his patrons and patronesses. In the first five years of this period, from 1670 to 1675, Charles was receiving money from the French king. Osborne's economies and the Catholic tendencies of the royal family were alike reprehended by a great majority of the members of the House of Commons. So fierce was their opposition that in 1673 the king not only withdrew a Declaration of Indulgence which he had promulgated, but even gave his consent to the Test Act that made it impossible for any Roman Catholic, even his own brother, to hold office. He continued, however, to accept money from Louis XIV as the price of putting off the meeting of Parliament, which was nearly certain to compel him to take the side of Holland in the great contest which was then going on in Europe. It was in the midst of this

155

religio-political warfare in England that Osborne, or Danby, as he now was, induced Charles to invite his kinsman, William, Prince of Orange, to England and marry him to Mary, daughter of James, Duke of York, almost without consulting her father and flatly against his known wishes (November 4, 1677).

Soon after the consummation of this marriage there came that most mysterious of all seventeenth century events, the Popish Plot (1678).[1] Who was behind it, whether it was the work of the Anglican hierarchy or of Danby himself, or of his chief political opponent, the Earl of Shaftesbury, are questions which can probably never be answered. It may be that it was nothing more than an attempt to extort money on the part of Titus Oates and those who lied with him. With a master stroke of genius, when everything seemed to be going to pieces and Danby had been put into the Tower, Charles confounded all his enemies. He assented to the Habeas Corpus Act (1679), which secured for Englishmen in England the right to a speedy trial before the court that properly had jurisdiction in each given case; but he refused to give his assent to the Exclusion Bill, which would have placed his brother James out of the line of succession to the throne. The royal brothers then undertook to remodel the constituencies, or electoral districts that returned members to the House of Commons, with a view to bringing it about that the members of that House should be persons in whom they could confide, or, at least, persons who might be less unfriendly to the Roman Catholic religion. When this work was only half done Charles suddenly died.[2]

---

[1] See J. Pollock's *The Popish Plot, a Study in the History of the Reign of Charles II* (London, 1903).

[2] Papers concerning the death of Charles and the accession of James are reprinted from the "London Gazette" in Massachusetts Historical Society's *Proceedings*, 1873–75, pp. 105–109.

The year 1679 was the turning point in this epoch. The reason why the English people did not rebel then instead of ten years later may be found partly in that sentimental attraction which has always bound the average Englishman to the reigning family with a tie which might almost be described as devotion. James I had done his work well and had made the dogma of the divine descent of the kingship almost an article of faith in the souls of a majority of the people of England. The experiences of the Civil Wars were still fresh in the memories of the older men and women; they dreaded a recurrence of intestine conflict and preferred the rule of a Roman Catholic king under Parliamentary guidance to the possibility of a military despotism like that which had followed the execution of the first Charles. Even more important than these reasons for accepting what was distasteful was the prosperity which had marked the last few years. The middle classes, upon whom the brunt of an armed conflict would fall, were making money; the new Stuart domination had not yet reached the point at which enthusiasm for religion and desire for political freedom triumphed over the greed for gain and the sentiment of allegiance to a personal king, although the unblushing shamelessness of court life had dealt such a blow to this sentimental attraction that four years of the second James were enough to overwhelm it.

The American colonists felt the increase of vigor which pervaded all branches of the administration after Osborne's accession to office. At this time the royal brothers regarded the colonies almost in the light of personal estates and wrote directly to the authorities in the plantations. In one instance, Charles commanded Sir William Berkeley to see that justice was speedily done in the case of a

friend.   In another, the Duke of York directed the Virginia governor to review a decision that had already been
made as to a planter who had influence at court.[1]   The
management of colonial business in 1675 was placed in
the hands of a committee of the Privy Council[2] that was
henceforth known as the Lords of Trade and Plantations
— an arrangement which continued until 1696.   The next
year, 1676, the government in England exhibited a renewed
interest in American affairs.   The needs of the royal exchequer prompted another attempt to enforce the navigation system, and London merchants trading to the colonies
were also insistent that their hoped-for profits should be
secured to them.   Moreover, the weakening of New England consequent upon King Philip's War made this a
favorable moment to coerce the recalcitrant colonists of
that section.   The Commissioners of the Customs and
William Blathwayt, secretary to the Lords of Trade, were
the moving spirits in this enterprise; but whether the
stimulus came from them or from those outside governmental circles, cannot be stated.   It was at about this
time that the captain of a royal warship reported that the
Massachusetts authorities had refused his offer of aid for
the seizure of an Ostend vessel lying at anchor in Boston
Harbor.   He also said that some of the people of that
colony stated that they preferred to have New Netherland
in the hands of the Dutch than in those of Colonel Lovelace and had refused the aid of his ship for the reduction
of Manhattan Island.   The royal authorities determined
to send an emissary to Boston to spy out the weak places
in the colonial armor and to advise them as to the best

---

[1] *Calendars of State Papers, America and West Indies, 1669-1674*, p. 187; *ibid., 1675-1676*, p. 148.

[2] *Ibid., 1675-1676*, pp. 183, 269, 355, 461, 603; *New York Colonial Documents*, iii, 228, 229; *Colonial Records of North Carolina*, i, 223.

way to proceed. The man selected for this difficult mission was Edward Randolph.

Of all the royal officials who represented English interests in America, not one more thoroughly won the hatred of the colonists than Edward Randolph. He was an honest, upright man, according to the standards of his day, but was possessed of a mania for compelling colonists to conform to English laws and regulations, utterly oblivious as to whether these rules were suited to their condition or no. He looked upon New Englanders as a grown man regards a set of naughty children and was fond of them, while he felt it his duty to chastise them. As he advanced in years the desire for the enforcement of English laws increased upon him, until at length he took an almost insane pleasure in seizing vessels. Little is known of Randolph's early life. He was connected with the family of John Mason, grantee of New Hampshire, and was a personal correspondent of several high-placed men, among them William Blathwayt. He may be described, indeed, as being hand in glove with the latter gentleman from 1676 until his death in 1703. Randolph had already been employed in Scotland to look after the estates which had come into the hands of the king in 1672 upon the death of Charles Stuart, Duke of Richmond and Lennox. It is possible that his success in this agency pointed him out as a fit person to represent the king's interests in New England, or it may be that Charles wished to have so faithful a servant out of the way that he might the more easily squander this inheritance. At all events, in 1676 Randolph appeared in Massachusetts with a letter from the king to the colonial authorities. He was also instructed to inform himself as to what laws of the colony were derogatory to those of England, as to the number and strength of the colonists, as to the observation of the trade and navigation acts, and as to the condition of religion. His mission, therefore, was of a twofold nature : ostensibly he was a messenger, in reality he was a spy.

John Leverett was then governor of Massachusetts. He simply told Randolph that he would send a reply to the royal missive by the captain of the ship that brought the messenger over and suggested that the latter might return at the same time. Randolph remained in New England for a month and gained much information from those who were disaffected to the government. Returning to London, he presented a " Narrative " of his doings to the Privy Council and, later, drew up a " Report." Many of the statements in these documents are interesting, rather as showing Randolph's prejudices than as giving a true picture of affairs in the colony. Among other things, he stated that there were then one hundred and twenty thousand inhabitants under the government of Massachusetts, of whom sixteen thousand were of military age and sex, which were gross exaggerations, and that there was not one beggar in the colony.[1] He was skillful in using phrases to arouse the prejudices of those to whom he addressed his reports and letters. In writing to the ministers, he constantly called attention to the use of the word " commonwealth," [2] by the men of Massachusetts — a word of evil omen to Charles, although not necessarily implying a republic or independence. To the ecclesiastical dignitaries

[1] *Calendars of State Papers, America and West Indies, 1675-1676*, p. 362; Royal Historical Manuscripts Commission's *Reports*, iv, 237. Bradstreet's " Answers to the Lords of Trade " (1680) may well be read in connection with Randolph's papers, *Calendars, 1677-1680*, p. 528.

[2] This word was then used almost synonymously with government, as in the title of Sir Thomas Smith's work, *The Commonwealth of England*, which is merely descriptive of the government of England in the time of Elizabeth.

he wrote of the Congregational system in New England and thereby aroused the ire of the bishops.

The heirs of Captain John Mason and Sir Ferdinando Gorges had, before this, complained of the encroachments of Massachusetts on their ancestral domains. As far back as 1671 Robert Mason had offered the province of New Hampshire to the king on consideration of being permitted to import three hundred tons of French wine free of duty.[1] That was the moment for Massachusetts to have silenced forever the Mason family, but probably the rulers of the Bay colony had no inkling of the low price at which the Masonian claims could be secured and also regarded their own title to the greater part of New Hampshire as indisputable. English judges thought differently and decided that the title to the soil was in the Mason family, while the jurisdiction belonged to the crown. The claims of Massachusetts to the province of Maine rested on less secure ground; Massachusetts, therefore, had an inquiry made as to whether the Gorges heirs would accept five hundred pounds sterling for their rights. The king, at this time, had an idea of buying both New Hampshire and Maine as an estate for his son, the Duke of Monmouth, and the colony thus came into direct competition with the crown. Other enemies of Massachusetts also appeared upon the scene : Captain Breedon restated his old assertions, and Randall Holden revamped the grievances of the Gortonists of forty years earlier. In 1679 Massachusetts sent over two agents to state the side of that colony.[2] They declared that they themselves were not old enough to remember the facts of which Holden made mention and that the question

[1] *Calendars of State Papers, America and West Indies, 1669–1674*, p. 272.

[2] The petition of Holden and Greene of 1679 is in Massachusetts Historical Society's *Proceedings*, ii, 339. The instructions to the agents are in *ibid.*, 1869, p. 92.

of the limits of Massachusetts was a matter of opinion. It seems, indeed, that the conditions of the early land grants were unknown to the Massachusetts authorities ;[1] or they may have thought that the royal letters patent superseded all earlier patents from the Council for New England. The agents furthermore suggested that in case Massachusetts retired from Maine, the Gorges heirs should repay that colony for the expenses which had been incurred in defending their province against the French — a matter of some seven thousand pounds sterling. This suggestion so frightened them that they consented to sell the province for twelve hundred and fifty pounds.[2] The sale was consummated and the Governor and Company of Massachusetts Bay became lord proprietor of the province of Maine, greatly to the chagrin of the king. Mason seized this opportunity of royal ill humor to press his claim to all of Massachusetts as far south as Salem. In 1682 he procured an order from the king,[3] directing the Massachusetts authorities to place him in possession of the unimproved lands in this part of the colony and to give him every facility for suing for the possession of the improved lands in the local courts with appeal to England. To this order, however, the Massachusetts rulers paid no obedience.

Edward Randolph was recompensed for his exertions by being appointed collector of customs in New England. He arrived at Boston in December, 1681, and at once found himself involved in controversies. The rulers declared his commission to be inoperative without their sanction, and stated that it was a capital offense to act under it without their permission.[4] Nevertheless he tried to perform his

[1] Letter of Peter Bulkly or Bulkley, one of the agents, dated London, 17th 11ᵐ, 1676-7, in Massachusetts Historical Society's *Proceedings*, 2nd Ser., xiv, 213.

[2] *Ibid.*, 1869-70, p. 201.
[3] *Calendars of State Papers, America and West Indies, 1681-1685*, p. 236.
[4] Massachusetts Historical Society's

duties and was compelled to give bonds to make good all damages in case his action should be held to be illegal, and his deputies were fined and imprisoned. When matters became too unpleasant in New England to be longer borne with, he sailed across the Atlantic to lay before the royal government a fresh series of complaints against the Massachusetts Bay Company. This brings us to the closing years of Charles's reign, when he was in effect an absolute king.

When Shaftesbury was forced to flee for safety to the Netherlands, when the house of Bedford could not save Lord Russell from the executioner, when the city of London could not maintain its privileges, when Virginia felt the weight of royal displeasure and royal favorites, there was little hope for the Governor and Company of the Massachusetts Bay in New England. Soon Randolph reappeared at Boston. This time he was armed with a writ of *quo warranto*, directing the Massachusetts corporation to come before the court of King's Bench in London and show why its charter should not be annulled. The magistrates and the deputies found it difficult to agree upon the action to be taken. Should the "Company" submit or should the king be defied to the uttermost? As was customary on such occasions, they "sought the face of the Lord." The ministers were called in and declared [1] it to be the duty of Massachusetts "to abide by what rights and privileges the Lord our God in his merciful providence hath bestowed on us"; if the king should take the charter, well and good, but every advantage should be taken of delay. The times were stormy in Eng-

Proceedings for 1899, p. 291; *Massachusetts Colony Records,* v, 338, 339; Toppan's *Edward Randolph,* i, 152. The Lords of Trade suggested that his salary should be doubled — so well were they satisfied with his exertions. "Journal of the Lords of Trade" Ms., iii, 260.

[1] Massachusetts Historical Society's *Collections,* Third Series, i, 78, 81.

land; no one could tell what a year or a month might bring forth. They must put their "trust in the God of their fathers, which is better than to put confidence in princes. And if they suffer because they dare not comply with the wills of men against the will of God, they suffer in a good cause." The Company, therefore, retained counsel to represent it before the court of King's Bench. The storms of the Atlantic fought for the colony and with other things delayed Randolph so that he could not make return of the writ within the specified time. Suit was then entered in the King's Bench against the officers of the Company by name and was dismissed on the ground that it should have been made against the Governor and Company, and not against individuals. Thereupon a writ of *scire facias* was moved for in Chancery for the avoiding of the charter, and the time for making return of the writ and for entering the decree was made so short that the colony could not make a proper defense. In this manner the king took to himself the government of Massachusetts Bay (1684).[1]

Randolph next secured writs of *quo warranto* against the other chartered colonies.[2] Pennsylvania alone was exempt, but even in the case of Penn, Randolph proceeded against Delaware, as he termed the Territories which the Quaker promoter held from the Duke of York. It is said that at one time Randolph had as many as five

---

[1] The best account of these proceedings is that by Charles Deane in the *Memorial History of Boston* (i, 369–380). Especially valuable is a long note on pp. 378, 379. The easiest way to gain an understanding of the matter is to read the "Exemplification of the Judgment vacating the Charter" in Massachusetts Historical Society's *Collections*, Fourth Series, ii, 246, especially pp. 262, 278.

[2] The *Colonial Records of North Carolina* (i, 353) contain an Order in Council directing the Attorney General to move for these writs; but this does not necessarily imply that the royal brothers were specially interested in the matter. The impulse seems to have come from the Lords of Trade, *Calendars of State Papers, America and West Indies, 1685–1688*, p. 173.

writs in his pocket. For one reason or another, it proved
to be impossible to bring any of these suits to a conclusion, and judgment was not entered against any colony
except Massachusetts. It is an interesting question as
to whether Randolph acted for himself and a few leading
men, or was carrying out the directions of the king.
There can be no doubt that the commissioners of the customs were greatly annoyed at the non-observance of the
commercial laws in New England. In 1675 they had
reported to the Lords of Trade that goods were being
brought into New England contrary to law and had
suggested that colonial governors should take an oath to
seize all vessels trading contrary to law, and to take bonds
of all ship masters loading enumerated goods requiring
them to unlade their goods in England or else pay duties.[1]
In 1676 English merchants engaged in European trade
had called attention[2] to the commerce which was carried
on by New Englanders directly with Europe. They declared that this was contrary to the navigation acts,
prejudicial to the royal revenue, lessened the prices of
domestic and foreign goods, decreased trade, and impoverished the king's subjects. Thus prompted, the Lords of
Trade had written letters[3] which were almost threatening
in tone to the colonial governors, but without producing
any tangible results. It seems evident from these scattered
facts that English mercantile interests were constantly
putting pressure upon the English government to enforce
the commercial laws, and it was impossible to do this
so long as the plantations were not directly under the
control of the crown.[4]

---

[1] *Calendars of State Papers, America and West Indies, 1675–1676*, p. 231.
[2] *Ibid., 1675–1676*, p. 337.
[3] *Ibid., 1675–1676*, pp. 369, 371.

[4] Professor Andrews in his *Colonial Self-Government* has called attention especially to this phase of the subject.

Other reasons were urging on the royal brothers to the same conclusion. Until the navigation system was enforced as to the enumerated commodities, the royal exchequer and with it the king's privy purse necessarily suffered. Moreover, the cutting up of the plantations into so many governments was in itself disadvantageous from an administrative point of view, and the size and distribution of these governments made the carrying out of any particular line of policy very difficult. These considerations were perfectly legitimate and might well have affected the action of the most liberal of governments and of kings. Charles and James, however, were far from realizing any such criterion. They believed in personal rule and did not regard themselves as despots. They were sorely tried by the contumacy of Massachusetts and Connecticut. James, also, had a personal interest in the destruction of these governments, because his grant from the king gave him land as far east as the Connecticut River. There is a hint in a letter from James to Andros, written as early as 1676,[1] that the dissolution of the New England governments had even then been determined on, for he tells Andros that he need not push his designs on western Connecticut, because other means would be found to attain the same purpose. Two years later Andros himself appeared before the Privy Council and advocated a general consolidation of colonial governments. It is impossible to say how far the royal brothers were actuated by fear of French aggression in America; but it is well to recall the fact that the Duke of York's territories included the region between the Kennebec and the St. Croix as well as New York, and that French expeditions and missionaries were constantly threatening these two districts which were separated from

1 *Calendars of State Papers, America and West Indies, 1675-1676*, p. 339.

each other by the New England colonies. It was entirely natural, therefore, that Charles and James should wish to get this whole region into their hands, not only for ease of administration, but as a means of protecting and defending the Duke's property in America. In saying all this it is not at all necessary to regard Charles and James as unscrupulous tyrants or as intending to advance the Roman Catholic religion, or to stamp out Puritanism. Similar considerations might well have actuated the most liberally minded Protestant monarchs.

After the judgment had been entered against the Massachusetts corporation, but before arrangements had been completed to take over the new royal province, Charles died and James became king.[1] The second Charles was not an admirable historic figure, but he shines in comparison with his younger brother. The two had in common their attachment to the Roman Catholic religion, their sensuality, and their belief in the divine right of kings to do as they pleased with their subjects and their subjects' property; in other respects they were quite different. Charles was a happy-go-lucky man of ability, who was willing to sacrifice his convictions to his love of ease and pleasure. "They will not kill me to make you king," he said to James, and he was quite right. The second James was a serious-minded man, who thought it his duty to save the souls of his subjects by reuniting England to Holy Mother Church, whether Englishmen disliked the reunion or not. He was entirely lacking in that good nature which redeemed so many faults in his brother's character. Torture[2] seemed to him a natural and proper

---

[1] Wednesday, February, 4/14, 1684/5.
[2] If any one doubts this, let him read of James's doings in Scotland in the histories of the time and see also Royal Historical Manuscripts Commission's *Reports*, xv, Part viii, p. 105 (Drumlanrig Mss.).

means of coercion, and constitutional scruples never entered his head. The crown lawyers informed him that the New England planters continued to enjoy the rights of Englishmen after the downfall of the Massachusetts Bay corporation,[1] but he made arrangements for their government as though the New England settlements were provinces conquered from the enemy.

Charles's demise, Argyll's expedition to Scotland, and Monmouth's Rebellion in England combined to defer the execution of the royal will for some months; the last also contributed to relieve New England from the imposition of Colonel Percy Kirke as the first royal governor. Edward Randolph, curiously enough, fought manfully against this appointment. He had a strange affection for the New England people, although his way of showing it was somewhat out of the ordinary run. In 1689, from his cell in Boston, he declared that things had been pushed too far by "ill men from New York [Palmer and West] who have too much studied the disease of this people."[2] He likewise thought that Kirke was an unfit man for the delicate task of imposing the new régime on Massachusetts.[3] The decision to make Kirke governor was taken while Charles was still living. His commission as originally drafted had provided for a representative assembly, but the clause embodying this provision had been omitted by the express order of the king. Kirke would probably have come over as the first royal governor of Massachusetts had not the serving up the adherents of James's unfortunate nephew for royal vengeance, as dealt out by Judge Jeffries, occurred in the nick of time

[1] Chalmers's *Introduction to the Revolt*, i, 178 ; Macaulay's *History of England*, i, 212.

[2] Toppan's *Edward Randolph*, ii, 98.
[3] Massachusetts Historical Society's *Proceedings*, xiii, 224.

to act as a powerful reënforcement to Randolph's argument.[1]

The first representative of royal authority in Massachusetts under the new dispensation was Joseph Dudley, a
time-serving son of New England. The suggestion of his
appointment as provisional governor, until permanent arrangements could be made, came from himself. He had
been serviceable to Randolph in his machinations against
the Massachusetts Bay Company and now pointed out
that he and others who had abetted that emissary were
sadly in need of some mark of royal favor, which would
not only set them right in the eyes of their fellow-
countrymen, but might cause others to be friendly to the
new order of things. For his part, Randolph thought that
the time had come for conciliation. He dared not press
for Dudley's appointment openly lest it should be thought
that there was some private design in contemplation
between them, but he recited Dudley's merits upon all
fitting occasions and with his accustomed facility.[2] Ultimately Dudley was appointed President of New England,[3]
which included not only Massachusetts, but New Hampshire, Maine, and the mainland of Rhode Island west of
Narragansett Bay. With this commission, Randolph sailed
into Boston Harbor in the *Rose* frigate, Captain George, on
May 14, 1686. The English government made it known
that the new arrangement was only temporary and gave
Dudley limited power. With the assistance of seven councilors, he was to exercise executive and other powers, but
was to make no change in the laws; he also had a com-

[1] Kirke's commission had been ordered
by Charles, but either that king's death
had terminated it or it had not actually
been delivered.

[2] Toppan's *Edward Randolph*, iii, 317.

[3] Dudley's commission is printed in
full in Massachusetts Colonial Society's
Publications, ii; his speech on taking
office is in Massachusetts Historical
Society's *Proceedings* for 1863, p. 487.

mission as vice admiral. Randolph, besides being collector of the customs, was appointed secretary and register and also was armed with writs of *quo warranto* against the neighboring colonies.[1]

Among the members of Dudley's council were William Stoughton, Peter Bulkly, Wait Winthrop, and Edward Randolph. Dudley and his advisers endeavored to centralize the government of the province, but otherwise pursued a conservative course. The old government did not go out of existence without a final effort. Toward the end of May " Edward Rawson, Secretary " presented to Dudley and his council a paper protesting against their exercise of jurisdiction. This document asserted that by the new arrangements " the subjects are abridged of their liberties as Englishmen," both in the matter of legislation and taxes, " there being not the least mention of an assembly in the commission." Dudley and his associates were advised to consider whether such a commission "be either safe for you or us." Beyond terming this a libellous document and threatening to examine Mr. Rawson, the President and Council paid no attention to it. They acted more harshly to Lieutenant John Gould of Topsfield who had denied their authority. He was imprisoned until he apologized, paid sixty pounds, and gave bonds for one hundred pounds more.[2]

The supplying the treasury with funds proved to be difficult, since the old law which provided for a general assessment had been repealed and the exchequer was empty. Almost the only sources of supply were an excise

[1] Randolph was a persistent office seeker — possibly on account of his poverty. In 1687 he petitioned to be appointed secretary of all New England, having previously leased the office (excluding Connecticut and Rhode Island) to John West for one hundred and fifty pounds per annum for four years. *Calendars of State Papers, America and West Indies, 1685-1688*, pp. 364, 413.

[2] Massachusetts Historical Society's *Collections*, Third Series, vii, 150.

on wines and rum and receipts from fees. The total revenue amounted to only a few hundred pounds, which were doled out to the leading officials. Dudley does not seem to have received any salary himself; but if Randolph can be believed, he gained something from the enforcement of the trade laws — he, as judge of the vice admiralty court, and Captain George of the *Rose* seizing and condemning vessels and dividing the profits without giving any to the collector and secretary.

There was no more disappointed man in New England than Edward Randolph. For years he had been fighting the king's battles with slight pecuniary gain to himself, and now when a reformation had been made, he reported that the new government was as bad as the old, if not worse. He writes that he would not object to Captain George's receiving prize money for the capture of vessels carrying on illegal trade, provided the seizures were made outside the harbor and not while the frigate was lying quietly at anchor within the port. Another cause of grievance was Dudley's lukewarmness as to religion. Randolph had brought with him a minister of the Established Church, a certain Mr. Ratcliffe. There was no public money which Randolph could divert to Ratcliffe's support, and he was obliged to maintain him out of his own pocket, at the moment that President Dudley and Captain George were absorbing the fines and forfeitures which he regarded as a just reward for his own efforts. Randolph and Ratcliffe demanded the use of one of the three meetinghouses in the town for their services, but were informed that these edifices were private and not public property, which could not have been said in any other town of Massachusetts. The best that they could do was to use a room in the townhouse. At first this was crowded to suffocation by those who came out of curiosity to see a surpliced minister. In a short time, however, only Randolph and a few other communicants attended. He suggested to the Lords of Trade (July 28, 1686) that the new governor, when he should be appointed, should be authorized to regulate preaching at his discretion.[1] This letter was written only five weeks after he had reproved the Plymouth government for levying taxes for the support of religion in that colony.[2] In the dearth of good Episcopalians, Dudley found it necessary to employ Congregationalists in civil and military offices. This was the final straw; Randolph now called Dudley a " false president " and declared that he was worse than Mr. Danforth, the former deputy governor, which from Randolph was the height of disparagement.

New England Puritanism, as exemplified in Massachusetts, was at its very narrowest. The hard contest to keep body and soul together had destroyed that quality of cheerfulness which was the saving grace of the earlier day, and the spirit of subconscious humor, which is indigenous to the soil, had not yet taken its place. Even so worldly minded a man as Samuel Sewall could find nothing except condemnation for the scene which he describes under the date of Saturday, September 25, 1686.[3] It was on that day that the officers of the English frigate then lying in Boston Harbor and other royal officials celebrated the birthday of Mary of Modena, James's Roman Catholic queen. They landed on Noddle's Island, now East Boston, fired guns, pitched a tent, and hoisted a flag. After sundown, they had a great fire and made much noise.

---

[1] *Rhode Island Colony Records*, iii, 204.

[2] *Ibid.*, iii, 199.

[3] Massachusetts Historical Society's *Collections*, Fifth Series, v, 152.

Never since Thomas Morton and his Merry Mount Maypole parted company had the good people of Boston and its neighborhood seen such a sight, for the New England Sabbath began at sundown of the preceding Saturday evening. The townspeople were scandalized; in his prayer on the morning of the next day, Mr. Willard of the South Church expressed great grief for this profanation of the Lord's Day. In truth, the rejoicing marked a change in the affairs of New England which Parson Willard and Judge Sewall could do little to stop, however indignant they might be. The attempt of the chosen people to establish a new Canaan in the Western wilderness had been too successful. It had attracted the notice of the money gatherers of London and had been subverted to the uses of the men of Belial. On December 20, 1686,[1] the guns of the *Kingfisher* roared forth the fact of the arrival of Sir Edmund Andros, governor of New England.

Since leaving New York, in 1681, Andros had been a gentleman of the bedchamber of the Duke of York and had commanded a troop of horse in the suppression of Monmouth's Rebellion. He was a steadfast son of the Established Church and may have been sent across the Atlantic that he might be out of the way while English institutions from the Church to the boroughs were being remodeled or twisted for the benefit of Roman Catholics. He brought with him a small body of "redcoats," who, according to a New England writer of the time, began to teach the people to "drink, blaspheme, curse, and damn."[2] For their entertainment on landing, Dudley had provided

[1] Massachusetts Historical Society's *Collections*, Fifth Series, v, 161; Toppan's *Edward Randolph*, ii, 7; iv, 133. Andros was deposed on April 18, 1689, so that his tenure of office was less than two years and four months.

[2] *Andros Tracts*, ii, 50.

a pipe of wine [1] in a convenient place near the townhouse, which would seem to argue that drinking was not unknown before their advent.   With the redcoats appeared also the hated red cross, which had not been seen on shore, except on the fort in the harbor, since the time when John Endicott banished it from the Salem banner.   The strength of the feeling on this matter can be seen from the fact that so vainglorious a man as Samuel Sewall resigned his commission as captain of one of the Boston militia companies, rather than march under the detested emblem.

Andros's Episcopalian zeal brought him into conflict with the Bostonians before he had been on dry land three full hours.   Meeting the ministers at a luncheon given in his honor, he demanded the use of one of their meetinghouses for Mr. Ratcliffe's services, suggesting that if this were out of the question, two congregations might use one meetinghouse successively on Sunday mornings.   The ministers and four members of each church met soon after and agreed that they could not with a good conscience yield to this request.   For the time being, Mr. Ratcliffe continued to use the townhouse.   A few days later, Andros again offended the religious sense of the people.   To the Puritans the observance of Christmas savored of popery,[2] but Andros attended service on that day, morning and afternoon, "a redcoat going on his right hand and Captain George on his left," with sixty red-coated soldiers following on.   Sewall relates with some satisfaction that the shops, nevertheless, were generally open and the people about their occasions.   Again in the following spring, on the anniversary of the king's coronation day, albeit it was "Sabbath night,"

---

[1] "Dudley Records" in Massachusetts Historical Society's *Proceedings*, Second Series, xiii, 278.

[2] The laws of 1670 provided a penalty of five shillings for observing Christmas, either by forbearing labor, feasting, or in any other way.

there were bonfires and fireworks.   Four days later there
was public fencing on the stage, " and that immediately
after the lecture," or midweek service.   Four days after
that a Maypole was set up in Charlestown — " the Devil "
had begun his march of triumph, so records Increase
Mather.[1]

With two such earnest churchmen as Andros and Randolph in the saddle, it was not likely that the Boston
meetinghouses would long enjoy immunity from a surpliced clergyman.   In March, 1687, Andros sent Randolph
to demand the keys of the South Meetinghouse.   That failing, they frightened the sexton into giving up the keys.   A
compromise was made that the Episcopalians and Congregationalists should hold services in succession on Sundays,
but this arrangement soon led to friction.   Andros and
Randolph promised fair enough, but the Episcopalian minister did not always stop at the appointed moment, neither
did Parson Willard, for that matter.   When complaints
were made, Andros lost his temper, talked about defending
his doings with his soldiers, and complained that the Dissenters would not give money toward the building of a
church for the use of the Episcopalians.   Finally, with the
consent of the Council, he seized a bit of town land upon
which was erected the first of three King's Chapels; but
Andros and Randolph were deposed before the building
was completed.[2]

Besides taking their meetinghouse and celebrating Christmas, Andros did many other things to wound the religious
susceptibilities of the Puritans.   He compelled them to

---

[1] Massachusetts Historical Society's
Proceedings, Second Series, xiii, 410, 411.

[2] See Henry W. Foote's very interesting *Annals of King's Chapel* for the history of the building and the successive
congregations which worshipped therein.
The history of the South Church and
Meetinghouse has been written by
Hamilton A. Hill.

kiss the Book when taking an oath in court or accepting office, instead of holding up the hand. He provided that no one should be married except with the Episcopalian services unless bonds were given, which should be forfeited in case any lawful impediment should thereafter appear.[1] He directed that no one should teach school without his permission.[2] He ordered that shops should be closed on the anniversary of what he called the "martyrdom of Charles I,"[3] and, finally, he proclaimed a day of thanksgiving for the birth of the Pretender.[4]

Sir Edmund Andros's authority extended over Massachusetts, New Plymouth, New Hampshire, Maine, and the King's Province.[5] Before long other territory was placed under his jurisdiction. Randolph had come over armed with writs of *quo warranto*, summoning the corporations of Connecticut and Rhode Island into the courts of King's Bench. The time for the returns of these writs had long since lapsed and they were worthless. In writing to the governors of those two colonies, Randolph made no mention of this fact. On the contrary, he declared that their only hope lay in submission to his Majesty; "tho' the weather be warme," he wrote, "the writs will keep sound and as good as when first landed."[6] The Rhode Islanders did not give up their charter, but otherwise they yielded to the royal wish.[7] The Connecticut rulers

---

[1] Hutchinson's *Massachusetts*, i, 318.

[2] "Andros Records," American Antiquarian Society's *Proceedings*, New Series, xiii, 467; see also petition of Joshua Ratstock to teach (Massachusetts Historical Society's *Collections*, Third Series, vii, 186).

[3] "Diary of Samuel Sewall" (Massachusetts Historical Society's *Collections*, Fifth Series, v, 201).

[4] Massachusetts Historical Society's *Proceedings*, 1871–73, p. 110.

[5] His commission bears date of June

3, 1686, and is printed in Massachusetts Historical Society's *Collections*, Third Series, vii, 139; Massachusetts Colonial Society's *Publications*, ii; *Rhode Island Colony Records*, iii, 212.

[6] *New York Colonial Documents*, iii, 368.

[7] Foster says (*Rhode Island Towns*, 23) that when Andros seized the government, the colonial Assembly voted that the freemen of each town might meet together and make all needful provision for the management of the affairs of

were not so compliant; they desired to see the writ and ascertain its validity before they surrendered; they coquetted with Governor Dongan of New York and suggested that if he would aid them with the king, they might be joined to his government. They also petitioned the king to overlook whatever irregularities there might be in their government and to confirm their charter.[1] Soon after his arrival, Andros informed the Hartford government that he was authorized to receive the surrender of their charter, and Randolph wrote at the same time advising them to take advantage of the only " door yet open," and request Andros to annex them to the dominion of New England, as otherwise they might fall to New York. The Connecticut magistrates wrote to the secretary of state that if the king would not continue them as they were, they would prefer to be joined to New England rather than to New York.[2]   James at once ordered Andros to take possession of Connecticut, but the people of that colony managed to keep the letters patent out of his grasp.[3]   Andros extended his jurisdiction over Connecticut on the first day of November, 1687. Five months later (April 7, 1688), James added New York and New Jersey to his jurisdiction,[4] and the country between the Kennebec and St. Croix Rivers was already under his administration, so that now he was chief magistrate of all English North America, north and east of Pennsylvania and south of the territories of the Hudson Bay Company. James's friendship for Penn undoubtedly was what saved the latter's prov-

---

their respective towns. It is probable that Andros exercised no effective jurisdiction in either Rhode Island or Connecticut. For the vote of the Rhode Island Assembly, see *Colonial Records*, ii, 191.

[1] *Connecticut Colony Records*, iii, 209.
[2] *Ibid.*, iii, 378.

[3] C. J. Hoadly, *The Hiding of the Charter*, in " Acorn Club Publications," tells the story as to the Connecticut charter. See also *Rhode Island Records*, iii, 187 and fol.

[4] *New York Colonial Documents*, iii, 573.

ince from extinction at this time, although the mayor and corporation of the city of New York had declared that it was absolutely necessary to destroy that colony as well as the others, because their " trade was much decreased by the impetuous encroachments of East and West Jersey, Pennsylvania, and Connecticut." [1] The Dominion of New England, after these consolidations, covered a territory imperial in extent and quite beyond the government of one man in the existing condition of transportation and lack of cohesion among the people of its several parts.

The power conferred on Andros with the consent of his Council, or the major part thereof, was quite in keeping with the grandeur of the domain over which he ruled. His commission [2] empowered him to make laws, levy taxes and rates, and administer justice. Appeals could be taken from the decisions of the provincial courts to the King in Council in cases which involved the amount of three hundred pounds sterling or more, but security must be given for the payment of costs, and executions were not to be suspended pending the prosecution of the appeal. Andros was commander in chief of the armed forces of the Dominion of New England, including both the soldiers whom he had brought with him and the local military forces. With the advice of his Council he was to " agree " with the inhabitants concerning such lands as might be " in our power to dispose of " under such moderate quit-rents, services, and acknowledgments as from time to time should be appointed. He was to take all possible care to discountenance vice and encourage virtue, and to see to it

---

[1] *Calendars of State Papers, America and West Indies, 1685-1688*, p. 367.

[2] The commission of 1686 is in Massachusetts Historical Society's *Collections*, Third Series, vii, 139; *Rhode Island Colonial Records*, iii, 212. The commission of 1688 is in *New York Colonial Documents*, iii, 537.

that " liberty of conscience be allowed to all persons and
that such specially as shall be conformable to the rites of
the Church of England be particularly countenanced and
encouraged."

The constitution and powers of the councilors are contained in the Instructions which were issued in September,
1686.[1] At first there were twenty-seven councilors ; others
were added as the territory under Andros's jurisdiction increased in size, until finally there were forty-two members
of the board. The records of eighty-four meetings are preserved in the archives ; at fifty-three of these, only ten members or less were present, sometimes only five. The assiduity
of the councilors in attending the meetings was in exact
ratio to their official position ; Randolph, the secretary,
Joseph Dudley, the chief justice, William Stoughton, a
justice, John Usher, the treasurer, and Francis Nicholson,
Andros's military representative who was later placed in
charge of affairs at New York, formed a clear majority at
thirty-four meetings. The Instructions provided that
the councilors should enjoy freedom of debate and vote,[2]
but this provision was soon disobeyed on more than one
occasion and was constantly disregarded after the first six
months. The reason for the cessation of interest on the
part of the ordinary councilors was Andros's arbitrary
actions, one example of which was the declaration of the
passage of an order for levying taxes upon which no formal
vote was taken, although there had been a heated debate
on the subject.[3] Andros's enemies state that the order restraining emigration from the dominion was passed at

---

[1] Massachusetts Colonial Society's
Publications, ii. The Instructions which
were issued in April, 1688, are similar.
Rhode Island Colonial Records, iii, 248.

[2] Andros's " Instructions," §§ 4, 10.

[3] This statement is made on the au-

thority of " A Narrative of the Proceed-
ings of Sir Edmond Androsse and his
Complices," which was written by
Stoughton, Hinckley, and Wait Winthrop
(*Andros Tracts*, i, 140).

New York at a slimly attended meeting, because a favorable vote could not be got at Boston and the records show that grants of land were made to Randolph and other favorites and sentences of fine and imprisonment given at meetings which were attended by eight members or less. It is difficult to see how Andros's administration can be viewed in any other light than as an illegal despotism, especially when one remembers that the commission itself was contrary to the laws of England, according to the opinion of the law officers of the crown. It will be well to examine, more at length, one or two examples of Andros's exercise of arbitrary power.[1]

His money and his lands have always been sacred to the Anglo-Saxon. To take either one or the other or both without his express consent given personally or by some one whom he regarded as his representative has always excited the utmost resentment. In dealing with the New Englanders, Andros performed his task in so tactless a manner that he aroused double or treble the amount of irritation that was inevitable under any circumstances. His instructions directed him to collect money only by existing law until he had communicated to the king plans for new levies,[2] while his commission authorized him to levy all necessary rates, but only with the consent of his Council. Appended to a copy of the Instructions of 1688, which is preserved in the Record Office at London, are certain notes made by Andros in answer to criticisms of his conduct on the part of the colonists. In one of these he

---

[1] The late Mr. William Whitmore in the introduction to the *Andros Tracts*, and in his chapter in Winsor's *Memorial History of Boston* (ii, ch. i), attempted to show that Andros had been treated unjustly by other New England writers. Mr. Whitmore did not have access to the "Andros Records," a fact which goes far to account for the different opinions expressed by him and the present writer.

[2] Andros's "Instructions," § 15; Massachusetts Historical Society's *Collections*, Third Series, vii, 141.

states that the taxes were levied by the advice and act of
the Council and that the Additional Imposts were levied
only after the king's pleasure had been signified.[1]   The records, however, show quite a different state of affairs.   There
were no existing laws for the collection of money, for they
had all terminated in 1684.[2]   Nevertheless, Andros put the
old machinery in motion, and that without a vote of the
Council.   The treasurer issued his warrants for the assessment and collection of the rates " according to former
usage."   In most of the towns the officials performed
their assigned tasks without a murmur, but when the
order for the collection of the tax reached the town of
Ipswich, there was trouble.   Several of the leading men
assembled and voted " that it was not the Towns Duty
any way to assist that ill method of raising Money without
a general Assembly."[4]   The townsmen agreed with them,
and " considering that the said act did infringe their liberty
as free-born English subjects," they refused to pay the
tax.   A few other towns also resisted, but as the men of
Ipswich were well known throughout the colony, they were
brought to Boston and tried by a "special commission" for
refusing to pay their rates and for making and publishing
factious and seditious votes and writings, while less important objectors were bound over for trial at the Superior
Court.   Charles Bedford, William Browne, John Hawthorne,
and Phillip Nelson were also commissioned[5] to make inquiry
in the towns of Gloucester, Haverhill, and Boxford, and to
examine and bind over such persons as had been factious

[1] Massachusetts Colonial Society's
Publications, ii.

[2] Whitmore's *Laws of 1672*, p. 23;
Massachusetts Colony Records, v, 414.

[3] Act of March 3, 1686, in *Connecticut
Colonial Records*, iii, 405. Andros did
practically the same thing in New York,

with the consent of his Council.   *Ibid.*,
iii, 447.

[4] *Andros Tracts*, i, 83; **Palfrey's** *New
England*, iii, 525.

[5] " Andros Records " in American
Antiquarian Society's *Proceedings*, New
Series, xiii, 478.

and seditious and had refused to obey the warrants of the treasurer.

Dudley presided at both the "special commission" and at the regular term of the Superior Court. In the course of the proceedings he declared that "the laws of England would not follow them [the colonists] to the ends of the Earth. . . . The king's subjects in New England did not differ much from slaves, and that the only difference was, that they were not bought and sold." [1] Some of the jurors were strangers in the colony. With a hostile judge and a packed jury, the result was not long in doubt. John Wise, the Ipswich minister who had borne a prominent part in the affair, was suspended from his ministerial functions, fined fifty pounds, and forced to give a bond in the sum of one thousand pounds for good behavior for one year. The fines, fees, prison charges, etc., for Wise and the other men of Ipswich amounted in all to between three hundred and four hundred pounds. Another man from the same town, Major Samuel Appleton, was ordered by Andros and six councilors to give bonds for one thousand pounds to appear when wanted and meantime to be of good behavior. He refused to give bonds and was committed to the common jail.[2] In this way constitutional opposition to the levying of taxes without representation was crushed out. Rebellion or submission was the only alternative.

Andros's commission directed him to "agree with the inhabitants" concerning such lands as now are or hereafter shall be "in our power to dispose of" under such

[1] *Andros Tracts*, i, 82; see also Palfrey's *New England*, iii, 526 note.

[2] See "Andros Records" in American Antiquarian Society's *Proceedings*, New Series, xiii, 481, 486 and note. See also cases of Shadrach Wilbore, Dudley Bradstreet, and Thomas Leonard in "Andros Records," *Andros Tracts*, and Palfrey's *New England*.

"moderate quitrents" as shall be appointed by us, but the "Instructions" direct that "no man's life, member, freehold, or goods be taken away or harmed . . . but by established and known laws not repugnant to . : . the laws of our kingdom of England."[1] This looks fair enough on paper, but Andros and his followers used their power in a most unjust and irritating manner.[2] Granting that the charter had been legally taken away, which Attorney General Powis said was not the case, the unsold lands in Massachusetts reverted to the crown, and might be granted by the king through such agents as he deemed proper and to such persons as he desired. Under the Company, lands had been granted outright and not on a quit-rent tenure, and the imposition of such a charge in itself was certain to arouse resentment. Andros exceeded his instructions; he regarded as royal lands all those to which a perfect title could not be proved under English law. It turned out that very little land was held in strict conformity to the requirements of English law.[3] The towns held large quantities of common land for the use of the inhabitants as pastures. All of this land Andros affected to regard as

---

[1] Andros's "Instructions," §§ 19, 30.

[2] This subject is treated in a long note to the "Letter-Book of Samuel Sewall," in Massachusetts Historical Society's *Collections*, Sixth Series, i, note to pp. 68–73.

[3] Professor P. S. Reinsch points out the great laxness as to legal procedure that prevailed in the colonies, especially in the seventeenth century. See his "English Common Law in the Early American Colonies" in *Bulletin of the University of Wisconsin*, No. 31. For a discussion of land titles in Massachusetts, see Massachusetts Historical Society's *Collections*, Sixth Series, i, 68 note; the same society's *Proceedings* for 1899 (p. 223) contains an extract from the opin-

ion of Sir Thomas Powis, attorney general in the reign of James II, that "the Massachusetts charter had been illegally vacated." Dr. S. A. Green has a very clear account of the New England land system in his *Records of Groton;* a more formal description is Egleston's *Land Systems of New England* ("privately printed" and reprinted in *Johns Hopkins Studies*). A most excellent discussion is in Gray's *Massachusetts Reports,* ix, note to pp. 503–528 (case of the Commonwealth *vs.* Roxbury). Randolph declared in 1687 there was not a councilor who understood "the laws peculiar to the Courts of England." *Calendars of State Papers, America and West Indies, 1685–1688*, p. 349.

ungranted and at his disposal. The bane of English colonial
management has always been the tendency to apply principles of law and methods of legal procedure which had
been developed in England to its colonies, with a sublime
disregard of the wishes of the colonists and of conditions
which necessarily prevail in frontier settlements. Conscious that he held the colonists in the palm of his hand,
so far as legal title to their lands was concerned, Andros
offered to confirm their deeds on certain conditions which
required the making of surveys and the payment of fees.
Moreover, these confirmations could only be obtained at
Boston, and a survey and confirmation were required for
each separate parcel of land, with the payment, of course,
of corresponding fees. The English officials were expert
in spying out bits of common land. Randolph asked for
half an acre of Boston common for a house lot,[1] for all
of the peninsula of Nahant for a farm, and for seven hundred acres in Cambridge and Watertown. Nahant was
connected with the mainland near Lynn village by a
narrow strip of beach. The Lynn people had built a
fence across this narrow isthmus and had in this way
found Nahant an excellent pasture for the town herd.
When the Lynn authorities showed Andros the town
records, he informed them that they were not " worth a
rush," that there was no such thing as a town in Massachusetts, and that their pleas were insignificant. At
another time he told Joseph Lynde of Charlestown,
whose lands had been purchased from the Indians, that
his deeds from the aborigines were of " no more worth
than a scratch with a Bears paw." [2] A few weeks before his downfall, Andros had a conference with the
venerable and venerated John Higginson, minister at

---

[1] Hutchinson's *Massachusetts*, i, 322.   [2] *Andros Tracts*, i, 92.

Salem, in which the latter was forced to take refuge in the book of Genesis to justify the colonists' rights to their farms. Andros on his part declared to the Salem minister that the colonists were either subjects or rebels,[1] subjects if they did what he ordered, otherwise they were rebels to be treated accordingly. All of Andros's conferences with the people ended in displays of anger on his part. When tact and patience were needed, there was threatening and loss of temper ; when quiet, strong action was required, there was vacillation and weakness. It was when the people were aroused to high indignation that news came to Massachusetts of the landing of William of Orange on the coast of England on the anniversary of Guy Fawkes Day, November 5, 1688.

---

[1] *Andros Tracts,* i, 88, 90.

NOTES

I. Bibliography. — This period of New England history presents an entirely new aspect since the publication of Robert Noxon Toppan's *Edward Randolph*[1] and the printing under his editorship of the "Dudley Records"[2] and the "Andros Records."[3] The original matter in Toppan's *Randolph* is preceded by an elaborate and discriminating memoir. This is written in the spirit of modern scientific historical investigation, but unfortunately reflects the lack of literary skill on the part of the author. It occupies nearly a volume and a half and is difficult to use, owing to the lack of chapters and to there being no table of contents. The notes to these pages are of equal value with the text, and students must be grateful to the author, notwithstanding the defects in his literary method. Previously, the Prince Society had published three volumes of *Andros Tracts*,[4] under the editorship of William H. Whitmore. Mr. Whitmore takes a very favorable view of Andros, but he made no use of the records of the Andros Council. The Andros laws to January, 1687–88, are printed in *Connecticut Colonial Records* (iii, 402 and fol.). These records and the *Colonial Records of Rhode Island* also contain matter on those colonies in this period. The Massachusetts Historical Society, besides the "Andros Records," has printed many documents relating to this period. Among them may be mentioned Sewall's "Diary"[5] and "Letter Book"[6]; the "Mather Papers,"[7] the "Winthrop Papers,"[8] and "Usurpation Papers."[9] The commissions and instructions to Dudley and Andros will be printed in the second volume of the *Publications* of the Colonial Society of Massachusetts. In the *Andros Tracts* (ii, p. xxxi) is a list of the places where many isolated documents may be found in print.

[1] *Edward Randolph including his Letters and Official Papers with historical illustrations and a Memoir* (Boston, Prince Society's *Publications*, 1898–99, 5 vols. — 250 copies only printed).

[2] Massachusetts Historical Society's *Proceedings*, Second Series, xiii, 222–286.

[3] American Antiquarian Society's *Proceedings*, New Series, xiii, 237–268, 463–499.

[4] Prince Society's *Publications*, 1868, 3 vols.

[5] Massachusetts Historical Society's *Collections*, Fifth Series, vol. v–vii; N. H. Chamberlain in his *Samuel Sewall and the World he Lived In* brings together topically the more dramatic and humorous entries in this work.

[6] *Ibid.*, Sixth Series, i.

[7] *Ibid.*, Fourth Series, viii.

[8] *Ibid.*, Sixth Series, iii and v.

[9] *Ibid.*, Third Series, vii, 150–195.

The best secondary accounts of the administrations of Dudley and Andros, and the events of the preceding years, besides Toppan's "Memoir of Edward Randolph" and Whitmore's "Introduction" to the *Andros Tracts,* are those in Hutchinson's *Massachusetts* and Palfrey's *New England.* Hutchinson used documents, some of which are no longer available, and Palfrey studied the manuscripts preserved at London and at Boston which have recently been printed. Whitmore also wrote the chapter on "The Inter-Charter Period" in Winsor's *Memorial History of Boston.*

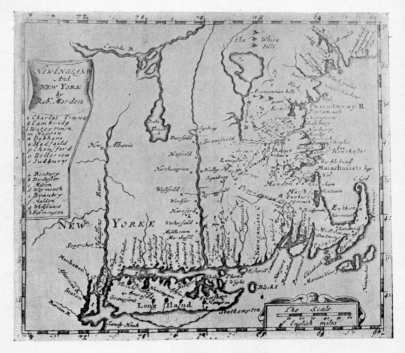

NEW ENGLAND, 1686–1688

(From Richard Blome's *Present State of His Majesties Isles and Territories in America*, London, 1687.)

CHAPTER VII

THE ENGLISH REVOLUTION IN AMERICA, 1689–1690

JAMES's course was run. The birth of a son to his Roman Catholic queen made it certain that, barring rebellion, his successor would be a Roman Catholic like himself, and that his daughter Mary, who had been reared in the Protestant faith by her mother, James's first wife and Clarendon's daughter, would never reign as queen in England. The English nation was Protestant to the core. To avoid civil strife and a disputed succession, it had endured the despotic rule of the second Charles; it had put up with the atrocities following Monmouth's Rebellion; but when it became assured that James was turning the government to the uses of the Catholic reaction, the leaders of English political life and the English people shut their eyes to the fact that he had a son born in wedlock. They declared the child to be a pretender, and nothing that James could do was of any avail. They drove the king from the throne and placed thereon his eldest daughter, Mary, and her husband, William of Orange. At the same time they exacted certain conditions which made a repetition of the misdeeds of the second Charles and the second James well nigh impossible.

The Revolution of 1688–89 was a Whig-Dutch conquest of the English empire carefully concealed under constitutional contrivances. It confirmed to Englishmen rights and liberties for which the Puritans had struggled in vain.[1] For the colo-

---

[1] The ecclesiastical side of this epoch is related in J. Stoughton's *Religion in England* (vol. v, "The Church of the Revolution").

nists the Revolution meant nothing of the kind. Their consent to the change of dynasty was not asked, their interests were not considered ; they were simply ordered to proclaim the new monarchs. The effect of the Revolution was to hand them over to the English landowning oligarchy to be exploited for the benefit of English industry. The remedial statutes which made the movement memorable in English constitutional history did not extend to the colonies.[1] Moreover, the new government exhibited an energy in colonial administration which the Stuarts had never shown. After 1689 the colonists were in a worse plight than they had been in the reigns of Charles and James. It will be well to look somewhat closely into the mode by which this Revolution was consummated with a view to note the processes by which its promoters sought to conceal its true character.

On December 17, 1688, William, Prince of Orange, entered London with his followers. By the advice of the leading men about him, he invited [2] (December 23) all persons who had sat in any of the Parliaments of Charles II to meet him at St. James's Palace (on Wednesday, December 26), at which place the lord mayor, aldermen, and fifty of the Common Council of the city of London would likewise attend him. Upon the advice of this assemblage of notable persons he summoned a Convention [3] to meet at Westminster on January 22, 1688–89. In the election of delegates to the Convention, the changes in the boroughs and other corporations, which Charles and James had brought about, were disregarded; the franchise was exercised by the classes

[1] See opinions of Henley and Yorke (1757) in Chalmers's *Opinions*, i, 197; Northey (1713), *ibid.*, i, 130; De Grey and Wills (1767), *ibid.*, i, 200.

[2] Grey's *Debates*, ix, 1 and fol.

[3] For the historical meaning of the word "convention," see a paper entitled "The Early Political Uses of the Word Convention," by J. F. Jameson, in American Antiquarian Society's *Proceedings*, New Series, xii, 183.

which had held it before the surrender of the charters, and
the time allowed for the polling was very brief.   In short,
the election was held without due notice, and many persons
who by law were entitled to vote were unable to exercise
their rights.   When the Convention met, many seats in the
Lower House were vacant ; those which were filled were
occupied for the most part by friends of the Revolution,
although there were some members who doubted the legality of the election.   One gentleman declared that " the
fourth part of the people of England are not represented
here " ; but his objection was insolently set aside with the
assertion, " If we sit here till he finds a way to sit better
than you are, you may sit here till Doomsday." [1] This body
then proceeded to vote itself " a full and free representation
of the Nation"; to declare the throne vacant, and to offer
it on certain conditions to William and Mary as " King
and Queen of England, and all the dominions thereunto belonging." The terms upon which this prize was offered to the
new monarchs were embodied in a document which was entitled " A Declaration of Right."   William and Mary, having
accepted the throne, united with the Convention in passing
what was termed a law,[2] declaring the Convention to be a
parliament.   The Parliament thus constituted then enacted
the Declaration of Right as a law, with the title of " An Act
declaring the Rights and Liberties of the Subject and Settling the Succession of the Crown." [3]   The monarchs now
" constitutionally " enthroned   dissolved this Parliament
and summoned another, which passed a bill declaring all
the acts of its predecessors to be laws — all of which sol-
emn proceedings savor somewhat of comic opera.   The
justification of the Revolution is the support which the

[1] Grey's *Debates*, ix, 23.
[2] 1 William and Mary, Cap. 1 (*Statutes of the Realm*, vi, 23).
[3] 1 William and Mary, Second Session, Cap. 2 (*ibid.*, vi, 142).

great body of Englishmen at the time and since have given to the doings of the Convention Parliament. Moreover, there is some evidence of popular pressure at the time. Mobs assembled in the avenues leading to the place of assemblage and hissed the Tory peers while the names of the recalcitrant lords were printed and hawked about the streets.[1] At the moment the Bill of Rights was hardly more than a party platform ; it has come to be regarded as the palladium of English liberty, as a " cornerstone " or " coping stone," as the foundation or sometimes the roof of the English constitution. It is worshipped with a degree of veneration almost equal to that with which Americans reverence the Declaration of Independence. Its genesis, however, shows a persistent disregard of the rights of the English colonists in America.[2]

In the thirteenth section of the first draft of the Declaration of Right there was a clause [3] securing the colonies " against *Quo Warrantos* and Surrenders and Mandates," and restoring to them their " ancient rights." For some reason, which cannot be traced, this clause disappeared ; but the words " New England and other plantations " were added to an order directing a committee of the Lower House to bring in bills to restore corporations to the state and condition they were in on May 16, 1660, and to confirm their liberties and franchises.[4] A bill for this purpose passed the Commons in January, 1689–90 ; but failed in the Lords because of an acrimonious discussion as to the legality of the surrender of the charters of English municipal corporations.[5] The mood changed to

<hr>

[1] Somerville's *Political Transactions*, 278 ; *Lords Journals*, xiv, 123 ; Grey's *Debates*, ix, 45.

[2] The colonists were regarded as " entirely dependent upon the crown of England," their consent was not asked or permitted as to changes of the succession.

See opinion of Attorney-General Harcourt, advising the disallowance of a Maryland law recognizing Queen Anne, Chalmers's *Opinions*, i, 343.

[3] *Commons Journals*, x, 17.

[4] *Ibid.*, x, 51.

[5] *Ibid.*, x, 253, 330 ; *Lords Journals*,

one of hostility to colonial privileges. For years the Lords Committee of the Privy Council had been trying to consolidate the colonial governments ; it was now represented to William that the present opportunity was most favorable for bringing the proprietary and chartered colonies "under a nearer dependence on the crown."[1] William, with the conquest of England and the overthrow of James and Louis still on his hands, had other things to think about than subjecting friendly colonists three thousand miles away. Fortunately, too, Mary was still under the influence of clergymen who were favorable to New England religious interests. The opportunity was allowed to slip away, never to return. On the other hand, no bills restoring the liberties and franchises of the New Englanders ever made their appearance. Finally, when William had time to take up the subject, he gave an energy to colonial administration that it had never known before and that lasted well into the next century.

In America, William's progress was watched with interest and his success was hailed with rejoicing. The colonists, with the exception of a small minority in Maryland, were all of them Protestants, although of many divergent sects. They had seen with dislike the increasing employment of Roman Catholics in military and civil offices in the colonies and in England. James's flight to the French court still further aroused their apprehensions. They soon began to suspect that he was plotting with Louis XIV to subject them to his will with the aid of the Canadian French and their Indian allies. James allied himself with the French and the Irish in Europe for the

xiv, 410 and fol.; Royal Historical Manuscripts Commission's *Reports*, xii, Part vi, p. 422; *Andros Tracts*, ii, No. 2.

[1] Chalmers's *Introduction to the Revolt*, i, 223.

purpose of regaining England; why should he not ally himself with the French and the Indians in America to preserve his colonial empire? In the plenitude of his power he had used the colonial service to reward his Roman Catholic followers, but it is improbable that he had matured any design to reconquer the colonists by the aid of the French; all of his energies were fully occupied with affairs on the eastern side of the Atlantic. Whether true or false, the charge of conspiracy between James, the French, and the Roman Catholics was useful in molding colonial opinion, and events shaped themselves to urge the colonists to fall in line with their fellow-countrymen in England.

On January 12, 1689, about a month after his arrival in London, but before the assembling of the Convention, William issued a circular letter,[1] directing all colonial officials who were not Roman Catholics to retain their places. Increase Mather, who was then in England as agent for Massachusetts, brought it about that no copy of this order was sent to Boston.[2] It is doubtful if the letter reached the other colonies. A month later the Council ordered all colonial governors to proclaim King William and Queen Mary and to administer the oath of allegiance to officeholders. Penn and Baltimore were called in; they promised to obey and dispatched orders to their agents in America to proclaim the new sovereigns.[3] The messenger died at Plymouth, England, before embarking for America, and William and Mary were not proclaimed in Pennsylvania and Maryland.

[1] New York Historical Society's *Collections*, 1868, p. 36; *Calendars of State Papers, America and West Indies, 1689-1692*, p. 4.

[2] In 1693 Elisha Hutchinson prevented a letter from Phips to the king reaching the government — by what means he does not say. Massachusetts Historical Society's *Proceedings*, First Series, ii, 297.

[3] *Calendars of State Papers, America and West Indies, 1689-1692*, pp. 7, 8.

In the Carolinas there was no discontent with the royal government as exemplified by Stuart rule ; there the uneasiness was on account of the proprietary system.   The Carolinians, however, were well content to follow the lead of England and proclaimed William and Mary, without so much as an attempt to overthrow the proprietors, who had all of them been followers of the Stuart monarchy.[1]   In Virginia the planters were in a complaining mood, owing to the usual reason, — the low price of tobacco.   In the spring of 1689 petitions came from them asking the Revolution government to moderate the exactions on tobacco.[2]   The first of these was presented to the House of Commons on April 16, and purported to represent divers planters of Virginia and Maryland.   The other petition, which was presented to the House on May 20, 1689, had a more official position in that it was said to be in the name of the Virginia Burgesses.   It recited that the impositions on tobacco had impoverished the Virginians and aroused disaffection among them to the hazard of the peace.   Furthermore, they stated that the late governor had revived by proclamation a law which had been repealed by the Assembly, that he had imposed exorbitant fines, had imprisoned people without trial, had refused to admit them to bail, had paid no attention to writs of *habeas corpus*, and all this in a colony which brought in one hundred thousand pounds annual benefit to the " Nation."   Trusting in the justice of the new govern-

[1] South Carolina Historical Society's *Collections*, i, 122. In July, 1688, the proprietors recommended the Carolinians " to testify their joy " over the birth of the prince, in the following February (1688–89) they order the new monarchs to be proclaimed. See also McCrady's *South Carolina as a Proprietary Government*, 229.

[2] *Commons Journals*, x, 89, 138; see also the vote of the Burgesses in the *Magazine of American History*, x, 57 ; Bancroft, citing Ms. letters, states that Virginia applied for a charter in 1691. *History of the United States* (ed. 1883), vol. ii, p. 17.

ment, the Virginians promised to accept the change in England without further demur. In Pennsylvania, also, there was no overt act of rebellion against constituted authority. In England, however, the finger of suspicion pointed strongly at William Penn. He was the friend of the fugitive king, and he and his fellow-Quakers had not the social and political strength which had made the new rulers necessarily tolerant of Presbyterians and Independents. He was arrested several times, was forced into hiding, and was believed by some people to have gone to France.[1] In 1692 the government of Pennsylvania and Delaware was taken from him, but was restored to him in 1694. In the northern colonies and in Maryland, religious and political conditions forbade so simple a settlement.

Sir Edmund Andros already had trouble enough in dealing with a fractious and stubborn people to occupy the time and energies of the most skillful of colonial governors. In 1688 the French and the Roman Catholic Indians of Canada began a series of attacks on the English settlements and thereby strengthened the suspicions of the English colonists. On August 16, 1688, a party of northern savages assaulted the little hamlet of Northfield [2] in the Connecticut Valley. Nicholson was promptly sent to the rescue and the governor of Canada disavowed all responsibility for the raid. Complications which had arisen with the French and the Indians to the eastward were not so easily arranged. A Frenchman, the Baron Castine, had settled on the shores of a little harbor on the eastern side of Penobscot Bay and had been rudely dispossessed by the

---

[1] Royal Historical Manuscripts Commission's *Reports*, xiv, Part ii, 474.

[2] Temple and Sheldon's *Northfield*, 115; *Calendars of State Papers, America and West Indies, 1685–1688*, p. 608.

New York officials before Pemaquid had come under
Andros's authority.[1] Whenever Frenchmen felt aggrieved,
Indian attacks were sure to follow. So it was in this
case. In November, 1688, Andros led a body of soldiers
to the Penobscot to overawe the natives. On this occasion, colonists were dragged into the military service, were
commanded in some cases by Roman Catholic officers,
and, on a few occasions, were inhumanly treated. Under
these circumstances the news of the success of William of
Orange proved to be the signal for the outbreak of popular
indignation.

In Massachusetts and elsewhere in New England, political motives played the leading part in the movements of
1689; but the astute leaders of the revolt against James's
minions used religious prejudices to intensify the resentment of the people against the Stuart officials. Armed
opposition had been long in the minds of the leaders and
the details of the movement had been carefully worked
out in advance. As was the case in later days, the actual
leaders succeeded in concealing their identity. Whoever
they were, they made their plans with great skill. Rumors were set on foot to the effect that Andros was a
"papist," and no more damaging allegation could have
been preferred against a man at that time and place.
Again, it was asserted that he was intriguing with the
French and designed delivering Boston into their hands,
and he was also charged with inciting the Indians to
slaughter the English settlers. These and other insinua-
tions were brought to the attention of the people in most
roundabout and ingenious ways. On one occasion a
paper, which was said to have been found on the highway,

---

[1] *Calendars of State Papers, America and West Indies, 1685–1688*, pp. 207, 239,
249, 522.

was handed to one of the justices. It bore the words:
" New England Alarmed arise and be warned, Let not
Papists you charm I mean you no harm." At another
time, an Indian was taken into Andros's presence and
charged with saying that " the Governor was a Rogue
and had hired Wohawky [an Indian] to kill Englishmen,
and had given the said Wohawky a gold Ring, which was
his commission, which gold Ring the said Wohawky sold
to Jonathan Prescott for two shillings in money." Again,
information was brought to Benjamin Bullivant, the attorney general, that another Indian had heard the governor
declare the French and Irish would come in the spring,
destroy Boston, and ravage the country. Furthermore, an
Indian declared that Andros had given him a book " containing a picture of the Virgin Mary," which the governor
had said was better than the Bible. In taking these
measures to arouse discontent, the leaders were acting
with the knowledge of the course of events in England
and that James had taken refuge in France.[1]

In December, 1688, the ship *Belcher* sailed into Boston
harbor with the news of the probable invasion of England
by William of Orange and his Dutch troops.[2] In January
1688–89, by order from England, Andros issued a proclamation announcing the invasion and directing the people
to be on their guard against surprise by a foreign enemy.[3]
The success of the Prince of Orange and the flight of
James were known in Boston before the end of the following March, for the " Addresses of the Nonconformist
Ministers " to William were printed at Boston before that

[1] Miss Jennie C. Watts kindly called
my attention to these entries in the Ms.
Massachusetts Archives.

[2] See on this general subject Massachusetts Historical Society's *Collections*,

Fifth Series, viii, 486, and Sixth Series,iii,
495.

[3] *Calendars of State Papers, America
and West Indies, 1689–1692*, p. 5.

time, and on March 25, John Nelson, the military head of
the movement, wrote to a friend that James had been
defeated and had fled.   The immediate and inciting cause
of the actual outbreak was the " Declaration," which William had issued on undertaking the invasion of England.
In this paper he had declared that " all Magistrates who
have been unjustly turned out, shall forthwith resume
their former Employments; as well as all the Boroughs
of *England* shall return to their ancient Prescriptions
and Charters." [1]   There is not a single word in this document as to colonies or colonists, and the section in which
the above-quoted sentence occurs has to do with the
election of " a free and lawful Parliament."   There is no
reason to suppose that William had the colonists in mind
in issuing this declaration.   Nevertheless, it imparted the
needed impulse to colonial revolt in that it gave or seemed
to give a quasi-legal sanction to the rising.

The Declaration was brought to Boston from the West
Indies by John Winslow. [2]   Andros at once clapped him
into prison without bail and seized his papers; but the
terms of the Declaration soon became known and inflamed
the people.   The leaders of the old colonial government now
consulted together and resolved to place themselves at the
head of the movement, which either " the outragious mad-
ness of our Foes or the impatient motion of our Friends "
might bring forth with a view " to prevent what ill effects
an Unformed Tumult might produce."   Conscious of the
coming crisis, Andros sought safety in the fort.

On the morning of April 18, 1689, bands of young men
and boys ran about the streets of the South End of Boston, shouting that the people of the North End had risen,

[1] *Commons Journals*, x, 4.
[2] Hutchinson's *Massachusetts*, second edition, i, 373; Toppan's *Randolph*, ii, 89 note; *Andros Tracts*, i, 77.

while similar bands rushed about the North End, crying
out that the Southenders were in arms. A signal was
also hoisted to let the country people know that the hour
of revolution had come. Randolph had bestirred himself
betimes on that eventful morning and was in his office.
He was in the act of taking a bond from Captain Everton
of the *Lark*, obliging that shipmaster "not to carry out
passengers without a tickett of leave," when something
occurred to alarm him.[1] He hastened to the fort, where
he found Andros and others of his henchmen. Joseph
Dudley happened to be out of town at the moment; but
Captain George of the *Rose* frigate, which was yet lying
at anchor in the harbor, sought the shore to see what was
going on and was promptly seized.[2] By noon some two
hundred armed men had assembled under the command
of John Nelson[3] and John Foster. Simon Bradstreet, the
last governor under the charter, Thomas Danforth, the
former deputy governor, Elisha Cooke, the ablest politician in the colony, William Stoughton, who had changed
sides in time, and some others of the old leaders, were
deep in consultation as to what should be done. A Declaration[4] was produced, stating the case of the colonists and
was read to the assembled people. The leaders then sent
a letter to Andros, advising him to surrender. While
these measures were being concerted by the revolutionists,
Andros at the fort had requested the ministers to attend
him, but they had refused on grounds of personal safety.
Under the circumstances he could think of nothing better
than to flee to the frigate; but the militia, under Captain
Nelson, appeared just in time to prevent his escape, and

---

[1] Toppan's *Randolph*, ii, 90.

[2] Hutchinson's *Massachusetts*, second
edition, i, 374, 375; Toppan's *Randolph*, ii,
91 note.

[3] There is an account of Nelson in
Massachusetts Historical Society's *Proceedings*, 1863–64, p. 370.

[4] *Andros Tracts*, i, 11.

the redcoats who had come with him from England seemed disinclined to fire on the Bostoners. Surrender appeared to be the wisest thing, and Andros with his followers marched to the townhouse where the leaders were awaiting them. No insult was offered to Andros on the way and he was consigned to the care of Mr. Usher, the treasurer of the Dominion, whose wife was a daughter of Lady Alice Lisle,[1] a victim of James's brutal ferocity. Randolph and other prisoners of lesser note were placed for safe-keeping in the town gaol, with the gaoler, whose office was intrusted to one "Scates, the bricklayer." In this bloodless way the Stuart domination in New England came to an end.

It is true that the castle in the harbor still held out and that the frigate possessed power of mischief; but the next morning the castle was surrendered by order of Andros or of Randolph. The guns of the shore batteries and castle were now trained on the frigate; but an arrangement was entered into with Captain George by which the surrender of the *Rose* was avoided, since that would deprive her officers and men of their arrears of pay and prize money. She remained in the hands of her officers, but her topmasts were lowered and her canvas was sent on shore for safe-keeping.[2] She was unable to sail for French succor, had her officers so wished.

The country people now swarmed to Boston. They hated Andros more intensely than did the townsfolk, because he had sought to deprive them of their lands, while the shopkeepers of the capital had benefited from

---

[1] Massachusetts Historical Society's *Proceedings*, Second Series, ii, 254; Palfrey's *New England*, iii, 494 note.

[2] On the seizure of Andros and his co-workers, see a brief but contemporaneous entry in the "Diary of Lawrence Hammond" in Massachusetts Historical Society's *Proceedings*, Second Series, vii, 150. See also "John Marshall's Diary" in *ibid.*, Second Series, i, 161, 162; Toppan's *Randolph*, ii, 92; *Andros Tracts*, i, 9.

the expenditures of the royal governor. The countrymen
demanded that Andros should be placed in chains, but
they were quieted by being permitted to escort him to
the fort, in which place of confinement he bore more of
the aspect of a prisoner than while living in custody in
a private house. Essaying to escape from his prison in
woman's garb, he was detected by the size and shape of
his boots, which he had neglected to change.[1] From that
time on he and his followers were confined within the
castle on an island in the harbor which now was called
Castle William. Later he managed to evade his guards
and flee to Newport; but there the people held him until
soldiers from Boston appeared and escorted him back in
triumph. The prisoners suffered from the cold, from
each other's society, and from their own sad reflections.
They complained[2] bitterly of their lot; but the fact that
one of their greatest grievances was the refusal of the
authorities to permit Andros's French cook to dress their
meat, diminishes the force of their contentions. The revolutionary leaders would gladly have released their unwel-
come guests, but every sign of relaxation on their part
brought forth unmistakable marks of popular disapproval which could not be neglected in their own interests
or in that of their captives. At length in February, 1690,
in consequence of orders from England, the prisoners were
placed on board the *Mehitable* bound for London.

No sooner were Andros and his minions securely incarcerated than a division of opinion appeared among the
people. The leading men, with the responsibility on their
shoulders for the downfall of Stuart rule in the province,
expressed themselves decidedly as faithful to the gov-

[1] *Andros Tracts*, i, 8.

[2] The statement of the colonial officers in command at the "castle" during
the period of Andros's imprisonment is in
Massachusetts Colonial Society's *Publications*, ii.

ernment which had been established in England. They formed themselves into a Council of Safety and asked (May 2, 1689) the people of Massachusetts to send delegates to Boston.[1] The voters, however, were clearly of the opinion that the charter should be reassumed as having been illegally annulled.[2] The lukewarmness of the magistrates as to the colony charter was probably due to a consciousness of the inadequacy of that instrument for the needs of the hour. Its provisions were so imperfect that it was impossible to conduct a legal government under it; at any time a new writ of *quo warranto* might be brought against them to show by what right they levied taxes on the non-freemen, and no effective answer could be made to such a demand. In obedience to the people's wishes, however, the magistrates acted as if it were still in force and asked for its confirmation; but they made no adequate effort to secure that result.

In New York, Andros was represented by Captain Francis Nicholson as lieutenant governor.[3] Like his chief, he was an army officer, and, like him, possessed little tact in dealing with men ; but he had not those sterling qualities which arouse interest in Andros, even when one disagrees with the latter's policy and the modes by which he sought to accomplish his purposes. Nicholson ruled New York and New Jersey with the assistance of the local members of Andros's Council, although the legality of this exercise of power on their part, under the commission of 1688, except as to purely executive matters, may well be questioned. The elements of racial, social, political, and

---

[1] Hutchinson's *Massachusetts-Bay* (ed. 1760), i, 382.

[2] Documents relating to this period are printed in the second volume of the *Publications* of the Colonial Society of Massachusetts.

[3] There is an article on Nicholson by Worthington C. Ford in the *Magazine of American History*, xxix, 499.

religious discord were strong in New York. There were the Dutch and the English settlers, who were descended from the early colonists. There were also many new-comers from New England who were impregnated with the political prejudices of the New English, as the Tory historian, George Chalmers, not inaptly terms the inhabit-ants of the country east of the Hudson. These were also skilled in the methods of political opposition, which were so strongly developed in Massachusetts and Connecticut. Finally, there were the English officials and their friends, who were largely of the Roman Catholic faith, or, like Nicholson, were willing to take part in Roman Catholic services even in that time of intense political and religious excitement. These lived by themselves and had little to do with the Dutch and the New English, whom they looked upon as "colonials." The settlers returned their dislike and, besides, believed that they were plotting with the Canadian French to overturn the Protestant govern-ment. Thomas Dongan, Nicholson's Catholic predecessor, was still in the colony; he had great influence with the Indians, large military experience, and forceful tact in dealing with men. No more fitting instrument could be found to carry out the policy of James and Louis on the American continent. It was, indeed, unfortunate at such a crisis that, with Dongan in the colony, the commander of Fort James on Manhattan Island, the commander at Albany, the collector of the revenue at New York, the officers of the troops which Andros had brought from Boston, and some of the soldiers stationed at the fort should have been Roman Catholics.[1] A much less suspi-

---

[1] The Roman Catholics were so nu-merous in New York at this time that a school was opened for the education of their children. Shea's *Catholic Church in the United States*, ii, 27.

cious set of men than the New York colonists might well seize the first opportunity to put it out of the power of Nicholson and his followers to work mischief. The deputy governor by his childish petulance and the members of his Council by their ill-timed timidity provided the opportunity. The news of William's success in his enterprise, which certainly spelled war between England and France, was definitely known in New York in February or March, 1688–89. That province was peculiarly exposed to attack from the French in Canada and from any French fleet that might escape from the Dutch and English seamen and put across the Atlantic, or from English ships of war that might have remained faithful to James. Nicholson, his advisers, and the colonists were agreed as to the necessity of repairing the defensive works on Manhattan Island: Nicholson because he wished security against an attack from New England; the Dutch and the New English because they feared a counter revolution. It was while the work on the fort was in progress that Nicholson's hot temper and unguarded tongue played the game of his antagonists. Stung by the ignorance or presumption of a Dutch militia subaltern, Nicholson exclaimed that he would rather see New York on fire than serve under such an ignoramus. Rumor, helped on by suspicion, soon twisted this hasty remark into an assertion that the deputy governor would like to see New York burning and, finally, that he would set fire to it himself. Jacob Leisler at this juncture pushed to the front; for two years he was the central figure in New York, and for a generation his name was the rallying cry of a strong political party.

Born at Frankfort-on-the-Main, Leisler was, strictly speaking, a German; but he was closely akin in blood and habits to his Dutch neighbors and had come to New

Netherland as a soldier in the service of the Dutch West India Company. For thirty years he had lived and labored in the colony and had accumulated a fortune, as money was estimated in those days. He now led the movement to secure New York for William and his English Protestant allies. Honest, patriotic, and strenuous, he had little education and possessed a strong, coarse temper, which prevented him from seeing the other side of a question or realizing that his opponents might be as patriotic and as honest as himself. He and his followers had no confidence whatever in the good intentions of Nicholson or in the good faith of Nicholson's advisers. The most important of these latter was Nicholas Bayard, a nephew of Peter Stuyvesant, and of French extraction on his father's side. He was colonel of the New York militia regiment and the chief man among Nicholson's supporters. He possessed a temper as hot as Leisler's and had aristocratic tendencies which stand out in sharp contrast to the democratic inclinations of his opponents. Bayard and the other councilors were as strongly opposed to "popery" and to Frenchmen as Leisler himself; and Nicholson erred through stupidity and ignorance, and not through malice. Under the circumstances it was essential that Leisler, Bayard, and Nicholson should keep their passions and fears under control; but this was the last thing in the world that any of them could do. Leisler, having the power, seized the fort and proclaimed William and Mary. On this Nicholson shiftily returned to England to make sure of his interests there. Bayard and the other two councilors could not, or at all events would not, act loyally with Leisler. They hesitated to proclaim the new monarchs, and their delay gave the control of the Hudson Valley to the revolutionists.

The first mutterings of the prolonged contest with France in the New World were now heard on the New England frontier and in the valleys of the Hudson and the St. Lawrence. On the close of the opening chapter in the hostilities between the French and the Iroquois in the time of Nicolls, the Carignan regiment, which had come out from France instead of returning home, was disbanded and its members turned into colonists. These were given lands along the Richelieu River and on the southern bank of the St. Lawrence. The officers became seigneurs and the men became the tenants of these feudal lords. These military colonists were the backbone of the expeditions which raided the English frontier. When the war broke out between the English and the French in Europe, it extended to America. On June 27, 1689, a party of French Indians attacked Cocheco Village, an outlying settlement near Dover, New Hampshire. They killed Richard Waldron and several more English colonists and carried others away into captivity. At the other end of the line the Iroquois seized the moment to deal a blow at their enemies, the Canadians, white and red. Without warning, fifteen hundred of them attacked the French settlements on the St. Lawrence. On the night of August 4 and 5, 1689, they entered La Chine Village on the upper end of Montreal Island, killed the men at once, slaughtered the women and children at their leisure, and regained their forest homes without incurring serious loss.[1] On this expedition they killed a thousand Canadians, both French and Indians.

December 9, 1689, was a glad day in Jacob Leisler's life, for then a letter from William was brought to New York

---

[1] Désiré Girouard's *La Vieux Lachine et le Massacre du 5 Aout, 1689* (Montreal, 1889).

addressed to " Francis Nicholson, Esquire, Our Lieutenant Governor and Commander-in-Chief of our Province of New York in America, and in his absence, to such as for the time being take care for the preserving the peace and administering the laws in our said Province of New York." [1] Nicholson had long since abandoned his government; but two of his three councilors claimed the dispatch as addressed to them. They had no power to administer the laws and would not have kept the peace for one instant if they could have fought with any chance of success. On the other hand, Leisler was keeping the peace as well as he could and was administering whatever laws were in force in the province. He drove the claimant councilors from his presence as " Popishly affected, Dogs and Rogues," [2] claiming that the letter was an acknowledgment of his right to rule.

Up to this time the people at Albany, inspired by the presence of Nicholas Bayard who had escaped from New York, had held aloof from the Leislerians. The officials at Albany seem to have been quite independent of those at New York and to have acted on their own responsibility. Their chief was Robert Livingston. He ventured to predict that the present movement in England would be no more lasting than Monmouth's Rebellion had been. When the accession of William and Mary could no longer be questioned, the Albany officials acknowledged their authority, but refused to recognize the rightfulness of Leisler's rule. In February, 1690, an event occurred which

---

[1] The same phraseology was used by the revolutionary government in England in addressing other colonial governments; for instance, the order commanding that Andros and his companions should be sent to England was addressed " To such as for the time being take care for preserving the peace and administering the laws in Our Colony of Massachusetts Bay in New England in America." See Massachusetts Colonial Society's *Publications*, ii.

[2] Brodhead's *New York*, ii, 597.

induced them to welcome the aid of almost any one. Frontenac was now again at the head of affairs in New France. Recognizing that the easiest way to overawe the Iroquois was to strike at them through the English, he dispatched a party in midwinter to deal a blow at New York. Eluding the Iroquois patrols, two hundred and ten men, of whom ninety-six were Indians, on the night of February 9, 1690, entered the open gate of the frontier village of Schenectady which was guarded only by two dummy sentries made of snow. The inhabitants were all in their houses, entirely unsuspicious of danger. In a short time sixty human beings were dead and the invaders marching away with twenty-seven prisoners. A score or so of the colonists escaped to Albany.[1] This disaster made the Albany settlers more conciliatory; they surrendered to Leisler's agent and son-in-law, Jacob Milborne. The revolution in New York was complete.

In New England social and political causes may be said to have dominated the movement; in New York racial heterogeneity had much to do with the unfortunate course of the Revolution in that province; in Maryland religious and economic as well as political factors were the cause of divisions of public opinion. Looking backward, one of the most memorable features in Maryland history is the religious freedom which prevailed there under the rule of Cecil and Charles Calvert, second and third Barons Baltimore; but this toleration was distasteful to the majority of her people. The great mass of the Maryland colonists were Protestants of one kind or another, varying from Church of England men to members of the Society of Friends. The Quakers there, as elsewhere, were advocates of religious

[1] Brodhead's *New York*, ii, 608; *Andros Tracts*, iii, 114; New York Historical Society's *Collections*, 1869, p. 165; Massachusetts Historical Society's *Proceedings*, 1878, p. 104; *Documentary History of New York*, i, 297-312.

freedom ; but the rest of the Protestants were strongly opposed to the toleration of Roman Catholics, for this was the precise form that religious freedom assumed in Maryland. It was likely that the first news of the Protestant Revolution in England would band the Protestants of Maryland together in opposition to their Roman Catholic rulers.

Another cause of grievance was the unrepresentative character of the Maryland Assembly. Originally the right to vote had been enjoyed by practically all the free male inhabitants of the colony ; but in 1670, Cecil Calvert, now approaching the end of his life, by an instruction to his governor restricted the franchise to those who possessed a freehold of fifty acres or forty pounds of visible estate. The apportionment also was extremely irregular. In 1670 Baltimore had directed that each county of the province should elect four delegates,[1] but that of the four only two should be summoned to the Assembly. This arrangement was eminently favorable to the lord proprietor, but was greatly disliked by the freemen.

The Baltimores enjoyed the distinction of being the most successful of the few English proprietors who made colonization pay ; but they were absentee landlords for the most part, and absentee landlordism was not accordant with American economic and political conditions. Everywhere, throughout the colonies, the settlers wished to own their farms outright. The Baltimores had been liberal landlords, but the Marylanders might well contrast the conditions on which they held their farms with those

[1] *Maryland Archives* (Council, 1667–87), p. 77; F. E. Sparks's "Causes of the Maryland Revolution of 1689" in *Johns Hopkins Studies*, xiv, Nos. xi–xii, p. 77. This qualification was recognized by law in 1688 and continued throughout the colonial period with the addition that in 1718 Roman Catholics were disfranchised. As to the apportionment, see Mereness's *Maryland as a Proprietary Province,* 201

which governed the holdings of the planters of Virginia or of the farmers of Pennsylvania. Moreover, wise and liberal as they were, the Baltimores manipulated the franchise and apportionment of representation in their province with a view to maintaining that political supremacy which seemed to be a necessary safeguard for their interests and the well-being of their fellow-religionists. It now unmistakably appeared that the rule of a Roman Catholic feudal proprietor was distasteful to the mass of the people of the province.[1]

In the first part of the month of January, 1688, the Maryland Assembly had debated with some degree of heat the question of taking an oath of fidelity to the lord proprietor. Later on, they had passed an act providing for an anniversary day forever in celebration of the birth of the Prince of Wales. The inhabitants of the Roman Catholic hundreds of St. Mary's County had voted an address to the king, congratulating him upon the birth of the Old Pretender. "We have," they said, "beheld and admired your Majesty like the sun in the firmament, not only dispersing all malicious and threatening clouds of disloyalty, but also making us and our posterity happy by the prolific virtues."[2] When William's success seemed assured, the Protestants in the colony took the matter into their own hands.

The governor of Maryland, or president, to give him his official title, was a singularly inefficient person, named William Joseph. Rumors of a Popish plot were now pertinaciously diffused throughout the colony; these generally took the form of an assertion that the "Popish administration, supported by Papists" and leagued with the Indians,

---

[1] See on this point a letter from Baltimore written in July, 1681, in Scharf's *Maryland*, i, 285.

[2] *Calendars of State Papers, America and West Indies, 1685–1688*, p. 616.

intended to massacre the Protestants. President Joseph
caused the dispensers of these reports to be arrested, which
only gave them added verity. Kenelm Cheseldyn, several
times Speaker of the Assembly, and Colonel Henry Jowles
were the leaders of the opposition, but the movement generally takes its name from John Coode. He had long been
in opposition to the Roman Catholic government and had
been arrested in 1681 on the charge of sedition in declaring
that the " Papists and Indians were joined together." [1] He
now became the head of an Association for the Defense of
the Protestant Religion and was the first signer of the Protestant Declaration.[2] His true character is hid amidst
the vituperation of Maryland writers. In 1696 he was
dismissed from his office of lieutenant colonel of militia on
account of blasphemy and was reported to be " a man of
most flagicious life and conversation, as to Drunckenness,
Swearing & all such debaucheries " ; [3] but this seems to
be the only evidence of the badness of his character.
Whatever their failings may have been, Coode, Cheseldyn, and Jowles were successful revolutionists, possibly
because the opposition was feeble, owing to the Protestants outnumbering the Roman Catholics, ten to one.
The Associators seized St. Mary's in July, 1689. They
captured or dispersed such Roman Catholics as sought to
resist them. They addressed William and Mary in loyal
phrase, declaring that they had seized the government for
their Majesties' service. They held an assembly which was

---

[1] *Maryland Archives* (Council, 1671–
81), p. 389; for other matter on this
subject, see pp. 269, 301, 383, of the same
volume. For the trials of Coode and his
companions, see *ibid.* (Assembly, 1678–
83). His name is frequently written
" Coad " or " Code " in contemporary
documents.

[2] *Ibid.* (Council, 1687–93), p. 99. This
volume contains a mass of documents
many of which repeat one another. The
doings of the Associators' Assembly are
described in the same publication (General Assembly, 1684–92, p. 231). The
most important documents are given by
Scharf in his *Maryland*, i, 308 and fol.

[3] *Ibid.* (Council, 1693–96), p. 488.

much more truly representative than the Convention Parliament which made William king or any that had met in Maryland for a generation. During the interval between the overthrow of the proprietary government and the coming of the first royal governor, they ruled the province with a moderation that was quite unusual at that time.

The new rulers of England might well have recognized their partisans in the plantations and have rewarded their faithfulness to "Revolution principles" by continuing them in the possession of those governments which they had wrenched from James's adherents. Instead of so doing, William and his advisers proceeded on the assumption that colonists followed the condition of the mother country and were as amenable to misrule after the overturn in England as they had been before it. In place of inaugurating a new policy, they merely reorganized the colonial administration on the lines of the old system.

NOTES

I. The Revolution in England. — The course of the "Glorious
Revolution of 1688–89" can best be traced in the *Lords Journals*
(vol. xiv); *Commons Journals* (vol. x); Grey's *Debates*[1] (vol. ix);
and the *Manuscripts of the House of Lords*.[2] Of the diaries and
contemporary writings the following are useful: Gilbert Burnet's
History of His Own Time (ed. 1833, vols. iii and iv); H. C. Fox-
croft's *Supplement to Burnet's History ;* Narcissus Luttrell's *Brief
Historical Relation of State Affairs* (vols. i, 1678–89, ii, 1690–
92) ; and Thomas Somerville's *Political Transactions* (Dublin,
1793). *A Collection of Papers Relating to the Present Juncture of
Affairs in England, 1688, 1689* (twelve parts entitled "A Second
Collection"), contains contemporary reprints of very many of the
most important papers of the time. Many pamphlets were published in the Netherlands which have never been properly corre-
lated with the English documents.

II. The Deposition of Andros. — There are several original accounts
of the events of April 18 and 19, 1689, in Boston. They are generally brief; but from them a connected story can be constructed with
very few doubts as to the accuracy of the main points. Of these
Byfield's *Account of the Late Revolution*[3] is the best known. Prince's
letter to Thomas Hinckly[4] is earlier in time, but not so detailed.
Palfrey prints,[5] "for what it may be thought worth," an account by
John Riggs, a "servant" of Sir Edmund Andros, which was presented to the Lords of the Committee of Trade on July 22, 1689,
and also descriptive matter from Captain George of the *Rose* frigate
and from Edward Randolph. Of the secondary accounts, that in
Palfrey's *New England* (iii, 576–590) is the best; but he gives the
impression that the Massachusetts people acted without knowledge
of William's success, which was not the case. The accounts in
Hutchinson's *Massachusetts* and Toppan's *Edward Randolph* are also
full and important.

[1] Anchitell Grey's *Debates of the
House of Commons from the year 1667
to the year 1694*, London, 1763.

[2] Royal Historical Manuscripts Commission's *Reports*, xi, Part ii (1678–88);
xii, Part vi (1689–90).

[3] *Andros Tracts*, i.

[4] Massachusetts Historical Society's
Collections, Fourth Series, v, 192; Hutchinson's *Massachusetts*, third edition, i,
334; Toppan's *Randolph*, ii, 90 note.

[5] *History of New England*, iii, 587
note.

III. The Revolution in New York. — The " Leisler Papers " in the New York Historical Society's *Collections*, 1868, pp. 241 and fol., contain a mass of information on this episode and should be supplemented by the third volume of the *New York Colonial Documents*. On p. 641 of the·latter work is printed Bayard's "Narrative of Occurrences in New York" (April–December, 1689), which gives an anti-Leislerian view. With these should be studied the volume of the *Calendars of State Papers* for the year 1689. The account in Brodhead's *New York* (ii, 564 and fol.) is vigorous, but is exceedingly prejudiced. The language employed by the principals in the conflict as to one another is so harsh and their denial of the truth of each other's statements so frequent and so pointed, that it is exceedingly difficult to come to a decision as to the relative merits of the Leisler and Bayard sides to the controversy. There is an interesting letter by Dongan to the Lords of Trade describing New York in 1687, *Calendars of State Papers, America and West Indies, 1685–1688*, pp. 326–336.

(From Richard Blome's *Present State of His Majesties Isles and Territories in America*, London, 1687.)

216

CHAPTER VIII

THE RECONSTRUCTED COLONIAL SYSTEM

GRANDSON of the first Charles, William of Orange was by blood partly an Englishman; but in those qualities that set him above the rest of mankind he was essentially a Dutchman. He had slight sympathy with English political ideas or modes of action; he was a great administrator rather than a great political leader. Given a free hand, he would have reformed the organization of the empire to secure greater vigor in government;[1] but the insecurity of his situation in England and his activity in continental wars prevented this. Obliged to let matters within the empire take their course, he necessarily sought to continue in office the best administrators whom he found there, unless they had been too friendly with James and had not repented in time. The most notable of these officials who had to do with colonial affairs was William Blathwayt, whose highest recommendation is that he was the trusted servant of three such different personages as Charles, James, and William, although according to Bolingbroke he was the poorest tool " that ever dirtied paper." [2]

---

[1] The colonial policy of William III is summarized by Egerton in his *British Colonial Policy*, 115.

[2] Royal Historical Manuscripts Commission's *Reports*, " Welbeck Abbey," v, 202.

William Blathwayt first becomes prominent at the time of the Popish Plot, when his skill in reading cipher dispatches introduced him to leading men. He had begun official life in the service of Sir William Temple and had transacted business for the English government in Italy, Sweden, and Denmark. He had long been interested in colonial affairs as secretary of the Committee of the Privy Council on Trade and Plantations. In 1687 he was also one of the clerks of the Privy Council and secretary at war, which position at that time seems to have been of a clerical nature. These offices yielded him above two thousand pounds [1] annually, besides what he took in as presents and fees. In addition to his other offices, Blathwayt was surveyor and auditor general [2] of the colonies. As auditor general, it was his duty to approve the expenditures of the royal provinces, and we find him receiving a grant of one hundred pounds from Massachusetts for " passing the accounts," [3] which is probably only one of numerous payments of the kind. As surveyor general, he was the official head of the customs service in the plantations. Blathwayt's administrative abilities and linguistic

[1] The secretaryship of the Committee of the Privy Council on Trade and Plantations alone yielded him a salary of nearly fifteen hundred pounds per annum, the equivalent of twenty-two or twenty-three thousand dollars at the present day. See Royal Historical Manuscripts Commission's *Reports*, xiv, Part vi, p. 166.

[2] Blathwayt's commission as " Surveyor and Auditor General of all our revenues arising in America " is printed at length in *Massachusetts Colony Records*, v, 521, and is followed by Blathwayt's " deputation " to Edward Randolph. A better view of the duties attached to this office can be obtained from the instructions which Horatio Walpole, Blathwayt's successor, gave to Paul Dudley in 1717 as deputy surveyor and auditor of his Majesty's revenue in Massachusetts and New Hampshire (Ms. in the library of the Massachusetts Historical Society). Dudley is instructed to examine all accounts of public revenue in these provinces; to acquaint himself as to all " Rents, Revenues, Duties, and Profits " which have accrued or shall accrue to the king, and to transmit to Walpole all acts relating to public revenue, etc. A detailed discussion of the duties of the surveyor and auditor general is in *A Miscellaneous Essay Concerning the Courses pursued by Great Britain in the Affairs of her Colonies* (London, 1755), 104-118.

[3] *Massachusetts Province Laws*, vii, 435; Mr. Goodell, the editor, thinks that this was a payment made out of gratitude; probably it was in the nature of a bribe.

talents commended him to William, who attached him to his person and advanced him in position and fortune. He was a good example of the influential, permanent under official who has always exercised great power in the actual operation of the English constitution, sometimes unhappily.

On his accession to power, William found colonial affairs in the hands of the Lords Committee of the Privy Council. He replaced the members of this committee by those who were in his interest, but Blathwayt continued to serve as its secretary. In 1691 William found a moment to attend to colonial affairs. The Lords of Trade advised him that it was an opportune time to bring the colonies into a closer dependence upon the crown, but he was deaf to the suggestion. On the other hand, he did not give his confidence to those colonial leaders who had secured the Protestant succession in America at considerable risk to themselves. By a wise use of the opportunities which events had placed in his hands, William might have laid the foundations for lasting concord between the two great portions of the English people; but the outcome was quite different. In recent years, English writers have united in objurgating George III and the stupid, ignorant politicians who guided England's affairs in the fifteen years before 1775; on their shoulders have been laid the faults which brought about the American Revolution; but the causes of that cataclysm lie farther back and may be largely found in the settlement of the imperial constitution in the years immediately following William's accession to power.

The imperial constitution might have developed in three ways: the plantations might have been governed directly from England, they might have enjoyed local self-government, or they might have been ruled on a composite system. Colonial affairs were so dislocated in 1689 that charters and precedents might easily have been abandoned and a system of absolute control established which would have enjoyed a long and prosperous existence — from a material point of view. A less capable and less self-assertive race of colonists would perhaps have developed in America; but on the other hand, England would probably have continued to enjoy the profits to be derived from the development of the resources of North America for many years after 1775. Some such scheme was actually proposed at this time, but was set aside by William. The second solution of the problem would have given the administration to the colonists themselves, relying upon the shackles of interest and the bonds of kinship to maintain the connection between the mother country and her sturdy offspring; but any such policy was impossible at the end of the seventeenth century, because it was opposed to the teaching of the mercantilist school of economists and to the political instincts of the members of the Whig aristocracy and of the great Tory families. To the mercantilists, colonies existed for the material benefit of the mother country; to the aristocracy, their principal recommendation was the comfortable offices which they provided for the dependents of the English ruling classes. The policy which was adopted harmonized with English political ideas in recognizing existing facts and in proceeding by a series of compromises. The plan was to reëstablish colonial representative institutions substantially on the footing of 1670, before Charles and James began their "reformations," to bring the colonies more within the scope of Parliamentary legislation, and to increase the power of the royal governors.

The "Glorious Revolution" and attendant legislation greatly limited the royal power in England; but in the colonies, the king's prerogative remained as great as ever, since the Triennial Acts, the Habeas Corpus Act,[1] and the remedial portion of the Act of Settlement did not extend to them. Meantime, ever since the Restoration, colonial institutions had been developing in a direction contrary to those of England.

The divergence which already existed between the institutions of the mother country and those of the colonies is clearly discernible from a consideration of the position of the holder of a high executive office in England and in the plantations. The Act of Settlement of 1701 [2] provided for the succession to the crown, conferring it upon the house of Hanover, and also provided that, in the future, English judges should hold office during good behavior. The law furthermore declared that no officeholder could sit in the House of Commons. This requirement was found to be so incompatible with English institutional ideas that within a few years this disability of executive officials was modified and certain of them were permitted to occupy seats in the House of Commons upon reëlection after the acceptance of an office.[3] Following on this, the cabinet system was established in England, the ministers being drawn from that party which was in a majority in the House of Commons and acting together as a body. It was in this way that the executive government and the representative element in the legislative branch were kept

[1] See on this point A. H. Carpenter's paper on "Habeas Corpus in the Colonies" in *American Historical Review*, viii, 18. On p. 24 he prints the proclamation of Governor Spotswood of 1710, extending the writ to Virginia. Colonial bail laws often provided the safeguard associated with the writ of *habeas corpus*, as that of Virginia of 1645. Hening's *Statutes*, i, 305.

[2] 12, 13 William III, Cap. 2 (*Statutes of the Realm*, vii, p. 636). The importance of this act in the history of American institutions was pointed out to me by Mr. A. Lawrence Lowell.

[3] 6 Anne, Cap. 41, §§ 24, 25 (*Statutes of the Realm*, viii, p. 742).

in harmony — with the added aid of an elaborate system of bribery. In the colonies the case was radically different, for there the executive officers represented the authority of England, — always excepting Connecticut and Rhode Island,[1] — while the elected branch of the colonial legislatures represented the wishes of the voters in the several plantations: in England, the interests of the two great branches of government were identical; in the colonies, they were in opposition.

In the reign of William the colonies were no longer infant communities, but had already attained the proportions of many full-grown states, as they contained more than two hundred thousand inhabitants. In 1695 the population of New York City was about five thousand;[2] in 1697 Penn thought that there were twelve thousand people living within the limits of Philadelphia;[3] and Boston was a thriving port of seven thousand. As to the colonies themselves, Virginia contained nearly sixty thousand inhabitants and Massachusetts nearly fifty thousand.[4] All the English settlements along the coast were rapidly growing in population and in wealth. The words " colonies " and " plantations " hardly describe their circumstances. Nevertheless, Englishmen in England still

---

[1] These were practically self-governing colonies; in the following constitutional discussions regard will be had only to the royal and proprietary provinces except where Connecticut and Rhode Island are specifically mentioned.

[2] John Miller estimated the number of families in the city at 855, which gives a population of 4275. See Miller's *New York Considered and Improved*, p. 54.

[3] " Journal of the Board of Trade " Ms., November 1, 1697 (" Philadelphia Transcripts," x, 333).

[4] George Bancroft in his *History of the United States* (original edition, ii, 450) estimates the population in 1688–89.

His figures are adopted with some changes by Franklin B. Dexter in his " Estimates of Population in the American Colonies " in the American Antiquarian Society's *Proceedings*, New Series, v, 22. They are approximately as follows: New Hampshire, 6000; Massachusetts, including Maine and New Plymouth, 48,000; Rhode Island and Providence Plantations, 5000; Connecticut, 20,000; New York, 20,000; New Jersey, 10,000; Pennsylvania and Delaware, 12,000; Maryland, 20,000; Virginia, 58,000; Carolina, 5000. By sections: New England, 79,000; Middle Colonies, 42,000; Chesapeake Colonies, 78,000, and Carolina, 5000.

regarded them as settlers and as subjects of England; Englishmen in the colonies looked upon themselves as possessing the rights of Englishmen, which had been guaranteed by Magna Charta and a long succession of memorable statutes.[1] The former regarded the colonial governments as public service corporations;[2] the latter looked upon them as having the same attributes as the government of England. The former regarded the colonial assemblies as similar to the council of an English city; the latter looked upon them as possessing powers similar to those which were exercised by the English House of Commons. Nevertheless the colonists generally acknowledged the binding force of laws passed by the imperial legislature.[3]

After 1689 the colonists claimed those rights which Englishmen in England had secured in the Bill of Rights and the Act of Settlement; but the royal authorities refused to acknowledge that colonial rights had in any way increased.[4] In the earlier day, in the time of James I

---

[1] The distinction is well seen in the action of the Maryland Assembly in passing a bill to recognize Magna Charta as a part of the law of the province and the disallowance of this measure by the king, because the attorney general expressed himself as uncertain "how far the enacting thereof will be agreeable to the constitution of this colony or consistent with the royal prerogative" (Chalmers's *History of the Revolt*, i, 259). Sir John Somers advised the disallowance of the Massachusetts Habeas Corpus Act because the right to that writ "had never been conferred on the colonists by a king of England," evidently regarding the guarantee of a speedy trial in Magna Charta as inapplicable to the colonial status.

[2] Soame Jenyns stated in 1765 that the charters empowered the colonies to make by-laws like those of corporations,

"Objections to the American Tax Considered" in *Works*, p. 425.

[3] Chalmers (*Introduction to the Revolt*, i, 284, 285 note) gives two instances in 1698 and 1701 of the colonists denying the validity of acts of Parliament in the colonies because the settlers sent no representatives to Whitehall; but Chalmers and the officials whom he quotes were on the lookout for colonial opposition.

[4] The most notable example of this non-extension of the remedial statutes to the colonies is the famous clause in the Act of Settlement, that judges should hold office during good behavior instead of during pleasure. The assemblies of the royal provinces time and again, by various means, tried to secure this reform; but the Lords of Trade resisted because permanent colonial judicial tenure would tend "to lessen that just Dependence which the Colonies ought to have upon

and Sir Edward Coke, the king had governed the newly settled plantations by force of the prerogative, and the great chief justice had denied the absolute supremacy of Parliament. Now that the legislative branch clearly dominated the executive in England, was it reasonable to expect that the colonists would quietly submit to the domination of the legislative by the executive in America, especially when the legislative represented their interests and the executive those of England? The course of constitutional controversy was further complicated by the fact that any victory which the colonists might win over the representative of the king could be set aside by act of Parliament. The king's power was limited, for, as Sir William Jones had informed James II, the monarch could no more grant a commission to levy money on his subjects in the plantations " without their consent by an assembly than they could discharge themselves from their allegiance";[1] but Parliament by act could legislate for the colonies in all cases whatsoever, including taxation. Theoretically, the royal prerogative flourished with undiminished vigor in the plantations; the governors were expected to obey the royal commands; but if they went beyond the legal exercise of their powers, they were practically irresponsible. It is true that they had to take oaths of office and were amenable to the court of King's Bench for oppression or for any offense which they had committed contrary to the laws of England;[2] but they could not be impeached in the colonies[3] or brought to

the Government of the Mother Country," *New York Colonial Documents*, vii, 475.

[1] Brodhead's *New York*, ii, 418.

[2] Act of 11 William III, Cap. 12 (Ruffhead's *Statutes at Large*, iv, 49). See also Note I, p. 250, for the case of Fabrigas *vs.* Mostyn.

[3] In 1703 Northey gave an opinion to the effect that colonial governors might be arrested and prosecuted in the colonies after the expiration of their term of office by individual colonists for arbitrary and illegal imprisonment; but there are no instances of this in the continental colonies. *New York Colonial Documents*, iv, 1033.

justice there for stealing; nor could they be tried anywhere for offenses which were regarded as crimes in the
colony over which they ruled, but were not so regarded by
English law.

Almost at the close of the colonial period, Lord Chief
Justice Mansfield, in the famous case of Campbell *vs.* Hall,[1]
laid down the general rule that the king having once parted
with a portion of his prerogative could not resume it, except by the authorization of an act of Parliament. Earlier
in 1705 Attorney General Northey had declared that the
government of the chartered colonies "cannot be arbitrarily assumed except by act of parliament or by due process
of law."[2] The king could, however, exercise power even
in chartered colonies, which certainly nullified portions of
the royal letters patent. In southern New England were
the two self-governing colonies of Connecticut and Rhode
Island, which had quietly resumed their charter governments
upon the downfall of Andros. For years the representatives of English authority had looked with eager eyes on
the military strength of New England. Massachusetts and
New Hampshire, by an abuse of power, had been put directly
under a semi-royal government; might not the strength and
resources of the two remaining chartered governments likewise be brought within the sweep of royal action? William appointed Colonel Fletcher, governor of New York, to
command the Connecticut military forces and Governor
Sir William Phips of Massachusetts to command those of
Rhode Island. The Connecticut people protested and
pointed to their charter; but the law officers of the crown
declared that, although the charter gave the ordinary administration in civil and military affairs to the Connecticut
corporation, the king, nevertheless, might appoint a com-

[1] See Note II, p. 250.   [2] Chalmers's *Opinions*, i, 351.

mander in chief of the military forces of that colony. Again Governor Dudley of Massachusetts was appointed to command the military forces of Rhode Island. He repaired to that colony to publish his commission, "whereupon the Inhabitants showed little respect to Her Majesties authority," and paid no regard to Dudley's declaration "that the militia is by act of Parliament vested in the crown,"[1] all of which impelled the Lords of Trade to advise the appointment of a royal governor for Rhode Island.

The "Revolution" government was even more destructive of chartered rights in its dealings with the proprietors of Maryland and Pennsylvania. Inasmuch as Lord Baltimore was a Roman Catholic and William Penn was a personal friend of the fugitive king, their continuance in power seemed to be dangerous. Lord Holt, the chief justice, was applied to and declared it to be his opinion that the king, on the ground of necessity, might appoint a governor to exercise jurisdiction in Maryland who should nevertheless be responsible to the proprietor for the profits which might be derived from lands and other sources.[2] Instead of ap-

[1] "Report of the Board of Trade and Plantations," 1703, in *New York Public Library Bulletin*, 1907, p. 469. Cornbury made a similar statement when asking for the command of the militia of Connecticut and New Jersey. See *New York Colonial Documents*, iv, 912. The act of 13 Charles II, which was law in 1760, begins as follows: "Forasmuch as within all His Majesties Realmes and Dominions the sole Supreme Government Command and Disposition of the Militia and of all Forces by Sea and Land . . . is and by the Lawes of England ever was the undoubted Right of His Majesty." The remainder of the act clearly refers to the home lands alone. 13 Charles II, Stat. i, Cap. vi (*Statutes of the Realm*, v, 308). See also Blackstone's *Commentaries*, Book i, ch. vii (fourth edition, i, 262). Thomas Trevor, the solicitor general, gave the following opinion: "That notwithstanding anything in the said Charters or Grants [of Connecticut and New York] that their Majesties by virtue of their Prerogative and Soverainty over those Colonies, which is not granted from the Crown to the Gov[r] and Company, nor to the proprietors by any of the Chart[rs] may appoint Governors for those places with such powers and authorities for the Government thereof, and for raising men and furnishing Provisions for the necessary defence of his subjects and the neighbouring Colonies against their Enemies as their Majesties shall in their great wisdom judge reasonable." *New York Colonial Documents*, iv, 1. Fletcher's commission as commander of the Connecticut militia is in *ibid.*, iv, 29.

[2] His words were "The king may by his commission constitute a governor [for

pointing Kenelm Cheseldyn, or some other leader of the Protestant Association in the colony, the king selected an Englishman, Lionel Copley, to serve as chief executive in this crisis. He was a member of the Established Church. On his arrival in the colony he threw his influence on the Protestant side and Maryland definitely passed out of the list of Roman Catholic colonial enterprises. In 1692 Benjamin Fletcher, governor of New York, was directed to take over the administration of Pennsylvania and the Territories on Delaware. Penn soon cleared himself of the charge of undue friendship to the king in exile and his American possessions were restored to him. Maryland, however, remained under royal rule for many years, until the accession of a Protestant to the Baltimore inheritance in 1715 removed further excuse for the sequestration of the jurisdiction and the proprietor was restored to his full rights.[1] Maryland was not again removed from the rule of that family until the American Revolution. Under the circumstances, the seizure of the government of these provinces may have been necessary as a matter of policy; but the further proceedings are hard to justify from any point of view.

Considering the temporary nature of the royal governments in the sequestrated provinces, the least possible interference with existing forms should have been made. Instead of recognizing the institutions peculiar to these proprietary governments and directing the interim governors to administer the laws which they found in force in Maryland and Pennsylvania,[2] the commissions issued to

Maryland] whose authority will be legal, though he must be responsible to Lord Baltimore for the profits." Chalmers's *Opinions*, i, 30, and see also the same author's *History of the Revolt*, i, 257.

[1] Scharf's *Maryland*, i, 381.
[2] Even Attorney General Northey, who was a great stickler for form, said that as to the civil government, "such governor is not to alter any of the rules

Copley and Fletcher were similar to those of the governors of the royal provinces of Virginia and New York. Fletcher, upon his arrival at Philadelphia, declared that all the laws of Pennsylvania were null and void, and summoned an assembly like that of New York without paying any attention to Penn's constitutional arrangements. Naturally, the people were alarmed and opposed him in every possible way; but the further history of Fletcher's dealings with the Quakers will be treated elsewhere.

The conditions which obtained in Maryland were very unlike those which prevailed in Penn's province, because the religious system and the political system were both disliked by the majority of the colonists. It fell out, therefore, that when Copley summoned an assembly like that of Virginia, the people joyfully acquiesced and joined with him in passing laws to give permanence to the new order of things. Copley died in 1693, but his successors, Nicholson, Blakiston, and Seymour, were in full accord with his policy. The legislation of the next few years remodeled the institutions of Maryland. One act authorized the confirmation of titles to granted lands as fully and absolutely "as if a patent from his Lordship had been granted for the same";[1] another organized a land office,[2] another repealed all the laws made before the Revolution.[3] The system of representation was reorganized according to colonial ideas,[4] public education also received attention,[5] the Church of England was established,[6] and the Toleration Act recognized as law within the province.[7]

William pursued a middle course as to Massachusetts:

---

of propriety or methods of proceedings in civil causes, established pursuant to the charters." Chalmers's *Opinions*, i, 31.

[1] Bacon's *Laws of Maryland*, 1692, ch. viii.

[2] *Ibid.*, 1692, ch. xxx.

[3] *Ibid.*, 1692, ch. lxxxiv.

[4] *Ibid.*, 1692, ch. lxxvi.

[5] *Ibid.*, 1694, ch. i; 1696, ch. xvii.

[6] *Ibid.*, 1702, ch. i; 1704, chs. xxviii, lvi.

[7] *Ibid.*, 1706, ch. viii.

its old government was not restored, a royal governor was
not sent over to administer affairs until permanent arrangements could be made ; but a new charter was issued, establishing a hybrid organization which will be described later
when treating of the political contests in that colony.
In New York a royal government was established which
became typical of the later royal provinces. The people
of New Jersey were permitted to struggle on with their
anomalous institutions ; but the governors of New York
continued to throttle the commerce of the colony on the
western side of the lower Hudson in the interests of the
treasury of their own province. This led to a collusive
suit in 1700,[1] between Jeremiah Basse, who claimed to be
governor of a part of New Jersey, and Lord Bellomont,
governor of New York. The case was tried in England
before Lord Chief Justice Holt and was the occasion of
some interesting remarks by that distinguished jurist.
Among other things he said that the question of whether
New Jersey was a separate colony or not rested upon its
having an independent assembly, and that the king could
resume the government of proprietary provinces at will.
Deeds of lease and release and royal letters from deceased
Stuart monarchs seem to have little interest for him. He
acted quite in the spirit of Attorney General Northey and Solicitor General Harcourt, who were of the opinion that there
was nothing in the charters of Connecticut and Rhode Island
to "exclude your majesty (who have a right to govern all
your subjects) from naming a governor on your majesty's
behalf for those colonies at all times." [2] Charters, indeed,
were a frail support for colonial rights. Ministers, parliaments, and judges, as well as colonial assemblies, were

[1] The essential extracts from the re-   399) are reprinted in the *Harvard Law
port of the case (*Modern Reports*, xii,   Review*, xviii, 483.
                                     [2] Chalmers's *Opinions*, i, 32.

guided by the actualities of the situation more than by theoretical claims. Had colonial affairs been conducted in a less haphazard way in England, and had better officials been sent to safeguard imperial interests in America, the free institutions of the colonies might have been crushed under the weight of the bureaucracy in London.

In 1695 an effort was made to reform the colonial administration by taking the control of colonial affairs away from the Committee of the Privy Council and giving it to an outside board. For a time the matter was in suspense when the bill to establish a Council of Trade by act of Parliament[1] was introduced into the House of Commons. The members of the new board were to be named in the law, as was the practice in many money bills. This aroused the king's interest and William appointed eight Commissioners of Trade and Plantations, May 15, 1696. Among the members of the new board were John Locke and William Blathwayt, both of whom had been long interested in the management of colonial affairs. The first commissioner was John Egerton, third Earl of Bridgewater, who had shown great abilities in administration and stood high in the confidence of the king. In addition to the eight appointed members, the Keeper of the Great Seal, the First Lord of the Treasury, the First Lord of the Admiralty, the Lord High Admiral, the Principal Secretaries of State, and the Chancellor of the Exchequer for the time being were authorized to attend when necessary and when other public service permitted. The board might ask the advice of the Attorney and Solicitor Gen-

[1] For the action in Parliament, see Chandler's *History of the House of Commons*, iii, 19, and Hansard's *Parliamentary Debates*, v, 977. See also Narcissus Luttrell's *Brief Historical Relation of State Affairs*, iii, 560, 563, 568; iv, 7, 11, 58; Abel Boyer's *History of King William III*, iii, 173; Burnet's *History of My Own Times* (second edition), iv, 294; Fox Bourne's *John Locke*, iii, 348.

erals, or of other law officers of the crown. The great officers of state seldom attended the meetings of the board, except when, as in the case of the Earl of Bridgewater, they held one of those important positions in addition to their place on this body. The board[1] frequently consulted the law officers of the crown until 1718, when its legal business became so heavy that special counsel was assigned to it. The quorum of the board was five; for the first thirty or thirty-five years of its existence it met three or four times in each week. It speaks well for the attention which its members paid to business that in all that time it seldom adjourned for lack of a quorum. As the years went by, however, inferior men were appointed, fewer meetings were held, fewer members attended those that were held, and less and less important business was transacted. After 1740 membership on the board was regarded as a joke: at one time an unusually assiduous member went by the sobriquet of "Trade," while his fellow-commissioners were referred to as "The Board."[2] The commissioners were generally denominated the Lords of Trade, thus perpetuating the title of the older organization, although nearly all of its members were commoners.

The matters committed to the new Board of Trade and Plantations were important.[3] The commissioners were to examine the state and condition of the general trade of

[1] There is a convenient list of members of the Board of Trade, with dates, in *New York Colonial Documents*, iii, pp. xiii–xix.

[2] The Lords of Trade were a consultative body only after 1766, as appears from the following Order in Council: —

"For the future also all measures relative to commerce and the colonies shall originate and be taken up in the *Ministerial executive* offices of Gov'm't their Lordships acting as a Board of Advice upon such points only as shall be referred from His Majesty," etc. *Calendars of State Papers, Home Office, 1766–1769*, No. 256.

[3] The commission is printed at length in *New York Colonial Documents*, iv, 145–148; it is also transcribed at length in the "Board of Trade Journals" (Ms.) in the Library of the Pennsylvania Historical Society, and is in *Lords Manuscripts*, New Series, ii, 416.

England, of the several particular trades in all foreign parts, and how the same are advanced or decayed and the occasion thereof ; what trades are hurtful, what beneficial, how the beneficial trades may be improved or extended and the hurtful ones discouraged. They were to ascertain the principal obstructions to trade and the means of removing the same and how trade might be secured and protected. They were to inquire how useful manufactures might be further improved and new ones introduced. They were to ascertain the proper methods of employing the poor and promoting the fisheries. They were to inform themselves of the condition of the plantations, of the administration of government and justice therein, of the "Limits of Soyle," and the products of the colonies. They were to determine how the colonies might be improved and made more useful to the mother country. They were especially to ascertain what staple commodities and manufactures were likely to be useful, and what would probably be harmful, and how the useful ones might be encouraged and the harmful ones discouraged or destroyed. Finally, they were to oversee the government of the colonies, advise as to the approval or disallowance of colonial laws, hear complaints of oppression and maladministration in the plantations, and require an account of the expenditure of public moneys. In the carrying out of these functions they might examine witnesses under oath and report in writing to the king or to the Privy Council.

The number and extent of the matters committed to the new board were too numerous and too important to be successfully handled by any one set of men, however assiduous they might be in the performance of their duties. The trade of England and colonial legislation

were often intimately related, but each formed a vast
subject for investigation and regulation. As exhibiting
the multifariousness of the tasks set for the new Lords of
Trade, it may be said that they undertook to inquire into
the whole system of levying duties on imports and exports
with a view to improving the royal revenue; this they did
by perusing as a committee the "Book of Rates." To
comprehend this system might well have occupied the
time of any body of men for several years — in 1757
Henry Saxby needed nearly seven hundred octavo pages
occupied with tabulations and synopses to describe the
British customs in existence at that time. In the early
years of the century, the commissioners began an investigation of the conditions of life in Ireland, with a view to
the amelioration of poverty in that country; this was a
most worthy enterprise and one which has unsuccessfully
occupied much of the time of England's rulers from that
day to this. The improvement of the lot of the poor in
England also occupied their time and attention. Occasionally they read memorials and petitions and heard
witnesses as to the conditions of trade to the coast of
Africa and to the Far East. The greater part of their
time, however, was taken up with the affairs of the
American colonies. It must be remembered in this connection that they were interested in the administration
and prosperity of Jamaica, Barbados, Nevis, and other
West Indian islands, as well as with the colonies on the
continent. In point of fact their time was in many years
more taken up with the affairs of the islands than with
those of the continent. This was quite natural, because
many of the sugar plantations were owned by residents
of England and all of the islands were more directly under
the control of the English government than were the con-

tinental colonies. Moreover, the commerce of the sugar islands was nearly equal to that of the northern colonies in the earliest years.[1] In their attempt to exercise colonial administration, the Lords of Trade exhibited great zeal, as, for example, when they undertook to peruse the journals of the colonial assemblies and the minutes of colonial councils.[2] They listened to complaints of the acts of colonial governors on the part of aggrieved colonists and under officials; they heard the evidence of merchants interested in colonial trade and that of returned royal officials; and they listened to the suggestions of those who were supposed to be experts in affairs of trade and plantations, and read letter after letter from well-meaning officials in the colonies.[3] It may well be questioned whether William expected so great a display of energy on their part; if he had intended that the board should accomplish any important results, he would certainly have organized it differently and given it more power. Locke and some other members of the board may have received salaries of a thousand pounds apiece.[4] The commissioners also had a little money at their disposal for clerk hire, since the methods of that day as well as of this required an immense amount of letter writing and copying of documents — sometimes even of those which were presented to

---

[1] Exports from Great Britain to America and the West Indies.

	1739-56 average		1756-73 average
N.A.	£1,000,000	N.A.	£2,300,000
W.I.	700,000	W.I.	1,100,000

[Richard Champion] *Considerations on the Present Situation of Great Britain and the United States* (London, 1784), 31-33.

[2] In 1697 the board spent two days in examining the Journal of the Massachusetts House of Representatives and the Minutes of the Council of that province. "Journal of the Board of Trade" (Ms.), May 19, 20, 1697.

[3] On one occasion (May 23, 1704) the Lords of Trade wrote to a colonial officer that his "Letters contain mostly the same matter over and over again, and in such a method as renders them very difficult to us to understand; Wherefore we must advise you for the future onely to write plaine matter of fact, and in such a manner as may be less obscure." Board of Trade Mss. New England 40, Entry Book, E. 328.

[4] Fox Bourne's *John Locke*, ii, 349; but Locke's words may have referred to another office.

the board in printed form. In 1707 the office force of the board received salaries amounting to eleven hundred and fifty pounds,[1] of which the secretary received five hundred. The remaining six hundred and fifty pounds were divided between eight clerks, three doorkeepers and messengers, and " one necessary woman." The salary list shows that the Lords of Trade had an organized force of employees and that this was so small that the business of the board was at best very slowly performed.

The result of the attempt to do too much work with an insufficient force was that papers were often not read until weeks or months, and sometimes almost a year, had elapsed since their reception.[2] Acts of colonial assemblies and sometimes other documents were referred to the law officers for their opinion. These were usually busy men, who took time in answering the requests of the board. Moreover, the commissioners had no executive power themselves ; they acted through the King in Council or through a secretary of state. After they had made up their minds on any point, they stated their desires in the form of a " representation," which was considered by the Council and usually made the basis of action ; but the process was lengthy. As an example of the delays which constantly occurred, William Bollan, agent for Massachusetts, in 1759, communicated the fact of the disallowance of certain laws to his employers. One of these was an act for the dissolution of the marriage of two unhappy colonists which had been passed in 1755.[3] The act in question had found its way to England and to the Lords

---

[1] " Journals of the Board of Trade " (Ms.), January 22, 1707/8 (" Philadelphia Transcript," xx, 23).

[2] For instance, a letter from Alexander Cummins, naval officer at Boston, is in-

dorsed, " Rec[d] Dec. 17, 1722, Read, Nov. 26, 1723."

[3] The Lords of Trade stated this to be the first colonial divorce act.

of Trade, who referred it to their counsel, Sir Matthew Lamb. Upon receiving his advice, they drew up a " representation " to the Lords Committee of Council for Plantation Affairs, and they in turn referred it to the Attorney and Solicitor Generals for their opinion and finally advised its repeal, which was done by Order in Council. This slowness of procedure produced inefficiency of action and often was the cause of great hardship. Naturally the colonists grasped at any means to avoid the exercise of the royal veto.

In those days of low salaries to subordinate officials, it was difficult to get a paper drawn up or authenticated except by the payment of money to clerks whose business it was to formulate documents and present them to the proper officials for attestation. Jonathan Belcher, governor of New Jersey, could not get his instructions until he had paid down two hundred pounds; but this " unexpected supply set the wheels in motion." [1] A clerk in those days simply would not copy a document unless and until he was paid for so doing. Under these circumstances two years was the normal time required for getting an answer to a letter from a colonial governor or action on colonial legislation.

The most fatal defect in the new organization, however, was its lack of power to compel obedience to its orders, or even to secure compliance with the directions of the King in Council. The functions of the board as a consultative body were enormous; but the execution of what seemed desirable to it was shared between the Lords of the Treasury, the Commissioners of the Customs, the Admiralty, and the Secretaries of State.[2] It was difficult

---

[1] Greene's *Provincial Governor* (Harvard Historical Studies, No. vii), 47 note.

[2] Provincial governors corresponded directly with the Secretary of State and

to recommend or to take action without wounding the susceptibilities of one or more of these boards or of some eminent personage. In 1697, for instance, Colonel Robert Quary, being in England, stated to the Lords of Trade that he could not afford to execute the office of admiralty judge in the colonies unless a salary should be attached to the place and also suggested means by which the illicit tobacco trade of Delaware Bay might be prevented. The Lords of Trade advised him to state his case to the Lords of the Treasury and the Commissioners of the Customs.[1] He did so and received a severe rebuff from those authorities because he had first consulted the Lords of Trade. In making new arrangements for colonial governments as, for example, in appointing Bellomont governor of the three colonies of New York, Massachusetts, and New Hampshire, so much conference was required in the settlement of his salary and power that two years elapsed between the first notification of his appointment and the sealing of his commission. With the accession of the House of Hanover, the ministry became more closely organized, the ministers themselves became more active in the discharge of their offices, and abler men had to do with colonial affairs. As was natural, the power of the board constantly declined until it ceased to have any useful function and was replaced by a colonial secretary in 1768. Of the Secretaries of State before 1760, none took a more active part in colonial affairs than Thomas Pelham-Holles, Duke of Newcastle, — the borough monger

received orders from him; he was their superior, not the Lords of Trade. Jonathan Belcher often sent two copies of the same letter, one to Newcastle, another to the commissioners. The "Belcher Papers" in Massachusetts Historical Society's *Collections*, Sixth Series, vi, 102, 160, 172, etc.

The letters printed in this volume give an interesting insight into the working of the colonial system.

[1] "Journal of Board of Trade" (Ms.), September 22, 1697 ("Philadelphia Transcript," x, 274).

of his time, — whose ability and "brute votes" in the House of Commons kept him in office for nearly half a century and made him one of the most powerful men in England. There are many letters from him in the records of the Board of Trade, and many other letters of his dealing with colonial matters have been printed in recent years. It has been the custom of English writers to sneer at Newcastle and to describe him as possessing little force, intelligence, or education. Any one reading these papers must be convinced that, ignorant as he was as to the geography of America and the writings of classical authors, he showed a good deal of common sense in dealing with colonial administrative problems.[1] Such administrative machinery as has been outlined in the preceding paragraphs was able to effect little in restraining the growth of constitutional freedom and personal liberty in the colonies. As the case stood, the authorities in England were practically powerless to enforce the supremacy of Parliament over the colonies, to keep colonial laws and institutions in harmony with those of England, to preserve intact the royal prerogative in the plantations, or to carry out the policy of the mother country as to commerce and navigation. What could be done by "representations" to the king, instructions to governors, and letters to recalcitrant officials, the Lords of Trade certainly did; but even the best-drawn Orders in Council proved to be of slight avail three thousand miles away.

Almost from their first meeting the Lords of Trade strove to convert all the chartered governments into royal provinces, for this seemed to be the first step toward administrative harmony. In this endeavor they had a measure of success: in 1696 there were only three royal

---

[1] See, for instance, below, p. 433.

provinces on the continent, — Virginia, New York, and New
Hampshire ; in 1760 their number had increased to seven,
New Jersey, North Carolina, South Carolina, and Georgia
having in the meantime been added to the list, while
Massachusetts possessed a mixed government partaking
of the royal and chartered types. Bills for the destruction of all or some of the colonial charters were introduced
into the House of Commons on several occasions ;[1] but
not one of them passed into law. Nevertheless, as Bancroft
justly observes,[2] the possibility of such action was a constant menace to colonial self-government. At this time
there was no doubt either in England or America as to
the theoretical supremacy of Parliament[3] over king and
colonists ; the question of exercising this power was one
of expediency rather than of right.

Although Parliament did not suspend or destroy any
charter government before 1774, it legislated for the colonies with increasing frequency after 1696. The post office
act, the naturalization laws, the acts for the deportation
of convicts to the colonies, the laws declaring the " Bubble
Act " to be in force in the plantations, and those forbidding experiments in finance will be mentioned later. In
this place two or three other laws may be noted as illus-
trating the supremacy of Parliament. One of these acts
appropriated to the use of the royal navy all trees fit
for masts not growing on private lands in New Hamp-

---

[1] For instance, in 1700, 1701, 1702,
1706, 1709, 1715, 1720. See *Colonial Records of North Carolina*, i, 535, 539, 552 ;
H. E. Egerton's *British Colonial Policy*,
118 ; Chalmers's *Introduction to the Revolt*, i, 303 ; Dummer's *Defence of the
Charters* (ed. 1765), p. 3.

[2] *History of the United States*, iii, 69,
108.

[3] See, for instance, Lord Chief Justice

Vaughan's declaration in 1720, " The
Colonies are of the dominions of England, and may be bound by laws made
for them by an English Parliament."
Vaughan's *Reports*, 400. Attorney General York and Solicitor General Wearg
in 1725 gave an opinion to the effect that
the royal prerogative extended to the
plantations. Chalmers's *Opinions*, i, 12 ;
Forsyth's *Cases*, 40.

shire, Massachusetts, Maine, Rhode Island, Connecticut, New York, and New Jersey.[1] Considering the corporate rights which the freemen of Connecticut and Rhode Island had under their charters and the mode in which the Massachusetts Bay Company had been destroyed, this act can be regarded in no other light than a bit of confiscation. Moreover, the grantees of New Hampshire and New Jersey had not forfeited their property rights. An atrocious feature of this law was that offenses under it could be proved by one witness. Another act,[2] which was passed in 1729, provided that every tar kiln in North Carolina should be confiscated, unless its owner made one half of its contents into pitch free from dross. Other laws limited the number of apprentices a hatmaker could employ,[3] limited the colonial manufacture of iron,[4] and forbade colonial-made woolens to be carried from one place to another in the plantations.[5]

The principal means adopted to keep colonial laws and institutions as nearly as possible in harmony with those of England was to negative colonial laws which were contrary to acts of Parliament, the common law, the instructions of the royal governors, or such as seemed to be inexpedient. This was done either by vetoing the laws of those colonies that regularly presented their legislation for approval or by declaring the laws of other colonies null and void on cases of appeal from colonial courts to the

---

[1] 8 George I, Cap. 12, § v (Ruffhead's *Statutes at Large*, v, 369).

[2] 2 George II, Cap. 35, § iv (Ruffhead's *Statutes at Large*, v, 716).

[3] 5 George II, Cap. 22, § vii (Ruffhead's *Statutes at Large*, vi, 90).

[4] 23 George II, Cap. 29 (Ruffhead's *Statutes at Large*, vii, 260) ; 30 George II, Cap. 16 (*ibid.*, viii, 36). See also Royal Historical Manuscripts Commission's *Reports*, xii, Part vii, p. 357.

[5] 10 and 11 William III, Cap. 10, § 19 (Ruffhead's *Statutes at Large*, iv, 12). At about the same time the duties on woolens exported from England were removed. The net result of this legislation was to lower the price of woolens to the colonists while forbidding them to engage in that manufacture themselves.

King in Council.[1] The veto power was extensively used in
the colonies long after it had ceased to be exercised in
England. An attorney general like Northey scented danger in trifling matters and advised the veto of all laws
which contained untechnical language. Others, as Francis
Fane, who acted as counsel for the board, were willing
to pass all laws which did not seriously threaten English
rights. A few examples of the use or abuse of the royal
veto will not be out of place. In 1705 Queen Anne
negatived at one time fifty-three laws of Pennsylvania;[2]
in 1754 George II disallowed eight acts of North Carolina, some of which had been passed as far back as 1715.[3]
William vetoed fifteen Massachusetts laws which were

[1] See Order in Council of March 9,
1698 (American Historical Association's
Reports, 1894, 315), directing the Connecticut authorities to permit certain persons to appeal to the King in Council if
they so desired. In 1701 Attorney General
Trevor and Solicitor General Hawles gave
their opinions to the effect that although
the Connecticut charter makes no mention of appeals to his Majesty, "yet that
an appeal doth lye to his Majestie in
his Council as a right inherent in the
Crown." His Majesty, therefore, may
act on appeals whether allowed in Connecticut or not. "Board of Trade Papers,
Proprieties" (Ms.), G. 18 ("Philadelphia
Transcripts," vi). The leading cases are
those growing out of the contest over the
Winthrop lands in Connecticut and the
"Church lands" in Rhode Island. These
will be examined at length in the third
volume of the present work in treating
of the right of state and federal courts to
declare acts of state legislatures and of
the federal Congress null and void. The
papers relating to them are in the Massachusetts Historical Society's *Collections*,
Sixth Series, iv, v; *Proceedings*, 1873,
p. 100; Connecticut Historical Society's
Collections, iv; Rhode Island Historical
Society's *Collections*, iii; the "Torrey
Papers" Ms. See also a luminous article by C. M. Andrews on the "Connecticut Intestacy Law" in the *Yale Review*

for 1894 and Hazeltine's "Appeals from
Colonial Courts" in American Historical
Association's *Reports*, 1894. Appeals
were heard by the Privy Council or rather
by a committee of that body. See Order
in Council of October 1, 1714, appointing
"the Whole Privy Council, or any three or
more of them . . . to be a Committee for
the Affairs of *Guernsey* and *Jersey*, hearing of Appeals from the *Plantations*, and
other Matters that shall be referred to
them." *A Miscellaneous Essay Concerning the Courses pursued by Great Britain
in the Affairs of the Colonies* (London,
1755), p. 54.
    The colonists sometimes paid slight
attention to orders of king and Council.
See A. McF. Davis's article on the case of
Frost *vs.* Leighton in *American Historical Review*, ii, 229.
    [2] See *Pennsylvania Statutes at Large*,
ii, 454–456.
    [3] *Colonial Records of North Carolina*,
v, pp. vi, vii, 115, 116. This action is the
more noteworthy because in 1737–38 the
Attorney and Solicitor Generals had reported that old laws of North Carolina,
which had been in force for many years,
were good, although they had not been
assented to in form. The last veto of a
bill that had passed both houses of Parliament was in 1707. See Massachusetts
Historical Society's *Proceedings*, Second
Series, v, 156.

passed after the establishment of the government under the province charter.[1] Some of these merely repeated the provisions of Magna Charta. One of them, however, provided that existing arrangements should continue for six months, so far as they were not repugnant to the laws of England or inconsistent with the new charter. This law would appear to be innocuous; but it was repealed by the king three years after its passage, and more than two years after its expiration.

The exercise of the royal veto was irritating, but was ineffective. Colonial authorities sometimes disregarded the royal mandate; as, for instance, in the North Carolina case that has just been mentioned, the governor did not dare to publish the orders of the king.[2] Frequently colonial legislatures passed a new act essentially like the vetoed one which went into force at once and remained in vigor until the royal government could get hold of it and repeal it. This practice almost nullified the king's prerogative. Charter provisions also aided the colonists. The Massachusetts Province Charter[3] required that all " Orders Lawes, Statutes, or Ordinances " should be sent to England " by the first opportunity " and might be rejected at any time within three years;[4] but they were to

[1] *Massachusetts Province Laws*, i, 40; and see index under Privy Council. Toppan, in his *Edward Randolph* (ii, 164 note), prints an extract from a letter of Chief Justice Wait Winthrop on the veto of the law as to judicature. He writes that letters came repealing the law while the Supreme Court was in session and "dissolved us, which was a great disappointment to many people there being near forty actions depending." The reason alleged for the destruction of the judiciary system of Massachusetts was that the law in question provided for jury trial in admiralty cases.

[2] In an earlier instance, the Attorney and Solicitor Generals in England in 1729 declared all the laws passed by the provincial legislature since the sale by the proprietors to be null and void, but these acts were regularly printed as valid laws in all the revisals of North Carolina statutes, *Colonial Records of North Carolina*, iii, p. iii. See another instance noted by Andrew McF. Davis in *American Historical Review*, ii, 236.

[3] *Charters and Constitutions*, i, 952.

[4] The time limit dated from the submission of the law to the Council; see Chalmers's *Opinions*, i, 349.

go into force when assented to by the governor.[1] The
charter, however, was silent as to "resolves." The General
Court therefore fell into the habit of including obnoxious
legislation among the resolves, and these were never submitted to the king. In the case of Pennsylvania, the
charter required that all acts of assembly should be transmitted to England within five years of their passage, when
the king had six months in which to veto them. Laws
that were likely to be vetoed, therefore, were passed for a
period of less than five years and were not sent to England
at all. The colonists so generally fell into the practice
of passing acts for limited periods that Attorney General
Northey declared the royal veto to be of no importance.[2]

The Lords of Trade frequently instructed the governors
in the name of the king to veto certain kinds of legislation ;
as, for example, acts for the emission of paper money, for
laying duties on European goods in English shipping,[3] or
for giving preference to colonial creditors over those residing in England. In 1721 Joshua Gee suggested that no
colonial law should be valid until it was approved in
England.[4] The Lords of Trade did not fall in with this
idea, but in 1723 an "additional instruction"[5] was issued
prohibiting governors of royal and proprietary provinces
from assenting to private acts unless a clause was appended

[1] In 1715 Colonel Burgess was instructed to pass no act of "an extraordinary nature" unless the draft of the
law had first been approved in England
or the bill contained a clause suspending
its operation until the royal pleasure
was signified. Massachusetts Colonial
Society's *Transactions*, ii. Burgess did
not come to the colony; but the instruction was repeated to later governors.

[2] Chalmers's *Opinions*, i, 350. In 1717
Governor Shute of Massachusetts was
instructed to give his assent to no law
which was so limited in point of time

that royal action could not be had
thereon. "Belknap Papers," Ms., 1665–
1745, No. 73.

[3] Order in Council, 1724; see "Board
of Trade Papers" (Ms.) ("Philadelphia
Transcripts," x, 52, 53).

[4] Joshua Gee's *Trade and Navigation
of Great Britain Considered* (third edi-
tion), 108. "Board of Trade Papers,
Plantations General" (Ms.), Bundle M,
No. 40 ("Philadelphia Transcripts," xi,
No. 40).

[5] *Ibid.*, Bundle L, No. 45 (vol. x, No.
45).

suspending their operation until the king's pleasure could be ascertained; in 1724 this was extended to acts laying duties on European goods, and in 1732 they were forbidden to pass any laws which gave the colonists advantages over residents of England. Finally, governors of royal provinces were required to negative all laws, including those repealing existing acts, unless they contained a suspending clause.[1] According to Franklin, a bill was introduced into Parliament somewhere about 1737 to make royal instructions laws in the colonies, but was defeated in the Commons.[2]

The veto power of the king was used in at least one instance at the request of the colonists themselves against the action of their own legislature. In 1749–50 the Massachusetts General Court passed a law levying duties upon tea, coffee, arrack, snuff, and other "unnecessary commodities" imported into the colony. As most of these articles were imported through Boston, the merchants of that town regarded this as an unjust attack upon their trade. The town petitioned the General Court to repeal the law, urging, among other things, that tea and coffee were mainly retailed by widows and other necessitous persons. They also declared that coffee was "one of the easiest, readiest, and cheapest refreshment the Inhabitants can take in the Morning."[3] Upon their peti-

[1] The Virginia Committee of Correspondence on November 5, 1760, wrote that "the Instructions to the Governor of this Colony were given by King Charles the Second soon after the Restoration, and have had little alteration since. By the 16th Article of those Instructions the Governor is directed to pass no act of a less continuance than two years, and no Act repealing or amending any other Act whether the same has or has not received his Majesty's assent unless a clause be inserted suspending the Execution thereof until his Royal Pleasure shall be known." *Virginia Magazine of History*, xi, 15. The words of the letter are explicit enough; but the instruction as to the "suspending clause" did not come into use until long after 1660.

[2] Bigelow's *Franklin*, i, 367.

[3] *Boston Town Records*, 1742–57, p. 221; for other matter on this subject, see *ibid.*, pp. 178, 180, 183, 185, 221, 241.

tion being dismissed, the town appointed an agent to appeal to the King in Council to disallow the act. This he successfully accomplished in 1752, being aided by the opinion of Mr. Lamb, counsel for the Board of Trade, that the law in question would be manifestly prejudicial to British commerce, presumably by lessening the demand for goods imported through England.

Colonial governments are generally grouped under several heads, but for our purposes it matters little whether a province was governed under the royal or proprietary form. In all of them the framework was very nearly the same. There was a governor who was usually selected by the Board of Trade and was always appointed by the king in the royal provinces, while the proprietary provinces were ruled over by a deputy governor to whose appointment the approbation of the king was required after 1696. In all there was a council whose authority came nominally from the same source as did that of the governor; but, as a matter of fact, the councilors were ordinarily the leading men in the several colonies with a constantly growing proportion of royal officials.[1] There was also an assembly which was called by different names, as House of Representatives in Massachusetts, House of Burgesses in Virginia, and House of Commons in South Carolina. Everywhere the members of these representative assemblies were elected in accordance with a general law. The apportionment was on the basis of the town or county, and was

[1] After 1733 the Surveyors of the Customs in the Plantations were *ex officio* members of the Councils. "Board of Trade Papers" (Ms.) ("Philadelphia Transcripts"), xi, No. 45. The governors of the royal provinces originally were members of the Council; by 1725 their functions had become so differentiated that Mr. West, counsel for the Board of Trade, ruled that a governor could not act as a councilor when that body was exercising legislative functions. See "Board of Trade Papers, Plantations General" (Ms.), viii, 55. See also O'Callaghan's "Historical Introduction" to *Journal of the Legislative Council of the Colony of New York*, p. xxvii.

being constantly readjusted by the establishment of new towns or counties on the frontier or by the division of existing towns and counties as these increased in population and wealth. The suffrage was exercised according to general regulations, which usually conferred it upon those men who possessed a certain amount of property, — landed property in the South, and real and personal estate in the North. There were, of course, many differences as to the precise power and functions of the voters and representatives in the different colonies; but the general fabric of government, so far as the executive and legislative branches were concerned, was substantially similar in all.

The governor was expected to exercise the royal prerogative [1] in his province, unshorn of those attributes which had been wrested from it in the course of the constitutional contests of the Stuart epoch. Thus he was to summon, prorogue, and dissolve assemblies at will, and adjourn them to any place within his province for any length of time that he might see fit.[2] No money could be drawn out of the colonial treasury except on his warrant, and his assent was absolutely necessary to the passage of any act by the colonial assembly.

The governor ruled by virtue of a commission which was issued under the great seal. By this instrument he was authorized to exercise very sweeping powers; but the wording of the commission is really of slight importance

[1] Prerogative describes those powers which the king can exercise of his own initiative, without seeking or receiving parliamentary sanction. It extended to the colonies except as limited by acts of Parliament, colonial laws, or royal action. Powers which the king had parted with could be resumed by act of Parliament. See Lord Mansfield's decision in the case of Campbell vs. Hall, Howell's *State Trials*, xx, 239, and opinion of the law officers of the crown in Chalmers's *Opinions*, i, 351.

[2] In 1738 Francis Fane, counsel to the Board of Trade, advised the repeal of a New York act regulating sessions and elections of the provincial Assembly on the ground that it was a " very high infringement upon the prerogative of the Crown," although similar laws had been in force in England for many years. Chalmers's *Opinions*, i, 188.

since the powers conferred upon the governor in his commission were excessively limited in his instructions. At the time of his appointment, besides his brief commission, he was given a long and detailed set of instructions which were added to from time to time and also modified and amended. In the end, this document ran into between one and two hundred sections. Moreover, the Board of Trade and the Secretaries of State were constantly sending out "additional" instructions to all the governors, ordering or forbidding them to do this or that ; but the governors were entirely unable to obey them.[1]   In point of fact, the governors of the royal and proprietary provinces possessed very little more authority than their personal character and position conferred upon them ; they were everywhere thwarted by the provincial assemblies.

Had the governors been persons of force, independent means, and character, they would have exercised an important influence upon colonial life and constitutional development.   Fortunately, they were usually persons of quite opposite qualities, although Huske's characterization[2] of them as broken members of Parliament and valets-de-chambre is overdrawn.   Some of them were needy adventurers, like Lord Cornbury, governor of New York; others were persons of no experience in affairs, like Gabriel Johnson of North Carolina ; while others were well meaning but inefficient men, like Burnet of New York and Massachusetts. The colonies were regarded as a hospital for the poor relatives or dependents of those who occupied high office in England.   No matter how covetous or inefficient a gov-

[1] Franklin relates that Lord Granville, President of the Privy Council, told him in 1757 that the king's instructions to colonial governors, "so far as they relate to you, [are] the law of the land, for the king is the legislative of the colonies," Bigelow's *Franklin*, i, 366.

[2] Phillimore's *Memoirs of Lyttleton*, ii, 604, quoted by Mahon in his *History of England*, v, 240.

ernor might be, he was always protected in England so long as his party remained in power — " the most nefarious crime a governor can commit is not by some counted so bad as the crime of complaining of it." [1] Of course, once in a while a man of ability was appointed to office in the colonies, but in the few instances where this was the case, there was always some peculiar circumstance which made it impossible for him to accomplish much in the way of upbuilding the royal power.

From the English Revolution in 1688–89 to the American Revolution in 1775–83, the constitutional development in all the royal and proprietary provinces was substantially the same. Everywhere the Assembly claimed for itself the powers and privileges of the House of Commons, and everywhere it denied that the Council bore any resemblance to the House of Lords. Everywhere the Assembly used its control of the purse to compel the representative of English authority to disobey his instructions, or, at all events, to pay no regard to them. The mode of compulsion varied slightly in the several colonies, owing to the different constitutional arrangements that prevailed in them : in Massachusetts the salary of the governor was the matter about which the contest was waged ; in New York the levying of taxes in general ; in Pennsylvania the paying tribute to the proprietary. It made little difference whether the governor represented king or proprietor ; everywhere the colonists demanded greater control of their affairs than the governor's instructions permitted. How strenuously the authorities in England would have insisted on their constitutional rights may well be doubted had not the enforcement of the

---

[1] So wrote Lewis Morris, the discharged Chief Justice of New York.

imperial commercial system been more or less involved
in the control of the colonial government. The phrase
" more or less involved " in the preceding sentence is
used because under the circumstances of the time it
would probably have been impossible to carry out the
navigation laws and acts of trade with the means at the
command of William, Anne, or the first two Georges.
Piracy, smuggling, and illicit trading could only have
been put an end to by armed naval and military forces
which were entirely out of the reach of these monarchs
and their advisers.

NOTES

I. Fabrigas *vs*. Mostyn. — This case[1] arose out of troubles in Minorca, an island in the Mediterranean then possessed by England of which Mostyn was governor. He caused Fabrigas, a native of that island, to be arrested, imprisoned, and deported. Fabrigas sued him for damages in the Court of Common Pleas at Westminster, alleging that the assault was committed " at Minorca, (to wit) at London aforesaid, in the parish of Saint Mary-le-Bow, in the ward of Cheap." The jury awarded damages to Fabrigas, whereupon the matter was carried before Chief Justice Mansfield on questions of law. He decided that the case could be maintained because "if the king's courts cannot hold plea in such a case there is no other court upon earth that can do it," since a governor could not be sued in the court of the colony over which he ruled. The fiction of law in " transitory actions" like this one was also made use of in citing colonial corporations into court; thus Connecticut was supposed to be in the "Parish of St. Michael, Cornhill," for *quo warranto* purposes, although the people of that and other colonies were held to be outside the realm when they laid claim to " the rights of Englishmen."

II. The Supremacy of Parliament. — This is stated in clearest phrase in Lord Mansfield's decision in the case of Campbell *vs*. Hall[2] (1774). The case arose out of the collection of the four and a half per cent duty on the products of the plantation which Campbell had acquired in the island of Grenada, soon after its conquest by the English. The island was ceded to England, February 10, 1763. In October, 1763, the king by proclamation established a government for the island with the usual provision for an assembly. In March, 1764, by another proclamation, he invited settlers, and on April 9 of that year he commissioned a governor with power to summon an assembly. On July 20, 1764, the king, by letters patent, extended to Grenada the four and a half per cent duty which was levied on exports from the Leeward Islands. The judges of the court of King's Bench, by the chief justice, Lord Mansfield, decided that the king by his commission of April 9 had divested himself of his legislative power and could not resume it as he tried to do in July, and that the tax could now be levied only "by the assembly of the island, or by an Act of the Parliament of Great Britain."

[1] Howell's *State Trials*, xx, 81.
[2] *Ibid.*, xx, 239 ; Thayer's *Cases on* *Constitutional Law*, Part i, p. 40 ; see also Brinton Coxe's *Judicial Power*, 190.

CHAPTER IX

THE LAST NAVIGATION ACT, 1696

THE navigation laws of Charles II were amply sufficient for the carrying out of the policy of upbuilding
English prosperity, could they have been enforced.[1] In
the chaotic commercial conditions of the time the innocent
trader was at the mercy of the covetous customs official
on shore and the equally covetous pirate at sea; when the
laws were only sporadically enforced, the lawful ship
owner or navigator was nowhere protected.[2] England,
at the turn of the seventeenth century, exercised no such
control of the sea as she maintained in after years. Some
of the war ships flying the naval ensign were owned and
navigated by private persons under commissions from the
admiralty; naval vessels, privateer, pirate, smuggler, and
innocent trader shaded, almost imperceptibly, one into
another. Moreover, the meaning, even the phraseology
of the navigation laws, was obscure; a man might well
find it difficult to know whether, in undertaking what
promised to be a profitable venture, he was breaking the

[1] Even Edward Randolph testified
before a committee of the House of
Lords that with a few changes and the
establishment of admiralty courts in the
colonies, the existing navigation acts
would be adequate.

[2] The troubles of a shipmaster of that
period are vividly set forth by an English captain in two letters to Wait Winthrop, Massachusetts Historical Society's
Collections, Sixth Series, v, 31. The
writer's vessel was captured by a French
privateer and recaptured by an English
one. The latter sued for salvage and
lost — all in the year 1694.

law or not; one might sail on a privateering voyage and return home, having unwittingly committed piracy. The extent and character of the Atlantic coast was in favor of the illicit trader, while the administration of the colonies by many different governments, only three of which were directly under royal control, added to the difficulties of zealous officials like Edward Randolph and Robert Quary[1] in the discharge of their duties. Furthermore, the home government expected the service to pay for itself by means of fines and forfeitures, but these were seldom ordered and almost never collected.

The effect of the navigation laws and the tonnage and poundage acts was to put a great premium on direct trade to Europe in those staple commodities which were produced in the colonies and required by law to be laid on the shore of England before reaching the markets of the continent. Tobacco was the only one of these enumerated goods which was largely produced in the continental colonies.[2] The effect of English laws was to add several pence to the price at which tobacco that reached European markets through England could be sold. It is true that the duty which was levied at importation was repaid if the tobacco was reëxported within eighteen months; but the fees, profits of merchants, expenses of handling, and warehousing probably doubled the original cost of the commodity so that tobacco that was carried direct to Europe, regardless of acts of Parliament, could be sold at least twenty-five per cent cheaper and leave a good profit. Chalmers, who had access to the custom house

[1] His commission as surveyor general in succession to Randolph is printed in Massachusetts Historical Society's *Proceedings*, Second Series, iv, 148.

[2] The duty levied at importation in accordance with the act of 1 James II, Cap. 4, was five pence per pound, all of which was repaid upon reëxportation within eighteen months. This law was made perpetual by 9 Anne, Cap. 21, § I (Ruffhead's *Statutes at Large*, iv, 472).

books, gives the amount of tobacco annually imported
into England in the years 1689–93 at fifteen million
pounds, of which two thirds " were supposed to have
been reëxported." [1] The duties paid at importation were
about three hundred thousand pounds sterling, of which
two hundred thousand pounds would have been repaid
on reëxportation, leaving a net annual revenue of over one
hundred thousand pounds sterling. These figures give
an idea of the size of the traffic and go far toward
justifying the zeal of the royal officials in the enforcement
of the law.

The navigation acts forbade colonial markets to Scots
and to goods imported through their country ; but it was
no easy matter to exclude the shrewd natives of North
Britain from a profitable commerce. Moreover, the laws [2]
of Scotland provided that goods which were reëxported
within twelve months should be free of duty. The Scots
were a thrifty and economical race and probably conducted
their commerce at less expense than the English. The
ease with which sailing ships from Glasgow could gain
the ocean in comparison with the delays incident to the
voyage down Channel, also greatly aided Scottish commerce. Scotch traders and goods imported through Scotland were met with frequently in the colonies. These
examples of the ill-working of the colonial system might be
much extended, but further facts will appear in connection with the following description of the difficulties of
enforcing the laws in America.

[1] George Chalmers' *History of the Revolt*, i, 218 note.
[2] See *Acts of the Parliaments of Scotland* (ed. 1820), vii, 563; x, 38. The act referred to was passed in 1669, but was still in force in 1696. George Muschamp, collector for Carolina, reported in 1687 that merchants of Scotland and Ireland claimed that the charter of that province gave them the right to trade directly with the Carolinians; the Attorney General was of the contrary opinion. *Calendars of State Papers, America and West Indies, 1685-1688*, p. 353.

In 1692, soon after his appointment as surveyor general of the plantations on the American continent, Randolph repaired to the Chesapeake, where he found that the navigation laws were as little regarded as they had been in New England in the earlier days. He came upon shipmasters who were loading tobacco without any thought of giving bonds or paying the penny duty required by the Act of 1672 ; he found that no records of entrances and clearances were kept, and that no attempt whatever was made to enforce the conditions of such bonds as had been taken. At St. Mary's, in Maryland, he ordered suit to be begun on fourteen bonds and then sought the Eastern Shore. When he returned, he found that nothing had been done on these suits and that several New England ships had meantime sailed with cargoes which had been laden in direct contravention of the law. On the other side of the Chesapeake he had seized two ships which were freighted with Scottish goods ; but he could not secure a condemnation because, as he said, the sheriff was a Scotch-Irishman, while the jury were Scotchmen and their friends. He asserted that vessels loaded with goods from Scotland, Holland, and France secured immunity by means of forged certificates, and added, that at Glasgow " they have false seals of the Custom houses of Whitehaven, Beaumaris, etc., and also blank certificates." [1]

In March, 1697, Randolph presented to the House of Lords certain definite statements [2] as to the infractions of the trade laws. He gives the names of fifteen vessels which loaded tobacco in Pennsylvania for England and did not land it there ; these carried, according to his statement, 1080 hogsheads of tobacco, besides some in

[1] Calendars of State Papers, America and West Indies, 1689-1692, p. 660.   [2] Lords Manuscripts, New Series, ii, 462-466.

bulk. Furthermore, he gives the names of twenty-two vessels trading between the plantations and Scotland contrary to the acts, in each case giving details as to dates, tonnage, master, and often as to lading, which make it difficult to think that even Randolph could have invented them all. In one specific instance he offers evidence that in 1692 a Dutch vessel anchored in the Delaware, transferred between two and three thousand pounds' worth of goods to Maryland boats and with the proceeds purchased one thousand hogsheads of tobacco.[1] Another vessel which he seized was laden with brandy and wine from Norway. These allegations were made before a committee of the House of Lords. In reply to some of them, William Penn observed that if tobacco was carried from Maryland to Pennsylvania in contravention of law, Randolph " ought to answer for that for suffering it; and if he can't, how can I ? The crime lies on the side of Maryland, where he chiefly resides." [2]

Quantities of Virginia tobacco were surreptitiously laden within her limits, where it was customary for the vessels to fill their holds at the plantations and sail thence directly for the northern colonies, the West Indies, or Europe, without complying with any part of the navigation acts as to tobacco. A good deal of it was taken to North Carolina, either overland or in small vessels, and there placed on seagoing ships. The limited number of ports of entry in comparison with the great extent of the navigable waters of Albemarle and Pamlico sounds, and the rivers which flowed

[1] *Lords Manuscripts*, New Series, ii, 465. At an earlier day he had given in a list of thirty-four vessels irregularly trading to New England between April, 1689, and February, 1690; but this period covered the time of his imprisonment. Nevertheless he gives so many details that an air of verity is given to the statement. Massachusetts Historical Society's *Proceedings*, 1871, p. 115.

[2] *Lords Manuscripts*, New Series, ii, 456; Penn also declared that Randolph was " not worth five hundred pounds, if one in the whole world."

into them, greatly facilitated illegal trading. It was no un-
common thing in the North Carolina sounds and in the
Chesapeake for a vessel to unload a portion of her cargo
before entering at the custom house and to add to it after
having obtained clearance papers. It was in the interest
of economy and efficiency that she should do so; but the
practice interfered greatly with the enforcement of the
colonial commercial system.

The profits which were derived from the plantation trade
were very large, especially those gained from traffic carried on in defiance of law. In 1702 the Lords of Trade
declared that every pound of wool exported from England
for manufacture elsewhere produced above ten times the
value of its first cost.[1] Goods which could be purchased
for sixpence in England could be exchanged " for a bushel
of wheat in North Carolina, and those costing eighteen
pence could be bartered for a barrel of tar." [2] Profits of
this magnitude invited the smuggler; in 1734 a ship laden
with French goods and tea, which had not been " laid on
the shore of England," anchored at Ocracock Inlet.[3] Her
cargo was transferred to light draft vessels of the country
which distributed the goods to ports on Pamlico and Albemarle sounds, and connecting waters as far as Virginia.
This vessel was doubtless fully laden with tobacco, some
of it from Virginia. If everything went well, and she
gained a French port in safety, she must have netted her
owners several hundred per cent profit. It was not alone
on the unfrequented sounds of North Carolina or the broad
bays of Virginia and Pennsylvania that illegal traders
flourished; New York and the New England colonies were

---

[1] " Report of Board of Trade," 1702,
Bulletin of New York Public Library,
x, 278.

[2] *Colonial Records of North Carolina*, iii, p. xvii.
[3] *Ibid.*, iii, p. xvi.

equally the abode of the smuggler and the receiver of piratical plunder.

Merchants and shipowners living on Manhattan Island had never paid much attention to trade regulations of any kind. In Governor Fletcher's time, he himself, the customs officials, and those engaged in unlawful traffic were in collusion to break down the force of the navigation acts. When Bellomont succeeded Fletcher, he found Chidley Brooke collector of the customs at New York. Bellomont ordered Brooke to seize the ship *Fortune*, which was laden with East India goods that had not been landed in England. Brooke delayed so long that most of the cargo was discharged and distributed.[1] Bellomont dismissed him from office and undertook to enforce the laws himself with the lieutenant-governor acting as marshal; but they accomplished very little in the way of enforcement. Men would not serve as tide waiters unless they were permitted to compound with the importers; they could not perform their duties except with every chance of being knocked in the head for their pains.[2] Nevertheless, the merchants were so annoyed by Bellomont's endeavors, unsuccessful though they were, that they waited upon him and informed him that he would speedily be recalled or they would make his life such a burden that he would ask to be relieved.[3] Robert Quary has generally received an unfavorable character from writers on American history, but some suggestions which he made in 1708 show him in a better light. In that year he visited New York and New England in the prosecution of his official duties and described the condition of affairs, as he viewed it, from his official station. He declared that the people living on

---

[1] *New York Colonial Records*, iv, 302.
[2] *Ibid.*, iv, 516.

[3] For New York, see *New York Colonial Documents*, iv, 324, 354.

the eastern end of Long Island could hardly help breaking the customs regulations because " it is almost impossible for the vessels that trade there to enter and clear at New York." [1]   At New London, in Connecticut, he found a collector whose habit it was to certify that tobacco which had been run out of the Chesapeake in contravention of law had been exported in conformity with the navigation acts.   Quary also tells of a certain Jno. Redwood who lived at Harbor Island in the Bahamas and was " a great rogue " in that he certified that certain cargoes of " enumerated goods " had been landed there which, as a matter of fact, had never left the ship and had been carried thence to Madeira and ports of Europe.

Notwithstanding the recorded infractions of the trade laws, colonial commerce was much more restricted to the channels designed for it by Parliament than it had been in the earlier time.   This was due, in great measure, to the employment of a few armed vessels to patrol the coast and to convoy ships laden with colonial staples from the plantations to English ports.   A " list of ships appointed for the care of the plantations and the trade in those parts against the enemy " [2] contains the names of eleven or twelve vessels which were stationed in the northern colonies or had recently been there, and twelve other vessels protected the commerce of the West Indies.   Occasionally one of them would stray northward from Barbados, Nevis, or Jamaica to recruit her crew or to replenish her stock of supplies.   The captains of naval vessels were nominally under the orders of the plantation

[1] *New York Colonial Documents*, v, 30 ; Massachusetts Historical Society's *Proceedings*, New Series, iv, 149.   See also Quary's " Memorial " to the Lords of Trade in 1703; *Collections* of the same

Society, Third Series, vii, 223.   There is a notice of Quary in the *Memoirs of the Pennsylvania Historical Society*.

[2] *Lords Manuscripts*, New Series, ii, 342.

governor, wherever they might happen to be; but they
paid little heed to the wishes of their civil superiors and
were a perennial source of complaint to the home authorities. At least one of the governors fitted out a vessel to
enforce the law relating to the exportation of tobacco.
The name of this revenue cutter was the *Speedwell* and her
commander was Thomas Meech. He cruised from the
10th of June to the 30th of November, 1695, and had some
success. Among other vessels, Captain Meech seized a
Scottish brigantine on the Jersey coast. She had brought
goods from Scotland under false papers, so he asserted;
but Governor Andrew Hamilton of New Jersey took the
vessel out of Meech's hands [1] and she was not condemned.
In a communication to the Lords of Trade, which Nicholson made in connection with the cruise of the *Speedwell*, he
stated that he could not secure convictions by juries in
cases relating to navigation and requested to be informed
as to how juries might be attainted,[2] but he gave no details
as to the failure of juries to do their duty.

Nicholson, Randolph, and Quary were united in their
complaints as to the refusal of colonial juries to give verdicts in their favor, which they attributed either to bribery
or to hostility to themselves; but the few reported cases
do not bear out their assertions. The most interesting of
these cases was that of Captain Trout, master of the
brigantine *Dolphin*.[3] From the affidavits presented it
appears that Randolph on espying the brigantine at anchor in the Delaware hailed her as he passed in another
vessel, boarded her without disclosing his identity, and

---

[1] Toppan's *Randolph*, v, 157.

[2] *Calendars of State Papers, America
and West Indies, 1693–1696*, pp. 654, 655;
Lords Manuscripts, New Series, ii, 465.
It is interesting to note that the former
of these citations is from the papers of
the Board of Trade, while the latter is
from evidence presented to the House
of Lords.

[3] Toppan's *Edward Randolph*, v, 107–
116.

closely questioned the master and crew. Their answers not being satisfactory, he seized the vessel by
marking the " broad arrow " on her mainmast, on the
ground that her master and crew were not Englishmen
as the law required. It also appears that Randolph had
stated he was about to depart for New York, which gives
to the affair something of the aspect of blackmail. Captain Trout was equal to the occasion ; he rowed upstream
to Philadelphia, twenty miles away, and presented a
petition for a special court to try the case on the ground
that his cargo of flour and wheat was on board and might
be damaged by delay. In this instance, Randolph was represented by David Lloyd, the attorney general of Pennsylvania and one of the ablest lawyers in the province.
After some discussion, the date of the trial was fixed for
two weeks ahead, which would give Randolph time to
transact his business in New York and return to Pennsylvania. When the day came, a jury was impaneled, evidence was offered to show that Trout and his men were
all of them subjects of England, and therefore very properly a verdict was brought in in favor of the defendant.
In this instance, Randolph seems to have been treated
with absolute fairness, and the verdict of the jury to have
been entirely in accord with the evidence. Randolph was
not satisfied and appealed to the provincial court of Pennsylvania ; his appeal was allowed provided he could give
security that he would prosecute it, which apparently he
could not do. Captain Trout now turned on his perse-
cutor. An old law of Elizabeth, still unrepealed and
presumably in force in the colonies, provided that an
informer who lost or failed to prosecute his suit should
pay the costs and damages. On the petition of Trout, the
costs and damages were assessed at forty-four pounds, and

a warrant was issued to the sheriff directing him to arrest
Randolph in case of his failure to pay. That, probably,
was the end of the case, and certainly is the end of it so
far as the records go. It shows clearly the difficulties of
Randolph's position and the harshness of his methods.
The last two seizures made by him before his death in
April, 1703, confirm the impression gained from Trout's
case. One of these was of a ship which was seized in
Maryland and was the occasion for more damages assessed
on Randolph. The other seizure was made on the eastern
side of Chesapeake Bay: as to this, after Randolph's death,
Quary wrote, "I have examined into the matter and can't
find the least color for it: the pretence was a parcel of
Irish linen for which there is a true and full certificate
that the duty was paid in England." [1] The most charitable way to account for Randolph's doings in the last
years of his life is to suppose that difficulties and disap-
pointments had injured his judgment; but he had acted
in an equally unjustifiable manner in his earlier career in
New England. Randolph's disregard for the feelings of
others not only worked hardship to innocent traders, but
also aroused against him the animosities of powerful men.
Among these was Lionel Copley, whom William had
appointed governor of Maryland. Copley complained to
the Lords of Trade [2] of Randolph's " exorbitant and malignant temper " and " scurrilous haughty deportment."
He states that the surveyor general had seized two or
three ships for no other reason than because they belonged
to those whom Randolph termed " New England rogues
and pitiful damned Scotch pedlars." He had impressed
people, horses, and boats into his service without any sug-

---

[1] Toppan's *Randolph*, v, 294.
[2] *Calendars of State Papers, America and West Indies, 1689–1692,* p. 679.

gestion of payment and, in a few months, had "made the country weary of him." Randolph, on his part, declared that the Pennsylvanians and Virginians were as bad as the New Englanders, if not worse, and described North Carolina as "a place which receives Pirates, Runaways, and Illegal Traders."[1]

Independent of Randolph and his co-workers, there is evidence of illicit trading on a large scale. Some years earlier (June 10, 1679), Robert Holden had informed the Commissioners of the Customs that a large trade was carried on between the Canary Islands and the colonies contrary to law. It was the custom, so he said, to load a ship at those islands and then touch at Madeira or the Azores, where one or two tuns of wine were taken on board and placed in the hatchway. On arrival in a colonial port, these casks were sampled by the gaugers and the whole cargo was passed without further inquiry. He also reported that vessels sailed from England partly laden, completed their cargoes in Scottish ports and entered in the colonies under their English papers.[2] Another way in which the navigation laws were evaded was to import goods into the continental colonies by way of Newfoundland, for the fishery of that island was given exceptional privileges by English law. Brandy, wine, and other European goods were carried to that island from France in French vessels and were taken thence to New England by the fishermen of Boston and Gloucester.[3]

---

[1] *Colonial Records of North Carolina*, i, 527. There is a long list of infractions of the navigation laws in the Carolinas from Randolph's pen in *ibid.*, i, 545.

[2] *Ibid.*, i, 245.

[3] Massachusetts Historical Society's *Collections*, Third Series, vii, 174. As far back as 1687 this trade had attracted the attention of the English customs authorities. See "Instruction" to Andros in Massachusetts Colonial Society's *Publications*, ii, and letter from the Commissioners of the Customs to Andros. *Calendars of State Papers, America and West Indies, 1685–1688*, p. 309.

Another route by which tobacco found its way to Europe and uncustomed goods reached the colonies was by means of a contraband trade to the Dutch colony of Surinam, on the northern coast of South America. At certain times in the year the fleets of the Dutch East India Company anchored off the island of Curaçoa on their way from India to Europe, or from the Netherlands to the East. At that place they were met by vessels from Philadelphia and other continental ports, and the goods of Europe and the East were exchanged for the tobacco of Virginia and Maryland.[1] Most of this was carried in bulk, but some of it, for appearance' sake, was packed in barrels with flour at either end, since these vessels were supposed to be engaged in carrying food stuffs from the continent to the sugar islands of the West Indies.

Besides these regular smugglers of one sort or another, there was a good deal of what might be termed irregular smuggling carried on through the pirates of Madagascar who formed a class by themselves. These seafarers were not of the regular pirate type, like those who frequently appeared off American shores in the reigns of William and Anne. Of the latter the most famous was Edward Teach, or Thach, who is better known under his sobriquet of Blackbeard. He was a pirate of the ship-scuttling, walk-the-plank variety. His beard was done up into ringlets and he had fourteen wives, of whom he personally throttled only three.[2] When business was slack or time hung heavily on his hands, he invited his

---

[1] *Calendars of State Papers, America and West Indies, 1693–1696*, p. 510.

[2] From the extent of his matrimonial ventures he was sometimes confounded with "Bluebeard," as in *Colonial Records of North Carolina*, ii, p. viii, where the editor notes that the secretary of that colony was commonly supposed to be in league with him. See also Charles Johnson's *History of the Pyrates* (second edition), p. 70.

companions to the hold of his ship and there set fire to sundry pots of brimstone, giving them and himself a taste of that future world to which they all were surely bound. Great was the rejoicing when a ship sailed into the James River with his head adorning a pikestaff stuck at the bowsprit end. In comparison with Blackbeard, Stede Bonnet,[1] and others of that ilk, the Madagascar pirates were courteous gentlemen. Their careers are equally well attested and cast an even stranger light on colonial conditions.

In 1696 several pirates were captured in England and the depositions of two of them are preserved. The deponents were Philip Middleton and John Dann ;[2] by combining their testimonies one can get a good idea of the way in which the business was carried on. They sailed from England in an ordinary and regular manner, but at Coruña, in Spain, with sundry companions in crime, they seized a ship and sailed in her to Johanna Island and Madagascar. By the time of their arrival at that rendezvous they had collected a crew of one hundred and seventy persons — fourteen of whom were Danes, fifty-two Frenchmen, and one hundred and four Englishmen. At Madagascar they were joined by several other vessels, and the fleet sailed for the Red Sea and Arabian Gulf. Every, or Avery, was in chief command. Other vessels in the squadron were the Philadelphia ship, *Dolphin*, Captain Want ; the Rhode Island ships, *Portsmouth Adventure*, Captain Faro, and *Pearl*, Captain William Mues ; and the New York ship, *Amity*, whose captain was the notorious Thomas Tew. She was so slow that she soon fell out of sight of the rest and the *Dolphin* was accidentally burned. The others

---

[1] Charles Johnson's *History of the Pyrates* (second edition), p. 91.

[2] *Calendars of State Papers, America and West Indies, 1696–1697*, pp. 260, 262.

drove prosperously on. Off Surat they captured a Moorish ship from which they extracted fifty thousand pounds in silver and gold, while another and larger vessel yielded them four times as much. After this good fortune, the ships separated. Captain Avery with his vessel and his share of the booty made for the island of New Providence in the Bahamas, where he secured the protection of Governor Trott by the payment of one thousand pounds. Eventually twenty-three of the pirates gained the coast of Carolina and disappeared from sight. Avery and a few others went to England to enjoy their ill-gotten gains, but found it difficult to dispose of their jewels and vessels of gold. Avery was plundered by the merchants of Bristol in as brutal a manner as he had ever looted Moorish ship. He died from fright and hunger, without leaving money enough behind to pay for a coffin. Captain Dann was betrayed to the mayor of Rochester, who discovered that his jacket was quilted with gold to the value, so Dann deposed, of one thousand pounds sterling. Although Captain Tew and the *Amity* were tardy on the occasion just described, it must not be supposed that he was negligent of such opportunities as came in his way. On the contrary he was reported by another witness to have returned to New York with booty to the amount of some eighty thousand pounds, and he himself is said to have received twelve thousand pounds as his personal share of one cruise.[1]

Pirates gorged with plunder sought the seclusion of the plantations in those vessels which returned after carrying supplies to the piratical station at Madagascar. These ships sailed from New York, Newport, or Philadelphia, with passes from Governor Fletcher or from some one in author-

---

[1] John Graves wrote to the Board of Trade and Plantations that Tew told him so. *Calendars of State Papers,* *America and West Indies, 1696–1697,* p. 379.

ity among the gentry of the black flag. Retiring pirates were willing to pay a good price for a peaceful home-coming, and in the colonial towns their money covered the nefariousness of their actions. The number of pirates in retirement or semi-retirement was large : in 1699 Bellomont reported that there were forty or more in custody in New York, Connecticut, and Philadelphia. Thomas Robinson in 1697 declared that pirates walked the streets of Philadelphia in perfect safety,[1] and Robert Snead, a substantial settler of Pennsylvania and a magistrate, was thwarted at every turn in his attempt to bring retired pirates to retribution by Penn's representative, William Markham, whose daughter was said to have married a pirate.[2] Penn was inclined to throw the blame for the condition of things in Pennsylvania on Markham and wrote to him that it was said in London that Pennsylvanians "not onlie wink att but Imbrace pirats, Shipps and men."[3] On the other hand, it should be said that the Council solemnly declared that no pirates had been harbored knowingly and that Markham's son-in-law was promptly expelled from the Assembly when it was charged that he had been engaged in piracy. In 1700 a stringent law was passed by the Pennsylvania Assembly for the suppression of piracy, trading with pirates, and harboring of returned sea-robbers.[4]

The profits of piracy and the trade connected therewith must have been very large. One vessel, the *Nassau* of New York, which carried supplies to Madagascar, is said to have

[1] *Calendars of State Papers, America and West Indies, 1696–1697,* p. 552. Governor Jeremiah Basse of New Jersey reported that colony to be a favorite resort of returned pirates. *Ibid., 1696–1697,* p. 557.

[2] *Votes of Pennsylvania,* i, Part i, p. 114; *Calendars of State Papers, America and West Indies, 1696–1697,* p. 613.

[3] *Minutes of the Council of Pennsylvania,* i, 527 ; see also *Calendars of State Papers, America and West Indies, 1696–1697,* p. 636.

[4] *Votes of Pennsylvania,* i, Part i, p. 115; *Laws of Pennsylvania,* ii, 100.

netted her owners thirty thousand pounds from one voyage. The New York Phillipses are stated to have cleared more than one hundred thousand pounds from business enterprises of this kind, and Stephen De Lancey, another rich New Yorker, is named among those who disposed of piratical plunder.[1] In 1699, Lord Bellomont reported that four vessels were cleared at one time for Madagascar; he had endeavored to exact bonds from them, obliging them not to trade with pirates, but was unable to do this as there was no law prohibiting the traffic.[2] The "Calendars of State Papers" contain the statement of a Jamaica governor that he had been offered twenty thousand pounds to pardon a piratical crew that had recently returned from the Red Sea with three hundred thousand pounds in goods and specie — and had refused![3] It is difficult to say how much of this traffic was what might be called "regular" piracy and how much of it was illegal trade carried on under this guise. Illicit commerce of one kind or another was so extensive that goods of European and Asiatic origin could be bought in some of the colonies at prices below those which were charged in London. Quary reported that at Newport, Rhode Island, there was "a greater plenty of European goods than in any place on the Main, tho' they have not so much as a vessel that goes from thence for England,"[4] although legally all European goods must be imported through England.

From 1689 to 1713 there was almost incessant warfare

[1] C. B. Todd's *Story of the City of New York*, 171; *New York Colonial Documents*, iv, 323, 542. "Captain Gough who keeps a mercer's shop at Boston, made a good estate" handling piratical booty — so one of Avery's men deposed. *Calendars of State Papers, America and West Indies, 1696–1697*, p. 314. See also Massachusetts Historical Society's *Collections*, Third Series, vii, 209.

[2] As to difficulties with pirates, see *New York Colonial Documents*, iv, 323, 325, 354, 385, 512.

[3] *Calendars of State Papers, America and West Indies, 1696–1697*, p. 20.

[4] Massachusetts Historical Society's *Proceedings*, Second Series, iv, 152.

between England and France. The days of Hawkins, Drake, and Cavendish seem to have returned except that now French victims replaced the Spaniards of the earlier time. Shipmasters, even those engaged in peaceful commerce, took out commissions from colonial governors, authorizing them to make spoil of the enemies of England.[1] Vessels were frequently fitted out for the express purpose of cruising against French and Portuguese privateers who sadly interfered with the commerce of the empire. When their regular prey was scanty, they seized upon whatever came in their way.[2] Privateering and piracy blend so imperceptibly into one another that it is often difficult to distinguish clearly between them.

The cases of William Kidd and Jonathan Quelch are instances of the difficulty referred to at the close of the preceding paragraph. Among the colonial governors who were charged with favoring pirates was Benjamin Fletcher of New York. He acknowledged, indeed, that he had entertained Captain Tew at table, and had given him a commission to cruise against the enemies of England; but he insisted that if Tew turned pirate, it was not his fault.[3] The outcry against Fletcher became so loud that he was recalled and Lord Bellomont was sent out to supersede him and commanded to put down piracy. While in England, before leaving for his government, Bellomont made the acquaintance of Robert Livingston, who at this time was prominent in New York affairs. He induced the newly appointed governor to confide the job of breaking up piracy to Captain William Kidd. This mariner had already

---

[1] *Calendars of State Papers, America and West Indies, 1696–1697,* pp. 260, 342; Rhode Island Society's *Publications,* vii, 195.

[2] See Goodell's "Notes" to *Massachusetts Province Laws,* xiii, 386.

[3] *Calendars of State Papers, America and West Indies, 1696–1697,* p. 518. Bellomont's prejudiced statement of his predecessor's misdeeds is in *New York Colonial Documents,* iv, 307.

been successfully employed by Massachusetts to drive off
a privateer hovering about the coasts of that colony; he
also had rendered services to the government of New York in
Sloughter's time, for which the Assembly of that province
had voted him one hundred and fifty pounds.[1] Six thousand pounds were subscribed by leading personages in England to fit out the expedition. Among the subscribers were
Lord Somers, the Earl of Oxford, and the Earl of Shrews-
bury. Bellomont,[2] Livingston, and Kidd also contributed.
The expedition was expected to be profitable, and one
tenth of the net proceeds was reserved for the king. After
recruiting and refitting at New York, Captain Kidd sailed
for the island of Madagascar.[3] Either the pirates had
news of his coming or his advent was ill-timed, for there
were no pirates to be captured. Balked of their prey,
Captain Kidd's ill-assorted crew took to piracy on their
own account and carried him with them, whether willingly or unwillingly depends somewhat upon whether one
sympathizes with Kidd or with his enemies. In the
midst of one of the debates between the captain and his
crew, Kidd becoming enraged at the discourse of William
Moore, his gunner, seized a bucket and dealt him a stroke
over the head from which he never recovered. On returning to Boston, Bellomont arrested Kidd, not without a degree of duplicity which ill befitted one of his station,[4] and
sent him to England. When Kidd came to trial, he

[1] Massachusetts Historical Society's
Collections, Third Series, i, 122; Journal of the Legislative Council of New
York, i, 3; New York Colonial Laws, i,
255.

[2] The agreement between Bellomont,
Livingston, and Kidd is in New York
Colonial Documents, iv, 762.

[3] Dr. E. E. Hale gives an interesting
account of Kidd's exploits in Memorial
History of Boston, ii, 173. There are

good articles in Hunt's Merchants' Magazine, xiv, 39; New England Historical
Genealogical Register for 1852, pp. 63,
77-84, and 1877, p. 332; and Essex Institute's Collections, iv, 29-37. See also
A Full Account of the Proceedings in relation to Captain Kidd in two Letters
written by a Person of Quality to a Kinsman of the Earl of Bellomont in Ireland,
London, 1701.

[4] Long extracts from the documents

asserted that the vessels which he had captured carried French passes and were, therefore, liable to seizure under his commission.[1] These passes, he said, he had given to Bellomont,[2] at all events he did not produce them in court. The evidence against him was so feeble and the bias of the judges so great that one's sympathies are aroused in his behalf. Besides being found guilty of piracy, he was condemned to death on the charge of murdering his gunner which could under no circumstances be justly regarded as more than manslaughter, the deed having been committed without premeditation and in anger. A victim was necessary, however, to save the honor of great personages, and Captain Kidd was executed at London. As is the case with so many historical problems, it is difficult to understand the place of William Kidd in ballad and legend. Probably the best way to account for his notoriety is to suggest that his name lent itself easily to poesy of a sort, and from the realm of imagination his misdeeds passed into the region of fact.

John Quelch, or Welch, sailed from Salem, Massachusetts, in a ship commissioned as a privateer under the command of Captain Ploughman. In due season the vessel returned with Quelch in command and without her captain, who had been thrown overboard, alive or dead. She was laden with the booty of several Portuguese ships. Meantime, while she was at sea, peace had been made

relating to Kidd's arrest are printed in Winsor's *Memorial History of Boston* (ii, 177) from the manuscripts in the Massachusetts Archives.

[1] The trial is in Howell's *State Trials*, xiv, 123–234. Kidd had a commission under the great seal, authorizing him to capture piratical vessels and a commission from the Admiralty empowering him to seize French ships, *ibid.*, xiv, 170.

[2] He stated this repeatedly at his trial, and also in a petition which is calendared in Royal Historical Manuscripts Commission's *Reports*, xv, Part iv, p. 17; and the House of Commons addressed the king, asking that the trial of Kidd might be postponed until Bellomont could send over the papers relating to Kidd. Chandler's *History of the Commons*, iii, 125.

between England and Portugal. Quelch and his comrades were, therefore, possibly not privateers, as they probably had supposed themselves to be, but pirates. At all events, they were tried by a special court, which was probably illegal, were convicted of piracy, and sentenced to be hanged. Their execution (June 30, 1704) was carried out at the water side of Boston in the sight of throngs gathered on the neighboring wharves and in one hundred and fifty boats and canoes. When the drop fell, a scream went up from the women spectators that was heard by Mrs. Sewall sitting in the entrance of her house fully a mile away. It is sometimes said that the eagerness of leading officials to share in the spoil was the cause of Captain Quelch's unhappy end.[1]

Much of the evidence given in the preceding pages relates to years subsequent to 1695, but it is confirmatory of the general thesis that colonial commercial and governmental systems were sadly in need of reorganization in the decade following the " Glorious Revolution." Such, certainly, was the opinion of Englishmen interested in colonial trade. In the winter of 1694–95, merchants of Bristol, Liverpool, and London petitioned the House of Commons[2] to provide a remedy for these continuous infractions of the navigation laws. In these petitions they especially mentioned the carrying of plantation goods to Scotland and Ireland without landing them in England, and the bringing of European commodities into England in vessels other than those allowed by law. It was at this time that the Scots showed an unmistakable inten-

[1] For an account of Quelch, see *Boston News Letter* for July 3, 1704, in New York Historical Society's library; Samuel Sewall's *Diary* in Massachusetts Historical Society's *Collections*, Fifth Series, vi, 103, 105–111. The admirable article by John Noble in Massachusetts Colonial Society's *Publications*, viii, 161, 162, gives valuable references.

[2] *Commons Journals*, xi, 195, 216; Hansard's *Parliamentary Debates*, v, 977.

tion of taking their share of the growing trade of the world. In 1693 the Scottish Parliament chartered a commercial corporation for foreign trade.[1] The intention of the leading men in this corporation appeared to be to trade to India and the African coasts. This attracted the notice of the English East India Company, which had powerful friends in Parliament. In December, 1695, protests and communications poured in upon the government and Parliament. The most effective of these were from the East India Company, but the Royal African Company also protested and also had great influence. The Commissioners of the Customs added their voices against the allowance of trading privileges to the Scots and asked to have the navigation laws rigorously enforced.[2] Colonial agents in London were asked for their opinion as to the effect of Scottish competition in the colonial trade; their replies were generally in favor of greater restriction, but the Jamaica agents must have somewhat startled Parliament by replying that the best way to prevent any mischiefs would be " to make the trade as easy as may be."[3] Parliamentary inquiries were now held,[4] motions were made in both houses, and in a few months this activity resulted in the passage of a new navigation act and the appointment of a new Council for Trade and Plantations.

As in the former time, so now Edward Randolph voyaged frequently across the Atlantic, partly perhaps to preserve his friendships and partly to enforce his ideas

---

[1] See Hiram Bingham's "Early History of the Scots Darien Company" in *Scottish Historical Review*, January, April, July, 1906.

[2] *Lords Manuscripts*, New Series, ii, 17; other papers of the same general character are in the same volume.

[3] *Ibid.*, ii, 19, 20.

[4] On December 17, 1695, a committee of the House of Commons was appointed to consider how the Scottish act had been obtained. Among its members was Lord Cornbury. *Commons Journals*, xi, 365.

as to the carrying out of the acts of trade and also as to colonial policy in general. He now vigorously seconded the efforts of those who were striving for a new act of Parliament relating to the trade and navigation of the colonies. He had no difficulty in citing numerous infractions of the laws, although he held that, generally speaking, the acts of Charles would be sufficient were they rigidly enforced.[1] At this time in his career, Randolph was especially bitter against the government of Pennsylvania, which was in an unusually chaotic condition. In the course of the discussion, Penn was asked why he should not give over the government of his province to the crown. He replied that he could not sell an acre of land unless he also possessed the jurisdiction, and suggested as a compromise that any deputy governor whom he should appoint should be approved by the king and should give bonds to the king for the faithful performance of his duties.[2] It was under these circumstances that the " Act for preventing Frauds and regulating Abuses in the Plantation Trade " was passed in the spring of 1696.[3]

The first section of this law provides that no plantation goods shall be carried from one plantation to another, shall be exported from, or imported into, the plantations except in vessels built and owned in England, Ireland, or the plantations and navigated by officers and crews, three fourths of whom must be subjects of the English crown,

[1] See his evidence in Lords Manu-scripts, New Series, ii, 233, and also his report of 1696–97 in ibid., ii, 440.

[2] Ibid., ii, 413.

[3] 7 and 8 William III, Cap. xxii (Statutes of the Realm, vii, 103). The legislative history of this measure can be traced in the Commons Journals, vol. xi. A bill was introduced in 1694 to better secure the plantation trade and to prevent the exportation of tobacco in bulk (ibid.,

xi, 188), but was not passed. Blathwayt was prominent in introducing the bill of 1695, which was passed, ibid., xi, 539. While the discussion of the resolution upon which this bill was based was going on, the measure for the establishment of a council of trade was brought forward, February 12, 1695, ibid., xi, 440. The royal assent was given to the " Act for preventing Frauds in the Plantation Trade " on April 10, 1696, ibid., xi, 555.

except prize ships and vessels employed by the Commissioners of the Navy. Plantation governors must take an oath to observe the acts under penalty of one thousand pounds sterling and removal from office, and officers appointed by them must give bonds to the Commissioners of the Customs for the faithful performance of their duties. The formalities of entering and clearing with the customs officials, which had been provided for England in 1662, were now extended to the plantations. Security must be given to land all enumerated goods in England, Wales, Berwick-on-Tweed, or other plantations. All colonial laws repugnant to this and other navigation acts were declared void, and ample penalties were provided for its infraction. In the future no plantation goods could be put on shore in Scotland or Ireland except in case of wreck or serious leakage, when they must be removed in other vessels to the shores of England. Those holding land and exercising jurisdiction by charter or letters patent from the crown must not sell land to aliens without the consent of the king, and the governors of proprietary colonies must be approved by the crown.[1] All vessels must be registered under oath and on changing names must be registered anew.[2]

[1] Section xi of this act reads as follows: "Provided always That all Places of Trust in the Courts of Law or what relates to the Treasury of the said Islands, shall from the making of this Act be in the Hands of the Native borne Subjects of England or Ireland or of the said Islands." The preceding sections mention "Islands, Tracts of Lands, and Proprieties and the said Plantations." Plantation governors were responsible for the enforcement of the navigation laws within their jurisdiction and were therefore included in the above category. The intention of the framers of this section was to exclude the Scots from colonial offices; but in 1699 when the Lords of Trade applied to Attorney General Trevor for a ruling which would prevent Governor Hamilton of New Jersey from acting in that capacity, he decided that Hamilton, although a native of Scotland, was a natural-born subject of the crown. See *Statutes of the Realm*, vii, 105 (7 and 8 William III, Cap. 22, § xi); Toppan's *Edward Randolph*, ii, 180 note; *New Jersey Archives*, First Series, ii, 250; "Journals of the Lords of Trade" (Ms.) xi, 341.

[2] See Note II, p. 280, for effect of this act on colonial trade.

In those days, before the functions of government had
come to be so efficiently organized as they now are, private endeavor and not official zeal was relied upon to
secure the enforcement of legal enactments. In the navigation acts of Charles II, ships and one third of the
goods forfeited for contravention of those laws were to go
to him or them that shall "Seize Informe or sue for the
same in any Court of Record by Bill, Plaint, or other
Action wherin no Essoigne, Protection, or Wager of Law
shall be allowed." [1]   These words are taken from the Act
of 1660, but similar language is to be found in the Act of
1663. The force of this clause was to confine the prosecution of suits for forfeiture under these acts to the common law courts, since they alone were technically termed
"courts of record." Moreover, the procedure mentioned
is that of the common law court and not of the courts of
admiralty. Randolph, in season and out, represented the
impossibility of securing convictions in revenue cases from
colonial juries, and urged the establishment of an admiralty court in every colony and the amendment of the law
so that cases might be tried in them. This was now done
in the Act of 1696 by substituting for the words, which
have been given above, the inclusive phrases, "any court
in his Majesty's plantations where such offence shall be
committed" or "in the court of admiralty held in his
Majesty's plantations respectively where such offence shall
be committed." Suits for penalties under the act might be
tried in any of these courts at the option of the officer or
informer who brought the suit; [2] this language is itself
not entirely clear, but it was construed to admit of bring-

[1] 12 Charles II, Cap. 18, § 1 (*Statutes
of the Realm*, v, 246).
[2] 7 and 8 William III, Cap. 22, § i, vi
(*Statutes of the Realm*, vii, 103). The
history of the matter is briefly sketched
in Chalmers's *Introduction to the Revolt*,
i, 275.

ing suits for the penalties mentioned in the act in colonial admiralty courts.

Admiralty law had its rise in the Mediterranean maritime codes, especially that of the Island of Rhodes. This body of law was adapted to more modern requirements by the Laws of Oleron, an island off the shore of southwestern France. These laws, relating to torts of the sea, embodied rules which were fitted to seamen of all nations, because the cases which were decided under them arose as to things and experiences which were common to all sea-faring people. They had developed in countries where the procedure of the Roman or civil code prevailed ; and in importing them into England for the settlement of cases relating to the sea, the procedure of the Civil Law was also brought in for use in that department of justice. It fell out in this way, that the procedure in the admiralty courts was unlike that of the common law courts and was opposed to the prejudices of the English people, mainly because there were no juries known to the civil law and also because the judge played the part of inquisitor as well as that of arbiter. A different set of lawyers practiced in the admiralty courts, and the trial of cases in them meant a diminution of influence and fees for the practitioners in the common law courts. This fact undoubtedly accounts for much of the jealousy of the common lawyers toward the admiralty courts. The colonists dreaded the establishment of this unknown jurisdiction among them, especially for the enforcement of laws which they believed to be opposed to their interests.[1]

Nothing was done immediately after the passage of

[1] On admiralty jurisdiction, see Edwin Edwards's *Admiralty Jurisdiction*, 21; Henry Spelman's *Admiralty Jurisdiction;* Emory Washburn's *Judicial History of Massachusetts*, 172 and fol.; Anthony Stokes's *View of the Constitution*, 166, 270; William Douglass's *Summary*, i, 483. Two volumes published at London in 1746 contain a mass of information on the topic chronologically arranged : *The Laws, Ordinances and Institutions of the Admiralty of Great Britain,*

the Act of 1696, but Blathwayt, Randolph, and Southwell pressed the matter upon the attention of the House of Lords, which, after prolonged inquiry, presented an address to the king, recommending the establishment of admiralty courts in the colonies, and this was done in the closing years of the century. The continental colonies were divided into two admiralty districts : the northern included New England, New York, and, after 1702, New Jersey;[1] while Pennsylvania and the colonies to the southward formed the other. An admiralty judge was appointed to each district, Wait Winthrop for the northern and Robert Quary for the southern. Each of these judges was authorized to appoint deputies and later the districts were made smaller and more judges were appointed. Quary tried to enforce the laws according to his lights,[2] and it must be said also according to his interests, since at one time he was both acting surveyor general and admiralty judge.

The early judges of the northern district were able to accomplish little, owing in part to the supineness of the collectors in that region. When, at length, collectors and judges bestirred themselves and began to secure convictions, the common law judges took a hand in the matter. They discharged from custody persons who had been imprisoned by the admiralty courts for not satisfying the judgments of those tribunals ; and they issued prohibitions restraining

civil and military, comprehending ancient naval laws, abstracts of statutes, marine treaties interspersed with dissertations.

[1] Draft of the surrender of New Jersey is in New Jersey Archives, First Series, ii, 452.

[2] An interesting case of conflict of jurisdiction occurred in Pennsylvania in 1698. Acting under orders from Quary as admiralty judge, the marshal seized certain goods. Thereupon Anthony Morris, a provincial judge, issued a writ of replevin, which was executed. David Lloyd, then attorney general of the province, advised Morris to take this action. Owing to certain technicalities, the royal authorities appear to have been in the wrong ; but Quary complained to England so loudly that Lloyd and Morris were dismissed from their positions and the former was suspended from his place at the council board. Minutes of the Council of Pennsylvania, i, 541 and fol., 565, 575, 603; W. R. Shepherd's Pennsylvania, 505.

the admiralty courts from an undue exercise of jurisdiction. Only a few prohibitions were actually issued, but those were enough to induce the admiralty judges to complain to the Lords of Trade, who secured from their counsel, Mr. West, an opinion as to the action of the common law colonial courts. This opinion was given in 1720,[1] and could not have been very satisfactory to those whose business it was to enforce the navigation laws. Mr. West declared that the prohibitions were legal, because if the common law courts in the colonies had no power to grant them, the colonists would have no remedy from the decisions of the admiralty judges. Moreover, an appeal from them would be to the High Court of Admiralty in England and not to the King in Council, but every colonist had the right to appeal to the king for justice; " for let an Englishman go wherever he will, he carries as much of law and liberty with him as the nature of things will bear." If the admiralty officials or any one in the colonies were injured by the grant of a writ of prohibition, these could appeal to his Majesty for redress. If on inquiry it should appear that the colonists were systematically endeavoring to abolish the due exercise of an admiralty jurisdiction in the provinces, Parliament by law might reduce the exercise of the admiralty jurisdiction in the colonies to a certainty. No such law was passed in the period covered by this volume, and the colonists, despite the efforts of royal officials and admiralty judges, and often in collusion with them, continued to carry on their commerce, greatly to their profit and in contravention of the navigation laws and other acts of the imperial Parliament.

In the matter of dealing with piracies, Parliament felt obliged to interfere and passed an act in 1700 for the establishment of Justiciary Courts of Admiralty for the

[1] Chalmers's *Opinions*, ii, 201–215.

trial of captured pirates.   This was a large body of commissioners with a quorum of seven and included colonial
governors, councilors, admiralty judges, captains of naval
vessels, and customs officials.[1]   It seems to have been
convened by special commission in each case and had its
own officers, who were distinct from those of the ordinary
admiralty courts, but the two had this in common,—
that in neither was there any provision for trial by jury.
Pirates, alone of the subjects of the English king, might
be put to death without the verdict of twelve good men
and true.

[1] On the establishment of these
courts see Emory Washburn's *Judicial*
History of Massachusetts, 173; *Works of*
John Adams, ii, 224.

NOTES

I. Bibliography. — The material on the subject-matter of the preceding chapter is contained in the *Calendars of State Papers, Colonial Series, America and West Indies,* beginning with the year 1689. This can be reached through the index under "privateers" and "piracy," the names of governors and other officials, of pirates,[1] and of the colonies. The second volume of the *Manuscripts of the House of Lords,* published under the supervision of the Royal Historical Manuscripts Commission, but not as part of their reports, contains extremely valuable matter which is printed in full. The reports of the commission on the *Manuscripts of the Duke of Portland at Welbeck Abbey* (viii, 65–83) also contain papers of exceeding interest as to Captain Kidd, including several letters from Lord Bellomont. The letters and other documents printed in the concluding volume of Toppan's *Edward Randolph* should by no means be neglected. The most important of this matter and of other reports and letters is noted on the pages of this chapter.[1]

II. Effect of the Act of 1696. — The Navigation Act and the efforts of Randolph, Quary, and those who worked with them brought about an important change in the commercial relations of England and the continental colonies, converting a balance in favor of the colonies to a balance in favor of England ; the difference being due to the fact that after 1696 the colonists were obliged, more and more, to import European goods indirectly through England instead of from the continent of Europe in contravention of the act of Charles. In 1696–97, from one Christmas to another, the continental colonies took from England goods to the value of £140,000 sterling and exported to that country commodities to the value of £279,852, the balance against England being almost £140,000. Virginia and Maryland sent to England tobacco to the amount of

[1] Captain Charles Johnson's *General History of the Pyrates* (second edition, London, 1724) has a good deal of the appearance of a romance, but is corroborated in many ways by the official documents and contains a convenient abstract of the civil and statute law relating to piracy. This book with Exquemelin's *History of the Bucaniers of America, from the first original down to this time : Written in several languages ;* and now collected into one volume (third edition, London 1704) form the groundwork of most modern accounts. S. C. Hughson's "Carolina Pirates" (*Johns Hopkins Studies,* xii, Nos. v, vi, vii) deals mainly with a later phase of the subject. John Fiske's chapter in his *Dutch and Quaker Colonies* (ii, 222–235) is extremely readable and so is Thomas A. Janvier's article on "New York Colonial Privateers" in *Harper's Magazine,* xc, 333.

£200,000 and took goods valued only at £58,000 in return. In 1699–1700 the continental colonies exported £399,961 and imported £235,488, an excess of exports of £164,472, and in the following twelve months the imports from England actually exceeded the exports to that country. "Chalmers's Papers," Ms. i, 16, 17.

III. Flag for Colonial Vessels. — In 1715 the following instruction was issued to George, Earl of Orkney, governor of Virginia for life; whether it was put into practice or not, does not appear. "Whereas great Inconveniences do happen by Merchant ships and other Vessels in the Plantations wearing the Colours born by our ships of war under pretence of Commissions granted to them by the Governors of the said Plantations, and that by Trading under those colours not only amongst our own Subjects, but also those of other Princes and States and Committing divers Irregularities they do very much dishonor our service. For prevention whereof, you are to oblige the Commanders of all such ships to which you shall grant commissions to wear no other Jack than according to the sample here described, that is to say, such as is worn by our Ships of War with a distinction of a White Escutcheon in the middle thereof and that the said mark of distinction may extend itself to one half of the Depth of the Jack and one third of the Fly thereof." Ms. in Virginia Historical Society.

CHAPTER X

BEGINNINGS OF CONSTITUTIONAL CONTROVERSY

WILLIAM SMITH, the historian of New York, declared that the colonies separated from England because they had outgrown their government half a century before 1776; an American assembly could not but discover " that themselves were the substance, and the Governor and Board of Council were shadows in their political Frame." [1] John Locke lays down the general proposition that in any government the legislative is supreme. The actions of executive authority frequently attract attention by reason of their brilliancy; but the slower-moving legislative in the end accomplishes its purposes and usually at the expense of its more spectacular partner. The history of the eighteenth century in the colonies is peculiarly illustrative of this proposition. The assemblies represented colonial desires in opposition to English control. They constantly gained power from the executive by the good old English method of tightening the grip on the strings of the purse, being greatly assisted thereto by successive French and Indian Wars, which placed the governors in constant need of money and compelled them to accede to demands in defiance of orders of king and proprietor.

[1] In a letter to Lord Dorchester, 1790, *Report on Canadian Archives*, 1890, p. 35. William Smith was a member of the New York Council for many years. At the Revolution he remained loyal to the king and at the time of writing this letter he was living in exile.

The peculiar construction of society in Virginia bound together the ruling classes by ties of self-interest. The constitution of that province had already become settled : the Burgesses controlled extraordinary expenditure through the appointment of the public treasurer, who was generally their Speaker ; they could not put pressure upon the governor by refusing to vote him his salary because that came out of permanent revenue. It was only on occasions of great stress that conflict between the representatives of royal authority and of Virginia voters was likely to arise. Ordinarily, a condition of constitutional calm prevailed in the Old Dominion. This was practically true also of Connecticut and Rhode Island, because in those chartered colonies both executive and legislative were appointed by the voters.

Throughout this period Massachusetts was a center of disturbance. Had the revolutionists reëstablished their government under the old charter, and asked for no confirmation of that patent, they might possibly have been permitted to go on. The downfall of Andros and Randolph accomplished, factions appeared among the successful colonial revolutionists, one party wishing the old charter renewed, the other desiring a new patent, and these parties in the colony were reproduced among the agents in London. Randolph was released from captivity, returned home,[1] and renewed his friendship with Blathwayt. They defeated the confirmation of the old charter, prevented the granting of a new patent like that of Connecticut, and forced the agents to accept a charter drawn by Blathwayt[2] with an important amendment

[1] Andros and the others were discharged from custody by order of the Privy Council in April, 1690. Massachusetts Colonial Society's *Publications*, ii.

[2] Hutchinson (*History of Massachusetts*, i, 364 note) declared that there were many inaccuracies in the Province Charter which probably " come from Mr. Blaithwait."

confirming the Massachusetts colonists in their lands. The destruction of the old corporation was a despotic act and the refusal of the Revolution government to renew it was unfair to those who had espoused that cause in America. Otherwise, the settlement was advantageous ; as long as the old charter was in existence, every conflict with the crown had imperiled the life of the corporation and had, therefore, to be avoided whenever it was possible. In the future, political contests would be hardly more than struggles with royal governors and could be entered upon with lighter hearts. The incessant controversies of the next seventy years bred a succession of political leaders who for adroitness and sometimes for statesmanship have rarely been exceeded in America. Moreover, the people of the Bay Colony, especially of Boston, were now forced to mingle, more or less, with officials sent over from England and with their families also. Although it was distinctly distasteful to them, this contact with the outer world forced upon them new ideas and thus broadened their outlook and made greatly for culture and freedom.[1]

The Massachusetts Province Charter of 1691 provided for the appointment of a governor and other executive officials by the crown and the election of a House of Representatives by the colonists on a moderate property qualification.[2] So far the new constitution resembled that of the royal province, but a novel feature was proposed as

---

[1] Samuel Sewall's interest in the Scots Darien scheme is an instance of this enlarged outlook. See Massachusetts Historical Society's *Collections*, Fifth Series, v, 488–490.

[2] The right to vote for representatives was conferred upon men who possessed a freehold to the annual value of forty shillings or personal property to the amount of forty or fifty pounds, the latter amount being in the engrossed charter in England, the former in the copy which was sent over to America. See *Massachusetts Province Laws*, i, 1, 21, 363 note, and a paper by Ellis Ames, in Massachusetts Historical Society's *Proceedings* for 1867, p. 370.

to the Council, since its members were nominated by the General Court and confirmed by the governor. The governor's consent was required to every act of the assembly, but only certain specified classes of documents were to be sent to England for royal approval. Liberty of conscience and of worship were guaranteed to all Protestants. The colonists were to have the liberties and immunities of natural-born subjects " as if they were born within the realm of England," and were to be permitted to appeal from the courts of the colony to the King in Council in personal actions, whenever the amount in dispute was over three hundred pounds sterling.

The new province included within its limits New Plymouth Colony, the islands off the southern side of Cape Cod, Maine, Nova Scotia, and the territory between them which had been granted to the Duke of York in 1664. New Hampshire was thus left as a distinct government. At the time of the deposition of Andros, New Hampshire had appealed to Massachusetts for aid against the Indians who had attacked her settlements, but the interim government had enough responsibilities at home and declined to give assistance. On January 24, 1690, twenty-two delegates met in convention at Portsmouth and adopted a " Form of Government," [1] or constitution, to which each man set his name. It never had any validity as the Convention also applied to Massachusetts to extend her government across the Merrimac, which she did and was governing that province in 1691. The failure to include New Hampshire in Massachusetts in the Province Charter was probably due to an opportune present which Samuel Allen, one of the Masonian proprietors, made to Blath-

[1] Massachusetts Historical Society's *Proceedings*, First Series, xvii, 218, where the document is printed in fac- simile. This was the first " constitutional convention " in our history.

wayt; and later Allen secured the appointment as governor, probably by similar means. Moreover, in the phrase which described the northern bounds of Massachusetts in the charter of 1691, the words "and every part thereof," which follow the phrase "three miles north of the Merrimac" in the charter of 1629, were omitted, probably by accident, and this discrepancy was later used to deprive Massachusetts of her right to southern New Hampshire and southern Vermont.

The first governor of Massachusetts under the Province Charter was Sir William Phips, a native of Maine and a daring and successful adventurer.[1] He was expected to be a popular first magistrate and to soothe the ruffled feelings of his fellow-colonists. He brought with him, however, instructions which were certain to make trouble in that he was directed to secure a settled support for the governor and the government, and to procure the building of several forts upon the northern frontier and the fortification of Pemaquid.

The colonists accepted the changed conditions of government; but this spirit of acquiescence was speedily dispelled. In common with the assemblies of other colonies, the Massachusetts General Court passed a series of laws securing to themselves many of the ancient rights of Englishmen and providing for the establishment of a system of courts.[2] These laws, however, were all annulled by the English government. In the case of the courts, this caused great inconvenience, and the exercise of the veto power in such a wholesale manner could hardly fail to arouse irritation. The political leaders at once saw that the most effective way to secure their rights was to keep the gov-

[1] On this part of Phips's career see Hutchinson's *Massachusetts* (ed. 1795), i, 352 note.

[2] *Massachusetts Province Laws*, i, acts of 1692-93, and editor's note on p. 109.

ernor and other royal officials dependent upon the good will of the General Court by making grants of money for salaries from time to time. Moreover, the colonists did not recognize the utility of the fortifications which were demanded. The assembly voted " five hundred pounds unto His Excellency, the Governor for his service and expence since his arrival "[1] and gave nothing for fortifications. Phips repeatedly besought the assembly to give him a settled support, but the utmost they would do was at the end of each year to vote him a sum of money. Acting on authority given him in the charter, Phips refused to confirm the election of Elisha Cooke, the senior of that name, as a councilor. He was obnoxious to the governor on personal grounds and also as a vigorous and shrewd politician and the leader in the contest over the salary and fortification dispute. Phips acted in so high-handed a manner in various directions that charges were preferred against him by other royal officials. He was recalled to England to answer these imputations and died at London in February, 1695. Lieutenant Governor Stoughton then acted as chief magistrate for two years until Lord Bellomont assumed the charge of the executive government of Massachusetts, New York, and New Hampshire. The assembly granted Bellomont two thousand pounds, but would make no permanent provision for his support.

After Bellomont's death, Joseph Dudley secured the wish of his life in being appointed governor of his native colony. Since 1692 he had resided mainly in England, where he had acted as deputy to Lord Cutts, governor of the Isle of Wight. He had been made colonel of an English regiment and had been returned to the House of Commons.[2]

[1] *Massachusetts Province Laws*, i, 109.

[2] In treating Dudley's career, I have drawn freely from an excellent doctoral

As governor of Massachusetts, his position was not so weak as at first sight one might expect it would have been. He had the support of the royal officials in the colony and of those colonists who advocated moderate measures and were opposed to radicals like Elisha Cooke and Thomas Oakes. Throughout his term of office, Dudley relied upon the support of the royal government and always received it. The experiences of his early life and his connections in England gave him an insight into the management of men and a degree of military support which few other natives of New England would have enjoyed. The military and naval expeditions of his term of office, which was coextensive with Queen Anne's War, necessitated the expenditure of considerable sums of money. The General Court kept a tight hand on the disbursement of colonial funds within the colony, but Dudley had the distribution of large contracts for furnishing supplies for the royal forces and these he could give to those who won his favor. He might have enjoyed a pleasant term of office had it not been for the instructions which he brought with him from England as to a permanent support of government and the fortification of the frontiers.

Dudley began his term of office by refusing to confirm several councilors and also by declining to accept Thomas Oakes as Speaker of the House of Representatives. When agent of the colony in England, Oakes had won the dislike of both Phips and Dudley. The former had denied him a seat in the Council and for this reason the House elected him as its Speaker. As Oakes was one of the most powerful politicians in the province, this action of Dudley's proved to be the beginning of an interesting contest as

thesis in the form of a memoir of Joseph Dudley, which was prepared by Professor Everett Kimball. Letters from Lord Cutts are printed in Massachusetts Historical Society's *Proceedings*, Second Series, ii, 171.

to the right of the governor to negative the election of a Speaker. As was the case in other provinces, so in Massachusetts since the inauguration of the government under the Province Charter the House had presented its Speaker to the governor for his confirmation.[1] This copying of English ceremonial in America was unnecessary and was unfortunate because it gave royal and proprietary governors a chance to interfere in the organization of the representative branch of the colonial legislature. Dudley contended that as the charter gave him the right to negative the acts of the assembly, he was within his constitutional right in refusing to ratify their election of a presiding officer. This dispute went on with varying degrees of vigor until 1726, when the king by an Explanatory Charter[2] decided that the choice of the Speaker by the House of Representatives must be confirmed by the governor of the province.

The main interest of Dudley's term, from the constitutional side, is as to the settlement of the salary for his support. The Representatives voted him five hundred pounds in each year.[3] Coupled with the instruction as to securing a settled support for himself and for the lieutenant governor was a demand for the rebuilding of the fort at Pemaquid and aiding New Hampshire in the construction of a fortification at the entrance to Portsmouth Harbor. The first of these was a sad reminder of the days of Andros, for the fort had been erected at Pemaquid when

---

[1] A good example of this is recorded in the *Minutes of the Council of Pennsylvania*, i, 617, where the speaker-elect declares his unfitness for the office to the governor, and, on being accepted, craves freedom of access, free speech, and freedom from arrest for the members of the assembly, which the governor grants.

[2] *Massachusetts Province Laws*, i, 21.

[3] *A Collection of the Proceedings of the Great and General Court of Massachusetts Bay, Containing Instructions for fixing a Salary on the Governour, and Methods taken by the Court for Supporting the several Governours*, 6; this work in the future will be cited as *Collection of Proceedings*.

that part of Maine belonged to the Duke of York. It was far beyond the settled frontier and was of no protection to the actual settlers in that region; but its existence was important as asserting the title of England to the territory east of the Kennebec River. It seemed to the colonists that this was an imperial rather than a local matter, and that the expense should therefore be borne by England instead of by Massachusetts. The case as to the Piscataqua fort aroused even more poignant grief, for the site of the fort at the entrance to Portsmouth Harbor was within the limits of New Hampshire, which had been separated from Massachusetts without any valid reason as it seemed to the inhabitants of the latter province. It must not be supposed that Massachusetts was niggardly in the expenditure of money for general purposes of defense. In 1704–05 the queen instructed the governor to bring these matters again to the notice of the assembly and to declare that the neglect of her command would demonstrate that the Representatives were "undeserving of her Majesty's Royal Favour and Bounty towards them." [1] In reply to this, September 15, 1705, the General Court drew up an address [2] to Queen Anne, in which they stated that they had already expended more than eighty thousand pounds in the prosecution of the war, a sum which before the war was ended swelled to over two hundred thousand pounds. Altogether they paid to Dudley sixty-nine hundred and fifty pounds as compensation for the fourteen years of his service as governor, but it was doled out in half-yearly sums.

The year following Dudley's removal, Lieutenant Governor Tailer ruled the province. In 1716 the next governor,

[1] *Collection of Proceedings*, 16. See also Palfrey's *New England*, iv, 254 note, for "Representation" of the Lords of Trade, April 2, 1703.
[2] *Collection of Proceedings*, 20–22.

Samuel Shute,[1] met his first General Court. In his speech at the opening of the session, he stated that he was commanded to acquaint the Representatives that Massachusetts was the only " Province in America under the Crown of Great Britain "[2] where stated salaries were not settled upon the governor; and also to remind them of the refitting of the fort at Pemaquid. They replied by voting him five hundred pounds "for his support in managing the Affairs of the Government"; but they would do nothing as to Pemaquid. In the next and two succeeding years they gave him a thousand and twelve hundred pounds, respectively; but in 1720 they cut him down to one thousand pounds, which he thought was insufficient. Probably at his own instigation he received an "additional instruction," forbidding him to assent to any bills for the issuing of paper money or for the payment of money to himself or the council or members of the assembly, except acts for raising a revenue for defraying the necessary charge of the government. The Council, however, advised that payment of salary was a necessity and, therefore, that the governor might consent to votes for the making of such payments. The close of Shute's career as governor was not happy, for he became involved in a violent dispute with the assembly over the publication of an attack upon himself in one of the newspapers and tried to use the incident to restore the censorship of the press. He left the colony rather hurriedly and for the remainder of his term of office resided in England. In these years, from 1722 to 1728, the General Court voted

[1] The appointment of Shute was the outcome of a curious intrigue. A certain Colonel Burgess had been selected for the office. Believing him to be hostile to the policy which they favored, Jeremiah Dummer and Jonathan Belcher, the colony's agents in England, paid him a thousand pounds to decline the office. See letter from Dummer in Massachusetts Historical Society's *Proceedings*, Second Series, iv, 192, and Palfrey's *New England*, iv, 386.

[2] *Collection of Proceedings*, 26.

money for the support of the lieutenant governor, but refused any for the absentee chief magistrate. This neglect of theirs forced the salary question again prominently on the attention of the English government, with the result that Shute's successor brought with him stringent instructions forbidding him to receive temporary gifts.

The new governor of Massachusetts was William Burnet. He was the son of Bishop Burnet, had been educated at Cambridge and Leyden, and had made a passable governor of New York and New Jersey. His instructions repeated the contentious demands as to Pemaquid and salaries. As to the latter, his attention was called to the fact that the General Court of Massachusetts had endeavored to secure the dependence of the royal governors by making them temporary grants, and he was instructed to demand that a fixed and honorable salary of at least one thousand pounds sterling per annum be immediately voted. The instruction closed with the statement that a disregard of this would be looked upon by the king "as a manifest mark of their Undutiful Behaviour to Us, and such as may require the Consideration of the Legislature." [1] This threat of applying to Parliament to provide a salary for the Massachusetts governor on the penalty of having the charter suspended or annulled, did not have its expected effect. The General Court came together in July, 1728, and voted Burnet seventeen hundred pounds, to enable him to manage the public affairs of the government and to defray his charges for moving his family, servants, and furniture to Boston. The sum was much larger than had ever before been voted to a governor at one time, but he informed the General Court that he was utterly disabled from assenting to the resolve containing this grant and he

[1] *Collection of Proceedings*, 41.

continued to give the same reply, although the assembly finally raised the amount to three thousand pounds.

Burnet endeavored to argue with the Representatives in written messages, which the Representatives were not slow in answering. In one of these papers he incautiously stated that by their charter they were to pass wholesome and reasonable laws, which were not hurtful to the British constitution. The Representatives seized upon this phrase as showing that he himself admitted them to have the rights of Englishmen. They then traced their rights back to Magna Charta, Henry III, and Edward I, as well as to the legislation of the Tudors and the Stuarts. Burnet endeavored to put pressure upon them by refusing to prorogue them or to dissolve them, and even went so far as to shift the scene of their deliberations from Boston to Salem, and later to Cambridge. He related their disobedience to the British government and received a communication from Lord Carteret, then Secretary of State, threatening the Massachusetts people with the loss of their charter by parliamentary action if they remained recalcitrant. Burnet also refused to consent to a bill for the payment of the salaries of the Representatives, hoping thus to starve them into compliance with the royal will. The House on its part dispatched agents to England to state its side of the case, and also to lay before the home government an account of such misdeeds on the part of Burnet as they had discovered. To supply himself with money, of which he stood in great need, he had extorted high fees for the clearance of vessels going to sea, both at New York and Boston. Before the Privy Council announced its disapproval of this action, Burnet was thrown into the water by the oversetting of his carriage on the way from Cambridge to Boston, and a week later died. Notwithstanding the stubborn resistance which he had made to what the Representatives regarded as their rights, they voted two thousand pounds to his children, which the latter were allowed to receive.

Jonathan Belcher, who had gone over to London as agent for the House of Representatives, now obtained the appointment as governor of Massachusetts Bay; but he brought the same orders as to a settled permanent provision for the support of the government. The leaders in Massachusetts fully realized that the political conditions which prevailed in the mother country were such that they could defy the orders of the government without danger. They refused to grant Belcher any fixed salary or to make any permanent provision for the support of government. Belcher requested the English authorities to permit him to receive annual grants. He was allowed to do so, provided the money should be voted at the beginning and not at the end of the sessions of assembly and would, therefore, lose the appearance of being presents for services rendered. In this way the long struggle came to an end. The Massachusetts General Court, however, was not so successful in securing control of the finances of the colony as was the Assembly of New York, which had gained the right to appoint the colonial treasurer, to audit the accounts, and to do away with the amendatory power of the council as to money bills; but as in New York, so in Massachusetts, the legislature fell into the habit of making specific appropriations.

In many ways the history of New York is the most interesting among colonial annals. There political parties were well organized and fought with great energy and achieved important results. In place of recognizing the revolutionary leaders in New York, William appointed

Colonel Henry Sloughter, otherwise unknown, as its first royal governor. He was instructed to exercise in New York substantially the same functions that were performed by the governor in Virginia. This was an important step in the constitutional development of New York, for from this time on that province was no longer treated as a crown colony, but was regarded as constitutionally equal to the only other royal government, the Dominion of Virginia. From this time on New York was to have a representative assembly, and from this moment begins the constitutional controversy between the assembly and the governor. No attempt was made in Sloughter's commissions or instructions to protect Jacob Leisler and his adherents from Bayard and their other enemies; [1] but the English authorities were probably unaware of the fierce factional feeling which prevailed in the province, and possibly it was inevitable that New York politics should run the course that they did. This, however, is all that can be said to absolve William from the responsibility of the tragedy which followed. At about the time that Sloughter sailed from England, a small body of soldiers was embarked for New York under the command of Richard Ingoldesby, who proved to be singularly unfit to handle the crisis which confronted him when he arrived. This force had been ordered to New York in the height of Dongan's controversy with the French governors in Canada; but their coming now was a misfortune. Had the soldiers arrived after Sloughter, or even had they come with him, all might have gone well. As it chanced, however, Sloughter and Ingoldesby pursued different courses across the Atlantic, with the result that the latter reached the colony first. He at once made friends with Bayard

[1] See above, pp. 203–209.

and his faction and demanded the surrender of the fort
on Manhattan Island from Leisler, but would not show him
any document authorizing this demand.[1]   When Sloughter
at length arrived, he, too, espoused the cause of the anti-
Leislerians.   He ordered the fort to be surrendered to
him, also without showing his commission.   Leisler hesitated just long enough to give his enemies the opportunity to brand him as a traitor.[2]   He was tried by a
special court, which was presided over by Joseph Dudley,
was convicted of treason, sentenced to death, and executed, and his property confiscated ; with him suffered
his son-in-law, Jacob Milborne.   It used to be said that
the death warrant was signed by Sloughter while intoxi-
cated ; the records indicate, however, that Leisler was executed in consequence of a resolution of the Council.[3]   These
executions took place in May, 1691.   Sloughter did not
long outlast the Revolutionary leaders, as he died in the
following summer, the victim of intemperance.

To understand the constitutional history of New York,
it is necessary to go back to the days of Colonel Dongan.
He was the first governor of that province who was
authorized by the Duke of York to establish representative institutions, and the ducal proprietor had been
brought to this distasteful determination by the fact that
the New Yorkers had roundly refused to pay taxes levied
by his fiat.   Dongan's commission and instructions[4] di-

[1] After Sloughter's death, Ingoldesby
exercised supreme executive power as
commander in chief.   Probably he had
a commission authorizing him so to act,
but it does not appear that he exhibited
any document of the kind to Leisler to
enforce his demand for the surrender
of the fort.

[2] The act of Parliament reversing
the attainder of Leisler states that
Leisler having notice of Sloughter's arrival " that same Night (though very
late) took Care to deliver the said Fort
to his [Sloughter's] Order, which was
done very early the next Morning."
*Journal of the General Assembly of
New York*, i, Appendix.

[3] *Journal of the General Assembly
of New York*, i, 14.

[4] *New York Colonial Documents*, iii,
328, 331.

rected him to cause the election of a general assembly of not more than eighteen members, who should be chosen by the freeholders of the province. The laws to which he and the assembly should consent were to go into force at once. They might be annulled at any time by the Duke, who stated, however, that he would confirm those that appeared to him to be for the manifest good of the country and not prejudicial to his own interests.

In September, 1683, Dongan issued writs for the election of the members of the first representative legislature in English New York. The Assembly met on October 17, 1683, and passed fifteen laws,[1] all of which went into operation at once. Among these was an act to settle the courts of justice and a second one provided for the holding of assemblies once in three years. A third, which was known in New York as the "Continuing Act," provided for the permanent support of the government. The most memorable of the fifteen laws was that which stands first on the statute book and was entitled "The Charter of Liberties and Privileges Granted by his Royal Highness to the Inhabitants of New York and its Dependencies." Notwithstanding the title, this was merely an act of assembly in the form of a declaratory law. It begins by declaring that the supreme legislative authority under his Majesty and the Duke shall reside in the governor, council, and the people met in a general assembly. The principles of English law, as they were understood at that time, were declared to be law in that province; freedom of worship and conscience was guaranteed to all Christians; and no taxes were to be levied without the consent of the representatives of the people. When this

---

[1] The laws of the Dongan Assemblies, including the Charter of Liberties, are printed in *Laws of the Colony of New York* (ed. 1896), i, 111–177. The Charter of Liberties is also in Brodhead's *New York*, ii, 659.

act came before the Duke in England, there was a good deal of debate. The phrase, "the people," in the charter attracted his attention, for it was a phrase that had seldom been used in a document presented to a Stuart ruler for his consent. Yet it was distinctly advisable to fall in with the mood of the New Yorkers. James's accession to the throne in February, 1684–85, put a different face on the matter and on the 5th of the following March he disallowed the Charter of Liberties.[1]

In 1689 Governor Sloughter was instructed to hold assemblies "acording to the usage of our other Plantations."[2] He met his first assembly in April, 1691. It at once showed its independence by declaring null and void all the legislative acts of Dongan's assemblies, including the "Continuing Act."[3] This resolution was not assented to by the Council and was probably not presented to it. The pre-

---

[1] The Order in Council, annulling the Charter of Liberties, is in New York Colonial Documents, iii, 357. In his "Introduction" to the Grolier Club reprint of Bradford's Laws of New York (p. lxvii), Mr. Fowler states that James had intended to confirm the charter — with some amendments of his own — and that it was signed and sealed for transmission to New York when Charles II died.

[2] The draft of this commission is printed in New York Colonial Documents, iii, 623, whence a portion is copied into the Laws of the Colony of New York (ed. 1896), i, 221.

[3] See Note II, p. 311. The existence of the assembly depended upon the governor's commission and instructions, which authorized him to summon, prorogue, and dissolve assemblies at will. He might keep a complaisant assembly in being, as was the case in Burnet's time, where no election was held for eleven years. The only way that an assembly could put pressure upon the governor was to keep him poor and this necessitated the destruction of the "Continuing Act." In 1726 and thereafter for years, assemblies passed bill after bill for more frequent elections. All such measures were disallowed in England until 1743, when an act limiting the life of an assembly to seven years was permitted to stand. The governors also regulated the apportionment of representation, which was most unequal. About 1710 Albany and the farming region to the southward contained about 1300 men, paid 600 pounds in each levy of 4000, and returned 10 members to the assembly; while New York City and Long Island, which contained 3400 men, paid about 3000 pounds in each 4000 levied, likewise returned 10 members. See on these topics, New York Colonial Documents, v, 783; Fowler's "Introduction" to Bradford's Laws of New York, p. lxxxv. The last figures in the note are taken from "A Memorial of Several Aggrievances and Oppressions of his Majesty's Subjects in the Colony of New York" in American Historical Association's Reports, 1892, p. 45. No date is given to the memorial, but the numbers of men correspond to an estimate of population in 1710 given in New York Colonial Documents, v, 339.

cise force of this declaratory resolution has been widely discussed. It certainly was not law, but in practice was more than an expression of opinion, because this and succeeding assemblies proceeded for the most part on the assumption that the declaration was true to the fact, and successive governors, by collecting money in accordance with new enactments, informally consented to it.[1] In whatever light it may be viewed, this resolution was one of the most important measures ever voted by a colonial assembly.

Colonel Benjamin Fletcher was appointed governor on the receipt of the news of Sloughter's death and remained chief magistrate of New York until the arrival of Bellomont in 1697. Little is known of Fletcher's antecedents or of his life after his return to England. Like so many Englishmen who achieved fame of one kind or another in America, he resembles in many respects the jack-in-the-box of one's youthful days : he pops into view, remains there for a short time, and then disappears. Moreover, our knowledge of his career as governor is derived in great measure from the letters of his rival and successor. Wherever we come across him in the legislative records of the provinces over which he ruled, his demeanor and doings seem to be rather above than below those of the average provincial governor. Fletcher's commission and instructions[2] were dated in March, 1691–92. They directed him to govern New York "according to such reasonable laws and statutes as now are in force, or hereafter shall be made and agreed upon by you, with the advice and consent of the Council and Assembly of our said Province." These laws should be agreeable

---

[1] There is a long discussion of this matter in Fowler's "Introduction" to the Grolier Club's reprint of Bradford's *Laws of New York*, pp. lxxviii–lxxxiii.

[2] *Lords Manuscripts*, New Series, ii, 431, where the commission is printed in full; *New York Colonial Documents*, iii, 827 ; the instructions are in *ibid.*, iii, 818.

to the laws of England "as near as may be," must be transmitted to London within three months of their making, and might at any time be disallowed by the king. All members of the assembly must take the oaths required by Parliament and subscribe the "test."

When Fletcher assumed control of affairs in New York, he found the treasury empty and the need for money urgent. There was in the first place, of course, the necessity of carrying on the government of the province; but at this time the needs went far beyond that because New York was exposed to constant attack by the French from the St. Lawrence Valley. Fletcher was also commissioned governor of Pennsylvania and was given the command of the militia of New Jersey and Connecticut. In all these colonies he had to do with stubborn and adroit political leaders. His task was one of great difficulty, and he acquitted himself as well as could be expected under the circumstances and without any unusual amount of corruption.

The position of the governor of New York as regards his salary was somewhat peculiar. Like the governor of Virginia, he was authorized in his instructions to take a stated amount (four hundred pounds in his case) for his own use from whatever sums were in the colonial treasury; but there the similarity ended, for the Virginia exchequer was kept filled by a permanent revenue, while the New York treasury, after the Declaratory Resolution of 1691, was generally bare of funds. In Massachusetts, as just narrated, the governor was expected to secure a definite permanent appropriation for his salary, and this was true also of other colonies. In these colonies the constitutional controversy was over the salary question; in New York, it necessarily took on the form of a controversy as to the granting of any money whatsoever.

It was in 1692 that the debate began in New York over
the question of the grant of money for the support of
certain troops who were supposed to be guarding the
frontier of that province against the French. The Assembly suspected Fletcher of appropriating to his own use
funds which they had voted to the support of the soldiers,
either by not employing as many men as they had voted
money for, or by not paying them the wages which it had
been expected he would pay them. The Assembly appointed a committee to inquire as to the reason for the
non-execution of the acts regarding the protection of the
frontier. It secured no success and in March, 1693–94,
the Assembly attempted to deal with the problem by
limiting the number of soldiers to nearly one half that
asked for by the governor. Thereupon he summoned
the members and stated that as his commission made
him captain general, it was their business to provide funds
for the employment of a sufficient force upon the frontier,
he to be judge of what force was competent for that
purpose. " It is true I have received a commission for the
command of the militia of Connecticut, but they refuse to
obey it. I have another commission for the government
of Pennsylvania, but you must first convert them before
they will be either concerned in the shedding of blood or
contribute to such as do it." [1] The Assembly was not converted by this reasoning and voted only enough money to
employ the number of soldiers which they thought necessary. In the same session, as one means of getting at the
truth in the matter, the Assembly appointed a committee
to see how the money which had been voted had been
used. This committee reported that it could find neither
vouchers nor muster rolls. The upshot of this report was

[1] *Journal of the Legislative Council of New York*, i, 54.

the appointment of a committee to inspect all the accounts. Fletcher, by the advice of the Council, agreed to
this, but the committee could not get satisfaction. In the
autumn of that year, 1694, the Assembly again approached
the matter and resolved " that the first thing that this
House goes upon shall be inspecting into the accounts of
revenue," a mode of action which takes one back to the
days of the struggle between king and Parliament, which
ended in the adoption of the Petition of Right. Fletcher
tried to hurry them by a declaration that he had not
diverted any of the money to his own use, except what
the king allowed him as his salary. He also caused to be
laid before them the accounts and vouchers of the receiver
general. Ultimately, the Assembly voted an " additional
duty " for one year, the money to be spent in rebuilding
the chapel within the fort and mounting sixteen guns
on the fortifications. The outcome of this dispute was
clearly favorable to the assembly. From this time it
regularly inspected the accounts, and ultimately the Lords
of Trade acquiesced in this exercise of power.[1]

The next controversy arose over the action of the House
in the following spring (April, 1695), when it voted to
raise one thousand pounds on certain conditions which
were stated in the act. The governor objected because by
his instructions all moneys were to be granted for their
Majesties' use; but the House refused to vote any further
funds except on these terms and was thereupon dissolved.
Thenceforward, Fletcher lived in amity with successive
assemblies, either because the New Yorkers felt that they
had gone as far as was prudent with the French on their

[1] The New York Historical Society
printed the " Argument before the Lords
of Trade as to the Act of New York compelling the Farmers of the Excise to lay
before the Representatives an Account "
in 1701 in its *Collections* for 1869, p. 177.

frontier, or because, as Fletcher's successor declared, he had packed the assemblies with his nominees.

The appointment of Richard Coote, Earl of Bellomont, in the Irish peerage as governor of New York was decided on in 1695,[1] but he did not reach America until 1697. Lord Bellomont was one of those characters peculiar to that epoch who possessed unbounded belief in their own capacity, a limitless lack of confidence in their opponent's good faith or abilities, and a vividness of expression which was common in those days. Coming to New York, he described Fletcher's government as "corrupted and debauched."[2] He at once ejected William Nicolls, William Pinhorne, and Chidley Brooke from the Council, asserting that Nicolls had acted as Fletcher's middleman in his dealing with pirates, while Pinhorne was a defaulter who had bought his office of judge. The third of these men, Chidley Brooke, Bellomont describes as "borne in one of my relations families in Ireland," and he had gone on his bond for two thousand pounds. Nevertheless, Bellomont describes Brooke, who was Collector of Customs and Receiver General of New York, as most careless, negligent, and backward; "a great Devote to Coll : Fletcher," who had made more money than the governor himself which he could not have done honestly. As to the lawyers of the province, Bellomont says that one was a dancing master, another a glover, a third had been condemned to be hanged in Scotland for burning the Bible ; these men "miserably mangled and prophaned" the noble English laws, while the chief justice was no lawyer, although the most gentlemanlike man that the noble

[1] His commission as governor of New York is in *New York Colonial* *Documents*, iv, 266; his instruction on p. 284.
[2] *Ibid.*, iv, 320.

governor had seen in the province.[1] These specimens of Bellomont's judgments as to his predecessors and fellow-workers are given to enable the reader to judge for himself as to the value of the governor's account of the assembly which met him shortly after his arrival. This included nineteen members, of whom eleven held their seats in spite of contests, and, being in a majority, refused to give a hearing to the other side. Bellomont describes the sheriffs who had been appointed by Fletcher as being " of the scum of the people, Taylors, and other scandalous persons."[2] In the city of New York the election had been held in an open field under the guard of soldiers. This display of force had caused the Leislerians to believe that Fletcher intended to impress them for service against the French, and they had therefore refrained from taking part in the election. He also charged that Fletcher had brought ashore the crew of an English naval vessel then lying in the harbor and that they with soldiers from Fort William Henry had voted. It is only right to say that Fletcher indignantly denied these charges, asserting that the only seamen who came ashore were those who had the right to vote by reason of possessing the necessary qualifications as freemen of New York.[3] Later, Bellomont was himself accused[4] of having appointed sheriffs from the meanest of the people, and with having held elections in several counties on the same day, thereby preventing those who held property in different counties from exercising their rights of suffrage. This testimony, to be sure, is more than usually suspicious because it

[1] *New York Colonial Documents*, iv, 442. Bellomont's letters and the report of the Board of Trade and such proof as was offered are in *ibid.*, iv, especially pp. 456, 479; Fletcher's reply is on p. 443.

[2] *Ibid.*, iv, 322.
[3] *Ibid.*, iv, 144, 178.
[4] *Ibid.*, iv, 620.

was made by sundry New York merchants who were intensely hostile to Bellomont on account of his attempted enforcement of the navigation laws.

Whatever the reason, Bellomont, after the beginning, had no trouble with his assemblies so far as obtaining money was concerned. The annoyances of his time were over the enforcement of the trade laws, the putting down of piracies, and the carrying on of the conflict between the Leislerians and anti-Leislerians. In the old times, in England, Parliaments had followed the whims of the sovereign; in New York, council after council was composed of the followers of Jacob Leisler or of his opponents for a decade after he had gone to his grave. Fletcher had been a vigorous anti-Leislerian. Possibly for that reason Bellomont was a Leislerian. Jacob Leisler and his son-in-law, Jacob Milborne, had been executed in 1691; the widow and the son of the Revolutionary leader promptly petitioned the king to reverse the attainder of their husband and father and they managed the case so well that Queen Mary, in 1694, when William was on the continent, ordered the estates of Leisler and Milborne to be restored to their families. Bellomont caused the bodies of the Revolutionary leaders to be disinterred and buried with great pomp,[1] the coffins being carried through the streets at the head of a procession of fifteen hundred men, chiefly Dutch, who were reviewed by the governor from a convenient window. The Leisler family, however, was not satisfied even with this measure of retributive justice, and redoubled their efforts until Parliament, in 1695, passed an act reversing the attainder.[2] The mode in which this act was obtained well illustrates the interlocking of

[1] *New York Colonial Documents*, iv, 620.

[2] *Journal of the General Assembly of*

New York, i, Appendix; *Documentary History of New York*, ii, 249.

colonial interests. The presiding justice at the trial of
Leisler and Milborne was Joseph Dudley of Massachusetts,
who was now an applicant for the governorship of his
native colony. His opponents sought to discredit him by
disparaging the part he played in the Leisler trial. They
joined those who were favorable to the reversal of the
Leisler attainder and carried the bill through the House of
Commons, but it is noticeable that the words, "arbitrarily,
illegally, and unjustly," which were in the original bill
before "convicted and attainted," were omitted.[1] The
Leisler family were still dissatisfied and applied to the
king for reimbursement of four thousand pounds, which
they alleged the Revolutionary leader had expended in
the service of the state, and they won. The letter stating
the king's wishes was dated at Whitehall, February 6,
1699–1700, and gave as a reason for the king's action his
gracious sense of Leisler's services and sufferings — a
somewhat tardy recognition. Eventually the Assembly
voted a thousand pounds in satisfaction of the king's
command.

Bellomont died in office in 1701[2] and was succeeded as
acting governor until the arrival of Lord Cornbury, first by
the senior councilor, Rip Van Dam, and later by John
Nanfan, cousin of Lady Bellomont and lieutenant governor.
The leader of the anti-Leislerian forces in the province was
Nicholas Bayard, who had been a personal enemy of the
doughty colonel before 1689 and had ineffectually opposed
him in that and the following year. In the flush of success after the coming of Sloughter and the debasement of

[1] *Lords Manuscripts*, New Series, i,
540.

[2] In the preceding year, Bayard, De
Lancey, Van Dam, Morris, and Schuyler,
and other leading men had petitioned
the king to appoint a new governor for
New York, to prevent "the decay of
trade." *New York Colonial Documents*,
iv, 624.

Leisler, he had secured the passage of an act to the effect
that whosoever endeavored by force of arms, or otherwise, to disturb the quiet of the province, should be deemed
a traitor and incur the penalties of treason. Bayard
had been in close relations with Fletcher and secured as
his part of the public plunder extensive grants of land,
which Bellomont had annulled. After the latter's death,
Bayard and some of his friends, among whom was Rip
Van Dam, circulated several addresses to the king, Parliament, and the newly appointed governor.[1] These asserted
that the disturbances of the last few years were the result
of corrupt designs; that Bellomont had appointed indigent
sheriffs, who returned whom they pleased to the Assembly;
and, finally, they declared that the last Assembly had
bribed the lieutenant governor and the chief justice. Nanfan did not relish these strictures upon his conduct and
that of his cousin's deceased husband. He caused Bayard
and the other leaders to be arrested and tried by a special
commission,[2] which was presided over by William Atwood,
who had recently come out from England as chief justice.
He bore with great harshness upon Bayard, who was convicted and sentenced to death under the act which he
himself had devised, but was reprieved until the king's
pleasure could be known. Upon the coming of Lord
Cornbury, the next governor, Bayard was released from
confinement and the Assembly which was now anti-Leislerian passed an act reversing the sentences which had been
passed upon him and his companions. This law was confirmed in England upon condition that those who had suffered should bring no suits against their prosecutors, and

---

[1] *New York Colonial Documents,* iv,
933.

[2] The Bayard case is given from his
side in Howell's *State Trials,* xiv, 471

and fol. See also the "Case of William
Atwood" in New York Historical
Society's *Collections,* 1880, 237.

this wise act of the English government put an end to political alignment in New York on the basis of friendship or hostility to Jacob Leisler; the misdeeds of Lord Cornbury, governor from 1702 to 1708, soon provided other grounds for political action.

Of all the governors who brought English authority into contempt in the colonies, none was more thoroughly disreputable than Edward Hyde, Lord Cornbury, grandson of the great Earl of Clarendon, cousin-german to Queen Mary and Queen Anne, and himself later the wearer of the ancestral title. He was a spendthrift, utterly dishonest, and without morals. Rumor even averred that he dressed publicly in woman's garb.[1] He was burdened with debts when he left England; he incurred more while he was governor; and, upon laying down that office, was at once arrested and remained in the custody of the sheriff, until the death of his father in 1709 gave him what remained of the family estates. With his eccentricities and failings of character, he combined a devotion to the Established English Church which would seem ludicrous in one of his temperament had it not led to confiscation and persecution.[2]

The main interest of Cornbury's administration, however, lies in his financial dealings with the colonists under his government. On his arrival, he found the city of New York entirely without defenses. Some few years before, the Canadian Frenchman, Lemoyne d'Iberville, had sailed into the harbor on an ostensibly peaceful mission, but it had been supposed with the intention of sounding the channels leading in from the sea. Later a French privateer had actually entered the harbor. As a means of protection, the Assembly voted money to fortify the Narrows; it also gave Cornbury a present of two thousand pounds

---

[1] *New York Colonial Documents*, v, 38. [2] See below, p. 446.

to pay the expenses of his voyage and to start his house-keeping in New York. The new governor took the present and also converted to his own uses all, or the greater part, of the money which had been voted for fortifications. After this the Assembly refused to vote any more money except on condition that whatever was collected should be paid into the hands of a treasurer appointed by itself and should be paid out only by him, this officer to be account-able to the governor and council, as well as to the Assembly. It was in vain that Cornbury insisted that his instruc-tions forbade him to assent to such an arrangement. The Assembly was inexorable; Cornbury laid the matter before the home government and was informed (1706) that the Assembly might appoint a treasurer to receive and disburse extraordinary grants of money. Under these circumstances it was quite natural that they should convert all ordinary grants to extraordinary ones.

The Assembly did not meet again until 1708, by which time the ordinary revenues had come to an end by limitation. By this time, also, Cornbury's financial irregularities were so notorious that the Assembly refused to continue the ordinary taxes. In place of so doing, they passed a series of resolutions to the effect that the levying of money upon the freemen in the colony " without consent in general assembly is a grievance." They also resolved that the ex-acting of fees, the " screwing " of excessive sums of money from the masters of vessels, and the compelling any man to pay fees for his prosecution were of pernicious conse-quence and contrary to justice.

Cornbury was removed from office by the queen, but succeeding governors had nearly as serious difficulties with the Assembly. The temptation to exact exorbitant fees was almost irresistible — a governor must live. Each

example of the compelling people to pay ruinous fees
served to make the Assembly more economical in its
votes of supply. Affairs were never so serious again as
they were in Cornbury's day; but several times there was
a deadlock. In 1710 the government in England proposed to tax New York by act of Parliament. This time
it was no idle threat, for a bill for that purpose was
actually drawn and approved by the law officers of the
crown;[1] when a change of government put off its actual
introduction into the House of Commons. The weakness
of successive governments in England and the military
necessities in America made the coercion of New York
impracticable. On the contrary, the Assembly could not
be resisted after it hit upon the idea of granting money
for one year only and of permitting no amendments to
money bills to be made by the Council. Successive governors protested against these proceedings. They appealed
to the Lords of Trade, who ruled that the Council had
full legislative powers. The Assembly paid no heed. The
councilors, so the representatives declared,[2] were appointed
by the mere pleasure of the Prince who issued the commission; they themselves got their inherent right to dispose of the people's money from the free choice and
election of the people, who ought not to be divested of
their property without their consent. This was in 1711
— fifty years before Otis and Henry made their great
arguments for the rights of the colonists!

---

[1] In 1711 Northey and Raymond, Attorney and Solicitor General, approved
such a proposed law. The bill is printed
with their indorsement in [William
Knox's] *Controversy between Great Britain and her Colonies Reviewed*, 185; see
also Chalmers's *Introduction to the Revolt*, i, 365.

[2] *Journal of the General Assembly of
New York*, i, 307. The assembly in South
Carolina also denied the power of the
Council to amend money bills, see S. C.
Hughson in *New York Evening Post*
for September 16, 1893, and McCrady's
*South Carolina under the Royal Govern-
ment*, 172, 181.

NOTES

I. New York. — The constitutional history of New York can be followed in the *Journal of the Proceedings of the General Assembly of the Colony of New York* (1691–1765); and the *Journal of the Legislative Council of the Colony of New York* (1691–1775). The latter work contains the legislative entries only; the executive entries are noted in *New York State Library Bulletin*, No. 58 (History 6), "Calendar of Council Minutes, 1668–1783," Albany, 1902. The *Report of the State Historian* for 1897 contains matter on New York history, 1691–1711.

The best history of New York in this period is William Smith's *History of the Province of New York to the Year 1732* (London, 1757). In 1829 and 1830 the New York Historical Society published as volumes iv and v of its collections Smith's *History* with a *Continuation* to the year 1760 from the original manuscript and a memoir of the author by his son. William Smith was the son of that Judge William Smith who is so graphically described by Bellomont; he was a lawyer, and was for many years a member of the council. Cadwallader Colden, for some time lieutenant governor of New York, severely criticised the earlier portion of this work in a series of letters which are printed in the New York Historical Society's *Collections*, 1868, p. 181; 1869, p. 203. Together the history and the criticism form a remarkable tribute to the keenness of New York political strife when their authors were prominent in politics.

II. The Declaratory Resolution of 1691. —

Die Veneris, 2 ho. P. M. April 24, 1691.

Upon an Information brought into this House, by several Members of the House, declaring, That the several Laws made formerly by the General-Assembly, and his late Royal Highness *James* Duke of *York*, &c. And also the several Ordinances, or reputed Laws, made by the preceeding Governors and Councils, for the Rule of their Majesties Subjects within this Province, are reported amongst the People, to be still in Force:

Resolved, Nemine Contradicente, That all the Laws consented to by the General Assembly, under *James*, Duke of *York*, and the Liberties and Privileges therein contained, granted to the People, and declared to be their Rights, not being observed, and not ratified and approved by his Royal Highness, nor the late King, are null, void, and of none Effect. And also the several Ordinances made by the late Governors and Councils, being contrary to the Constitution of *England*, and the Practice of the Government of their Majesties other Plantations in *America*, are likewise null, void, and of none Effect nor Force within this Province. *Journal of the General Assembly of New York*, i, 8, 9.

CHAPTER XI

PENNSYLVANIA politics in the first half of the eighteenth century had much the same aspect that we have seen in the colonies of New York and Massachusetts with the variations that arose from the fact that Pennsylvania was a proprietary province and that the rulers belonged, for the most part, to the Society of Friends. The issues fought over were important, the persons who led the conflict were themselves interesting and presented certain strong characteristics. In the first eighteen years of the century, William Penn was still living, but he was in Pennsylvania for only the opening year,[1] and after his return to England passed much of his time in the debtors' prison, owing to the machinations of those who had had charge of his property during his absence and had somehow secured a hold on him. He was so discouraged by the lack of financial support from his colonists that in 1703 he negotiated with the government of Queen Anne for the sale of the province to the crown.[2] At a later time the transfer was on the point

[1] Duration of William Penn's residence in America: arrived at Newcastle, October 27, 1682 ; sailed from the Delaware, August, 1684; arrived at Philadelphia, November 29, 1699; sailed from the Delaware, November 4, 1701. There is some question as to the exact date of his departure, depending upon whether one reckons it from the time of going on shipboard or of passing Cape Henlopen. The above dates are taken from W. J. Buck's *William Penn in America*, — one of the best books on early Pennsylvania.

[2] Royal Historical Manuscripts Commission's *Reports*, v, 320. The report of the Lords of Trade on this proposal is printed in *New York Public Library Bulletin* for 1907, p. 471.

of being made when he became incapable of executing a valid deed. In 1712 he became mentally unbalanced and remained so until his death in 1718. Until the American Revolution, therefore, Pennsylvania remained a proprietary province in the hands of Penn's children and grandchildren. Some of them did not belong to the Society of Friends, and all of them looked upon Pennsylvania as an estate from which revenue might be extracted, not at all as an "Holy Experiment." The Pennsylvanians had for these later proprietors not even the scanty affection which they bestowed upon "the Founder." Probably this condition of affairs was inseparable from the proprietarial relation. The Penns stood to their colonists, not merely as governors to the governed, but also as great landed proprietors, as landlords to tenants and owners of vast quantities of vacant lands which they were holding for a rise in price, while at the same time they derived revenue from those lands which had been conveyed to actual settlers. In the royal provinces the colonists never thought of taxing the unused portions of the royal domain; but there was something contrary to the genius of American institutions in having private individuals possess enormous tracts of land which were steadily rising in value, and also derive a steadily growing income from landed estates, and pay no taxes whatever. The leaders of the colonists were strong men, among whom Benjamin Franklin and John Dickinson rose to the positions of greatest prominence; the mere fact that these two statesmen regarded the position assumed by the Pennsylvanians as justifiable goes far to show either that the proprietarial relation was a defective form of colonial government, or that in this instance the proprietors themselves were undesirable.

The first important event in this time was the establish-

ment of the constitution of the province under the Charter
of Privileges of 1701.   In 1692 the jurisdiction of Pennsylvania had been taken away from Penn, owing to his
close relations with the deposed James, and Governor
Fletcher of New York had taken over the administration
with such powers as he was authorized to exercise in New
York.[1] Fletcher came to Philadelphia and proceeded to
govern the province as if the royal letters patent, the Frames
of Government, and the laws of Pennsylvania had never
had an existence. He summoned an assembly on the lines
of the New York legislature and demanded money for the
defense of the colonies against the French invaders and
their Indian allies. He also desired compensation for
himself and other government officials. While in Pennsylvania, Fletcher acted with entire propriety and some
tact. He sought to placate opposition by inviting the
Quaker leaders to his table, but they would not come because it seemed to be treason to their community to be
friendly with him. They would " rather die than resist
with carnal weapons," he declared, nor would they " dip
their money in blood." [2]   On their part, the Pennsylvanians
were desirous of securing a confirmation of their laws, which
Fletcher maintained had fallen bodily with the cessation of
the proprietary government. The laws were in a very precarious state because they had never been properly recorded
or enrolled, or submitted to the king for royal action.[3]
The Assembly asked Fletcher to confirm a hundred of them,
more or less, by title, and he very properly refused. He
obtained a small grant of money for the maintenance of
the New York Indians who were between the outlying

---

[1] His commission is printed in *Votes
of Pennsylvania*, i, Part i, p. 67.

[2] *New York Colonial Documents*, iv,
31, 56 ; other papers relating to Fletcher's

adventures in Pennsylvania are in the
same volume.

[3] See on this point *Minutes of the
Provincial Council*, i, 418.

Pennsylvania settlements and French marauders, and also a little for himself and then departed for New York, leaving Penn's kinsman, William Markham, behind him as lieutenant governor.

Markham was an Episcopalian and, therefore, out of sympathy with the aims of the Friends, nor was he a man of the force of character needed to cope with the "topping Quakers." In 1694 the jurisdiction was restored to Penn,[1] but he continued his cousin in office as his representative. The first question to arise after Penn's restoration was as to the organic law of the Province: did the revival of the jurisdiction under the royal letters patent revive the Frame of Government and the laws which had been made in the proprietary period; or was Markham, in default of specific instructions from Penn, administering the government as it was at the close of Fletcher's tenure of office? The ruling class in the colony was clearly desirous of retaining the advantages which they enjoyed under Penn's second organic law, but was not willing to be bound by its peculiar provisions. In the end, Markham was forced to give his consent to a constitutional act[2] of the Assembly's framing which embodied their ideas; but Penn's consent was never obtained to this instrument. A curious incident of this time is set forth in the records under date of 1695. It seems that certain members of the legislative body waited on Markham with two bills: one, the Act of Settlement, the other granting the tax of one penny in the pound. Markham charged them with presenting them together, "as if you meant to tack them" one to the other.

---

[1] *New York Colonial Documents*, iv, 108; Markham's commission is in *Minutes of the Council of Pennsylvania*, i, 473.

[2] The 1696 Frame of Government is in *Votes of Pennsylvania*, i, Part i, Appendix i, p. viii; *Charter to William Penn and Laws of Pennsylvania, 1682–1700*, p. 245.

He said that he could not assent to the former and asked them to pass the latter, leaving out of it all mention of compensation to himself. Upon this a member of the Council, probably David Lloyd, stated that in the Parliament of England the granting of privileges always preceded the voting of money, and "although Pennsylvania was a poor province then they were to proceed in a parliamentary way."[1] Upon this refusal, Markham dissolved the Assembly.

The constant complaints of Randolph, Quary, and other persons as to illegal trade and the harboring of pirates in the Delaware[2] brought Penn to the colony in the last years of the century. He intended to make a long stay in Pennsylvania and possibly to end his life there; but he was obliged to return to England in 1701 to defend his American possessions against his enemies. This part of his career exhibits Penn in the best possible light. His position was a most difficult one. He was greatly in need of money and was harassed by creditors. The colonial authorities in England urged on by Quary were demanding the enforcement of the navigation laws and the expulsion of pirates from Penn's domains. His colonists were expecting him to support the government out of his private funds and at the same time refusing to pay the rents which he regarded as his due. Colonel Quary

[1] *Minutes of the Council of Pennsylvania*, i, 494.

[2] Penn's irritation is clearly shown in a letter to Markham in 1697–98. He writes that Philadelphia is reported to be "overrun with wickednes, Sins so very Scandalous, openly Comitted in defiance of Law and Virtue: facts so foul, I am forbid by Comon modesty to relate them. . . .

"For my sake, your own sakes, and above all for God's sake, Let not the poor province Longer suffer under such grievous and offensive Imputations." *Minutes of the Council*, i, 527; the action of the Council is recorded on pp. 528–531.

The ill conditions which prevailed at Philadelphia may be partly accounted for by the fact that side by side with the Quaker population there was a large body of non-Quakers, especially of the lower classes. The Quakers kept themselves in order by reason of their strong social organization, but the lack of laws and courts left the non-Quakers with few curbs to their passions.

was not friendly to Penn, but he bore witness to the difficulties in which the proprietor found himself. "Governor Penn," he wrote to the Lords of Trade in 1700, "is reduced to this great streight, if he complys with his [colonists] here; then he must violate all his promises which he hath made at home, for supporting The King's Authority in his Government, and if he doth not comply with them, then he must not expect any money from them." [1] Although Penn felt deeply the ingratitude of his colonists, he nevertheless desired to place the government of his province on a secure foundation, which would safeguard the rights of his young children, who might at any time become proprietors by his death, and would also render it impossible for any future proprietor to oppress the "chosen people." He regarded Markham's organic law as in no way binding upon him because his assent had never been given to it. The colonists had no desire to return to the restriction of the Frame, and expressed their wishes in no uncertain way. Penn reasoned with them, argued with them, implored them if there is anything "that jars, alter it; if you want a law for this or that, prepare it; I advise you not to trifle with government. I wish there were no need of any, but since crimes prevail government is made necessary by man's degeneration." [2] To all of this the representatives replied that they wanted only the rights of Englishmen and "were willing to leave the rest to Providence." This settlement of the matter did not suit Penn and he pressed for the adoption of a new fundamental law. [3]

[1] *Pennsylvania Magazine of History*, xxiv, 65. Penn's idea of Quary is given on an earlier page of the same volume, where he describes him as "the greatest of villains and God will I believe, confound him in this world for his lies, falsehood, and supreme knavery." See also *Penn-Logan Correspondence*, ii, 289.

[2] *Minutes of the Council of Pennsylvania*, i, 596.

[3] *Ibid.*, ii, 36.

One of the principal obstacles in the way of any settlement was the constitutional relations of the three lower counties on the Delaware, or the "Territories," both to Penn and to the Province of Pennsylvania. Penn's right to govern the people of this region rested on deeds of lease and release similar to those of Berkeley and Carteret of New Jersey, about which a controversy was proceeding at this precise time. Undoubtedly Charles and James had intended to confer on Penn the jurisdiction over the Territories, and James was on the point of granting a royal charter to Penn, settling the matter in his favor, when the Revolution of 1688 put an end to this as well as to other plans. It was necessary for Penn to act circumspectly in this matter, or the people of the Territories might raise very inconvenient questions. Their relations to the Pennsylvanians were also puzzling. In 1682 an Act of Union had annexed the older settlements to Pennsylvania and provided that the people of the Lower Counties should be "governed by the same laws, and enjoy the same privileges in all respects"[1] as the inhabitants of the Province. At that time the settlers in the Lower Counties on the Delaware had outnumbered those of Pennsylvania and had exceeded them in wealth; but by 1700 the situation was reversed.[2] The former adopting the weapon of minorities now asserted that under the Act of 1682 the representatives of the Province must never exceed in number the representatives from the Lower Counties, since only in that way could the equal privileges guaranteed by the Act of Union be maintained.[3] They now

---

[1] *Votes of Pennsylvania*, i, Part i, Appendix i, p. i.

[2] In the tax levy of 1694 the Pennsylvanians paid 427 pounds to 332 paid by the settlers in the Lower Counties; in 1700 the Pennsylvanians paid 1575 pounds to 425 paid by the inhabitants of the Lower Counties. *Votes of Pennsylvania*, i, Part i, pp. 85, 139.

[3] *Minutes of the Council of Pennsylvania*, ii, 49.

refused to have anything to do with a new constitution except on their own terms.

There were other subjects of debate. Penn had thought out no well-conceived land system for his American possessions. No careful records had been kept and there was nothing which showed the exact obligations of his tenants to him or of him to them. At the outset, Penn probably did not expect to make anything from his American possessions. Pennsylvania seemed to be an almost unlimited estate, and he had offered lands on very easy terms.[1] Most of his tenants had agreed to pay quitrents; but in practice these could not be collected, and the colonists refused to give him money to carry on the government. They expected him to make enough from his lands and the collections of fees to defray all charges of administration. His affairs were so badly managed until James Logan assumed the agency of his colonial estates that this expectation proved to be entirely unfounded. Even after 1700 Logan could not make much financial return to Penn, whose affairs were now in a very bad condition.[2] There was right on both sides to this dispute, and on both sides there was a good deal of friendly obstinacy.

At the close of the session of the Assembly in June,

[1] The purchasers of large estates, for example, had been promised house lots in the great town; ten acres to those who bought five hundred acres and so proportionately. Philadelphia did not contain enough land to satisfy the purchasers and leave sufficient for Penn's legitimate use. He proposed, therefore, to cut down the amount to be given within the city limits making up the balance in the suburbs or "Liberties." Naturally, this aroused irritation.

[2] The *Penn-Logan Correspondence*, so far as it has been printed, gives some interesting details as to the financial relations of Penn and his colonists. In the years after 1700 there was no market for their produce and money was scarce (i, 66, 70, 75, 80, 278, 288, 301, 326, 340-343; ii, 423). Logan received some money; he paid out some of it on account of governmental expenses and in support of Penn's relatives in the province; another portion he invested in tobacco; but a fatality seemed to be on their business ventures. It is exceedingly probable that very small financial return was ever made to "the Founder." Later on his descendants gathered profit from the province. See, however, Shepherd's *Pennsylvania as a Proprietary Province*, 86, 92.

1700, after Penn had given his assent to eight laws that
the representatives presented to him, a general debate over
a new organic law ensued between the governor, councilors, and representatives met together in one room. No
conclusion could be reached because of the contention
between the deputies from the Province and the Lower
Counties as to the number of members from each section.
Thereupon Penn suggested that he should resume the government under the royal letters patent and administer it
in accordance with the Act of Union and the clause in
the Frame of 1683 as to property. By this last enactment, Penn had confirmed to all the inhabitants of the
Province and the Lower Counties " full and quiet possession of their respective lands," saving such rents and services as are reserved to the proprietary.[1] This settlement
would have left a reasonably clear field for the working
out of institutions in Pennsylvania; but Penn was not
satisfied, he wanted a new written organic law and recurred to the subject again and again at every subsequent
session of the Assembly.

At this juncture, Penn received information that a bill
had been introduced into Parliament to do away with all
proprietary governments — his own among the rest. His
immediate presence in England was absolutely necessary
for his own interests and those of his colonists, and he
urged them to come to some agreement as to government;
but the more urgent he became, the more they delayed,
hoping thereby to secure concessions. From all this labor
and contention there ultimately emerged the famous
Charter of Privileges for Pennsylvania, which remained
the fundamental law of the Province and of the Territo-

[1] *Votes of Pennsylvania*, i, Part i,
Appendix i, p. vi. The demands of the
Assembly were formulated in an Address
which was voted at a later session and is
printed in *ibid.*, i, Part i, p. 145; Penn's
reply is on p. 148.

ries for seventy-five years, from 1701 to 1776. It is the most famous of all colonial constitutions, because it contained in its provisions many of the most important features of all workable written constitutions. Its authorship is uncertain and always will be, owing to the imperfect state of the records. The Assembly formulated plans, Penn likewise produced plans; these were exchanged and revamped. Finally, in the last hour before Penn's departure, an agreement was reached. To bring this about, a provision was inserted, giving the people of the Territories the right to separate from the Province at any time within three years, and Penn accepted from David Lloyd a "Charter of Property," which was apparently intended by Lloyd to have the same force as the charter of government. Penn signed the latter and ordered the great seal of the Province to be affixed to it; the former he took with him to England, saying that he would sign it likewise within six months, if his counsel so advised. They did not so advise and the Charter of Property never became law; its provisions, indeed, are unknown.

The Charter of Privileges[1] provided that there shall be yearly chosen by the freemen four persons out of each county to form an assembly. This body shall choose its own speaker and other officers, be judge of the qualifications and election of its members, prepare bills, impeach criminals, and "have all other powers and Privileges of an Assembly, according to the Rights of the free-born subjects of England, and as is usual in any of the King's plantacions in America." There is nothing in the document concerning the appointment of a governor and council; but the proprietors appointed these officials, thereby establishing a

---

[1] *Votes of Pennsylvania*, i, p. 127; i, Part ii, p. i; *Minutes of the Council of Pennsylvania*, ii, 56.

government which resembled that of a royal province. Other clauses in the Charter of Privileges provided for freedom of conscience to all who believed in " one Al mighty God "; all persons who also professed "to believe in Jesus Christ, the Saviour of the World " could take part in the government of the Province upon making certain affirmations and declarations. It will be readily seen from the language just quoted that Jews were disqualified from holding office; the obligation as to allegiance and to sub scribing to the test also made it impossible for Roman Catholics to take part in the government.[1] Jews and Roman Catholics were tolerated, but there was never in provincial Pennsylvania complete religious liberty except possibly during the years 1700–05, and even this is doubtful. No clause of this law could be altered except with the con sent of the governor for the time being, and six sevenths of the Assembly, and the proprietor agreed for himself and his successors never to consent to any alteration of the clause guaranteeing freedom of conscience; but the Act of 1705 confining membership in the Assembly to Protestants was in direct contravention of this pledge.[2] The constitutional position of the Charter of Privileges is uncertain. A copy of it is among the papers of the Board of Trade.[3]

[1] It is also noteworthy that in suc cessive naturalization laws in 1708, 1729, 1730, 1734, 1737, and 1742, only Protestants who took the required tests were given the rights of citizenship. See Stillé's "Religious Tests in Provincial Pennsylvania" in Pennsylvania Maga zine of History, ix, 395. Queen Anne in 1702 directed that all holders of public offices in the colonies must take the oath and subscribe the test as required in the Toleration Act, ibid., ix, 390. Under this order no Quaker could serve as deputy governor or councilor in Penn sylvania. See Sharpless, Quaker Gov ernment, i, 126, 128.

[2] Pennsylvania Statutes at Large (ed. 1896), ii, 219. The oaths acted as a religious test in other colonies, Mary land for example. See petition of Quak ers in Ridgeley's Annapolis, 60.

[3] MS. Board of Trade Papers, Pro prieties E. 225. N. 50, November 2, 1705 ("Philadelphia Transcripts," vol. viii). Pennsylvania Statutes at Large, ii, 374. Chalmers (Introduction to the Revolt, i, 298), after mentioning the Charter of Privileges, says that "of the various grants of privileges hitherto conferred by Penn on his followers, none had been presented for the royal approbation." The use of the word "hitherto" seems

Probably, therefore, it was submitted to the crown for royal action and as there is no mention of its being disallowed, it may be regarded as having the force of law. It is unfortunate that the word " charter " was used in the title of this document, because this has led to confusing it with the letters patent which formed the fundamental law of Pennsylvania.

In 1702 the settlers of the Lower Counties refused to send members to the Assembly, which met at Philadelphia in that year. Two years later representatives appeared from the Lower Counties, but then the members from the Province declined to admit them to the Assembly. In this manner, Pennsylvania and Delaware separated, but the Charter of Privileges remained the constitutional frame for both until the Revolution, and both had the same governor.

Comparing the Pennsylvania chief magistrates with the run of appointed royal and proprietary governors, it cannot be said that those sent to Pennsylvania by Penn and his successors were worse than those appointed by the king and by the other proprietors. There never was so thoroughly disreputable a ruler of Pennsylvania as Lord Cornbury of New York; but John Evans, who came to Philadelphia in 1705, was certainly a peculiar man. He was a young Welshman, who filled the double position of governor and companion to William Penn, Jr., who came over with him. He seems to have had no respect for age, experience, or the susceptibilities of others. His youth and impetuosity told against him. It is reported that old William Biles, exclaiming in council " Let us kick him out," was brought into court and fined, and the young governor,

to imply that this one was so presented. See also Shepherd's *Pennsylvania*, 295 note.

instead of contenting himself with the humiliation of one of the oldest settlers, proceeded to collect the fine.[1] One evening he and the younger Penn fell into a debate with some Philadelphia officials in Enoch Story's Inn. From debating the disputants came to blows. In the uproar others interfered and arrested the governor and the son of the proprietor.[2] This affair increased neither the respect in which the governor was held by those whom he was sent to rule nor the love of the youthful Penn for his father's co-religionists, — shortly afterward he abandoned the Society of Friends.

The Quaker rulers of Pennsylvania were determined to maintain their position as to oath taking.[3] They consistently refused themselves to swear, either publicly or privately; and they refused to permit others to do so. During the first forty-five years of the eighteenth century a " common swearer," man or woman, might receive as many as five hundred and eighty-eight lashes distributed over seven years. The attempts to incorporate these ideas into the penal code of Pennsylvania met with strenuous opposi-

---

[1] *Pennsylvania Magazine of History*, xxvi, 202.

[2] Janney's *Penn*, 480; Watson's *Annals of Philadelphia*, i, 114.

[3] *Pennsylvania Statutes at Large* (ed. 1896), ii, 49, Acts of 1700, ch. xliv. Any person who "shall swear in his or her common conversation by the name of God, Christ or Jesus," for the first offense shall pay five shillings or five days at the house of correction at hard labor, "and to be fed with bread and water only during that time ;" second offense six shillings or six days ; third offense, ten shillings or ten days. For the fourth offense the convicted man or woman "shall be fined (at the discretion of the county court) not exceeding five pounds or be compelled to work in prison at hard labor, not exceeding two months, and shall be deemed a common swearer,

and be liable to be whipped and to receive twenty-one lashes once in every three months, during the sitting of the court, for seven years."

Swearing by any other name or thing cost half a crown or three days hard labor ; speaking profanely, ten pounds or three months imprisonment ; and cursing oneself or any other or anything five shillings for each offense.

This act was in force until 1745–46, when it was modified because it had proved ineffectual. The seven-year lashing was now done away with, and ten shillings or ten days hard labor in the house of correction provided as a punishment for the second and subsequent convictions (*Pennsylvania Laws*, v, 42) and so it continued throughout the colonial period.

tion from successive attorneys-general of England and led
to the disallowance of law after law.   In connection with
this general theme, it may be observed that the Pennsylvanians contended that laws which had been agreed to by the
Assembly and the proprietor's representative were the
supreme law of the Province, regardless of acts of Parliament and of the wishes of the proprietor, until such laws
were disallowed by the crown.   As the charter allowed five
years from the time of passing an act until its presentation
to the royal authority, it is clear that by passing successive acts the Pennsylvanians could legislate as they pleased,
despite proprietor, king, and Parliament, provided they
could buy the lieutenant governor's consent.[1]   The proprietors to protect themselves were finally obliged to place
their lieutenant governors under bonds not to assent to
certain specified classes of legislation.   Among the laws
that were disallowed by the royal authorities, whenever
they could get sight of them, were those permitting an
affirmation instead of an oath on the part of Pennsylvania
officials and in the provincial courts of law.

The British Parliament in 1696 enacted[2] that a member
of the Society of Friends might affirm instead of taking an
oath, when qualifying as a witness in civil cases ; but the
act especially declared that this privilege should not extend to giving evidence in criminal cases, to serving on

---

[1] The views of the home authorities
on the legislative power in Pennsylvania
are stated in a "Report of the Lords of
Committee of Council for Plantation
Affairs," June, 1760 (*Minutes of the Provincial Council of Pennsylvania*, viii,
524).   In 1705, when the sale of the
province to the crown was in agitation,
Attorney-General Northey gave an opinion that laws made by the Assembly and
the deputy governor did not require the
proprietor's consent, but were absolute
unless repealed by the king in the mode

prescribed in the charter.   *Pennsylvania
Statutes at Large*, ii, 373.

[2] 7 and 8 William III, Cap. 34 (*Statutes of the Realm*, vii, 152).   This act
was continued, with modifications, until
1714, when it was made perpetual for
England and Scotland and extended to
the plantations for five years.   The form
of affirmation in the Act of 1696 was : "I
A. B. do declare in the Presence of Almighty God, the witness of the Truth of
what I say."   For the oaths and affirmation see note on p. 455.

juries, or to exempting any public official from taking the oaths prescribed by law. The Pennsylvanians by acts of the local legislature sought to extend the exemptions under this law to all cases, much to the dismay of the law officers of the crown. The conditions of judicial procedure in Pennsylvania were without a parallel even in the colonies.[1] There were courts in the province which were presided over by judges who possessed more or less legal knowledge.[2] Many of these magistrates did not belong to the Society of Friends and had no prejudice against taking or giving an oath. The Quakers not only could not take an oath themselves; their consciences did not permit them to offer an oath to another person.[3] Could they conscientiously sit on the bench and suffer a Church of England or Presbyterian colleague to administer the oath to jurors and witnesses or, perhaps, have this done by the clerk? At times the Quakers' consciences permitted this practice;[4] at times forbade it, because by so doing they seemed to countenance the taking of an oath. For

[1] Quaker justice as seen by unfriendly eyes is set forth in *News from Pensilvania, or a brief Narrative of Several Remarkable Passages in the Government of the Quakers* (London, 1703).

[2] Sometimes the mode of procedure was extremely irregular. Quary, in 1703, described a gaol delivery in which persons were convicted and sentenced to death, whipping, and branding by justices appointed by a governor who had not been approved by the queen and without an oath being taken by judges, jurors, or witnesses. *New York Colonial Documents*, iv, 1045. See also *Penn-Logan Correspondence*, i, 192, 217.

[3] The Quakers were sensitive on the subject of perjury, as appears from the penalties affixed to it in successive laws: — an act of 1700 provided that a person convicted of bearing false witness should pay to the party grieved such damage as the said party shall sustain, be publicly exposed as a false witness, and never be credited in court. Repealed by the queen in 1705-06 (*Pennsylvania Laws*, ii, 47). In criminal cases the false witness " shall suffer and undergo such damage or penalty " as the convicted person, " make satisfaction to the party wronged," be publicly exposed, and never again be credited. Repealed by the queen in 1705-06. (*Ibid.*, ii, 133.) After 1710 the laws as to affirmation provided that the false witness should be punished as guilty of " willful and corrupt perjury " in Great Britain. (*Ibid.*, ii, 357, 426; iii, 40, 201, 210.) " Lying in common conversation " was half-a-crown or three days at hard labor by the Act of 1700. (*Ibid.*, ii, 48.)

[4] See Acts of 1705-06, § 3 (*Pennsylvania Laws*, ed. 1896, ii, 270).

years no courts were held in some parts of the province. This absence of judicial tribunals did not work hardship for the Quakers, because as between themselves justice was rendered in their Monthly and Quarterly Meetings. Where one or both parties to a dispute did not belong to the Society of Friends, the closing of the courts was unfair to the non-Quaker, since members of the Society must frequently have been in the position of defendants, could an action have been brought. Penn's comment is interesting. "It looks dirty," he wrote to Logan, "that one Quaker shall cozen a man, and the other refuse him justice; and where bias may be already, at least some dirt sticks." [1]

In 1716, in the time of Governor Gookin, the administration of justice temporarily ceased. In the preceding year there had been riots in Philadelphia which had a religious beginning, and a murder had been committed in the county of Chester. Gookin stated that the English law as to affirmation was in force in the colonies, and that therefore a murderer could not be convicted without a good deal of swearing. The magistrates who had jurisdiction for the trial of the alleged murderers refused to proceed under their commission, stating that as the governor who had appointed them had doubts as to the condition of the law regarding affirmation, they could take no action in opposition to his interpretation. In the end the murderers remained in prison until the Assembly voted Gookin enough money to enable him to return to England. His successor, Sir William Keith, had no such scruples. The accused murderers were tried, convicted, and sentenced to death. They asked to be allowed to appeal, as they had a right to do under the royal charter, but were executed without delay.

[1] *Penn-Logan Correspondence*, i, 247.

The members of the Established Church living in Burlington, New Jersey, presented a memorial to the home government in 1711. They vividly portrayed the results of Quaker justice, declaring that their lives and property were at the mercy of unsworn magistrates, jurors, and witnesses.[1] In 1718 the matter was brought to a final conclusion by the passage of a law in Pennsylvania adopting the bloody penal code of England as the law in the province.[2] The half century following the Restoration saw an almost constant increase in the savagery of dealing with crime in the mother country and an almost proportionate increase in the amount of crime, although it would not be safe to infer that either of these resulted from the other. The colonists had followed hesitatingly the example of the home land, but there was certainly no amelioration in the penal statutes or in the vindictiveness of magistrates. The Quaker legislature of Pennsylvania in 1718 adopted the whole penal code of England and extended the provision of the English law as to affirmation to criminal matters and to officers appointed under colonial laws. Up to this time only a very small number of crimes had been punished with death in Pennsylvania; now highway robbery, setting fire to house or barn, witchcraft, cutting out another's tongue, putting out his eye, or otherwise maiming him were capital crimes. The authorities in England were so rejoiced at the adoption of their savage code by the Quaker colony that now, at last, they permitted the law extending the right of affirmation in all cases to remain on the Pennsylvania statute book.

Another contest that runs through nearly the whole

---

[1] MS. *Board of Trade Records, Proprieties*, ix, Q, 17. Twelve years earlier members of a jury in Pennsylvania had been fined fifty shillings for casting lots as to their verdict. *Pennsylvania Magazine of History*, xxvii, 235.

[2] *Laws of Pennsylvania*, iii, 203; see also Sharpless, *Quaker Government*, i, 152.

period of Pennsylvania's provincial history was the result of the Quakers' scruples as to the use of "carnal weapons" in combination with the keen demand for funds and soldiers which the French wars of the time necessitated. The conflict began with Fletcher's administration; for he, as governor of New York, had the responsibility of defending the northern frontier. After long and patient negotiation with the Quakers, he secured a grant of three hundred pounds sterling to "feed the hungry and clothe the naked" New York Indians and small sums of money for the support of the government.[1] One of the devices by which the Pennsylvanians proposed to accomplish their purpose of securing Fletcher's consent to their bills at the least possible cost is recorded under date of 31st May, 1693.[2] A committee of four, among whom was David Lloyd, waited upon him with a bill which had been read twice, but had not been passed. This inchoate measure provided for a grant of money, one half of it for the governor's use. Fletcher declared that he would not look at it until it was signed by the Speaker. Later, he relented and sent to the Assembly already signed such bills as he could approve under his instructions, agreed to order other laws to be put into execution for the present, and asked for the money bill in return, and it was given to him.

The leader in these early contests with the representatives of proprietor and king was David Lloyd,[3] a Welsh-

[1] Votes of Pennsylvania, i, Part i, p. 97.

[2] On this interesting contest between Fletcher and the Pennsylvanians see Minutes of the Provincial Council, i, 398–433, especially 426–433; Votes of Pennsylvania, i, Part i, pp. 65–77. The "Petition of Right," with the accompanying laws and Fletcher's order to have them enforced until the royal pleasure were "further known," is in Charter to William Penn and Laws of the Province of Pennsylvania passed between the years 1682 and 1700, pp. 188–220. The same volume (pp. 539–551) contains an "historical note" on this matter.

[3] There is no adequate memoir of David Lloyd. The little sketch by

man, a Quaker and a lawyer, and a most successful officeholder. At one time he was attorney-general of the
Province; at another, chief justice, and he frequently combined these positions with membership in the Assembly, —
on occasion serving both as chief justice and Speaker.
He is the most interesting of early Pennsylvanians and
was hated thoroughly by Penn and Logan and other prominent men of the Province. In the dearth of material it
is impossible to state with anything like confidence whether
Lloyd or his critics were in the right. He was usually successful and led Pennsylvania away from the paternalism
of Penn toward the democracy of Jefferson and Duane.
At this time he talked so long and so earnestly that he
wore out even the stout Benjamin Fletcher.

In 1694, when Penn received back the jurisdiction from
William III, he pledged himself to " carefully transmit to
the Council and Assembly there [Pennsylvania] all such
orders as shall be given by their Majesties in that behalf;
and he doubts not but they will at all time dutifully
comply with and yield obedience thereunto . . . for the
supplying such quota of men, or the defraying their part
of such charges as their Majesties shall think necessary
for the safety and preservation of their Majesties' dominions in that part of America." [1] Penn certainly tried to
carry out his part of this agreement, but without much
success. Besides the Quakers' natural disinclination to
vote money for war, or to provide an efficient colonial
militia, the question of voting money for any purpose

Joseph S. Walton in *The Journal of the
Friends' Historical Society* (iii, Nos. 2,
3) brings together in convenient form
the better-known facts of his life. In
his *Life of William Penn* (p. 407), Janney states that Lloyd had been a captain
in Cromwell's army; but Walton says
that he was born in 1656.

[1] *New York Colonial Documents*, iv,
109; Sharpless, *Quaker Government*, i,
193; *Calendars of State Papers, America and West Indies, 1693–1696*, p. 316.
Penn's statement that " he doubts not "
the Pennsylvanians would obey their
Majesties' orders appears to Sharpless
to have been " disingenuous."

became complicated with the determination of the colonists to tax the proprietors' estates and, if possible, to put upon them the odium of refusing the demand of the English government for money to be expended for military purposes.

In 1701 the English government sent to Pennsylvania a demand for three hundred and fifty pounds for the purpose of erecting forts on the frontiers of New York. Penn " transmitted " the demand to the Assembly, but declined to give any advice, and the Assembly excused itself on the plea of poverty and asked Penn to assure the king of their readiness to answer his commands " so far as our religious persuasion shall permit," [1] — and nothing further was done. In 1709 a letter came from Queen Anne, directing Pennsylvania to furnish one hundred and fifty men at its own expense toward an army for the invasion of Canada. Governor Gookin suggested that the expense of raising such a force would be about four thousand pounds, and if the Assembly would vote money, he doubted not that he could find the recruits. The Assembly replied by voting five hundred pounds as a present to the queen " in point of gratitude . . . for her great and many favors to us," which Gookin refused to accept; but in 1711 two thousand pounds were actually voted.[2] There the matter rested for the time being. It was not until 1739 that the question was again a burning one, and by that time other men than the original settlers had risen to take the chief part in political affairs.

Foremost of the leaders in Pennsylvania politics was Benjamin Franklin, the first great American. He was

---

[1] *Minutes of the Council of Pennsylvania*, ii, 31. See also an article by H. V. Ames, in *Pennsylvania Magazine of History*, xxiv, 61.

[2] *Minutes of the Council of Pennsylvania*, ii, 558; Sharpless, *Quaker Government*, i, 198-202.

born in Boston, Massachusetts, in January, 1706.   He was
the youngest of sixteen children, being the youngest son of
youngest sons for five successive generations.[1]   The story
of his early life is derived mainly from the wonderful
"Autobiography," which he prepared at a time when
memory often becomes constructive as to the events of
one's former career.   He was always a leader, whether as
a journeyman in a printing office, member of a literary
club, or of an assembly; always, until age lessened his
vigor, wherever he might be, he was the first among equals.
Facility in the use of his fingers was joined with an
inventive faculty that amounted almost to genius.   As a
man of science, he was among the foremost of his time,
and received the extraordinary honor of an election to the
Royal Academy without his knowledge and without any
fee.   It is, however, to his literary gift that he owed the
greatest part of his success.   When he established a newspaper, he could easily write better than his competitors;
when he wished to make clear a scientific experiment, he
could describe it in print better than any of his contem-
poraries.   The desire for money is the spur to success; it
was eminently so in the case of Franklin : he labored, he
starved, he contrived, for money.   Above all and beyond
all, his distinguishing characteristic was the complete
adaptation of the means for the accomplishment of the
end to which he had set himself; to use a New England
country phrase, so long as Franklin was "law honest," he
did not trouble himself as to the precise moral significance
of a proposed line of action.   "When you come to a low
place, stoop," was a saying of "Poor Richard" and a rule
of Benjamin Franklin.

[1] An admirable brief characterization of the career of Benjamin Franklin
is the paper with this title in American Philosophical Society's *Proceedings*
(xxxii) by Dr. Samuel A. Green.

Franklin had scarcely established himself as an independent printer when he started a newspaper, " The Pennsylvania Gazette." In one of the earliest numbers he printed some remarks on the dispute between the Massachusetts Assembly and Governor Burnet, calling attention to the attitude of the Massachusetts representatives. They thought, so he explained, that there should be a mutual dependence between the governor and governed; and that to make their governor independent would be dangerous and destructive of liberty and the ready way to establish tyranny. He thought that their action would cause the people of the mother country to observe that even in the third and fourth generation of their colonial life, the colonists still retained that ardent spirit of liberty and undaunted courage which has so gloriously distinguished Britons and Englishmen.[1] These remarks struck the attention of the principal people of Pennsylvania and caused them to buy Franklin's paper. They also form an early example of the play of intercolonial forces which was rapidly to strengthen as the years went by; but, in truth, the people of Pennsylvania needed no such urging to impel them to maintain their rights and conscientious scruples against those who attempted to rule over them.

In 1739, on the approach of the war with Spain, the English government through the proprietors and the governor suggested the establishment of a militia in Pennsylvania; but the Assembly replied that the Province had prospered for many years without such an organization, nor would they vote money for the building of a fort to secure the navigation of the Delaware River. It was upon this issue that Franklin came to the front, setting

---

[1] Franklin's *Works* (Temple Franklin ed.), i, 66.

on foot an association of volunteer militia and providing by a lottery for the building of a fortification which was armed by gifts from New York and from the proprietors. In 1745, at the time of the French war, the government requested the aid of Pennsylvania for the conquest of Louisbourg on the Island of Cape Breton, and that place having been captured before any action was taken, they asked for money to supply it with provisions and powder. The Assembly replied that, owing to the peaceable principles of many of their number, they could not provide money for arms and ammunition, but they appropriated four thousand pounds for the purchase of " bread, beef, pork, flour, wheat or other grain." [1] The governor used this money or a portion of it in the purchase of gunpowder on the ground that " other grain " covered that commodity, and the Assembly never protested against this action.   Again, in 1746, the Quakers voted five thousand pounds for the king's use,[2] without further specification.

With the outbreak of the French and Indian War in 1754 the matter again came up and this time, owing to the seriousness of the occasion, assumed a phase it never had before. The questions at issue were the granting of money for military purposes and the passing of an act which would permit the authorities to punish mutiny and desertion in the militia, which they could not well do as long as that body was a volunteer organization. With this matter was now joined the question of taxing the proprietors' estates. According to the bills which were passed the Assembly proposed to tax not only the lands which had been granted on rental tenures, but also to tax the vacant land which had not been granted at all.[3] The

---

[1] *Votes of Pennsylvania*, iv, 14.
[2] *Ibid.*, iv, 39.

[3] *Colonial Records*, viii, 530. The land system from a proprietary point of view

proprietors do not seem to have been averse to having the rents which they actually received taxed, and suggested that to bring this about, the taxes on their properties should be paid by those who were using them, and that the tax should be deducted from the rent, but that their ungranted lands should not be taxed at all. This plan would have been very favorable to the proprietors as they would have paid a tax only on lands upon which a rent was actually paid and it would have been the interest, therefore, of every one to make sure that his neighbors paid their rents and by so doing lessen his own taxes. The Assembly upon this occasion voted ten thousand pounds, but attached conditions which the governor could not accede to under his instructions. The Braddock disaster made the case of Pennsylvania very serious, especially as the unfriendly Indians in the western and northern part of the Province at once went over to the French.

By this time the authorities in England had become thoroughly convinced of the danger of allowing the Pennsylvania government to remain longer in the hands of the Quakers. The members of the Society of Friends formed about one sixth of the total population of Pennsylvania, but they had maintained their hold upon the Assembly by the peculiar method of apportioning the representation which had come down from the days of William Penn. In the Charter of Privileges it was provided that each of

is described in a letter from John Penn to Shelburne written in 1767, *ibid.*, ix, 385. See also "Mr. Wilmot's Brief in behalf of the Proprietors in opposition to the Approval of Certain Acts of Assembly" in the *Pennsylvania Magazine of History*, vols. xxiii–xxv, and Shepherd's *Pennsylvania*, ch. v. A compromise was made in 1759, by which the proprietors' representative in the Province should have more control of financial matters and the proprietors' lands should be taxed on a reasonable valuation. See "Report" of the Lords of Trade to the Privy Council (*Minutes of the Provincial Council of Pennsylvania*, viii, 524) and its action thereon (*ibid.*, viii, 552).

the six existing counties should return four members, and Philadelphia sent two more, or twenty-six in all. The further provision was made that in case the Lower Counties separated from the Province, their members should be added to the three counties of Pennsylvania, thus preserving the number of the Assembly at twenty-six, which would be a good working number for such a body. The apportionment of representation for the counties which should be organized in the future was left to the Assembly for the time being. After 1701 Pennsylvania grew very rapidly, and three more counties were formed, but these were given only two members apiece.[1] The three original counties were the seats of the Quaker settlements; the newly settled portions of the Province were inhabited mainly by Germans and Scotch-Irish of varying beliefs, but few of them were members of the Society of Friends. The German settlers, who now outnumbered those of any other nationality, had come to America to better their condition, and especially to become owners of land which it was not possible for ordinary people to accomplish in Germany. They had no desire for political power and were quite willing to leave the management of affairs in the hands of those at whose invitation they had crossed the Atlantic. It cannot be said, therefore, that the Quakers were usurping the government; but it was nevertheless true that the Pennsylvania Assembly was in the hands of those who represented the minority in the colony.

The English government recognized clearly enough that the only possible course to be adopted was to secure the removal of the Quakers from the Assembly; but the members

---

[1] See an article by C. H. Lincoln on "Representation in the Pennsylvania Assembly prior to the Revolution" in *Pennsylvania Magazine of History*, xxiii, 23–34.

of the Society of Friends in England were such consistent
supporters of the existing government there that it hesitated to take action. The time had arrived, however, when
hesitation might be fatal. Accordingly, a bill was introduced into Parliament to exclude from the Pennsylvania
Assembly all persons who would not take the Oath of
Allegiance, which, of course, no Quaker could do. Before
anything definite was done the English Society of Friends
intervened. Some of their leading men sought out a "Noble
man in high station," who presumably was the Duke of
Newcastle. He could not give them much hope, but advised
them to wait upon other "principal persons in high stations" and endeavor to prevail upon them to join in suspending action on the understanding that the English
Society of Friends would use their utmost endeavors to
prevail upon their co-religionists in Pennsylvania neither
to offer themselves as candidates for reëlection nor to
accept of seats in the Assembly during the continuance of
the present war. Upon this advice they secured a suspension of action on the part of Parliament and sent a committee of two of their body to America to induce Friends
there to retire from public life.[1] Before their arrival, however, several Quakers, members of the Assembly, had already refused to be candidates for reëlection. The committee secured the retirement of enough more to give the
majority in the Assembly as then constituted to those who
were not of that sect. The majority thus passed to those
who had no conscientious scruples against the prosecution
of war, the voting of a strong militia act, or the giving of

[1] Sharpless, in his *Quaker Government* (i, 252–259), gives documents from
the "Friend's Records" from which the
above narrative has been drawn. See
also [William Smith's] *Brief State of*
the Province of Pennsylvania in which
the Conduct of their Assemblies is im-
partially examined (London, 2d ed.,
1755).

money for military purposes.   On their retirement, four of the Quaker members joined in a statement of reasons which had actuated them in taking this step, " Understanding," so they declare, " that the Ministry have requested the Quakers . . . to suffer their seats, during the difficult situation of the Affairs of the Colonies, to be filled by Members of other Denominations, in such manner as to prepare, without any Scruples, all such Laws as may be necessary to be enacted for the Defence of the Province." [1]   Retirement from public life under such circumstances and for such reasons is an act of public spirit and political disinterestedness that seldom has been paralleled in the history of legislative bodies.

[1] *Votes of Pennsylvania*, iv, 564, 626.

NOTES

I. The Contest as to Oaths. — Besides the entries in the *Votes of Pennsylvania, Minutes of the Council, Colonial Records*, and the *Statutes at Large*, the following articles and books are useful: Lawrence Lewis's " Courts of Pennsylvania in the Seventeenth Century " in *Pennsylvania Magazine of History*, v, 141; C. J. Stillé's " Religious Tests in Provincial Pennsylvania " in *ibid.*, ix, 365; Henry Budd's " Colonial Legislation in Pennsylvania " in Colonial Society of Pennsylvania's *Bulletin* for 1897; and Sharpless, *Quaker Government*, i, 144, 252. I have especially profited from an unpublished essay on " Procedure in the Courts of Pennsylvania " by Charles H. McIlwain, now Preceptor at Princeton University.

II. Control of Expenditures. — In Pennsylvania the Assembly carefully supervised all provincial expenditures. It audited the accounts and, instead of making permanent support for the governor and other officials, at the end of each session made grants to them. Following is an extract from the bill for " Incidental Charges " for 1751 which was signed by the Speaker and presented to the governor at the very close of the session: —

James Hamilton, Governor	£1000
William Allen, Chief Justice . . .	200
Richard Partridge, Agent	170 = 100 Sterling
For case of Province	340 = 200 "
Six Nations as Condolence on Death of Canassatego	100
Tench Francis, Attorney General . .	100
B. Franklin, Clerk and Printing . .	121
W. Franklin, Now Clerk	4 15 sh. 6 d.
Catherine Cox for bull killed by Indians in 1747	3
Dr. Thos. Graeme for physic for the Indians	1 11 " 6 "

The total, which included charges not given here, was 3799 pounds provincial money. *Votes of Pennsylvania*, iv, 201.

CHAPTER XII

CAROLINA IN COMMOTION, 1689–1750

LIKE Pennsylvania, Carolina was in the clutches of pro·
prietors. Her people had no objection to taking oaths,
or to voting money for military purposes, and they never
thought of taxing the estates of the proprietors. Nevertheless, their relations with their rulers were fully as
troublesome as were those of the Pennsylvanians with William Penn and his children. The Carolinians were not
more inclined to insurrection than were other settlers, but
their actions constantly led to commotions which closely
verged on rebellion. In these events, the southern colony
attracts more attention because the movements there were
more dramatic and led to more important results. It
would be hard to find more masterful spirits, even in our
colonial history, than William Rhett, John Barnwell, Ralph
Izard, Robert Gibbes, Nicholas Trott, and the Johnsons
in the southern colony and Culpeper, Carey, Pollock, and
Mosely in the northern colony. It is to the boldness and
courage of these men and their neighbors in resisting tyranny and misgovernment that the effervescence of Carolina
history was due.

The Carolinian proneness to activity was not lessened
by the quality of rule that was meted out to them by the
proprietors and their agents. At the best, the manage-

ment of a distant colony by eight persons bound together
by the Fundamental Constitutions of Carolina would have
been a precarious adventure.   In the reigns of William
and Anne, religion and politics were in an unsettled condition in England and these dissensions were reflected in the
debates of the proprietors.   Moreover, the relations of the
proprietors to their employees in Carolina were very peculiar.   Each proprietor in England was represented by a
deputy in the colony and, in addition, Nicholas Trott, the
chief justice of South Carolina, was the confidential agent
of the proprietors whose official representative was the
governor.   Each faction in the colony also had its agent
in London, as had the governor and the assembly.   Finally,
the Lords of Trade seized every opportunity to sow dissen-
sion between the Carolinians and their rulers in the hope
that the outcome would be the overthrow of the proprietors.

The first bitter contest in South Carolina turned on the
question of religion and toleration.   The charters authorized the proprietors to grant toleration, while, at the same
time, they contemplated the establishment of the Church
of England in the colony as the state church.   For a generation the proprietors promised religious freedom to all
who would go to Carolina, but neglected to provide for the
establishment there of the Church of England.   In 1704,
in the midst of the contest over the " Occasional Conformity Bill " in England, the Assembly, in South Carolina,
passed two acts [1] which reflected the political and religious
desires of the proprietors and of the governor, Sir Nathaniel Johnson, a high churchman and a Jacobite.   The first of
these measures, which was passed by a vote of twelve to

[1] Cooper's *Statutes of South Carolina,*   *lina under the Proprietary Government,*
ii, 232, 236; *Colonial Records of North*   406.
Carolina, ii, 863; McCrady's *South Caro-*

eleven at a special session of the assembly, provided that
no dissenter should be chosen a member of the Commons
House of Assembly.   The other act provided for the division of the settled part of the colony into parishes, the
building of churches, and the employment of ministers, all
at the public charge.   It contained also a clause providing
for a commission or committee composed of laymen to sit
in judgment on the ministers.   It is impossible to state
from accessible material the proportionate numbers of dissenters and adherents of the proposed establishment;[1] and
the matter is further complicated by the presence in the
colony of a considerable body of French Protestants who,
strictly speaking, would be regarded as dissenters, but who
in liturgy and ceremonial approached very closely to the
Anglican form and acted with the friends of a church
establishment.   The dissenters and others who objected to
the passage of these laws were ably represented in London.
At first they sent John Ash, who embarked from Virginia,
fearing that he might be stopped if he sailed from Carolina.
Upon his death in London, soon after his arrival there,
Joseph Boone was dispatched to England to act in their
behalf.

Boone was a Congregationalist, a man of property, who
had close business relations with influential merchants and
dissenters in London; he also possessed great adroitness
in the management of affairs.   He presented a memorial
to the proprietors, and upon Lord Granville's dismissing
him rather insolently, laid a petition before the House of
Lords.[2]   The latter paper was signed by Boone and several

---

[1] It is said that in 1706 "above two-
thirds of the people" of Carolina were
dissenters. Oldmixon's *British Empire
in America*, i, 486; McCrady (*South
Carolina under the Proprietors*, 440)
believes that "those who conformed to
the Church of England constituted very
nearly one-half of the population."

[2] *The Humble Address of the Right
Honourable the Lords Spiritual and
Temporal presented to Her Majesty . . .
and the Petition therein mentioned . . .*

leading English merchants and dissenters. In this paper the agent stated that he had already addressed the proprietors in the name of one hundred and seventy Carolina planters, and that they had nevertheless ratified two laws to which the people of the colony strongly objected. He declared that the election of the members of the assembly which had passed these laws had been managed with great partiality, and that "all sorts of People, even Servants, Negroes, Aliens, Jews, and Common Sailors" had been admitted to vote and that the laws had been passed at a special session, at which many of the dissenting members were not present. Passing to the acts themselves, he tactfully alleged that the ecclesiastical jurisdiction in the colony belonged to the Bishop of London, but that one of these laws had taken it away and instead had established a commission of twenty laymen with absolute power to deprive any minister of the Church of England in the colony of his benefice. Moreover, in the other act, the assembly had incapacitated every person from being a member of any General Assembly unless he had taken the sacrament according to the rites of the Church of England or, at all events, had not received it in any dissenting congregation. After debates, which are not recorded, the House of Lords presented a memorial to the Queen, rehearsing these facts very nearly in the language of the petition and advised the repeal of the laws on the ground that they would interfere with the settlement of the colony, be of advantage to the French, and injure the trade of Great

with Her Majesties Answer, London, 1705. Reprinted in American Historical Association's *Report*, 1892, p. 28. The address and proceedings leading up to it are printed, more or less modernized, as to spelling and punctuation, in *Lords Journals*, xviii, 130–151. The Petition and the Address are printed from the

Board of Trade Papers in *Colonial Records of North Carolina*, i, 637, 643. Defoe, in his *Party Tyranny*, prints the Church Act and Petition which are reprinted in *Colonial Records of North Carolina*, ii, 891. Most of these documents are in the Appendix to Rivers's *Early History of South Carolina*.

Britain. The government fell in with this idea, especially as the Lords of Trade suggested that the conduct of the proprietors should be looked into. The law officers of the crown, however, advised that the matter should not be pressed any farther, since several of the proprietors were peers, and it was not certain how far the prosecution could be carried without intrenching upon their privileges.[1] The proprietors consenting to the acts being repealed by another assembly in Carolina, the matter stopped at that point.

In 1706 the assembly repealed these laws[2] and passed another Church Act,[3] which contained none of these obnoxious features. By this law the settled part of the colony was divided into parishes, in each of which a church was to be erected and provision made for religious service at public expense. The ministers should be called by the inhabitants of the parishes who belonged to the Established Church, who should also choose vestrymen and wardens yearly. These and commissioners named in the act looked after the building and reparation of the ecclesiastical edifices. Expenses incurred for religious purposes were to be defrayed from the public treasury, but the vestries might levy an assessment on all the inhabitants of the parish.

Beside this contest over religion, the first twenty years of the eighteenth century witnessed many severe commotions of other sorts in the colony. In the first place there were Indian wars, the earliest of which in point of time was with the Tuscaroras in North Carolina in 1711 and 1712. The people of the southern part of the province

---

[1] *Colonial Records of North Carolina*, i, 644.

[2] Cooper's *Statutes of South Carolina*, ii, 281.

[3] *Ibid.*, ii, 282.

sent a force to the aid of their brethren in the north [1]
under the command of Colonel John Barnwell.[2] The
Indians were compelled to sue for peace, but again attacked the whites and another expedition was sent to the
aid of the North Carolinians in 1713, this time led by
Colonel James Moore. Later, in 1715, the Indians of
South Carolina who lived along the southern border, incited, or at all events aided by the Spaniards in Florida,
fell upon the whites and there followed a series of Indian conflicts which are known as the Yamassee War.[3]
In these conflicts the proprietors rendered no aid to the
colonists. The expeditions cost a good deal in men and
in money and seriously interfered with the prosperity of
the province.

In addition to enemies from within, the colonists were
also threatened by attacks from without. The first
part of this period covers the years of the War of the
Spanish Succession. This came to an end as to Europe
and as to northern America in 1713 by the Treaty of
Utrecht; but this settlement was not regarded by Spain
or France as applying to Carolina, Florida, and the
West Indies. In 1706 a combined expedition, led by Le
Feboure with five vessels, crossed the bar at the mouth of
Charleston harbor and anchored off Sullivan's Island.[4]
Governor Johnson assembled a body of armed men and
impressed all the vessels in the harbor to serve as a naval
force. He made so bold a show of resistance that the

[1] In 1711 the northern Carolinians had appealed to Virginia for aid; but Governor Spotswood would give none unless the northern Carolinians would give a mortgage on all the settled lands of their province to secure repayment of expenses. *Colonial Records of North Carolina*, i, p. xxx.

[2] The "Journal of John Barnwell,"

1711, is printed in the *Virginia Magazine of History*, v, 391.

[3] On the Yamassee War, see Rivers's *Sketch of South Carolina*, 260 and fol.; McCrady's *South Carolina under the Proprietary Government*, 531 and fol.

[4] So named for Florence O'Sullivan, the first surveyor of the province.

enemy forbore to attack and instead sent a summons to surrender, giving Johnson one hour in which to reply. Instead of taking the proffered time, he answered that it needed not a minute to reply that he would defend the town for the great Queen of England.[1] The enemy landed a party on the shore of the harbor, but beyond inflicting a small amount of damage to private property effected nothing. On the contrary, they were surprised by the Carolinians and driven away, leaving thirty-three of their number in the hands of the English. In 1719 news reached Carolina of a new expedition which was to sail from Havana for the conquest of the Bahamas and the southern continental colonies. This force never got beyond New Providence, for after vainly attacking that place it was dispersed by a storm.[2] Nevertheless, the imminence of danger aroused the Carolinians to a renewed sense of their insecurity and of the inefficiency of the proprietors' government.

Indian attacks from within and Spanish hostility from without were not all the woes to which the Carolinians were subjected in these years. Pirates of greater or lesser fame appeared off Charleston harbor from time to time and made valuable captures, and also used the shores and ports of Carolina for purposes of refitting. Many pirates came to the colony after the close of their plundering career and settled there, more especially, perhaps, in the northern part of the province. One pirate, the notorious Thatch, or Blackbeard, anchored off Charleston in June, 1718, and sent a boat up to the town for certain medicines of which he was in need. To insure the return of boat and men, he informed the authorities

[1] Alexander Hewatt's *Historical Account of South Carolina*, i, 184.   [2] *Ibid.*, i, 287.

that he had captured Samuel Wragg, one of the Council, and his son William, whose lives would be forfeited in case the Charlestonians did not obey his peremptory demands. The medicines were got together; but before they could be sent a storm arose. For a time the captives were in serious danger, for Blackbeard suspected treachery. He was induced, however, to postpone their execution, and before the time had expired men and medicines appeared. The Wraggs were set ashore and after suffering many hardships regained the town, whence they had sailed a few days before. They left behind them in Blackbeard's grasp goods and specie to the value of six [1] or eight thousand pounds sterling. Blackbeard then sailed northward along the coast and did not again appear off the shore of Carolina.

Another pirate, Stede Bonnet,[2] or Captain Thomas, as he chose to call himself in the last months of his life, sailed into the Cape Fear River in a vessel which at one time he had called the *Revenge*, but was now somewhat inappropriately named the *Royal James*. He was a man of property and education; perhaps he took to piracy from some latent Jacobitism, as the name of his ship would imply. He does not appear to have plundered the Charleston people on this cruise, but they had determined to clear the seas of the gentry of the black flag. Under command of William Rhett, who had been bred a sailor, but now held a military title, they sent a naval force to capture or sink Bonnet and his ship. The Carolinian vessel anchored near the pirate craft, whereupon Bonnet sought to run by her and so gain the open sea. The *Royal James* went aground and so, too, did the Charleston vessel

---

[1] S. C. Hughson's "The Carolina Pirates" in *Johns Hopkins Studies*, xii, 72.

[2] See Howell's *State Trials*, xv, 1231–1302.

when it sailed to the attack. For five hours the ships, which were stranded within pistol shot of each other, kept up a cannonade, but without doing much damage. The Carolina vessel floated first and Bonnet threatened to explode the magazine of the *Royal James;* but was prevented by his men, who preferred to take the chance of capture and trial to nearly certain death in their own ship. Bonnet and those of his crew who had not been killed were borne in triumph to Charleston, where twenty-two of them were tried, convicted, and hanged. Bonnet, himself, escaped from the marshal's house, where he was confined instead of being kept in irons in the gaol. He was recaptured and condemned. Then his courage forsook him and he implored the governor to send him to England. His letter of supplication is interesting, on account of the language which would have done credit to an Elizabethan seaman. "Now the God of Peace," he wrote to Governor Johnson, "that brought again from the Dead our Lord Jesus, . . . make you perfect in every good Work to do his Will, working in you that which is well pleasing in his Sight through Jesus Christ, to whom be Glory forever and ever." [1]   But Johnson was obdurate and Bonnet ended his exciting career on the gibbet. In the interval, while he was in hiding, another piratical fleet anchored off the harbor. This time Johnson placed himself at the head of a force composed of merchant vessels that happened to be in port, sailed boldly against the enemy's ships, and captured them. What with Indians, Spaniards, and pirates the South Carolinians enjoyed anything but an easy existence, and it is small wonder that they felt themselves to be quite deserted by the proprietors. It was while their

---

[1] Hughson's "The Carolina Pirates" in *Johns Hopkins Studies*, xii, 347.

minds were thus filled with indignation that their masters in England set themselves directly in opposition to
their wishes.

The expenses of the campaigns against the Indians and
the Spaniards had been met by issuing paper money.
The retirement of this had been provided for by laying
duties on goods imported into the colony, as well from
England as from other places. Up to 1716 the representative system of southern Carolina was anomalous in the
extreme. Representation was apportioned among the several parts of the colony and the franchise was very liberal;
but these advantages were overshadowed by the practice
of holding elections in Charleston, where the electors could
be more easily controlled by the stronger and richer men
of the colony. In 1716 the Assembly had provided that
elections should be held in each parish and should not continue longer than two days, which would prevent those
who owned lands in many parishes from voting in more
than a few of them. The franchise was now restricted
to white men professing the Christian religion and possessing thirty pounds current money, and the qualification of the
members of the assembly was raised to personal property of
five hundred pounds current money, or the possession of five
hundred acres of land.[1] In 1719 the assembly again amended
the qualifications so that a voter was required to possess a
freehold of fifty acres of land or pay taxes to the amount
of fifty pounds of current money, while the qualification
for the representative was raised to one thousand pounds
in the money of the province or the ownership of a settled
plantation of five hundred acres with six negro slaves employed thereon.[2] Another act of these years provided that
the receiver of the money derived from the Indian trade

---

[1] Cooper's *Statutes of South Carolina*, ii, 688.   [2] *Ibid.*, iii, 50, 52.

should be appointed by the Assembly instead of by the governor. In 1719 instructions came from the proprietors, directing the act levying duties to be repealed [1] by order of the king and disallowing the act for the appointment of the receiver. Furthermore, Governor Johnson was instructed to dissolve the assembly which had passed these measures and to hold an election for a new assembly according to the ancient usage, and a new council was appointed like those of the other provinces instead of being composed of deputies of the several proprietors.

This action of the proprietors was legal and according to the provisions of the charter, but the Carolinians, like other colonists, felt that when a law had been assented to by the representatives of the government in the colony, it should not be repealed by the authorities in England, either royal or proprietary. The repeal of the duty act was the most serious, because it left the colony without financial resources at a time when money was urgently needed; but the disallowance of the laws changing the mode of election aroused the most opposition. So keen was the resentment in the province that the governor and council sent one of their number, Mr. Francis Yonge, to England to represent to the proprietors the dangerous situation in the province. All the arguments of the envoy were in vain. The proprietors sent a dictatorial letter to Johnson, directing him to dissolve the assembly and to have a new one elected according to the old method.[2] As if deliberately wishing to add to the disaffection, they refused the further request which had been made as to the disposition of the lands

---

[1] Cooper's *Statutes of South Carolina*, iii, 68.

[2] On these proceedings, see Yonge's "Narrative" in Carroll's *Historical Collections*, ii, 141; and in the Appendix to Rivers's *Early History of South Carolina*. See also McCrady's *South Carolina under the Proprietary Government*, 630 and fol.

that the colonists had captured from the Yamassee Indians.
They now directed the governor to grant no land, not even
for fortification, but on the contrary to set aside certain
tracts for their own use. In this they broke the contract
which existed, at least impliedly, with those who had
recently emigrated to the colony.

At this moment of extreme tension, Governor Robert
Johnson found himself obliged to concert measures against
the threatened Spanish invasion. He summoned the
councilors and members of the assembly who were near
at hand, and sought their advice as to the best means of
securing funds. The assemblymen replied that the duty
act was still in force and that therefore no legislation was
necessary. The receiver had been ordered, so they said, to
enter suit against any one who refused to pay the duty.
Upon this Chief Justice Trott declared that no such suit
would be recognized in his court. He was already excessively unpopular in the colony and charges had been preferred against him by the Assembly for arbitrary and
tyrannical action on the bench. His removal had been
asked of the proprietors, who had replied by sending him
the letter of complaint with their thanks for a speech
which he had made, not long before. Under the circumstances the only thing that Johnson could do was to call
out the militia. The members of each company as they
came together were asked to sign certain articles of association, pledging themselves to oppose the measures of the
proprietors and to act as loyal subjects of the king. In
December, 1719, all the companies marched to Charleston
and were reviewed by the revolutionary leaders. Elections
to the assembly had meantime been held, but the members
chosen refused to regard themselves as forming an assembly
and, instead, called themselves a Convention. They asked

Robert Johnson to act as governor in the name of the king until the royal pleasure should be known. Johnson refused,[1] but after a brief and ineffectual resistance he allowed matters to take their course. It was in this way that proprietary rule came to an end in southern Carolina.

The Convention sent John Barnwell to London to represent the case of the Carolina people to the royal authorities.[2] Joseph Boone had been in London for some time and used the great influence which he possessed to aid the Convention's agent. As has already been said more than once, the Lords of Trade and the government itself had for years been hostile to the perpetuation of proprietary rule. Indeed, McCrady, the historian of South Carolina, thinks that the rulers in England may be regarded as having instigated the rebellion in Carolina. At all events, the king and his advisers at once hearkened to the wishes of the South Carolinians and appointed Sir Francis Nicholson governor. From the point of view of their charter, it cannot be said that the proprietors had done anything that was unauthorized or illegal. On the other hand, the king was obliged to govern and protect his subjects. If his appointed agents did not do so, it was his duty to perform the task by other agents, and, therefore, he was justified in governing Carolina, or a part of it, directly until better arrangements could be made. This had been clearly recognized as to Maryland and Pennsylvania in the time of William and Mary, as has already been shown. Nicholson was appointed provisional governor of South Carolina,[3] but his rule lasted

[1] F. Yonge's "Narrative" in Carroll's *Historical Collections of South Carolina*, 184.

[2] He informed the Lords of Trade that the population of "Carolina," probably southern Carolina, was 9000 whites and 12,000 blacks — adding that the

whites had annually decreased for the last five years while the blacks had increased. Royal Historical Manuscripts Commissions *Reports*, xi, Part iv, p. 254.

[3] This is the last of Nicholson's colonial service, which had begun as Andros's lieutenant when the latter was governor

for seven or eight years until the proprietors surrendered their rights of jurisdiction and most of them sold their title to the soil to the king.   At first the proprietors, after they had recovered from the shock of having the government of the southern part of their province taken from them, tried to sell their rights to the whole province to the South Sea Company, which at the moment was at the height of its career ; but this plan fell through.   It proved to be difficult to make a sale to the crown, because the titles to some of the proprietors' shares were in doubt and the bargain was not consummated until 1728.   By this arrangement the crown obtained title to seven eighths of the undivided lands of the province of Carolina, paying seventeen thousand five hundred pounds for it and five thousand pounds in addition for quitrents which had not been collected.[1]   The eighth proprietor, Lord Carteret, who in later years became Earl Granville, parted with his rights of jurisdiction, but refused to give up his rights to the soil.

For years the fate of the northern settlements hung in the balance : should there be one, two, or three jurisdictions set up in Carolina ?   The northern Carolinians were averse to outside control : in 1675, 1677, 1678, 1679, 1689, 1708, 1709, 1710, and 1711 there had been commotions in that part of the province ;[2] governor after governor had been driven out and the authority of others had been disputed.   The most noteworthy of these movements was that which is associated with the name of John Culpeper

---

of the dominion of New England and had been continued in Virginia and Maryland.

[1] This settlement was confirmed in 1729 by Parliament by act of 2 George II, Cap. 34 (Ruffhead's *Statutes at Large*, v, 708).

[2] On the history of this early time, see Saunders in the "Prefatory Notes" to the *Colonial Records of North Carolina*, i, pp. xxi, xxvii ; ii, p. ix ; on later rebellious proceedings, *ibid.*, viii, p. vii.

and the years 1677–79. This has attracted especial attention because Culpeper was tried on the charge of treason in the court of King's Bench in England.[1] On this occasion the proprietors interfered and stated that the rebellion was nothing more than a riot, or a series of riots, and could not be regarded as resistance to constituted authority. Sometimes the Assembly played a more constitutional rôle, as in 1715, when it resolved that laying taxes on the people "without authority from the Assembly, was unwarrantable, a great infringement of the liberty of the subject, and very much weakened the government by causing many to leave it."[2] In the greater part of this period the proprietors commissioned a governor for southern Carolina, who appointed a deputy for northern Carolina. A strip of unoccupied territory two hundred miles in width separated the settled portions of the province, and in 1713 the proprietors appointed Charles Eden as governor of North Carolina with a council; the definite separation into North and South Carolina may conveniently be dated from that year. At the time of the rebellion at Charleston, Eden and his council refused to recognize the revolutionary authorities in South Carolina, and the people of North Carolina did not take any action.[3] It fell out in this way, therefore, that the proprietors continued to exercise jurisdiction in North Carolina after the royal government had been established at Charleston, and it was not until the sale of the soil and the jurisdiction had been effected in 1728 or 1729 that North Carolina came

---

[1] The judges declared in this case that to take up arms against a proprietary government was treason against the king. Chalmers's *Annals*, i, 562.

[2] *Colonial Records of North Carolina*, ii, p. xi; see also *ibid.*, iii, 264.

[3] Saunders says that "in conscience and truth men might well be excused for not being in haste to get under Royal rule." The weaker their government was, the better the people of North Carolina liked it. *Colonial Records*, ii, pp. vi, vii.

under royal rule.[1] From time to time the southern Carolinians had wished that the northern settlements might be
annexed directly to their own government; this was especially true in the first years of the royal rule, when the
formation of the southern part of South Carolina into a
separate government was in agitation, but this plan was
never put into execution.

From the very beginning there had always been two
centers of colonization in Carolina, and as time went on the
conditions of life in the northern and southern parts of
the province became very different.   At first the products
of the two sections were similar, — lumber and furs; but
the trade relations of the southern region were with
Europe and the West Indies,[2] and not at all with the
other English continental colonies.   After rice came to be
the staple product of the country around Charleston, the
aloofness of South Carolina from North Carolina and the
other English continental colonies became more and more
evident.   That commercial town also served as the capital
of the southern government and as a place of residence for
the principal men.   In North Carolina there was nothing
of the kind, such towns as there were being mere villages;
the city of Bath in 1709 was the only " town " in the province and had only twelve houses: in short, population was
concentrated in southern Carolina and dispersed in northern Carolina.   Moreover, in the southern part of the province, negro slavery had already assumed an intensive
form, while in the northern settlements it played little
or no part in the life of the settlers.   Exact figures are

---

[1] The negotiations for the sale were
completed in 1728, and the authorities of
the northern province were directed to
communicate with the royal officials
and not with the proprietors in the same
year. The Act of Parliament establishing the agreement was passed in 1729,
and the formal deed of surrender was
signed in July, 1729. See *Colonial Records of North Carolina*, ii, p. i.

[2] McCrady's *South Carolina under
the Royal Government*, 264.

unattainable, but the best estimates show that in 1732 there were probably thirty thousand whites and six thousand negroes in North Carolina; in South Carolina, in 1734, there were fifteen thousand whites and twenty-two thousand negroes, and in the next four years more than ten thousand negroes were imported into the latter colony.[1] The leaders of South Carolina were men of force and ability, and the settlers of North Carolina were excessively independent; their environments were so dissimilar that in no short time social conditions in the two colonies became very dissimilar and have been so ever since.

The troubles of the proprietary period had interfered sadly with the material growth of both parts of the province. The Indian wars had not led to the killing of many whites, but in connection with threatened Spanish invasion, danger from pirates and constant disputes with the proprietors had undoubtedly diverted the current of emigration into other colonies, notably to Pennsylvania. In 1679, and again in 1705 and 1726, Virginia had aimed a deadly blow at the growth of North Carolina by prohibiting the bringing of tobacco into Virginia from outside the capes of the Chesapeake, except from her own county of Lower Norfolk.[2] This prohibition was undoubtedly intended to lessen the production of tobacco for export by the people of North Carolina, but tobacco was grown there and exported in considerable quantities. Not only was North Carolina tobacco carried away clandestinely, but tobacco was brought overland from the southern Virginia counties and shipped from Carolina ports in preference to those of the Chesapeake, owing to the immunity from the

[1] For a comparative statement of the population of the two colonies for a series of years, see Note at end of chapter.
[2] Hening's *Statutes*, ii, 445; iii, 253; iv, 175. See also *Colonial Records of North Carolina*, i, pp. xxii, 261, 628; ii, 636.

"penny duty" which was thereby gained since the aquatic condition of the Carolina seaboard forbade even the lax inspection that prevailed in Virginia.   It appears, therefore, that after 1700 Carolina tobacco in reality enjoyed more facilities for reaching the markets of the world than did the tobacco of Virginia.   The principal exports of North Carolina, however, were naval stores, — tar, pitch, and turpentine, — all of which were extracted from the pine trees that grew in the sandy soil of her lowland counties. Otherwise the energies of her people were devoted to clearing the land and growing food for home consumption.

The royal officials in North Carolina surpassed those of any other colony in powers of vituperation, and at least two of the missionaries, whom the Venerable Society for the Propagation of the Gospel sent across the Atlantic to convert the North Carolinians to the true faith, were not much better than the governors.[1]   The first governor to come to the colony after the change to the royal government was Gabriel Johnston.[2]   He arrived in 1734 and held the office for eighteen years.   He was not a profane man nor a drunkard, but he owed his appointment to his skill in defending his patron from attack and not to any approved ability in administration or knowledge of colonial

---

[1] Saunders (*Colonial Records of North Carolina*, ii, p. ix) states that Eden, Burrington, and Everard were "a cormorant brood in that day, at least, not equalled in America." The Council, after Burrington's departure, charged him with having "vilely prostituted" his office "in conjunction with a set of profligate tools" (*ibid.*, iv, 81). Burrington hated the chief justice, whom he called "Baby Smith," and said that he was an ungrateful, perfidious scoundrel and an egregious sot, while the attorney general did not know enough law to be clerk to a justice of the peace, and the admiralty judge was an infamous character.

As to the missionaries, one of them, Jonathan Urmstone by name, was indicted by the grand jury for being drunk, and another was described by Alexander Garden, the Bishop of London's Commissary, as "one of the vilest and most scandalous persons in the government," who was seen by many persons "lying dead drunk and fast asleep" on Sunday morning. See *ibid.*, i, 630; ii, 53–79, 271, 374, 401, 417, 431; iii, 344; iv, 33.

[2] *Ibid.*, iv, pp. i, v, vii.

affairs.   He was a typical Englishman, who believed that he
knew more than any " colonial " could possibly know.   Before he had been in Carolina six weeks, he wrote home to
the Lords of Trade that the people of that province were
not adepts in the art of making tar and that they might
well be compelled to alter their methods.   He was delighted
with the " balsamick " air of the province and doubted
not that he would acquire " a pretty good estate " without
doing any one harm.[1]   These expectations were not realized, as, at his death, he left only debts and his salary two
thousand pounds in arrears.   Johnston found that only
six of the laws of North Carolina had been confirmed by
the proprietors.[2]   He refused to regard any of the others
as in force whenever they interfered with the royal prerogative or revenue, and soon became involved in a vigorous dispute with the Assembly as to the collection of quitrents.

Land in Carolina had been granted subject to the payment of a quitrent of four shillings per hundred acres.[3]
Custom and law had sanctioned the payment of this ex-
action in money or in commodities at convenient places.
The people held that the rent should continue to be pay-
able at the plantation or at some agreed-upon spot.
Johnston contended that he himself could regulate the
place of payment and the rate of commutation when the
rent was paid " in kind."   He designated four places
where the rents must be paid either in sterling money or
its equivalent.   The Assembly took up the cause of their
constituents and addressed the Council, asserting that quit-

[1] Royal Historical Manuscripts Commission *Reports*, xi, Part iv, 258.

[2] *Colonial Records of North Carolina*,
iv, 24.

[3] On the controversy over quitrents,
see *ibid.*, iv, pp. xiv, xvi, 111, 132 and
fol.; v, 19, 77, 81, 447.   The " Great
Deed of Grant " of 1693 is printed in
ibid., iii, 292.   As to irregularities in
grants and surveys, see *ibid.*, v, 361.

rents always had been paid on the land unless there was an express agreement to the contrary. They declared that in Virginia the quitrent collectors went from house to house, gathering the tobacco, and that an allowance was made to those who paid in inspected tobacco. The Council, on the other hand, asserted that the bill which the Assembly presented to it was "so clogged" with objectionable matter that it was obliged to reject it, and, furthermore, denied that the practice in Virginia was as the Assembly had stated. The Council also called attention to the fact that the king had purchased Carolina of the proprietors for a valuable consideration and was clearly entitled to receive the quitrents. To this paper the Assembly rejoined by an appeal to what was termed the "Grand Deed," by which it was alleged that the quitrent was to be two shillings per one hundred acres in tobacco at one penny per pound, which rate might be commuted in other goods as agreed upon with the receiver general of the proprietors. The royal officials, under orders from the governor, now seized the goods of those who did not pay the rents as ordered by him. The Assembly, which was in session, directed its officers to arrest the collectors. Thereupon the governor dismissed the assembly, because when it was no longer in session all persons who had been imprisoned by its order would be at liberty. Not long after this, upon the rumor that a planter had been imprisoned at Edenton for resisting the quitrent collectors, five hundred planters marched to the outskirts of the town with arms in their hands and dispersed to their homes only upon being informed that the man had been set at liberty. Before going they declared that they would give "the most cruel usage to such persons as durst come to demand any quitrents of them

in the future." This occurrence seems to have taught
Johnston a lesson, for he desisted from pushing his own
interpretation of the law, and by "management" and concession secured the passage of a bill regulating the collection of quitrents, which was, however, disallowed in
England. It does not appear, indeed, that any considerable amounts of quitrents were collected in North Carolina before 1760.[1]

Lord Carteret, now Earl Granville, had refused to sell
his right to the soil of Carolina at the time that the other
seven proprietors parted with theirs, although he had
surrendered his rights of jurisdiction to the crown. The
difficulties of Gabriel Johnston were not in any way lessened by the decision of the royal authorities to set off
Lord Granville's tract wholly in North Carolina. This
they did by an Order in Council, which was dated May 9,
1744, and directed that the land extending from the Virginia line southward to the parallel of 35° 34′, and from
the Atlantic Ocean westward, should be set off for him.[2]
The quitrents arising from lands already granted within
this region and the profits to be derived from future sales
would go to him. It fell out in this way, therefore, that
the oldest settled and richest part of the colony paid no
quitrents to the royal government, while the expenses of
maintaining the jurisdiction there continued. There now
occurred one of the most curious contests in colonial constitutional history. The northern counties, which were
generally spoken of as Albemarle, returned the majority
of the members to the assembly. Being violently opposed
to Governor Johnston, the members from Albemarle re-

---

[1] *Colonial Records of North Carolina*,
iv, pp. xvii, 424. From a paper in another volume of the same series (viii,
161) it appears that the amount of quitrents collected in 1769 was only 1750
pounds sterling.

[2] *Ibid.*, iv, pp. x, 655, 674.

fused to vote taxes of which they themselves would pay
the greater part. In 1746 Johnston caused the assembly
to meet at Wilmington in the extreme southern part of
the province, with the expectation that the northern settlements would not be largely represented, and they were
not. The members who attended were easily persuaded
to pass a representation act, giving two members to each
county and to vote generous grants of money which would
be collected almost entirely from the northern residents.
These, however, refused to pay on the ground dear to
every Englishman of "no taxation without representation"; as these would not pay, the inhabitants of the
southern part of the colony also declined to contribute.
For eight years there was a legislative deadlock, so that
this cunning device of Gabriel Johnston produced little
except unpopularity in the province and a reprimand from
the Lords of Trade for his sharp practice.[1]

The royal government sought to limit the number of
representatives in the North Carolina assembly and asserted that it had the right to regulate the constitution of
the legislative body of the province. In 1754 the king
vetoed the "Representation of the People" act, which
had been passed in 1746, and also twelve laws, setting off
counties or incorporating towns — for these sent representatives to the assembly; but Governor Dobbs delayed
publishing the fact of the repeal of these twelve laws.[2]
Ultimately the home government conceded the right of
the Carolinians to regulate the apportionment of representation, but reserved the power to confer representation by
charter; but it does not appear that this was ever done.[3]

[1] The documents relating to this incident are in *Colonial Records of North
Carolina*, iv, 1152, 1154, 1223, and see also
ibid., iv, p. xviii, and vi, p. xxv.

[2] *Colonial Records of North Carolina*, v, 326.
[3] *Ibid.*, v, pp. vi, vii, 399, 405.

The protection of the southern boundary of Carolina against the Spaniards had long occupied the attention of the authorities. At one time they had established a post on the Altamaha River; but the maintenance of the garrison had been so expensive that it had been abandoned. In 1732 James Edward Oglethorpe,[1] with some philanthropic associates, obtained a charter from the king, giving them land between the Savannah and Altamaha rivers for the establishment of a " buffer " colony, to be known by the name of Georgia. Oglethorpe came of an old and distinguished family, but his politics interfered with his advancement in England. As a member of the House of Commons he had become interested in the amelioration of the condition of poor debtors, who were mercilessly consigned to the horrible prisons which then were a disgrace to England. He hit upon the idea of colonizing these unfortunates in the southern part of South Carolina. On January 13, 1733, he sailed into Charleston harbor with his first band of refugees. Thence proceeding southward, he founded the town of Savannah on the southern side of the river of that name. For the next few years he exercised paternal power over the settlers, acting as judge, lawgiver, and defender.

Oglethorpe and his associates were actuated by the highest and most honorable motives; but their regulations were not conducive to the success of the enterprise. They granted lands in such small amounts that the establishment of the plantation system was impossible, especially as the colonists were forbidden to own slaves. As the conditions of cultivation in Georgia were like those which pre-

---

[1] There are several lives of Oglethorpe, that by Robert Wright being the most authoritative; but Henry Bruce's sketch in the "Makers of America" series is the most readable. There is a good article by Austin Dobson in *Longmans' Magazine*, reprinted in Littell's *Living Age*, 1899, p. 538.

vailed in South Carolina, it was quite hopeless for the small farmers of the new colony, who were generally without capital, to compete with the rich landowners of the region around Charleston. The Georgia trustees soon modified the regulations as to land, and their settlers hit upon the expedient of hiring negro slaves for long terms of years or during life.[1] The trustees were so disheartened by the ill success of their schemes that in 1751 they surrendered their rights to the crown.[2]

In any case, living in Georgia in these early days would not have been pleasant, owing to the proximity of the Spaniards in Florida. The greater part of Oglethorpe's time in the colony was taken up with a succession of expeditions for the conquest of St. Augustine or in defending the English settlements from Spanish attacks. The history of these expeditions is a dreary tale of misfortune and incapacity ; but they undoubtedly exhausted the strength and resources of the Spaniards. The last one was in 1740, when the English marching overland actually came within sight of the town, but did not push the attack when it might have succeeded.[3]

As was natural under these circumstances, Georgia grew with phenomenal slowness ; in 1760 there were only five or six thousand white settlers within her limits. Of these the most interesting was a band of persecuted Protestants from the bishopric of Saltzburg in the Austrian Tyrol.[4] They founded the town of Ebenezer on the Savannah River ; but this in common with other early Georgia

[1] Charles C. Jones's *Georgia*, i, 420.

[2] The charter terminated by one of its provisions in 1753, the only example of limitation in point of time.

[3] Jones's *Georgia*, i, 326–369 ; Candler's *Records of Georgia*, iv, 614–627, and the biographies of Oglethorpe. The South Carolina view of the matter is stated in the *Collections* of the Historical Society of that state, iv, No. i.

[4] See Strobel's *The Saltzburgers and their Descendants* and Charles C. Jones's *Dead Towns of Georgia*.

towns died a natural death in competition with the profits from the plantation system. Higher up the river, near the site of the modern city of Augusta, there was established a fur-trading post which was at first on the Carolina side of the river, whence the peltries were taken overland to Charleston ; but later the fort was established on the Georgia side and the furs were taken downstream to Savannah. Georgia fulfilled its mission as a "buffer" colony, but only at the expense of depriving the South Carolinians of valuable lands and a lucrative fur trade.

NOTE

Population of the Carolinas. — The following tabulation shows
not only the increase in population, but also the marked contrast
between the two provinces : —

South Carolina		North Carolina	
1719,[1] 9,000 whites,	12,000 blacks	1717,[2] total whites and blacks, 9,000	
1734,[5] 15,000 whites,	22,000 blacks	1732,[3] 30,000 whites, 6,000 blacks	
1749,[6] 25,000 whites,	39,000 blacks	1754,[4] 62,000 whites, 15,000 blacks	
1763,[7] 30,000 whites,	70,000 blacks	1760,[8] 77,000 whites, 16,000 blacks	

[1] John Barnwell to Lords of Trade, Royal Historical Manuscript Commission's *Reports*, xi, Part iv, p. 254.

[2] John Pollock in *Colonial Records of North Carolina*, ii, xvii.

[3] Governor Burrington in *ibid*.

[4] Compiled from census of tithables in *ibid*., V, 320.

[5] McCrady, in *South Carolina as a Royal Province*, p. 184, from Governor Glenn's "Report."

[6] Governor Glenn in Carroll's *Historical Collections*, ii, 218.

[7] Dr. George Milligan in *ibid*., ii, 478.

[8] Bassett's "Slavery in North Carolina" in *Johns Hopkins University Studies*, xiv, 193.

CHAPTER XIII

SYSTEMS OF LABOR

UNSKILLED laborers for the exploitation of the resources of North America have always been in keen demand. Negro slavery played little part in the earlier days; but as the eighteenth century advanced, the employment of negroes became more and more marked in every decade. In the earlier time, white persons bound to service for a term of years[1] performed the hard work of field, forest, and farm, and there were also domestic servants who worked for a weekly wage.[2] Ordinarily, the necessary household service was performed by the women of the family and their collateral female relations in the North. In the Middle Colonies, indentured servants and negro slaves were employed in the household, but south of the Potomac this work was done by slaves.

Farm labor in New England and in the Middle Colonies was largely performed by the owner of the land and the members of his family; but " help " was sometimes employed on wages. Labor was scarce and wages were high. In the confusion of colonial currencies it is impossible to be pre-

---

[1] These were indentured or indented servants, so called from the name of the contract. They were of various classes, — free willers, redemptioners, convicts.

[2] In his diary, Lawrence Hammond mentions a maidservant by the name of "Trial." He also had in his employ a young girl who came into his family at the age of thirteen, to dwell there as a servant for six years and to be taught and provided for as should be meet. Many children were bound out in this way by guardians or town authorities in order that they might not become a public charge.

367

cise; but a " laborer " received the equivalent of two thirds of a bushel of corn for a day's work in New England in the decade before 1760,[1] and wages were higher in Pennsylvania.[2] Indentured servants of a good class were everywhere in demand, and after 1720 they came in constantly increasing numbers to all the colonies north of Maryland.

Besides apprentices who went into domestic service, it was the custom to bind out boys to masters for the purpose of learning a trade, as was the case with Benjamin Franklin. In Pennsylvania and south of it, agriculture was almost the only industry, and there the distinction between the apprentice and the indentured servant was only one of age. The terms of service and the conditions of apprenticeship were carefully regulated by the lawmakers, because their own children might come within that category. Of the indentured servants, the most interesting were the free willers or redemptioners, who sold their services for a limited term, generally five years, to provide their own passage money[3] or the price of transportation of those who were dependent upon them; among these were the Germans who came to Pennsylvania in the middle of the century.[4] Otherwise, the great mass of the servants in the colonies were English men, women, and children who had been forced to emigrate by the government or by kidnappers and hard-hearted kinsfolk; for these servitude was little removed from slavery.

Kidnapping, or "spiriting," was at its height in the reign of the second Charles, but it continued long after the death of that monarch. Most of the victims of the "spir-

---

[1] See tables in the Appendix to the second volume of Weeden's *Economic History of New England.*

[2] H. M. Jenkins's *Historical Sketches of Gwynedd*, 300.

[3] Franklin relates the case of an Ox-ford scholar who dissipated his property and sold himself into service in America. John Bigelow's *Franklin*, i, 172.

[4] See chapter XIV of the present work.

its" were boys and girls, who were gathered from the streets of London and Bristol and from the country round about. Usually they belonged to the poorer classes, but sometimes spiriting was made use of to extort money. In 1670 as many as ten thousand persons were spirited from England in one year.[1] A kidnapper stated in 1671 that for twelve years past he himself had annually sent five hundred persons to the colonies, while another declared that he had sent eight hundred and forty in a single year.[2] The records of the London courts give specific examples.[3] For instance, there was Jane Price, who was convicted of assaulting Richard Jackson, and conveying him against his will to a vessel, then at anchor in the Thames, with the intention of selling him in Virginia for her own gain, — she was fined one pound six shillings eight pence. The worst case recorded is that of Alice Deakins. She was a girl of sixteen years, who was spirited by a man and a woman, for which they were fined twelve pence each; had they stolen goods to the value of a few shillings, they would have been sentenced to death as felons. Judges, like other persons in those days, exhibited a callousness as to human suffering out of accord with modern humanitarianism; they were also influenced by the fact that unscrupulous persons sold themselves to colonial contractors, deserted at some of the outports while the ship was making her way down Channel, and then claimed to have been spirited away.[4]

Merchants engaged in the plantation trade complained to the government of these evil conditions. Bills were introduced into Parliament to prevent the "spiriting of

[1] Morgan Godwyn's *The Negro's & Indians Advocate*, 171.
[2] *Calendars of State Papers, America and West Indies, 1675–1676*, p. 521.
[3] *Middlesex County Records*, iv (index under "Spiriting" and Preface, pp. xli–xlvii). See also *Calendars of State Papers, America and West Indies, 1661–1668*, p. 555.
[4] *Ibid., 1661–1668*, pp. 98, 220, 233.

children " to the plantations, and at one time there was an official register.[1] Toward the close of the century the conditions of emigration had improved somewhat,[2] but the profits which the government and English merchants derived from the traffic made them close their eyes to many cruelties; " the plantations cannot be maintained without a considerable number of white servants " — so it was stated in Parliament.

Deportation from one's home land as the punishment for crime is as old as history. As a punishment of political or religious offenses, banishment was frequently employed in Tudor times; and in Elizabeth's reign rogues and vagabonds might also be expelled from the kingdom. With the beginning of colonization, transportation to America came to be regarded as a convenient means to reduce the expenses of looking after criminals in England, as well as a good method of providing the colonies with laborers; but it was not until the reign of the second Charles that transportation was recognized on the statute book. The first act was passed in 1662;[3] it authorized justices of the peace with the approbation of the Privy Council to send rogues, vagabonds, and " sturdy beggars "

[1] In *Calendars of State Papers, America and West Indies, 1675–1676* (p. 521), is noted the " Copy of an Act to prevent stealing and transporting other children, passed 18th March 1670 [-71]." Bruce (*Economic History of Virginia*, i, 618) makes a similar statement. No such act appears in the *Statutes of the Realm*, and the " Journals " of the Lords and the Commons show that every attempt to pass legislation of the kind met with failure. See *Commons Journals*, ix, pp. 137, 138, 140, 142, 166, 233, dealing with the bill noted above and also pp. 250, 251, 286, 558, 559, 561, which have to do with bills that were introduced in 1672, 1673, and 1676. In 1691 a bill passed the third reading, but was then dropped. See *ibid.*, x, 544, 546, 555, 562, 580, 589.

December 13, 1682, an Order in Council was issued forbidding any person under the age of fourteen to be bound over for the plantations unless his parents were present and consenting thereto, and even then he was not to be carried on shipboard until two weeks later, that any abuses might be remedied.

[2] As late as 1743 there is the case of the abduction of James Annesley and his sale in Pennsylvania. *Gentleman's Magazine*, xi, 110; xii, 386; xiii, 612.

[3] 14 Charles II, Cap. 12, § 6 (*Statutes of the Realm*, v, 402).

to the plantations; six years later the judges were authorized either to execute the " moss troopers" of northern England or transport them to the plantations.[1] Cromwell and Charles sent their captive enemies to the plantations, and the crushing of Jacobite hopes after the battle of Culloden induced hundreds of Scots to betake themselves to America without going through the formality of transportation.[2] The religious laws of the Restoration provided for the transportation of Quakers and for the sending of other dissenters to the colonies outside of New England and Virginia under pain of death as felons in case of return to England without permission.[3] These were to be sent to Barbados and Jamaica to work on the plantations.

The transportation of criminals, as the word is ordinarily used, was a matter of executive and judicial action until 1671. During the Protectorate and in the early years of Charles II, scores of convicted felons were pardoned on condition of going to the plantations; but in this case, also, most of them were transported to the West Indies. On one occasion, indeed, the "Middlesex Records" mention certain convicts who were to be sent "versus Virginie insulam seu insulas vocatas le Barbadoes aut aliquam aliam partem Americe"; but whether any of these reached the "island of Virginia" is unknown.[4] Convicts nevertheless must have been transported to Virginia at this time, because in 1670 the assembly of the Old Dominion prohibited the bringing in of felons.[5] In 1679 the

[1] 18 Charles II, Cap. 3 (*Statutes of the Realm*, v, 598).

[2] Bruce's *Economic History of Virginia* (i, 609–612) contains a useful summary of the facts on this subject. See also *Calendars of State Papers, America and West Indies, 1661–1668*, Preface, p. xxx.

[3] 14 Charles II, Cap. 1 (*Statutes of the Realm*, v, 350); 16 Charles II, Cap. 4, §§ 3, 4, 16 (*ibid.*, v, 517, 519); 22 Charles II, Cap. 1 (*ibid.*, v, 648). It is noteworthy that transportation was not provided in the last law, the Conventicle Act of 1670.

[4] *Middlesex County Records*, iii, 337.

[5] "Robinson's Notes" in *Virginia Magazine of History*, ix, p. 44; see also

English Habeas Corpus Act[1] provided that no person could
be imprisoned beyond the seas; but convicted felons in
open court might pray to be transported and could then
be carried to any plantation belonging to the king.[2] Previously, in 1671, Parliament had enacted that persons convicted of the willful burning of hay, grain, or buildings,
or destroying horses, sheep, or cattle in the night time,
might avoid judgment by transportation to the colonies
for seven years.

In 1717 the transportation of convicts was systematized
by act of Parliament.[3] This provided that persons convicted of crime who were entitled to benefit of clergy might
be transported to the plantations for seven years, those
who were excluded from benefit of clergy might be transported for fourteen years : in each case, return to England
before the expiration of the allotted period was punishable
with death. Persons contracting for the transportation
of felons could sell their services for the prescribed term.
Later other acts were passed to render more speedy and
effectual the transportation of convicts, and in 1768 Scotland was included with England notwithstanding the
vigorous protest of Dr. Franklin.

Convicted felons were sent to the West Indies, to the
colonies on Chesapeake Bay, and also to the settlements
on the Delaware.[4] The West India planters welcomed

*Calendars of State Papers, America and
West Indies, 1669-1674,* p. 63.

[1] 31 Charles II, Cap. 2, §§ 11-13 (*Statutes of the Realm,* v, 937).

[2] This act also provided that persons
who had agreed to transportation and
had received earnest money might be
transported. As early as 1662 bills for
the transportation of felons, vagrants,
and other undesirable persons had been
introduced into the House of Commons.
In 1669 a bill for this purpose passed

the Commons by one vote, but being
amended by the Lords was "laid aside"
upon its reappearance in the lower
House. See *Commons Journals,* viii,
438, 443; ix, 233; Grey's *Debates,* i, 236.

[3] 4 George I, Cap. 11 (Ruffhead's *Statutes at Large,* v, 174). This act was
made "more effectual" by 6 George I,
Cap. 23 (Pickering's *Statutes at Large,*
xiv, 292).

[4] See further on this subject, Note I
at end of chapter.

laborers of any kind, but the Virginians and Pennsylvanians disliked having English criminals unloaded upon them. They passed many laws to prohibit or limit the traffic. The English government vetoed every law of Virginia of the kind, but Pennsylvania was able to do something to moderate the influx of convicts. The Marylanders were not so strongly opposed to their importation[1] and probably had the greatest proportionate number of convicts of any colony. Many of these transported convicts were victims of misfortune; others were deported because they were married without the sanction of the Established Church.[2] Many convicts were educated persons and were employed by their masters in confidential positions, and upon the expiration of their terms of service became highly useful and reputable citizens. In Virginia, one penitent thief rose to the position of attorney-general; in Maryland, a majority of the schoolmasters in 1773 were transported convicts.[3]

Criminals did not then look upon transportation with the same feelings of horror with which the practice is now regarded. Those who were able to maintain themselves were not indentured and easily made their escape from the colony where they were landed. So many of this class returned to England that the government interfered and directed that no more of them should be transported

---

[1] J. V. L. McMahon (*Historical View of the Government of Maryland*, i, 314) states that before 1763 fifteen to twenty thousand convicts had landed in that province, the total white population of Maryland at that date being not over one hundred and ten thousand.

[2] 26 George II, Cap. 33, § 8 (Ruffhead's *Statutes at Large*, vii, 526).

[3] See J. D. Butler's "British Convicts shipped to American Colonies" in *American Historical Review*, ii, 12–33. Franklin strongly reprobated the practice of transportation, suggesting that a large number of rattlesnakes should be sent from Pennsylvania to England in the hope that the changed conditions of living might free them from their evil habits, — as the New World was said to reform English criminals. *Pennsylvania Gazette*, May 9, 1751; see *The Nation*, September 1, 1898.

without giving bonds[1] to the amount of one hundred pounds sterling, to be forfeited in case of return to England within four years. Sometimes convicts seized the ship conveying them to the plantations and made their escape.[2] The colonists, while reprehending the importation of criminals from other parts of the empire, had not the least objection to deporting their own vicious and idle inhabitants, partly as a means of punishment, but more particularly to lessen the public burdens.[3]

The condition of the indentured servant in the colonies was good until negro slavery degraded the position of the white laborer, although the fact that the servant's term was limited frequently induced the master to get all he could out of him while the servant was still under contract. The master was obliged to maintain his slave after the period of bodily vigor had passed; it was his interest, therefore, to prolong his period of useful labor; but the town or county authorities would take care of the servant, if he became disabled after the close of the contract period.

Legislation[4] was sometimes necessary to prevent cruel exactions on the part of the masters of indentured servants, and in the absence of positive enactment the justices often looked after their welfare. In one case, Virginia magistrates went so far as to release the servants of a cruel mistress and to forbid her to employ others. When a

---

[1] Egerton's *British Colonial Policy*, 40.

[2] Royal Historical Manuscripts Commission's *Reports*, xiv, Part ix, p. 77.

[3] In 1683 the Massachusetts magistrates ordered one William Batt, "an idle person that refuseth to work," to be transported to the West Indies, and the New York authorities sent Marcus Jacobsen, the "long Swede," to Barbados after being whipped and branded for seditious speeches. See *Boston Town Records*, 1660–1701, p. 162; Brodhead's *New York*, ii, 165.

[4] See the Massachusetts Law of 1758–59 (*Province Laws*, iv, 179), which provided a fine for abusive treatment and even for neglect to have youthful servants taught to read, write, and cipher.

servant's term was completed, he was not to " be sent
away empty," to use the words of the Massachusetts law,[1]
but was to be provided with competent clothing, agricultural implements, and sometimes with a gun and food.
Often, too, the government gave the freedman fifty acres
of land, and he was soon enabled to lay the foundations of future prosperity. The law, also, usually compelled a master who detained his servant beyond the
contract time to compensate him for so doing.

In a period when the whip was looked upon as an
effective weapon of reformation and was applied vigorously
to the bare backs of free white men, women, and children,
it was naturally used with even greater vigor and frequency
on the backs of indentured servants.[2] These were, as a
rule, subject to the same laws as any other white person;
but where a free white would pay a fine, a servant, like a
negro slave, for the same offense[3] would receive a flogging.
Thirty-nine lashes greeted the returning wanderer in Virginia, whether servant or slave.[4] The servant, furthermore,
was compelled to serve his master after the expiration of
his term double the time that he was gone or even more,
and also to reimburse the public for the expense of catching
him. These laws were especially severe in Maryland and
South Carolina,[5] since the wilderness to the southward of

[1] Whitmore's *Massachusetts Laws of
1672*, p. 105. The Maryland law of 1715,
ch. xliv, § 9, is very precise on this point.
See Bacon's *Laws* under this year.

[2] For instance, a Rhode Island law
of 1728 provided that children or servants striking their parents or masters
should be whipped, not exceeding ten
stripes. *Laws of 1767*, p. 65.

[3] See, for examples, *Pennsylvania
Statutes at Large* (ed. of 1898), v, 126;
Hening's *Statutes of Virginia*, vi, 360.
In Maryland, on the other hand, ser-
vants underwent imprisonment instead

of receiving a flogging, making good the
time to their masters at end of the contract periods (Bacon's *Laws of Maryland*, 1750, ch. v, § 1), and a master was
limited to ten lashes; if the servant deserved more, application must be made
to a magistrate. Bacon's *Laws of Maryland*, 1715, ch. xliv, § 22.

[4] Hening's *Statutes of Virginia*, ii,
278; vi, 363. See also *New York Colonial Laws*, i, 147.

[5] In Maryland, ten days' extra service
might be exacted for each day of freedom, Bacon's *Laws of Maryland*, 1715,

the latter and the province of Pennsylvania to the north-ward of the former offered extraordinary facilities for escape. Another cause for anxiety as to both servants and slaves was their tendency to pilfer, which was met by the enactment of stringent laws.[1]

Slavery and servitude in the early colonial period had no such distinctive meaning as they later came to have. In "King James's Bible" Joseph is described as "a servant in the land of Egypt,"[2] although he was a slave. In the dictionaries of that time servitude, slavery, and bondage are synonymous.[3] The status of a slave was unknown to English law, and this was a subject on which the colonists worked out their own legal system. Colonial laws as to servants and slaves shade imperceptibly into one another, but there is an evident distinction between them in the minds of the lawmakers. Slaves were regarded as property to be taxed and disposed of by will as other chattels;[4] servants were taxed by the poll, and the contracts under which they served, and not themselves, were inventoried as forming part of a man's estate. Moreover, children of

---

ch. xliv, § ii. A South Carolina law of 1686 provided twenty-eight days extra for each day's absence. In 1744 one week's service was required for each day of absence, not exceeding two years in all; and the captured fugitive might be whipped not exceeding twenty stripes. He had to satisfy the master for the costs of his recapture and flogging by extra service not exceeding one year, in addition to what he served on account of his absence. See Cooper's *Statutes of South Carolina*, ii, 23, 53; iii, 623. There was no law in those days requiring the rendition of fugitive servants; once in Pennsylvania the runaway was usually safe.

[1] *New York Colonial Laws*, i, 157; Hening's *Statutes*, ii, 118; Cooper's *Statutes of South Carolina*, ii, 22; *Pennsylvania Statutes at Large*, ii, 56; Whit-

more's *Massachusetts Laws of 1672*, p. 104, and innumerable later enactments in the same compilations. In 1693 in North Carolina a servant was convicted of petty larceny and sentenced to receive thirty stripes "on naked back, stripped to his wast, and severely whipt, and be bound to serve for his fees one year and a half from this day . . . besides his former indenture of five years," *Colonial Records of North Carolina*, i, 401.

[2] *Deuteronomy*, v, 15; see other instances in *ibid.*, v, 14; xii, 18; *Exodus*, xxi, 20, 26; *Leviticus*, xxv, 39.

[3] Minsheu's *Guide into Tongues*, London, 1617.

[4] Samuel Sewall objected to the taxation of slaves as property because doing so confounded men with hogs and cattle.

a slave mother were themselves slaves, but children of a
mother who was a servant were themselves free. Whenever a person was regarded as property by the tax gatherer
or the judge of probate, such person was a slave and not
a servant, no matter how leniently or severely he or she
might otherwise be treated.

Negro slaves were owned in all the colonies and in sufficient numbers to affect social and political institutions
even in New England. There were about six thousand
negro slaves in Virginia in 1700.[1] From this time they
increased out of all proportion to the white population,
until, in 1760, nearly one half of the inhabitants of the
Old Dominion were negro slaves. Some of the more far-
sighted of the Virginia planters lamented the increase of
slavery. One of them, Colonel William Byrd, the ever
famous Virginia planter and author, informed the Earl
of Egmont, the grandfather of Lord Rawdon of the Revolutionary War, that there are now (1736) at least ten
thousand " Ethiopians " in Virginia. " They blow up the
pride, and ruin the Industry of our White People who,
seeing a Rank of poor Creatures below them, detest work
for fear it shoud make them look like Slaves." Moreover, continues Byrd, the presence of so many " of these
descendants of Ham " makes severe measures necessary,
" these base Tempers require to be rid with a tort Rein,
or they will be apt to throw their Rider."[2] Twenty
years later, Andrew Burnaby, an English traveler, visited
Virginia and reported that the people of that colony
hardly looked upon Indians and negroes as belonging to

---

[1] Bruce's *Economic History of Virginia*, ii, 108. In 1670 Governor Berkeley had estimated the number of slaves
at 2000. Colonel Jenings, President
of the Virginia Council, informed the
Lords of Trade that there were 12,000
slaves in the Old Dominion in 1708,
Colonial Records of North Carolina,
i, 692.

[2] *American Historical Review*, i, 89.

the human species. The laws are such, he says, that it
is almost impossible to convict a white man for killing a
negro or an Indian.[1] Travelers are often inaccurate observers and worse reporters, but the laws of Virginia
strongly corroborate Burnaby in this instance.

In 1748, and again in 1753, the Virginia Assembly revised the laws relating to servants and slaves, which were
not again radically changed until the Revolution.[2] Slaves
were defined as those persons who were imported into
Virginia and were not Christians in their native country;
but Turks and Moors in amity with the British king, and
those who could prove that they had been free in England
or in some Christian country, were not regarded as slaves.
With a lack of consistency, for which lawmakers are
famous, it was further provided in the same law that
conversion to Christianity within Virginia should not
operate to set free persons already in the status of a
slave.[3] Children followed the condition of the mother
— if she were a slave, they were slaves. No free white
person could intermarry with a negro or mulatto, bond
or free, under penalty of six months' imprisonment and a
fine of ten pounds current money, the clergyman celebrating such a marriage to forfeit ten thousand pounds of to-

[1] Burnaby's *Travels through North
America*, p. 31, and note. An earlier
English writer, a philanthropist, informs
us that the Virginians cropped their
slaves' ears, " which they usually cause
the Wretches to broyl, and then compel to eat them themselves " but phi-
lanthropists are worse observers than
travelers. See Morgan Godwyn's *The
Negro's & Indians Advocate*, 41.

[2] The acts of 1748 and 1753 are in
Hening's *Statutes of Virginia*, vi, 104,
356.

[3] Douglass states that the law officers of the crown gave an opinion to
the effect that bringing a slave into
England, or baptizing him, did not set
him free, *Summary*, i, 219. Other assemblies also provided that conversion
to Christianity did not free a slave. Cf.
New York Laws, 1691–1718, p. 81. On
this general subject see McCrady's *South
Carolina under the Royal Government*,
49–52. In 1727 the Bishop of London, in
a pastoral letter, declared that " the em-
bracing of the Gospel does not make the
least Alteration in Civil Property . . .
it continues Persons just in the same
State as it found them." Dalcho's *Episcopal Church in South Carolina*, 109.

bacco.[1] Slaves could not be set free, except for meritori-
ous services which must be adjudged by the governor and
council in each case. No persons of color, no matter if
free and Christian, could at any time purchase any Christian servant nor any other except of their own complexion
and such as are by this act declared to be slaves. No person whatsoever could have any dealings with servants or
slaves, or receive from them any commodity except with
the consent of the master.

The law as to runaways in the act of 1753 applied to
both servants and slaves who were found off their master's plantation without a certificate, unless employed on
some errand, as going to the mill. All such persons upon
being arrested were to reveal their master's name or be
committed to the county gaol, when a description should
be published. If after two months' time no owner appeared, the runaway should be sent to the public gaol at
Williamsburg, being passed from constable to constable.
Each officer upon arresting or receiving a runaway could
whip him, not exceeding thirty-nine lashes; but this punishment did not relieve the servant of the obligation
of satisfying his master by extra days of service.[2] If a
claimant did not appear within three months after Williamsburg was reached, the runaway was to be "hired
out," a strong iron collar, with the letters "P. G."
stamped thereon, being first placed about his neck.
From the careful way in which the law is framed it
would seem to be probable that free blacks and mulattoes,
as well as poor white persons, might be arrested from time
to time and be entirely unable to prove that they were

---

[1] Laws of this type were frequent.
See, for instance, *Massachusetts Province
Laws*, i, 578.

[2] Hening's *Statutes of Virginia*, vi,
363.

free. The stealing of a slave was declared to be felony without benefit of clergy.[1]

These laws further provide that slaves conspiring to rebel should be put to death; likewise, those who prepared or administered any medicine whatsoever; but benefit of clergy was allowed where it was proved that no bad effects had followed the administration of the physic, and slaves might prepare such decoctions with the consent of the master. Incorrigible slaves who could not be reclaimed from their evil habits of going abroad at night or running away might be dismembered. The accidental killing of a slave during correction was not punishable, and slaves killed in the execution of the law should be paid for by the colony,[2] except where a dismembered slave died through the negligence of the surgeon, in which case the master might sue that person for his value. Thirty lashes well laid on, on the culprit's bare back, was the punishment for any negro who lifted his hand against a white person.

The planters of the Old Dominion were fearful lest the slaves should conspire with free blacks or white servants, and made drastic laws against meetings in which slaves took part. Negroes could not testify against a white person, but might give evidence against a slave in capital cases. Before the slave was put on the witness stand, the judge should warn him that in case he gave false testimony, he would be placed in the pillory for an hour, with one ear nailed to the board which would then be cut off, after which he would lose the other ear in a similar

---

[1] So, also, in Maryland. See Bacon's *Laws of Maryland*, 1737, ch. ii, § 4.

[2] When there was no express law, compensation for executed slaves was sometimes made, as in North Carolina in 1735, when the Assembly voted one hundred and fifty pounds to the master of a negro who had been executed at Cape Fear. *Colonial Records of North Carolina*, iv, 149.

manner and receive thirty-nine lashes at the public whipping post. Slaves were tried by special tribunals, which were composed of two or three justices and five freeholders, without the intervention of a jury.[1] This was also with some variations as to numbers of justices and freeholders the law in Pennsylvania[2] and South Carolina,[3] and, for a limited number of offenses, in New York.[4]

Slavery had developed more slowly in Maryland than it had in Virginia, owing to the fact that the plantations in the northern tobacco colony were much smaller than they were in the older province across the Potomac. Moreover, the northern and western parts of Maryland, which were settled in the eighteenth century, were suited to the production of breadstuffs and were, therefore, better fitted for the use of white laborers than they were for the employment of negro slaves. Baltimore, which came to be the commercial metropolis of the Chesapeake, did not assume great importance until near the middle of the century.[5] Then, negroes congregated there as they did at Philadelphia. North of Maryland, with the exception of the Hudson Valley and of a small section of Rhode Island, negro slavery was confined to the commercial towns. They were brought to all these ports mainly by vessels returning from voyages to the West Indies and seem to have practically remained in the place to which they first came. Negro slavery, one might say, was spo-

---

[1] Hening's *Statutes of Virginia*, vi, 106.

[2] *Pennsylvania Acts and Laws*, ii, 234.

[3] Cooper's *Statutes of South Carolina*, vii, 356.

[4] *Colonial Laws of New York*, ii, 684. In Maryland, slaves accused of offenses which entailed death or loss of limb were entitled to a jury trial, but were limited to twenty peremptory challenges. See

Bacon's *Laws of Maryland*, index under "Negroes." Maryland laws as to slaves were codified in 1715 and remained with little change until 1760.

[5] Negro slaves committing murder or arson were not burned at the stake in Maryland, but were to be hanged and quartered. Bacon's *Laws of Maryland*, 1729, ch. iv, § i; in 1751 this was changed to death as a felon, namely, by hanging.

radic rather than widespread north of Mason and Dixon's line. Slaves and free negroes formed a considerable proportion of the total population of northern seaports, although they formed only a small part of the total population of those colonies. The existence of slavery in this congested form in portions of the middle and northern colonies made it necessary for the legislatures of those colonies to enact very nearly as severe laws as we have found in Virginia. In every case they were developed directly from the English law as to servants and vagrants. The rapid growth of slavery in Philadelphia was, indeed, remarkable, although it must be borne in mind that the early Quaker colonists had no scruples on this subject — even William Penn owned negro slaves.[1] In 1693, ten years after the founding of that town, the governor and council felt it necessary to direct the constables to arrest all negroes, male or female, whom they found " gadding about " on the first day of the week, without a ticket. The culprits were to be placed in gaol, there to remain without meat or drink until Monday morning, when each of them should receive thirty-nine lashes well laid on, on his or her bare back, at the expense of the owner.[2] Moreover, in Pennsylvania, as in Virginia and South Carolina, negro slaves were tried for murder, burglary, and other offenses by special courts composed of justices and a limited number of freeholders, and might be sentenced to death or be whipped, not exceeding thirty-nine lashes, be branded, and deported from the colony under pain of death in case of return,[3] and transportation was provided for slaves who stole goods to the value of five pounds.

[1] W. J. Buck's *William Penn in America*, 399.

[2] *Minutes of the Council of Pennsylvania* (ed. 1852), i, 381.

[3] *Pennsylvania Statutes at Large* (ed. 1896), ii, 233.

Severe punishments were not only prescribed by law in Pennsylvania, but were actually inflicted. In 1707 certain negroes had been convicted of burglary and sentenced to death. As Pennsylvania masters could not recover the value of the slaves executed, they petitioned to be allowed to sell the convicts outside of the colony. This request was granted on condition that the negroes should be flogged on their bare backs at the cart's tail on three successive market days from the Market Place to Second Street, and thence down through Front Street to the bridge.[1] Whether they survived this ordeal or perished under the lash, is not stated.

There may have been two or three negroes on Samuel Maverick's plantation in Massachusetts at the coming of the Great Emigration in 1630; otherwise slavery in New England begins with the disposal of the captives who were taken in the Pequot War. Very few adult male Indians were captured, the women and children were divided between Massachusetts, New Plymouth, and Connecticut as the spoil of war.[2] In 1641 the Massachusetts General Court adopted a code of laws which is known as "The Body of Liberties." Among other provisions was one that there should never be any bond slavery in Massachusetts, except in the case of lawful captives and such strangers as willingly sell themselves or are sold to the colonists; but this should exempt none from servitude who should be judged thereto by the authorities.[3] The exact meaning of this law has been much disputed. New England writers have usually interpreted it to mean that no one could be born a slave within the colony, but one

---

[1] *Minutes of the Council of Pennsylvania* (ed. of 1852), ii, 406.

[2] Massachusetts Historical Society's *Collections*, Fourth Series, iii, 360.

[3] Massachusetts "Body of Liberties," section 91, in *American History Leaflets*, No. 25, p. 16.

author has stigmatized it as the first law in any English colony to recognize the condition of slavery.[1] It is certain that there were slaves in Massachusetts in 1641, but they could probably have been counted on the fingers of one's hands. Englishmen and English colonists in those early days had not the slightest objection to slavery as an institution. It does not seem likely, therefore, that the makers of this law intended to abolish slavery within the colonial limits ; probably they only sought to reduce Biblical precepts to English legal language and did not foresee the consequences of their action. In 1646 the Massachusetts magistrates sent some negroes back to Africa on the ground that they had been kidnapped ;[2] but after a time the judges did not inquire so closely into the antecedents of slaves. For a hundred years, indeed, they usually interpreted the law of 1641 to mean that a child followed the condition of the mother : if she were a slave, the child was a slave and entitled to maintenance by the owner of the mother. Negroes born in the colony were frequently sold ; but sometimes the purchaser was warned that he must run the risk of their "getting free."[3] In the early years of the Revolutionary epoch, persons who were held as slaves sued for their freedom under this law and obtained it.[4]

The records of the town of Boston contain convincing proof of the presence there of negroes in considerable numbers. In 1723 the selectmen, upon order from the town, drew up a set of regulations. They proposed[5] that any

---

[1] See Note III at end of chapter.

[2] *Massachusetts Colony Records*, ii, 168.

[3] A case of this kind occurred in 1765, the seller saying that he could only convey his right and title. Ms. in the cabinet of the Massachusetts Historical Society.

[4] The earliest case of a slave suing for freedom under this law is that noted by John Adams in his diary under date of 1766. See *Works* (ed. 1850), ii, 200.

[5] *Boston Town Records*, 1700–1728, pp. 173–175. These regulations were not adopted as drawn ; but their provisions, for the most part, became law in one way or another.

free negro or mulatto who sheltered any negro or mulatto
servant or slave should pay the sum of twenty shillings
and be severely whipped; for the enforcement of this provision any two freeholders might enter the house of any
free negro or mulatto. Furthermore, no free negro could
sell any strong drink, cakes, or other provisions on " public
days." All the children of free negroes must be bound out
to English masters. Any free Indian, negro, or mulatto who
received any stolen goods from any servant or slave should
be severely whipped, make restitution, and depart the province under pain of imprisonment at hard labor during
life in case he returned. No negro could carry any manner of arms, clubs, canes, or knives under pain of severe
punishment at the house of correction. Any negro striking one of his Majesty's subjects should be severely punished
and transported. Finally, no negro could work as a por-
ter,[1] except with the approval of the selectmen and upon
giving bonds of fifty pounds; and upon the breaking out
of a fire in the town none could leave his own or his
master's house unless such happened to be on fire or in
eminent hazard. Moreover, the newspapers frequently
contained advertisements of runaways and of negroes
offered for sale.[2] On the other hand, negroes in Massachusetts had the same rights and privileges as white men
as to trial and the giving of evidence.[3]

Probably there were more negroes in Rhode Island in
proportion to the total population than in any other New
England colony.[4] Many were brought to Newport on ves-

---

[1] The town records give one the impression that free negroes were regarded
with jealousy. See, for instance, *Boston
Town Records*, 1660–1701, p. 5, where the
employment of a negro as a cooper is
forbidden under penalty of twenty shillings for every day the negro works.

[2] See, for example, *Boston Weekly
News-Letter*, January 1, 1756; *Boston
Evening Post*, August 23, 1742.

[3] Quincy's *Massachusetts Reports*, p.
29.

[4] Slaves never formed a large proportion of the total population of Connecti-

sels returning from the West Indies, and there was a demand for slave labor on the large farms in the Narragansett country.[1] The most prosperous town of this region was South Kingston. In 1748 it contained 1405 whites, 380 negroes, and 193 Indians who were probably mostly slaves or life servants. This proportion of negroes to white inhabitants, many of whom were servants, obtained nowhere else in New England. Taking the by-laws of South Kingston[2] in connection with the general laws of Rhode Island,[3] it is possible to construct a slave code closely resembling that of Virginia of the same epoch. There were similar regulations against negroes keeping animals and traveling, and two justices, without a jury, could sentence negroes in all but the most serious cases. Any one could seize a suspected colored person found abroad after nine o'clock at night. One of the most attractive figures to greet the inquirer into the conditions of life which prevailed in the Narragansett country at that day was the Rev. James MacSparran, missionary of the venerable Society for the Propagation of the Gospel in Foreign Parts. His "Diary"[4] contains many valuable entries, among others one which informs us that he was in the habit of catechising the negroes as well as the whites. He had several negro slaves who gave him a

---

cut. In 1762 the total population was 146,520, of whom 4590 were negroes and 930 Indians. See "Answers to Lords of Trade," Ms. in Massachusetts Historical Society's library. The negroes had increased from 3587 in six years. See also B. C. Steiner's "Slavery in Connecticut" in *Johns Hopkins Studies*, xi, Nos. ix, x; and W. C. Fowler's "Historical Status of the Negro in Connecticut" in the *Historical Magazine*, xxiii (1874), pp. 12–18, 81–85, 148–153, 260–266; and also printed separately.

[1] There are brief descriptions of slavery in the Narragansett region by the present writer in *Johns Hopkins University Studies*, iv, 114–116, and by W. D. Johnston in Rhode Island Historical Society's *Publications*, New Series, No. 2, p. 113.

[2] See South Kingston Records (Ms.), 1714, pp. 49, 50; 1728, 113.

[3] *Laws of Rhode Island* (ed. of 1767), pp. 151, 152, 176, 195, 234.

[4] *Diary of James MacSparran*, pp. xxi, 52.

good deal of trouble.   August 29, 1751, he felt obliged to
chastise one of them named Hannibal who had spent the
night out.   When the slave was tied up MacSparran gave
him a few lashes.   As he was being untied " My poor
passionate dear [Mrs. MacSparran] saying I had not given
him eno', gave him a lash or two " at which he ran.   He
was captured at Block Island and being brought home,
was carried to a blacksmith, " where he had what is called
Pothooks put about his Neck."   A few months later,
owing to Hannibal's continued incorrigible conduct, Mac-
Sparran was obliged to sell him.

Slaves were also extensively used on the great farms
bordering the Hudson and as laborers in the city of New
York itself.[1]   Slavery had flourished as an institution in
New Netherland.[2]   After the English conquest, in the
"Duke's Laws," Colonel Nicolls caused a paraphrase of the
Massachusetts statement in the "Body of Liberties " to be
inserted, substituting the words "no Christian shall be
kept in Bondslavery "[3] for the more inclusive phrase of the
Massachusetts law that "none" shall be so kept.   Negroes
and their children were recognized as slaves in New York
from the earliest days of English rule, provided they had
not been baptized ; and a law of 1706 expressly provided
that every negro, Indian, mulatto, and mustee should follow the condition of the mother.[4]

In 1700 there were some six thousand slaves in New York
in a total population of forty thousand and a good many
free blacks, especially in New York City.   Either the slaves
in that city were of a turbulent disposition or some cir-

---

[1] On slavery in New York, see a
paper by Edwin V. Morgan in American
Historical Association's *Papers*, v, 337.

[2] In 1698 there were two thousand
negroes in New York out of a total population of eighteen thousand. *Documentary History of New York*, i, 687.

[3] *Duke of Yorke's Laws*, 12.

[4] *New York Colonial Laws* (ed. 1894),
i, 598.

cumstances, which have not come down to us, made the whites suspicious of them.   In 1712, and again in 1741, the whites were seized with a panic at what they believed to be conspiracies on the part of the blacks to burn houses and massacre white people.   How much truth there was in these surmises cannot be definitely stated from the evidence that is preserved ; but white persons were murdered and houses were set on fire.   Legislators and judges at the time thought that severe measures were necessary.   In 1712 it was provided by law that three justices with five freeholders, without the intervention of a jury, in cases of murder or arson, could sentence a slave to death " in such manner, and with such circumstances as the aggravation or enormity of their crime " in their opinion required.[1] The courts acted upon this authorization.   In 1712 a negro was hanged in chains while alive, another was broken on the wheel, and two more were burned to death ; in 1741 fourteen negroes were burned to death, eighteen hanged, and seventy-one transported.[2]

The condition of panic which was responsible for the cruel executions that have just been noted was undoubtedly due to the fact that there was no effective supervision of the black population in New York.[3]   In the southern colonies the plantation system with its attendant overseers and slave drivers made for an efficient condition of discipline.   Another circumstance which provoked severity in New York was the nearness to Canada.   In 1705 the As-

[1] *Laws of New York*, 1691–1718, pp. 141–144.

[2] B. F. Thompson's *Long Island*, 136. Daniel Horsmanden's *Journal of the Proceedings in the Detection of the Conspiracy* (New York, 1744) ; reprinted in 1810 as *The New York Conspiracy or a History of the Negro Plot with the Journal of the Proceedings.*

[3] Few persons in New York owned more than five slaves. Lewis Morris, of Morrisania, had twenty-nine adult negro slaves in 1755 ; but this was exceptional. *Documentary History of New York*, iii, 510.

Punishment January 11

sembly provided that any slave found forty miles north of Albany without his master should be arrested and put to death, the owner receiving compensation for his loss.[1] The absence of the plantation system also led the Assembly to provide for the appointment in each town of officials termed "common whippers," who should receive not more than three shillings for each slave flogged.[2] Enough has been said to show that negro slavery was an institution to be reckoned with in the tobacco colonies[3] and in the governments to the northward. The laws developed naturally out of the English law relating to servants, and their peculiar characteristics were due in each case to the intensity of slavery in the several colonies or in portions of them.

Slavery in South Carolina developed on its own lines and its slave code was built upon the laws of the sugar colonies and not on the Common Law of England. In fact, the life of southern Carolina was lived apart from that of the other English colonies on the continent. It had originally been settled from Europe by way of Barbados;[4] its commerce was almost entirely with Europe and the West Indies: in 1746, of two hundred and thirty-five vessels that cleared outward from Charleston, only thirty-seven sailed for the northern colonies.[5] The necessities of rice cultivation and the climatic conditions of the colony made negro slavery profitable in southern Carolina and the negroes increased out of all proportion to the white population, especially

[1] *New York Colonial Laws*, i, 582.

[2] *Ibid.*, i, 521.

[3] For slavery in North Carolina, see a valuable paper by Professor Bassett in *Johns Hopkins Studies*, xvii, Nos. vii and viii.

[4] It is interesting to compare the slave laws of Barbados with those of South Carolina; the former may con-veniently be found in the *Report of the Lords Committee of Council on African Trade* (1789), ii, Part iii.

[5] Ms. records of South Carolina, quoted in Schaper's "Sectionalism in South Carolina." American Historical Association's *Report* for 1900, vol. i, 297.

after 1730. After that date the slaves always outnumbered
the whites and in 1760 there were twice as many blacks
as whites, possibly more. Moreover, one quarter of the
slaves in the colony in 1740 had been imported within four
or five years, and from this time on the annual importations
were large. Few Indians were held as slaves in South
Carolina, but many of them were exported from Charleston to the Sugar Islands. These were captives whom the
tribes of the interior had sold to the fur traders and by them
had been driven to the coast and sold to the exporters [1] —
the whole transaction bearing a singular likeness to the
collection of negroes in Africa for sale to the white slave
traders. Slavery in one form or another may be said, indeed, to have already dominated the life of the older settled
parts of the province.

The South Carolinians realized the dangers to which
the presence of such large numbers of slaves exposed
them. In September, 1739,[2] their worst fears were justified by an outbreak of the slaves on a few plantations.
Before the insurrection was put down, twenty-one whites
and forty-four blacks had lost their lives. The ease with
which the negroes had begun the movement increased
the fears of the whites and led to a reconstruction of
the slave laws. The Assembly now sought to check the
importation of negroes and to improve the conditions
under which they lived and, at the same time, to make
conspiring and running away more difficult. To accom-

[1] Logan's *History of Upper South
Carolina*, i, 182. Professor Schaper, in
his excellent monograph on "Sectionalism in South Carolina," p. 292, repeatedly
mentions "slave-catching," but gives no
details of the export trade in Indians.
He informs me that the manuscript records at Columbia, South Carolina, contain much information on this subject

as well as on the fur trade of Charleston.

[2] McCrady's *South Carolina under
the Royal Government*, 186. He states
that the year was 1739 and not 1740, as
he had given it in his earlier essay on
"Slavery in South Carolina" in the
American Historical Association's *Report* for 1895, p. 656.

plish the first of these objects, it was provided that taxes varying in amount from ten pounds to one hundred pounds, according to the height of the negro and the date when purchased, should be paid every time a negro slave was bought or sold.[1] To keep out the stubborn and refuse negroes of other colonies, an additional fifty pounds was levied upon every slave imported into South Carolina by land or water from any other colony. To improve the conditions under which the negroes labored the Assembly declared that none should be worked more than fifteen hours in each day in summer time, or more than fourteen hours in the winter season; they should have Sunday as a holiday and should have sufficient clothing and food.[2] Provisions were also made looking to the prevention of abuses by negro slave drivers by requiring the presence of a white person when punishment was inflicted. To make conspiracy more difficult, the legislators provided that no slave should go off his plantation without a white person or a written pass. Any one finding a slave wandering or coming upon slaves consorting together could seize such slaves and, in case of resistance, fire upon them. Compensation for slaves who were killed under such circumstances was paid to the master out of the public treasury, and white persons suffering injury were given pecuniary compensation. Wandering slaves of unknown masters should be carefully examined for any brand or mark and full descriptions of them with the brands and marks published. As a further guarantee against conspiracy, it was forbidden

---

[1] Thus ten pounds should be paid within fifteen months for the purchase of any negro over four feet two inches in height who had not been six months in the province, and after that time one hundred pounds should be paid on the first purchase of every such negro during the ensuing three years. Cooper's *Statutes of South Carolina*, iii, 557, 561.

[2] *Ibid.*, vii, 411, 413.

to teach any slave to write, to cause one to be so taught, or to employ one in writing under the penalty of one hundred pounds.[1]

The next year after the revision of the slave code, which has been described in the preceding paragraph, a negro was convicted in South Carolina upon his own confession and also upon that of an accomplice of setting fire to a house inhabited by a white person. For this he was sentenced to be burned to death.[2] This punishment was not inflicted in accordance with an act of the Carolina legislature, but by virtue of the principles of the English Common Law, which made the setting fire to dwelling houses, administering poison, and killing one's master by a servant petty treason, the punishment of which was death in one of the more terrible modes.[3]

The cases of brutal punishment of negro slaves which have been noted in the preceding paragraphs were rather a mark of the time than the infliction of cruel and unusual punishments on any one particular portion of the community. Boring the tongue with a red-hot iron, while the culprit's head and hands were confined in the pillory, nailing his ears to the board while in the same position, cutting off of ears, branding on cheek or fore-

[1] Cooper's *Statutes of South Carolina*, vii, 413.

[2] McCrady's *South Carolina under the Royal Government*, 233.

[3] Cases of burning were not confined to South Carolina. In 1733 two negroes were convicted of murder in Virginia; the man was sentenced to be hanged, the woman to be burned. *Virginia Magazine of History*, i, 328. See also *ibid.*, iii, 308, 430; iv, 341; vii, 303. In Massachusetts in 1681, and again in 1755, negroes were sentenced to be burned for murder or arson, and in New York in 1707 two slaves, an Indian man and a negress, were condemned by a special court for the murder of their master and his family, the man to be hanged, the woman to be burned. *New York Colonial Documents*, v, 39 (letter from Governor Cornbury to Lords of Trade, dated at New York, February 10, 1707-08). The first Massachusetts case is detailed at length by John Noble in the *Publications* of the Colonial Society of Massachusetts, vi, 323. In a supplementary note, Albert Matthews mentions other cases in New York, New Jersey, Virginia, and South Carolina. See also on this subject, Massachusetts Historical Society's *Proceedings*, xx, 104, 122.

head, and the infliction of floggings of various degrees and continuances: all these were common in that time and had been for centuries. A few examples will serve to show the prevalence of these punishments throughout British America during the hundred years preceding the Revolution. In these respects the exposure to wilderness conditions had, as yet, wrought no amendment. In Massachusetts a law of 1711 provided that a highway robber should be burned on the forehead or hand, be imprisoned for six months, and render treble damages to the party robbed. Fifty years later [1] the penalty of death was provided for this offense and was inflicted as late as 1789. [2] Thieves were everywhere harshly dealt with; in 1722 William Doyle was convicted in North Carolina of stealing goods to the value of four shillings sixpence and was sentenced to be whipped at the cart's tail thirty-nine stripes on the bare back through Edenton and the same through Bath, and Hannah Davis in the same colony, for taking goods to the value of ten pence, was given nine lashes on the bare back. [3] Probably William Doyle was glad that he did his stealing in North Carolina, because, had he done it in England, he would have been hanged. Pocket picking is usually associated with a somewhat dense population, but the light-fingered gentry lived in Virginia and received a flogging [4] when they were caught in the act. Ignominious punishments, such as wearing a letter of different colored cloth upon one's

[1] *Massachusetts Province Laws*, i, 674; iv, 489.

[2] John Noble's paper on " Legislation in regard to Highway Robbery in Massachusetts," Massachusetts Historical Society's *Proceedings*, Second Series, xix, 178.

[3] *Colonial Records of North Carolina*, ii, 474, 478.

[4] *Virginia Magazine of History*, ix, 45. The fifth volume of the same series (pp. 23, 113) contains interesting excerpts from the decisions of the General Court of the Old Dominion of a somewhat earlier date than now under discussion.

garment, were frequent in the colonies; in Pennsylvania a more permanent mark was provided in the shape of a letter " A " burned on the forehead of him or her who was the third time convicted of adultery.[1] Horse stealing, as in all frontier communities, was severely punished. In Pennsylvania, in 1766, for the second offense, both the horse thief and the person knowingly receiving a stolen horse were to be whipped thirty-nine lashes, stand in the pillory for one hour, be committed to the workhouse for not more than three years at hard labor, pay the costs of prosecution and the full value of the animal, not only to the owner but also to the government.[2] These punishments appear ferocious to the modern reader. It may well be asked, however, whether in the less nervous condition of human beings in those days and the different standards of shame which prevailed they were not actually much less severe than they would be at the present time, when the human body and mind are more highly strung?

In 1760 the subject of free negroes and of the manumission of slaves had not assumed important proportions, although some laws had been already passed on that subject.[3] It is clear that slave owners had already begun to take advantage of manumission to save themselves from supporting their slaves in old age; and that the colonial assemblies had found it necessary to safeguard the purses of the taxpayers by providing that no master could free his slave except on condition of giving bonds to secure the town or parish from the obligation of supporting the freed negro in the event of incapacity.

[1] *Pennsylvania Statutes at Large* (ed. 1896), ii, 180. On the general subject of ignominious punishments in the colonies, see a paper by Andrew McF. Davis in American Antiquarian Society's *Proceedings*, x, pp. 97–126.

[2] *Pennsylvania Statutes*, vii, 91.

[3] *Massachusetts Province Laws*, i, 606. In 1723 free negroes, mulattoes, and Indians were disfranchised in Virginia (Hening's *Statutes*, iv, 133); but they were to pay taxes as before.

There were not lacking objectors to the employment of Indians and negroes as slaves. Some of these were actuated by humanitarian motives ; others saw danger in the presence of large numbers of negroes ; while a few were affected by both considerations. The earliest protest against human slavery on the part of the North American colonists is the vote of the delegates of Providence and Warwick,[1] which was passed on May 18, 1652, and declared that no one could be held in service in those plantations for more than ten years, at the end of which time he should be set free. The earliest argument against negro slavery was the work of Francis Daniel Pastorius, the brothers Op den Graeff, and Gerhard Hendricks, who were living at Germantown in Pennsylvania. In April, 1688, they presented to the Germantown Monthly Meeting a protest [2] against slavery, which was transmitted to the Quarterly Meeting of Philadelphia and was finally considered by the Yearly Meeting, which was then held at Burlington, New Jersey. The latter body set it aside on the ground that it was " not proper to give a positive judgment in the case, it having so general a relation to many other parts." The protesters declare, that in Pennsylvania there is liberty of conscience, which they think is right and reasonable, but there ought to be likewise liberty of the body, except in the case of evildoers. " In Europe there are many oppressed for Conscience sacke ; and here there are those oppressed wch are of a black Colour." How is it better to buy and sell negroes than it is for the Turks to buy and sell white people ? " There is a saying that we shall doe to all men, licke as we will

---

[1] *Rhode Island Colony Records*, i, 243. If a servant or slave was "taken in under fourteen," he might be compelled to serve until his twenty-fourth birthday.

[2] Pennypacker's *Settlement of Germantown*, 145.

be done our selves. . . . And those who steal or robb
men, and those who buy or purchase them, are they not
all alicke?" This makes an ill report in all those countries of Europe that "the Quackers doe here handel men,
Licke they handel there ye Cattle; and for that reason some
have no mind or inclination to come hither. . . . Pray!
What thing in the world can be done worse towarts us
then if men should robb or steal us away & sell us for
slaves to strange Countries, separating housband from
their wife & children." Five years later, in 1693, the
Monthly Meeting of Philadelphia formulated a protest
against slavery;[1] in 1696 the Yearly Meeting advised
"that Friends be careful not to encourage the bringing
of any more negroes"; and again, in 1711, on the representation that Quakers were still importing negroes,
repeated the advice and further suggested that merchants
should write to their correspondents discouraging the sending of any more negroes to Pennsylvania. Before this,
in 1706, the Assembly had already forbidden the bringing
in of Indian slaves and had laid a tax on all negroes
imported. Half a century later slaves were still being
brought into the province, as appears from a rule made
by the Yearly Meeting in 1755 that all Friends who imported slaves after that time should be disowned from the
religious communion of the Society.[2] Three years later
it further advised Friends to set their slaves at liberty,
"making a Christian provision for them"[3] and appointed
a committee to visit Friends who owned slaves and labor
with them to set them free. The committee was "largely

[1] *Pennsylvania Magazine of History and Biography*, xiii, 265.
[2] Bettles's "Notices of Slavery" in Pennsylvania Historical Society's *Memoirs*, i, 377, — an excellent paper.
[3] Sharpless's *Quaker Government*, i, 32, and Bettles's "Notices" as above, 378.

successful "; but there were many slaves in Pennsylvania in 1760 — and many still in Quaker hands. Moreover, there are instances, many of them, of Quakers selling their slaves, instead of setting them free ; but the Meetings labored earnestly with their members not to do this ;[1] and, undoubtedly, the mass of Quaker slave owners, sooner or later, carried out the behests of their organization.

The other notable protest against slavery in this period was the well-known tract of Samuel Sewall's, entitled "The Selling of Joseph,"[2] which was printed at Boston in 1701. The author asserts that the numerousness of slaves in Massachusetts and their uneasiness has awakened interest in their condition. He argues that all men, "as they are Sons of *Adam*, are Coheirs, and have equal Right unto Liberty and other outward Comforts of Life." Originally and naturally, he declares, there is no such thing as slavery. Ethically and morally, slavery is wrong; it is also wrong from the political and material standpoints. It would conduce more to the benefit of the province to have white servants than black slaves since the latter " can never embody with us . . . but still remain in our Body Politick as a kind of extravasat Blood." Sewall's discussion was rather of the academic order, but it reflected the opinions of other persons besides himself. In 1705,[3] four years after its appearance, the Massachusetts General Court laid a duty of four pounds on each negro imported into the colony, and in 1712 prohibited the importation of Indian servants or slaves under penalty of forfeiture.[4] South Carolina[5] and Maryland[6] passed sim-

---

[1] See H. M. Jenkins's *Historical Sketches of Gwynedd*, 349.

[2] Massachusetts Historical Society's *Proceedings*, 1863, p. 161; *The Historical Magazine*, viii, 193.

[3] *Massachusetts Province Laws*, i, 578.

[4] *Ibid.*, i, 698.

[5] Cooper's *Statutes of South Carolina*, ii, 154, 385, 647; iii, 6.

[6] See Maryland's acts of 1715, 1717, 1728, and 1763.

ilar laws for practically the same reasons, a prejudice against the presence of so many persons of the black race in their midst. Massachusetts and some other provinces also encouraged the importation of white male servants from Great Britain by promising a bounty of forty shillings for every such person brought into the colony.[1] The English government was unalterably opposed to the limitation of labor in the plantations. By the exercise of the veto power and by instructions to the governors, it forced negroes and convicts upon an unwilling people and fully justified Jefferson's indignant phrase in the original draft of the Declaration of Independence: " He has prostituted his negative for suppressing every legislative attempt to prohibit or to restrain this execrable commerce."

[1] *Massachusetts Province Laws*, i, 634.

NOTES

I. Destination of Convicts. — The colonies on the Chesapeake and the Delaware, and not New England, New York, or South Carolina, were the destination of the great mass of transported convicts, although why this should have been the case cannot be stated. It is possible, of course, that the people of the latter colonies refused to purchase convicts, but they certainly had no objection to the ordinary type of indentured servants.

The "Aspinwall Papers"[1] contain a "Representation" of the Board of Trade to the king in 1772, advising the repeal of a Virginia law of 1767. This required masters of vessels bringing convicts or servants to the colony to make oath that none of his passengers had been afflicted with gaol fever or smallpox within fifty days or to proceed to quarantine. The Board considered this enactment to be contrary to acts of Parliament and likely to bring hardship to contractors. Pennsylvania also tried to limit the importation of convicts by imposing a duty of five pounds per head, one half to go to the collector or informer, and further required that a bond of fifty pounds with sufficient security be given for the good behavior of the convict for one year.[2] Law after law was passed to limit the importation of negro slaves. In Pennsylvania this could be done by passing acts for so short a time that the royal veto could not be interposed. Governors of the royal provinces were forbidden to assent to laws limiting the importation of slaves.[3]

II. Deportation of Indian Captives. — The colonists generally approved of the transportation of Indian captives to the West Indies and their sale as slaves to the planters there. Even Roger Williams signed his name to an order for the sale of "a parcell of Indians" taken in King Philip's War;[4] and at that time the New Plymouth government sold one hundred and eighty-eight Indians for nearly four hundred pounds sterling.[5] Virginia laws of 1676 and 1679 distinctly authorize the enslavement of Indians by their captors, but

[1] Massachusetts Historical Society's *Collections*, Fourth Series, x, 691.

[2] *Laws of Pennsylvania* (ed. 1896), iv, 164, 360, and note on p. 171.

[3] *Ibid.*, iii–vii. McCrady (*South Carolina under the Royal Government*, 378 note) prints one of these instructions. As to the unwillingness of the colonists to accept convicts, see *Calendars of State Papers, America and West Indies*, *1696–1697*, Nos. 356, 530, 532, 541, 543, 544, 559, 560, 567, 570.

[4] Rhode Island Historical Society's *Publications*, New Series, i, 236.

[5] *Plymouth Colony Records*, v, 173; x, 401.

the government itself did not sell any Indians as slaves.[1] As late as 1713 the North Carolina[2] government sold eight Indians for ten pounds apiece for shipment to the West Indies.

III. The Massachusetts Act of 1641. — The most authoritative interpretation of this law is that by Horace Gray, at one time Chief Justice of Massachusetts and later Associate Justice of the Supreme Court of the United States: " Previously to the adoption of the State Constitution in 1780, negro slavery existed to some extent in Massachusetts, and negroes held as slaves might be sold, but all children of slaves were by law free."[3] On the other side, the best paper is George H. Moore's *Notes on Slavery in Massachusetts.* He takes a very hostile view, which was replied to in *The Historical Magazine* for 1866, Supplement.[4] The appendix to the "Belknap Papers"[5] contains the correspondence on slavery in Massachusetts between Judge St. George Tucker of Virginia and Dr. Belknap: most of the letters and documents have to do with a later period, but some of them are useful on this part of the topic.

[1] Hening's *Statutes*, ii, 346, 404, 440; *Virginia Magazine of History*, ii, 173.

[2] *Colonial Records of North Carolina*, ii, p. iv.

[3] Quincy's *Massachusetts Reports*, 29 note.

[4] See also the volumes for 1863, 1864, and 1869.

[5] Massachusetts Historical Society's *Collections*, Fifth Series, iii, 375–442. Abner C. Goodell's paper on " John Saffin and his Slave Adam " in the *Publications* of the Colonial Society of Massachusetts (i, 85) contains many references.

CHAPTER XIV

THE COMING OF THE FOREIGNERS

In 1700, and indeed for twenty-five years thereafter, the English formed the great majority of the inhabitants of the colonies ; but there were thousands of settlers from the other parts of the British Islands. There were the Welsh, who came more especially to Pennsylvania and founded the settlements of Gwynnyd, Bryn Mawr, and Merion near Philadelphia. There were many Welshmen in that town itself and in other parts of the colony. Scots, both Lowlanders and Highlanders, came after the rebellions of 1715 and 1745. The breaking down of the clan system in the Highlands also sent thousands more to the New World. Many of the Scots were political prisoners and were sold into service, but others came on their own resources and founded separate settlements. Three hundred and fifty of them came in a body to North Carolina, where they were so well regarded that their leading men were appointed magistrates and they were all freed from taxes for ten years.[1] The Scottish immigrants had suffered greatly at the hands of the Hanoverian dynasty, but with typical Scottish dourness remained faithful to the Royalist cause in the Revolution. Thousands of immigrants came from Ireland, both Protestant and Roman Catholic. The former

---

[1] *Colonial Records of North Carolina*, iv, p. ix.

of these came from the northern part of the island and were of Scottish, English, French, and German descent, most numerously of the first-named.[1]   There were hundreds or thousands of Roman Catholic Irish in Maryland and in Pennsylvania, and there were Irish servants in nearly every colony,[2] but the great migration of this portion of the Irish race came in the nineteenth century.

In no colony were the people solely of English descent or even of British, Irish, and Scottish extraction. Everywhere there were " foreigners " [3] or their children, everywhere there were negroes. The most picturesque of the foreigners were the French Protestants, or Huguenots, whose ancestors fled from France at the time of the revocation of the Edict of Nantes by Louis XIV. Most of the Huguenots went first to England and thence found their way to American shores; but some of them came by way of Holland, and a few may have come directly from France. They settled in many colonies, but most numerously in South Carolina. At Charleston their descendants flourished as merchants,

---

[1] There is interesting information on this theme in C. A. Hanna's *The Scotch-Irish or the Scot in North Britain, North Ireland, and North America* (2 vols., New York, 1902); Samuel Swett Green's article on "The Scotch Irish in America" in the American Antiquarian Society's *Proceedings* for April, 1895, is the best study of the subject that has yet appeared and has an important "bibliographical note." The Scotch-Irish Society of America has held sundry "congresses" and has printed the proceedings thereof. The vigorous sounding of the praises of the "Scotch-Irish" has not been pleasing to the "Irishman proper," as may be seen from J. C. Linehan's *The Irish Scots and the "Scotch-Irish"* (Concord, New Hampshire, 1902); there is also some matter on this part of the subject in an appendix to the "separate" of Mr. Green's paper.

[2] See, for example, Barber's *Historical Collections of Connecticut* (p. 166) reprinting from the "Connecticut Gazette": "Just imported from Dublin, in the brig *Darby*. A parcel of Irish Servants both Men and Women, to be sold cheap, by Israel Boardman at Stamford." The outflow of Irish laborers was sufficiently large to alarm the landlords in Ireland according to John Stewart. In a letter dated at Dublin in 1736 he says that the landlords brought the "runners" for the emigrant ships into court and tried by every means to embarrass the ship masters, *Pennsylvania Magazine of History*, xxi, 485.

[3] This word was used at the time (1760) to denote European immigrants; the English legal term descriptive of them was "alien."

while in the country they prospered as planters. They settled to a considerable extent in adjoining districts and held fast to their own religion and, for a time, to their own language. Many of the best-known names in South Carolina history belong to the people of this industrious, intelligent, and upright race. Many Huguenots settled in tidewater Virginia, five hundred of them coming in a body in 1700 ;[1] they soon acquired land and became tobacco growers on a large scale. In New England they were especially numerous in Rhode Island. In Massachusetts they were less numerous, but left behind them three of the most famous names in the history of that state : James Bowdoin, Peter Faneuil, and Paul Revere. In New York Nicholas Bayard, Stephen DeLancey, and John Jay were men of the first importance ; the Maurys and Fontaines figure largely in the annals of Virginia ; in South Carolina few names are more illustrious than Laurens, Légaré, and Marion.

With 1710[2] the great outpouring from German lands which has continued ever since had its beginning. For generations the central portion of the Rhine Valley had been the scene of repeated campaigns and devastations. Military necessity knows no law of mercy and the Palatinate with the neighboring Rhenish provinces had been utterly ruined, that they might not support armies for the invasion of France or for the defense of the German fatherland. The social system of Germany operated to hold down the working classes ; no matter how industrious a man might be, he could not hope to rise above the condi-

[1] Virginia Historical Society's *Collections*, v, 9. Ann Maury's *Memoirs of a Huguenot Family* is a book of exceeding value. C. W. Baird has traced the story of the French in America in his *Huguenot Emigration to America* (2 vols., New York, 1885); but much material has come to light since he wrote.

[2] For the earlier settlement at Germantown, see the present work, p. 116.

tion of his parents.   From time to time a longing for
variety has come over sections of the German race.   Possibly the migration of the eighteenth century was due rather
to this last cause than to the French devastations which
had occurred years before.

Joshua von Kocherthal, a German minister, presented a
petition to the English government, asking permission for
himself and others to go to England.   They arrived in
1708 and in the same year sailed for New York with Lord
Lovelace.   In the summer and autumn of 1709 no less
than thirteen thousand Germans arrived in London.[1]
They were mainly from the Palatinate and being wretchedly poverty-stricken were generally spoken of as the "poor
Palatines."   Nearly one thousand of them were Roman
Catholics, which seems to show that religion had little
if anything directly to do with this particular exodus.
Queen Anne took a personal interest in making provisions
for the wanderers.   A thousand tents were taken from the
Tower and pitched on Black Heath.   These accommodated
many of the strangers, others were lodged in vacant warehouses.   The government and charitable persons provided
food and clothing for the newcomers, but notwithstanding
all these efforts the question of the disposal of the Palatines soon became pressing.   Those of the Roman Catholics
who could not be persuaded to change their religion were
sent back to Germany, each with a small amount of
money for the expenses of transportation.   Some of the
Palatines found employment in England and three thou-

---

[1] On this movement see F. R. Diffenderffer's "German Exodus to England"
in Pennsylvania German Society's *Proceedings*, vii, 257–413.   It has been said
that Queen Anne instigated this movement by issuing some kind of invitation;
but no such document has ever been produced.   It has also been stated that the
passage of an act for naturalizing foreign
Protestants was the leading cause of
their coming ; but the act in question
was passed so near in point of time to
the migration that this suggestion does
not seem to be worthy of much weight.

sand of them were sent to Ireland, whence some of their descendants came to America a century and more later.

Five hundred or more of the Palatines emigrated to North Carolina, with a smaller band of Swiss immigrants under the auspices of Baron Christopher de Graffenreid.[1] He had procured from the Carolina proprietors a grant of thousands of acres of land, with the promise of other thousands when these should be settled. They called their principal town New Berne, in memory of that older Berne in far-off Switzerland. Their early years were not happy. Graffenreid, venturing into the interior, was set upon by the Tuscaroras, who were still living in that southern region, was captured, and only saved himself from death by torture by declaring that he was "King of the Palatines." Graffenreid soon afterward returned to Europe; but the Palatines remained in Carolina. Many of them worked back from the seaboard to the interior valleys, where they were joined by others of the same stock who had penetrated southward from Virginia,[2] Maryland, and Pennsylvania.

More than three thousand Palatines accompanied Governor Hunter to New York in 1710. Lord Bellomont had warmly advocated the making of tar from the pine trees which lined the banks of the Hudson and its affluents. He had proposed to employ English soldiers in this task, when they were not engaged in their more warlike business of protecting the northern frontier. Hunter suggested that the starving Germans might be usefully employed in this work and in this way reimburse the government for trans-

---

[1] Graffenreid's "Manuscript" and other material as to this colony are printed in *Colonial Records of North Carolina*, i, 718, 905. Professor Julius Goebel has many interesting papers in his possession on this and other phases of the German migration.

[2] There was also a small settlement of Germans in the older settled part of Virginia, at Germanna. See *Virginia Magazine of History*, vi, 385.

porting them to America and maintaining them while engaged in this labor. Governor Hunter was a well-meaning, honest man, but he involved himself in this scheme without having first gained the requisite information, and without making certain that the Palatines understood what was expected of them. After their arrival at New York, four months were expended in seeking a suitable spot for the prosecution of the "great design," during all of which time the laborers had to be supported in idleness. In fact, Hunter's funds were exhausted before the Palatines had cut down a single pine tree. He drew upon the government for more money, and his bills came back protested, for the administration in England was no longer in the hands of his friends. The Palatines had no heart in the work and labored only under compulsion. Somehow they had become imbued with the idea that certain Indian chiefs, whom they saw in London, and Queen Anne, herself, had given them a tract of land in America called Schoharie. After preparing tens of thousands of trees for burning they struck, demanding to be taken to Schoharie. By this time Hunter's private credit was exhausted, and in the summer of 1712, he told them to shift for themselves.[1]

The Palatines then sought the valley of the Schoharie River, which empties into the Mohawk from the south not far from the confluence of the latter river and the Hudson. They bought the land of the natives, but did not secure

[1] The failure of the plan was inevitable, for the pine trees from which so much was expected were of the white pine species that is remarkably free from resin. Also a miscalculation had been made as to the price of Finland tar, which could be bought for one half of the price that Hunter supposed would have to be paid. See Jacobs's "German Emigration to America" in Pennsylvania-German Society's *Proceedings*, viii, 114. An interesting letter as showing the desire of the British government to promote the production of "naval stores" is in the *Journals* of the Lords of Trade, November 2, 1711 ("Philadelphia Transcripts," xxiii, 6). In it the British ambassador at St. Petersburg is requested to ascertain how tar is made in Muscovy. See also Royal Historical Commission's *Reports*, "Welbeck Abbey Mss.," v, 190.

a confirmation from the governor. Rival claimants soon appeared and were followed by a sheriff with legal notices. The Palatines defended themselves most sturdily; but a few of them venturing to Albany were seized and held as hostages. Some of the Schoharie settlers yielded and others procured a good title to lands on the Mohawk.[1] The irreconcilable Palatines took up the line of march to the southward and settled on Tulpehocken Creek, near the modern city of Reading. Again they failed to secure a grant of land from the proprietor of the soil, which brought new troubles upon them. The best known of them was Conrad Weiser. His father was the foremost of those who came from New York; the son lived for many years in Pennsylvania, greatly assisting successive governments in their negotiations with the Indians, whose language and customs he thoroughly understood.[2]

The coming of an earlier colony of Germans to Pennsylvania has already been narrated. The great German migration to that province begins about 1717 and continues with almost unabated vigor until the Revolutionary period. The emigrants were got together in Germany by mercenary men who were sometimes called "Newlanders," because they sang the praises of the New World; they were also known as "soul stealers," because they made away with the hapless emigrant, body and soul. The Newlanders averred they had been in America, had there ac-

---

[1] The Germans who came with Erghimer, father of the heroic Herkimer, and settled the German Flats, belonged to a later migration.

[2] The colonial records of Pennsylvania in the years 1731–60 contain a great mass of matter on the career of Conrad Weiser; the "Journal" of his trip to the Ohio in 1748 is reprinted in *Early Western Travels* (vol. i). Joseph S. Walton's *Conrad Weiser and the Indian Policy of Colonial Pennsylvania* is the clearest exposition of the latter subject and the best biography of Weiser. C. Z. Weiser's *Life of [John] Conrad Weiser* contains numerous letters that throw much light on the Indian troubles of Pennsylvania. W. J. Buck's *Indian Walk* (Philadelphia, 1886) is also useful.

quired money and good clothing, and were anxious to bring a share of these benefits to their oppressed country-men. In reality they received so much for every person whom they brought to the ship's side for embarkation to America. Coming from the interior of the Rhine country the emigrants journeyed down that river, passing thirty-six customhouses and being fleeced at every turn by hungry and avaricious officials. On shipboard they were packed away like herrings in a box ; food was scarce, of poor quality, and unusual sort, while the water was un-drinkable.[1] Some of the ships and captains made several voyages, and the reputations of vessels, commanders, and their owners and employers were important ; it was in their interest to land as many passengers in as good health as was possible.[2] Considering the long previous journey and the poverty of the emigrants, the loss of life was not excessive in comparison with that of the early comers to Virginia and the Carolinas.

The cost of transporting one person from the Palatinate to Pennsylvania was about one hundred and twenty-five dollars, the voyage from Rotterdam to Philadelphia cost-ing fifty dollars. These amounts should be multiplied by three to bring them into the present standard of money. As few families numbered less than four persons, it re-quired considerable capital to transport a family from the Palatinate to the interior of Pennsylvania. Many were unable to pay their passage money, others ran in debt for

---

[1] The hardships of this migration have been dwelt upon at great length by writers on the Germans in America. These base their accounts on letters and journals, but probably the documents have been accepted too literally. These journalists were not accustomed to the ways of the sea and must have suffered great hardships in any event.

[2] See an interesting paper by Andrew D. Mellick entitled "The German Emi-gration to the American Colonies, its causes and the distribution of the Emi-grants" in *Pennsylvania Magazine of History*, x, 241, 375, especially p. 391; and the "Narrative of the Journey of the Schwenkfelders to Pennsylvania" in *ibid.*, x, 167.

delicacies and medicines on the voyage. Upon arrival at Philadelphia, they were obliged to sell their services for a term of years and, oftentimes, when the older members of the family were ill or infirm, they were obliged to sell the services of their children in order to satisfy the claims of the captains upon them. In this way families were separated and parents and children never saw each other again. These German indentured servants are usually referred to as " redemptioners," but the term applies to others equally as well. The German redemptioners were purchased of the ship captains by contractors who were called " soul drivers " ; [1] these conducted the newcomers to the interior and there sold them to the farmers. This is the dark side of the picture. There is a bright side which equally deserves description. In Germany, the peasant had no chance to rise beyond his station in which he was born or to see his children shine in careers for which they were fitted by talent or disposition ; life was one hopeless round of labor with nothing to look forward to except a poverty-stricken old age. In America, the redemptioner was usually employed by persons of his own race who understood his requirements and prejudices. At the end of three or five years the redemptioner became free ; received fifty acres of land from the proprietor, and often had a small stock of money which he had gained by doing odd jobs out of time while still in service. He could acquire more money by another year of service and then begin to clear his farm and establish himself as a land-owner. It is said that many well-to-do German immigrants voluntarily served for

[1] Day's *Historical Collections of Pennsylvania*, 209. In 1730 all sales or assignments of servants within the city of Philadelphia were required to be made before a magistrate. The records were carefully kept and accessible. *Pennsylvania Statutes at Large*, iv, 170. See on this general subject E. E. Proper's "Colonial Immigration Laws" in *Columbia Studies in History*, xii, No. 2.

a year or so that in this way they might acquire the experience which was necessary for a successful start in life under new conditions.

The Germans spread diagonally through the colony from the western bounds of the counties of Bucks and Philadelphia to the Maryland line. Everywhere they picked out the choicest lands, especially the limestone valleys.[1] They cleared their lands slowly but thoroughly, so that when their farms began to yield, the harvest was bountiful. They built solid houses, at first of logs and later of stone, and provided themselves with great barns and other outbuildings. They kept together for the most part and were mainly occupied in farming, although there were also many good mechanics and artisans among them. They kept to their German speech and customs and to the religion which they had brought with them from the fatherland. This clinging to language and customs was in some respects a serious disadvantage because it deprived them of that weight in the management of affairs to which their numbers and general intelligence entitled them. For a generation, the Germans willingly intrusted the affairs of government to the English who were in control at the time of their coming; they even chose Englishmen and Scotch-Irishmen to represent them in the General Assembly.[2] It was in this way that English institutions remained the dominant institutions in Pennsylvania, long after the English as a race had ceased

---

[1] Day's *Historical Collections of Pennsylvania*, 416.

[2] In the list of the members of the Assembly in 1744 there is not one German name (*Votes of Pennsylvania*, iv, 1). In 1748 among the members was Derick Hogeland (*ibid.*, iv, 91); he was probably of Dutch descent, but may have been a German. Peter Worral was in this and succeeding assemblies; he was a Quaker but may have been a German. Not a German was elected to succeed the outgoing Quakers in 1756; but in 1757 (*ibid.*, iv, 757) there are several non-English names: Daniel Roberdeau, Denormandie, Gabriel Vanhorne, Isaac Wayne, David McConnaughy, and Colonel John Stanwix.

to be in the majority. The Germans not only added greatly to the wealth and prosperity of Pennsylvania; they protected the older settled counties from Indian attack. It has been said that Quaker blood was never shed by the North American Indian; to this the historians of the German migration reply that the Indians sheathed their knives in the bodies of the German frontiersmen. These settlers came from a martial race and when the time of war required their services in defense of freedom and of right, they have always been freely given. In later days, also, the descendants of these Germans have won renown in politics and business.

No account of the German migration to Pennsylvania would be complete without some statement as to their religious and communal ideas. They belonged to many sects; there were, for instance, the Mennonites, the Dunkards, who are more properly called Dunkers or Tunkers,[1] the Moravian Brethren, and the Schwenkfelders, — a good many Germans were Roman Catholics. The question of the rite of baptism marked the Protestant sects, one from the other, religiously. For instance, the Mennonites believed in baptism by sprinkling, the Dunkers by dipping, while one of the sects practiced triple immersion. Each, as a rule, had its own peculiar forms and services. Ecclesiastically, their ideas were harmless, but some of their theories on the mode of living were rather unusual.[2]

---

[1] George W. Falkenstein's *German-Baptist Brethren*.

[2] J. F. Sachse's *German Sectarians of Pennsylvania, 1708–1800* (2 vols., Philadelphia, 1899) and the same author's *German Pietists of Provincial Pennsylvania* (Philadelphia, 1895) contain a mass of interesting matter rather loosely put together. Most of the travelers who passed through Pennsylvania in the latter part of the eighteenth century visited one or more of the German communities. Christopher Sauer's edition of the *Bible*, which was printed at Germantown in 1743, was the first edition of that book to be published in any European language in the English colonies; but Eliot's "Indian Bible" had been printed at Cambridge eighty years earlier.

At one time Germantown sheltered one of the earliest of American radical reformers. This was Peter Cornelius Plockhoy, who came from the Netherlands and was, strictly speaking, a Dutchman. His plan for the happiness of the poor and ridding nations of idle persons and also of capitalists was printed at London in 1659.[1] He argued for equality and collective housekeeping. Whenever a hundred families lived separately, he says, one hundred women were required to perform the necessary household tasks; by combination the number could be reduced to twenty-five, thus setting free seventy-five women for productive labor. In his community, he would have four kinds of people, agriculturalists, merchants, sailors, and artisans, all of whom were to work ten hours each day. Housekeeping was to be in common, the meals being taken together, the males sitting on one side of the table, the females on the other. In this household all should be taken care of, there should be no rich and no poor, and the evening of life should be passed in calm security. Plockhoy obtained a piece of land on the southern side of Delaware Bay and settled there with a score of Mennonites; but was rudely uprooted by Sir Robert Carr, in whose sight Utopian plans for the extinction of capitalists found no favor. Years afterwards, blind and infirm, Plockhoy came to Germantown and was cared for by the Mennonites at that place.

Instances of intercolonial migration have been repeatedly given in the preceding pages. Especially noteworthy has been the spreading of colonists from Connecticut and, to a less degree, from the other New England colonies into New York, New Jersey, and northern Pennsylvania.

---

[1] Pennypacker's " Germantown " in Pennsylvania-German Society's *Proceedings*, ix, 232, 245.

Emigrants from New England also followed the coast southward to Carolina. New Yorkers settled in the southern colonies, and the migration of the Palatines from Schoharie to Pennsylvania has just been described. Toward the middle of the century an important flow of intercolonial migration began and continued for some years with ever increasing strength. Philadelphia was the landing place of crowds of immigrants besides those who settled in Pennsylvania. Hundreds and perhaps thousands of Irish of Scottish parentage and Germans proceeded from Philadelphia through Lancaster and York to Winchester, crossed the Potomac, followed the Shenandoah Valley to Staunton and thence across the Dan to the Carolinas. Many of these did not proceed the whole distance but stopped, some in Maryland, many in Virginia, and others in North Carolina. They were an extremely desirable set of colonists, and their coming was made easy for them by the suspension of the religious laws in their favor and by the appointment of some of their own people as magistrates. It was in this way that communities grew up in the western part of these colonies which were quite distinct as to race and manners from the older communities in the tidewater and piedmont regions.[1]

According to the ideas of nationality which prevailed in all European countries at the time of the settlement of the colonies, allegiance was indelible; once an Englishman or once a Frenchman, always an Englishman or always a Frenchman. An alien in a foreign country was subject to many disabilities to which the native was not liable ; he could not own land, exercise trading privileges, bequeath or inherit property. To obtain these civil rights of the

---

[1] Governor Tryon of North Carolina stated that in the autumn and winter of 1765–66 more than 1000 wagons passed through Salisbury with families from the northward, *Colonial Records of North Carolina*, vii, 248.

natural born subject of England, it was necessary for the foreigner to be given the rights of a denizen, which might be done by the king and might confer only limited rights. Or an alien might be naturalized by act of Parliament, in which case he usually enjoyed all the rights of a native-born subject, excepting perhaps that he might not be able to occupy certain offices. The grant of denizenship or of naturalization conferred upon the person civil rights only and had nothing whatever to do with the franchise. To obtain the right to vote for a member of the British House of Commons, it was necessary for the naturalized subject resident in Great Britain to acquire the requisite qualifications for an elector in a county or a borough.

In the beginning of English colonization, persons carried to the plantations were generally regarded as possessing civil rights; none of the colonists had political privileges and duties except under some special grant as, for instance, being freemen of the Massachusetts Bay Company. In the articles of capitulation of New Amsterdam in 1664, it was provided that those Dutchmen who continued to live in the conquered settlements should have the rights of Englishmen as to property, commerce, and inheritance.[1] With the eighteenth century, there came a great inflow of foreign-born immigrants. To them were given by act of the English government or of the provincial proprietors and legislative bodies, the civil rights of native-born Englishmen. In 1740, Parliament passed an act[2] for the naturalization of foreign Protestants in the American colonies. To take advantage of this act the alien must

[1] This is probably the first naturalization of aliens in the colonies; the act of the Maryland Assembly passed in 1666, naturalizing Augustine Herman of Prag and his family, was probably the earliest colonial law of the kind, Bacon's *Laws of Maryland*, under date.

[2] 13 George II, Cap. 7 (Ruffhead's *Statutes at Large*, vi, 384).

have resided in the colonies for seven years or more and
not have been absent from them for a longer space than
two months at any one time. Such persons must also
take certain prescribed oaths and partake of the sacrament
according to the English form.[1] Quakers, however, might
affirm instead of taking an oath and Jews might omit the
words " on the true faith of a Christian," and neither of
these classes of persons was required to partake of the
sacrament. Such naturalized persons enjoyed the civil
rights of native-born subjects of the English king, but
could not be Privy Councilors, members of Parliament,
or hold any office of profit or trust or receive grants from
the crown in Great Britain or Ireland, but might hold
offices and grants in the plantations. This act with some
minor changes remained the general law for the rest of
the colonial period and was the basis of the first naturalization act passed by the United States Congress. Other
acts naturalized certain specified classes of foreign Protestants as, for example, those who had served for two years
in the Royal American Engineers. Bands of immigrants
of certain religious societies [2] were also naturalized without regard to residence in the colonies and, indeed, sometimes before emigration from Europe.

Long before 1740, the separate colonies had naturalized
foreign-born immigrants, either by special act or by
general law.[3] In these colonial laws, the period of residence was usually much shorter; in the case of Massachusetts, in 1730–31, the required period was reduced to

[1] It is to be noticed that one result
of this act was to prevent Roman Catholics holding land in Pennsylvania;
see *American Catholic Historical
Researches*, xiv, 95.

[2] See, for instance, An Act for encouraging the People known by the Name of
Unitas Fratrum, or *United Brethren* to

Settle in his Majesty's Colonies in America (22 George II, Cap. 30, Ruffhead's
Statutes at Large, vii, 155).

[3] A Virginia naturalization paper issued in 1712 is in Hening's *Statutes*,
iv, 548; another, dated 1722, is in *William and Mary Quarterly*, iii, p. 11.

one year.[1] Many interesting questions arose as to the rights conferred by colonial legislation. Did these acts, for instance, confer any rights in England, or in the other colonies? In 1718 Solicitor General Thomson[2] gave as his opinion that a colonial law applied only to the province or colony in which it was passed. It fell out in this way, therefore, that a foreign-born resident of Massachusetts who was possessed of the requisite amount of property might own land and vote in that colony and be treated as an alien upon going to the neighboring province of New Hampshire.[3]

With the increase of population and growth of industry and commerce there came the attendant poverty, distress, and concomitant vagabondage. In dealing with this problem, as it arose successively in different sections of the colonies, local conditions played a more important part than they did in any other respect. The demand for unskilled labor was intense in the colonies which were settled after 1660 and could only be partly satisfied by the importation of negro slaves because it was felt to be desirable, even in South Carolina, to have white men on every plantation as a precaution against servile insurrection. The legislators

---

[1] *Massachusetts Province Laws*, ii, 586.

[2] Chalmers's *Opinions*, i, 344.

[3] Sometimes complications arose, even within a colony. The Maryland Assembly, for example, had provided by law that any one could become a member of it who could be elected to the House of Commons. The Naturalization Act of George II, however, forbade persons who were naturalized under its provisions from occupying seats in Parliament; it followed from this that naturalized Marylanders could not be elected to the Assembly of that province. Governor Eden assented to an act of the Maryland Assembly, removing this disability. He was censured by the home government for so doing, because the English authorities disliked any broadening of colonial representative systems. There were many other peculiarities which grew out of the different legislation of England and the several colonies. Enough has been said, however, to show that naturalization in a liberal form was prevalent in the colonies in 1760. Massachusetts Historical Society's *Collections*, Fourth Series, x, 695. There are valuable papers on this subject in the same society's *Proceedings*, 1858–60, p. 337; *American Historical Review*, ix, 288; American Historical Association's *Report* for 1893, p. 319.

in the colonial assemblies were nearer to the mass of the people than were the members of the House of Commons in England. Moreover, in Pennsylvania, humanitarian motives, which have always actuated the Society of Friends, tended to bring about an amelioration of the lot of the more unfortunate classes in that community. As a result of these causes a well-defined tendency is observed to deal with poverty and vagabondage in a more lenient manner than was the case in England. On the other hand, the poor free whites and the indentured servants naturally merged one into the other, although the tendency of legislation was to treat the two classes as distinct.

In Virginia and the other colonies to the south of the Potomac, newly arrived immigrants were protected by law from their foreign creditors for a period of five years, or for longer times [1] from the time of their landing. Throughout the colonies there was more consideration shown to the poor debtor than in England. Imprisonment for debt was generally disliked, and an insolvent or bankrupt by taking the poor debtor's oath [2] and surrendering whatever property he still possessed could secure his personal freedom — although in some colonies subsequent prosperity laid upon him the obligation of pay-

---

[1] The Virginia act of 1642 prohibiting suits for debts contracted in foreign countries appears to be the first law of the kind; in 1663 this law was declared in force except as to goods imported into the colony; see Hening's *Statutes of Virginia*, i, 256; ii, 189. Carolina laws of a similar nature are noted in *Colonial Records of North Carolina*, i, pp. xxxiii, 183, 674; ii, 836, 838; Cooper's *Statutes of South Carolina*, ii, 124. Jamaica also protected immigrants from foreign creditors; see *Calendars of State Papers, America and West Indies, 1675–1676*, pp. 219, 396. The North Carolina act of 1707 excepted the following classes

of debts: those due to the Queen, to Virginians, for goods brought into the colony, debts made within six months, etc. The governor of Maryland complained of this law, and the Lords of Trade advised its repeal. Parliament in some sort replied to this and other colonial enactments by the passage, in 1732, of An Act for the more easy Recovery of Debts in his Majesty's Plantations and Colonies in America (5 George II, Cap. vii, Ruffhead's *Statutes at Large*, vi, 74).

[2] *North Carolina Laws* (Davis's Revisal, 1773), pp. 538–541; *Colonial Laws of New York* (ed. 1894), iii, 1099.

ing the debts which were in existence at the time of his
bankruptcy.

In dealing with the hopeless poor, local conditions
came more into play. Each administrative unit was
usually responsible for the support of all persons within
its boundaries. This practice led to the adoption of many
laws and local regulations [1] which have a queer look in
these days of unrestricted movement [2] and show how far
we have departed from the ways of our ancestors. It also
led to the forcible ejectment of intruders, often after a
sound whipping as an earnest against return.[3] Sometimes,
it proved to be difficult for a son or daughter to enter-
tain the older members of the family when these latter
had acquired a domicile elsewhere : the records contain
entries of the refusal of the authorities to allow a mother
to visit her daughter until the selectmen of the former's
town had given satisfactory assurances that they would
receive the poverty-stricken parent back again after she
had worn out her welcome at her son-in-law's house.

In New England and the Middle Colonies almshouses
were often constructed in the more densely settled towns [4]
and counties; but in the country districts the poor
were still "auctioned off" to him who would care for
them at the lowest cost per head. In the Southern

[1] *Rhode Island Laws of 1767*, p. 228;
Laws of North Carolina of 1755, p. 172.

[2] For instance, see *Boston Town Records*, 1660–1701, 67, where the authorities order certain persons to bind out
their children to service within one
month. On p. 135 of the same volume is
an agreement between the town and an
employer in which the latter agrees to
receive a child and keep her until she be
eighteen years of age, and pay the town
its charges and " forty shillings to clothe
her."

[3] See a case in Rhode Island, in 1748,
which is recorded in F. Denison's *Wes-
terly and its Witnesses*, 139.

[4] See, for an instance, *Minutes of the
Common Council of New York*, ii, 85:
" Ordered that the Mayor agree with
some person for the keeping of an hospital for the maintenance of the poor of
this city upon the most easy terms that
may be." This entry was made in 1699;
it is also interesting for the use of the
word "hospital" to designate a house
for the poor — following the earlier English usage.

Colonies, licenses to beg were sometimes given, as was the
case in Virginia, but the able-bodied vagrant was usually
bound out to service, while the vagrant pauper who could
not find a master was generally turned loose after a whipping with a threat of worse treatment in case he was again
found wandering.[1] Precautions were also often taken
against the landing of impotent poor persons by the captains of immigrant ships ; but there was no regular inspection of incoming immigrants, except at Philadelphia.

The care of indigent sick persons was generally left
to private charity, or was handed over to the local authorities. In times of epidemics, as the frequent ravages
of the smallpox, pesthouses were frequently established
at public cost, where those suffering from infectious diseases could be segregated from the community, but, in
general, each family was expected to take care of its
members in its own way and at its own expense. In
1751[2] the Pennsylvania Assembly incorporated the trustees of the Pennsylvania hospital, which was the first institution of the kind to be established on a permanent
basis. This hospital was to be open for the entertainment
and care of the sick and distempered from any part of
the province without partiality or preference, and was
free to the sick poor, so far as the funds at the command
of the managers would admit; but this did not apply
to those who were afflicted with incurable or contagious

[1] *Laws of North Carolina* (ed. 1773),
p. 172 (Act of 1755). The New York Act
of 1756 was especially severe: no house-
holder could maintain a stranger for
more than three days without giving
bonds to save the city or county from
all charges on his or her account. Otherwise a wanderer should be carried from
constable to constable to some place
where he or she had remained forty
days, or to place of nativity, or to border
of province. Returning without permission, the vagrant was whipped on the
bare back 31 lashes if a man, 25 if a
woman, "and so as often as he or she
shall return after such transportation."
Laws of New York (ed. 1894), ii, 58. The
laws of Virginia were very similar, Hening's *Statutes*, vi, 29–31.
[2] *Pennsylvania Statutes at Large*
(ed. 1896), v, 390.

diseases. The space not needed for the poor could be devoted to paying patients. In return for this service, the colony permitted the trustees to solicit subscriptions and to receive certain penalties which were levied for the prevention of the exportation of unmerchantable goods. In 1761 one hundred and fifty-three patients were admitted to the hospital, which number rose, in 1774, to four hundred, of whom only about one sixth were paying patients.

Pennsylvania also led the way in the establishment of prisons on modern lines, where those incarcerated were confined separately and treated with some degree of humanity.[1] In the other colonies, places of detention were usually termed houses of correction, which name reflects the opinions of that time that crime was wickedness and not disease. In conclusion, it may be remarked that while the colonists in 1760 had advanced beyond the ideas that were then prevalent in England and on the continent of Europe, they had only just begun to feel the impulse of modern philanthropy.

[1] Similarly, while in other colonies the stocks or the lash was the fate of the drunkard who could not pay the five-shilling fine, in Pennsylvania he should work in the House of Correction for five days for the first offense, and ten days for each succeeding conviction, *Pennsylvania Statutes at Large*, ii, 99.

NOTES

I. The German Migration. — Writing many years ago, George Bancroft remarked that neither the Germans nor their descendants "have laid claim to all that is their due"; but this reproach can no longer be made. In 1891 the Pennsylvania-German Society began the publication of its *Proceedings and Addresses,* of which fifteen volumes had been issued up to 1906. The papers printed in this series are naturally of uneven merit. Among the most useful are S. W. Pennypacker's "Settlement of Germantown" (Vol. ix), H. E. Jacobs's "German Emigration to America" (Vol. viii), J. F. Sachse's "The Fatherland: in the Discovery, Exploration, and Development of the Western Continent" (Vol. vii). See also F. R. Diffenderffer's *German Immigration into Pennsylvania.* This volume bears the sub-title "II. The Redemptioners," but it is all that has been published. It is of great value, not only to the student of racial migration, but also to one interested in colonial labor problems. K. F. Geiser's "Redemptioners and Indentured Servants" in the *Yale Review,* x, Supplement, is a very useful compilation. On the Germans in New York reference may be made to F. Kapp's *Die Deutschen im Staate New York* and S. H. Cobb's *Story of the Palatines; *L. F. Bittinger's *The Germans in Colonial Times.* On the Germans in Virginia see an article by Herrmann Schuricht in the *Annual Reports* of the Society for the History of the Germans in Maryland, ix and x.

II. Racial Origins. — In recent years historical societies have been founded for the express purpose of exploiting the virtues of immigrants of particular races and creeds, to secure for this element or that "its due place in history." A recent writer, indeed, contends that Julia Ward Howe's descent from General Marion "made a battle hymn her natural expression." It is difficult to define American or Irishman. Is the place of a man's birth the determining factor? Is any man born in Ireland an Irishman? Was the Duke of Wellington an Irishman? The case of James Logan, Penn's agent, is to the point: he was born at Lurgan in the northern part of Ireland while his parents were temporarily residing there; they had come from Scotland and passed the remainder of their days in England, while he lived and labored in America for more than half a century, — was he a Scot, an Irishman, a Scotch-Irishman, or an American?

The American nation is composed of so many elements that one man may be descended from half a dozen different stocks and as many religions. Shall an historical society belonging to each one of these races and religions claim the distinguished personage for its own? Names are an insecure guide in tracing ancestry. For instance, a Frenchman named Blondpied settled in New England; his sons became respectively Blumpey and Whitefoot; and Israel Israel of Pennsylvania was not a Jew at all, but a Quaker. The following table shows that a prominent man might be descended from eight or more different racial stocks and have ancestors of as many religions:

SCOTTISH [Presbyterian]	IRISH [Roman Catholic]	FRENCH [Huguenot]	SPANISH [Roman Catholic]	HEBREW [Jewish]	GERMAN [Lutheran]	DUTCH [Reformed]	ENGLISH [Church of England]
great grand- father	great grand- mother	great grand- father	great grand- mother	great grand- father	great grand- mother	great grand- father	great grand- mother

grandfather   grandmother   grandfather   grandmother

father   mother

distinguished personage

CHAPTER XV

RELIGION AND TOLERATION, 1689-1760

The Toleration Act[1] was passed by the English Parliament in 1689 to free English and Welsh dissenters from the penalties of the religious laws. It was not designed to alleviate in any way the condition of the Roman Catholics. Several interesting questions at once arose : did the act extend to the colonies, and thus suspend the religious laws of Virginia in favor of Protestant dissenters, or exclude Roman Catholics from office, even in Maryland. Whatever answer might be given to these questions, the Toleration Act commended itself to the colonists; many of the assemblies[2] repeated its provisions and the royal

[1] 1 William and Mary, Cap. 18 (*Statutes of the Realm*, vi, 74): "An Act for Exempting their Majestyes Protestant Subjects dissenting from the Church of England from the Penalties of certaine Laws." It will be noticed that the phrase "dominions thereunto belonging" is omitted from the title, but the colonists were certainly "subjects." The oaths as they stood in the middle of the eighteenth century are printed in the *Bulletin of the New York Public Library*, i, No. 2, p. 44: *Virginia Magazine of History*, v, 102.

The Toleration Act provided that neither the law of 23 Elizabeth, Cap. 1, nor half a dozen other laws, "shall be construed to extend to any Person or Persons dissenting from the Church of England, that shall take the oaths made" in Cap. 1 of 1 William and Mary and make the declaration provided in 30 Charles II, Statute 2, Cap. 2 (the Test Act). Since "bare non-conformity

is no sin at common law," to use Lord Mansfield's words, relieving Protestant dissenters from the penalties imposed by statutes was equivalent to tolerating them. See on this subject "The Christian Religion and the Common Law," by P. E. Aldrich in American Antiquarian Society's *Proceedings* for April, 1889. The oaths required by the Toleration Act are printed in the Note at the end of this chapter.

[2] Virginia in 1699 provided that Protestant dissenters who qualified according to the Toleration Act should be exempted from attending the services of the Established Church (Hening's *Statutes*, iii, 171 and 360). A New York law of 1691 guaranteed religious toleration to Protestants (*Colonial Laws of New York*, i, 248). The Massachusetts Province Charter of 1691 granted "liberty of conscience in the worship of God to all Christians, except Papists" (*Massachusetts Province Laws*, i, 14).

government directed that all colonial officeholders must take the oaths therein provided as well as subscribe the "test." The importance of this legislation may be seen from the fact that there were thirty or forty dissenters to every Church of England man in the colonies.[1] The Roman Catholics were not numerous in any colony; even in Maryland they formed less than one twelfth of the total population.

Small as was the number of the Roman Catholics, the colonists feared them as intensely as did the people of England. This jealousy and suspicion was mainly due to the rising spirit of nationalism that made English Protestants resent the assumption on the part of the Pope that he had any right or power to determine the relations of Englishmen to their rulers. The severest anti-Catholic laws were made in Maryland.[2] From 1704 to the Revolution no Roman Catholic service could be celebrated except in a private house; but this was not so much of a hardship as it would have been in other colonies because in the missionary establishments and in the houses of the richer Roman Catholic planters there were often large rooms that were designed for religious purposes. No Roman Catholic could teach school under penalty of transportation to England for trial there; children of Roman Catholic parents upon attaining their majority must take the oaths under penalty of being deemed incapable of inheriting lands, which should go to the

---

[1] Caleb Heathcote to the Earl of Oxford, Royal Historical Manuscripts Commission's *Reports*, v, 199. He added that if the people were not instructed in "better principles" and the charter governments regulated, the northern colonies would surely separate from the rest of the empire. Heathcote was at one time mayor of New York.

[2] The principal anti-Catholic laws of Maryland are given in Bacon's *Laws* as follows: 1704, Chap. lix; 1715, Chap. xxxvi, § vii; 1716, Chap. v, § viii; 1717, Chap. x, § ii. These acts are summarized in McMahon's *Maryland*, 243. This legislation was partly based on the English law of 11 William III, Cap. 4, § iv (*Statutes of the Realm*, vii, 587).

nearest of kin who was a Protestant; and Roman Catholics could not purchase lands. In 1717 Roman Catholics who would not take the oaths were disfranchised and later they were compelled to pay a double tax and, of course, also contributed to the support of the Established Church of the province. It was intended to proceed further and confiscate the property of the Jesuit missionaries as well as entirely prohibit the exercise of priestly functions on the part of Roman Catholics, but the project fell through because the two houses could not agree as to the precise limit of persecution.[1] In 1708 there were probably about three thousand Roman Catholics in a total population of forty thousand.[2] In 1756 the number was not over four thousand[3] and they then formed only about one thirteenth of the total population.[4]

There were few Roman Catholics in Virginia, but the people of the Old Dominion were so fearful that persons of that faith would cross the Potomac from Maryland that they forbade Roman Catholics to possess arms, give evidence in a court of law in any case whatsoever, or hold any civil or military office unless they took the oaths prescribed by the Toleration Act and supplementary Virginia laws.[5] In Pennsylvania there was no anti-Roman Catholic legislation. Persons of that belief enjoyed freedom of conscience and of worship in the Quaker colony and could also hold land and engage in any business.

---

[1] In 1746 a proclamation of Governor Bladen directed that all Papists who were suspected of trying to pervert subjects from their allegiance should be arrested, and, if need be, imprisoned, Shea's *Catholic Church*, i, 406.

[2] *American Catholic Historical Researches*, viii, 177. J. G. Shea has some interesting remarks on Maryland intolerance in his *Catholic Church in the United States*, i, 351 and fol.

[3] *Ibid.*, ii, 52.

[4] See report of Governor Sharpe to Lord Baltimore in 1758, *Sharpe Correspondence*, ii, 316.

[5] See especially the Act of 1699, Hening's *Statutes*, iii, 299. The later laws of 1748 and 1756 are in *ibid.*, v, 480; vii, 35. The laws as to dissenters in general, which also apply to Roman Catholics, are in *ibid.*, ii, 45, 48, 51; iii, 171, 360.

Few of them found shelter there, however, possibly because they could not take part in political life as they could not take the oaths required by the English government.[1]

In New York and in New England there were very few Roman Catholics, but the proximity to Canada and the attempts of French priests to convert the Indians to the Roman Catholic religion led to severe laws against the priests and missionaries of that church. In 1699 the English Parliament by law directed all Roman Catholic priests to depart the realm before the 25th of the following March.[2] This act was repeated by the legislatures of New York and Massachusetts[3] and remained on the statute books of those colonies until the Revolutionary epoch. One other colonial law must be mentioned. On the Rhode Island statute book, under date of 1663–64, are these words: "All men professing Christianity and of competent estates and of civil conversation, who acknowledge and are obedient to the civil magistrate, though of different judgments in religious affairs (Roman Catholics only excepted) shall be admitted freemen and shall have liberty to choose and be chosen officers in the colony, both military and civil." This sentence has given historians hostile to Rhode Island the opportunity of accusing the rulers of that colony of inconsistency. The act was never

[1] In 1757 Lord Loudoun reported that there were 1365 Roman Catholics in Pennsylvania, Scharf and Westcott's *History of Philadelphia*, i, 253; ii, 1366. Mass was first publicly celebrated at Philadelphia in 1707, *American Catholic Historical Researches*, xii, 39.

[2] 11 William III, Cap. 4, § iii (*Statutes of the Realm*, vii, 586). In 1705 Attorney-General Northey declared that this act extended to the colonies, Chalmers's *Opinions*, i, 3.

[3] *Laws of New York, 1691–1718*, p. 41;

Massachusetts Province Laws, i, 423. See the present work, vol. i, pp. 246–249. J. G. Shea, in his *Catholic Church*, i (p. 356), says that the passage of these laws was due to Bellomont, whom he characterizes as "a fierce anti-Catholic zealot, son of a Colonel Coote whose butcheries of Catholics in Ireland stand out horribly"; but Shea gives no authority for this statement. In 1696 there were only ten Roman Catholics in New York City, *American Catholic Historical Researches*, v, 93.

passed in 1663–64, or at any time during the life of Roger Williams; it first appears on the statute books in 1719: how it got there no one knows. It remained law in that colony and state until 1783, when Roman Catholics were given full political rights.[1]

The lot of the Roman Catholics in the colonies was so difficult and disagreeable that Charles Carroll of Maryland, father of John Carroll, the first Roman Catholic bishop in the United States and uncle of Charles Carroll of Carrollton, signer of the Declaration of Independence, applied to the king of France for a grant of land in Louisiana, with the design of removing the Maryland Roman Catholics, or many of them, to that region; but the project was not approved by the French government, owing to the nationality of the members of the proposed colony, and it fell through. Considering the general harshness of their treatment by the assemblies of the English colonies, and, on the other hand, the considerate treatment of the French in Canada by the English authorities after the conquest, it is indeed memorable that the pride of race and spirit of patriotism kept the Roman Catholics of Maryland and Pennsylvania loyal throughout the French and Indian wars and attached them fixedly to the cause of independence at the time of the Revolution.

The Church of England was established by colonial law in Virginia, Maryland, and the Carolinas.[2] Each of these

---

[1] At least one Roman Catholic had earlier been enfranchised by special act. On this general subject see *Rhode Island Laws of 1719* (Rider's reprint, p. 3, and "Introduction," 14). The clause is also in the Widow Franklin edition of *Rhode Island Laws of 1745*, p. 4. See Rider's "Inquiry concerning the origin of the clause disfranchising Roman Catholics" in *Rhode Island Historical Tracts*, Second Series, No. 1; Arnold's *Rhode Is-*land, ii, 490; *American Catholic Historical Researches*, xi, 14; Charles Deane in Winsor's *America*, iii, 379; *Records of the State of Rhode Island*, ix, 674.

[2] The Church was definitely established by law in North Carolina in 1758, but not much had been accomplished under its provisions to 1760, judging from Tryon's statement that in 1765 there were only five clergymen of the church in the province and that four of

colonies was divided into parishes ruled over by vestries and provided at public charge with a church, glebe, and parsonage. [2] In each the minister was licensed by the Bishop of London and the governor and paid by public contributions, and the services were those prescribed by the Canons. In Virginia[1] the vestries were close corporations, the vestrymen, as vacancies occurred in their body, filling them by election ; in Maryland the vestrymen were chosen by the freeholders[2] and in South Carolina they were annually elected.[3]   In these three colonies the clergy were supported out of public funds, every one contributing whether he attended the services of the church or not.   In Virginia and South Carolina the salaries were arranged by the vestries, but in Maryland the ministers were supported by a tax of forty pounds of tobacco per head on every taxable inhabitant of the parish.   In Virginia the ministers were employed by their vestries on yearly contracts and were therefore responsible to their leading parishioners; in point of fact, they were rather the companions than the spiritual guides of the richer planters.   In South Carolina a commission appointed by law exercised some oversight of the clergy who were selected by their parishioners.   In Maryland the proprietor enjoyed the right of presentation.

them were missionaries sent out by the "Venerable Society," *Colonial Records of North Carolina*, vii, 102. See also an excellent paper by S. B. Weeks on "Church and State in North Carolina" in *Johns Hopkins Studies*, xi, Nos. v and vi.

For the South Carolina church act see the present volume, p. 345. In 1706 (Cooper's *Statutes*, ii, 288) the Huguenots were placed on the same footing as the Episcopalians.

[1] The most important laws as to the Church in Virginia are printed in Hen-

ing's *Statutes*, iv, 205, 206; *ibid.*, vi, 90; vii, 302. For the oath of a vestryman in 1761, see *Virginia Magazine of History*, ii, 215.

[2] The laws establishing the Church in Maryland are in Bacon's *Laws*, 1692, ch. ii; 1702, ch. i. See also McMahon's *Maryland*, i, 243. As to the clergy, see also F. L. Hawks's *Contributions to the Ecclesiastical History of the United States*, ii, 187.

[3] Cooper's *Statutes of South Carolina*, ii, 282.

The Established Church in South Carolina came into severe and direct competition with the dissenting sects; that colony was a mission field and its clergymen were largely provided by the Society for Propagating the Gospel. They were usually persons of good character and the condition of the Church was distinctly creditable. As to Virginia, Bishop Meade, writing in the next century, says that a regard to historic truth forces him to acknowledge that at no time, from its first establishment, was the moral condition of the Church even tolerably good.[1] He makes this statement not from his own knowledge, but from what he had heard from old men and from what he had read. As to Maryland, we have the evidence of a contemporary, Dr. Chandler, a strenuous defender of the Episcopacy, who visited that province in 1764. He writes to the Bishop of London that he thinks it his duty to inform him of the wretchedly bad character of the clergy of the Established Church in the colony. There are some whose behavior is exemplary, he declares, " but their number seems to be very small in comparison, they appearing here and there, like lights shining in a dark place. It would really, my Lord, make the ears of a sober heathen tingle to hear the stories that were told me by many serious people of several clergymen in the neighborhood of the parish where I visited."[2] Of course the good people of Maryland may have enjoyed making the ears of a New England parson burn by telling him stories of his fellow-clergymen which perhaps were not entirely true, but there seems to be good evidence from other directions to the effect that drunkards and

---

[1] Bishop Meade's *Old Churches, Ministers, and Families of Virginia*, ii, 351.

[2] F. L. Hawks's *Contributions to the Ecclesiastical History of the United States*, ii, 249.

persons of immoral character were too frequently occupants of benefices in the provinces on Chesapeake Bay.[1]

In Virginia no one could be legally married except by the minister of the Established Church. This was not the case in South Carolina or Maryland, but in all three colonies the dissenters equally with the members of the Established Church contributed to the support of the minister recognized by law, no matter how much they disapproved of his religious ideas or his personal character; they also paid for the building and repairing of the public church and the minister's dwelling — if they had any money left they might devote it to the support of their own religion and minister.[2] The Maryland Act Concerning Religion of 1649 was repealed in 1692. From 1723, for nearly a century, Maryland possessed the most ferocious of laws against blasphemers,[3] which was repealed in 1820 in time to save the Unitarians from being stigmatized and hanged.

The care of the spiritual concerns of colonists was generally regarded as vested in successive bishops of London.[4] The origin of this custom seems to have been the fact that John King was Bishop of London and a

---

[1] For an example, see W. S. Perry's *Historical Collections Relating to the American Colonial Church*, iv, 128.

[2] W. H. Foote's *Sketches of Virginia, Historical and Biographical*, 50; H. R. McIlwaine's "Struggle of Protestant Dissenters for Religious Toleration in Virginia" in *Johns Hopkins Studies*, xii, No. 4, and W. T. Thom's paper in *ibid.*, xviii, Nos. 10, 11, 12. This subject will be further treated in volume iii of the present work.

[3] The Act of 1649 is summarized on p. 501 of volume i of the present work; the repealing act is in chapter 84 of the acts of 1692. The act against blasphemers of 1723 (Bacon's *Laws of Maryland*, 1723,

ch. xvi) continued without amendment until 1820. According to its provisions, whoever shall wittingly blaspheme or curse God or deny the divinity of Christ, or "utter any profane Words concerning the Holy Trinity or any the Persons thereof" for the first conviction shall be bored through the tongue and fined twenty pounds; for the second be "stigmatized by Burning in the Forehead with the Letter B" and be fined forty pounds; for the third, be put to death.

[4] As to this matter see A. L. Cross's admirable essay in the *Harvard Historical Studies*, No. ix, entitled "The Anglican Episcopate."

member of the Virginia Council at the outset of English American colonization. Moreover, the chief ecclesiastic of the commercial metropolis of the realm was naturally brought into contact with the mercantile companies and became interested in the spiritual welfare of seamen who went on long voyages to foreign parts in their ships, and also of English merchants who settled in foreign ports for commercial reasons. However it originated, the bishops of London from the beginning saw to the licensing of candidates for the colonial ministry. One of them, Bishop Gibson, performed these functions by reason of a commission from the king.[1] Another, Bishop Sherlock, sought to refuse to exercise these functions with a view to compelling the appointment of a resident American bishop or more than one. At the end of the seventeenth century the Bishop of London was represented in Maryland and Virginia by officials who were termed commissaries,[2] of whom Commissary Bray[3] of Maryland and Commissary Blair of Virginia were persons of force and character. The commissary was the agent or deputy of the Bishop and performed all episcopal functions except that of ordaining priests. The commissaries found, wherever they went in the colonies, that the governor was already exercising many of their functions and was disinclined to part with his powers; for example, with that of licensing clergymen to preach who already held letters from the Bishop of London.[4] The

[1] Printed in Colonial Society of Massachusetts' *Publications*, v, 112.

[2] Cross (*Anglican Episcopate*, 294) gives a form for the " Appointment of a Commissary " and "Directions " for his guidance. These are taken from an interesting pamphlet entitled *Methodus Procedendi contra Clericos irregulares in Plantationibus Americanis*, which is

printed in the same volume, pp. 294–309.

[3] Bernard C. Steiner has an article on Bray in Maryland Historical Society's *Fund Publications*, No. 37.

[4] Cross prints a license on p. 309 of his *Anglican Episcopate*; T. C. Gambrall prints a letter of induction on p. 189 of his *Church Life in Colonial Maryland*. Governor Burnet of New York

commissaries had very little power to punish clergymen for offenses against the rules of the Church or social order because the assemblies nowhere gave them punitive authority or the right to summon or examine witnesses. Once in a while the commissaries held a trial, but the results were unsatisfactory because the incriminated ecclesiastic could not be compelled to attend or the witnesses to testify even to facts of common notoriety. The personal influence of the commissary was constantly exerted for good, but they accomplished little.

As the eighteenth century advanced, the desire for the appointment of a resident American bishop became keener. The presence of so high placed an ecclesiastic would increase the dignity of the clerical profession. Even in Virginia and Maryland the better men among the clergy desired such an appointment, but many ecclesiastics were against it and so were the planters of Virginia, who did not wish to be deprived of their control of the parish priests. In Maryland it was also opposed because the proprietarial authority would have been diminished by such an appointment. The failure of the project was made certain, however, by the opposition of the dissenting sects in New England and the Middle Colonies. They refused to believe that an American bishop would confine himself to the exercise of his strictly ecclesiastical function; he would, they thought, strive to obtain those powers which in England were exercised in the diocesan courts. They induced their non-conforming brethren in England to put pressure upon successive Whig governments by reminding the Duke of

took a serious view of his ecclesiastical functions, possibly because he was the son of a bishop. Richard West, for a long time Counselor of the Lords of Trade, declared that Burnet would give no one the right to preach who could not produce a satisfactory sermon on the spot. W. A. Whitehead's *Contributions to the History of Perth Amboy*, 162.

Newcastle of the evil political effect of displeasing the voters of their religious persuasion.   It fell out, therefore, that when Bishop Sherlock approached Newcastle on the subject, the latter replied that the matter was one of national consideration which had long been under deliberation by great and wise men and by them laid aside. Horatio Walpole, the successor of William Blathwayt, as auditor general of the colonies, was asked for his advice and wrote a long letter (May 29, 1750)[1] to Bishop Sherlock, which was also designed to be a reply to many things which Thomas Secker, Bishop of Oxford, had said in sermons and probably also in correspondence with Newcastle.   Walpole declared that the colonists do not want resident bishops, have required priests to be ordained in England according to the Canons, and have exhibited jealousy against the exercise of ecclesiastical jurisdiction in the plantations. He informed the Bishop that the support of the dissenters is very necessary to the present government and reminded him that the High Church party formerly had occasioned great mischiefs and that the matter could not be discussed in Parliament without great danger. He concluded by expressing the hope that when Sherlock had coolly weighed the consequences of his plan, he would await with patience the decision of the Privy Council.   Walpole sent a copy of this letter to Newcastle, who read it with great attention and wrote that he always had very "good doubts" about the measure and had so told the Bishop of London.   Newcastle agreed with Walpole that reviving old disputes and creating new divisions among those who sincerely mean the good of their country was a matter which should not be lightly undertaken — and that was the end of the business for the

[1] This correspondence is printed in full from the "Newcastle Papers" Ms. in Appendix xi to Cross's *Anglican Episcopate*, pp. 320–332. Walpole's letter begins on p. 324.

time. The episode is important, not only in itself, but as showing how careful the English government was of the feelings and desires of the colonists.

The Venerable Society for Propagating the Gospel in Foreign Parts [1] had been founded in 1701 largely through the efforts of Dr. Bray and Bishop Compton. It performed a very good work in sending a succession of able and upright missionaries to those colonies where the church was not established. The society contributed to the salaries of these missionaries or paid them itself, and it also had in its employ, from time to time, colonists who had taken holy orders. The activity of its missionaries was especially noticeable in New England, where, although the soil must have seemed somewhat stony at first, in the end it produced good fruit. This was especially the case in Connecticut in the twenty years before 1760. Many graduates of Yale College were converted to the Established faith — among them Samuel Seabury, the first bishop of the Episcopal Church in the United States, and Samuel Johnson, the first president of King's College in New York. In the middle of the century, Dean Berkeley,[2] afterwards Bishop of Cloyne, settled in Rhode Island in furtherance of his scheme to found a college for the education of colonists to be priests of the Established Church. He was a remarkable man, full of enthusiasm, but lacking in those qualities which make a successful founder. All avenues of pecuniary assistance for his plan closing to him one after another and the appointment to a bishopric becoming probable, he returned to England. Before going he presented a large

---

[1] See *An Account of the Society for Propagating the Gospel in Foreign Parts*. The charter is in a *Collection of Papers of the Society for Propagating the Gospel in Foreign Parts*.

[2] See A. C. Fraser's memoir in his edition of the *Works of George Berkeley*; A. G. Balfour's *Essays and Addresses*. The American part of Berkeley's career is described by W. E. Foster in American Antiquarian Society's *Proceedings* for April, 1892.

collection of valuable books to Yale College at the instance, mainly, of Dr. Johnson, who, it has been surmised, may have suggested to Berkeley the possibility that Yale might become an Episcopalian institution.

Religion in New York[1] has a complicated history. After the English conquest, in view of the different religious beliefs of the Dutch and the English settlers, Colonel Nicolls found it necessary to establish entire freedom in religious matters; this remained, so far as freedom of conscience to Protestants was concerned, but did not confer political rights or do away with the necessity of taking certain oaths on assuming office or giving evidence. The Duke of York's laws stipulate that provision for religious services shall be made in every town; but the character of those services was left to the people of the several divisions of the colony. This arrangement continued throughout the proprietary period, each governor bringing with him a chaplain who conducted services within the fort. These in Dongan's time were performed by "two Romish priests,"[2] and at other times by those of the Established Church of England. With the reorganization of the province after the Revolution of 1688 the first important attempts to secure preferential treatment for the Established Church were made, and curiously enough the man who was most concerned was Benjamin Fletcher, whom one would not ordinarily regard as a religious person. It was in 1693 that the Assembly of New York passed a law for settling a ministry and raising a maintenance for them in New York and three counties of the province.[3] This act provided that a good sufficient Protestant minister should be appointed in each county, to be paid from forty to one

[1] There is much valuable matter in the *Ecclesiastical Records, State of New York*.

[2] Shea's *Catholic Church*, i, 91.

[3] *Laws of New York, 1691–1718*, p. 19.

hundred pounds per annum by public contribution. Ten
vestrymen and two churchwardens were to be annually
elected by the freeholders of the county. These with
two or more justices of the peace might levy the tax
for the support of the minister who was to be called by
the vestrymen and churchwardens. While this measure
was under discussion the Council amended the bill to
give the governor the power of appointing the minister,
but the Assembly refused to accept any amendment of
the kind. Fletcher resented this refusal on the part
of the Assembly, calling the amendment "very imma-
terial,"[1] and declaring that by his commission he had a
right to appoint the ministers in the province. The act
was hardly passed before disputes arose as to its meaning, and the Assembly, upon being asked, ruled that the
vestrymen and churchwardens had the power to employ
dissenting Protestant ministers if they wished and to levy
a tax for their support. Fletcher, acting under the interpretation which the Council gave to the law, incorporated
the wardens and vestrymen of Trinity Church[2] and gave
them much valuable land which up to that time had
formed a part of the "king's farm." This action of his
aroused considerable indignation; but eventually a compromise was made by which the Reformed Dutch Church
also secured recognition.

Lord Cornbury was the most discreditable governor
New York ever had and also one of the firmest adherents
of the Established Church in the province. An infectious
disorder in the city obliged him to reside at the town of
Jamaica on Long Island. The Act of 1693 had not ex-

[1] *Journal of the Legislative Council
of New York*, i, 48.
[2] Morgan Dix has a brief and interesting account of Trinity Church in W.
S. Perry's *American Episcopal Church*,
ii, 473.

tended to that part of the province and the Long Islanders had kept on managing religious affairs to suit themselves. They were Congregationalists or Presbyterians and employed ministers of their own way of thinking and paid them out of the public levy. This fact angered Cornbury; by a disreputable ruse he secured the meeting house and parsonage at Jamaica and established a conformable minister therein. He also tried, but vainly, to induce the Assembly to provide for the salaries of ministers of the Established Church by public levy.

In New England there had been important changes in the religious outlook.[1] The forfeiture of the charter of the Massachusetts Bay Company destroyed the intimate connection between Church and State that had existed in that colony; and the provisions of the Province Charter of 1691 completed this separation by conferring the franchise on those holding a certain amount of property regardless of their religious affiliations. Moreover, the governor was appointed by the crown and was usually an adherent of the Established Church. The disunion of Church and State in the Bay Colony gave the more liberal elements in the population a chance to express their opinions and even to put their opinions into practice without loss of political power, although, perhaps, with a certain degree of social ignominy. These liberals were strongest in Boston and Cambridge and possessed sufficient power to oust the Mathers from the control of Harvard College and to found the Brattle Street Church in Boston, which was presided over by a non-conformist minister who was called from England and did not receive ordination in the colony.

[1] Williston Walker, of the Hartford Theological Seminary, has an interesting paper on this theme in the *Yale Review* for May, 1892, entitled "Why Did Not Massachusetts Have a Saybrook Platform?"

In Connecticut the development was in precisely the opposite direction, for there Church and State were one and the Rev. Gurdon Saltonstall was elected governor, the only time that a clergyman occupied that position in any colony. The most important event in the religious history of Connecticut in these years was the adoption of the "Saybrook Platform" in 1708.[1] This body of ecclesiastical doctrine was formulated by a synod which was held at Saybrook in conformity with an act of assembly and was composed of four laymen and twelve ministers,[2] eight of the latter being members of the Yale corporation. The assembly approved it and thus changed the religious system of Connecticut from a Congregational basis to a semi-Presbyterian one, and at the same time extended the benefit of the English Toleration Act to those who qualified themselves before a county court; but all such persons must continue to contribute to the support of the regular minister. Connecticut and Massachusetts had definitely separated religiously.

The Congregational churches may still be regarded, in 1760, as being "established" in both of the larger New England colonies, but the severe laws as to outsiders had been relaxed[3] and Episcopalians, Baptists, and Quakers[4] now enjoyed religious toleration. They were no longer obliged to contribute to the support of the regular ministers or to the building and reparation of the town's

[1] *Public Records of Connecticut* (1706–1716), p. 87.

[2] Trumbull's *Connecticut*, i, 482, where the Platform is printed at length; see also Williston Walker's *Creeds and Platforms*, ch. xv.

[3] Abner C. Goodell has a luminous paper on this subject in the *Publications* of the Colonial Society of Massachusetts (i, 140). In this instance, as in others which are noted elsewhere in the present volume, the minority appealed to England with the result that practices which were desired by the majority of the people or by the ruling classes were frowned upon in England partly because they were contrary to English law.

[4] *Massachusetts Province Laws*, ii, 494; iv, 67, etc.; see also *Public Records of Connecticut*, 1706–1716, p. 50, and *ibid.*, 1726–1735, p. 237.

religious edifice ; but every one was still obliged to attend
some religious service on the Lord's Day.   The operation
of the laws embodying these arrangements left much to
be desired.   These outsiders were properly enough debarred from voting in town meeting on questions relating to the regular religious organization ; but Connecticut
went beyond this and forbade them to vote at all in
town meeting.[1]   It was difficult to decide who should
receive the benefits of this arrangement, and the town
records give one the impression that this was frequently taken advantage of to avoid making any contribution whatever for the support of religion.   Selectmen
also were sometimes overstrict as to the proof of membership in outside religious organizations.   As the number
of members of these other religious societies increased, the
town's revenue for religion declined and had to be made
good by a tax upon the pews in the regular church.   Up
to this time, voluntary contributions for religious purposes
seem to have been very rare, possibly because of the great
jealousy which prevailed as to the establishment of corporations.

The middle of the eighteenth century witnessed in New
England and the other colonies a religious revival which is
known as the Great Awakening.[2]   Earthquake and pestilence had something to do with preparing the minds
of the people for emotional excitation ; but that it came
when it did was due to the presence and exhortations of

[1] *Public Records of Connecticut*,
1726–1735, p. 211 (Act of October, 1728,
still in force in 1760).

[2] The leading facts in this movement
are well set forth in Joseph Tracy's *Great
Awakening*.   G. L. Walker's *Some Aspects of the Religious Life of New England* contains a brief statement of this
episode.   Jonathan Edwards's *Thoughts*
on the Revival of Religion in New England, 1740*, and his *Faithful Narrative
of the Surprising Work of God in the
Conversion of Many Hundred Souls in
Northampton* should be read, in part at
least, by any one desirous of taking a
sympathetic view of this important
epoch in the religious development of
the American people.

two remarkable men, Jonathan Edwards and George Whitefield. The former came of good New England stock, was
trained at Yale College, and was a mental prodigy.   In his
earlier years he had written sundry essays on logic and
on scientific subjects which, had he lived a century later,
would doubtless have prepared him for the highest walks
of science.[1]   In New England, in the first half of the eighteenth century, such mental endowments as Edwards possessed could find a field for display only in the ministerial
profession. With this keen intellect, Edwards united wonderful skill in the use of language and remarkable power
of expression.   There had, of course, been religious excitement from time to time, but it was not until the winter of
1734-35 that anything which can be called a general revival took place.   This followed on notable sermons which
Edwards preached at Northampton in the Connecticut
Valley in Massachusetts, and it spread thence down the
river and somewhat to the eastward and westward.

George Whitefield was an Englishman, an ordained
priest of the Established Church, and, in some sort, a companion of the Wesleys in arousing renewed interest in
Christianity.[2]   In 1740 he came to Boston from Georgia
and traveled thence through the colonies, preaching as he
went, frequently in the fields. With the ground prepared
by the earlier exhortations of Edwards, his ministrations

---

[1] See E. C. Smyth in American Antiquarian Society's *Proceedings*, October, 1895, p. 212. Edwards's essay
on "The Will," which was prepared at
a later time, is still regarded as a work
of distinction. On his philosophical
ideas see I. W. Riley's *American Philosophy, the Early Schools*, ch. iii; on his
scientific achievements see Huxley in
Encyclopædia Britannica (9th ed.). The
best concise account of Edwards's career
is A. V. G. Allen's small volume in the

" American Religious Leaders " series;
Samuel Hopkins's *Memoir of Edwards* is
an old-time book that is still readable.
Edwards's writings have been many
times reprinted. Dwight's edition (Boston, 1829) is the one referred to in the
present volume.

[2] The Methodists were not strong in
colonial days. On the history of that
sect see J. M. Buckley's *Methodists in
the United States* and J. J. Tigert's *The
Making of Methodism.*

aroused great excitement in New England, where fifteen thousand persons are said to have " experienced religion " through his influence in a few weeks.   Whitefield then proceeded on a pilgrimage of preaching throughout the Middle and Southern Colonies.   Even Benjamin Franklin felt the spur of his eloquence and joined with others to build a great hall in which he and other preachers of any denomination might express their religious views. Of his influence, Franklin tells an amusing story that he himself went to hear Whitefield at a later period when he had ceased to be so strongly affected by his eloquence. When the sermon began,[1] perceiving that a collection was to follow, he resolved not to give a penny to further certain schemes which Whitefield had much at heart and of which Franklin did not entirely approve.   As the speaker warmed to his discourse, Franklin decided to give the copper change which he had in his pocket, later he determined to give the silver also, and when the dish finally came round, he put into it all the money he had about him, — gold, silver, and copper combined.   When a religious revivalist could produce such an effect on Benjamin Franklin, it must be conceded that he possessed remarkable power of stirring human souls.

Edwards seized the opportunity of Whitefield's progress and delivered a series of sermons which in America have seldom been surpassed.   Of these discourses, the most famous perhaps are those upon the " Punishment of the Wicked " and as to the "Eternity of Hell Torments," which he preached in 1741 and 1739, respectively.[2]   For the wicked, so he told his hearers, there will never be any rest or respite in hell, for they will be tormented with fire and brimstone

---

[1] Franklin's *Works* (Sparks's ed.), i, 138.

[2] Edwards's *Works* (ed. 1809), vii, 393, 419.

day and night forever and ever. " You have often seen a spider," he asked of his audience, " . . . when thrown into the midst of a fierce fire, . . . There is no long struggle, no fighting against the fire, no strength exerted to oppose the heat, or to fly from it ; but it immediately stretches forth itself . . . and is burned into a bright coal. — Here is a little image of what you will be the subjects of in hell." From this torment there was no escape. It went on forever, day and night, year after year, age after age, for thousands and millions of ages, " when after you shall have worn out the age of the sun, moon, and stars, . . . without rest day or night, or one minute's ease yet you shall have no hope, but shall know . . . that still there are the same groans, the same shrieks, the same doleful cries, incessantly to be made by you, and that the smoke of your torment shall still ascend up for ever and ever ; and that your souls, which shall have been agitated with the wrath of God all this while, yet will still exist to bear more wrath." The effect produced by one of Edwards's sermons was described by a neighboring diary-keeping colleague.[1] He relates that before the sermon was done there was a great moaning and crying : "What shall I do to be saved — Oh, I am going to Hell — Oh, what shall I do for Christ? " The shrieks and cries were so piercing that for a time Edwards was obliged to desist. Men and women could not support themselves, but grasped the pillars of the church or were kept from falling by those about them, while some groveled on the floor or lay inert on the benches.

These " manifestations " or " bodily effects " were the least evil part of the results which accompanied the revivals. There cannot be the slightest doubt of the sincerity

---

[1] Ms. Diary of the Rev. Stephen Williams, quoted in O. W. Means's *Strict Congregational Church of Enfield*, p. 19.

or good faith of men like Edwards, Whitefield, and the lesser preachers who worked with them. Edwards tells us with evident sincerity of the results of his ministrations : how great numbers were led to religion ; and Whitefield gives us the same impression, only his converts numbered thousands where those of Edwards were estimated in hundreds. Many strongly religious men in New England and elsewhere doubted the goodness of the work which the revivalists were doing. Later Edwards himself seems to have come to a realizing sense of the insufficiency of the work and to have admitted that bodily pain and excitation were not true religion. In point of fact, the Great Awakening resulted in the formation of two groups of Congregationalists in Connecticut and in the lessening of the hold which religion had on the people throughout the colonies. So far as the breaking down of the barriers between denominations denoted a diminution of the influence of religion, these results are to be deplored ; for it must be remembered that religious liberalism has ever gone hand in hand with religious indifference ; the religious enthusiast is always intolerant.

Edwards's later life was fruitful in literary production, but was full of misfortune. His parishioners at Northampton fell away from him and dismissed him from his pastorate, the first time that such a thing had happened in New England.[1] The ecclesiastical cause of their differences turned on the question of the admission to full religious privileges of the grandchildren of church members who had themselves been in the highest odor of sanctity. According to the Puritan idea of the early seventeenth century, a church member had the right to offer

[1] One of the earliest signs of this slipping away from Puritan grace was the substitution of Watts's hymns for the Psalms. See Massachusetts Historical Society's *Proceedings*, Second Series, x, 429.

his child for baptism and it was generally held that this baptism gave to the child the right of being admitted, without a confession of faith, to certain privileges of church membership, including that of offering his child for baptism. This arrangement was called the Half-Way Covenant. Jonathan Edwards's predecessor and grandfather, the Rev. Solomon Stoddard, had gone one step farther and had admitted to the communion table those who were church members by baptism, but not by confession of religious experience. It is said that Stoddard was led to do this because intense religious conviction had come to him while at the communion table. For years Edwards made no objection to this arrangement, but the outward manifestations and spiritual changes wrought in human beings by the revivalist preachers could hardly fail to direct his attention to the inconsistency of the Half-Way Covenant, let alone the Stoddard development of it — what was the use of converting adults, if they could already be in full communion? At all events, he determined to admit no more members to communion who did not make an express confession of religious belief.[1] At the same time he also displayed a singular lack of tact in dealing with a question of social morals which had arisen. It is supposed that copies of Richardson's *Pamela* had come into the hands of some of his parishioners and had been circulated among them. Stating that he understood the young people were reading an obscene and indecent book, Edwards called for an inquiry and even read out from the pulpit the names of those who had it in their possession. In the days of John Cotton and Thomas Shepard the incriminated families would have bowed

---

[1] The best brief discussion of the Half-Way Covenant and its results is in O. W. Means's *Strict Congregational Church of Enfield*, pp. 11–14.

their heads and accepted the reproof. Now they did nothing of the sort, but asked for the summoning of an ecclesiastical council to give them permission to dismiss their overzealous pastor. The council was held and by a majority of one vote authorized the parish to dismiss their pastor, if they were still so inclined, which they did by a vote of two hundred to twenty. Later, in town meeting, they further decided that he should not preach in town even in the absence of other ministers. For some time he officiated as missionary to the Indians of Stockbridge and was then called to the presidency of the college at Princeton, New Jersey, in succession to his son-in-law, Rev. Aaron Burr, and died there soon after from the effects of inoculation for smallpox. The close of Edwards's career has been thus told in detail because it marks a distinct epoch in the history of religion in New England.

The religious reaction which followed on the Great Awakening was favorable to the growth of dissent throughout the colonies. In Connecticut the ecclesiastical constitution went to pieces because in so many towns " Separatist " churches, or Strict Congregationalist churches as their members preferred to be called, were established; the Baptists and the Episcopalians also made many converts, but this took place after the period covered in the present volume.

Toward the close of the first half of the eighteenth century, Presbyterians [1] and Baptists [2] assumed considerable

---

[1] C. A. Briggs's *American Presbyterianism: its origin and early history* (New York, 1885); R. E. Thompson's *History of the Presbyterian Churches in the United States.* On the Presbyterians in the Carolinas, see George Howe's *History of the Presbyterian Church in South Carolina* and W. H. Foote's *Sketches of North Carolina*, 77 and fol. (in a " condensed form " in *Colonial Records of North Carolina*, v, 1193 and fol.).

[2] H. C. Vedder's *History of the Baptists in the Middle States;* Isaac Backus's *History of New England with particular reference to the Baptists* (3 vols., 1784; reprinted in 2 vols., 1871); David Benedict's *General History of the Baptist Denomination* (2 vols., New York, 1848).

importance, not only in New England, but in Maryland, Virginia, and North Carolina. There had been Presbyterians and Presbyterian ministers in Virginia from an early time, but the man who gave the stimulus which resulted in the rapid growth of Presbyterianism in the English colonies was Francis Makemie. He was born in Ireland of Scottish parents and studied for the ministry at Glasgow. He had originally come to the colonies in 1683 and plied the twofold occupations of itinerant Presbyterian preacher and West Indian merchant, traveling through the Chesapeake colonies and making voyages to Barbados. In 1707 Makemie appeared in New York on his way to Boston and was invited to preach, the Dutch offering him their religious edifice for the purpose. This shocked the religious sensibilities of Lord Cornbury.[1] He forbade the loan of the church and Makemie preached to those who came to him in a private house. This was on Sunday, in January, 1707 : on the following Tuesday he went to Newtown, Long Island, to preach to the people there and was arrested by a warrant from the governor for preaching without a license. Makemie had a license from the governor of Barbados and evidently supposed that under the Toleration Act this would be sufficient anywhere in the colonies. At first he was released on bail and was afterward tried, returning to New York for that purpose. He was defended by three able lawyers, James Reigniere, David Jamison, and William Nicholl. The case was never properly reported [2] and our knowledge of it is derived

---

[1] An anonymous account of the trial is in the library of the Massachusetts Historical Society; it is reprinted in Force's *American Tracts*, iv, No. iv. There is a good description in W. H. Foote's *Sketches of Virginia*, p. 63. See J. Maclean's *College of New Jersey*, i, 38.

[2] In the indictment it was averred that he endeavored to subvert the queen's ecclesiastical supremacy; that he had unlawfully preached without the governor's license; that he had preached in an unlawful conventicle, all of which was contrary to the laws of England. See Force's *American Tracts*, iv, No. iv, p. 23.

mainly from the side of the defendant.   It is certain, however, that he was acquitted by the jury and was then condemned by the court to pay all the costs of his prosecution,
which amounted to some eighty-three pounds sterling!
The American Presbyterians with the members of the
other dissenting Protestant sects complained bitterly of
Cornbury's doings, and the Assembly of New York also
making representations against him on account of his
arbitrary proceedings, he was recalled.   This incident
marked the end of the prosecution of Protestant dissenters
in New York; but it was after this time that Jews were
disfranchised in that colony.[1]

As the eighteenth century advanced, Presbyterianism
gathered increasing strength and, outside of New England,
attracted to itself practically all those of the Congregational Church.   There were very many Presbyterians in
central Pennsylvania, mostly Scotch-Irish immigrants.
Groups of these streamed across Maryland into the valley
of Virginia and were encouraged in this migration by the
Virginia governor, William Gooch, who promised them
religious toleration, because they served as a bulwark for
the frontier.   As long as they confined themselves to the
Shenandoah Valley, they were permitted to elect a vestry
of their own numbers and to manage their parish affairs
to suit themselves.   The coming of the itinerant revivalist
preacher changed completely this attitude.   The rulers of
the Old Dominion belonged entirely to the Established
Church and were, as a matter of fact, almost without exception vestrymen or churchwardens.   The social fabric
of the province was bound up with the maintenance of
the Established Church and the existing parish organization.   When, therefore, Presbyterians, Methodists, and

---

[1] In 1737; *Journal of the General Assembly of New York*, i, 712.

Baptists began to make converts in the old-settled part of Virginia, the ruling class at once demanded that the laws should be strictly enforced. The English Toleration Act, which was the law in Virginia, required that Nonconformist places of worship should be registered and those who ministered in them licensed. The enforcement of any such law of course destroyed the efficiency of the itinerant missionaries and bore hardly upon many of the regular Nonconforming clergy, who sometimes preached in half a dozen different churches in the course of a month. The missionaries were sometimes indicted, as were those in whose houses they preached; but the juries were loath to convict and the government was obliged to try other measures, such as fining those who did not attend the services of the Established Church. This attempt was unsatisfactory and indirectly caused the modification of the law so that any one who could prove that he attended any religious service could go free.[1] The dissenters continued to make numerous converts until the outbreak of the French and Indian War, which put all other matters out of mind; in 1760, those who did not go to the regular services in Virginia probably outnumbered those who did attend.

Baptist congregations were scattered widely throughout the colonies. Their missionaries had appeared in New England in the earliest days, and for a few weeks Roger Williams himself had embraced that belief. In 1760 there were many of them in New England, but the colony

---

[1] Hening's *Statutes of Virginia*, v, 226; see also on this general subject, H. R. McIlwaine's "Struggle of Protestant Dissenters for Religious Toleration in Virginia" in *Johns Hopkins Studies*, xii, No. iv. Foote's *Sketches of Virginia*, chs. x, xi, admirably set forth this matter from a dissenter's standpoint. Samuel Davis, *The State of Religion among the Protestant Dissenters in Virginia* (Boston, 1751), gives a good account of these hardships, especially p. 18 and Appendix, pp. 41–44.

in which they formed the largest proportion of the total population was North Carolina, where they had been almost from the beginning and where they had at one time formed with the Quakers the only religious organizations. With the growth of the dissenting faiths the Baptists became noticeable in the Old Dominion, but did not become a strong fighting body until the Revolutionary period.

Where there were so many different sects as there were in the colonies, there was more or less attempt at conversion, especially through the working of the marital relation. It was a rule of the Roman Catholic and Anglican faiths, as well as of the Quaker, that children were born into the religious organization to which the parents belonged. In the case of the two former organizations, infant baptism and confirmation at adolescence were also required. In these religious bodies a policy of segregation was pursued. This was also true of the peculiar sects like the Dunkards and the Mennonites. The young people of each religious order were kept by themselves and precautions were taken to prevent their marrying outside of their respective folds. In some instances this was done by virtue of unwritten law; in others by reason of written regulations. In the case of the Quakers, for instance, the Monthly Meetings often inquired several times a year of each young man in the Meeting whether he was consorting with a young woman outside of the fold with a view to marriage; if such were found to be the case, considerable pressure [1] would be put upon the erring swain to induce him to mend his ways. In mixed marriages where one party was a Protestant and the other a Roman Catholic, it was customary to enter into prenuptial contracts as

[1] There is an excellent chapter on this subject in Caroline Hazard's *Narragansett Friends' Meeting*.

to the spiritual education of the children in the Roman
Catholic faith; or, as in Maryland, where it was arranged
that the girls should be brought up as Roman Catholics,
the boys being reared as Protestants.

In Virginia the English law was followed. This required that all marriages must be celebrated by a clergyman of the Established Church, no matter what the beliefs
of the marrying pair might be.[1] Afterward, or before,
they might also be joined in the bonds of matrimony by a
clergyman of their own faith, but unless they were married according to law, their children would, of course, be
regarded as illegitimate. In no other colony was this
requirement made by law. The Roman Catholic and
Established Churches had this in common, that they regarded marriage as a sacrament to be celebrated only by
ecclesiastics. The dissenting sects held that marriage was
a civil contract and should be carried out according to the
colonial law. It followed from this that in the colonies
where the dissenters were in a majority or, indeed, where
they formed a large minority of the total population, marriage was regulated by law as a civil contract. In New
England any "settled minister" might marry within the
town where he preached, and any justice might marry
within the county where he resided,[2] and a similar practice was followed in New York[3] and New Jersey.[4] In
Pennsylvania, Quaker marriages were recognized by law,
but people of other denominations could be married by

---

[1] Hening's *Statutes*, ii, 49; iii, 150,
441; vi, 81.

[2] *Massachusetts Province Laws*, i, 61,
209, 216, 354; ii, 60; iii, 622; *Connecticut
Code of 1702*, p. 73.

[3] *Laws of New York, 1684-1719*, i,
151. The marriage laws of New Netherland and New York are summarized
in the New York Genealogical and Bio-

graphical Society's *Records of the Dutch
Reformed Church*, i, pp. vi-xii. John
Miller, chaplain of the English garrison
at New York in Fletcher's time, is very
severe on the morals of that city. See
Paltsit's edition of Miller's *New York
Considered*, pp. 59-62.

[4] Leaming and Spicer's *Grants, Concessions . . . of New Jersey*, 332.

their own clergymen.   In 1701 the law required that the
marriage of Quakers[1] should be solemnized by the parties
"taking one another" before witnesses, and the marriage
certificate must be signed by twelve persons, one of them
a justice of the peace of the county where the parties resided.   Persons belonging to other religious organizations
might be married according to the rule of their respective
societies.   In North Carolina, where clergymen were
scarce, it was early provided that persons wishing to be
married could go before the governor or any one of the
Council, taking with them three or four neighbors and
make a declaration that they join together in the holy
state of wedlock.[2]   In all the colonies, ample provision was
made for previous publication of marriage intentions and
for filing the necessary certificates, either in the parish
records or in the office of the county clerk.

In the conditions which necessarily prevailed in wilderness settlements to which there was a constant and large
influx of immigrants and also numerous deaths by accident,
it was necessary to make provision for dealing with big-
amy; and where women were scarce and bachelor life disagreeable, of providing for remarriage.   There can be little
doubt that many persons came to the colonies to free
themselves from wives and husbands who were no longer
pleasing.   To guard against these dangers, the colonists
enacted severe laws.   In South Carolina and Massachusetts, for instance, a bigamist was punished by death,[3] while
in Pennsylvania he or she was flogged and imprisoned for

[1] *Laws of Pennsylvania*, ii, 21; the
editorial note on p. 23 says that this act
was never considered by the crown. A
Quaker marriage certificate is printed
in *Pennsylvania Magazine of History*,
xviii, 256. There is some interesting
matter on this topic in Bolles's *Pennsylvania*, ii, 310, 313–317.

[2] *Colonial Records of North Carolina*, i, 184.
[3] Cooper's *Statutes of South Carolina*, ii, 508; *Massachusetts Province
Laws*, i, 171.

life.[1] On the other hand, where one party to a marriage contract disappeared, it was generally provided that the other might lawfully marry after the expiration of a certain number of years, generally three or five.

The colonists did not have the same fear of the Jews that they had of the Roman Catholics, probably because the former were not under the domination of a foreign potentate as was the case with the latter. The religious freedom which obtained in the Netherlands attracted the Jews thither, and some of them were shareholders in the Dutch West India Company. It fell out, therefore, that the first Jews to emigrate to North America came to New Amsterdam between 1650 and 1660. It cannot be said that Peter Stuyvesant welcomed them, but he was ordered by the directors of the Company to give them protection and encouragement, as appears by a letter which was written in 1655.[2] They came from Holland and from Brazil, whence Jews were ejected about 1655. The best known of these early Jewish residents in New York was Asser Levy,[3] who stood up manfully for his rights and was naturalized as a citizen before the end of the Dutch period. Far different was the welcome which was accorded to Jacob Lumbrozo, " the Jew doctor " from Lisbon, who came to Maryland in 1656, and, two years later, was tried for blasphemy under the provision of the famous so-called " Toleration Act " of 1649, which provided death for him who denied the divinity of Christ. For some reason nothing was done to Lumbrozo, the Jewish writers say because his professional knowledge was too valuable to be dis-

---

[1] *Laws of Pennsylvania*, ii, 183.

[2] *New York Colonial Documents*, xiv, 315; see also M. J. Kohler's article on Jews in New York in American Jewish Historical Society's *Publications*, No. vi.

[3] He took the oath as a citizen after the English conquest. *New York Colonial Documents*, iii, 76.

pensed with. At all events, in 1663 he was given letters
of denization and subsequently received a grant of land. [1]

The Jews were never very numerous in the colonies before 1760, because there were comparatively few of them
living in the colonizing countries of Europe and practically
none in England. Although few in number, they were
widely scattered throughout the plantations.[2] There was
a settlement of German Jews at Lancaster [3] in Pennsylvania
and others in and about Philadelphia. The Jews also settled at Charleston, South Carolina,[4] and at Newport, Rhode
Island, they mustered in considerable numbers. It will be
seen from this that they were attracted to the commercial
centers. Synagogues were erected at Charleston in 1757,
at New York and Philadelphia in 1760, and at Newport in
1762. Probably these were all small buildings, and their
erection does not necessarily prove that the Jews were
numerous in those places or were rich.

Most of the members of the Hebrew race, whose coming has been noted, remained faithful to their religion.
In 1722 Judah Monis [5] was appointed instructor in Hebrew at Harvard College, but only after he had been
baptized as a Christian. For thirty-nine years, until his
death in 1761, he maintained his place. In 1735 he
issued the first Hebrew grammar which was printed in

---

[1] See J. H. Hollander's articles on
the Jews in Maryland in American Jewish Historical Society's *Publications*, i,
25; ii, 38.

[2] The Georgia Charter prohibited
toleration to "Papists" while guaranteeing "liberty of conscience . . . in the
worship of God to all persons inhabit-
ing" that province (*Charters and Constitutions of the United States*, i, 375).
On the settlement of Georgia, Jews came
to the province in sufficient numbers to
alarm the trustees, who felt it necessary to issue a letter declaring that

Georgia was not intended to be a Jewish
colony.

[3] American Jewish Historical Society's *Publications*, ix, 29.

[4] B. A. Elzas, *History of Congregation Beth Elohim* and numerous articles
by the same author; N. Levin's "Historic Sketch of the Congregation Beth
Elohim" in *Charleston Year-Book* for
1883; and Leon Hühner in American
Jewish Historical Society's *Publications*, xii, 39.

[5] See article by Joseph Lebovich in
Jewish Comment for August 22, 1902.

North America. Four days in the week every student except those of the freshman class attended his instruction. He also was the author of two essays, which show how thoroughly he had embraced Christianity. One of these discovers the true reason why the Jewish nation is not as yet converted and proves the divinity of Christ. The other likewise proves the doctrine of the " Ever Blessed and Adorable Trinity." Monis was so zealous in his new faith that it was deemed expedient to advise him " not to judge too hastily of his neighbor and exclude from salvation everyone that differs from him in the explication and belief of the article of the Trinity."

The sternness of religious belief, which had strongly marked the period of early colonization, in 1760 had given way to mental excitation over questions of the political rights of the colonists and of the connection between those rights and constitutional limitations. It is not until the time of the Stamp Act that these considerations come out prominently; but the breaking down of religious beliefs, or the lack of interest in religion, which plainly appears in the reaction from strictness in religious observances, may be regarded as leaving the colonial mind open to new impressions, to that new train of thought which was so sedulously cultivated by the political writers of the ten years before 1775. It is for this reason that the religious condition of the colonies in 1760 has been so fully treated at this place. Philosophy, which up to the middle of the century had concerned itself mainly with religion, from this time has to do chiefly with politics. To this the ever widening opportunities of intellectual improvement powerfully contributed.

NOTE

The Oaths and the Declaration.—

THE OATH OF ALLEGIANCE

I A. B. Doe sincerely Promise and Sweare that I will be Faithfull and beare true Allegiance to Their Majestyes King William and Queene Mary Soe helpe me God.

THE OATH OF ABJURATION

I A. B. Doe Sweare that I doe from my Heart Abhorr Detest and Abjure as Impious and Hereticall that damnable Doctrine and Position That Princes Excommunicated or Deprived by the Pope or any Authoritie of the See of Rome may be Deposed or Murthered by their Subjects or any other whatsoever And I doe Declare that noe Forreigne Prince, Prelate State or Potentate hath or ought to have Power Jurisdiction Superiority Preeminence or Authoritie Ecclesiasticall or Spirituall within this Realme Soe helpe me God.

1 William and Mary, Cap. 1, § 4 (*Statutes of the Realm,* vi, 24).

THE DECLARATION OR TEST

I A. B. doe declare That I doe beleive that there is not any Transubstantiation in the Sacrament of the Lords Supper, or in the Elements of Bread and Wine, at, or after the Consecration thereof by any person whatsoever.

25 Charles II, Cap. 2, § 8 (*Statutes of the Realm,* v, 784).

THE AFFIRMATIONS

By the provision of the Toleration Act (1 William and Mary, Cap. 18, § 10, *ibid.,* vi, 75) "dissenters from the Church of England who scruple the taking of any oath" might substitute for the phrases to which they objected ("I doe swear," "so help me God") the words "sincerely promise and solemnly declare before God and the World" but these must make the above declaration and also subscribe the following :—

I A. B. professe Faith in God the Father and in Jesus Christ his Eternall Sonne the true God and in the Holy Spirit one God blessed for evermore And doe acknowledge the Holy Scriptures of the Old and New Testament to be given by Divine Inspiration.

CHAPTER XVI

THE MARCH OF EDUCATION, 1690–1760

THE second half of the seventeenth century witnessed the lowest stage of colonial culture. The witchcraft persecutions of its last decade closed this epoch of progress downward; beginning with 1700 educational diffusion everywhere worked for intellectual enfranchisement. With the knowledge that is at present available as to the structure and working of the human brain, it is not difficult to account for episodes like the witchcraft delusion in Massachusetts and the religious revival of fifty years later throughout the colonies. History is rich in reproductions of the characteristics of remote progenitors; thus, after the manner of the ancient Druids, men and women, even at the present time, delight to venerate trees and stones, and occasionally to return to the thoughts of those early peoples who believed in the reality of ghost-like apparitions that nowadays are regarded as childish. By long dwelling on things supernatural, the mind compels itself to believe in them, and one human brain by concentration affects another without the medium of ordinary physical action. When the results are beneficent or are not harmful, they are denominated spiritualism, hypnotism, telepathy, mental suggestion; when, in times past, they were malevolent, manifestations of unknown forces were termed witchcraft.[1]

[1] See a thoughtful paper on this theme by Barrett Wendell, "Were the Salem Witches Guiltless?" in which he maintains that some of them were not

456

From the time of the " sorceress Medea" to this hour there have been manifestations of psychical phenomena. Medea

> " In moulten wax, tho' absent, kills by Art,
> Arm'd with her needle, gores a tortured heart."

Likewise, in 1323, John de Nottingham of Coventry in England worked his charms by means of a bodkin thrust into different parts of the waxen effigy of Richard Sowe ; [1] when he put it into the figure's forehead, the real Richard had dreadful thoughts ; when he thrust it into the figure's heart, his victim died. This is the evidence, as it comes down to us ; but the jury of Englishmen, twelve good men and true, would not convict.[2] Scotland had been direfully oppressed by witches. It was natural, therefore, when James VI of that kingdom became James I of England, that Parliament should pass an " Acte against Conjuration Witchcrafte and dealinge with evill and wicked Spirits," [3] which provided the penalty of death for such baleful crimes. This law remained on the statute book for a century and more, as it was not repealed until 1735. One of the last persons to be tried under it was Jane Wenham, " the Hertfordshire witch," who was convicted of " conversing with the Devil in the shape of a cat." [4] Her case has a peculiar interest,

(*Historical Collections of the Essex Institute*, xxix, 129). See also E. S. Morse in *Science*, vii, 749. Some of the " witches" noticed in history were undoubtedly insane persons, while others were criminal in intention.

[1] So also did Bridget Bishop or some one else of Salem, Massachusetts — at least several puppets with pins sticking into them were found in the cellar of her house, Woodward's *Records of Salem Witchcraft*, i, 163.

[2] Mary D. Harris's *Life in an Old English Town*, p. 66. J. B. Thayer printed an interesting and stimulating paper on " Trial by Jury of things supernatural " in the *Atlantic Monthly* for April, 1890.

[3] 1 James I, Cap. 12 (*Statutes of the Realm*, iv, Part ii, 1028).

[4] For the case of Jane Wenham see Francis Bragge's *Full and Impartial Account of the Discovery of Sorcery and Witchcraft practis'd by Jane Wenham of Walkerne in Hertfordshire* (London, 1712) and *Witchcraft Farther Displayed*

because, in the course of the testimony, two clergymen of the Church of England testified to the efficacy of the Book of Common Prayer in the exorcism of the bewitched. This was in 1711. One hundred years later, in 1808, the Rev. Isaac Nicholson, curate of Great Paxton in the county of Huntingdon, England, preached a sermon against witchcraft, in which he gave an account of the attacks on the person of Ann Izzard, who was reputed to be a witch.[1] Not quite one hundred years later (March 7, 1901) evidence was given in court in a New England town in behalf of a young woman who sued for damages from a man who was said to have hypnotized her, reputable persons testifying that when in the hypnotic state the thrusting of pins into her body produced nothing more than smiles.

The end of the seventeenth century saw a recrudescence of the belief in witches and witchcraft in the colonies from Virginia northward to New England. In Maryland[2] a woman was executed on this charge and in Virginia the belief in witchcraft was widespread and sincere, but there were no executions. In Pennsylvania,[3] also, there were those who believed in witchcraft and a jury was induced to bring in a verdict of "Guilty of haveing the Comon fame of a

---

(London, 1712). The first of these was examined in *The Case of the Hertfordshire Witchcraft considered; A Full Confutation of Witchcraft;* and *The Impossibility of Witchcraft.* These were published in 1712 and stirred Mr. Bragge to write *A Defense of the Proceedings against Jane Wenham* (London, 1712). The case is summarized by W. B. Gerish in his *A Hertfordshire Witch; or the story of Jane Wenham* (Bishop's Stortford, 1906) and also in the same author's *Sir Henry Chauncy, Kt.* (London, 1907, pp. 50–54).

[1] See Isaac Nicholson's *Sermon against Witchcraft*, London, 1808. Two other interesting English books on witchcraft are John Beaumont's *An histori-*

cal, physiological and theological Treatise of Spirits, Apparitions, Witchcrafts, and other Magical Practices (London, 1705); Richard Boulton's *A Compleat History of Magick Sorcery and Witchcraft* (London, 1715, 1716). The latter work (vol. ii, pp. 51–165) contains many amazing sorceries, one of which bears a very close resemblance to the case of the Parris children at Salem. It will be noticed that the books mentioned in this note were all published in England after 1700.

[2] Scharf's *Maryland*, i, 297.

[3] *Minutes of the Provincial Council of Pennsylvania*, i, 40. See also Sharpless, *Quaker Government*, i, 39.

Witch," but it would go no farther.   The most attractive
of these witches was Grace Sherwood of Virginia, whose
very name compels attention.   She and her husband were
unpopular with the neighbors and possessed litigious dis-
positions.   In 1698 they sued John and Jane Gisburne for
slander, setting the damages at one hundred pounds sterling because the Gisburnes had declared that Mrs. Sherwood had bewitched their pigs and their cotton.   She
also wanted one hundred pounds from Anthony Barnes
and his wife, Elizabeth, for saying that she came into their
house and went out of it through the keyhole like a black
cat.   Again she sued Mr. and Mrs. Luke Hill; they struck
back and brought the matter to the attention of the higher
authorities.   In the course of all these proceedings, Grace
Sherwood was twice examined for witch's marks by a jury
of women, who reported that she had two such marks.   She
was also ducked to see if she would float, and floating she
was taken out of the water, put in irons, and locked up in
gaol.   She eventually got out of prison and died quietly,
leaving a small property.[1]

With the Restoration in England there had been a revival of witchcraft persecutions.   The most famous of the
witch trials of this time was that which was held before
Sir Matthew Hale in 1664.   He charged the jury that
there was no doubt whatever as to the existence of
witches.   The jury agreed with him, convicted the four
persons on trial, who were sentenced to death and were
executed.   An account of this trial was printed in 1682 [2]

[1] See the "Record of the Trial of
Grace Sherwood in 1705, Princess Anne
County, for Witchcraft" in the Virginia
Historical and Philosophical Society's
Collections, i, 73–78 (Richmond, 1833).
There is a good deal of matter on
witchcraft in Virginia, including the
Sherwood case, in Virginia Magazine of
History, v, 331, and William and Mary
Quarterly, ii, 58; iii, 96, 190, 242.   Howe's
Historical Collections of Virginia, 436.
In 1698 a Virginia jury fully believed
that John Byrd and his wife Anne were
witches.

[2] A Tryal of Witches at the Assizes
held at Bury St. Edmunds for the County

and was widely read. Two other books containing cases
of witchcraft and information as to the best modes of de-
tecting witches were also printed at about the same time
with the names of two royal chaplains on their title pages.[1]
These works, with others, came into the hands of Cotton
Mather, one of the ministers at Boston. They were used
by him in the preparation of a work [2] on witchcraft,
which had great influence in preparing the minds of the
people of New England for the appearance of witches in
their midst. When eminent judges, members of the Royal
Society, prominent ministers of the Established Church,
and high-placed Puritan clergymen all believed in the
existence of witches, persons of common clay might well
have held the same opinions.

The outbreak of the witchcraft delusion which has
given an unhappy notoriety to Salem, one of the leading
towns of Massachusetts, began in the family of Samuel
Parris, minister at Salem Village, who was on bad terms
with some of his neighbors. He had in his possession
a work on witchcraft written by William Perkins, preacher
at St. Andrews in Cambridge, England, and published in

of Suffolk on the Tenth Day of March,
1664, before Sir Matthew Hale, Kt., London, 1682, reprinted London, 1838. The
trial is also chronicled in Howell's State
Trials, vi, 687.

[1] One of these, entitled Saducismus
Triumphatus or Full and Plain Evidence concerning Witches and Apparitions (London, 1681), was written by
Joseph Glanvil, who had been Chaplain
in Ordinary to Charles II and was a
member of the Royal Society. John
Hale (pastor of Christ's Church at
Beverly, Massachusetts) published at
Boston in 1702 A Modest Enquiry into
the Nature of Witchcraft. He states (p.
28) that the "witchcraft judges consulted
the following books: Keeble's Common
Law (chapter on conjurations); Hale's
Tryal of Witches; Glanvil's Collection

of Sundry Trials in England and Ireland; and Bernard's Guide to Jurymen." On the general subject of the
relation of the Salem witchcraft delusion
to the prosecution of witches in England,
see G. L. Kittredge's "Notes on Witchcraft" in American Antiquarian Society's Proceedings, xviii, 148–212.

[2] The Wonders of the Invisible World.
Observations . . . upon the Nature, the
Number, and the Operations of the Devils
(Boston, 1693). An excellent reprint is
in S. G. Drake's The Witchcraft Delusion
in New England, vol. i. The title may
possibly have been suggested by George
Sinclair's Satan's Invisible World Dis-
covered, or a choice Collection of Modern
Relations proving that there are Devils,
Spirits, and Witches (Edinburgh, 1685).

1608. This was entitled "A Discourse of the Damned Art of Witchcraft." Parris's children either at his instigation or else prompted by curiosity schooled themselves to simulate the antics of bewitched persons as described in this work. They charged certain persons whom they disliked and other persons whom their father disliked with bewitching them. The Salem magistrates thought the matter should be looked into, and a panic seized the minds of the people. At this moment, Sir William Phips, the new governor, arrived at Boston. He was an ignorant, superstitious, well-meaning person, who was extremely ill fitted to cope with such a crisis. Writing to William Blathwayt, he described the province as miserably harassed by a most horrible possession of devils. "Some scores of poor people were taken with preternatural torments," he wrote, "some were scalded with brimstone; some had pins stuck into their flesh ; others were hurried into the fire and water, and some dragged out of their houses and carried over the tops of trees and hills for many miles together." [1] There was no doubt of witchcraft in Phips's mind. He at once appointed a special court to take cognizance of these cases.[2] On this court were several of the most enlightened men of the province, like Samuel Sewall, who in after years were heartily ashamed of their share in the transaction. Scores of people were accused and many were led into confession of guilt, since that seemed to be the easiest and often the only way to secure immunity. Then the people began to be dissatisfied ; it became certain that innocent persons were being accused. Phips put an end to the court and the delusion speedily came to an end. There can be little doubt that in the

[1] *Calendars of State Papers, America and West Indies, 1689–1692,* 720.
[2] As to the legality of this commission, see Peleg W. Chandler in Massachusetts Historical Society's *Proceedings,* xx, 395.

course of these persecutions the charge of witchcraft was used for purposes of private revenge and also to get rid of unpopular persons.   On the other hand, some of those who were condemned had doubtless employed mental suggestion or hypnotic influence to worry those whom they disliked. When the court adjourned on September 22, 1692, nineteen persons had been convicted and hanged and one had been pressed to death [1] for refusing to plead to the indictment; fifty-five had confessed to being witches and had been pardoned; one hundred and fifty were in prison awaiting trial.[2]

With the opening of the eighteenth century new forces came into play, not only to enlarge the settler's material outlook, but to liberalize his mind.   Among these were the constant discussion in political gatherings, the establishment and spread of newspapers and magazines, and the great enlargement of the means for literary and scientific education.   Schools and colleges were everywhere founded and improved, but perhaps the most potent influences were the assemblings of professional men, merchants, and agriculturalists in the colonial legislative bodies, the town meetings, and the open elections which were the rule in the colonies to the south of the Hudson. In the town meetings of New England, men of education contributed their knowledge; but their determination was stiffened by the strength which the farming members brought from the soil; these in turn gained ideas from their more cultured political allies and opponents.   The elections to the colonial legislatures outside of New England were held after the manner of the English hustings, the elector's vote being recorded in a book which was

[1] On the *peine forte et dure*, see the present work, i, 184.

[2] The leading authorities on the Salem witchcraft delusion are mentioned in the Note on p. 490.

open to inspection and of which a transcript might be had at slight expense. These meetings were attended by the able men and the men of means who exercised all their power to bring the voters to their side; the personal contact between a small Virginia planter and George Washington, or George Mason, was an educative influence of the highest importance. The more open, prolonged, and controversial these electoral meetings were, the greater was their effect upon the mental development of the average voter.

The democratization of society in the colonies gave to the workers as distinguished from the merchants and professional men a degree of personal freedom that was unknown in older countries. The abundance of land and its easy acquisition tended to upset the social relations which the settlers brought with them from Europe. In many colonies there were large estates, and in some colonies, notably in New York, there was an established landlord class.[1] But the intense demand for labor and the ease with which a working man, who was dissatisfied with his condition as a tenant, could acquire a farm of his own, made it impossible for colonial legislatures to tie the laboring classes to fixed places of residence as they were in Europe. On the other hand, these classes exercised great political power, owing to the low property qualification which generally prevailed. This, in turn, led to a demand for educational advantages and also to the trying of experiments which nowadays would arouse animadversions in most of our cities and towns. For example, the Boston town meeting voted the public money for the building of a " grainery " and the storing therein wheat and corn

---

[1] There is an interesting article on the New York aristocracy in *American Historical Review*, vi, 260.

when it was low in price with a view to its subsequent sale in small quantities at cost to the poorer classes.

In New England, education at public expense was well established before the middle of the seventeenth century. Every town in Massachusetts and Connecticut [1] was obliged to provide a school where children could learn to read and write, and the larger towns must also provide facilities for fitting boys for the " University." These schools were not comparable to the primary and grammar schools of the present day; but they were creditable institutions for their time and place. The townspeople often clung to the bare requirements of the law, and sometimes delinquent towns were presented by the grand jury for not complying with the law at all.[2] The word "free" did not necessarily imply that the parents were not to pay toward their children's education when they could, but only that no class was debarred from the town school.[3] The teachers were approved by the ministers of the neighborhood [4] and their salaries were fair for the epoch. Sometimes the parents were discontented with the opportunities placed before their children. The Boston town records, under date of 1711, contain a memorial complaining of the

[1] Although there was no public school system in Rhode Island until after 1760, there were many private and semi-private schools in that colony. See T. W. Higginson's *History of the Public School System of Rhode Island;* Fuller's *History of Warwick*, 143; Staples's *Annals of Providence*, 492. Burnaby (*Travels through North America*, ed. 1775, p. 118) states that there was a Jewish school at Newport in 1759.

[2] *Early Records of Lancaster*, 172.

[3] In Sandwich, Massachusetts (1713), all parents paid for the instruction of their children in reading, writing, arithmetic, Latin, and Greek, according to the subject taught. Freeman's *History of Cape Cod*, ii, 89.

[4] *Massachusetts Province Laws*, i, 470, 1701. Teachers in private schools were to be approved by selectmen. *Ibid.*, i, 681, 1711. It must be remembered that education was then everywhere closely connected with religion: in the royal provinces, the instructions to the governors usually provided that no one should be allowed to teach who was not a member of the Established Church. See, for instance, Instructions to Burrington of North Carolina in 1730 (*Colonial Records*, iii, p. 111). In those colonies where the church was established by law, acts of assembly frequently prescribed the same condition. See an example in Bacon's *Laws of Maryland*, 1723, ch. xix, § 8.

time spent in the study of Latin and Greek, which "hath proved of very Little, or no benefit as to their after Accomplishment," [1] they therefore pray that some "more easie and delightfull methodes" be put in practice for the training of those who are not "designed for Schollars." This request was referred to the "inspectors" and that seems to have been the end of it. The townspeople also once in a while questioned the competency of a master. In 1734 the writing masters in the town were requested to present some of their own performances in writing at the next general town meeting for the inspection of the voters. An approach was made in colonial days to the manual training of more recent times by the establishment of a "spinning school," primarily for the training of poor children ; but any parents might send their children to these classes upon the payment of a small fee. The experiment did not work very well in practice and was soon abandoned, but the fact that it was made is noteworthy as giving added proof that the townspeople were interested in general educational matters as increasing the efficiency of the individual and not necessarily as giving him book learning which would fit him for the study of theology.

There are many references in the law books to "free schools" in the other colonies. There were schools attached to the Dutch churches in New York, but in the Middle Colonies the great diversity in religious beliefs prevented the establishment of any general school system. Pennsylvania parents were directed by law to teach their children to read and write under penalty of five pounds, and there were several schools in Philadelphia and other towns. The most notable of these was the Penn Charter School, which

---

[1] *Boston Town Records*, iii, 78 (Boston City Document, No. 137, 1711).

was founded by public money in 1697.[1] In Maryland the law required the establishment of a school in each county; but the fact that the teacher must belong to the Established Church damped public interest, since most of the inhabitants were dissenters; but some schools were established.[2] Many Virginians left money for the founding of schools, but the dispersed condition of the plantations prevented the children resorting to any one place for instruction. Otherwise there would doubtless have been a school in each parish or county; and as it was, there were a dozen free public schools in the Old Dominion in 1724 and probably twice as many private ones.[3] The richer planters provided private tutors for their own children, who were often joined by others from the neighborhood and by relatives from a distance. Efforts were made to establish free schools in the Carolinas, but these did not produce any large results in colonial times.[4] Considering the condition of life in frontier communities and the large number of immigrants, it is surprising how many colonists could read and write, especially outside of the servile classes.

The colonies north of Carolina, with the exception of Maryland, Rhode Island, and New Hampshire, already (1760)

[1] Sharpless, *Quaker Government*, i, 37; *Minutes of the Council*, i, 531; Gabriel Thomas's *An Historical and Geographical Account of Pensilvania and West-New-Jersey*, 40; *History of Chester County*, 302.

[2] Bacon's *Laws of Maryland*, 1696, ch. xvii; 1723, ch. xix; 1728, ch. viii. Education was also retarded in North Carolina for the same reason; as late as 1769 Governor Tryon vetoed a bill for establishing a school because it did not require the schoolmaster to belong to the Established Church. *Colonial Records of North Carolina*, viii, 6; see also *ibid.*, v, pp. xviii, xxv.

[3] W. S. Perry's *Protestant Church in Virginia*, 261–318.

[4] Mayor Courtenay (*Charleston Year-Book*, 1880, p. 255) states that the Venerable Society established a school at Charleston in 1711; later (*ibid.*, 1886, 173) he gives 1710 as the date of the establishment of a free school in Charleston. The church school was probably the one referred to by Dalcho (*Episcopal Church in South-Carolina*, p. 93). See also McCrady's "Education in South Carolina" in South Carolina Historical Society's *Collections*, iv, and the same author's *South Carolina under the Proprietary Government*, 701. The school acts are in Cooper's *Statutes of South Carolina*, ii, 342, 376, 389.

contained, each of them, an institution of collegiate rank. Apart from the "Academy" at Philadelphia, these were designed primarily for the education of ecclesiastics. The oldest was Harvard,[1] which had been founded in 1636, six years after the coming of the Puritans to Boston. The next in point of time was William and Mary[2] in Virginia, which was chartered by the monarchs whose names it bears. Its founder was James Blair, who went to England in 1691 and succeeded in procuring an act of incorporation and funds.[3] The province also contributed public money, and individuals in Virginia made liberal subscriptions. As is still the case with some American collegiate institutions, the new establishment contained a preparatory department which flourished out of all proportion to the other parts of the college. William and Mary College resembled an English public school of the type of Rugby or Eton and performed a useful service in facilitating the education of the sons of all but the richest planters.[4] Students who enjoyed

---

[1] Quincy's *History of Harvard University* (2 vols., 1840). W. R. Thayer's article in *The History of Middlesex County* (i, 77) is brief, well arranged, and satisfying.

[2] There is much material relating to the founding and early history of William and Mary College in the *Quarterly* published by that institution under the able editorship of its president, Lyon G. Tyler, who has briefly related the story of the institution in chapter iii of his *Williamsburg*. See also *Virginia Magazine of History*; Hening's *Statutes*; American Historical Association's *Reports*, iv, Part iv. A somewhat meager account with a bibliography was printed by the United States Bureau of Education in 1887. Hening (*Statutes*, ii, 30) states that a petition for the establishment of a college was formulated in 1660-61.

[3] Franklin relates that when Attorney-General Seymour objected to the

giving of money for this purpose, Blair declared that Virginians "had souls to be saved as well as the people of England," to which Seymour replied: "Souls! Damn your souls! Make tobacco!" — but Franklin was fond of a good story. Sparks's *Works of Benjamin Franklin*, x, 111.

[4] Isaac Weld, an English traveler, who dined with the president of William and Mary in 1797, states that "half a dozen or more of the students, the eldest about twelve years old, dined at his [the president's] table one day that I was there; some were without shoes or stockings, others without coats. . . . A couple of dishes of salted meat, and some oyster soup, formed the whole of the dinner." *Travels through North America*, 96. Of Princeton, he writes (*ibid.*, 149) that the students "from their appearance, however, and the course of studies they seem to be engaged in, like all the other American colleges I ever

free tuition and maintenance were bred for the ministry of the Established Church to which all the teachers were required to belong. There were also always several Indian students in the college who were supported by funds left in trust by the English scientific man, Robert Boyle. Blair found it easier to obtain grants of public funds and private subscriptions than it was to collect the money.[1] He had difficulties with successive governors, — Andros, Nicholson, and Spotswood, and in each case secured the removal of his opponent. Although the results were by no means commensurate with the effort, Blair's name must always be held in grateful remembrance by all chroniclers of education in America.

Many Virginians, before and after the founding of William and Mary, may fairly be described as cultured gentlemen. Of them Colonel William Byrd is the best known. He was the second of that name in American history and inherited the great estate which his father had accumulated, not always with entire credit. The younger man was educated in England and traveled on the Continent before his return to Virginia in the early years of the eighteenth century. His house at Westover was one of the finest in the province. In his library were over three thousand volumes, of which seven hundred were on historical subjects, nearly five hundred on scientific themes, and over six hundred on the classics.[2] It

---

saw, it better deserves the title of a grammar school than a college."

[1] The president, masters, and students were exempted from the payment of taxes, and the proceeds of duties on hides and skins exported were given to the college. See entries in Hening's *Statutes*. The teachers and students at Yale College were likewise exempted from taxation, *Connecticut Records*, viii, 131.

[2] On libraries in Virginia, see *William and Mary Quarterly*, ii, 169, 247. One is sometimes surprised at the number and size of colonial libraries. For instance, the printed catalogue of the library of the Rev. Samuel Lee, which was offered for sale at Boston in 1693, contains about one thousand titles, of which not more than eight were books printed in America, Massachusetts His-

was as an author, however, that he won fame. His *History of the Dividing Line, Progress to the Mines*, and *Journey to the Land of Eden*, describing the life and manners in Virginia in the first half of the eighteenth century, are valuable historical material and give their author a place in American literature. Parts of them, as well as of his letters, are often too coarse for modern print, but they are typical of their time.[1]

The next collegiate establishment to be founded was the institution which, after a few years of itinerancy, was in 1716 finally located most appropriately at New Haven, for the leaders of that settlement ever since 1647 had agitated the founding of a college in their town.[2] It took its name from Elihu Yale, a native of Massachusetts, who had acquired riches in India, and was then residing in England.[3] Cotton Mather, embittered by the treatment of his father and himself by Harvard College, wrote to Elihu Yale that the new institution might be called for him Yale College, if he would make it a grant of money, and so it fell out. The growing liberality of Harvard College was one of the causes for the establishment of the Connecticut college ; but the increasing population and wealth of that colony powerfully contributed to that end.[4] The ruling body of Yale was composed entirely of clergymen ; at its meetings, besides strictly college business,

torical Society's *Proceedings*, 1896, p. 340. S. B. Weeks gives facts as to libraries and literature in North Carolina in American Historical Association's *Reports* for 1895, 169.

[1] An excellent edition of William Byrd's writings in one volume was published at New York in 1901, with notes and a memoir by Professor John Spencer Bassett. The inventory of his library forms Appendix A of this publication.

[2] *New Haven Colony Records*, ii, 141, 370.

[3] Some interesting facts in Elihu Yale's career are set forth in Bernard C. Steiner's "Two New England Rulers of Madras" in the *South Atlantic Quarterly* for July, 1902 (also issued separately). On the raising of money in England, see *Publications* of the Colonial Society of Massachusetts for 1899, p. 177.

[4] Williston Walker in *Yale Review* for May, 1892, p. 79.

religious measures were concerted which were later carried into effect by ecclesiastical councils and the legislature of the colony.   Curiously enough, one of the first presidents of Yale became an Episcopalian, which led to the adoption of a rule that no one impregnated with " prelatical corruption " should, in the future, have anything to do with the government of the college.   After 1707, for one hundred years, all officers of the college were obliged to consent to the confession of faith as stated in the Saybrook Platform.[1]

Six other collegiate institutions were established in the colonies before the beginning of the Revolutionary War. Of these, the colleges at Princeton, New York, Providence, and New Brunswick in New Jersey were primarily for the education of prospective ministers;[2] Dartmouth college at Hanover, New Hampshire, was designed mainly for the training of Indians to be missionaries of the faith to their tribesmen;[3] alone the "Academy" at Philadelphia represented the "higher education" in its wider aspect.

Apart from theological differences, all these collegiate institutions, excepting William and Mary and the "Academy" at Philadelphia, were carried on in the same way, and the life in them was practically similar.   Harvard College may be taken as a type, since its records have been largely printed.   The age of students at admission was low, boys of eleven to fourteen frequently being admitted; but on the other hand there were always some old freshmen,

[1] Bernard C. Steiner's *History of Education in Connecticut*, 74. On the founding and early history of Yale, see Clap's *History of Yale College*.

[2] On the general subject see Charles F. Thwing's *History of the Higher Education in America*. For particular colleges see John Maclean's *History of the College of New Jersey* and J. De Witt's chapter in the *Memorial Book of the Sesquicentennial of Princeton*, p. 317; Moore's *Historical Sketch of Columbia College* and Beardsley's *Life and Correspondence of Samuel Johnson*; Guild's *History of Brown University*.

[3] F. Chase's *History of Dartmouth College*.

even as old as thirty years. Until 1773 classes at Harvard were "placed" according to the rank of the student's family. This was a delicate operation and often led to serious complaints. The students not only were ranked in their classes according to their social eminence, or lack of it, but also sat at Commons in the same order and were sometimes punished by being degraded four or five numbers or even placed at the foot of the list. The admission examinations were very different from the modern system: in 1751, when John Adams applied for admission, he was placed in a study with paper, pen and ink, a Latin dictionary, and a grammar, and told to translate a bit of English into Latin, taking as much time as he pleased; he also wrote out the rules of the college in his own hand. The studies were almost entirely classical, each class being placed in charge of a tutor who heard recitations in all branches. The text-books were venerable in age and forbidding in appearance, like Burgersdicius's *Logic*, Heereboord's *Meletemata*, and Wollebius's *Divinity*. The students also recited in mathematics and astronomy and were carefully trained in rhetoric and elocution by means of frequent "disputations." Some attempt was made at scientific training, but it was very rude at best. It was not until 1766 at Harvard that the tutors were placed in charge of separate branches of instruction. In the earlier years whipping had been the principal means of discipline, but in 1734 fines were substituted. The list is rather interesting as showing the academic appraisal of crimes: absence from prayers cost the culprit twopence, but "going on skating" cost one shilling; absence from recitation, gambling, lying, drunkenness, and many other transgressions were rated at one shilling sixpence, but profane cursing or firing off a gun within the college pre-

cincts cost two shillings sixpence.   Where so much attention was paid to social distinction, it was quite natural
that dress should be strictly regulated.   We find, therefore, that in 1754 every candidate for a degree must
appear at commencement in dark clothes, and that no
one should wear "any silk night-gowns" on that occasion.
The students were to attend morning and evening prayers,
which were conducted by the president, and also services
on the Lord's day, and were strictly charged to be of good
behavior on these occasions.

The "Academy" at Philadelphia had a very different
origin in that its establishment was due mainly to Benjamin Franklin, whose religion was somewhat noticeable
for its modernity; he and his fellow-trustees even proposed to secure the services of an Episcopalian as the
first head of their institution.   Franklin also desired to
broaden the curriculum by placing the study of the English language and of those which he termed the dead
languages on a footing of equality and to have science
given a prominent place.   The traditions of scholars were
too fixed for even Franklin to make head against them ;
but the "Academy" at Philadelphia was the first American
institution in which any marked attention was paid to
these subjects which now occupy so prominent a place.
It was opened in 1749 and attracted students from the
beginning.[1]   It had its vicissitudes and did not fully come
up to Franklin's desire, but it certainly went a good way
toward the realization of his wishes and in time became
the University of Pennsylvania.[2]

[1] On the founding of the University
of Pennsylvania, see a paper by George
B. Wood in the third volume of the *Memoirs of the Historical Society of Pennsylvania.*   See also T. H. Montgomery's
History of the University of Pennsylva-
nia from its Foundation to A.D. 1770;
"Benjamin Franklin and the University
of Pennsylvania" in the Bureau of Education's *Circulars of Information,* 1892,
No. 2.

[2] Before 1760 professional training,

Another influence which affected most powerfully the mental and political development of the settlers was the increased facility of communication between the different parts of the several colonies and between the colonies themselves. The roads would not be regarded as good according to the notions of the present time, but they were passable for wheeled vehicles and a decided improvement over the Indian trails and horse tracks of the earlier day. In 1760, what might be described as a trunk road passed from Boston southward toward Providence and thence through the length of Connecticut to the city of New York. From the mainland opposite that place, another road ran to the Delaware, and from Philadelphia connections were made with Baltimore in Maryland which had been founded some years previously and was fast rising into a thriving commercial port. South of Baltimore there were no intercolonial roads on the seaboard. Indeed, the transportation of those Southern Colonies was almost entirely by water; this applied not only to travel within those colonies, but also between them. Inland from Philadelphia, a road passed westward and southward by York, Pennsylvania, and Frederic, Maryland, to the valley of Virginia, and thence southward to the "Upper Regions" of the Carolinas. Along this line of communication went large bands of emigrants in the thirty years before the outbreak of the Revolutionary War. Most of the transportation of goods from colony to colony was carried on by water in small vessels plying along the coast. To this fact was due the commercial importance of an island town like Newport, which in the exist-

other than in theology, was obtained by study in the office of an established lawyer or physician, but degrees in medicine or physic were conferred in Pennsylvania and New York before the outbreak of the Revolution.

ing modes of communication was as well fitted for the distribution of goods as a mainland town like Boston. The export trade of Philadelphia was largely in the products of the farms within a radius of forty or fifty miles from that town, which necessitated the construction of suitable roads for heavy wagons.

The establishment of the postal service in the colonies began with the settlement of Connecticut, because the relation of that colony to Massachusetts necessitated frequent communication. After the conquest of New Netherland the governors of New York were desirous of establishing a postal service to connect the outlying settlements with their headquarters, and the consolidation of all the Northern Colonies under Andros made such a system almost necessary. In 1692, when governor of Virginia, Andros established a postal service in the Old Dominion,[1] and Maryland followed in 1695.[2] By the end of the century, a system for carrying letters was in operation from Boston to Williamsburg, for Pennsylvania and New Jersey had already established systems of their own.

In 1710 Parliament passed an act for "establishing a General Post-Office for all Her Majesties Dominions."[3] This provided for a central post office and a postmaster general in London with chief letter offices in Edinburgh, Dublin, New York and other places in the plantations. The rates of postage are significant: a letter or packet weighing an ounce was charged four shillings from Lon-

---

[1] Bancroft's *United States* (author's Last Revision), ii, 18.

[2] Scharf's *Maryland*, i, 361.

[3] The post office in the modern sense of the word dates back in England to the Act of 12 Charles II, Cap. 35 (*Statutes of the Realm*, v, 297). The Act of 1710 is 9 Anne, Cap. 11 (*ibid.*, ix, 393, Cap. 10, of the ordinary editions); Chalmers (*Introduction*, i, 347) prints an extract from a letter from Spotswood to the Board of Trade, dated June, 1718, saying that the Virginians regarded the law of 1710 as a grievance because "Parliament could not lay any tax (*for so they call the rates of postage*) on them, without the consent of the general assembly."

don to New York, or the other way; from the West Indies to New York, or the other way; but from New York to any place within sixty English miles the rate was one shilling fourpence; while from New York to Boston or Annapolis the rate was the same as from New York to London. A peculiar feature of the law was that which provided that the mail should be carried across all ferries without charge. The office of deputy postmaster general in America was a valuable one not only for the salary which it brought in, but also because it gave the holder the first opportunity to get news of what was going on in other places.[1]

The connection between the post office and the newspapers was very intimate. In 1696 John Campbell came to Boston as postmaster. He used the advantages which his position gave him in the writing of newsletters that were sent to many persons in different parts of New England. As there were several printing-presses in Boston and in Cambridge, it soon occurred to Campbell to have his communications printed; the *News Letter*, which appeared in print at Boston on April 24, 1704, was the first regular newspaper to be issued in America. It bore the words, "Published by Authority" under its title, and, at the outset, received support from the government.

When printing was first introduced into England, the government encouraged the art, but before long the tendency of printing to emphasize facts to which the rulers in

[1] In 1755 a fortnightly service of "Pacquet-Boats" was established between London and New York (*Boston News Letter*, January 15, 1756). The rates remained the same from London to New York, but letters now were carried from London to all the continental colonies for the same sum: 1*sh.* for a "single letter," 4*sh.* for one ounce. See further on the history of the post office before 1710 Mary E. Woolley's article on the "Colonial Post Office" in Rhode Island Historical Society's *Publications*, i, No. 4; and see also Massachusetts Historical Society's *Collections*, Third Series, vii, 48.

Andrew Hamilton, deputy postmaster, stated that he received a salary of fifty pounds from New York, and a similar sum from Massachusetts. *Votes of Pennsylvania*, i, Part i, p. 101.

Church and State were hostile, became apparent. Then printing was strictly regulated by executive orders, which required the licensing of all but a few books before publication. This remained the policy of the English government and was recognized by Parliament in a succession of laws, the last of which expired by limitation in 1695.[1]

The earliest printing-press in America was set up in Mexico before the middle of the sixteenth century.[2] The Jesuit fathers on their ever memorable voyage to Maryland in 1633 may have brought a press with them, but no vestige of it or of its productions is known. The first press in the English colonies from which issued books that have survived to the present day was brought to Massachusetts in 1638,[3] owing in part to the fact that Archbishop Laud had made Puritan printing in England an extremely hazardous undertaking. The new press was directed by the presidents of Harvard College and was not likely to print anything unsuited to the ecclesiastical atmosphere of the Puritan commonwealth. It was not until 1665 that a private printing office was opened in the colony. At once the General Court established a board of censors and confined printing to the town of Cambridge. The licensers and the General Court did not always agree as to

---

[1] The Long Parliament continued the policy of the royal government, which led John Milton to write the "Areopagitica." In 1649 Gilbert Mabbott resigned his office of licenser with the statement that it should be lawful to print anything without previous license, provided the author's and printer's names were attached to it that they might be punished for publishing libellous matter. Gardiner's *History of England*, vii, 51, 130; viii, 225, 234; Gardiner's *Commonwealth and Protectorate*, i, 63, 194; Masson's *Life of John Milton*, iv, 118; Duniway's *Freedom of the Press*, pp. 1–16. For contemporary French practice, see G. B. Depping's *Correspondance Administrative Sous Louis XIV* (Paris, 1851), ii, 724–727, 861.

[2] See Winship's "Earliest American Imprints" in *American Book-Lore* for July, 1899, and in Massachusetts Historical Society's *Proceedings*, xii, 395.

[3] The history of printing in the Bay Colony is admirably set forth in George E. Littlefield's *The Early Massachusetts Press, 1638–1711* (2 vols., Boston, 1907), and in S. A. Green's article on the "Early History of Printing in New England" in Massachusetts Historical Society's *Proceedings*, Second Series, xi, 240.

what was desirable; in 1669, the latter stopped the printing of "a booke, that Imitations of Christ, or to that purpose, written by Thomas à Kempis, a Popish minister," [1]
although it had been licensed by the board of censors. In
1674 printing was permitted at Boston as well as at Cambridge.

The overthrow of the Massachusetts Bay Company
placed the control of the press in the hands of the representatives of the crown; Randolph acted as licenser in
addition to his other duties. Andros when he became
governor of New England interfered actively with the
operation of the colonial printing-presses, as he was
obliged to do by his instructions.[2] The overthrow of the
Stuart domination brought no freedom to the press.[3]
This was not at first apparent to the colonists for, on
September 25, 1690, there appeared a three-paged double-
columned pamphlet, entitled "Publick Occurrances, both
Foreign and Domestick." [4] The Revolutionary government ordered it to be suppressed and directed that for the
future no person should set forth anything in print without
permission in writing first obtained. The commission given
to Sir William Phips and later royal governors substan-

---

[1] *Massachusetts Colony Records*, iv,
Part ii, p. 424.

[2] "And forasmuch as great inconveniencies may arise by the liberty of printing within our said territory under your
government, you are to provide by all
necessary orders that no person keep any
printing press for printing, nor that any
book, pamphlet or other matters whatsoever be printed without your especial
leave and license first obtained," *Publications of the Colonial Society of Massachusetts*, ii.

[3] *Andros Tracts*, iii, 107.

[4] The only known copy of this first
American newspaper is in the British
State Paper Office. It is reprinted in the
Historical Magazine, i, 228; see also
ibid., v, 90. The order for its suppression is in Massachusetts Historical Society's *Proceedings* (Second Series, viii,
54) and American Antiquarian Society's *Proceedings* for April, 1892.
There is a valuable article on early
broadsides by Nathaniel Paine in *ibid.*,
1899, p. 457. A broadside, entitled "The
Present State of the New-English Affairs," which was printed at Boston in
1689, is sometimes regarded as a newspaper; but it would appear to have been
rather in the nature of a governmental
statement of fact than a "newspaper."
Both of these are reproduced in S. A.
Green's *Ten Fac-simile Reproductions*
(Boston, 1903).

tially renewed the clause in Andros's instructions until
1730, when it was dropped. Similar instructions [1] were
given to the governors of the other royal provinces ; but
the colonial assemblies everywhere refused to attach any
penalty to disobedience of king and governor.

The first printing-press to be set up outside of Massachusetts [2] of which we have tangible information is that
which William Bradford established at Philadelphia, about
the year 1686.[3] Before long he became involved in trouble
with the authorities of the Quaker colony, owing to his
publishing a pamphlet by George Keith, once a Quaker
preacher, but now a schismatic.[4] On his way to Pennsylvania, Keith had visited New England to his physical dis-
comfort, and had there also gathered something of the
Puritan respect for the outward manifestations of Christian belief. Arrived at Philadelphia, he endeavored to
reform Quakerism, insisting that "there was too great a
slackness therein." He argued for stricter church organization, less attention to the spirituality of religion, and
more to its external form. In the furious flow of denun-
ciation [5] that followed it is difficult to ascertain the exact

[1] See that to Cornbury as governor of New Jersey in Smith's *New Jersey*, 259.

[2] Jefferson told Hening, according to Thomas (*History of Printing*, revised edition, i, 331), that John Buckner was placed under bonds in 1682 by Lord Culpeper, governor of Virginia, "not to print any thing hereafter, until his majesty's pleasure shall be known," and that the king, in 1683, directed Lord Howard of Effingham "to allow no person to use a printing press on any occasion whatsoever." No issue of Buckner's press is known, and printing is usually supposed to have been begun in Virginia by William Parks in 1727. "William Nuthead at the City of St. Maries" is the imprint on "The Declaration of the Reasons and Motives for the Present Appearing in Arms of their Majesties

Protestant Subjects in the Province of Maryland," which was licensed by "J. F." on November 28, 1689. The only extant copies also have the words "Reprinted in London" on the title page. See Thomas's *History of Printing*, i, 320 note.

[3] C. R. Hildeburn's *The Issues of the Press in Pennsylvania* (the first volume covers the period 1685–1763).

[4] On this dispute see Proud's *Pennsylvania*, i, 363, 365 note; Sharpless's *Quaker Government*, i, 79, 81; *Pennsylvania Magazine of History*, xxvii, 283.

[5] Thomas Lloyd, the scholarly first President of Pennsylvania, denounced Keith as "being Crazie, turbulent, a decryer of magistracie, and a notorious evill Instrument in Church and state,"

truth. The major part of the Friends in Pennsylvania adhered to the doctrines of George Fox; but some eminent men, as Thomas Budd, Francis Rawle, and John Hart, espoused the Keithian cause. Twenty-eight of the "Foxians" drew up a "Testimony," in which they charged Keith with "publishing openly several times, that there were more doctrines of devils, and damnable heresies, among the Quakers, than in any profession among the Protestants." Calling his opponents "rotten Ranters" and "Muggletonians," he wrote a pamphlet which Bradford printed with the title of "An Appeal from the twenty-eight Judges [the signers of the 'Testimony'] to the Spirit of Truth." Keith charged his opponents with condemning him in their "spiritual court," and declared that they had deserted Quaker principles in commanding men to fight a band of pirates who had appeared in the Delaware.[1] Keith, Bradford, and MacComb, who had distributed copies, were indicted for publishing a seditious pamphlet vilifying magistrates and having a tendency to weaken the hands of authority. The only account of the trial which followed comes to us from Bradford. According to this statement, the presiding justice, Arthur Cook, must have learned his manners on the English bench, for he asked, "What bold, impudent, and confident men are these to stand thus confidently before the Court?" Bradford in reply claimed the rights of "every free born English subject"; to which Cook answered that if he had been in England, he would

---

Minutes of the Provincial Council of Pennsylvania, i, 366, 378. See also Pennypacker's "Germantown" in Pennsylvania-German Society's *Proceedings,* ix, 203; he gives a proclamation against Keith on p. 207.

[1] Proud's *Pennsylvania* i, 370, and Thomas's *History of Printing,* revised edition, i, 212, contain very different accounts of this whole affair. The latter is derived from Bradford's description in "New England Spirit of Persecution, transmitted to Pennsilvania." His selections are in quotation marks, but are not literal transcripts. See also Brodhead's *New York,* ii, 437.

have had his back lashed already. The magistrates declared that the act of Parliament, which required a printer to affix his name to every book published by him, was law in Pennsylvania, although that colony was not mentioned by name in the act nor had the law been reënacted in the colony. David Lloyd prosecuted for the government and laid down the general rule that the jury had to determine only the fact of the publication of the pamphlet by Bradford, the question whether it was a seditious publication or not was to be decided by the court. This was undoubtedly law in England at the time, and the further assertion that the jury were entitled to base a verdict on the evidence presented, or on their own knowledge, was also correct.[1] As part of the evidence, the prosecution offered the "chase" or frame containing the type from which the pamphlet was alleged to have been printed, but it was not brought into court nor proved to be Bradford's. It is related on tradition that it was shown to the jury in their room and that upon one of the jurymen accidentally pressing against it with his cane, the mass of type fell to the floor. The jurymen were out for forty-eight hours and then not agreeing upon the verdict, the judge ordered them to be kept without meat, drink, fire, or tobacco; but this treatment not bringing compliance with the court's wish, they were dismissed. The experience, however, was one which Bradford did not care to have repeated. Leaving his son in Philadelphia with a printing outfit, he himself transferred his own printing business to New York

[1] Lord Chief Justice Sir John Holt declared that to endeavor to possess the people with an ill opinion of the government is to publish a libel. (1704, Howell's *State Trials*, xiv, 1128.) Lord Chief Justice Raymond held that falsehood was not an essential feature of a libel and refused to admit evidence to prove the truth of the statement which was alleged to be libellous. (1731, *ibid.*, xvii, 625.) Lord Chief Justice Mansfield asserted that it rested with the court alone to determine whether the matter complained of was or was not libellous (Campbell's *Chief Justices*, ii, 478, Woodfall's case, 1770).

in 1693. There no one was likely to care whether he was
a Foxian or a Keithian, and there he was well received and
given encouragement.[1] George Keith somewhat justified
the suspicions of the Quakers, for he abandoned the
Society of Friends and reappeared in Philadelphia as a
clergyman of the Established Church and pioneer missionary of the Society for Propagating the Gospel in Foreign
Parts.

The earliest case of prosecution for libel in Massachusetts was that of Thomas Maule, December, 1695. He
was a Salem Quaker, who already had earned ten stripes
for stigmatizing the minister of that town, the Rev. John
Higginson, asserting that he "preached lies" and that his
sermons contained the "doctrine of devils." The name of
the book which got Maule into trouble at this time was
Truth held forth and maintained. As no printer would
set up the work at Boston, he had employed William Bradford to print it for him at New York ; but when copies appeared in Massachusetts, the Council and House of Representatives speedily took action, and an indictment was
brought against Maule for publishing a scandalous book as
well as for maintaining that there were as many errors in
the Bible as there were in his book. He appealed to the
jury with a skillful reference to the witchcraft persecution,
which had recently come to an ending, and was declared
not guilty. Upon this he published another work, entitled
New England's Persecutors Mauled with their own Weapons.[2]

Like all the early colonial newspapers, those of Boston
were colorless productions, but on August 17, 1721, James
Franklin, the elder brother of the greatest mental prodigy

<hr/>

[1] See C. R. Hildeburn's *Printers and
Printing in Colonial New York.*
[2] This case is carefully set forth from

the manuscript sources in Duniway's
Freedom of the Press in Massachusetts,
pp. 70–73.

ever produced in America, began the publication of the *New England Courant*. This sheet was edited by certain gentlemen, whom the Rev. Mather Byles denounced as "Profane Sons of Corah," "Children of the Old Serpent," and collectively as forming the "Hell-Fire Club of Boston." At first the writers in this paper directed their shafts against the theologians; it was not until they animadverted upon the motives of the governor and General Court that the authorities became alarmed at their language. In 1722, however, an article in the *Courant* insinuated that the government was not doing everything possible for the capture of a pirate who was then known to be hovering off the coast. It is not at all necessary to suppose that this charge had in it any element of truth, but colonial governments of that time were peculiarly sensitive to such allegations. The General Court now denounced the publication as a high affront and directed the sheriff to imprison James Franklin. After a week in durance, he confessed the "Inadvertency and Folly" of the publication, but was kept in prison for three weeks longer, in order further to drive the conviction home. However, he had not been at liberty a week when the *Courant* contained a poem satirizing the assembly. These events occurred in the administration of Governor Shute, who was distasteful to the Representatives on account of his actions concerning the salary question and for other reasons. His flight removed the one cause for dealing delicately with the publisher of the *Courant*. The next time that an article appeared in that paper denouncing religious hypocrites and giving ironical advice to the House of Representatives, James Franklin was forbidden to issue his *Courant* or anything of a like nature "Except it be first Supervised, by the Secretary of this Province." Disobeying, he was arrested on the charge of contempt of the General Court. The paper, however, went on appearing under the name of Benjamin Franklin, who was then an apprentice in his brother's office. The grand jury, when the matter came before it, refused to indict James Franklin for publishing without a license, and with this failure anything like the censorship of the press came to an end in Massachusetts.

The most famous libel case in colonial times, and one of the most famous in the history of English law, was that of John Peter Zenger in 1735.[1] He was a German who had come to America with the Palatines in 1710 and had learned the trade of printer with William Bradford. He had then gone to Maryland and not succeeding there had returned to New York and had begun the publication of a paper entitled *The New York Weekly Journal*, the first number of which appeared in 1733. The new publication was received with rejoicing by the opposition leaders in the colony, for the existing paper which was printed by Bradford was devoted to the interests of the government. Among the older politicians, or leaders in politics, was Rip Van Dam,[2] who a third of a century earlier had gone to prison with Nicholas Bayard and had ever since been prominent in the government. As senior councilor, he had been acting governor for thirteen months between the death of Governor John Montgomerie and the arrival of Governor William Cosby. A lively dispute at once arose between Van

---

[1] See *A Brief Narrative of the Case and Tryal of John Peter Zenger* (New York, 1738); *Remarks on the Trial of John-Peter Zenger* by "Indus Britannicus" (London); Peleg W. Chandler's *American Criminal Trials*, i, 151; Howell's *State Trials*, xviii, 675. Livingston Rutherfurd's *John Peter Zenger, his Press, his Trial* (New York, 1904) reprints the "Brief Narrative" and gives in addition all that is known of Zenger and his case.

Among the articles on Zenger and his trial may be mentioned that in *Pennsylvania Magazine of History*, xx, 405, and a notice of Hamilton in *ibid.*, xvi, p. 1.

[2] There is an excellent notice of his career in *New York Colonial Documents*, vi, 153 note.

Dam and Cosby as to the division of the emoluments which had accrued during the former's incumbency of that office. As they could come to no agreement, the matter was taken to the courts.   The feeling in the colony was distinctly against Cosby, who had aroused public indignation by speaking contemptuously of a gift of seven hundred and fifty pounds which the assembly had made him, soon after his arrival, for his efforts in behalf of the colony in England before his departure for his government.   He therefore decided to have the case tried before the judges sitting as a court of exchequer, where it would be decided without the intervention of a jury.   The question at once arose as to whether the governor had the right under his commission to establish such a court or to confer such an authority upon the existing judges.   The chief justice of New York at that time was Lewis Morris, who had held the office for some eighteen years acceptably to all concerned, but now he declared against the governor's right to confer this power and was dismissed from office.   He appealed to the public through the press and with others wrote several articles which were printed in Zenger's paper, and it was for this that Zenger ultimately found himself in court on the charge of publishing a false and scandalous libel.

The two leading lawyers in New York at that time were James Alexander and William Smith.   They had defended Rip Van Dam and had been disbarred by the new judges, De Lancey and Philipse, for their vigorous conduct.   The court had appointed a young man named Chambers to defend Zenger, but Morris and those who were really being prosecuted through him secured the services of Andrew Hamilton of Philadelphia.   Hamilton was a very able lawyer and an extraordinary man.   Born in Scotland, he had come to the colonies and settled in Virginia as a planter, had then moved to Maryland, and finally had come to Pennsylvania and taken up the practice of law.   Curiously enough, that Quaker colony from the beginning had been the abode of successful and vigorous legal practitioners, of whom it is only necessary to call to mind David Lloyd whose name has been so often mentioned in these pages. Hamilton had also performed many public services in his chosen city.   Now he was nearly eighty years of age and physically weakened, but his mind was fresh and vigorous. His coming into the case was kept secret until the moment of his appearance.   His standing in the profession, his age, and his great and deserved reputation made it impossible for the judges to refuse to hear him, as they had refused to hear Smith and Alexander. Hamilton at once admitted the fact of printing and publishing and said that that did not constitute a libel, for the words complained of must be false, scandalous, and seditious, or else the article was not libellous.   To this the attorney-general objected and endeavored to show that the words complained of were libellous.   Mr. Chambers then contended that it was incumbent on the government to prove that the words complained of were false, seditious, and scandalous.   Hamilton followed with a very long address, in which he sought to diminish the force of the attorney-general's argument by showing that the cases which he had relied on had been before that " terrible Court " of Star Chamber and had been adjudged in earlier days. The judges laid down the rule that it was for the court to decide whether a writing was libellous, and that it was not necessary for the government to prove the passages complained of to be false.   Hamilton then offered to prove by evidence that they were true and therefore not scandalous, but this was not permitted, for, to use the words of the chief justice, " a

Libel is not to be justified; for it is nevertheless a Libel that is true." Hamilton stated that he had never met with an authority saying that it was inadmissible to give evidence as to the truth upon an information for libel. But the judges would not change their ruling and informed him that he was not to be permitted to argue against the opinion of the court. They even assumed a somewhat threatening tone.

It was at this juncture that Hamilton turned to the jury for witness to the truth of the facts that he was not allowed to prove. They were from the neighborhood, and therefore knew of their own knowledge that the facts were true as stated ; moreover, he declared that it was a standing rule in law that the suppressing of evidence ought always to be taken for the strongest evidence. He then asked the attorney-general to define a libel, and, that having been done, enticed the chief justice into an argument in which De Lancey laid down the rule that " All Words are libellous, or not, as they are understood. Those who are to judge of the Words, must judge whether they are scandalous or ironical, tend to the Breach of the Peace, or are seditious : There can be no Doubt of it." Hamilton thanked the chief justice for his opinion and declared that it was for the jury to decide how the words should be understood ; and if they understood the words complained of by the attorney-general to be scandalous and false, then they should say that Zenger was guilty of publishing a false libel, and not otherwise. To this interpretation of the law or practice of the courts De Lancey at once objected ; but Hamilton went on to say that he knew it was so and made an impassioned appeal, citing historical facts and cases from the time of Tarquin and Brutus down to that of the " seven Bishops." The information presented by the attorney-general against

Zenger was one of those legal documents in involved phraseology which seems formidable to a layman.   To diminish the
weight of this, Hamilton paraphrased it by a text from
the fifty-sixth chapter of Isaiah : " His Watchmen are
all blind, they are ignorant, etc.   Yea, they are greedy
Dogs, that can never have enough."   This, he declared,
the attorney-general with his skill could turn into *" His
Watchmen* [*innuendo* the Governour's Council and Assem-
bly] *are blind, they are ignorant* [*innuendo*, will not see
the dangerous Designs of His Excellency] *Yea, they* [the
Governour and Council, meaning] *are greedy dogs, which
can never have enough* [*innuendo*, enough of Riches and
Power]."   By this sally he raised a laugh and seriously diminished the force of the attorney-general's efforts.   Hamilton closed in a different vein, stating that the case before
the jury was not that of a poor printer, nor of New York
alone, but might affect every freeman in the English
colonies.   It was the cause of liberty, and he made no
doubt but that the jury by their conduct would win the
love and esteem, not only of their fellow-citizens, but of
every man who prefers freedom to slavery.   By baffling
this attempt at tyranny, and by their uncorrupt verdict,
they would secure to posterity, " that, to which Nature
and the Laws of our Country have given us a Right, —
The Liberty — both of exposing and opposing arbitrary
Power (in these Parts of the World, at least) by speaking
and writing Truth."   After this exposition of the law it was
no use for the attorney-general to state that all the jury had
to do was to find that Zenger had printed and published
the journals as set forth in the information, nor for the
chief justice to try to diminish the weight of Hamilton's
remarks as to the conduct of judges in former times ; for
the jury retiring at once returned with the verdict of not

guilty, the announcement of which was followed by three huzzas in the court room.

It was in the decision of the Zenger case that an American jury broke away from what was then and for fifty-six years afterward the established rule in English courts, that it was for the judge to decide whether a publication complained of was or was not libellous, the jury being concerned only with the decision of the fact as to the printing and publishing. For America, the outcome of the Zenger case was of the utmost significance. Only eleven years before, in the trial of John Checkley at Boston,[1] the jury had brought in a verdict of guilty if the book in question " be a false and scandalous Libel. . . . But if the said Book . . . be not a false and scandalous Libel. Then we find him not guilty." Checkley's counsel sought to have his client acquitted on the ground that the jury should have found whether the book was libellous or not, but the judges decided the book to be libellous and the defendant guilty. After 1735 there were unjust libel suits,[2] and the example of the jury in the Zenger case was not always followed; but Gouverneur Morris was nevertheless correct when he said that the trial of Zenger was " the morning star of that liberty which subsequently revolutionized America."

The importance of this decision lay in the fact that the newspapers which were printed in the colonies after that time came to be the vehicle of instruction on the constitutional status of the American colonists and on the rights of the Americans as men in the light of the law of nature

[1] See Slafter's *John Checkley*, ii, 1–50 (Prince Society's Publications).

[2] One of the most interesting libel suits was that of Knowles *vs.* Douglass, which was repeatedly tried in Massachusetts courts in 1748 and 1749 and appealed to the King in Council, but apparently not decided. See John Noble's paper in Colonial Society of Massachusetts' *Publications*, iii, 213.

and of theory. These articles were written by the ablest politicians and literary men of the day in America. The discussions which constantly took place in assemblies, town meetings, and committees were also published in the newspapers. They kept alive and directed the forces of liberty and finally brought about the inevitable separation from the mother country sooner than it would otherwise have occurred. Had the newspaper press been muzzled, it is possible that the Declaration of Independence might have been written, but it certainly would not have been adopted by a Continental Congress in the year 1776, or, in all probability, for many years thereafter.

NOTE

The Salem Witchcraft Delusion. — Upham's *Salem Witchcraft* (2 vols., 1867) is the standard work on this theme; but this author's views are so strong that it is well to read the evidence copied from the originals in W. E. Woodward's *Records of Salem Witchcraft* (2 vols., Roxbury, 1864). See also some interesting papers noted in Massachusetts Historical Society's *Proceedings* for 1867, p. 163, and *ibid.*, Second Series, i, 339. Other matter is listed in Winsor's "Literature of Witchcraft in New England" in American Antiquarian Society's *Proceedings*, 1895, p. 351, and Moore's bibliography of the subject in *ibid.*, 1888, p. 245. There is an exceedingly interesting series of papers by George F. Chever in the "Historical Collections of the Essex Institute," i, 162; ii, 21, 73, 133, 185, 237, 261; iii, 17, 67, 111, and the succeeding volumes of the same series contain much that is valuable on this episode. There is a long discussion between G. H. Moore and A. C. Goodell in the *Proceedings* of the Massachusetts Historical Society, First Series, xx, 280; Second Series, i, 65, 77, and two letters by Peleg Chandler in *ibid.*, First Series, xx, 328, 395. These papers deal especially with the legality of the court and are supplied with abundant citations. Two interesting essays are S. A. Green's *Groton in the Witchcraft Times* and Henry Ferguson's paper in his *Essays in American History*.

CHAPTER XVII

COLONIAL INDUSTRY AND COMMERCE

THE year 1760, the date of the capitulation of Montreal and the surrender of Canada, marks the close of the colonial period and the beginning of the Revolutionary epoch. At that time there were one and one half million human beings living in the territory which in 1783 came to be known as the United States. The settlements extended in an almost unbroken line from Penobscot Bay to beyond the Altamaha River and inland into the valleys of the Appalachian Mountains; and the old French settlements west of the mountains now belonged to England. In comparison with the map of 1660 that of 1760[1] gives an impression of colonial maturity, and almost suggests the change which a few years would witness.

Of the million and a half colonists, 473,000 lived in New England, 405,000 in the Middle Colonies, or 878,000 north of Maryland; while in Maryland and the colonies to the southward there were 718,000 more. These totals include both whites and blacks. Subtracting the slave population,[2] it appears that there were 791,000 whites in the

---

[1] See the map at end of volume.

[2] In 1760 the total negro population was not far from 386,000, of whom 87,000 were in the colonies north of Maryland and 299,000 in Maryland and the colonies to the southward. The latter were distributed as shown in the following table: —

COLONY	TOTAL	WHITES	BLACKS
Maryland,	164,000	108,000	56,000
Virginia,	315,000	165,000	150,000
North Carolina,	130,000	110,000	20,000
South Carolina,	100,000	30,000	70,000
Georgia,	9,000	6,000	3,000
	718,000	419,000	299,000

North and 419,000 in the South, the northern boundary of Maryland being taken as the dividing line. If Maryland is regarded as belonging to the North, the totals are 1,042,000 for the North and 554,000 for the South. Again subtracting the slave population from the totals of each section, the white population of the North was 899,000 and that of the South 311,000 — almost exactly the proportion which prevailed one hundred years later between the states which seceded and those which remained in the Union.[1] About one third of the colonists in 1760 — white and black — were born outside of America.[2]

Agriculture was the chief employment of the colonists. The Middle Colonies produced wheat and corn in abundance and exported large quantities of flour and meal to the West Indies and also to New England. The New

The distribution of whites and blacks in the two Carolinas and in the Chesapeake Bay colonies seems puzzling at first, but is in strict accord with other facts than estimates of population. These estimates of the population of the colonies are based on the correlation of multitudinous figures taken from many sources. Franklin B. Dexter has brought together a mass of facts on this subject in American Antiquarian Society's *Proceedings*, New Series, v, 22.

[1] The total population of the North in 1760 was 1,042,000; in 1860, 18,000,000. The white population of the colonies south of the Potomac in 1760 was 311,000; the white population of the seceding states in 1860 was 5,500,000.

[2] In making this computation, reliance has been placed on the statements of Benjamin Franklin and Edward Wigglesworth. The former thought that when not molested by the enemy, the population doubled every twenty-five years " by natural generation only, exclusive of the accession of foreigners " (Franklin's *Works*, iv, 24). Wigglesworth states that it had doubled every twenty-five years, partly from the great accession of foreigners (*Calculations on American Population*, Boston, 1775, p. 1); thirty years has therefore been taken as the period for doubling by natural increase. It is interesting to note, in passing, that Wigglesworth prophesied that the population of the United States would reach the eighty million mark in 1900 — the census figures for that year were 76,000,000, excluding the island possessions.

Large families were the rule in colonial days. Governor Dongan mentioned a New York woman who had three hundred and sixty descendants living (*New York Colonial Documents*, iii, 391); and a Rhode Island matron could count a progeny of five hundred, of whom two hundred or so were living at the time of her death (Updike's *Narragansett Church*, 320). The mortality was also very great, whole families being carried off by smallpox and throat and lung disorders. Lawrence Hammond relates that down to 1689 when he made the entry he had had four wives, the last three being widows; the four had borne him eight children, of whom two only were then living (Massachusetts Historical Society's *Proceedings*, Second Series, vii, p. 150).

Englanders exported thousands of bushels of potatoes, turnips, and other roots to the sugar plantations, besides fish by the barrel and quintal. The Southern colonists fed themselves and exported tens of thousands of hogsheads and barrels of tobacco, rice, and indigo.

The preparation of agricultural products for the market sometimes consumed so much capital and labor that it may well be regarded as manufacturing. Tobacco, after being picked, was dried and otherwise cured, sorted into different grades, and packed for exportation; but the further manufacturing of it into smoking tobacco and snuff was carried on in England or the continental countries. Rice had to be cleaned, polished, and carefully packed in barrels for exportation. The indigo plants were placed in a vat and fermented with water under pressure. The resulting liquid went through two or three other processes before the coloring matter could be secured which was then pressed into cakes and dried for exportation. The making of naval stores demanded the gathering of the resinous matter of the Carolina yellow pine, boiling it, and subjecting it to a number of refining processes to produce the tar, pitch, and turpentine of commerce. In North Carolina twenty-six sawmills were established within twelve months for the shaping of logs for use in the colony and exportation to England. In the North the manufacture of wood was carried farther. Numerous small articles were produced for consumption at home as well as for exportation to the islands and, not infrequently, the frames of houses were prepared and sold to the sugar planters. Besides these activities which were incidental to agricultural pursuits and to the clearing of the land, there were many industries which would more strictly come within the meaning of the word "manufacture."

The preparation of coarse cloth for domestic uses was carried on in the household. In the North the women and children of the family combed the fleeces, spun the yarn, and sometimes wove the fabric which was often fulled and finished in mills, one of which was established at Watertown, Massachusetts, as early as 1662. In the South, cotton, wool, and flax were worked up into cloth by the household slaves and servants and, in the intervals of plantation work, by the outdoor employees. On a large plantation, one of the servants or slaves might be a weaver ; but there were many itinerant weavers in the South as well as shoemakers who went from county to county or from parish to parish, plying their trades at the different plantations. The shoe industry had been established in New England at an early date, especially at Lynn. It was customary for one man to provide leather and other materials which were worked up in the intervals of farm labor. Other household manufactures were the making of small articles of iron, such as nails, and the finishing of small wooden implements, spools, and bobbins. Even the children joined in these homely pursuits.

The manufacture of iron in Pennsylvania at one time bade fair to assume considerable proportions; but the hostility of English iron masters being aroused, Parliament (1750) by law prohibited the manufacture of iron in the plantations beyond the early stages.[1] This law put an end to the exportation of manufactured iron to Great Britain ; but the working up of the metal for domestic uses continued in the colonies. In New England, bog iron, or ore extracted from the mud of ponds, was made into anchors, chains, and fastenings for vessels which were built in that section. Altogether, from this brief survey

[1] 23 George II, Cap. 29 (Ruffhead's *Statutes at Large*, vii, 261).

it is evident that manufacturing was going on as a matter of daily life in the colonies, and that only lack of capital and labor prevented its extension.[1]

The imperial Parliament did a good deal toward promoting colonial industry by establishing a monopoly in the carrying trade of the empire and thus protecting the shipbuilding interests of the colonies as well as of England, and also by the payment of bounties and premiums on the production of rice, indigo, naval stores, and timber suited to the purposes of the royal navy. Chalmers[2] states that in the four years from 1713 to 1717 ninety thousand pounds were paid as premiums on naval stores. Colonial industries were also protected by the geographical situation of the colonies, for the transportation across the Atlantic and into the interior, for any distance from tide water, added very greatly to the price which must be charged on European goods. The colonists were in favor of what has since come to be known as "protection." As early as 1721 the Boston town meeting instructed the representatives of that town to promote the passage of legislation for the encouragement of the trade, husbandry, and manufacture of the province by providing premiums on the raising of wheat and flax and the manufacture of the latter, and by discouraging the purchase and use of French silks and stuffs.[3] The distillation of molasses into rum probably presents the nearest approach to modern systems of manufacturing then found in the colonies. This industry was carried on mainly in Philadelphia, New York, Newport, Boston, and Medford. The amount of rum

---

[1] A report to the Lords of Trade in 1728 stated that it cost fifty per cent more to manufacture silks, linen, and woolen goods in the colonies than in England, and that there was no available labor in America for any extensive manufacturing of these goods. "Board of Trade Papers," x, Nos. 103, 104.

[2] *Introduction to the Revolt*, i, 323.

[3] *Boston Town Records*, iii, 154, 156.

produced was very large.[1] It was consumed in the colonies, where it came to be regarded almost in the light of a necessity, in the fur trade with the Indians, and in the trade to the west coast of Africa, replacing Spanish and Portuguese wines and French brandy.

The small extent to which intensive manufacturing processes had been carried was due to the fact that the colonies were still frontier communities, that capital was limited, and that credit was only slightly developed. The colonists generally were indebted to English merchants and were desirous of trying new financial expedients in the hope that the weight of this indebtedness might be lessened. There was no scarcity of metallic money, but the volume of the currency was entirely inadequate for the needs of the settlers in the absence of banking facilities. The colonists sought to remedy these inconveniences by making commodities, as tobacco, wheat, corn, and cattle, legal tender, by the establishment of banks which should loan their credit on the basis of mortgages, and by the issuing of paper currency.

In Virginia almost from the beginning tobacco had been used in lieu of money. In 1730 the Virginia Assembly provided for the establishment of warehouses and for the inspection of tobacco stored therein. The inspectors were directed to issue transfer notes, which might be used in the satisfaction of debts, public and private, in the county or district where they were issued. This system was later more efficiently organized and improved by authorizing the issuing of " crop notes," which called for the delivery of certain hogsheads of tobacco instead of

[1] McPherson (*Annals of Commerce*, iii, 176) states that " there have been 20,000 hogsheads of French molasses manufactured into rum at Boston in one year," making 1,260,000 gallons of rum. This is on the authority of a tract which was written in 1731.

any tobacco of suitable grade in the warehouse. These notes passed from hand to hand, were good for a year or eighteen months, and formed a safe and convenient currency.[1] In Pennsylvania, at one time, wheat certificates[2] were also used. In New England the colonial legislatures, from time to time, authorized public dues to be satisfied by the payment of hemp, rye, pork, or other specified commodities at rates which were fixed in the law.[3] This was called country pay, and private debts were often contracted and satisfied by the tender of goods, as were the public levies.

The metallic currency of the colonies was not English guineas, crowns, shillings, and pence, because only small amounts of English coin ever found their way to America, owing to the balance of trade between Great Britain and the colonies being almost constantly in favor of the home country, and also because English law forbade the exportation of coins out of the realm; but the settlers nevertheless followed English nomenclature in making up their accounts and setting prices. The words "pounds," "shillings," and "pence" were applied to Spanish and Portuguese coins and not to English, and had different meanings in dif-

[1] In 1742 the laws relating to tobacco inspection were reduced to one enactment (Hening's *Statutes*, v, 124). This provides that all tobacco exported after November of that year must be inspected at a public warehouse. After the examination the inspector shall deliver to the person bringing the tobacco as many promissory notes as shall be required, "which notes shall, and are hereby declared to be current in all tobacco paiments whatsoever . . . within the county wherein such inspectors shall officiate and in any other county next adjacent thereto, and not separated therefrom by any of the great rivers or bay hereinafter mentioned" (*ibid.*, v, 132). See

also the act of 1748 in Hening, vi, 154; 1761 in *ibid.*, vii, 387. Early enactments are in *ibid.*, iv, 32, 247, 380, 478. On Virginia money problems see W. Z. Ripley's "Financial History of Virginia" in *Columbia University Studies*, iv, No. 1; W. L. Royal's "Virginia Colonial Money" in *Virginia Law Journal* for August, 1877.

[2] Pennsylvania *Statutes at Large*, ii, 225; iii, 86, 181.

[3] See, for example, *New Hampshire Provincial Papers*, vi, 151, where twenty commodities at fixed values can be tendered to the treasurer in payment of the year's tax levy.

ferent colonies. The Spanish piece of eight reals or ryals, usually termed the "piece of eight," was the metallic basis of the colonial monetary system. Unfortunately, these coins were minted at different places, contained somewhat different amounts of silver, and decreased in coin value as the century advanced. In 1728 the Spaniards began the coinage of the "milled dollar," which took the place of the old piece of eight and was adopted by Congress in 1786 as the basis of the United States coinage.[1] The subsidiary coins in the Spanish system were the half dollar, or four-real piece, the quarter dollar, or two-real piece, which was often called the pistareen, the eighth or one-real piece and the sixteenth and thirty-second. The gold coins were the Portuguese "johannes" or "joe," which was the equivalent of sixteen Spanish milled dollars, the half joe, and the quarter joe. Another Portuguese coin was the "moidore," which was equivalent to about six dollars, and there were Spanish and French pistoles, which were equivalent to something under four milled dollars.[2]

A further complication in the colonial monetary system is to be found in the fact that, while the words "pounds," "shillings," and "pence" were used, they were nowhere given the value of the English coins, and varied in the several

---

[1] W. G. Sumner's "The Massachusetts Coin Shilling" in *American Historical Review*, iii, 607; H. C. Lea's "Spanish Experiments in Coinage" in Appleton's *Popular Science Monthly* for September, 1897; Robert Chalmers's *History of Currency in the British Colonies* (pp. 4–18); R. Ruding's *Annals of the Coinage of Great Britain* (vol. ii); S. S. Crosby's *Early Coins of America.* Simon L. Adler's paper on "Money and Money Units in the American Colonies" in the *Publications* of the Rochester Historical Society gives an excellent, concise view of the subject.

[2] Maryland's delegates to the Stamp Act Congress of 1765 acknowledge the receipt of these gold coins in payment of their expenses and compensation : —

	£	s.	d.
409 Spanish pistoles at 27s.	532	3	—
5 half johannes at 57s. 6d.	14	7	6
4 French pistoles, 26s. 6d.	5	6	—
1 moidore,	2	3	6
1 half ditto,	1	1	9
	575	1	9

See *Authentic Account of the Stamp Act Congress*, p. 31.

groups of colonies. In 1652 Massachusetts had established a mint at Boston for the coinage of shillings, which were worth only about seventy-five per cent of the English shilling in the hope thereby that these "pine tree shillings" would remain in the colony. The piece of eight in the Massachusetts standard represented six shillings [1] instead of four shillings sixpence, which was its value in English shillings. The English government confirmed a Massachusetts law of 1697, thus perpetuating the Massachusetts rating for the piece of eight. In 1704 Queen Anne, in a proclamation, provided that the piece of eight should not pass in the colonies for more than six shillings, and this arrangement was ratified by Parliament [2] three years later — this being the origin of the phrase " proclamation " money, which is used so often in colonial laws.

Each colony had its own standard of value for the piece of eight: in New England and Virginia, it was six shillings; in South Carolina and Georgia, four shillings eightpence; in New York and North Carolina, eight shillings; in New Jersey, Maryland, Pennsylvania, and Delaware, seven shillings sixpence; and it may again be stated that the piece of eight was equivalent to four shillings sixpence in sterling money.[3] This variation extended, not only to the milled dollar or piece of eight, but also to its parts;

---

[1] *Massachusetts Province Laws*, i, 296.

[2] This act is given in different editions of the statutes as 6 Anne, Cap. 8, 9, 20, 30, 57. It is in the *Statutes of the Realm*, viii, 792; Cooper's *South Carolina Statutes*, ii, 563.

[3] Israel W. Andrews, in the *Magazine of Western History*, iv, 141, has expressed this matter with great clearness. Taking 100 as the value of the English pound sterling, the Georgia and South Carolina pound would be 90; the New England and Virginia pound, 75; the Pennsylvania, Maryland, New Jersey, and Delaware pound, 60; and the New York and North Carolina pound, 56¼. Jefferson's " Notes on the Establishment of a Money Unit and of a Coinage for the United States " in *Writings* (Ford's ed.), iii, 446, contains much useful information on this subject in a brief compass. Bullock's note on the depreciation of the colonial metallic currency in his edition of William Douglass's *Discourse Concerning the Currencies of the British Plantations* (p. 300) is an intelligible statement on a very difficult theme.

thus the "eighth" or ryal was a shilling in New York, ninepence in Virginia and Massachusetts, and eleven and one quarter pence in Pennsylvania where it was known as the "eleven penny bit," "levy," or "bit." This metallic currency was often badly clipped or reduced in weight by "sweating." [1]   All in all, commercial dealings and personal intercourse between the colonies were greatly hindered by the financial systems therein prevailing.

The first paper currency was issued by Massachusetts in 1690 to pay the expenses of the Quebec expedition of that year. A committee had actually been appointed to distribute the spoil of the Frenchmen when the expedition returned without any loot. There was no money in the provincial treasury wherewith to satisfy the just demands of the soldiers and sailors, and the Massachusetts government issued paper notes in payment of wages and supplies. These notes were to be received by the colony in payment of taxes and other public dues. They at once depreciated, but soon reached par again because the government that was established under the Province Charter accepted them at their face value plus five per cent. This was the origin of paper money in Massachusetts, in the American colonies, in the British Empire, and almost in the Christian world. From this beginning the use of paper money continued in Massachusetts. The temptation to anticipate taxes by the issue of notes was especially great because of the large expenditures that were incurred in successive French and Indian wars. The number of issues is bewildering to the modern student, as it was to those who handled them. In the fifty years after 1700 silver rose to a premium of eleven hundred per

---

[1] To sweat coins was to remove small particles of silver or gold by shaking a number of coins together in a bag.

cent.[1]   An influential faction in the colony and the government in England saw with dismay this overwhelming
torrent of paper money in Massachusetts and other colonies.   The capture of Louisbourg[2] by Massachusetts, in
1745, almost unaided by the English government, and its
subsequent restoration to France by the Treaty of Aix-la-
Chapelle, furnished an opportunity for the imperial authorities and the friends of sound money in the colony to
bring about the resumption of specie payment.   Parliament voted one hundred and seventy-five thousand pounds
sterling for this purpose.   It was brought to Boston in
silver and copper coins and used to redeem the colonial
paper at the rate of seven and one half for one.   The operation was carried out with singular wisdom and success.
There was, inevitably, some inconvenience, but values soon
righted themselves.[3]   In 1751, by another act,[4] Parliament
forbade the issue of paper money in the New England colonies except for certain stated objects ; but these exceptions
were sufficiently broad to cover the flotation of paper money
in time of war and often even in time of peace.

South Carolina, at the other end of the slender line of
English continental colonies, soon followed in the footsteps
of Massachusetts in issuing bills of credit ; for as New England was exposed to peril from the French and Indians

---

[1] Thomas Hutchinson graphically describes the beginning of paper money
in his *History of Massachusetts* (3d ed.,
i, 357).   The history of later issues is
related by Andrew McFarland Davis in
his *Currency and Banking in Massachusetts*, and in many papers read before
the Massachusetts Historical Society,
the American Antiquarian Society, and
the Colonial Society of Massachusetts.

[2] See the present work, p. 547.

[3] Alexander Del Mar, in his *History of
Money in America* (p. 83), makes the
extraordinary statement concerning this

resumption : " The effect was frightful.
Ruin stalked in every home ; the people
could not pay their taxes; and were
obliged to see their property seized by
the sheriff," etc.   Del Mar probably
referred to a later time, but the picture
is overdrawn.   The best account of
this transaction is in Davis's *Currency
and Banking*, i, 203, 252.

[4] 24 George II, Cap. 53 (Ruffhead's
Statutes at Large, vii, 403).   It is said
that this act was passed at the instance
of the hard money men in Massachusetts ;
but the evidence is vague.

of Canada, so southern Carolina was likewise constantly threatened by the Spaniards and their Indian allies in Florida.   The first bills issued by South Carolina were put forth in 1702[1] to pay the expense of an expedition against the Spaniards.   These were only six thousand pounds in amount, bore interest at the rate of twelve per centum per annum, and were made legal tender in payment of private debts.   Other small issues were made in 1706 and 1707. The first large issue of paper currency in South Carolina was in 1712, when fifty-two thousand pounds of so-called " bank bills " were issued.[2]   These were given in exchange for securities based on lands and crops.   They bore interest, one twelfth part was to be repaid annually, and they might be tendered in payment of debts.   The Yamassee War led to new issues and they, in turn, to the inevitable depreciation, until in 1722 the bank bills were rated by law at four for one in silver.[3]

Massachusetts and South Carolina had some excuse for their dalliance with paper money; but Rhode Island[4] issued paper money as a political speculation.   It issued over half a million pounds to private individuals in proportion to their political influence.   The bills found their way into Massachusetts and interfered with the restoration of credit in that colony.   The depreciation of the Rhode Island bills is almost incredible.   In 1752 the legislature enacted that one Spanish milled dollar should pass for fifty-six shillings in " old tenor " bills of credit,[5] which

[1] Brevard's *Digest of Statute Law of South Carolina*, i, xi; Cooper's *South Carolina Statutes at Large*, in the " Notes " at the end of the second volume (pp. 708–713), has a concise essay on the monetary system of South Carolina, including the passages from Brevard's " Introduction," which are noted above.

[2] Cooper's *Statutes of South Carolina*, ii, 389.

[3] *Ibid.*, iii, 174.

[4] See E. R. Potter's " Paper Money in Rhode Island," extended and illustrated by Sidney S. Rider in *Rhode Island Historical Tracts*, First Series, No. 8.

[5] *Acts and Laws of Rhode Island, from 1745 to 1752*, p. 105; *Acts and Laws of Rhode Island* (ed. 1767), p. 168.

amount ten years later was raised to one hundred and forty shillings.   Ezra Stiles, later President of Yale College, was minister at Newport in 1760.   With a diarist's minuteness he sets down his "incomes" for the year ending October 22, 1760, at twenty-three hundred pounds Rhode Island currency, or ninety pounds sterling, the exchange being given at twenty-six for one, which rose to thirty-two for one in 1762.[1]

Pennsylvania issued paper money as a matter of economic policy, which was advocated by so shrewd and successful a business man as Benjamin Franklin.[2]   He lays down the general proposition that "There is a certain proportionate quantity of money requisite to carry on the trade of a country freely and currently ; more than which would be of no advantage in trade, and less, if much less, exceedingly detrimental to it."   From this proposition, to which there is necessarily agreement, Franklin argues that bullion and land are valuable by so much labor as it costs to procure that bullion or land, and currency has an additional value in proportion to the time and labor that it saves in the exchange of commodities.   He sets aside all objections drawn from the depreciation of the paper money of New England and South Carolina, with the remark that this is nothing to the purpose unless it can be shown that their currency was emitted with the same prudence and on as good security as that which he advocated.   Pennsylvania had already issued paper money ; in 1723 the Assembly had authorized the emission of £15,000 in paper bills,[3] to be loaned

[1] At the darkest hour of the Civil War exchange was a little under three for one.

[2] *A Modest Inquiry into the Nature and Necessity of a Paper Currency.* This was printed anonymously in 1729, when Franklin was in his twenty-third year. He at once acknowledged the authorship and received the job of printing the paper currency which was issued in the later part of that year.

[3] *Statutes at Large of Pennsylvania,* iii, 324.

on security of land or silver, and bearing interest at the
rate of five per cent.   The interest and one eighth of the
principal were to be paid.annually.   This experiment met
with such favor that later in the same year the Assembly
authorized the issue of £30,000 more on the same terms.[1]
From this beginning, Pennsylvania slowly followed the lead
of the other colonies: in 1729 another issue of £30,000 was
authorized, to be redeemed in sixteen years [2] instead of in
eight ; in 1731 irredeemable bills were issued and many
bills that came back to the loan office were again
emitted instead of being destroyed.   Nevertheless Pennsylvania acted in a conservative and cautious way compared
with some colonies and paper money cannot be said to have
worked evil in her case.[3]   Other colonies [4] issued paper
currency, and the exchange of commodities between the
colonies was hampered by these varying standards and
scales of depreciation.

Besides the financial expedients that have just been described, the colonies experimented with banks, both public
and private.   The most interesting of these were the land
banks, which were not unlike the mortgage investment
companies of 1880.   The objection to both was very

[1] Statutes at Large of Pennsylvania,
iii, 389.

[2] Ibid., iv, 98.

[3] See articles by C. W. Macfarlane in
Annals of American Academy of Political Science, viii, 50; Henry Phillips's
An Historical Sketch of the Paper
Money issued by Pennsylvania (Philadelphia, 1862, 40 pp.), also in the first
volume of his larger work. Any one
convicted of counterfeiting in Pennsylvania in 1767 was punished with death,
and any one tendering counterfeit coin
was to stand in the pillory with his or
her ears nailed for the space of one hour,
then have the ears cut off, be publicly
whipped on his or her bare back with
twenty-one lashes well laid on, and for-

feit the sum of one hundred pounds lawful money (Statutes at Large of Pennsylvania, vii, 91, 103).

[4] See Henry Phillips's Paper Currency of the American Colonies. John
Wright's American Negotiator or the Various Currencies of the British Colonies
reduced into English Money (third edition, London, 1767) is a very useful book.
C. J. Bullock in his Monetary History of
the United States goes over the whole
subject of colonial currency and treats
at length the financial history of North
Carolina and New Hampshire. For the
former of these colonies see also Colonial Records of North Carolina, ii, p. v;
v, pp. xxii, 419; viii, 211.

nearly the same ; namely, the individual holder of the note or security of the land bank or the mortgage company had no lien on any particular piece of land or mortgage. In the case of the public loan offices of Pennsylvania, South Carolina, and Rhode Island, the credit of the colony came to the aid of the investor. The most notable private land bank was the one which was established in Massachusetts in 1740.[1] This bank issued its own notes in exchange for mortgages and promised to repay the notes in goods at the end of twenty years ; those who received notes for mortgages agreed to receive the notes of the bank in payment of debts due to themselves. The institution started out with vigor and the plan seemed so promising that the formation of county banks on a similar basis was proposed and perhaps begun. Capitalists, merchants, and many political leaders objected to the establishment of this institution. The governor, Jonathan Belcher, a native of the province, threatened dismissal to all officials who aided or abetted the enterprise. The opponents of the bank petitioned Parliament, which responded by passing a law declaring the so-called " Bubble Act "[2] of 1720 " did, do, and shall extend," be in force, and be executed in the colonies.[3] The participators in the Massachusetts land bank had done nothing illegal nor were they strictly within the category of offenders mentioned in the Bubble Act. The threat of Parliamentary intervention, however, was enough ; the whole scheme collapsed, bringing ruin to many who had taken part in it, among others to the father of Samuel Adams of Revolutionary fame.

[1] Davis's *Currency and Banking in Massachusetts*, vol. ii. A good deal of this matter was previously printed in the publications of the American Antiquarian Society and other learned associations.

[2] 6 George I, Cap. 18, §§ 16–29 (Ruffhead's *Statutes at Large*, v, 308).

[3] 14 George II, Cap. 37 (Ruffhead's *Statutes at Large*, vi, 430).

Besides all these forms of money there were other obligations, such as merchants' notes and bills of exchange. Merchants' notes were simply promises to pay, issued by merchants in good standing and were negotiable, but seldom were used as currency properly so-called; that is to say, they passed through few hands. From time to time, the temptation to issue notes of this character, based upon private credit, was made use of by associations of merchants or capitalists, as was the case in New Hampshire, where leading men associated and secured an act of the New Hampshire legislature to permit the carrying out of their scheme. In this case the design was to use these notes in Massachusetts; but this was promptly stopped by a prohibitory act of Massachusetts and the subsequent disallowance of the New Hampshire law by the king. The public loan offices were in reality state banks issuing notes in exchange for mortgages and guaranteeing the payment of the notes at certain specified times, and often accepting the notes for public dues and sometimes even making them legal tender in the settlement of private debts. In a colony like Pennsylvania, where the loan office and paper money issues were managed in a conservative way, the public banking enterprises were beneficial; but in most colonies they were far otherwise.

Occasionally British merchants were unfavorably affected by the depreciation of colonial currency and the passage of laws in the colonies affecting the payment of debts. In 1748, for example, a Virginia law provided that sterling debts could be paid in " current money," or the ordinary coins in circulation, at twenty-five per cent advance.[1] This law was confirmed in England and was

[1] Hening's *Statutes of Virginia*, v, 540. As early as 1734 (*ibid.*, iv, 436) the treasurer had been authorized to borrow money to discharge the public debts; in

distinctly unfavorable to merchants, for current money
sometimes depreciated forty per cent in sterling exchange.
In 1755 the Virginia Assembly modified this law to provide that the colonial courts in awarding execution for
sterling debt should fix the rate of exchange in each case.[1]
The "Two Penny Acts" also affected adversely British
merchants as well as the parsons and other colonial creditors.[2] London merchants presented a memorial against
the confirmation of the second of these laws, pointing
out that large quantities of tobacco were owing them in
Virginia, which debts could be commuted in money at the
rate of twopence per pound if this law went into effect,
although tobacco was then bringing a much higher price.
The king instructed the governors to refuse their assent to
any laws of the kind and Parliament legislated[3] for the
protection of British merchants; but it is nevertheless
probable that they often found it very difficult to collect
debts due them in many colonies.

From the beginning the colonists had been dependent
upon commerce for everything except the bare necessities
of life. The tobacco and rice of the Southern Colonies
formed the great reason for their existence; the Northern
Colonies based their prosperity upon a flourishing trade
with the sugar islands of the West Indies. Throughout
this period the handling of the tobacco of Maryland,
Virginia, and North Carolina was confined by law to England. Joshua Gee, the ablest writer on colonial trade of
that time, states that the royal exchequer profited very
little from the "enumeration" of tobacco. Three fourths

1755 the issuing of "treasury notes"
was systematized (ibid., vi, 467, 529).
These notes were legal tender for all
debts except the quitrents.
  [1] Hening's Statutes, vi, 479.

[2] Beer's British Colonial Policy, 1754-
1765, p. 186; Hening's Statutes. vii, 240.
See the present work, vol. iii.
  [3] 14 George II, Cap. 37; 5 George III,
Cap. 7.

of the duties which were levied at the time of the importation into England were repaid on the reëxportation of
the better grades of tobacco to the ports of northern Europe. The poorer grades could not be sold in the Mediterranean markets in competition with native-grown tobacco,
owing to the increased cost which the payment of two
freights entailed; the result was that the poorer tobacco
was destroyed by fire on the London docks.[1] The enumeration of rice placed the planters of Carolina and Georgia
at such a disadvantage in the Mediterranean markets that
they were permitted to export their rice directly to ports
south of Cape Finisterre upon payment of one half the
duty which would be levied upon the rice if it were
landed in Great Britain.[2]

The colonists imported manufactured goods in constantly
increasing amounts from Great Britain, so that by 1754
the annual adverse balance against the continental colonies
and in favor of England was nearly two hundred thousand
pounds sterling. This constantly increasing adverse balance was made good, partly by the freight money, which
the colonists received for carrying a very large portion of
this commerce, and partly by an extremely profitable trade
to the West Indies.[3] A most interesting essay might be

[1] *The Trade and Navigation of Great
Britain Considered shewing that the
surest way for a Nation to increase in
Riches is to prevent the Importation of
such Foreign Commodities as may be
raised at Home.* The references in the
present volume are to the third edition,
London, 1731. The memorial of 1721 is
in "Board of Trade Papers," Ms. ("Philadelphia Transcripts," vol. x).

[2] 3 George II, Cap. 28 (Ruffhead's
Statutes at Large, vi, 35).

[3] The trade between the colonies and
the mother country had about balanced
in 1700 (see above, p. 281). In the three
years, 1714–17 the balance against the

colonies was £48,000; in 1724–26, £53,000;
in 1754–55, £173,444; and in 1759–60,
£1,847,965. These figures are taken
from the "Chalmers Papers" (Ms. i,
No. 14); they were compiled from the
customhouse returns. Considerable allowance should be made in any deduc-
tions founded on these returns because
McPherson (*Annals of Commerce,* iii,
340) states that the customhouse figures
were based on a valuation that was
settled in 1697 and adhered to despite
great fluctuations in prices and a great
general increase in the value of goods
which continued under an old name.
Dr. John Mitchell (*The Present State of*

written on the education of the European palate for foreign foods and drinks, and especially on the part played by tea, coffee, sugar, and rum in molding the fate of races and of empires. The production of the last three articles in the West Indies brought about the importation of negro slaves in great numbers, while the climate and unusual labor conditions swept them away with frightful rapidity, especially in the first five years after their arrival.

Barbados was the oldest English plantation in the West Indies and had been famous for its sugar ever since the Restoration. At a later time, Jamaica disputed with Barbados for the primacy of the British sugar islands, which ultimately included Grenada, Guadeloupe, Nevis, Antigua, and several smaller islands.[1] Sugar raising was carried on very largely by "planting attorneys," or agents for the absentee owners who passed most of their lives in England; at one time Barbados was said to yield a clear net profit of ninety-five thousand pounds per annum.[2] Almost nothing else was produced in the sugar islands; the food for the laborers was imported from the continental colonies; without these supplies the slaves would have starved.[3]

The New Englanders sent to the islands their poorest fish,

Great Britain and North America, London, 1767, p. 280) gives the annual excess of exports from England to the Northern Colonies in the years 1756–61 as £1,292,806. There can be no doubt that there was a large annual balance in favor of England which had to be liquidated by the exportation of specie from the colonies, although the exact size of that balance cannot be definitely stated.

[1] The essential characteristics of "tropical colonization" are admirably set forth by G. L. Beer in chapter viii of his *British Colonial Policy, 1754–1765*.

[2] *Importance of the British Plantations in America to Great Britain* (London, 1732), p. 27.

[3] This is strikingly set forth in a letter from St. Croix, written in 1769, and printed in the *Providence Gazette* for August 26 of that year. The writer states that the Danish government has forbidden the importation of any goods into its West Indian possessions in British vessels, except flour, lumber, fish, pork, and beef. On the last two articles there is a duty of twenty-five per cent, and the products of the islands must be exported in Danish vessels; "if these restrictions are carried into effect, they [the Danish colonists] cannot subsist; for without America they cannot live."

which sometimes bore the trade name of "Jamaica fish."
New York and the Delaware colonies, especially the latter,
exported great quantities of corn, peas, beans, oats, bread,
and flour.   The Northern Colonies also sent beef, pork,
poultry, horses, oxen, sheep, and hogs.   Of these the horses
and oxen were to be used for riding and for working the soil;
even the oxbows and yokes for the latter were imported from
the Northern Colonies.   The sugar islands could not even
supply the lumber and shingles for their dwellings: these
were imported from the North; sometimes even "house-
frames" prepared for speedy erection were sent from New
England.   Staves, hoops, and other materials for the hogsheads, puncheons, and casks to contain the crop were also
brought from the North and so, too, were the candles and oil
for illumination and the soap for household use.[1]   This trade
was not only between the continental colonies and the British sugar islands, it was carried on equally with the French,
Spanish, and Danish islands, contrary to the laws of England, France, Spain, and Denmark.   The means for the
evasion of the law were ample.   One way was to lose
one's identity, or rather the identity of one's ship, by converting her into a foreign bottom by obtaining a French or
Dutch register.   Moreover, by "a little greasing" permits
to trade in the French and Spanish islands might be obtained.   Or, having in mind the scarcity of naval vessels,
the enterprising Northern trader might sail to an alien

---

[1] A specimen cargo is that of the
Volant, which cleared at Salem in 1742
for "Barbadoes and elsewhere." She
carried 54,000 feet of board, 34,500 shingles, 3500 staves, 10 barrels of shad, 16
horses, 78 bags of corn, 20 bags of rye,
32 empty hogsheads for water. For this
bill of lading I am indebted to Mr. R. E.
Peabody. For a list of goods imported
into the British sugar islands from the
continental colonies, see Note II, p. 523.

In 1720–21, 68 vessels cleared at Barbados
for England, and 429 for other plantations ("Chalmers Papers," Ms. i, No. 26).
Richard Hockley paid 18 shillings per
barrel for flour in Philadelphia and sold
it for 25 to 30 shillings at Jamaica; but
the profit he regarded as only "tolera-
ble"; in a preceding letter he gives 11
shillings as a high price for flour. See
Pennsylvania Magazine of History,
vols. xxvii, xxviii.

island under his own name and without any disguise or permit. Of course, upon arrival at his home port with a cargo of French molasses and rum, the tide waiters might ask inconvenient questions; but these could usually be answered by the same means that West Indian permits were obtained. Sometimes a few hogsheads of English grown sugar or molasses, suitably marked, were stowed near the hatchway and the bill of lading of these few extended to cover the whole cargo. This trade was so profitable that the loss of a vessel now and then could easily be borne.

The illicit trade with the alien sugar islands was profitable because of the heavy taxes levied on the products of the British sugar plantations at exportation. These were the four and one half per cent duty [1] on all goods exported from Barbados and the other islands excepting Jamaica, which levied duties of its own.[2] In addition, there were the "enumerated duties"[3] on sugar exported from the British islands to the Northern plantations. On the other hand, only one per cent was levied on the exports of the French islands. Furthermore, the processes of refining were carried much farther on the French plantations than they were on the English, owing in part to the stimulus given to the refining industry in England by legislation.[4] The southern bound cargoes were usually sold for a good deal more than was necessary to purchase the molasses and other commodities

[1] *Laws of Barbadoes*, 121. This act was passed in 1663 to secure the royal confirmation of their lands; it was not repealed until 1838. The proceeds were not used to maintain the government of the island, but were covered into the exchequer and used for general purposes, greatly to the dismay of the Barbadians. See *Groans of the Plantations*, 1689.

[2] *Acts of the Assembly of Jamaica*, 1756, p. 159. By this law (1728) Jamaica guaranteed to pay into the royal exchequer at least £8000 per annum, exclusive of quitrents; but raised the money in any way that seemed best.

[3] 25 Charles II, Cap. 7 (*Statutes of the Realm*, v, 792).

[4] See "The Irregular and Disordered State of the Plantation Trade," which was written about 1696 (American Historical Association's *Papers* for 1892, p. 36).

for the homeward voyage. The balance was paid in coin and bills of exchange, which were brought home and soon found their way to England to pay for the manufactured goods which were imported into the Northern Colonies from that country.

Another trade which brought in profit to the Northern Colonies was the roundabout or triangular trade. A vessel would sail from Boston or Salem or some other northern port for Lisbon, or a Mediterranean port, dispose of her cargo there, take on another for the West India islands, and thence return with a hold full of sugar, molasses, and rum, and the ship's chest well filled with bills of exchange and silver. The most profitable long voyages were those which were made to the west coast of Africa, either directly from the home port or by way of the sugar islands. On the coast of Africa the captain of the vessel would exchange his cargo of rum and short iron bars for palm oil, gold dust, and negroes. The slaves he would take to the West Indies and with the proceeds of their sale fill his vessel with sugar, molasses, and rum, and sail for home.

By far the greater part of the slaves brought to America in the eighteenth century came in English ships,[1] especially those which sailed under the flag of the Royal African Company,[2] which was incorporated in 1672. In the reign of William III the trade was thrown open,[3] and it is stated that from 1698 to 1707 twenty-five thousand negroes

---

[1] In a *Treatise upon the Trade from Great Britain to Africa* by "An African Merchant" (London, 1772, Appendix) it is stated that in 1752 eighty-eight ships sailed from England to Africa for 25,920 negroes, and that in 1771, 195 ships carried 47,146 negroes.

[2] This was not the first African Company; there were two before the Great

Rebellion, and a joint stock corporation was organized in 1662. There is an interesting article on the "Royal African Company of England" by W. R. Scott in the *American Historical Review*, viii, 241.

[3] 9, 10 William III, Cap. 26 (Ruffhead's *Statutes at Large*, iii, 710).

were annually landed in the English colonies, mostly in the islands, but many of these were sold to the Spaniards.[1] In those days a slave could be bought on the coast of Africa for about twelve pounds and sold in America for from twenty to forty pounds;[2] but the profits were not excessive when one bears in mind the inevitable loss and the heavy expenses of the voyage across the Atlantic.

Colonial traders, especially those of Newport and Boston, engaged in the slave trade, among them Peter Faneuil, one of whose vessels, the *Jolly Bachelor*, by her name reflected the genial character of her owner. Colonial slave vessels were small in size, seldom being over one hundred and fifty tons, more often under ninety tons. The larger ships, besides captain and surgeon, carried a crew of from ten to

[1] In conformity with the "Assiento" or contract with the Spanish government to supply the Spanish colonies with a certain number of slaves each year, see an interesting brief account in Douglass's *Summary, Historical and Political, of the British Settlements* (ed. 1747), i, 75–79. The outbreak of war with Spain in 1739 put an end to this contract.

[2] These figures are deduced from the *Report of the Lords of the Committee of Council of Trade and Foreign Plantations*, 1789, ii, Part iv, Appendix, No. 25, which is entitled "A Chronological Account of the Prices . . . of Negroes."

DATE	COST OF NEGRO ON COAST	SELLING PRICE AT JAMAICA
1676 to 1679	£3	£17
1698 to 1707	£10	£20
1760	£12	£35

In this report (vol. ii, Part iv, No. 18) the total value of the slaves in the English West India islands is computed at twenty-two and one half millions sterling, while houses, lands, vessels, tools, etc., are valued at forty-seven and one

VOL. II. — 2 L

half millions. In this computation, slaves are estimated at fifty pounds each, as negroes have been "commonly sold in parcels at that sum." These figures give some idea of the intensity of slavery in the West Indies just after the American Revolution. A study of prices of negro slaves in the continental colonies gives nearly the same average figure, but these computations are so involved, owing to the varying colonial currencies, that the details are not worth stating; the net result, however, is probably not far out of the way. Slaves born in the colonies and those imported who had been trained brought higher prices.

As to numbers, nearly three hundred thousand negroes were imported into Jamaica alone in the first half of the eighteenth century, the largest number in any one year being 13,000 in 1732. One third of these were exported mainly to Spanish colonies. In 1730 the negro population of Jamaica was 84,000; in 1758, 150,000. See *An Inquiry concerning the Trade, Commerce, and Policy of Jamaica* (1759). The Appendix besides the table, from which the above figures are taken, has also "curious and useful remarks" upon the marketing of sugar and rum.

twenty men; but the smaller vessels had no surgeon, and only five or six men in all. Captain and surgeon, where there was one, received wages and a bonus proportionable to the number of slaves landed in health[1] and were often permitted to import a few slaves on their own account. It was thus for the interest of the ship's officers as well as of the owner to bring as many negroes as possible across the Atlantic. Every possible care was taken of the slaves, they were got on deck in the daytime in good weather and their quarters washed and sprinkled with vinegar. They were also well fed, being given African and American food on alternate days. Their movements were necessarily confined and the men were chained day and night, but this could hardly be avoided. One of the most successful captains, who made voyage after voyage with the loss of less than two per cent, reported that he had on his last voyage lost thirty out of one hundred and thirty slaves because the weather had been so bad for three successive weeks that he could not get the negroes on deck. Sensational writers on slavery and the slave trade have dilated upon the "horrors of the Middle Passage," but in colonial days the slaves were treated with greater humanity than were the first comers to Jamestown or the German redemptioners. In later years, when the slave trade was regarded as criminal, the profit on each slave was so large that the loss of half a cargo would not ruin a voyage; then it was that cruelty and hardship abounded.[2]

[1] On one voyage the arrangement was that the captain should receive £100 and the surgeon £50 if the loss of slaves was under two per cent, and one half of these sums if it did not exceed three per cent.

[2] The foregoing account is based on papers by George C. Mason in *American Historical Record*, i, 340; William B.

Weeden in American Antiquarian Society's *Proceedings*, October, 1887, p. 107; and Charles Deane in *ibid.*, October, 1886, p. 191. W. E. B. DuBois in his monograph on "The Suppression of the African Slave-Trade," *Harvard Historical Studies*, i, has a convenient summary of the rise of the traffic. James Bandinel's *Some Account of the Trade in*

Most of the slaves imported into the continental colonies came by way of the West Indies, but occasionally a cargo would be brought from Africa direct. In 1708 Governor Cranston of Rhode Island informed the Lords of Trade[1] that within his recollection only one vessel had come to Newport directly from Africa, and she brought only forty-seven negroes. Most of the slaves who came to the Northern Colonies were brought from the islands. They were either the unsalable part of the cargo, being too old or too young or sickly, or were sometimes slaves who had been taken in payment of balances due from the planters to Northern merchants. The negroes throve and multiplied in Carolina and the Chesapeake colonies.[2] In the islands the case was very different, for there the mortality was very great in the five years after importation, and the number of births was not greatly in excess of the deaths. It fell out, therefore, that the great mass of the negroes imported from Africa were sold in the islands.

Until 1717 Barbados was extraordinarily prosperous; she not only produced abundantly herself, but owing to her geographical position was the shipping center of the sugar islands. In that year the Barbados Assembly laid a duty on sugar, molasses, and rum imported and gave the deathblow to this important business.[3] At this time the French sugar islands were more prosperous than the English, partly owing to the causes which have been noted in a preceding paragraph, but more especially to the fact

---

Slaves from Africa (London, 1842) is based on the report of the Lords Committee noted above. Most modern works reproduce the facts contained in these two. The examples of brutality that are constantly recounted can be traced back to a few captains, and the worst stories are told of one whom the life on the coast had probably driven insane.

[1] Rhode Island Colony Records, iv, 54.

[2] See Governor Glen's *Description of South Carolina*, p. 57, and an interesting report by Colonel Jenings, President of the Virginia Council in 1708. *Colonial Records of North Carolina*, i, 694.

[3] *Laws of Barbadoes*, 303.

that the obligation of a second voyage due to the "enu meration of sugar" and molasses raised the cost of land ing English grown sugar at a continental port fully twenty-five per cent over that at which French sugar could be sold.[1] The stagnant condition of the sugar plan tations attracted attention in England because many fami lies prominent in politics and society drew revenue from those plantations, and the prosperity of the islands also interested the official class because the exchequer drew a direct revenue from the tropical colonies. In 1720 the Lords of Trade were informed that foreign sugar, molas ses, and rum were exported from the continental colonies directly to Europe in very large amounts, enough sugar being sent from New York alone in each year to bring one thousand pounds into the royal exchequer had it been landed in England. In 1730 the British sugar plant ers petitioned Parliament to give a distinct measure of protection to their industry, and the exports of sugar for that year were less than those for 1729.[2] The House of Commons passed a bill to prohibit the importation of alien produced sugar, rum, and molasses into the North ern Colonies. The agents of the mainland provinces and

[1] *Present State of the British Sugar Islands Considered in a Letter from a Gentleman of Barbadoes* (London, 1731).

[2] "Plantations General," Bundle M. No. 35 ("Philadelphia Transcript," xi, No. 35). Bryan Edwards, however, in his *History of the British West Indies* ii, 508), states the imports of British sugar into Great Britain as follows: —

1729	994,761 cwt.
1730	1,024,078 cwt.
1731	818,277 cwt.
1732	822,844 cwt.
1733	1,001,784 cwt.
1734	695,679 cwt.
1735	903,634 cwt.

The apparent disagreement between these figures and the statement in the text is due to the fact that sugar exported from the island in one year would appear, to some extent, in the table of importations into Great Britain in the following year. It may be added that the total annual productions of the British sugar plantations was stated by one authority as high as 1,500,000 pounds sterling, see "A—r Z—h," *Considerations on the Dispute now depending before the House of Commons* (London, 1731), p. 5. This amount included pimento, cotton, and dyeing woods in addition to products of the cane.

Colonel William Cosby, who had been appointed governor of New York, now opposed the bill so vigorously that in the Lords it was "put off," or indefinitely postponed.[1]

This defeat incited the sugar planters to renewed efforts. They printed many tracts and presented more petitions. They asserted that £121,000 invested in goods in England and sold in the West Indies showed a profit of £79,600, including freight;[2] that twenty pounds in every hundred of goods sold in the colonies went into the royal exchequer; and that British sugar planters imported their machinery from England and bought tens of thousands of negroes from the English slave dealers.

The Northern colonists were not idle. In 1731 Pennsylvania merchants remonstrated against the passage of "a sugar act as petitioned for by the sugar islands,"[3] frankly acknowledging that they carried on a large trade with the alien islands because the English sugar colonies could not take nearly all the provisions which the "Bread Colonys" exported. Another memorial[4] pointed out in addition to the usual arguments that the profit from the West India traffic "centers in *Great Britain*, by means of the Ballance of Trade; For their Industry chiefly centers in this, *viz.* to make Returns to *Great Britain* to purchase its Manufactures; and the more they are enabled to make Remittances home, the greater their Demand will be of those Commodities." The General Assembly of New York declared that if the

[1] *Lords Journals*, xxiii, 696; *Commons Journals*, xxi, 641; other references may be found through the indexes. See also *Journal of the General Assembly of New York*, i, 633; *Correspondence of the Colonial Governors of Rhode Island*, i, 34.

[2] *Importance of the British Plantations*, London, 1731, p. 66.

[3] "Board of Trade Papers, Proprieties," Ms. Bundle S. 13 ("Philadelphia Transcripts," xiii, No. 13).

[4] This is entitled *The Case of the British Northern Colonies* (apparently printed for use of members of Parliament). It is also copied in the "Board of Trade Papers, Plantations General," Ms. Bundle M. 1 ("Philadelphia Transcripts," vol. xi), where it is ascribed to John Sharpe.

Northern colonists were cut off from this trade they " must be reduced to Nakedness or to make our own Cloathing." [1] Sir John Barnard presented a petition [2] against the new bill from the Governor and Company of Rhode Island and Providence Plantations which was not received because it was a petition against a money bill, and, moreover, seemed to deny the right of Parliament to tax the colonists and legislate for them. The Lords of Trade and both houses of Parliament fell in with the wishes of the sugar planters and passed the Sugar Act of 1733.

The title of this measure is " An Act for the better securing and encouraging the Trade of his Majesty's Sugar Colonies in America." [3] The preamble recites that the welfare and prosperity of the British sugar colonies are of "the greatest consequence and importance" to the trade, navigation, and strength of "this kingdom," and declares that the sugar planters of late years have fallen under such great discouragement that they no longer are able to compete on an equal footing with the planters of the foreign sugar islands. For these reasons the following duties shall be paid on all rum, molasses, and sugar imported into the continental colonies from the foreign islands: ninepence on each gallon of rum, sixpence on each gallon of molasses, and five shillings on each hundredweight of sugar. These duties were to be paid in ready money before the goods were landed. The penalty for disobedience was forfeiture of goods, — one third for the support of the government of the plantation where the forfeiture should be recovered, one third to the governor of the plantation personally, and one third to the informer or prosecutor.

---

[1] *Journal of the General Assembly of New York*, i, 628. See also *Minutes of the Provincial Council of Pennsylvania*, iii, 423.

[2] Hansard's *Parliamentary Debates*, iii, 1261.

[3] 6 George II, Cap. 13 (Ruffhead's *Statutes at Large* vi, 116).

The burden of proof was placed on the owner of the suspected goods.   Persons who should assist in bringing on
shore foreign rum, sugar, or molasses before the duty was
paid were to forfeit treble the value of the goods ; persons
resisting customs officers engaged in enforcing the law
were to pay fifty pounds, which was also the sum forfeited by any customs officer who connived at fraudulent
importations ; the master of the ship importing condemned
goods should pay one hundred pounds.   There was also
a section in the act which provided that all duties should
be drawn back on sugars which were reëxported from
Great Britain within twelve months.

The English statute book does not contain a more unjustifiable law relating to the colonies before the famous
legislation which is associated with the name of George
Grenville.   The statements made in the preamble to justify its passage are false, although they no doubt were
believed to be true ; it was not the sugar islands that
were the mainstay of British commerce and in so far as
they were, the mainstay was the trade in negro slaves.

It is difficult to trace the interaction of industrial and
legislative factors on the course of prices.   This is especially the case in a problem like the present, when
wars, droughts, and hurricanes seriously affected the production of sugar in the West Indies and successive emis-
sions of paper money in the continental colonies destroyed
the stability of monetary values.   On the one hand,
there is evidence of innumerable voyages from Northern
ports to the alien sugar islands and back, and more molasses was distilled into rum in the Northern Colonies than
was produced in the British sugar islands.   On the other
hand, the course of prices of rum and other commodities
in New England and the Middle Colonies would give the

impression that the law was somewhat observed in the latter and that no attention was paid to it in the former. The manuscript accounts of two New England merchants throw light on this point. From 1719 to 1729 the price of New England rum in eastern Massachusetts varied from four shillings to five shillings per gallon; in 1734 the price was five shillings, threepence; and in 1735 six shillings, sixpence. In these years, however, the price of silver had risen from eighteen shillings in Massachusetts currency to twenty-seven shillings, so that reduced to silver values it would seem that rum had declined in price rather than increased. The same deduction cannot be made from the tables of prices at which commodities were sold in Philadelphia, for these would seem to show that the price of rum, sugar, and molasses increased, although perhaps not in proportion to the duty.[1]

[1] C. W. Macfarlane points out that one difficulty in compiling the figures given below lies in the fact that tables of prices current were regarded by newspaper editors in the eighteenth century as "padding," which could be omitted when there was anything else to print. To understand the significance of these figures, it should be recalled that the Act of 1733 laid a duty of ninepence per gallon on rum imported into the continental colonies from alien plantations, sixpence per gallon on molasses, and five shillings the hundredweight on sugar. C. W. Macfarlane's tables are in the *Annals of the American Academy of Political and Social Science*, viii, 68, 88.

	1715–19	1724–29	1735–39	1750–54	1755–59	1765–69	1770–75
	s. d.	s. d.	s. d.	s. d.	s. d.	s. d.	s. d.
Rum (W. I.) .	2 4– / 3 4	1 10– / 4	2 1– / 2 10	2 10– / 4 6	2 6– / 5 7	2 7– / 3 10	2 10– / 4 6
Sugar . . .	40– / 55	21– / 40	25– / 50	30– / 60	35– / 77	35– / 66	40– / 60
Molasses . .	15– / 18	14– / 20	17– / 24	18– / 26	21– / 38	19– / 24	19– / 24
Flour . . .	7– / 9 6	9– / 13 3	7– / 13	10 6– / 15 4	10 6– / 16 6	12 6– / 18 00	13 6– / 21 6
Corn. . . .	1 6– / 1 10	2– / 3	1 3– / 2 6	2– / 3 9	1 6– / 3 7	2 4– / 3 6	2 8– / 4 6
Tobacco . .	13 6– / 22 6	10– / 40	10– / 20 00	8– / 28	8– / 35	10– / 37 6	15– / 40

No sooner was the act passed than the sugar planters realized that it was the prohibition to take their sugars directly to the ports of the European continent that affected them.[1] In compliance with their petitions, they were now permitted to send their sugar directly to Europe. This exemption was not made as to molasses and rum, but the acts of 1739 and 1742[2] satisfied the cravings of the sugar planters and they do not seem to have taken any interest in the constant disregard of the Sugar Act of 1733.

Notwithstanding the attempts to regulate colonial commerce, which have been noted in this chapter, the trade of the Northern Colonies was exceptionally prosperous in the years 1720 to 1760. Colonial vessels visited all parts of the Atlantic seashore, but did not as yet pass the capes at the southern extremities of Africa and South America. In reading the commercial papers of the American merchants of that time, one is impressed with the dangers constantly to be expected from pirates, privateers, and rapacious officials; but one is equally struck by the absence of fear of the regular customs officers who were supposed to be enforcing the navigation laws and the Sugar Act. Before Pitt's famous letter of 1760[3] it may even be doubted if merchants and tide-waiters were actually conscious of their duties and obligations; when they at length realized what was expected of them, rebellion on the part of the colonists was not far off.

[1] See *The Miserable Case of the British Sugar Planters*, especially pp. v–vii.

[2] 12 George II, Cap. 30 (Ruffhead's *Statutes at Large*, vi, 368); 15 George II, Cap. 33 (*ibid.*, vi, 476). To enable the British sugar refiners to continue in business, Parliament granted a bounty on all British grown refined sugar exported and a drawback of the whole duty which was paid on importation, 21 George II, Cap. 2, § 7 (*ibid.*, vii, 89).

[3] See below, p. 567.

NOTES

I. The Sugar Act of 1733. — A standard work on the West Indies is Bryan Edwards's *The History, Civil and Commercial of the British Colonies in the West Indies* (2 vols., London, 1794; 3 vols., London, 1801, — the additional matter in the third volume is descriptive of the alien sugar islands). Edwards gives figures of exports and imports, but they relate to a later date than is covered in this chapter. Edward Long's *History of Jamaica* (3 vols., London, 1774) and R. H. Schomburgk's *History of Barbados* (London, 1848) are also scholarly and useful works; otherwise, the formal histories of the West India islands have generally little attraction for the seeker of facts. A most useful book for the student is *An Abridgement of the Laws in force and use in Her Majesty's Plantations* (London, 1704), which points the way to a study of the laws of the islands.[1]

The prolonged contest which ended in the passage of the Act of 1733 brought forth many petitions and more tracts from both sides. These are ordinarily controversial in tone, but contain here and there valuable information. Among them may be mentioned two letters from a "Gentleman of Barbadoes to his Friend in London;" "A—r Z—h's" *Considerations on the Dispute now depending before the House of Commons;* and *A Comparison between the British Sugar Colonies and New England.*[2] This last is an interesting and bitter attack on the Northern Colonies in the course of which some impor-

[1] *Acts of the Assembly passed in the Island of Jamaica for 1681–1737* (London, 1738); *Acts of Assembly passed in the Island of Jamaica, 1681–1754* (London, 1756); *Acts of the Assembly of the Island of Jamaica, 1681–1768* (2 vols., Jamaica, 1769); *Acts of Assembly passed in the Island of Barbadoes from 1648–1718* (London, 1721).

[2] *The Present State of the British Sugar Colonies Considered: in a Letter from a Gentleman of Barbadoes to his Friend in London* (London, 1731); *The British Empire in America considered in a Second Letter from a Gentleman of Barbadoes to his Friend in London* (London, 1732); A—r Z—h, *Considerations on the Dispute now depending before the Honourable House of Commons, between the British, Southern and Northern Plantations in America* (London, 1731); *A Comparison between the British Sugar Colonies and New England as they relate to the interest of Great Britain* (London, 1732). Other tracts on this side are *A True State of the case between the British Northern-Colonies and the Sugar Islands* (1732); *The Importance of the British Plantations in America to this kingdom* (London, 1731); *The Importance of the Sugar Colonies to Great Britain stated and some objections to the Sugar Colony Bill answered in a letter to a Member of the House of Commons* (London, 1731); *Proposals offered for the Sugar Planters Redress and for reviving the British Sugar Commerce* (London, 1733); *Some Considerations humbly offer'd upon the Bill now depending in the House of Lords . . . In a Letter to a Noble Peer* (London, 1732).

tant statements are made as to the course and conduct of trade. Several tracts printed after the passage of the act also throw light on the conditions prevailing before that time, especially those which are usually associated with the names of John Ashley and John Campbell.[1]

On the side of the Northern Colonies two tracts are worth noting: *A Letter to the West India Merchants by a Fisherman* (London, 1751) and *Considerations on the Bill now depending in Parliament concerning the British Sugar-Colonies* (London, 1731). The legislative course of the bills can be followed in the "Journals" of the two Houses, and brief notices of the discussions in Parliament are in Hansard's *Parliamentary Debates*, viii, 918, 992–1002, 1195–1200, 1261–1266.

[1] John Ashley's three pamphlets are entitled : *Sugar Trade with the Incumbrances thereon, laid open* (London, 1734); *Some Observations on a direct Exportation of Sugar from the British Islands with Answers to Mr. Toriano's Objections* (London, 1735); *Memoirs and Considerations on the Trade and Revenues of the British Colonies in America* (London, 1740. A "Second Part" was published in 1743). Campbell's useful tract is entitled *The Candid and Impartial Considerations on the Nature of the Sugar Trade; The compara-* *tive Importance of the British and French Islands in the West Indies.* Other tracts of this same nature are *The Miserable Case of the British Sugar Planters wherein is contained . . . the Advantages of a Direct Exportation from the Sugar Islands to Foreign Markets* (London, 1738); William Perrin's *Present State of the British and French Sugar Colonies* (London, 1740); *The State of the Sugar Trade shewing the dangerous consequences that must attend any additional Duty thereon* (London, 1747).

II. Statistics of Trade. — The following figures have been compiled from various sources and are useful for purposes of comparison : —

COLONIAL TRADE [1]

	Imports into England Annual Average 1714-17	Exports from England Annual Average 1714-17
Continental Colonies	£ 382,576	£ 431,027
Sugar Isles	1,102,219	348,318
West Indies (general)	3,391	26,986
Bermudas	412	1,396

EXPORTS FROM ENGLAND [2] TO —

	Annual Average	
	1744–48	1754–58
Northern Colonies	£ 697,253	£ 1,482,811
West India Islands	672,667	753,568

QUANTITIES OF GOODS PRODUCED IN THE BRITISH PLANTATIONS IN AMERICA AND EXPORTED THENCE, YEARLY [3]

Newfoundland	£ 115,000
Quebec	80,000
Maritime Provinces	6,500
Total Conquered French Possessions	£ 201,500
New England	£ 134,000
New York (flour and biscuit, £ 150,000)	228,000
Pennsylvania	228,000
Maryland and Virginia (including 100,000 hogsheads of tobacco) .	870,500
The Carolinas (rice, £ 200,000)	286,500
Georgia	16,200
Total Continental Colonies	£ 1,763,200

[1] "Chalmers Papers" (Ms.), i, 14.
[2] [B. Franklin] *The Interest of Great Britain Considered with regard to her Colonies* (London, 1761), p. 58. Dr. John Mitchell (*The State of the Colonies*, p. 280) gives the annual average of exports from Great Britain to the continental colonies in the years 1758–61 at £ 2,045,144.

[3] *Impartial Observations to be considered on by the King, his Ministers, and the People of Great Britain.* It is signed "Impartiality" and dated March 25, 1763. A copy is in the John Carter Brown Library.

[West India Islands]

Jamaica (sugar, 560,000 ; rum, 100,000) . . . . £ 709,500
Barbados (sugar, 220,000) 277,000
St. Kitts 229,000
Tobago 277,000
Grenada 249,800
Antigua 268,000
Minor Islands 375,400

Total Sugar Plantations . . . . £ 2,385,700

Total English Colonies . . . . £ 4,148,900

[French Colonies]

Guadeloupe . . . . £ 837,000
Martinique 632,000
St. Domingo 2,923,333
St. Lucia 93,300

Total French Islands . . . . £ 4,485,633

ACCOUNT OF ENTRANCES AND CLEARANCES FOR 1760 [1]

COLONIES	INWARD			OUTWARD		
	From British Ports	From Foreign Ports		To British Ports	To Foreign Ports	
	Ships	*Ships*	*Tons*	*Ships*	*Ships*	*Tons*
South Carolina . .	200	46	15,628	228	133	17,686
North Carolina . .	304	None	10,915	313	1	11,423
Virginia	512	23	48,099	502	4	41,097
Maryland . . .	330	11	25,853	329	None	25,630
Pennsylvania . .	525	69	33,234	605	31	34,978
New York . . .	122	56	9,901	167	80	14,222
New England . .	643	203	44,932	1047	83	56,577

[1] Ms. in Massachusetts Historical Society's Library. See also "Ship Registers of the Port of Philadelphia" in *Pennsylvania Magazine of History*, xxiii–xxviii.

GOODS IMPORTED INTO THE BRITISH SUGAR ISLANDS

An account of Lumber, Provisions, &c. imported into all the British West India islands from the colonies in North America, between the 1st day of January and the 31st of December, 1772, with an average valuation thereof at the ports of delivery, calculated in Jamaica currency.[1]

	£	s.	d.
17,211 hogshead packs, 7s. 6d. each	6,454	2	0
21,160,461 staves, £10 per M.	211,604	0	0
27,138,507 feet of lumber, £7 per M.	189,969	10	11
20,936,188 shingles, at 45s. per M. (on an average) . . .	47,106	8	6
1,169,086 hoops at £5 per M.	5,845	8	7
365,300 bushels of India corn, 3s. 9d. per bushel . . .	68,493	15	0
26,280 bushels of peas and beans, 5s.	6,545	0	0
126,300 barrels of flour of 2 cwt. each, at 18s. per cwt. .	227,340	0	0
4,960 tierces of bread of 1½ cwt., at 20s. per cwt. . .	7,440	0	0
7,656 half tierces of rice of 2½ cwt. each, 15s.	14,375	0	0
5,377 tierces of rice of 5 cwt. each, 15s.	20,163	15	0
12,575 barrels of pork, at £3 5s.	40,868	15	0
2,220 horses at £20, on an average	44,400	0	0
1,296 oxen, £12	15,552	0	0
3,693 sheep, £1	3,693	0	0
21,185 hogsheads of 8 cwt. of salted fish, and			
30,062 quintals of 1 cwt. of salted fish, £1, p. ct. . . .	199,542	0	0
939 dozen of poultry, 35s.	1,643	5	0
Total	1,111,036	0	0

[1] Brian Edwards's *Thoughts on Proceedings of Government Respect-* *ing Trade of West India Islands,* p. 66.

CHAPTER XVIII

ENGLAND AND FRANCE IN AMERICA, 1684-1754

LA SALLE's great expedition down the Mississippi ends the history of the exploration of the eastern part of North America. Instead of seeking to discover new regions, La Salle[1] now endeavored to colonize the northern shore of the Gulf of Mexico; his design was to plant a colony of Frenchmen in the vicinity of the Mississippi, to monopolize that river basin for France, to absorb the fur trade of that region, and to dispossess the Spaniards of the mines of New Biscay. The last part of the project fell in with the plans of Louis XIV, who, at that moment, was deeply resentful of Spanish pretensions and Spanish deeds. He aided the enterprise, and La Salle sailed from France for Santo Domingo and Louisiana in the summer of 1684. The expedition included one ship of war, three smaller vessels, and less than two hundred persons, soldiers, and colonists, both men and women. The contrarieties of La Salle's nature are so great that it is difficult to state his expectation, but it seems probable that he intended to secure the aid of thousands of Indians in his projects against the dominions of Spain. Moreover, he possessed those qualities of enthusiasm which have enabled many another man to achieve wondrous results with scanty

[1] Parkman has treated the close of La Salle's career at length in his *La Salle and the Discovery of the Great West*, chs. xxiii-xxix. The sources are printed at length in Margry's *Découvertes et Établissements des Français*, ii, 374-613; iii, 1-582. The most interesting document is the "Relation de Henri Joutel"; it is in *ibid.*, iii, 91-507. See also Shea's translation of Le Clercq's *First Establishment of the Faith*, ii, 199-283.

means. It is not at all improbable that he really expected to attack the Spanish settlements, and had he done
so with anything like the impetuosity that impelled the
raiders on the New England frontier, he might have succeeded. The event was far otherwise.

From the outset, misfortune came upon La Salle.[1] The
voyage across the Atlantic was dreary enough; at Santo
Domingo, he took to his bed and the whole force became dis-
organized. Ultimately a new start was made, but the fleet,
instead of entering the Mississippi, anchored off Matagorda
Bay on the coast of Texas to the south of Galveston
(January, 1685). The entrance to the port was narrow
and tortuous; one of the vessels ran aground and was
lost with a large part of the stores of the expedition.
Possibly La Salle purposely selected this extreme western
position on account of its nearness to the Spanish settlements whose conquest he had in hand; as soon as the
expedition was partly established on shore, La Salle's chief
anxiety was to find the Mississippi and communicate with
his lieutenant, the ever faithful Tonty, in the Illinois country. This action was compatible with raising a force of
Indians for an attack on the Spaniards, but it seems likely
that La Salle had nothing more in mind than to move his
headquarters to the lower Mississippi and to get fresh supplies from the French posts in the interior. While on one
of these explorations he was murdered by his own men,
March 19, 1687. Beaujeu with the naval vessel regained the
coast of France, and La Salle's elder brother with his
nephew and a few followers found their way to the St.
Lawrence. All the rest perished of disease, shipwreck, or
Indian attack, with the exception of a few who were seized

[1] Formerly his disasters were attributed largely to the action of Beaujeu, the
naval commander of the expedition; but
the evidence is so indistinct that it seems
fairer to ascribe his tragic ending to bad
fortune as well as to treachery.

by the Spaniards ; two of these escaped to France and told
of the last days of the settlement and of its ending.   In
some respects, La Salle's sad fate seems appropriate to his
adventurous career.   Other Frenchmen having not a tithe
of his intrepidity or greatness of soul were to succeed
where he failed and to create a new center of French influence in the lower Mississippi Valley.   The story now
turns to the northern region and to La Salle's friend and
protector, Comte de Frontenac, in his second period of
power as governor of New France.

The Glorious Revolution in England seemed to be the
Frenchman's opportunity in America.   Although the Iroquois could not be overwhelmed directly, they might be
reduced to obedience through the humiliation of their
English allies by the conquest of New York.   This would
not only deprive them of their supplies of firearms, gunpowder, and lead, but the occupation of the Hudson River
to its mouth would place the heretical English colonists at
the mercy of the faithful.   There was nothing chimerical
in the scheme, for, at the moment, New York was in the
midst of the Leislerian tumult.   In any event, that colony
was weak, owing to the dispersal of its settlements and
the openness of its principal city to attack from the sea.
The plan required the coöperation of a military expedition
from the St. Lawrence and a naval armament from France.
In approving it, Louis XIV also gave his approbation to
the removal of all the English settlers in the colony except,
of course, those who were Roman Catholics and who swore
allegiance to France.   The scheme was an alluring one,
but the moment Frenchmen embarked upon the sea, misfortune was their lot.   Long before Frontenac reached
Quebec to make preparations for the conquest of New
York, all opportunity for a successful surprise was gone.

In place of this great operation, he shrewdly planned three small expeditions whose success would restore prestige to French arms, but whose failure would pass almost unnoticed.

The first band of raiders passed through the unguarded gates of Schenectady on the night of February 9/19, 1690.[1] The second party assailed Salmon Falls, a settlement on the boundary between Maine and New Hampshire, in March, 1690, and then joined the third expedition in an attack on Fort Loyal, on the site of the present city of Portland. This post was surrendered on promise of good treatment, which was at once broken. These expeditions were successful from the French point of view, but in one respect their result was not hopeful, because they led to the holding of an intercolonial congress at New York in May, 1690. To this meeting came delegates from Massachusetts, New Plymouth, and Connecticut. They and the New Yorkers agreed upon an intercolonial expedition against Montreal by the way of Lake Champlain. New York was to furnish four hundred men, the other three colonies together three hundred and fifty, while the Iroquois were to join them with a formidable body of warriors. In addition, Massachusetts was to send a strong naval expedition with an adequate land force to attack Quebec. John Winthrop was appointed to the command of the joint land force. The undertaking was unfortunate from the outset. Dissensions were followed by ravages of the smallpox, and the expedition came to a standstill at the southern end of Lake Champlain. With twenty-nine white men and more than a hundred Indians, John Schuyler pushed on to the village of La Prairie on the St. Lawrence, opposite Montreal. They killed or captured those who were work-

[1] For an account of this exploit, see above, p. 209.

ing in the fields, destroyed great quantities of provisions, and retreated without loss.

In the spring of this year an expedition left Boston for the conquest of Acadia. The commander was Sir William Phips, who had won his title and fortune by despoiling a wrecked Spanish galleon in the West Indies and carrying his treasure safely to England — the latter feat being more perilous than the former. In May he attacked Port Royal, occupied it without difficulty, and returned to Boston laden with loot and glory. In the summer he sailed at the head of a more formidable force for the capture of Quebec. He had more than two thousand soldiers, poorly disciplined and inadequately supplied with ammunition.[1] The voyage up the St. Lawrence was safely accomplished; but when Phips arrived in front of the capital of New France, the energy and courage which he had shown so conspicuously in his earlier voyages deserted him. He delayed the attack and when made he did not push it home, and abandoned the enterprise at the moment when it might have succeeded. We know now, what he could not have known, that practically the entire military force of New France had been gathered in Quebec, and that the garrison could not have clung to the fortress for more than a few days longer on account of lack of food. In extenuation of Phips's conduct, it should be said that he was poorly seconded by his subordinates. The martial spirit which had carried New England through so many early conflicts had temporarily departed, while the ambition to accomplish great results remained. The Peace of Ryswick[2] in

---

[1] Original papers relating to this expedition are in Massachusetts Historical Society's *Proceedings* for November, 1901, pp. 281-318 ; Massachusetts Society of Colonial Wars, *Year-Book* for 1898, 111-282 ; others are in Ernest

Myraud's *Sir William Phips devant Quebec* (Quebec, 1893) ; there is a manuscript journal of the expedition in the "Chalmers Papers."

[2] Du Mont's *Corps Diplomatique*, vii, Part ii, p. 400. Chalmers notes the

1697 left the combatants and their boundary disputes where they were in 1688 ; but France was the gainer because she still maintained a foothold on the two great river valleys of North America.

Of the famous families of New France, few won greater renown than did that of Le Moyne ; of them Pierre Le Moyne d'Iberville ranks easily first, although his brother, Jean Baptiste Le Moyne de Bienville is more closely connected with American annals. Iberville led the raiders to Schenectady, served in forays against the English posts on Hudson's Bay, and commanded several successful naval expeditions.[1] In 1698 he petitioned the king for authority to establish a post near the mouth of the Mississippi River to secure that region for France and to provide a new outlet for the fur trade of the interior. At almost the same moment, Sieur de Rémonville published a memoir, calling attention to the importance of Louisiana and to the danger of its being seized by the English who were even then engaged in fitting out an expedition for the purpose of making a settlement in the Mississippi Valley. Louis XIV replied favorably to Iberville's request, and he sailed from Brest on October 24, 1698, with two hundred soldiers and colonists, among them his brother Bienville and Father Douay, who had been with La Salle on his last expedition.

Iberville was an experienced sailor and had no trouble in reaching the Gulf shore near Pensacola (January, 1699). There, however, was a Spanish post which had been founded, perhaps, in anticipation of his coming. Proceeding westwardly, the vessels anchored off Ship Island, one of the group that forms the eastern extension of the delta of the Mississippi. Establishing a temporary post at this

faults of this settlement in his *Introduction to the Revolt*, i, 276.

[1] Heinrich in his *La Louisiane* (pp. 285–289) has an interesting account of the Le Moyne family.

point, Iberville and Bienville entered the mouth of a great river which they ascended for a considerable distance. On the return journey the natives gave the explorers a letter which Tonty had left for La Salle a dozen years before. This convinced the brothers that the stream which they had found was, indeed, the Mississippi. They established a post on its bank below the site of the later New Orleans to guard against English encroachments ; the bulk of the colonists moved from Ship Island to the shores of Biloxi Bay on the mainland. Leaving Bienville in the colony, Iberville returned to France.[1]

The history of the early years of Louisiana[2] is one unbroken record of disagreement, starvation, and misfortune. The fur trade did not turn out to be as profitable as had been expected, because a good deal of it was diverted to the English settlements. For years there was great lack of food in the colony. On two separate occasions, in this early time, bands of marriageable girls arrived from France and gave opportunity for a merry round of marriage services ; otherwise, the early years of the colony were not cheerful. In 1713 there were four hundred white settlers and twenty negro slaves in Louisiana.

[1] Iberville made two other voyages to the Mississippi. Upon the outbreak of war in 1701, he took command of a fleet to ravage the English settlements and to protect those of France and Spain. He died at Havana in 1706.

[2] C. E. A. Gayarré's *History of Louisiana* (revised ed. 1885) is the standard history of Louisiana; for the early period it is necessarily founded on F. X. Martin's *History of Louisiana from the Earliest Period* (2 vols., New Orleans, 1827). Grace King in her *Bienville* ("Makers of America" series) and her *New Orleans, the Place and the People*, has retold the story briefly and attractively. Pierre Heinrich's *La Louisiane* *sous la Compagnie des Indes* (Paris, 1907) is the best account of the early years of the Colony and has an excellent bibliography. Villiers du Terrage gives a few pages to the early time in his *Les Dernières Années de la Louisiane Française* (Paris, 1904). A useful list of early maps is in Thomassy's *Cartographie de l'Ancienne Louisiane* (in his *Geologie Pratique de la Louisiane*, pp. 205–226, also issued separately). Many documents are printed in the *Louisiana Historical Collections*, vols. ii, iii. Chapter II of P. J. Hamilton's *Colonial Mobile* deals with the first years of Louisiana history from the point of view of a local antiquary.

In 1712 the king granted the trade of Louisiana to Sieur Antoine Crozat for fifteen years.   Louisiana is described in this patent as the land between New France and New Mexico and bounded on the east by Carolina.   Crozat infused new life into the undertaking, but as it soon appeared that the profits, if there were any, were certain to be small, he lost interest and transferred his patent to the crown.   In 1717 the king conferred upon the Company of the West the commercial rights which Crozat had surrendered, together with the title to the soil.   This company, which was then generally known as the Mississippi Company, was the famous speculative body that was connected with John Law's banking schemes.   For a time the profits of the Mississippi Company were large, or seemed to be so, but they were derived from speculation in France and not from the commerce and agriculture of Louisiana.   The history of the colony at this time is instructive, nevertheless, because it shows the working of an ineffective monopoly.   Enjoying the sole rights of trade within Louisiana, the Company undertook to carry on the whole commerce, charging what it pleased for the things that it sold, and paying what it pleased for those that it bought.   Had Louisiana been an island cut off from all intercourse with the outer world except through the employees of the Company, and had these been honest, such a policy might have been carried out.   As it was, the proximity of English and Spanish settlements and traders made the enforcement of the Company's regulations an absolute impossibility.   English traders brought goods into the back country and undersold the Company's agents, while the fur dealers at Pensacola and Charleston paid higher prices for peltries than did the French, and thus diverted to those ports a large part of the fur trade of Louisiana.[1]

[1] Pierre Heinrich's *La Louisiane sous la Compagnie*, Book i, ch. ii.

The early Louisiana colonists had been mainly recruited from the military service, and the military element for a long time predominated in the colony. Crozat and the Mississippi Company sent over colonists in considerable numbers; but the death rate was very heavy, both on the voyages and in the first years of residence in America. Moreover, the settlers constantly disappeared into the wilderness. There they would be free from the exactions of the Company and also from the moral, religious, and legal restraints of civilization; among the natives also they could enjoy the delights of outdoor life and accumulate wealth from the prosecution of the fur trade which was prohibited to them while they were living in the settled parts of the colony. Social and governmental conditions were very different in Louisiana from those which prevailed in New France. In the southern colony the land was not parceled out into seigniories as it was in the northern, and there was never a body of feudal proprietors answering to the seigniors and habitants of Canada. The Jesuits were brought into competition with the clergy of other orders, as well as with the secular priests in Louisiana, as they were not in New France. Possibly for this reason the relations of the Louisianians to the Indians were very different from those of the Canadians to the natives who did not belong to the Iroquois confederacy. French writers declare that English traders from Carolina and Virginia incited the natives against the French settlers in the lower Mississippi Valley; but there is no reason to suppose that the governments of the English colonies did anything of the kind, or, indeed, had any settled policy as to the French colonists in these early years.

The founding of the city of New Orleans (1718) on the eastern side of the Mississippi River, and some hundred miles from its mouth, was the most important event in the first twenty-five years of Louisiana's history. There had been a fortified post below this point in earlier years, and settlements had been made farther up the river, but the government had been administered from the settlements on Biloxi Bay and on Mobile Bay. Probably there were Frenchmen living on the site of New Orleans before 1718, but in that year streets were laid out in regular order and several buildings were erected. Four years afterward (1722) the new settlement became the capital of the province. Pierre F. X. de Charlevoix gives an unfavorable description of it in that year. He says that the city comprised about one hundred " barraques " placed in no very great order, a wooden storehouse, and two or three " maisons," which would be no ornament to a village of France.[1] He estimated the population of the entire province at about fifty-five hundred, of whom six hundred were negro slaves.

In 1722 the administration of Louisiana was reorganized by the division of the province into nine districts, each of which was under the jurisdiction of a commander, but there was an appeal from his decisions to a Superior Council, which was appointed by the authorities in France. In the same year the colony was parceled out for religious purposes between the Capuchins and the Jesuits: the former having charge of the spiritual concerns of those living south of Natchez; the latter having religious supremacy north of that point. This arrangement was made by the Bishop of Quebec, for the limits of civil and ecclesiastical rule were not coincident. It is hardly worth while to follow the later history of Louisiana in detail. In 1731 the

[1] Charlevoix's *Histoire de la Nouvelle France*, iii, 430 (" Journal d'un Voyage fait par ordre du Roy dans l'Amerique Septentrionale; adressé a Madame la Duchesse de Lesdiguîeres ").

Company surrendered its rights to the crown; but there was no great change in the government. During the next fifteen years the population of the province remained almost stationary; in 1745 there were seventeen hundred white men, fifteen hundred white women, and two thousand negro slaves in Louisiana. The large proportion of slaves to the white male population and the harshness of the slave code, which was based on that of Santo Domingo, in no long time led to an insurrection. By the middle of the century, besides the settlements on the lower Mississippi at New Orleans, at Natchez, and near the mouth of the Arkansas, there was a post at Natchitoches, near what is now the boundary between Louisiana and Texas, and a number of settlements in the Illinois country besides the colony not far from the site of the modern St. Louis, and one or two other posts on the western bank of the Mississippi. It is now necessary to return to the narrative of the international relations of the English and French colonists, and for the present the dispute is confined to the seaboard.

The Treaty of Ryswick in 1697 gave a breathing space of four years to the combatants in Europe and America; but in 1701 the conflict began anew ostensibly over the question of the succession to the Spanish throne, but in reality over the old question of the supremacy of Protestant or Catholic. The twelve years' war which followed is known in European history as the War of the Spanish Succession; in American annals it is called Queen Anne's War.[1] Frontenac was no longer living; his successor was Philippe de Rigaud, Marquis de Vaudreuil. In Frontenac's time the defense of Canada against the Iroquois and the raising the martial spirit of its people had been the main object. Now

[1] This part of the story is treated by Parkman in his *Half-Century of Conflict*, vol. i.

the case was altered. The Iroquois seemed to be more amenable to French influence than at any earlier day. Large numbers of the Mohawks had been converted to Christianity and had been settled in Canada at Caughnawaga on the right bank of the St. Lawrence above Montreal. The Iroquois seem to have felt that it was well to have the French as a makeweight to the English, and that it would not do to carry hostilities with them too far. At the moment they appeared to be bent on peace, and the French were equally desirous of doing nothing that would stir them into harmful activity. The case of the Indians of northern New England was very different. They were hesitating between the English and the French; the French missionaries had great influence among them, but so also had the English traders. At this time there was talk in Canada and also in France of the conquest of New England. It was known, of course, that the New Englanders were numerous, but they were looked down upon as farmers and shopkeepers. Iberville proposed to lead a force to attack the capital city of New England, his idea being to approach it at nightfall, and, from the edge of the surrounding forest, surprise the inhabitants, entirely oblivious of the fact that that hated center of Puritanism was situated on what was practically an island. These were wild ideas. Vaudreuil's plan was much less picturesque and as much more practical. It was, in brief, to raid the New England frontier with bands composed of Christianized Indians operating with a few Frenchmen and every now and then with parties of New England Indians. It would be impossible in this way seriously to diminish the military resources of New England; but, on the other hand, the New England Indians would be brought to the side of the French, and the Roman Catholic Indians of New

France would secure a supply of Puritan captives for conversion or ransom. How far conversion entered into the plan may not be clear, but it is certain that when they were once in Canada, no effort was spared to bring captive New Englanders to the Faith.

Of all the events of this trying time, none stands forth better recorded than the attack on Deerfield in February, 1704. Two hundred Indians and fifty Canadians stole through the wilderness in the dead of winter. From the afternoon of February 28 until two o'clock the next morning they shivered in the gloom of a pine forest about two miles from the town. The night was harsh and the sentries, thinking that no one would be abroad in such inclement weather, went into their houses and, it is said, to bed. No one was on the lookout when the enemy climbed the palisades. Suddenly they broke into the houses, such of them as were not securely guarded, and killed those who resisted or who did not find safety in flight. One house held out to the end and preserved its occupants, seven men, four or five women, and a number of children. In all, fifty-three English people were killed on the spot and one hundred and eleven were dragged away into captivity, while one hundred and thirty-seven escaped in the confusion of the attack or defended themselves until the raiders left. Among the captives was John Williams, the minister of the town. With his wife and five children he started on the long journey to the St. Lawrence. Mrs. Williams struggled on for a day or two, when she became so feeble that her Indian captor killed her. For the next few days one captive after another, who could not keep up with the party, was put out of misery; in all some seventeen were killed on the march, and others died of hunger. At length Williams reached Chambly, but his suffering was by no means at an end. The priests and the Indians made a most determined effort to convert him. He was dragged into the church, was ordered by his Indian master to make the sign of the cross, and was told to kiss the crucifix. To hasten his conversion, the Indian threatened him with his tomahawk and tried to bite off one of his thumbnails. Vaudreuil bought him of his Indian captor, but he was not permitted to have his children about him. These the Jesuits incessantly tried to convert, sometimes even whipping them. In after years, Williams and about one half of the captives were ransomed and exchanged for Frenchmen captured in Acadia. Williams's daughter, Eunice, when seven or eight years old, was converted to Catholicism.[1] She afterward married an Indian and lived the life of a squaw to the end, although she visited her relatives in Deerfield no less than four times. They asked her and her husband to settle down in New England, but she refused, declaring that it would endanger her soul. For years war parties, large and small, harassed the frontier until scarcely a town from Wells on the Maine coast to Northampton in the Connecticut Valley was free from its tale of woe. Bands of bushrangers were sent out from time to time by the Massachusetts authorities, but little could be done in this way; the only practical mode of meeting the difficulty was to attack it at its source and to conquer New France.

These raids on New England had their origin in the St. Lawrence Valley. The logical thing to do would be to attack Montreal and the near-by settlements, whence these war parties proceeded. This, in the existing condition of affairs, was a matter of difficulty. The Iroquois were luke-

[1] This part of the story is graphically told by Charlotte A. Baker in her *True* *Stories of New England Captives,* 133-249.

warm; the New Yorkers were engaged in a fierce contest over constitutional limitations with their masquerading governor, Lord Cornbury; the Pennsylvania Quakers would not give money for war unless, as Governor Fletcher remarked, they were first converted; and the Jersey men, secure in their position, would give no money under any conditions. The wilderness between the settlements in New York and New England and the French hamlets on the St. Lawrence at once protected the French settlers and gave opportunity for the warfare of the forest. Under these circumstances, Acadia was bound to atone vicariously for the sins of the larger French colony.

In 1704 a hastily gathered expedition under Benjamin Church, the old Indian fighter now sixty-five years of age and so corpulent that he required an assistant to push him over the hard places in the woods, undertook to inflict retribution upon the French settlers and the Indians in the East. Accomplishing nothing in Maine, the expedition sailed for Port Royal in Acadia, but was so poorly commanded that it returned discomfited, without having accomplished anything whatever except to secure a few prisoners for purposes of exchange. In 1707 a more formidable expedition was sent from Boston for the conquest of Acadia. It included nearly fifteen hundred soldiers and sailors and was convoyed by an English frigate and the "Province Galley." The commander was Colonel John March, who had already performed valuable service on the frontier, but proved to be entirely incapable for the work in hand. The troops landed, but after a few days on shore, reëmbarked and returned. They were sent back again and after some skirmishing on shore finally returned to Boston. In 1709 a more formidable attempt was made against New France. This time there was to be an expedition by way of Lake Champlain, with the aid of the Iroquois Indians under the command of Francis Nicholson, once governor of New York and later of Maryland and of Virginia.   In connection with it, an attack was to be made on Quebec this time by a naval force and soldiers sent from England, with some recruits from Boston.   The inland expedition ended in failure.   The Iroquois were indisposed, a pestilence made its appearance, and a military force from Canada appeared to dispute the progress of the expedition.   The fleet which was to have come from England for the conquest of Quebec in 1709 actually appeared in 1710.   After taking on board supplies and recruits at Boston, the expedition sailed for Port Royal instead of for Quebec.   The invaders landed, nearly two thousand strong, and in due season began regular siege operations against the town.   After a few days of cannonading, Subercase, the French commander, surrendered.   When taken the garrison numbered but two hundred and fifty-eight men ; but some had doubtless escaped from the place before the end.   Nicholson changed the name from Port Royal to Annapolis Royal.   The town had already been captured by Argall in 1616, by Sedgwick in 1654, and by Phips in 1690, but it was now to remain permanently in English hands.[1]   As it was the only place of any importance or of military strength in Acadia at that time, its possession meant that of the whole province.

The next year (1711) another attempt was made to capture Quebec.[2]   This time a formidable fleet with a large force of land troops on board came from England, and

[1] Parkman's *Half-Century of Conflict*, i, 142–149; *Year-Book* of the Massachusetts Society of Colonial Wars for 1897, 81–126.

[2] Hovenden Walker's *Journal: or Full Account of the late Expedition to* *Canada with an Appendix containing Commissions, Orders, Letters*, etc. (London, 1711) ; *Year-Book* of the Society of Colonial Wars in Massachusetts for 1897, pp. 127–141; Parkman's *Half-Century of Conflict*, i, 157–175.

after recruiting men and provisions at Boston sailed for the St. Lawrence. The land commander was John Hill, brother of the queen's favorite, Mrs. Masham. The naval commander was Admiral Sir Hovenden Walker. It is difficult to say which was more incompetent, because Hill never had a chance to show the extent of his inefficiency; but as to the unsuitability of Walker for chief command of so great a naval force, there could be no question. The fleet consisted of eleven ships of war, with about sixty transports and attendant ships. They carried twelve thousand fighting men, of whom fifty-five hundred were British regulars and fifteen hundred were provincials. Well led, the expedition should have conquered Quebec and all Canada. As it was, it never came within sight of the capital of New France. The navigation of the lower St. Lawrence is exceedingly dangerous, and Walker had more confidence in his own capacity than in that of a bribed French pilot. At all events, in a fog and strong wind the fleet sailed directly into the breakers and might well have been utterly destroyed. Ten ships went on the rocks with the loss of nine hundred lives. The loss in ships and men was heavy, but the force was so large in comparison with any that could be brought against it that its hasty return after this disaster was inexcusable and discreditable to the men responsible for it. This was the last military event of importance in America in the course of the war. In 1713 at Utrecht was signed a treaty which may well be regarded as the beginning of the diplomatic history of the United States. By this instrument,[1] France ceded to England Acadia with its ancient limits, and acknowledged the Iroquois to be subjects of the dominion of England. Moreover, Newfoundland was also given to England, but the French

[1] Du Mont's *Corps Diplomatique*, viii, Part i, p. 341.

were to be allowed to dry fish on the coast from Buena Vista to Cape Riche. Hudson's Bay and Straits, with an undefined amount of territory, were also acknowledged to be English.

The Peace of Utrecht left the French nearly prostrate in Europe and America. They had almost reached the determination of abandoning their American colonies. A few years sufficed to bring new vitality, and by 1720 they were once more embarking on the path of colonial expansion. This now took the form of denials of the plain meaning of the treaty of 1713. At that time, for the sake of peace, they had been willing to sacrifice all the territory east of the province of Maine, but now they declared that Acadia meant only the eastern part of the peninsula which now forms the province of Nova Scotia; this, with Port Royal, was all that the treaty gave to the English. In 1713 they had acknowledged the Iroquois to be subjects of England; now they endeavored to confine the Iroquois territory within the smallest possible dimensions.

This renewed activity of the French took the material form of the fortification of a port on the island of Cape Breton, which was named Louisbourg,[1] and the renewal of Vaudreuil's policy of attaching the Indians of northern New England definitely to the French cause, and also of trying to induce the Acadians to emigrate from their beloved peninsula to the island stronghold of Cape Breton. The posture of affairs in Acadia was, indeed, peculiar. Port Royal, now Annapolis, was in English hands, but sometimes it seemed that the home authorities regretted its possession. They did little to insure its defense, and gave the commander no adequate force with which to

---

[1] Parkman describes the founding of Louisbourg and its capture in 1745 in his *Half-Century of Conflict*, i, ch. ix, and ii, chs. xviii-xx.

impress the French colonists with the desirability of being faithful to their new masters. On the other hand, the French authorities dispatched emissaries, especially priests, to seduce the Acadians from their new allegiance and to impress upon them the thought that their duty to God required them to remain good Frenchmen. For their part, the Acadians might well have felt doubtful as to their position. They had been required to take an oath to be faithful subjects of their new king, but at the same time had been given some kind of assurance that they would not be obliged to bear arms against those of their own race and religion. They regarded themselves as " Neutrals." Under the circumstances this arrangement was distinctly advantageous to the English, because the Acadians, believing themselves secure, resisted the approaches of French emissary and Roman Catholic priest, and neither repatriated themselves nor attacked the English garrison. The English were therefore able to maintain their hold on the country at very slight cost to themselves ; but at the same time they made no attempt at an effective occupation of Acadia.

The case of the New England Indians was more serious. The emissary chosen by the French authorities in Canada to secure the Indians of Maine for France was Father Rale, a well-meaning French cleric. He established himself with the Norridgewock Indians on the Kennebec, and there lived as spiritual guide and leader in what the French now affected to regard as territory which had not been surrendered in 1713. There could be only one issue, and that was the dispersal of the Indians by Massachusetts troops and the death of Father Rale himself. Following on this the frontier was harassed by Indian raids, which led to renewed irritation on the part of the English with the loss of valuable lives and much human suffering and with no resultant political advantages.   Yet it must be said that the French authorities in Canada should not be held to too strict an account.   Their position with the ever increasing strength of the English colonies was most precarious.   The northern New England Indians were to them like a modern "buffer state," and their hold upon them was worth much human suffering on the part of their growing enemy.

In 1744 there began in Europe another of those dynastic wars which marked the first sixty years of the eighteenth century.   In this contest the English and the French became involved on opposing sides, and the conflict thus begun necessarily extended to their American colonies. The governor of Massachusetts at this time was one of the few remarkable Englishmen who occupied high office in America in that century.   William Shirley[1] had many annoying peculiarities, but he possessed that imaginative prescience which forms one of the attributes of statesmanship.   The stronghold of Louisbourg on Cape Breton Island attracted his attention and he determined to wrench it from the grasp of its builders.   The means at his command were absurdly inadequate for the performance of so great a task; but in war, enterprise and good will often have outweighed guns and preparations, no matter how elaborate. New England provided the men and material for the land attack almost unaided, but an English naval force arrived in the Gulf of St. Lawrence just in time to give that command of the sea which the enterprise demanded.   The commander of the English colonial attacking force was William Pepperrell, a substantial merchant of the town of Kittery in the province of Maine and one of the richest men in the colonies.   He had not enjoyed much military experi-

---

[1] There is no adequate memoir of Shirley. J. A. Doyle's article in the *Dictionary of National Biography* brings together the events in Shirley's career, but it is very brief.

ence in the field, but he possessed the businesslike faculty of securing harmonious action from men of such varying characteristics as a Massachusetts farmer and an admiral in the British navy.[1] On the 24th of March, 1745, ninety transports, more or less, many of them fishing vessels, escorted by three colonial cruisers, sailed from Boston for the conquest of the second strongest fort in North America. Four thousand men, who had been recruited in seven weeks, with a few light cannon, was the force which Pepperrell had for storming the citadel; but he expected to capture a detached battery in which were thirty heavy pieces and with these take the town.   The spirit of this adventure is well illustrated by a letter which Mr. Parkman prints in the first volume of his "Half-Century of Conflict."   It is from John Payne of Boston, whoever he may have been, to the colonel of one of the Massachusetts regiments.   As Parkman says, it gives no sign of the religious feeling of the New England people, but well illustrates their ardor in this enterprise.   The writer says he hopes that this will find "you" at Louisbourg "with a bowl of punch, a pipe, and a pack of cards," and whatever else you desire.   He concludes with the statement that if drinking to your success would take the fort, it must now be in your hands, and asks for arrack with which to celebrate the victory.

The siege was not so soon concluded as the writer of the letter, noted in the preceding paragraph, hoped, but it was not long continued after the letter had reached its destination.   Six days after it was written, on April 30, Pepperrell landed his men on the shore to the westward of the town.   Two days later, May 2, four hundred of the New Englanders marched around Louisbourg Harbor and

[1] There is a good sketch of Pepperrell's career prefixed to the volume of "Pepperrell Papers" in Massachusetts Historical Society's *Collections*, Sixth Series, x.

entered unopposed the grand battery which contained the coveted thirty heavy guns. Under the superintendence of Seth Pomeroy, a gunsmith by trade and now a major by profession, the touchholes of the captured ordnance were soon drilled out, the guns were dragged to the land side of the town, and fire opened. There was suffering among the soldiers, lack of food and clothing, and the inevitable sickness; but, nevertheless, the work went steadily on. For forty-nine days the siege continued. A combined attack by sea and land was on the point of being made when Louisbourg surrendered; but not until nine thousand cannon balls had been fired into the town.[1] It was the fortune of war, rather than valor and discipline, which gave this signal triumph. None the less, Louisbourg fell, and Pepperrell became an English baronet.

Few disasters in the eighteenth century so overwhelmed the French with shame as did this catastrophe. They set on foot a great expedition to sail across the Atlantic, reconquer Louisbourg, seize Acadia, and burn Boston. In June, 1746, sixty-five or sixty-six ships sailed from Brest under the command of the Duc d'Anville. Ten or eleven of them were ships of the line, while thirty-four were transports which conveyed three thousand men. Calms and sudden squalls succeeded one another, and then came pestilence. As they neared the American coast they were enveloped in fog which broke away as a gale burst upon them. D'Anville died of apoplexy or poison, his successor killed himself, and what was left of the expedition returned to France.[2] The next year, 1747, the French tried again,

---

[1] " Pepperrell Papers " in Massachusetts Historical Society's *Collections*, Sixth Series, x, 300. There is other matter in the same society's *Proceedings* for 1867 and 1897. Parkman's account in his *Half-Century of Conflict* will amply serve the needs of most readers.

[2] Parkman has related this episode in detail in his *Half-Century of Conflict;* see also American Antiquarian Society's

but this time their fleet met a stronger English squadron on the open sea and suffered defeat. On the other hand, a well-concerted expedition which Shirley organized for the conquest of Canada was disbanded in 1746, either because the king had employment for his troops elsewhere, or possibly because of English jealousy of colonial military prowess.[1] In 1748 the Peace of Aix-la-Chapelle put an end to this conflict. Louisbourg was restored to the French, but New England, by act of Parliament, was repaid a part of the money which she had expended in the war.

From 1713 to 1754, apart from the struggle for Acadia and Cape Breton, the principal interest in the relations of Englishmen and Frenchmen in America lies in the exploitation of the fur trade of the interior by the people of these two nationalities. The year of the settlement of Louisiana witnessed the attempt of three nations — England, France, and Spain — to occupy the country on the northern shore of the Gulf of Mexico. The French expedition, which resulted in the settlement of Louisiana, has already been described. Simultaneously, the Spaniards sought to occupy the Gulf coast of Florida. They were, in point of time, before the French, and Iberville, sailing along the northern shore of the Gulf, found them already ensconced at Pensacola. From that time for sixty years and more the Spaniards retained possession of that town and gradually extended their posts to connect that settlement with the older Spanish town of St. Augustine. These settlements were never very strong, but they served the purpose of maintaining the Spanish

Proceedings, New Series, xvii, 5. Hugo Paltsits, the author of the latter paper, gives the number of D'Anville's fleet at ninety-seven, including fifty-six transports and twenty-four "privateers and other vessels."

[1] See opinion of the Duke of Bedford printed in *ibid.*, p. 8. Shirley's account of these campaigns is in his *Memoirs of the Principal Transactions of the Last War* (London and Boston, 1748).

hold on that territory and on the Indians living in that region.

The English occupation of the country from the Gulf to the Ohio and between the Alleghanies and the Mississippi is more difficult to trace, but it was none the less effective. La Salle, on his trip down the Mississippi in 1682, saw English goods in the possession of the natives living on the banks of the great river, and Iberville, or rather his brother Bienville, found an English ship at anchor in that stream. The Indians of the region, now comprised in the states of Mississippi, Alabama, western Georgia, Tennessee, and Kentucky, were divided into four great tribes. Of these the northernmost were the Cherokees, who lived in what is now Tennessee; westward of them, nearer the Mississippi and in the northern part of the state of that name, were the Chickasaws; south of them were the Choctaws. South of the Cherokees and east of the Chickasaws and Choctaws lived the Creeks, their tribes extending southeastwardly into Florida. The Cherokees were the most civilized of North American Indians, but the Chickasaws and Choctaws were also beyond the hunter stage. They lived in villages and had rather advanced ideas as to government.

Of the Indians mentioned in the preceding paragraph, the Choctaws as a rule were amenable to French influence, although occasionally they gave the French colonists a good deal of anxiety. The other tribes were all friendly with the English, the Cherokees especially so, and the Creeks least of all. In 1730 Sir Alexander Cuming arrived in Carolina to negotiate with the Cherokees and succeeded so well that he took a number of their chiefs to England that they might gain an added sense of British power and strengthen the league of friendship.

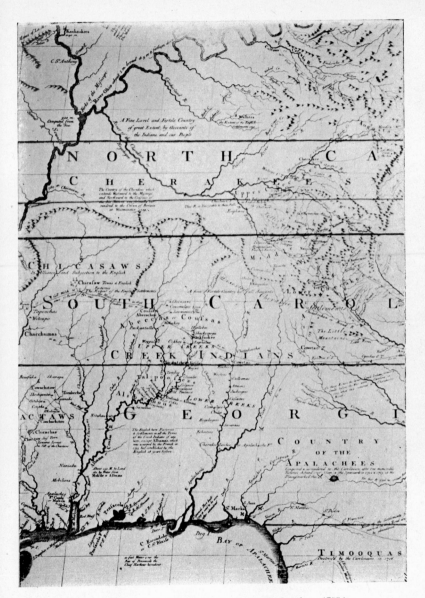

(From Mitchell's *Map of North America*, London, 1755.)

The Chickasaws and Choctaws were often at war with one another and were incited thereto by the whites. The Chickasaws took their captives to Charleston, as did other Indian tribes, and they were shipped from that port to the West Indies, where they were sold as slaves. The Carolina fur trade with these Indians assumed very large dimensions about 1720; and throughout this period, notwithstanding Indian wars, continued to be a source of wealth to the merchants of Charleston, to South Carolina, and to English merchants, for some of the Southern fur traders were in the employ of persons residing in England.[1] The traffic was carried on by regular routes. Fort Moore on the Savannah River, opposite the site of the present Augusta, was the headquarters of the traders. From that point a road led to Charleston and another westwardly to the Indian villages. Later, another post was established on the Congaree, near the present city of Columbia; and still later, frontier posts were established at Ninety-six and Fort Prince George. In the beginning the furs were brought down to the coast and the trade goods were taken west on the backs of carriers, but later mules were utilized and trains sometimes containing eighty of them journeyed eastward and westward; nearly a quarter of a million deerskins were brought into Charleston in the year 1731, and doubtless other furs besides.[2] These facts have been given in some detail because they show that the English influence was very strong in the southwest in the first half of the eighteenth

[1] This statement is made on general grounds; but it has a slight confirmation in the following extract, which is taken from an anonymous tract entitled *The Importance of the British Plantations in America to this Kingdom* (London, 1731), p. 66, "The Indian Trade there [South Carolina] being of such exceeding Advantage, and frequently carried on by the Servants of those who live here."

[2] J. H. Logan, *History of Upper South Carolina*, 382; this valuable work has been freely used in discussing this subject. McCrady has brought together the leading facts in his *South Carolina under the Royal Government*, 270, 297.

century. The tendency was for the French gradually to push the English northwardly from the Gulf and east wardly from the Mississippi. But in all this time the English seem to have been more successful in their dealings with the Indians of this region than were the French.

In the extreme north dwelt the Iroquois, who are now called the Six Nations, since the Tuscaroras, driven from Carolina, joined their kindred tribes north of the Ohio. From the beginning of European colonization the Iroquois[1] had held close relations to the settlers of New York, whether Dutch or English. In 1684, Dongan, with their consent or desire, had taken them under English protection, and this fact had been emphasized and confirmed at many subsequent conferences. Especially on July 19, 1701, in a conference held at Albany between Lieutenant Governor Nanfan and representatives of the Five Nations, they gave and rendered up "all that Land where the Bever hunting is w[ch] we won with the Sword 80 years ago & pray that He (the King) may be our Protector & Defendor there; and desire that our Secretary may write an Instrument w[ch] we will Sign & Seal that it may be carried by him to the King."[2]   In 1713, by the Treaty of Utrecht, the French acknowledged the Iroquois to be English subjects. What this phrase meant to the parties to the treaty cannot possibly be stated, nor does it make much difference, because the limits of the Iroquois

---

[1] On the Iroquois, see L. H. Morgan's *League of the Iroquois* (New York, 1851, reprinted with additional matter, 1901); H. R. Schoolcraft's *Notes on the Iroquois* (Albany, 1847). There are valuable papers in the publications of the local historical societies of the Iroquois country, especially the Oneida Historical Society.

[2] Peter Wraxall's *An Abridgment of the Records of Indian Affairs contained in Four Folio Volumes, transacted in the Colony of New York from the year 1678 to the Year 1751*, folio 37. The manuscript of this work is at Albany, a copy was placed at my disposal by Mr. C. H. McIlwain. The treaty is printed in *New York Colonial Documents*, iv, 908.

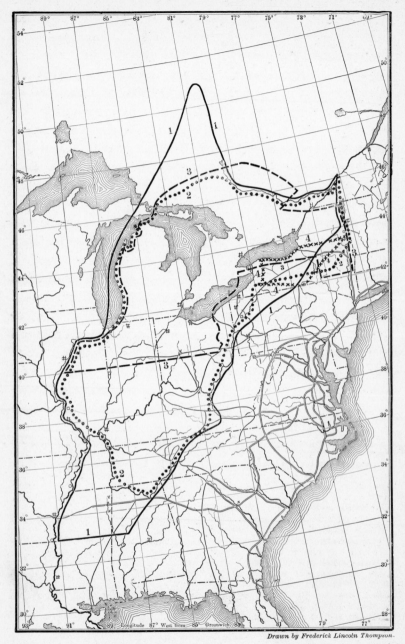

THE LIMITS OF THE IROQUOIS ACCORDING TO CONTEMPORARY MAPS

(1, Huske, 1755 ; 2, Jeffreys, 1755 ; 3, Kitchin, 1769 ; 4, Palairet, 1759. Roads and
trails are marked by double and single lines.)

country are absolutely unknown now and were then.[1]

The Iroquois had a somewhat divided allegiance. On the one side, they feared greatly the power and insinuating ways of the French ; on the other, they constantly complained of the high price of English goods and of the failure of the English authorities to perform their promises. At one time they protested against the sale of rum, but at another time demanded that the prohibition, which the New York governor had placed on this traffic, should be at once removed. They do not seem to have understood the working of the forces of supply and demand upon the price of commodities, nor to have realized that war naturally increased the price of gunpowder and lead. In one conference, when it was suggested that English missionaries should be sent to their villages to convert them to Christianity, they replied that the white people of Albany wore good clothes on Sunday, but owing to the low price of beaver and the high price of English goods it was difficult for them to clothe themselves at all, much less to have an extra suit for Sunday ; when they were able to appear in proper garments on that day, then they would welcome the missionaries,[2] but not before. They

---

[1] Upon the accompanying sketch the limits of the Iroquois as given in several contemporary maps are laid down on modern topography as near as may be. The line of the greatest extent is that given on a map which was compiled by Ellis Huske, an Englishman, who served as postmaster at Boston, published the "Boston Weekly Postboy," and acted as deputy postmaster general of the colonies. He was brother of John Huske, a distinguished general in the British army, and this map is generally ascribed to the latter. Mr. T. N. Hoover has shown, however, that it was the work of Ellis Huske, who had good opportunities for acquiring information. The smallest area allotted to the Iroquois is on a French map of 1746, which was made by the noted cartographer D'Anville. Both of these maps reflect the patriotic motives of their makers. Probably the most accurate expression of the territorial rights of the Iroquois is that given by Peter Bell on his map of 1763 and by Kitchin on his of 1769; but the southern boundary of the Iroquois homeland might well follow the forty-second parallel to Lake Erie; and the influence of the Six Nations extended far to the south and west of that lake.

[2] Wraxall's *Abridgment of Indian Affairs*, Ms. fol. 94.

frequently alleged that the English traders sold goods to the Frenchmen at Montreal cheaper than they sold them to the Indians. This may have been true, because there undoubtedly was a large trade in Indian goods between Albany and the French settlements. The regulation of this traffic was one of the burning questions in New York politics in that period. It was carried on contrary to the interests of the growth of English power on the continent, but was so profitable that laws were of slight use in checking it.

Westward of the Iroquois lived various tribes, who were generally grouped together under the phrase " the Farr Indians " or " the Wild Indians." Of these the " Twich Twicks," " Twightwees," or Miamis and the Wagenhaes most frequently appear in the records of conferences. The New Yorkers desired to have these Wild Indians come to Albany with their furs; but the Iroquois preferred to act as middlemen. The relations between the western tribes and the Iroquois were very complicated. The latter regarded the former as tributaries; the English desired the Iroquois to keep the peace with the Farr Indians; while the French were always stirring the remoter savages to do what they dared not do themselves, — make war upon the Five Nations. Altogether the problem was an interesting one, full of complications and difficult of solution. The extent to which the English traded directly with the western Indians or, indeed, with the western Iroquois, is another difficult matter. So far as the evidence of the maps tells us anything, there were several English posts on or near the southern shores of the Great Lakes or on the head waters of the rivers flowing from the north into the Ohio. Some of these posts were Indian villages, others were forts that were occupied for

a few months only in each year. By 1750, however, it
seems reasonably certain that there was considerable
trade going on between the English and the Indians of
the interior, and that a good many English traders resided
permanently in those regions.

South of the Iroquois and the Wild Indians, and north of
the territory inhabited by the Cherokees, was another group
of Indian tribes who inhabited the southern and central
portions of what are now the states of Ohio, Indiana, and
Illinois. Among these, except those living on or near the
banks of the Mississippi, English influence was strong.
When Céloron de Bienville made his famous journey
down the Ohio, he kept coming across English traders.
For instance, at an abandoned village of the Shawanoes,
he found six English traders, the next day at another village he came across six more; at Logstown there were
ten of them,[1] and at the mouth of the Scioto there was
another party of Englishmen. These entries in Céloron's
"Journal" are the best evidence of the activity of English traders in the western country. South of the Ohio,
in what is now the state of Kentucky, the country was
uninhabited save by wild game, and was hunted over by both
the Ohio and southern Indians. From this brief statement it will be seen that the English influence was strong
beyond the mountains in the first half of the eighteenth
century, and that many Englishmen had been to that
region and some of them had resided there; but it does
not seem that there were any persons who can properly
be called English settlers west of the mountains in 1750.
The French, on the other hand, had already established
several permanent settlements in the western country,
especially along the line of the Mississippi and its near-by

---

[1] Parkman's *Montcalm and Wolfe*, i, 47.

affluents. There was the settlement at Cahokia and others in the vicinity, at Kaskaskia and at Vincennes, the last named on the Wabash River. In these and other scattered French hamlets there might have been, perhaps, five hundred white persons — men, women, and children — north of the settled parts of Louisiana and south of the Great Lakes. In addition, there were the settlements at Detroit, St. Joseph's, and perhaps other places which might be dignified by the term "village" and not be regarded strictly as trading posts or mission stations. To sum up, it appears that the French were entitled by right of occupancy to the lands along the Mississippi and the Great Lakes and the St. Lawrence so far as these did not properly belong to the Five Nations. On the other hand, the English were as clearly entitled to the Atlantic seashore from Lake Champlain and the Penobscot southward to Spanish Florida. They had not occupied the interior region between the Alleghanies and the Mississippi, but their extensive fur trade and influence with the natives may be said to have given them a better right to a large part of this country than the French enjoyed by reason of their few settlements on the middle Mississippi and its affluents. The country was open to the first occupant and it was a legitimate prize to fall to him who displayed the greatest activity.

On the 15th of June, 1749, Céloron de Bienville, sent by the Marquis de la Galissonière, governor of Canada, set out from Montreal to take possession of the Ohio Valley for France.[1] He had with him two hundred and fourteen white men, soldiers, and Canadians, and a body of Indians

---

[1] "Céloron's Journal" is printed in *Catholic Historical Researches*, ii, 61–76, 103–117. A map of "Céloron's Route" is in *Frontier Forts of Pennsylvania*, ii, frontispiece.

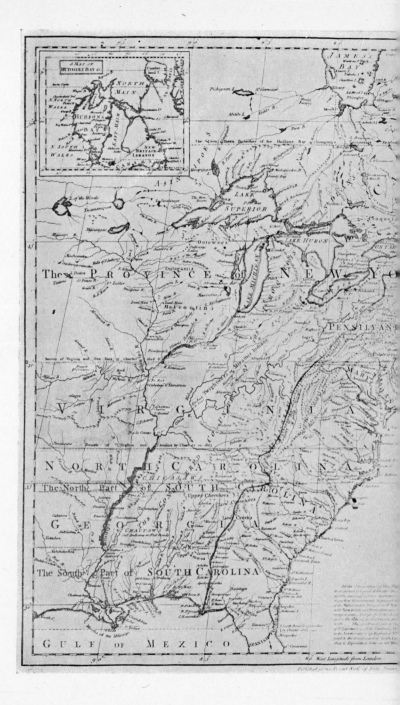

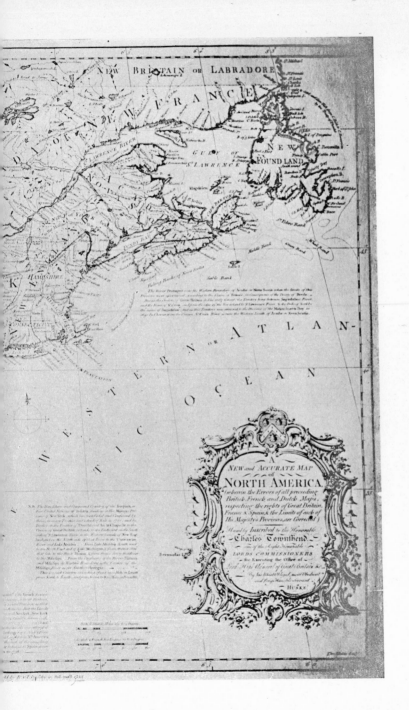

in twenty-three canoes. Leaving Lake Erie, they carried
their canoes overland to Chautauqua Lake in southwestern New York, less than ten miles away. This led them
to the Allegheny, down which they floated, stopping every
now and then to warn off a group of English Indian traders, to palaver with the natives, or to deposit a leaden plate
suitably inscribed. On they went past the confluence of
the Monongahela and down the Ohio to the Great Miami
and up this stream and back to Canada by the way of the
Maumee and Lake Erie. This ceremonial taking possession was a favorite way with the French. By itself, it
conferred no rights, but when followed by settlement, it
did not in any way diminish the right conferred by the
latter.

For years traders had pressed over the Alleghanies from
Will's Creek, where Cumberland now stands, and also
through central Pennsylvania to the junction of the Monongahela and Allegheny rivers, and thence westwardly. At
this time it was uncertain whether this part of the Ohio
Valley was within the limits of Pennsylvania or Virginia,
and this doubt interfered with the English occupation
either by traders or more permanent settlers. In 1749,
however, leading Virginia gentlemen, among them Lawrence and Augustine Washington and George Mason, determined to take the initiative. They procured from the
king a grant of two hundred thousand acres, to be picked
out and settled south of the Ohio and between the Monongahela and the Kanawha rivers, with a promise of three
hundred thousand more if a hundred families were settled
within seven years and a fort built and maintained. In
1750 the company dispatched Christopher Gist, an Indian
trader, to explore the Ohio country and select lands for
them. He reached Logstown, on the Ohio, in November;

he went as far north as Pickawillany on the Great Miami, not very far from the site of the present Bellefontaine, Ohio.   In the following spring he returned to the Ohio River and, following up the Kanawha, regained the settled parts of Virginia.   At about the same time the Loyal Land Company was given eight hundred thousand acres west of the mountain by the Virginia Assembly.   It sent Dr. Thomas Walker[1] across the mountains, by way of Cumberland Gap, to select and survey the lands.   He built a house somewhere on the upper waters of the Cumberland River, and, if we may believe the maps, lived there for some time.   Nothing more was done by either of these land companies, the activity of the French shortly afterward discouraging them.   Such was the condition of affairs when, in 1752, the Marquis Duquesne de Menneville became governor of Canada and proceeded to carry out a more aggressive policy in the Ohio Valley.

The new governor was instructed to build whatever forts on the Ohio he might think were absolutely necessary, but he was informed that the expense of the French colonies in America was already enormous.   In the spring of 1753 he sent a thousand men to the Ohio country.   Passing by the landing place of Céloron, the expedition occupied Presque Isle on the southern shore of the lake, where the city of Erie now stands.   Thence they cut a road to the Rivière aux Bœufs, where they built a fort which they named Fort Le Bœuf.   This stream led to the Allegheny and thence to the Ohio.   Much more was intended, but disease and discouragement prevented.   Three hundred men re-

[1] On these expeditions see J. S. Johnston's *First Explorations of Kentucky*, forming No. 13 of the Filson Club Publication. Besides "Doctor Thomas Walker's Journal" and "Colonel Christopher Gist's Journal," the volume is supplied with excellent notes and introductions, and also has a " Map showing Routes of Walker and Gist," facing p. 33.

mained to garrison the two forts; the rest returned to the settlements on the St. Lawrence.

The governor of Virginia at that time was Robert Dinwiddie, a Scotchman and a man of ability and patriotism, although perhaps given to over-energetic action. Being informed by the traders of the presence of the French, he determined to send a written protest and warning and to demand their retirement from the Ohio Valley. The person whom he selected for this dangerous mission was George Washington, a young surveyor who was already favorably known to many influential persons.

Of all men in history, not one so answers our expectations as Washington. Into whatever part of his life the historian puts his probe, the result is always satisfactory. Washington was a strong, vigorous human being, with a strong, vigorous mind, and an amount of will power which was always equal to the task of compelling his mind and body to perform the part to which Providence set them. He grew up with the expectation of making his own way in the world, and in youth enjoyed the inestimable advantage of close contact with the wilderness. He was trained as a surveyor and was also taught the rudiments of the military art. Descended from Robert and Lawrence Washington of Sulgrave Manor in Northamptonshire, England, he possessed that fairness of mind which had led them in the early years of James's reign to sign a petition in favor of certain Nonconformist ministers who had been driven from their cures.[1] Coming to Virginia, we find his grandfather, John Washington, of so fiery a disposition that he

---

[1] This was the famous "Northampton Petition," in favor of the Nonconformists. The judges assembled before the Privy Council declared that the presenting it was an offense "very near treason, . . . tending to the raising of sedition, Rebellion, and discontent among the people," see Croke's *Reports*, ii, 37; *State Papers, Domestic*, Ms., James I, vol. xii, No. 69. As to the ancestry of Washington see H. F. Waters' *An Examination of the English An-*

was known to the Indians as the "Devourer of Villages," from the completeness of the way in which he did his appointed work. The young surveyor came honestly by that fair-mindedness and military capacity which were forever his distinguishing characteristics. Accompanied by Christopher Gist and six other white men, Washington followed the well-known trading route from Will's Creek to Logstown, and thence to Venango at the confluence of the Allegheny and French Creek; here was an English trading house which the French had seized with its occupants and converted into Fort Machault. Washington was well received at the conquered post and at Fort Le Bœuf. The French commander sent Dinwiddie's letter to Duquesne, and Washington returned to Virginia. This journey occupied the months of November to January, 1753–54.[1]

Dinwiddie now decided to send a force of Virginia militia to the forks of the Ohio to seize and fortify that strategic point and also to incite the Indians to oppose the French. His activity, in turn, induced the Frenchmen to renewed exertions. An English fur trader, Captain Trent, had already gone to the forks of the Ohio in February, 1754, to build a fort there and thus forestall the French; but before the post had been made defensible, the Canadians appeared in much larger numbers than the English and compelled the latter to evacuate the unfinished post. They themselves then constructed on the same spot a much more important work, which they named Fort Duquesne. Meantime Dinwiddie had been setting on foot

cestry of George Washington, Boston, 1889, reprinted from New England Historical and Genealogical Register, 1889. See also E. D. Neill's "Ancestry and Early Years of George Washington" in Pennsylvania Magazine of History, xvi, 261. Washington's personal habits are shown in his "account books," excerpts from these are printed in ibid., xvi, 77.

[1] Washington's Writings, ii, 427 and fol. (Sparks ed.); i, 10 and fol. (Ford ed.); Gist's "Journal" is in Massachusetts Historical Society's Collections, Third Series, v, 101–108.

an expeditionary force to cross the mountains and garrison the fortification which Captain Trent had begun. He now redoubled his efforts, but without much result. Virginia had no efficient military force, and Pennsylvania with its Quaker majority in the assembly was worse off in this respect than Virginia.[1] The best that Dinwiddie could do was to raise a few hundred men who pressed to the point of danger under the command of Colonel Joshua Fry and Washington, the latter commanding the advance. The traders' routes across the Alleghanies and in the western country were bridle paths used by pack trains, but not suitable for artillery and wagons. To move any considerable number of men it was necessary to cut a road from Will's Creek, and this took time. It was thus that Washington found himself at a place called Great Meadows on the western slope of the Alleghanies (May, 1754). Understanding that there was a party of Frenchmen in the vicinity, Washington with a detachment set out to oppose them. He came across the Frenchmen suddenly in the forest and ordered his men to fire. The commander of the French force, Coulon de Jumonville, and a score of his men were killed,[2] and the remainder, twenty or more in number, were captured. This conflict is generally regarded as the beginning of hostilities, but

---

[1] The failure of North Carolina to give effective aid has been the subject of disputation, see *Colonial Records of North Carolina*, v, pp. x–xix, 110, 124 and fol. The papers printed in the text do not always support Saunders's contention in the "Prefatory Note" that North Carolina did her full duty.

[2] French writers almost uniformly refer to this as the "Murder of Jumonville." See Villiers du Terrage, *Les Dernières Années de la Louisiane Française*, 61. As to numbers see Ford's *Writings of Washington*, i, 90. Din-

widdie's letter to Lord Albemarle describing this episode is in *Colonial Records of North Carolina*, v, 368. The *Virginia Magazine of History* (xviii, 43) has an interesting account of this expedition from the pen of Adam Stephen, one of the officers of Washington's force. He declares "it is uncertain whether the English or French fir'd first," which assertion is borne out by a contemporary letter which is attributed to Stephen and printed in the *Pennsylvania Gazette* for Sept. 19, 1754, and given in extract in a note to p. 46 of Stephen's account as above.

the first blow had been struck when the French seized the English trading house at Venango.[1]

Washington returned to Great Meadows and ultimately constructed a rude fortification at that point, which he called Fort Necessity. There on July 3, 1754, he was attacked by a larger French force, commanded by Jumonville's brother, Coulon de Villiers. After defending himself for a time until some of his men were killed and all were disheartened, Washington surrendered upon condition of marching out with the honors of war. The articles of surrender also contained the words "l'assassinat du Sieur de Jumonville," which Washington is supposed to have understood to have signified "death of Jumonville," but which French writers have regarded as an acknowledgment on his part of the assassination of the French commander. The articles were signed about midnight of July 3–4, 1754, but the actual surrender was made on the latter date. In this way in the forests of Virginia began the imperial war between Great Britain and France that was to end with the expulsion of the French from the eastern half of North America.

[1] The most interesting document connected with this portion of Washington's career is the "Journal du Major Wasington," which was first printed at Paris by the French government in 1756 in a volume entitled *Mémoire contenant le Précis des Faits avec leurs Pieces Justificatives*. This compilation is supposed to have been made by J. N. Moreau, who did work of the kind; the original is not known, nor is there any hint of the method by which the French authorities got possession of this copy. It was printed several times in French and has been thence retranslated into English and many times printed as in the appendix to W. Livingston's *Review of the Military Operations in North America* (Dublin, 1757). The most convenient reprint is Sparks's *Washington's Writings*, ii, Appendix, p. 432. J. M. Toner's *Journal of Colonel George Washington, 1754*, is overloaded with annotations. As a source the "Mémoire" and its accompanying documents need authentication. Papers relating to the surrender of Fort Necessity are printed in *Virginia Magazine of History*, vi, 268.

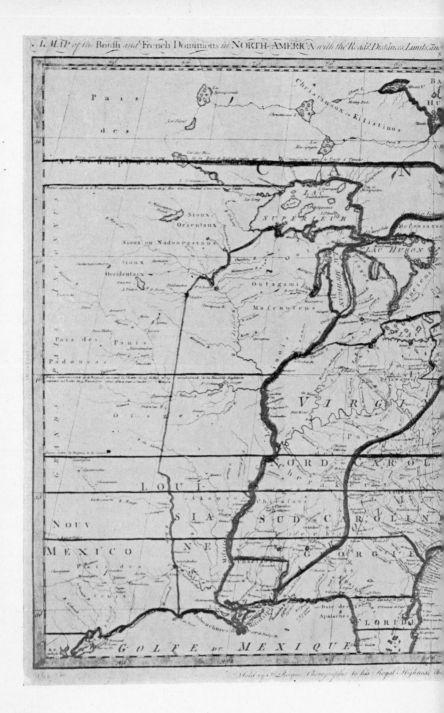

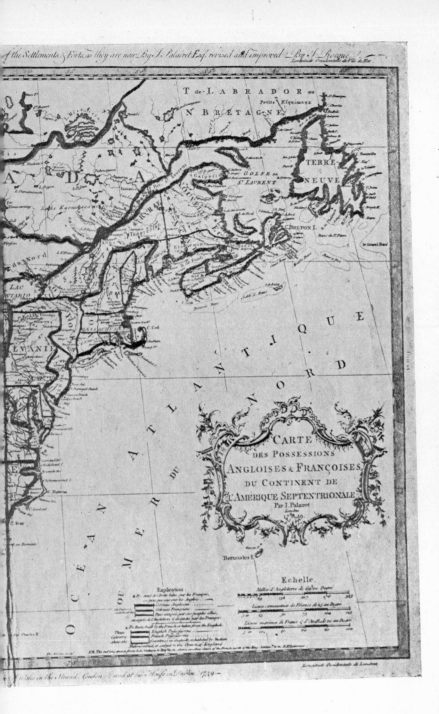

T de LABRADOR ou
N BRETAGNE
Petits Esquimaux

TERRE
NEUVE

GOLFE DE
St LAURENT

BRETON I.

le Grand Banc

ATLANTIQUE NORD

OCÉAN ATLANTIQUE DU MER DU

Carte
DES POSSESSIONS
ANGLOISES & FRANÇOISES,
DU CONTINENT DE
L'AMÉRIQUE SEPTENTRIONALE
Par I. Palairet

Bermudes I.

Explication

Echelle

LAC
ONTARIO

LVANIE

CHAPTER XIX

THE EXPULSION OF THE FRENCH

THE conflict which began in the American wilderness in 1754 spread to Europe and became merged in the world-wide struggle for existence and power that is known to English historians as the Seven Years' War. In America the contest was denominated the French and Indian War and cannot be thoroughly understood apart from the contest in Europe, for, as Pitt observed, "America was conquered in Germany." The strength of the combatants cannot be gauged from an American continental colonial standpoint; but regard must be had to the fact that the forces of both England and France were directed more especially to the eastern side of the Atlantic, to the West India Islands, and to the lands bordering on the Indian Ocean. Thus Pitt was obliged to provide an extensive fleet to keep the French within their harbors of Brest, Rochefort, and Toulon, or, in military phrase, to "contain" them, while combined naval and military expeditions seized Canada, Guadeloupe, Martinique, Pondicherry, and Havana. The great fleets of Hawke, Boscawen, Saunders, and Keppel in the Bay of Biscay and Straits of Gibraltar were as truly fighting for the possession of Canada as the smaller squadrons in the St. Lawrence; the armies which England gave to Frederick in Germany were fighting the battles of England in America as were the armies of Amherst and Wolfe at Louisbourg and Quebec. The English colonists on the mainland outnumbered the French in Canada and Louisiana many times; but France was relatively much stronger in the West Indies, where she possessed Grenada, Dominica, Guadeloupe, Martinique, and Haiti, or the western half of the island of Santo Domingo, besides many smaller islands advantageously situated for commerce protection. In the later years of the contest, Spain brought into the conflict besides Mexico and the lands of the Spanish Main the island of Cuba and the rest of Santo Domingo. The armies of France were large and admirably trained, her navies were supplied with splendid ships, excellently armed. Whenever matters seemed unusually grave, projects of invasion of the British islands at once served to divert formidable portions of England's military and naval forces from the conquest of the colonial possessions of the French king in America and India to the defense of Great Britain and Ireland. The fact that the contest was prolonged for eight or nine years, notwithstanding the brilliancy of England's war minister and the victories of her forces in America and India, shows that the combatants were more evenly matched than the outcome of the war in America when taken by itself would indicate.[1]

The military capacities of the colonists of France were out of all proportion to their numbers and wealth as compared with the English settlers. Possibly because the French colonists had never been self-sustaining, the home government had been more liberal in furnishing them

[1] The strategy of this great war is admirably set forth by Julian S. Corbett in his *England in the Seven Years' War, a study in combined strategy* (2 vols., London, 1907). He pays a great and well-deserved tribute to Admiral Saunders for the splendid service he rendered in the Quebec campaign. A smaller book, but one equally worth reading, is William Wood's *The Fight for Canada, a Naval and Military Sketch* (1 vol., Westminster, 1904).

with defenders than had the English government with
its colonists on the continent. The Indians of New
France also for generations had been accustomed to fight
in company with their white neighbors. Finally, the
government of New France was a feudal military oligarchy directed from Paris. Fortunately, the administration in Canada was honeycombed with corruption and
was weakened by the lack of harmony among the higher
officers. The English continental colonies had taken care
of themselves from the beginning. Ordinarily, they had
provided for their own military necessities, although from
time to time England had sent out expeditions or had
reimbursed the colonists for their expenses. The English
government had taken a direct interest in the frontier
warfare of Georgia, providing both men and money for
that purpose; but up to this time the protection of the
continental colonies had not come into the system of imperial defense, and the conquest of Canada and Louisiana
had not been thought of by English statesmen as being
within the realm of practical international policy. On
the other hand, the islands of the West Indies had long
been looked upon as being within the imperial system;
the protection of English sugar plantations and the conquest of foreign sugar islands had been regarded as next
in importance to the protection of the shores of England
and the acquisition of European naval stations like Gibraltar and Minorca. These tasks absorbed the larger portion of British military and naval strength and deducted
just so much from that which was applicable to the conquest of French possessions on the American continent.

The soldiers engaged in the contest in America were
necessarily drawn mainly from the home countries; the
naval armaments entirely so, and the military forces to a

greater and greater extent as the conflict assumed more formidable proportions; thus Wolfe's Quebec expedition comprised eight thousand English soldiers and possibly five hundred colonial rangers, the naval force and the transports being entirely drawn from England. The colonists often performed notable service, as in Bradstreet's campaign, but their chief contribution was providing the means for fitting out naval fleets and land expeditions. At first sight it would seem that the English colonies should have given England an overwhelming advantage; and had it been possible strictly to blockade the American possessions of France, the strength of the English colonists as providers of food would have worked greatly against the French.

None of the French colonies produced enough food for the need of their inhabitants; their sugar islands, like those of England, depended almost entirely upon the Northern Colonies for the food consumed by the servants and slaves who labored on the plantations. Of course in time the people of these islands could divert a part of their strength and time from the making of sugar to the production of bread and meat, but even then they would not have been able to fit out and supply the expeditions and fleets which used their harbors. Had the British government been able to stop all trade between the English continental colonies and Canada and the French sugar islands, their conquest would have been greatly simplified; but this proved to be impossible. For fifty years and more, in defiance of law, the continental colonists had traded with the French West India Islands; perhaps it was the fact that this commerce was always illegal that made it seem not so heinous and unpatriotic in war time as it really was — and trade with the enemy has gone on unchecked in every great war. This traffic was contrary not only to English law, but was also illegal under the statutes of Pennsylvania, New York, South Carolina, and other colonies.[1]

The commerce between the bread colonies and the French sugar islands at first was carried on as it always had been by means of certificates and bills of lading which were not true to the fact. When this commerce became dangerous, vessels engaged in supplying the enemy's islands with food were provided with licenses to sail to St. Pierre or some other French port for the purpose of exchanging prisoners. Governor Denny of Pennsylvania sold these licenses for twenty pounds or even less, so it is said. On the other hand, Governor Fauquier[2] of Virginia informed Pitt that four hundred guineas had been offered him if he "would license a Flag of Truce"; prisoners under these circumstances had a commercial value. When this commerce was suppressed the colonists traded indirectly through some neutral port, especially by way of the roadstead of Monte Christo, off the northern coast of Santo Domingo, not far from the boundary of the French part of the island. Sometimes there were as many as fifty vessels lying at anchor there — most of them from the continental colonies, but a few were from the British islands. In 1760 Pitt directed the governors of the English colonies to "put the

[1] See, for instance, *Pennsylvania Statutes at Large*, v, 184; *Laws of the Colony of New York* (ed. 1896), iv, 84, 96; Cooper's *South Carolina Statutes*, iv, 109. The act of Parliament prohibiting the exportation of food stuffs (except fish, roots, and rice to southern Europe) was passed in 1757 (30 George II, Cap. 9, Ruffhead's *Statutes at Large*, viii, 19).

[2] Fauquier to Pitt, Oct. 28, 1760, Kimball's *Correspondence of William Pitt*, ii, 350, and James Hamilton to Pitt, Nov. 1, 1760, *ibid.*, ii, 351; Stephen Hopkins to Pitt, *ibid.*, 373. The last letter gives a remarkably clear account of the illicit trade and also of the ordinary course of commerce. He hints that if this trade is stopped, the Northern colonists will necessarily turn to manufacturing. The author of *A State of the Trade carried on with the French, of the Island of Hispaniola, by the Merchants in North America, under Colour of Flags of Truce* (London, 1760) declares that a cargo of cotton, linen, and woolen cloth, and other European goods, would yield 50 to 100 per cent profit and the return cargo of sugar would bring in another inordinate profit; for £400,000 invested in New York or Boston a shipowner might earn in one voyage £3,200,000!

most speedy and effectual Stop to such flagitious Practices." [1]

While the French colonies formed an excellent military engine so far as their strength permitted, the power of the English plantations was distributed between twelve or thirteen separate governments, all of which were unfitted for the performance of strenuous military tasks and were jealous of one another.[2] This weakness of the English colonies was due to the ascendency over the executive branch which the assemblies had gained in them. The voting of the smallest sum of money or the authorizing the mobilization of the militia always resulted in days and weeks spent in debate and often in constitutional controversies between the two branches of the administration. The strength of these governments for the solution of the peace problems was unfavorable to the transaction of military business. Moreover, the several colonies were jealous of one another and indisposed to united effort. The New Englanders habitually acted together, but they were very suspicious of the New Yorkers, and this feeling was fully reciprocated. It originated in differences in settlement and institutions and was intensified by long-continued commercial rivalries. The passiveness of Pennsylvania angered the New Yorkers, Marylanders, and Virginians, who felt that the great Quaker-German colony was not doing its part. The Carolinas had grown rapidly in population and resources, but possessed little military strength, owing to the prevalence of slavery in an intensive form in South Carolina and to the dispersal of the settle

[1] Kimball's *Correspondence of William Pitt*, ii, 320. At one time, Amherst reported that so much flour was sent from New York to the West Indies that it was difficult to obtain enough to feed the English forces operating against Canada.

[2] On this point see Dinwiddie's letters in Hamilton's *Letters to Washington*, vols. i and ii.

ments in North Carolina. The Carolinians also had their own problems to face in the shape of threatened Indian war and probable conflict with the Spaniards in Florida. Taking everything into consideration, the strength of the English colonies, save under exceptional circumstances, should be rated at only about one half of its nominal value.

In the approaching contest, the attitude of the Iroquois was of great importance, fully as much as it had been in the earlier French wars. In September, 1753, therefore, the Lords of Trade directed the governors of New Hampshire, Massachusetts, New York, New Jersey, Pennsylvania, Maryland, and Virginia to hold a conference with representatives of the Six Nations in order that a joint agreement might be made between all the English colonies, north of Carolina, and the Iroquois. Accordingly, on June 19, 1754,[1] commissioners from these colonies, excepting New Jersey and Virginia, and from the two other New England colonies of Rhode Island and Connecticut, met at Albany. The commissioners proceeded to discuss not merely the conduct of Indian affairs, but a union of all the colonies for their security and defense. Among the commissioners was Benjamin Franklin, and the document which is known as the Albany Plan of Union came from his pen. He was not the only one to propose plans of union at that conference or Congress, as it is usually termed. Indeed, the idea of intercolonial union seems to have been widespread at that time. Thomas Hutchinson of Massachusetts, Meshech Weare[2] of New Hampshire, and the Rev. John Peters of Pennsylvania have also left plans of union in their handwriting. The consideration of the

---

[1] *New York Colonial Documents*, vi, 853; Franklin's *Writings* (Smyth's ed., iii, 197; Bigelow's ed., i, 308).
[2] Weare's plan of union is printed in

subject at Albany appears to have been due to Governor Shirley of Massachusetts, but it is not clear that he acted on the initiative of the English government. The plan that was agreed to demanded so great a surrender of power by the several colonies that none of them adopted it, although it had received the vote of every one of their commissioners. As the scheme was unacceptable to the colonists, it never came before the royal government for action; but there is no reason to suppose that the authorities in England would have approved it.[1] They preferred a scheme which the Lords of Trade prepared in August, 1754, and presented to the king for his consideration.[2] This plan provided that a circular of instruction should be sent to all the governors of the continental colonies, setting forth the necessity of a union for military purposes. Each colony was to appoint one person to represent it at a conference, at which the general defense of the colonies should be considered and the quota of troops and the amount of money to be raised by each colony should be settled. The king would appoint a commander-in-chief, who was to have the expenditure of the money so raised; but the colonial assemblies might make representations as to military affairs to the commander-in-chief as occasion arose. These commissioners also were to formulate a project of a General Convention for joint colonial action on military subjects which, with the approbation of the assemblies, should be submitted to the king for his confirmation. Nothing was done in furtherance of this

---

Bulletin of the New York Public Library, i, 149; Peters's plan in *American History Leaflets,* No. 14, and Carson's *Hundredth Anniversary of the Constitution,* ii, Appendix; Hutchinson's plan in Frothingham's *Rise of the Republic,* Appendix.

[1] As to this point, see G. L. Beer's *British Colonial Policy,* 22 and note.

[2] *New York Colonial Documents,* vi, 903; *American History Leaflets,* No. 14. The whole subject of colonial union will be considered at length in the third volume of the present work.

scheme, probably because the adoption of Franklin's plan of colonial union by the commissioners at Albany convinced the authorities in England that further agitation of the subject was not advisable at the moment. Later, in appointing Governor Shirley of Massachusetts commander-in-chief of all the forces on the continent, the English government may be regarded as acting in conformity with the project of the Lords of Trade.

The British government regarded the French aggressions in the interior as justifying reprisals on land and sea, and this without giving any just cause for war. An elaborate plan of action was proposed for 1755 ; one army operating from Virginia was to capture Fort Duquesne, other expeditions from New York and from New England were to attack Crown Point and Niagara and dispossess the French of their posts in Acadia. To add to the chance of success, a fleet under Boscawen was sent to the Gulf of St. Lawrence to seize a French fleet convoying troops and supplies to Canada. Boscawen bungled his part of the business in capturing only one or two of the French ships ; but this was enough to induce the French government to look upon war as existing, although they probably would have endured the inconvenience of many attacks upon their land forces in America before proceeding to that extremity.

For the enterprise against Fort Duquesne,[1] two regi-

---

[1] Winthrop Sargent's *History of an Expedition against Fort du Quesne* (Pennsylvania Historical Society's *Memoirs*, v, also issued separately) is still the standard work on the subject ; but much new material has been discovered since Sargent edited the documents which are printed in this volume. Among the papers in the *Pennsylvania Magazine of History* may be mentioned an account from French sources (xx, 409), contemporary accounts from British newspapers (xxiii, 310), and a list of killed and wounded (xxvii, 499). Dinwiddie described the retreat in a letter to Shirley, which is printed in *Colonial Records of North Carolina*, v, 429. There are papers in the *Proceedings* of the Massachusetts Historical Society for 1857, p. 230; 1879, p. 118; and Second Series, v, p. 3.

ments of British regulars were sent out from England under the command of General Edward Braddock, an Englishman, who was assisted by a staff of English officers. Braddock was a trained soldier of experience in warfare and of undoubted courage. His age of sixty years and his lack of tact are sufficient to account for his refusal to respect colonial conditions,[1] but he also appears to have been deficient in administrative ability. The expedition proceeded through the unsettled portions of western Virginia, which was almost inevitable, since it may be said to have grown out of the policy of Virginia's governor in attempting to forestall the French on the Ohio. It is useless to speculate upon the might-have-beens, and England has almost always suffered defeats in the beginnings of wars and has almost as invariably succeeded in the end; it was with the British as it was with Washington — failure was necessary to bring forth the highest effort.

In the conditions of ocean transport and wilderness road cutting, Braddock made commendable speed. He sailed from England in December, 1754, reached Virginia in the following February, held a council with the colonial governors in April, was at Will's Creek on May 10th, and on July 9, 1755, fought the battle in which his expedition was wrecked and himself mortally wounded. The English soldiers and their brave officers were done to death in

[1] In 1818 William Findley repeated in print the substance of what Washington, when President, had said to him as to Braddock's expedition. The recollection of one old man as a source of history is often deplorable — let alone that of what one old man averred that another old man had said years before. The statement attributed to Washington is so interesting, however, that it is here repeated for what it is worth: Braddock, said Washington, " was unfortunate, but his character was much too severely treated. He was one of the honestest and best men of the British officers with whom I was acquainted; even in the manner of fighting he was not more to blame than others." Niles's *Register*, xiv, 179. This extract from Findley's letter is quoted at length in Boyd Crumrine's *History of Washington County, Pennsylvania*, p. 52 note. This book contains an excellent account of the Braddock expedition, based upon local depositions and an intimate knowledge of the country.

an open space on the east side of the Monongahela, some seven or eight miles from Fort Duquesne. Braddock's only thought was to keep his soldiers in line and compact formation and send them thus against the enemy, mostly Indians sheltered behind trees and partly protected by some sort of defensive works. Some of the Virginia soldiers essaying to fight the enemy frontier-fashion broke ranks and deployed in skirmish line, utilizing every bit of cover; but Braddock with many a good military oath called them back to the ranks; some of the regulars also trying to do the same thing, he beat them back to their close formation with his sword. Attacked on three sides, the Englishmen stood this treatment as long as human nature permitted and then fled.[1] The most gratifying thing about the whole affair was the bravery and utter disregard of self shown by the old general in this his last fight on earth. For the time being this was the end of attempts to seize Fort Duquesne. The interest of the war now turns to the North.

For a quarter of a century the French had occupied a post at Crown Point, where Lake Champlain narrows into riverlike proportions, and thus held a firm grasp on the route from the Hudson to the St. Lawrence. Even earlier the French had built a fort at Niagara, which gave them a certain measure of control of the lake route from Montreal

[1] Mr. J. K. Lacock of Amity, Pennsylvania, has communicated to me the following extract from a letter from Hermanns Alricks to Governor Morris of Pennsylvania, dated Carlisle, July 22, 1755, and preserved in the Pennsylvania Archives at Harrisburg: "This morning our Sheriff Mr Potter came to this Town, he informs me, that the French and Indians had cast an Intrenchment across the road before our Army which they Discover'd not Untill the[y] came Close up to it, from thence and both sides of the road the Enemy kept a Constant fireing on them, our Army being so confused, they could not fight, & they would not be admitted by the Genl or Sr John St Clair, to break thro' their Ranks and Take behind trees." Lowdermilk (History of Cumberland, Maryland, 158) gives a graphic description of "a most singular ditch" and ravines forming an ideal position for an ambuscade.

to the West.   On the other hand, the English had for many years held a post at Oswego at the southeastern corner of Lake Ontario.   For the possession of these important points of strategic advantage and the English forts between Lake George and the Hudson River, the contest was prolonged.   Up to 1758 the course of events was generally in favor of the French.

With the signing of the Treaty of Aix-la-Chapelle in October, 1748, the English government for the first time displayed an active interest in the affairs of the Acadian peninsula.   Having restored Louisbourg to France, the English ministry determined to build a stronghold and establish a naval base at Chebucto Bay, where Halifax now stands.   Thither in June, 1749, came twenty-five hundred settlers, who laid out a town to which other colonists were attracted, so that in 1752 it numbered four thousand inhabitants.   This settlement of Halifax in Nova Scotia was also memorable for being the only English colony founded by direct royal endeavor on the North American continent.   In addition to this fortified town there were a few scattered posts in the peninsula and a feeble garrison at Annapolis near its southwestern end; but away from Halifax and its immediate vicinity there was no effective English occupation of Acadia.   The French inhabitants of the peninsula numbered about nine thousand.   They were agriculturists, were devoted to their religion, and were strong in their racial prejudices.   Unfortunately for them, they lived in one of the most important strategic points on the Atlantic coast, holding the southern entrance to the Gulf of St. Lawrence.   Moreover, the French authorities in Canada refused to accept the cession of Acadia as a finality. They disputed as to its boundaries and stationed a force at the most northerly point of the Bay of Fundy in a fort which they named Beauséjour. Not far to the east at Beaubassin the English established a fortified post which they named Fort Lawrence, in honor of the governor of Nova Scotia.

One part of the general scheme of offensive operations against the French in 1755 was the expulsion of the garrison at Beauséjour, which the English held to be wrongfully occupied. Lieutenant Colonel Monckton commanded the expedition, which was composed in part of two thousand Massachusetts troops enlisted for one year and led by Colonel John Winslow. No effective resistance was made and the French fort was surrendered by its commander, Duchambon de Vergor, in June, 1755. Before the month was out all the other French posts on the mainland east of the St. Croix were abandoned by their garrisons.

The French Acadians had taken the side of their compatriots and co-religionists in these preliminaries. The English resented their conduct and stood in fear of them — not without reason, considering their numbers and the nearness of the French garrison at Louisbourg. These communities might prove a serious menace to any expedition to the St. Lawrence that was conducted from Halifax as a base unless a considerable garrison was left at that post. The Acadians could be neutralized by seizing and holding as hostages the leading men among them, or by settling an overwhelming number of English colonists in their country;[1] they could be eliminated from the military problem by distributing them throughout the old English settlements to the southward. The last was likely to be the most efficacious solution of the difficulty, as well as the easier and cheaper from a military point of view. So

[1] Governor Shirley of Massachusetts had earlier suggested the substitution of a population that could be trusted in place of the disaffected Acadians, and had advocated bringing over settlers from Great Britain.

it seemed to Governor Lawrence and his advisers, among whom was Commodore Boscawen. The deportation of the Acadians was ordered and such papers as have survived do not contain any suggestion that Lawrence's action was disapproved by his superiors in England. The Acadians were unfortunate in living within the field of military operations; had their homes been a hundred miles farther south or north, they might have lived placidly and died peacefully where they were born.

The deportation was conducted under Lawrence by Monckton and Murray and Winslow, but the chief part fell to the last named, who had charge of sending the settlers away from Grand Pré and the Basin of Minas. He left a detailed journal of his doings and of the impression which the sad business made on his mind. The Acadians had already been disarmed,[1] but they were so numerous that Winslow thought it necessary to place as many of the men as possible on five vessels, which he had at his disposal, while awaiting the arrival of transports to carry the exiles to their new homes. There were delays inevitable to such operations, and the Acadians did not assist Winslow to make easier his difficult and distasteful duty. While awaiting the arrival of the transports those who were confined on shipboard were fed by their families by means of boats, which came to the shore and collected supplies. " When the wind blows, the people on board are starving," so wrote Winslow on September 20, 1755.[2] At length the transports arrived. In the harsh autumn weather there was much confusion, families were not kept together, and, no doubt, there was loss of property; but these accidents were inseparable from the cir-

[1] Parkman's *Montcalm and Wolfe*, i, 261; Richard's *Acadia*, ii, 6–9.   [2] Nova Scotia Historical Society's *Collections*, iii, 136.

cumstances of the case. The Acadians were carried to the colonies from Massachusetts to Georgia. The English settlers were not at all rejoiced[1] at their coming, and, in some cases, were as frightened at the apparition of an Acadian as they would have been at the sight of a wild Indian in full war paint. Many of the exiles escaped from their new abodes, some of them going to Louisiana, others to Canada. A good many of them found their way back to Acadia and rejoined those of their former neighbors who had been fortunate enough to elude capture.[2]

In 1757 a new chapter opened in the history of England and America, for it was then that William Pitt became the ruler of England, which position he held for four eventful years. This remarkable man had begun official life by refusing to handle the nation's money as his own when he occupied the office of Paymaster of the Forces. With a tendency toward theatricalism, William Pitt possessed the imaginative enthusiasm which marks the great statesman. He also was fearless of criticism when he felt that what he was doing was for the benefit of king and country, which is one of the attributes of the man of power. He now infused some of his own faith and energy into military and naval commanders. Acting on the initiative of others, he completely changed the policy of the empire as to America.[3] Up to this time the idea had

---

[1] See *Virginia Magazine of History*, vi, 386.

[2] As to numbers, see Winsor's *America*, v, 463.

[3] The arguments for the conquest of Canada are set forth at length by Dr. John Mitchell in a tract entitled: *The Contest in America . . . giving an Account of the Views and Designs of the French, with the Interests of Great Britain, and the Situation of the British* and French Colonies in all parts of America (London, 1757). See also *Occasional Reflections on the Importance of the War in America. . . . In a Letter to a Member of Parliament* (London, 1758).

Major Wood (*The Fight for Canada*, 45) names De Lancey and Pownall as the men who influenced Pitt to adopt the new policy; but probably the moment had come for a change in the

been simply to hold back the French; now, the plan was
to expel them from the continent, and the difference was
great. In carrying out this policy, Pitt[1] also departed
from tradition. He sought out the best men in military
and naval life, regardless of their years, and gave them
responsibility and stood behind them. He concentrated
English military and naval forces in America upon one
field of activity at a time, abandoning for the moment
the conquest of the West India Islands for the occupation
of Canada. He recognized that the colonists could supply
men and food, but could not unaided withdraw much
labor and what was equivalent to capital from ordinary
occupations. He provided, therefore, that the colonists
should pay the wages of the soldiers raised by them and
supply them with arms and with clothing, but that all
other expenses should be borne by the crown.[2] In later
campaigns the home government also provided arms, ammunition, tents, and part of the other expenses.[3] The
first result of the new policy was the capture of Louisbourg in 1758.

Since its restoration to them in 1748 the French had
reconstructed and extended the fortifications of Louisbourg
until it deserved the title of "the Dunkirk of America";

attitude of the English government, regardless of the efforts of individuals.
Corbett's chapter entitled "Inauguration of Pitt's 'System'" treats the
problem in its larger relations (*England
in the Seven Years' War*, i, 179–196,
254–262, 267–272). See also an article by
Hubert Hall on "Chatham's Colonial
Policy" in *American Historical Review*,
v, 659. An interesting *Scheme to Drive
the French out of All the Continent of
America* signed by "T. C." was published at London in 1754 and Boston in
1755.

[1] This part of Pitt's career is set forth
in great detail by A. von Ruville in his
William Pitt, Earl of Chatham, vol. ii,
London, 1907.

[2] Pitt to colonial governors, Feb. 4,
1757, Kimball's *Correspondence of William Pitt*, i, 3, 5.

[3] *Ibid.*, i, 138. Parliament had already voted £165,000 as a "free gift"
to the colonies, excepting Pennsylvania
(29 George II, Cap. 29, and 30 George II,
Cap. 26). In 1758–63 nearly one million pounds sterling were voted to the
North American colonies as "compensation." See acts of 31 George II, Cap.
33; 32 George II, Cap. 26; 33 George II,
Cap. 18; 1 George III, Cap. 19: 2 George
III, Cap. 34; 3 George III, Cap. 17.

it was now a much more formidable fortress than when
Pepperrell and his New Englanders had captured it in 1745.
In place of the small force which then defended it, more
than three thousand disciplined soldiers now formed its
garrison, while twelve warships, carrying over five hundred
guns and three thousand men, lay at anchor in the harbor.
For the conquest of Louisbourg,[1] Pitt provided a fleet of
twenty-three ships of the line and eighteen frigates under
Admiral Boscawen and eleven thousand regular soldiers,
besides a few hundred provincials, under the command of
Jeffrey Amherst with whom as brigadiers were Charles
Lawrence and James Wolfe.   Of these the last was to win
the greatest fame.   Born in 1727, James Wolfe was now
thirty-one years of age, but already he had had a long
military career, since he had entered the army at the age
of fourteen ; at eighteen he was a brigade major, and at
twenty-two commanded a regiment.   In person he was
tall and slight and in health the reverse of robust, but he
possessed a spirit as enthusiastic as Pitt's own.   Landing
at almost the same spot at which the New Englanders[2] had
gained the shore thirteen years earlier, the English advanced overland while Boscawen with his powerful fleet
held open their communications.   Once on shore and with

---

[1] Amherst's letters in the *Correspondence of William Pitt*, i, form the
best account of this exploit; see also
Parkman's *Montcalm and Wolfe*. It
is interesting to compare Amherst's letters with those of Loudoun and Abercromby — greatly to the advantage of
the first named.

[2] Wolfe on two occasions, and probably on others, displayed a lack of confidence in New Englanders which is
worth noting.   In 1758, writing from
Louisbourg, the scene of Pepperrell's exploit, he declares: "The Americans are
in general the dirtiest most contemptible
cowardly dogs that you can conceive.
There is no depending upon 'em in

action.   They fall down dead in their
own dirt and desert by battalions, officers and all.   Such rascals as those are
rather an incumbrance than any real
strength to an army "(Royal Historical
Manuscripts Commission's *Reports*, ix,
Part iii, p. 77).   Nevertheless in 1759 we
find him applying for some of the "Boston Militia" stationed at Louisbourg:
"the Men were asked if they chose to
go, and as it seldom happens, that a New-
England man prefers Service to a lazy
life, none of them seem'd to approve of
the proposal "—which was quite natural, if Wolfe's opinion of them was
known (Kimball's *Correspondence of
Pitt*, ii, 119).

his base secure, Amherst pushed the siege with vigor and success. The descriptions of life within the fortress are among the most vivid that we have. Ere long the French ships were set on fire, buildings within the walls destroyed or greatly damaged, and a breach opened through which an assault could be made.[1] Then, on the 26th of July, 1758, Louisbourg finally passed out of the hands of France into those of England. The defense had been admirably conducted by Drucour and his subordinates, and the surrender at last was made at the intercession of the civil governor. While the siege of Louisbourg was drawing to a close, Brigadier General Forbes, commanding a new expedition against Fort Duquesne, lay ill at Carlisle on the frontiers of Pennsylvania.

Braddock's defeat was the signal for the Delawares and Shawanoes to attack the frontier settlements of Pennsylvania, which were utterly unprotected, the settlers lacking even powder and lead, although they had frequently petitioned the Assembly for supplies of these and other warlike stores. The sufferings of the frontier families became so intense that in 1755 the Assembly voted fifty-five thousand pounds for the king's use,[2] to which the proprietors added five thousand pounds more. These funds were used to build a chain of forts on the Blue Mountains between the Delaware and the Susquehanna, to which the settlers could resort, and the garrisons of which would afford them some degree of protection in their houses.[3] In the next year the Quakers retired from the

[1] An excellent account of this siege is in the "Journals of Capt. John Montresor" in New York Historical Society's *Collections for the Year 1881*, pp. 151–188.

[2] *Pennsylvania Statutes at Large*, v, 201.

[3] See *Report of the Commission to* locate the Site of the Frontier Forts of *Pennsylvania*, i, 3–347 (map precedes the article); ii, 79–114 (maps at pp. 65, 80). The authorities not only fortified the frontier; they departed further from early Pennsylvania policy in offering a reward of fifty dollars for the scalp of every woman belonging to a hostile Indian tribe

Assembly and thereafter Pennsylvania took a more active part in the conflict. Besides the capture of Louisbourg, the plan of operations for 1758 included the sending of an expedition against Fort Duquesne and extensive warfare on the northern frontier.

The command of the Duquesne expedition was given to Brigadier General John Forbes, who had begun life as a physician, but had now been in the military service for some years. He had twelve hundred Highlanders besides colonial troops from Pennsylvania and the colonies to the southward, numbering in all about six thousand men. His leading subordinate was Lieutenant Colonel Henry Bouquet, a Swiss from Canton Berne. Contrary to Washington's advice, Forbes decided to proceed through Pennsylvania, Braddock's road being circuitous and over-grown with brush.[1] He advanced by short stages, every-where fortifying as he went. This slow rate of progression turned out to be in favor of his success, for the Indian allies of the French, disgusted at having nothing to do, deserted their employers. What made most in Forbes's favor, however, was a treaty of peace, which the Pennsyl-vanians were able to make with the Delaware and Shawa-noe Indians who had been attacking the frontier settlements for several years. During the whole campaign Forbes was so ill that he had to be carried in a litter. The command of the advance fell to Bouquet. Unfortunately he per-mitted one of his subordinates, Major Grant, to reconnoitre

---

and one hundred and thirty for that of a man. *Pennsylvania Archives*, ii, 619; *Minutes of Council*, vii, 74–76. The prac-tice was not unusual; in 1760 the Georgia Council offered the following reward for every enemy's scalp, a "Trading Gun, three Pound of Powder, six Pound of Shot, a Blanket, a Flap, a pair of Indian Boots, and a Cag containing four Gallons of trading Rum." Candler's *Georgia Rec-*

ords, viii, 248. See also *Massachusetts Province Laws*, iii, 1145; *Laws of New York*, iii, 540; Hening's *Virginia Statutes*, vi, 551, 565; vii, 121.

[1] Forbes to Pitt, Kimball's *Corre-spondence of William Pitt*, i, 295. Forbes's letters in this volume form the best narrative of the expedition; see also Parkman's *Montcalm and Wolfe*.

out of supporting distance from the main body. This detachment was set upon by the French and Indians and badly defeated. So slow was Forbes's advance that November found the army still at some distance from the fort and a decision was reached to stop further progress for the year. Information then came to Forbes that the French were in a critical condition. With twenty-five hundred men he now pushed rapidly forward, Washington being in command of his right wing. When they reached the vicinity of the fort, explosions were heard and a reconnoissance showed that the French had blown up their defenses and abandoned their stronghold (November 24, 1758). In this way the French possession of western Pennsylvania came to a close.

The operations in northern New York were less successful. The command there fell to General Abercromby.[1] In July, 1758, he had at Fort William Henry, at the southern end of Lake George, an army of more than fifteen thousand men — the largest force that had been assembled at one place in the course of the war. Of these, six thousand were regulars. Brigadier General Lord Howe, an able officer and a gentleman, was the second in command. The force advanced to the vicinity of Ticonderoga, but there found itself confronted by an advanced work consisting of a series of field entrenchments and fallen timber ; the French force defending the place was commanded by the Marquis de Montcalm, an able, disinterested, and patriotic French soldier. The English attacked, to be met by a murderous fire which killed Lord Howe and hundreds of soldiers, Abercromby's loss being given as nineteen hundred and forty-four officers and men, killed, wounded, and missing. The

---

[1] His account of his failure is in Kimball's *Correspondence of William Pitt,* i, 297.

disaster was great; but the worst thing about the affair was the poltroonry of Abercromby himself, who fled from the scene, although even with this loss he still was greatly superior to the French. A supplementary expedition under Lieutenant Colonel Bradstreet turned out better. He had with him some three thousand men, almost all colonists. Proceeding by the way of the Mohawk, he gained the southern shore of Lake Ontario, built boats near the site of the destroyed Oswego, crossed the lake to Fort Frontenac, and within a week after landing captured that stronghold with its garrison and all the French vessels in the vicinity. Destroying the fort with its supplies for the French posts on the Ohio, he recrossed the lake and returned to the Hudson. The operations of this year as a whole were distinctly in favor of the English and showed what could be accomplished by intelligent direction, concentration of effort, and the good-will of the colonists.

For the year 1759, Pitt planned a formidable campaign. He contemplated a simultaneous attack on Canada by two forces, — one operating up the St. Lawrence from the sea, the other advancing northward from the Hudson. If all went well, Wolfe in command of the former would capture Quebec in combination with the latter army under command of Amherst, but either was supposed to be strong enough to work without the other.[1] It was expected that Wolfe would have twelve thousand men under his orders, besides an adequate naval force. The actual numbers proved to be less than nine thousand soldiers,[2] but the naval armament was ample. Amherst with eleven thousand men was to seize the forts guarding the Lake Champlain route to the St. Lawrence, while Colonel John

[1] See letter from Wolfe of May 19, 1759, in Doughty's *Quebec*, ii, 53.
[2] *Grenville Correspondence*, i, 305.

Prideaux with five thousand soldiers and a body of Indians under Sir William Johnson should attack the French fort at Niagara. Prideaux reached Niagara in safety, having left a strong force at Oswego to rebuild and garrison a fort at that place. Niagara was defended by some six hundred men commanded by Captain Pouchot, and a large body of Indians had been summoned from the interior to his aid, together with the scattered forces of the French from the posts in the upper Ohio Valley and at Presque Isle. The latter, numbering a thousand whites and a few hundred Indians, gained the vicinity of Niagara while the siege was in progress and were defeated by Johnson with his Indians and a few white soldiers. This disaster to the French settled the fate of Niagara, which surrendered in July, 1759; Prideaux had been killed early in the siege, and the command at the end was exercised by Sir William Johnson. Amherst sent Gage to take over the command, to hold Oswego and Niagara, and to descend the St. Lawrence. This last task was too formidable to be attempted with the force at his command, but Gage successfully held Oswego and Niagara. This in itself, with the destruction of Fort Frontenac, meant the partial isolation of the French posts at Detroit and Michillimackinac and at other points in the interior, although communication was still possible by way of the Ottawa River and Georgian Bay. Amherst only partly succeeded in the execution of his advance northward to the St. Lawrence by way of Lake Champlain. At his appearance the French abandoned Ticonderoga and Crown Point, but halted at Isle aux Noix at the northern end of the lake. He was obliged to build boats to transport his troops and to combat a fleet of French vessels. By the time this was accomplished the season was too far advanced to permit of

further pursuit.   Amherst's failure left Wolfe to struggle
alone against nearly the whole remaining force of New
France.[1]

Fortunately the strength of France on both sides of the
Atlantic was now distinctly on the wane.   Her campaigns
in Europe against Frederick the Great had exhausted her
vitality.   The French government was able to send only
five hundred men with limited supplies to Canada in
1759, and could afford no naval force that could hope to
oppose successfully that which Admiral Saunders had for
the protection of Wolfe's army and supplies.   The small
French fleet eluded the English squadron sent to intercept
it and played an important part in the ensuing operations.
In Canada the condition of affairs was disheartening.
The governor, Pierre François Rigaud, Marquis de Vaudreuil, was the son of that earlier Vaudreuil who had set
the Indians on the unprotected New England frontiers.
Born in Canada, he loved the land of his birth and strove
vigorously for its safety.   He had some of the elements of
greatness, but was oppressed by a sense of his own importance and constantly undervalued the talents and
services of Montcalm.   While Pitt was at the head of
English affairs, the whole strength of the British empire
was thrown by one hand ; Vaudreuil and Montcalm were
responsible to two masters, the colonial ministry and the
ministry of war, and the governor was supreme in military
as well as in civil matters.   This in itself was a great
loss of power to Canada.   Moreover, the government of
the province, like that of the home country, was honeycombed with corruption.   Vaudreuil himself made no

---

[1] The bibliography of the siege of
Quebec is noted at the end of the chapter; the Quebec campaign is admirably
set forth with due attention to the events
of 1759 in Europe, Asia, and the West
Indies by Julian Corbett in his *England
in the Seven Years' War*, i, 396–476; ii,
1–70.

money out of his country's distresses ; at all events he was acquitted of the charges brought against him. The other civil officers were guilty of peculation on a large scale ;[1] but Montcalm and the leading military men seem to have had the defense of the province solely at heart without thought of illicit pecuniary gain.

In the spring of 1759 the French authorities in Canada were straining every nerve to make head against the expeditions which they were informed were to be led against their posts on Lake Champlain, the Great Lakes, and the Ohio. Then the news came that a great fleet was on its way to attack Quebec. At once the whole plan of defense was changed and all possible troops were concentrated for the protection of that fortress. In all, Vaudreuil and Montcalm gathered to the defense of Quebec about fifteen thousand white soldiers, including Canadians and more than a thousand Indians.[2] Between one thousand and two thousand men were stationed in Quebec itself; the rest, fourteen thousand in number, were encamped below the town, on the bank of the St. Lawrence, their flanks being protected by the St. Charles and the Montmorenci rivers. Wolfe had with him less than nine thousand soldiers, amply supplied with artillery and protected by a formidable fleet.[3] The disparity of force so

[1] The condition of affairs in New France is excellently described by Major Wood in the third chapter of his *Fight for Canada*.

[2] As to numbers see Parkman's *Montcalm and Wolfe*, ii, 202; Doughty's *Quebec*, ii, 52.

[3] According to a statement printed by Doughty (*Quebec*, ii, 22), Wolfe sailed from Louisbourg in the first days of June, with 76 transports, having on board 8535 soldiers, including infantry and artillery, and practically no reënforcements reached him during the campaign. The naval force enabled Wolfe to move his troops up and down the river and from one side to the other with great facility ; this mobility was of great advantage to him and partly offset the smallness of his force. For some reason, Wolfe was very poorly supplied with money. After the fall of Quebec the officers in the fleet loaned £3000 to Murray for the use of the garrison in the purchase of provisions and other supplies during the coming winter. See Kimball's *Correspondence of William Pitt*, ii, 182.

far as numbers went was great, but in quality the French
army, or the larger part of it, was hardly more than a
gathering of men, while the English soldiers formed a
thoroughly disciplined force. The natural defenses of
Quebec were unparalleled in the western world and hardly
exceeded anywhere. They were impregnable against direct attack. Unless Amherst pressed forward from the
interior, the task to which Wolfe set himself might well
have disheartened the stoutest soul; but there was no
thought of drawing back in the mind of that intrepid
leader.

The expedition reached the Isle d'Orleans without mis-
hap. Once there, Wolfe realized for the first time the
serious nature of the problem. It was not the number of
the enemy which was serious, but the fact that it was impossible to get at the French army unless it came out
of its defenses. For weeks and months, from June to September, the two armies confronted one another, the French
lining the river bank below Quebec and later occupying
posts above the town. The English maintained one force
on the eastern side of the Montmorenci River, another on
the Isle d'Orleans, and a third at Point Levis on the southern bank of the St. Lawrence opposite Quebec. From
these positions it was possible to destroy the houses
within the walls of Quebec and to annoy the French army
in its camps on the other side of the Montmorenci gorge.
Beyond this and the destruction of French villages nothing
was accomplished. The delay, however, made in favor of
the English, for thousands of the Canadians deserted and
returned to their homes, but in September, Montcalm's
force still outnumbered that of the English. In all this
time there was but one direct attack made by the English.

The river between the St. Charles, which empties into

the St. Lawrence just below Quebec, and the Montmorenci was bordered by high and steep banks which were crowned by entrenchments. The strand in front of these bluffs was laid bare at low tide for a considerable distance, and at those times the Montmorenci could be forded at its mouth. Wolfe conceived the plan of a combined attack on the bluff by troops landing from vessels in the river to be joined by others marching across the mouth of the Montmorenci from the English camp. Probably the scheme was impossible of execution in any event. As it was conducted there was lack of coöperation between the soldiers who were landed from the shipping and those who forded the Montmorenci. An inopportune rainstorm also rendered the slope of the bluff so slippery that scaling it was well-nigh impossible. It was under these adverse circumstances that the English were repulsed with the loss of over four hundred in killed, wounded, and missing, and these among the best soldiers in the English army. After this repulse, Wolfe changed his plan of action and sought to gain the level ground above Quebec.

The banks of the river from Quebec upward for thirty miles were high and precipitous, but were broken, here and there, by ravines up which in peaceful time people could make their way. As soon as the English showed signs of operating in this direction by some of the war vessels running the batteries of Quebec and anchoring above the town, Montcalm detached portions of his force to guard all these points of approach, until at length he had a thousand soldiers above the town. As a last hope, Wolfe determined to make an effort in this direction. This idea was first suggested to Wolfe by his brigadiers,[1]

---

[1] Wolfe to Pitt, Sept. 2, 1759 (Kimball's *Correspondence of William Pitt*, ii, 157); *Dominion Archives*, 1898, Note A.

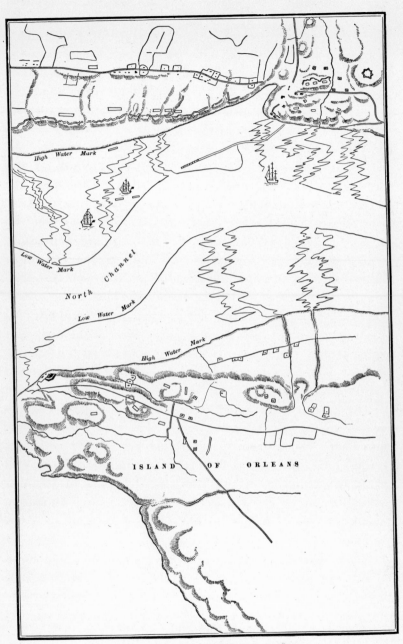

THE OPERATIONS BELOW QUEBEC

(From a sketch of the "British Engineers' Map" made in 1857. The map is reproduced on a large scale in colors in Doughty's *Siege of Quebec*, vol. i, and in Wood's
Fight for Canada.)

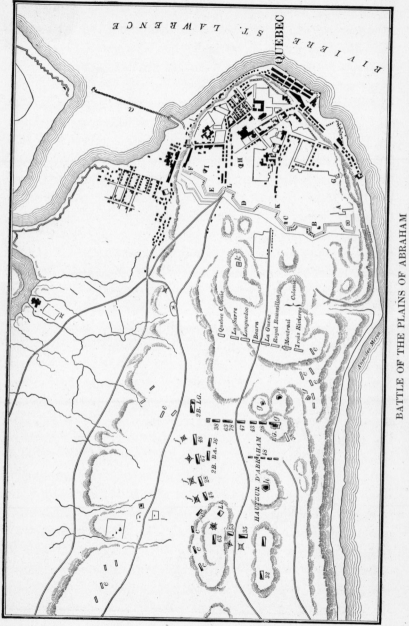

BATTLE OF THE PLAINS OF ABRAHAM

(From a sketch of the "British Engineers' Map" made in 1857.)

but the plan of operations was his own, and the execution of it was also his. Montcalm expected that the attack in this quarter when it came would be delivered at some distance from Quebec. The upper posts, therefore, were more strongly defended than those nearer the city. It was by one of the latter that Wolfe determined to hazard all. A mile and a half from Quebec a ravine, called Anse du Foulon, led from the river to the level ground near the Plains of Abraham. It was at this place that Wolfe and his men made their way in the early morning of September 13, 1759. He had with him something more than four thousand men, but of these a few hundred were left behind to guard the landing place. At the top of the pass there was a French post of not more than two hundred soldiers, commanded, as fate would have it, by that same Vergor who had been charged with surrendering Fort Beauséjour too soon. The path up the ravine had been obstructed by fallen trees and entrenchments. The vanguard of the British force, composed of twenty-four volunteers, scrambled up the almost impassable face of the cliff and, gaining the French post, routed Vergor and his men from their beds. This in itself was one of those fortunes of war that decide the fate of empires. At other points, while drifting down the stream, the English had been challenged, but had been allowed to pass, owing to the good French accent of one of their number. Here, however, no sentry had challenged them and they gained the top of the bluff practically unopposed. The ravine once in their hands, it was soon made passable for men and later for the passage of two small cannon.

Both Wolfe and Montcalm had that presage of doom which spurs some men to duty and others to despair. Before embarking in the boats, Wolfe took from his neck the miniature of his betrothed and gave it to John Jervis, later Earl St. Vincent, to be forwarded to her. Montcalm could not sleep in his camp on the other side of Quebec. Acting with Wolfe, Saunders, the British admiral, the preceding evening and well into the night had cannonaded the shore in front of Montcalm's line while his rowing boats had been lowered and filled with men from the vessels as if about to attack. At length the ship's batteries grew silent and some hours afterward Montcalm heard the sound of firing from above the town. Mounting his horse, he rode toward Quebec and from the high land on the eastern side of the St. Charles saw the red coats of the British soldiers as they stood on the high ground on the other side of the stream, some two miles distant. "This is a serious business," he said to his aide-de-camp, and sent him back to bring the soldiers forward to Quebec.

The position of the English was most critical, for Wolfe had too few men to properly occupy the open ground between the St. Lawrence and the St. Charles. Sharpshooters gathered in the underbrush and opened fire so that a portion of the small English force on the left of the line had to be "refused" to meet this danger. Filled with the idea that it was a detachment of the English army that he had before him, and that the whole force was not in position, Montcalm deployed his available men, who were about equal in number to those that Wolfe had on the ground, and attacked. Now drill and discipline told. The volley firing from some of the British regiments was described by a French officer as like the discharge from a heavy gun. The soldiers of the French veteran regiments were valiant, disciplined men, but there were many with Montcalm who had not that steadiness which long service alone can give. The French line wavered, then broke, and, pursued by the English, the defenders of New France fled to the shelter of the walls. In this moment of victory and defeat, when an empire was passing, Wolfe and Montcalm were mortally wounded.[1]

Vaudreuil still had a force of men superior to the English, who were now commanded by Townshend, Wolfe's second brigadier, his first, the gallant Monckton, having been wounded. Instead of holding his men in the camps across the St. Charles and acting in concert with Bougainville, who commanded the posts up the river, Vaudreuil fled on the evening of the day of battle (September 13, 1759), by inland roads around the English army and thence to Montreal. The Chevalier de Lévis now took command of the army in the field and hastened to the succor of Quebec. Before he could communicate with the garrison it had surrendered to the English (September 18, 1759). De Lévis then returned to Montreal. Leaving Murray with seven thousand men to hold Quebec for the winter, Admiral Saunders, with the remainder of the expedition, sailed for England in October. Murray was an able, faithful officer, but his task was a difficult one.[2] The town was in ruins; supplies, especially firewood, were scanty. Scurvy attacked his men until at length he had less than three thousand available. De Lévis strained every nerve to attack the town in the following spring in the interval between the resumption of navigation and the arrival of the British fleet with reënforcements; but Murray maintained his hold on the town until the coming of the fleet in May, 1760, compelled the French to retire up the river to Montreal.

[1] Wolfe was first struck in the wrist, then a bullet pierced his body, but still he pressed on to the charge, when a third struck him to the ground. Borne away in the rush of fugitives, Montcalm was fatally wounded. Vaudreuil with charac-teristic pettiness wrote that he was shot while running away.

[2] On the affairs of the winter see Murray to Pitt, May 25, 1760, Kimball's *Correspondence of William Pitt*, ii, 291.

The English plan of campaign for the year 1760 included three distinct operations. It was proposed that the main force of the English under Amherst should gain Montreal by way of Lake Ontario and the St. Lawrence River; a second force under Haviland should advance by the way of the Richelieu River; and Murray with all that could be spared from Quebec, together with the garrison of Louisbourg, should proceed up stream. All three armies combining before Montreal would compel the surrender of that town and of the remaining French soldiers. The plan was a pretentious one, but in making it due weight was given to the exhausted condition of the French. Everything turned out as designed, and on September 8, 1760, Vaudreuil signed articles of capitulation by which Canada and all its dependencies passed into the hands of England. By these articles the French forces throughout Canada were to lay down their arms and were not to march out with " the honors of war." De Lévis objected strenuously to these terms; but Amherst was insistent. Recalling the disgraceful massacres which followed French victories in the early part of the " half-century of conflict," he declared that he was determined by this requirement to manifest his " detestation of such practices" — and he did so.

With the capitulation of Montreal, New France passed into English hands; the scene of war had already been transferred to the Gulf of Mexico and the Caribbean Sea. In 1761 the English redoubled their efforts in that direction and in June captured the island of Dominica, having taken Guadeloupe in 1759. In August, 1761, the Bourbon monarchs of France and Spain entered into an agreement which is called in English " The Family Compact." This obliged one member of that family to come to the aid of another member upon the latter's request, and to be entitled to compensation in case of losing territory in consequence of rendering this assistance. Another treaty of the same date provided that if France and England should still be at war in May, 1762, Spain should come to the assistance of France. As war was going on between England and France at the appointed date, Spain took the side of France. This was England's opportunity. In the summer of 1762 a strong English fleet and a powerful land force appeared off Havana. The soldiers were set on shore and, after suffering greatly from the climatic conditions, carried Morro Castle by assault and thus gained possession of Havana and with it Cuba.[1] On the other side of the globe, Manila surrendered to the English General Draper (October, 1762);[2] but the knowledge of this success did not reach England in time to secure the insertion of the Philippine Islands among the places to be retained by England, and they were restored to Spain. Meantime, in 1760, George II had been succeeded by his grandson, the third English king of that name. His policy was to free the monarchy from the control of the great Whig families, and to this end peace was necessary. The carrying out of this determination led to the resignation of Mr. Pitt and to the making of a treaty less advantageous to England than Pitt and his partisans thought the sacrifices and victories of the British nation demanded.

The Peace of Paris of 1763[3] provided that the French

[1] E. E. Hale reprinted two reports of the siege under the title of *The Capture of Havana in 1762 by the forces of George III* (Boston, 1898). Other accounts are in the *Year-Book* of the Massachusetts Society of Colonial Wars, 1899, p. 125. Julian Corbett has an excellent account of this campaign, largely from manuscript sources in his *England in the Seven Years' War*, ii, 246–284. See also Duro's *Armada Española*, vii, 39–82.

[2] *Ibid.*, vii, 83–99.

[3] Julian Corbett has given a fresh account of the negotiations of 1763 from manuscript sources in his *England in*

should retire from North America, giving that portion of it east of the Mississippi and of the island on which New Orleans stands to the English; that island and Louisiana west of the great river, by another agreement, went to Spain. This latter sacrifice was made to recompense Spain for her cession of Florida to the English as the price of the restoration of Havana. England, on her part, gave to France two small islands in the Gulf of St. Lawrence to serve as fishing stations and not to be fortified or garrisoned. She also restored many of the sugar islands, but retained Grenada, St. Vincent, Dominica, and Tobago.

Many Englishmen thought that all the conquered West India Islands should have been retained and Canada restored to France — if the relinquishment of any conquest was necessary to secure peace. One of the arguments for this policy was stated by the Duke of Bedford to Newcastle in May, 1761. " I don't know," wrote Bedford, " whether the neighbourhood of the French to our North American colonies was not the greatest security for their dependence on the mother country." [1] This idea was seized upon by those Englishmen who had interests in the West Indies and was so strongly stated that Franklin wrote a pamphlet setting forth the comparative importance of the continental and insular possessions of Great Britain.[2] Even before this Dr. John Mitch-

the Seven Years' War, ii, 327–365. The earlier negotiations are described in the same volume. There is a good deal of original matter on the negotiations of 1761 in Thackeray's *Pitt*, i, 496 and fol. The French side was stated by Choiseul in a *Mémoire Historique* (Paris, 1761; reprinted at London in the same year as *An Historical Memorial of the Negotiation of France and England from the 26th of March, 1761, to the 20th of September of the same Year, with the Vouchers*).

The treaty is in Martens et Cussy's *Recueil de Traités*, i, 30; the paragraphs relating to America are printed in French and also in translation in *American History Leaflets*, No. 5.

[1] Quoted by Corbett from the " Newcastle Papers " Ms. in his *England in the Seven Years' War*, ii, 173. For the opinions of Choiseul and Vergennes, see Note IV, p. 600.

[2] *The Interest of Great Britain considered with regard to her Colonies and*

ell [1] had adverted to " the false and groundless notion that seems to influence many people's opinions and conduct with regard to the colonies is the fear of their rebelling, . . . to let the French have a power nigh them to keep them in awe." Again, on another page, he refers to " lame and designing politicians, who pretend to tell us, that it is the interest of *Britain* to allow *France* a considerable power in America, in order to keep the British colonies in subjection ! " The idea of colonial rebellion was certainly widespread in England at the time, and the thought that the presence of the French was the necessary curb to American ambitions was also prevalent, not only in England, but in France, although the oft-quoted remark of Choiseul to Stanley that Canada in the hands of the French would always be of service to England to keep the " Colonies in that dependence which they would not fail to shake off the moment Canada should be ceded," needs confirmation. Looking backward, it is clear that Bedford and Choiseul and those who thought with them were wrong and Franklin and Mitchell right. The absence of pressure from Quebec and Montreal had nothing to do with bringing about the American Revolution, nor can it be proved that a desire for revenge was the leading motive which induced Louis XVI to give aid to the Americans in their struggle for justice and then for independence.

the *Acquisitions of Canada and Guadaloupe* (London, Boston, and Philadelphia, 1760).

[1] *The Contest in America between Great Britain and France* . . . ; *giving an Account of the Views and Designs of the French, with the Interests of Great Britain, and the Situation of the British and French Colonies in All parts of America* (London, 1757), pp. xxi, xxii, 206. Other pamphlets on this subject are: *The Importance of Canada considered in Two Letters to a Noble Lord* (London, 1761); *Considerations on the Importance of Canada . . . addressed to the Right Hon. William Pitt* (London, 1759); *A Detection of the False Reasons and Facts contained in five Letters (entitled, Reasons for keeping Guadaloupe at a Peace, preferable to Canada) . . . by a Member of Parliament* (London, 1761).

With this great accession of colonial interests a new chapter opened in the history of the British colonial empire. Would the rulers of Britain continue to permit the people of the continental colonies to develop their industries and their institutions with the minimum of control, or would they establish effective governments in them and strive to make them directly contributory to the imperial treasury? Upon the answer to this question depended the future of the British empire. The differentiation between the people of the continental colonies and those of the home land had already gone so far that one might describe the British empire as made up of two nations. It has been well said that in the long run and barring exceptional circumstances one nation cannot profitably rule another, although it is impossible to predicate the precise occasion for the breaking up of empires. What constitutes nationality? Community of race, language, religion, institutions must be present in the make-up of a nation. The people must be of one racial stock; they must have a common mode of speech; their religious aspirations must find expression in common lines; their institutions for government and for the protection of person and property must be substantially similar. In 1660 the people of England and of the English colonies in North America may be said to have formed parts of one nation; in 1760, this was no longer true. The absorption of Dutch New Netherland, the great flowing in of immigrants from Germany and from France and the importation of thousands of negroes from Africa had given to the colonies racial elements that were not present in England. Moreover, although there was as yet no considerable amalgamation of the white elements in the colonial population, it may be said that changed climatic conditions and environments had already begun to alter the racial characteristics of the descendants of the first comers from England.   In religion in England, the church establishment had bound itself more firmly to the State ; while in America dissent had thriven under radical conditions of living — not one colonist in forty owed fealty to the colonial representative of the Established Church of England.   Above all, colonial institutional ideas had developed on lines which were opposed to those prevailing in the home lands.   Finally, the commercial interests of the two great divisions of the British empire were now distinctly different.   In all that constitutes nationality, two nations now owed allegiance to the British crown.   The colonists were patient and long-suffering ; only prolonged misgovernment on the part of the rulers of Britain compelled them to declare themselves independent of that empire from which they had sprung.

NOTES

I. Bibliography. — The French and Indian War in its larger aspects has been admirably treated in recent works. Of these Julian Corbett's *England in the Seven Years' War* (2 vols., London, 1907) is the longest, the most philosophical, and is based largely on manuscript sources. William Wood's single volume entitled *The Fight for Canada ; A Naval and Military Sketch from the History of the Great Imperial War* is a most stimulating work. So many documents have been brought to light and so much study has been given to these campaigns by competent men since Parkman wrote his *Montcalm and Wolfe* that this book must now be regarded as partially obsolete, — as to the Quebec campaign at least, — and the same thing is even truer of Kingsford's *History of Canada* and of all earlier works. The elaborate bibliographies in Winsor's *America* (v, chs. vii, viii) are still useful for the earlier phases of the struggle. The letters and reports in Gertrude S. Kimball's *Correspondence of William Pitt, when Secretary of State, with Colonial Governors, and Military and Naval Commissioners in America* form a most useful history of the important portion of the war (2 vols., New York, 1906).

II. Quebec. — The standard work on the operations which culminated in the capture of Quebec and the cession of New France is by A. G. Doughty[1] and G. W. Parmelee, entitled *The Siege of Quebec and the Battle of the Plains of Abraham* (6 vols., Quebec, 1901). The first three volumes contain an elaborate narrative, the last three denominated " Appendix," Parts I–III, give the documents, — correspondence of Wolfe, Montcalm, Bougainville, the "Townshend Papers," etc., and an extended bibliography by "A. Doughty and J. E. Middleton, with a list of plans of Quebec by R. Lee-Phillips of the Library of Congress, Washington." Notwithstanding this extensive collaboration, or, probably, because of it, the work has some curious limitations; there are no page numbers given in the lists of illustrations, some of which are printed without any title and out of relation to the immediate text. Among these illustrations

---

[1] Mr. Doughty's other works on this theme are "The Probable Site of the Battle of the Plains of Abraham " in the *Transactions* of the Royal Society of Canada (Second Series, v, § II, pp. 359– 425); *The Fortress of Quebec, 1608–1903* (74 copies, Quebec, 1904); *Report of the State of the Government of Quebec* by General Murray, June 5, 1762 (25 copies, Quebec, 1902).

are two plans of the siege of Quebec, one in colors after the original manuscript in the British Museum (vol. i, p. 264), the other Jefferys's *Correct Plan of the Siege*[1] (vol. ii, p. 272). These with Doughty's map in the third volume (p. 96), showing the action on the Plains of Abraham in connection with the streets of modern Quebec, give a very clear view of the progress of the campaign. The documents printed in these volumes, with Captain John Knox's *Historical Journal of the Campaigns in North America in the Years 1757, 1758, 1759, and 1760* (London, 2 vols., 1769), will serve the needs of all but the closest investigator. The reports of Wolfe, Saunders, and Townshend to Pitt have been several times printed: J. Wright's *History of the Late War*, 199, 206, 214, 218; Thomas Jefferys's *French Dominion in America*, 131, 133, 137; Kimball's *Correspondence of William Pitt*, ii, 149, 159, 164, 170; in the last named from the originals. Winsor (*America*, v, 603) gives a list of the original papers, which is, in some respects, more available than the longer enumeration in Doughty's *Siege of Quebec* (vol. vi); the more important sources are noted in William Wood's *Fight for Canada*, Appendix; Parkman gives a list in his *Montcalm and Wolfe*, ii, 436–441. Many documents relating to this siege are printed in the publications of the Literary and Historical Society of Quebec.

III. The Deportation of the Acadians. — This subject has attracted great attention, mainly owing to its poetic exploitation and to the race and religion of the sufferers. Edouard Richard,[2] Rameau de Saint-Père,[3] and Abbé Casgrain[4] have espoused the cause of the Acadians with ardor and have lost no opportunity to flay those who do not agree with them. The best brief statement on this side is by Francis W. Grey in *American Catholic Quarterly Review*, xxii, 787–808. The English side is stated by Parkman in his *Montcalm and Wolfe*[5] (i, ch. viii) and by Sir Adams G. Archibald in a paper

---

[1] A facsimile of *An Authentic Plan of the River St. Laurence from Sillery to the Fall of Montmorenci with the Operations of the Siege of Quebec drawn by a Captain in his Majesties Navy* and dedicated to Pitt by Thos. Jefferys is bound in at the end of the second volume of Kimball's *Correspondence of William Pitt*. These Jefferys maps have been extensively reproduced, see Winsor's *America*, v, 542 — the facsimile on that page is too small to be serviceable.

[2] *Acadia, Missing Links of a Lost-Chapter* (2 vols., Montreal, 1895).

[3] *Une Colonie Féodale en Amerique, L'Acadie, 1604–1881* (Paris, 3 vols., 1889).

[4] *Un Pèlerinage au Pays d'Evangeline* (Quebec, 1887).

[5] With this should be read chapter ix of his *Half-Century of Conflict*, which was written after the discovery of new material, although dealing with events earlier in point of time.

which he read before the Nova Scotia Historical Society in 1886 and printed in their *Collections*, v, 11–97. See also a brief article by Archibald MacMechan, entitled " Evangeline and the Real Acadians" in the *Atlantic Monthly* for February, 1907.

The original documents relating to the Acadians and their misfortunes are printed in Thomas B. Akins's *Selections from the Public Documents of the Province of Nova Scotia* (Halifax, 1869) and the "Journal of Colonel John Winslow" in Nova Scotia Historical Society's *Collections*, iii, 71–196. Governor Lawrence's Instructions to Colonel Winslow are on p. 78; Winslow's declaration to the "French Inhabitants" on p. 94; his descriptions of the difficulties of the task on pp. 108, 126, 136, etc. The manuscript is in the library of the Massachusetts Historical Society. The *Halifax Morning Herald* for October and November, 1886, contains a series of interesting articles by Sir Adams Archibald and Archbishop O'Brien on the two sides of this controversy. The *Quebec Morning Chronicle* for April, 1889, and the *Halifax Morning Herald* for April 10, 1890, have interesting articles by Abbé Casgrain and Mr. Akins.

IV. Choiseul's Prophecy. — The French prophecies as to the effect of the cession of Canada on colonial dependence were first published, a dozen years later, in two anonymous tracts: *Three Letters to Dr. Price*[1] and *Second Thoughts or Observations upon Lord Abingdon's Thoughts on the Letter of Edmund Burke to the Sheriffs of Bristol.*[2] The author of the former (pp. 136, 137 note) writes that " the French seem to have been better acquainted with the temper of the North American colonies than we ourselves. Upon looking over some rough draughts of letters I had written to some friends in England from Constantinople, (where I was at the close of the last war,) I find in one of them an account of a conversation I had at that time (viz. early in the year 1763) with Mr. de Vergennes, then Ambassador from the court of France at the Porte, and

[1] *Three Letters to Dr. Price, containing Remarks on his Observations on the Nature of Civil Liberty* (London, 1776). This is often attributed to John Lind, an industrious hack writer of the time.

[2] A copy of the second edition of this exceedingly rare tract is in the John Carter Brown Library at Providence. It was placed at my disposal by Mr. George Parker Winship, to whom I am greatly indebted for assistance in many ways.

I also wish gratefully to acknowledge the aid which many other friends and students have afforded me. The names of some of them are given in the notes to the preceding pages. Here I wish especially to thank Miss Eva G. Moore, Miss Marion F. Lansing, and Mr. J. R. H. Moore for their aid in verifying citations and extracts and making many valuable suggestions.

now secretary of state for foreign affairs : — 'You are happy,' said he, 'in the cession of Canada : we, perhaps, ought to think ourselves happy that you have acquired it. Delivered from a neighbour whom they always feared, your other colonies will soon discover, that they stand no longer in need of your protection. You will call on them to contribute toward supporting the burthen which they have helped to bring on you, they will answer you by shaking off all dependence.' "

After giving the above anecdote of Vergennes, the author of *Second Thoughts* writes, " May we be allowed to shew further the French opinion of American independence, by mentioning another anecdote, for the truth of which we think we can venture to vouch ? When Mr. Stanley waited upon Choiseul with the ultimatum [in 1761], the Duke, during their interview, expressed his wonder that our great Pitt (votre grand Pitt) should be so attached to the cession of Canada ; for the inferiority of its population, he observed, would never suffer it to be dangerous in the hands of France ; and being in the hands of France, to us it would always be of service, to keep our Colonies in that dependence which they would not fail to shake off the moment Canada should be ceded."

INDEX

Abercromby, Gen., his Ticonderoga campaign, 582.

Acadia, attack on, 1690, 531; attack and conquest of, 1704–1707, 541, 542; English settlement in, 544.

Acadians, the, their position, 545, 575; deportation of, 575–577; bibliography, 599.

Acts, etc. (*see also* Laws), Navigation, 9–13, 27; Uniformity, 15 *n.*; Conventicle, 15 *n.*; Five Mile Act, 15 *n.*; Massachusetts Franchise, 69; against Quakers, 98 *n.*; of Union (between Penna. and Delaware), 120, 319; of Settlement (Penna.), 121; Test, 155; Habeas Corpus (1679), 156, 372; not law in America, 221 and *n.*; "Bill of Rights," 191; of settlement, 221, 223 *n.*; last Navigation, 1696, 251–279; New York Charter of Liberties, 297; Declaratory Resolution of New York, 298; text of, 311; Penna. Blasphemy Act, 325 *n.*; English, as to affirmation, 326 and *n.*; Church Acts of South Carolina, 342–345; for transportation of criminals, 372; Massachusetts, 1641, 383, 400; English Naturalization, 414; English Toleration, 423; Post-office, 474; Sugar, of 1733, 515–519 (bibliography, 522).

Admiralty Courts, 276–278; bibliography, 276 *n.*

Aix-la-Chapelle, Peace of, 549.

Albany (Fort Orange), renamed, 40; conference, 1684, 146; Revolution of 1689 in, 208.

Albany Plan of Union, 569–571.

Albemarle, Duke of, *see* Monk.

Alexander, William, Earl of Sterling, grants to, 32.

Allen, Samuel, and New Hampshire, 285, 286.

Amherst, Gen. J., captures Louisbourg, 579; commander-in-chief, 583, 584; ends the war, 594.

Andros, Edmund, bibliography, 186, 214; governor of New York, 52–60; early career, 52, 53; and William Penn, 56; and Philip Carteret, 57, 58; and

the French, 143, 151; governor of New England, 173–185; overthrow of, 196–202 (bibliography, 214).

Anne, Queen, and the Palatines, 404; proclamation as to money, 499.

Anti-slavery, sentiment and protests, 395–398.

Anville, Duc d', 548.

Appeals from colonial courts, 240–241 *n.*; Leisler appeal, 305, 306; Bayard appeal, 308; South Carolina Church Acts, 342–345.

Arlington, Lord (Henry Bennet), 4; and Virginia grant, 63, 64.

Articles of Capitulation, of New Netherland, 38, 39, 41.

Ashley, Lord, *see* Cooper, A. A.

Assemblies, colonial, rise and power of, 282 and fol.

Attorneys General, Opinions of English, *see* Opinions.

Atwood, William, 307.

Bacon, Nathaniel, Jr., 84–89; his family connections, 84 *n.*

Bacon's "Laws of Virginia," 85.

Bacon's Rebellion, 84–90; bibliography, 92.

Baltimore, Third Baron, *see* Calvert.

Bancroft, George, his *United States*, 26 and *n.*

Banking, colonial, 504.

Baptists, the, 438, 445, 448.

Barnwell, Col. John, 346, 353.

Bayard, Nicholas, anti-Leislerian leader, 206–209; his trial, 306–308.

Beauséjour, Fort, captured, 575.

Belcher, Jonathan, 236, 291 *n.*; governor of Massachusetts, 294.

"Belcher Papers," 237 *n.*

Bellomont Earl of, *see* Coote, Richard.

Berkeley, Dean, 434.

Berkeley, John (Lord Berkeley), 4; proprietor of Carolina, 13; receives grant from Duke of York, 44, 45; granted part of Virginia, 63.

Berkeley, Sir William (governor of Virginia), proprietor of Carolina, 5; and navigation acts, 12; opposes Dutch, 49;